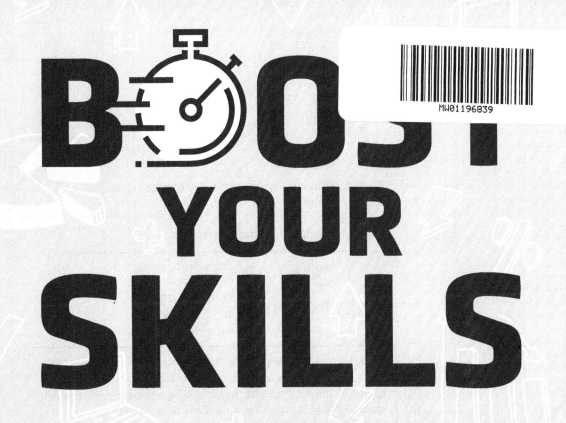

BOOST YOUR SKILLS

in Accounting and Bookkeeping

Eric A. Weinstein, MBA, CPA

LABYRINTH

LEARNING®

Boost Your Skills in Accounting and Bookkeeping
By Eric A. Weinstein, MBA, CPA

Copyright © 2024 by Labyrinth Learning

LABYRINTH
LEARNING®

Labyrinth Learning
PO Box 2669
Danville, CA 94526
800.522.9746
On the web at: lablearning.com

Co-Founder:
Brian Favro

Product Manager:
Jason Favro

Learning Solutions Architect:
Laura Popelka

Production Manager:
Debra Grose

Senior Editor:
Alexandra Mummery

eLearning Specialist:
Lauren Carlson

Indexing:
BIM Creatives, LLC

Cover Design:
Sam Anderson Design

All rights reserved. No part of this material protected by this copyright notice may be reproduced or utilized in any form or by any means, electronic or mechanical, including photocopying, recording, scanning, or by information storage and retrieval systems without written permission from the copyright holder.

Labyrinth Learning® and the Labyrinth Learning logo are trademarks of Labyrinth Learning. Intuit® and QuickBooks® are registered trademarks of Intuit, Inc. For technical assistance with QuickBooks, contact Intuit at www.intuit.com. Other product and company names mentioned herein may be the trademarks of their respective owners.

The example companies, organizations, products, people, and events depicted herein are fictitious. No association with any real company, organization, product, person, or event is intended or should be inferred.

Screenshots printed with permission.

PRINT ITEM: 1-64061-575-X
ISBN-13:   978-1-64061-575-5

Contents

Preface

Boost Your Skills in Accounting and Bookkeeping uses Labyrinth Learning's proven step-by-step approach to teach introductory accounting concepts and how to complete the key financial statements. Aimed at serving future bookkeepers, the text is optimized for students with little or no prior accounting knowledge. Straightforward guidance and examples address the most common questions students ask in the classroom. The logical progression and clear narrative set this exciting text apart from similar offerings currently in use for this course.

Key features include measurable chapter objectives and self-assessment quizzes, real-world examples, an engaging design and clean graphics, progressive discussion of the accounting cycle, video tutorials, reinforcing practice sets, and a comprehensive project.

Certification and This Course

This learning solution aligns with the Intuit Certified Bookkeeping Professional certification requirements, distinguishing this courseware as a trusted and critical part of preparing for this exam.

About the Author

Eric A. Weinstein (MBA, CPA) is a Professor of Business Administration at Suffolk County Community College on Long Island, NY. Eric graduated Summa Cum Laude from Georgetown University in 1999, where he earned a BS in Business Administration and majored in Accounting. In 2004, he earned an MBA from the Fuqua School of Business at Duke University. Eric has received many awards in his career, including the State University of New York Chancellor's Award for Excellence in Teaching. Eric and his beautiful wife, Cara, are the proud parents of sons Tyler, Lucas, and Noah. The family lives in Dix Hills, NY, where they enjoy being bossed around by their mini-dachshund, Molly.

Acknowledgements

Many individuals contribute to the development and completion of a comprehensive learning solution. We are grateful to the many instructors and subject matter experts who have assisted with this manuscript. Many thanks to Firecakes Donuts (firecakesdonuts.com, nationwide shipping) in Chicago, IL for the use of their images. Additionally, a special thanks to Angela Azzara, Comsewogue High School, for her thorough review and insightful feedback. This textbook has been greatly improved as a result of her assistance.

This learning solution has benefited from the feedback and suggestions of the following:

Lori Allemand, *Pearl River Community College*

Jay Anders, *Beaufort County Community College*

Dolores Archibald, *New York City College of Technology*

Lisa Banks, *Mott Community College*

Elaine Barnwell, *Bevill State Community College*

Robert Barta, *Suffolk County Community College*

Mary Barton, *Meridian Technology Center*

Sheryl Bertrand, *Hennepin Technical College*

Terrence Bethel, *Professional Certifications Bahamas*

David Bland, *Cape Fear Community College*

Kathy Bowen, *Murray State College*

Kim Braun, *Braun Business Solutions*

Erin Brokel, *Kirkwood Community College*

Marilyn Brooks-Lewis, *Warren County Community College*

Jonee Callahan, *Nash Community Center*

Elim Carpenter, *Roybal Learning Center*

Deborah Carter, *Coahoma Community College*

Laura Chang, *Collin College*

Eleanor Charltoln, *Washtenaw Community College*

Christina Chavez, *Elk Grove Adult and Community Education*

Marilyn Ciolino, *Delgado Community College*

Diana Clarke, *Pasadena City College*

Cathy Combs, *Tennessee College of Applied Technology, Morristown*

Carla Crutchfield, *College of the Ouachitas*

Mary L. Darling, *Wilber Wright College*

Milt Cohen, *Los Angeles Unified School District*

Martha Cranford, *Rowan Cabarrus Community College*

Patrick Cunningham, *Dawson Community College*

Annette Davis, *Glendale Community College*

Steven E. DeWald, *University of Wisconsin, River Falls*

Larissa Dias-Lizarraga, *Brewster Technical Center*

Monica Edwards, *Wayne Community College*

John Fasler, *Whatcom Community College*

Debbra Finney, *Turlock Adult School*

Brenda Fisher, *Raritan Valley Community College*

Jerry Funk, *Lonestar College*

Evangelina Garner, *South Texas Vocational Technical Institute*

Carlysle George, *New York Institute of English and Business*

Jeanne Gerard, *Franklin Pierce University*

Lorie Goodgine, *Tennessee College of Applied Technology, Paris*

Pat Granger, *Lamar State College, Port Arthur*

Amy Grice, *Bevill State Community College*

Barker Hale, *Kilgore College*

Rosemary Hall, *Bellevue College*

Michele Hand, *Dickinson Lifelong Learning Center*

Gail Harmon, *The Accounting Academy*

Craig Harness, *North Arkansas College*

Kelley Butler Heartfield, *Ivy Technical Community College*

Lyle Hicks, *Danville Area Community College*

Joyce Hill, *Mississippi Band of Choctaw Indians*

David Hollomon, *Victor Valley College*

Chris Hood, *Tehachapi High School*

Delbert Hoskins, *Spencerian College*

Dorothy House, *Huntington Beach Adult School*

Carol Hughes, *Asheville Buncombe Technical College*

Fred Intondi, *OCM BOCES*

Judy Jackson, *Northeast Texas Community College*

Rex Jacobsen, *Lake Washington Institute of Technology*

Jodie Lynn Johnson, *First Coast Technical College*

Anita Jones, *West Georgia Technical College*

Daniel Kerch, *Pennsylvania Highlands Community College*

Dave Kiley, *Muskegon Community College*

Donna Kilburn, *Tennessee Technology Center, Ripley*

Cedric Kirton, *Technical Learning Center*

Lynne Kemp, *North Country Community College*

Kathy Kolar, *Marion County Technical Center*

Lynn Krausse, *Bakersfield College*

Marypat Lee, *Vista Adult Education*

Sherry Laskie, *Milan Institute*

Greg Lauer, *North Iowa Area Community College*

S.D. Lewis, *Stanly Community College*

JoAnne Lloyd, *Wayne Community College*

Sue Lobner, *Nicolet Area Technical College*

Teresa Loftis, *San Bernardino Adult School*

Angelo Luciano, *Columbia College, Chicago*

Sandi Lyman, *Rocky Mountain Business Academy*

Kevin Lynch, *Training Unlimited*

Gwyneth MacArthur, *Business Education Technologies*

Richard Mandau, *Piedmont Technical College*

Michelle Masingill, *North Idaho College*

Karen McGuire, *Mid-Michigan Community College*

Tammy Metzke, *Milwaukee Area Technical College*

Linda Miller, *Northeast Community College*

Trent Miller, *San Antonio College*

Cynthia Moody-Paige, *Erwin Technical Center*

Shahrzad Moshiri, *CDC-Quaboag Valley Community Development Corp.*

Larry Murphy, *AIB College of Business*

Michael Murphy, *Unified School District #1*

Christopher O'Byrne, *Cuyamaca College*

Mari Oliver, *Western Carolina University*

Monika Olsen, *Acalanes Adult Education*

Arleen Orland, *Santa Clarita Technology/Career Development Center*

Sharon Ota, *Mission Veijo High School, Oceanview High School*

Terri Peoples, *Seventy-First High School*

Joanne Perez-Arreola, *Maricopa Skill Center*

Heather Perkins, *Traviss Career Center*

Troylene Perry, *Arkansas State University, Mountain Home*

Denise Plesniarski, *Hudson Country Schools of Technology*

Kathy Powell, *Colorado Northwestern Community College*

Kelly Powers, *Pickens Technical College*

Howard Randall, *Mission College*

Deana Ray, *Forsyth Technical Community College*

Carol Riley, *Mashpee High School*

Brad Rivers, *Gaston College*

Cynthia Robertson, *Remington College, Shreveport*

Carol Rogers, *Central New Mexico Community College*

Rex A. Schildhouse, *Miramar College*

Doris Scott, *Traviss Career Center*

Harley Sherman, *Oakland Community College*

William Simmons, *Austin Community College*

Joan Simpson, *Bainbridge State College*

Denise Skivers, *Manatee Technical Institute*

Lauren Smith, *Front Range Community College*

Sally Solum, *Lake Area Technical Institute*

Eric Stadmol, *Santa Rosa Junior College*

Gina Stephens, *Georgia Northwestern Technical College*

Michelle Stobnicke, *Santa Fe Community College*

Susan Takesian, *Timberlane High School*

Terry Tipsord, *Mt. Hood Community College*

Lee Ann Wall, *Monroe County Area Technology Center*

Laura Way, *Fortis College, Ravenna*

Deborah Welch, *Tyler Junior College*

Michele Wilkens, *Minnesota State Community and Technical College*

Mary Wilson, *Garden City Community College*

Kelly Winters, *College of Southern Maryland*

Marjorie York, *Kennebec Valley Community College*

Peter Young, *San Jose State University*

Julie Zevchek, *Cuyahoga Valley Career Center*

1 Evaluating Transactions

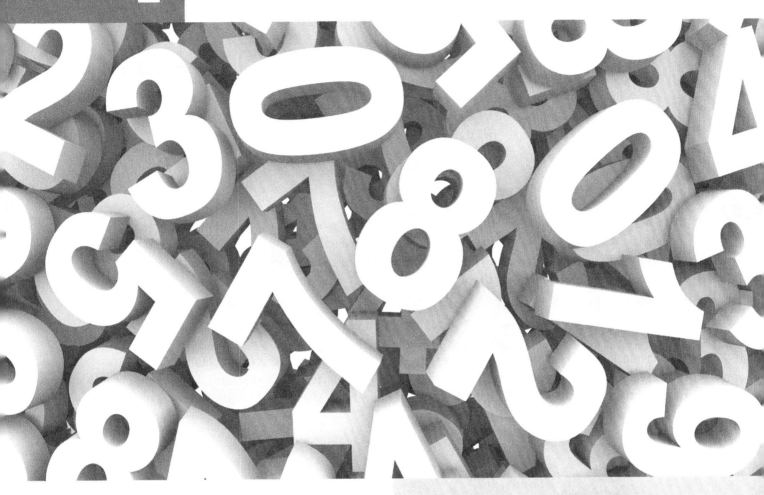

Accounting allows a business to both convey how well it has performed and evaluate how it can improve. Understanding the language of accounting allows you to communicate with the accountants and financial professionals in any organization. In this chapter, you will be introduced to the accounting equation. You will also learn about a number of important accounts and how to evaluate transactions.

LEARNING OBJECTIVES

‣ Describe the accounting equation
‣ Differentiate between account types
‣ Evaluate a transaction
‣ Convey transaction details

Project: Opening Nathan's Donut School

Nathaniel H. Spencer has loved donuts since he was very young. His love of donuts led him to pursue a culinary degree and then to open Nathan's Donut School, a cooking school focused on gourmet baking. He consulted with a lawyer to open his business, but now he's unsure how to track the activity of the school. Nathaniel knows you are studying accounting and has asked you to help with the accounting work for his new business.

You know that the best way to help Nathan is to start at the beginning, with the accounting equation. You then consider the best way to evaluate business activities, using the language of accounting. Lastly, you practice expressing the business activities of Nathan's Donut School using this language.

Before You Begin

Go to **boostyourskills.lablearning.com** and download the resources for this course. These resources include the starting files needed to complete some of the exercises, an answer key, and links to helpful videos. Throughout the course, when you see the cloud icon, go to the Video Launchpad file in your resources and click the link to watch the video.

The Accounting Cycle

The accounting cycle is a series of steps that helps a company properly keep its accounting records for a fiscal period, which can be any length of time (month, quarter, entire year, etc.). Once the cycle is complete at the end of one fiscal period, it begins anew for the next fiscal period. Throughout this course, we will reference and study the accounting cycle.

Ask Yourself 1-1:   The accounting cycle begins at the start of each fiscal period. True or false?

> **NOTE!** Compare your answers to those in the key at the back of the book to check your understanding of the concepts presented.

Accounting and Bookkeeping Defined

Accounting is the process of recording a business's financial transactions. It provides a way of expressing individual business events, and the cumulative impact of those events. This is important so the business can keep track of its own activity and so this activity may be summarized for those outside of the business, such as potential investors, bankers, and governmental agencies.

> **NOTE!** A single business event, such as the purchase of an item, is referred to as a **transaction**.

The United States Bureau of Labor Statistics describes the duties of a **bookkeeper** as recording financial transactions, updating statements, and checking financial records for accuracy. Key qualities of these professionals include the following:

- **Confidentiality** is one of the most important responsibilities of a bookkeeper. As a bookkeeper, you will access a variety of information about a business, including payroll data, corporate profits, etc. Bookkeepers are expected and trusted to maintain the confidentiality of this information unless they are given proper authority to disclose it.
- **Security** is a related responsibility, as the bookkeeper must both keep corporate information in confidence and also protect it so others cannot access it without authorization.
- An important quality of a bookkeeper is **integrity**. Bookkeepers must act in accordance with both applicable professional standards and all applicable laws. They also must be honest and fair in all professional dealings and complete their work in a timely manner.

Now that you understand some high-level qualities of a bookkeeper, let's start examining the accounting concepts that impact a bookkeeper's day-to-day activities.

The Accounting Equation

View the video "The Accounting Equation."

The most fundamental accounting concept you will learn is the **accounting equation**:

Assets = Liabilities + Owner's Equity

Assets are items of value within the business. Examples include cash, accounts receivable (monies owed to the business from a customer), supplies, equipment, and land.

Liabilities represent the portion of assets owed to entities outside of the business, such as outstanding loans, mortgages, and monies received in advance of services rendered (for example, a sports team receiving season ticket revenue before the actual games are played has not yet earned the money, and therefore it owes entertainment to its fans).

Owner's equity is the portion of assets not owed to entities outside of the business and to which, as a result, the business owner(s) can lay claim. For example, when the owner of Nathan's Donut School invested money to open the business, that money was not owed to anybody else and therefore increased the owner's equity in the business.

The accounting equation dictates that all items of value (assets) equal the portion of assets owed to others (liabilities) plus the portion of assets not owed to others (owner's equity).

> **TIP!** Another perspective on the accounting equation is that funds are raised to purchase assets in two ways: either borrowed from individuals outside the business (liabilities) or contributed by the business owners (owner's equity). Again, assets must equal liabilities plus owner's equity.

Ask Yourself 1-2: Which of these is a liability?
   A. Land
   B. Supplies
   C. Outstanding Loan
   D. Equipment

👀 A CLOSER LOOK

What Are the Differences Between Business Types?

Businesses can be formed as one of three different primary types of legal entities: sole proprietorships, partnerships, or corporations.

Sole proprietorships are owned by one individual. There are many benefits of a sole proprietorship, including that it's the simplest form of business and easier to start than other entities. In a sole proprietorship, the owner can make decisions without consulting others and profits are taxed only once (on the owner's individual tax return). One significant drawback is that the owner has unlimited liability, which means their personal assets could be jeopardized in a legal proceeding. Also, the owner must rely entirely on his own experience to run the business. A small business such as Nathan's Donut School could be organized as a sole proprietorship.

Partnerships are owned by two or more individuals. They're similar to sole proprietorships in that profits are taxed once and the owners have unlimited liability. However, decisions must be agreed upon by all owners, and profits must be shared. Often the benefits of having multiple owners, each with a particular expertise, can outweigh the drawbacks.

Corporations issue shares of stock to their owners and can be public (any investor may purchase an ownership stake) or private (only certain investors are permitted to purchase an ownership stake; these are often family owned). The primary benefit of corporations is they offer limited liability to each owner, which means that although an owner's investment could be lost if the business fails, each owner's personal assets are fully protected. The primary drawback is that profits are subject to double taxation, first on the business tax return and again on individual tax returns when distributed to the owners in the form of dividends.

Throughout this course, the Case in Point sections provide examples that illustrate the concepts just introduced. Review these sections to confirm your understanding of the topic before moving to the next section.

In this first Case in Point example section, we will determine the missing amounts in a series of accounting equations.

Assets = Liabilities + Owner's Equity

The accounting equation is a basic algebraic equation. In these examples, we are simply solving for "X."

1. Assets: $7,500. Liabilities: $3,000. Owner's Equity: $X.

   The accounting equation dictates that $7,500 = $3,000 + $X. To determine the value of X, subtract $3,000 from both sides of the equation.

   $7,500 − $3,000 = $3,000 + $X − $3,000

   $4,500 = $X

   Owner's Equity equals $4,500 in this example.

2. Assets: $13,000. Liabilities: $X. Owner's Equity: $9,250.

   In this example, $13,000 = $X + $9,250. Subtract $9,250 from both sides to arrive at X.

   $13,000 −$9,250 = $X + $9,250 − $9,250

   $3,750 = $X

   Liabilities equal $3,750 in this example.

3. Assets: $X. Liabilities: $24,500. Owner's Equity: $45,000.

   In this example, $X = $24,500 + $45,000, so simply add together the components on the right side of the equation to arrive at X.

   $X = $24,500 + $45,000

   $X = $69,500

   Assets equal $69,500 in this example.

Account Names and Descriptions

Within each category of the accounting equation are a variety of accounts. Asset accounts include Cash, Accounts Receivable, and Supplies, as well as Prepaid Insurance, Buildings, and Patents.

Liability accounts include Accounts Payable (monies owed for purchases usually made in the past few months), Notes Payable (similar to Accounts Payable; monies owed for which a formal document has been signed by both parties), Salaries Payable (monies owed to employees), Loans Payable (monies owed to repay loans), Taxes Payable (monies owed to governmental entities for taxes), and Interest Payable (monies owed for interest payments).

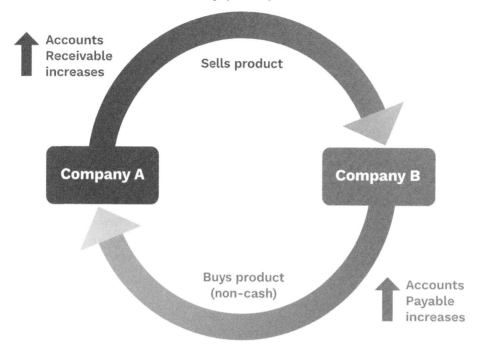

When Company A sells a product to Company B (which doesn't immediately pay), accounts receivable is impacted for one company, while accounts payable is impacted for the other company.

Owner's equity accounts include expense accounts such as Rent Expense and Utilities Expense (costs of doing business), revenue accounts such as Sales Revenue (monies earned from the sale of goods as part of the typical operations of the business) and Service Revenue (monies earned from providing services as part of the typical operations of the business), and Drawing (withdrawals made by the owner).

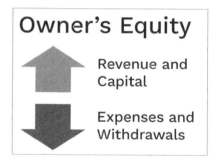

While revenue and capital increase owner's equity, expenses and withdrawals decrease it.

Owner's equity also includes accounts that reflect the ownership share of the owners. These accounts differ from one organization to another; for example, a sole proprietorship has one capital account (John Doe, Capital), while a partnership has multiple. On the other hand, the ownership interest in a corporation is included within the **Common Stock** account (or **Preferred Stock** account, which is an ownership class that includes benefits beyond those of common shareholders) and the **Additional Paid in Capital** account. In this course, we examine sole proprietorships and, therefore, will use a capital account here.

Corporations use other equity accounts, including **Retained Earnings** (portion of corporate earnings not distributed to owners and, therefore, retained for future investment) and **Treasury Stock** (portion of common stock a company has repurchased and is, therefore, not presently in the hands of investors).

COMMON ACCOUNTS BY TYPE		
Assets	**Liabilities**	**Owner's Equity**
Cash	Accounts Payable	Sales Revenue
Accounts Receivable	Notes Payable	Service Revenue
Supplies	Salaries Payable	Rent Expense
Prepaid Insurance	Unearned Revenue	Utilities Expense
Merchandise Inventory	Mortgage Payable	Telephone Expense
Equipment		John Doe, Capital
Buildings		John Doe, Drawing
Land		

TIP! Companies may use different account names. Although the overall list of account names is far too long to memorize (or even identify), you'll find that there is a core list of accounts used in most transactions.

It's important to identify the correct accounts when recording transactions. Therefore, you should focus heavily on understanding what each account represents.

Ask Yourself 1-3: Which of these is an owner's equity account?
  A. Sales Revenue
  B. Telephone Expense
  C. William Harris, Drawing
  D. All of these

CASE IN POINT 1-2

In this example, we will identify a series of accounts as being an asset, a liability, or an owner's equity account.

1. Rent Revenue
   The Rent Revenue account represents revenue earned from renting out a facility. For example, Nathan's friend is a local coffee roaster. She rents out space in Nathan's Donut School's parking lot and sells coffee to his students. All revenue accounts are owner's equity *accounts.*

2. Buildings
   The Buildings account represents the cost of all buildings that have been purchased. Buildings are valuable to a business, and therefore this is an asset *account.*

3. Accounts Receivable
   The Accounts Receivable account represents monies that are owed to a business and due in the short term (typically within a few months). Accounts receivable are typically generated when goods are sold, or services are provided, and payment is not immediately made. As accounts receivable are valuable to a business, this is an asset *account.*

   The Notes Receivable account is similar to Accounts Receivable but is due to be paid at least 12 months later (long-term), is associated with a formal document signed by buyer and seller, and typically requires the payment of interest.

4. Telephone Expense

   The Telephone Expense account represents expenses incurred for telephone usage. All expense accounts are owner's equity *accounts.*

5. Accounts Payable

   The Accounts Payable account represents monies owed to others by the business and that are due in the short term (typically within a few months). Accounts payable are typically generated when goods are bought or services are received and payment is not immediately made. As accounts payable amounts are funds owed to others, this is a liability *account.*

6. Nathaniel H. Spencer, Drawing

   The Nathaniel H. Spencer, Drawing account represents monies withdrawn from the business by the owner. Similar to revenue and expenses, all drawing accounts are owner's equity *accounts.*

7. Supplies

   The Supplies account represents the cost of unused supplies currently held by the business. Because supplies are valuable to the business, this is an asset *account.*

Evaluating Transactions

☁ **View the video "Evaluating Transactions."**

The **Financial Accounting Standards Board (FASB)** establishes and maintains the **Generally Accepted Accounting Principles (GAAP)**, which all U.S. businesses follow for financial reporting. A concept underlying GAAP is **double-entry bookkeeping**. This means that when a transaction takes place, at least two accounts must be impacted. A transaction represents a single business event that has occurred, such as the purchase of a machine, the payment of a debt, or the withdrawal of cash for personal use. Many more than two accounts can be impacted by a single transaction, but for the accounting equation to remain in balance, there always must be at least two.

> **TIP!**   Search online for GAAP and FASB to learn more about the guiding principles of accounting.

Evaluating a transaction is a three-step process:

1. Determine which accounts are impacted. For example, if Nathaniel purchases a commercial oven for $1,500 cash, then the two accounts impacted are Cash and Equipment.

2. Determine whether the balance (expressed in terms of monetary value) in each account increases or decreases. Nathaniel purchased equipment, so the Equipment account balance increases. He paid in cash, so his Cash account balance decreases.

3. Determine by how much each account is impacted. If only two accounts are affected, then they will both be affected by the same amount. However, if more than two accounts are affected, you'll need to look more closely to determine by how much each account has changed.

When evaluating a transaction, it's important to view the transaction from the perspective of *your* business. In the example, cash was received by the other company, but for Nathaniel's purposes, this has no consequence. He is only concerned with the fact that *his* business now has *less* cash than it did before. That's why his Cash account balance decreased.

Accounts Impacted	Balance Change	Amount
Equipment	↑	$1,500
Cash	↓	$1,500

Ask Yourself 1-4:   GAAP establish and maintain the FASB. True or False?

CASE IN POINT 1-3

In this example, we will evaluate transactions, determining the accounts impacted and by how much each increases or decreases.

1. Nathaniel invests $35,000 to open Nathan's Donut School.

   - *Step 1:* Nathaniel invested cash in the business, and since none of the $35,000 is owed to anybody, he can claim ownership of the entire amount. Therefore, the accounts affected are **Cash** and **Nathaniel H. Spencer, Capital** (represents Nathaniel's share of the equity).

   - *Step 2:* As a result of the investment, the company has more cash than it did before. Nathaniel's ownership interest has also increased, as he is now the owner of more assets. Both accounts **increase**.

   - *Step 3:* Since the $35,000 was invested by Nathaniel, both accounts increase by **$35,000**.

Assets	=	Liabilities	+	Owner's Equity
$35,000		$0		$35,000

2. Nathan's Donut School pays $20,000 for baking equipment.

   - *Step 1:* Cash was paid to complete the purchase of the baking equipment, so the **Cash** and **Equipment** accounts are impacted.

   - *Step 2:* Nathan's Donut School now has less cash and more equipment than it did before. The Cash account has **decreased** and the Equipment account has **increased**.

   - *Step 3:* The baking equipment cost $20,000, so the Cash account decreases by **$20,000** and the Equipment account increases by **$20,000**.

Assets	=	Liabilities	+	Owner's Equity
−$20,000		$0		$0
+ $20,000				
$0				

   Both affected accounts appear on the same side of the accounting equation. That's okay as long as the equation stays in balance.

3. The company purchases $500 of supplies and $1,000 of furniture on account.

   When an asset is purchased on account, cash is not paid when the asset is acquired but, instead, is owed. The debt owed is a liability.

   - *Step 1:* Supplies and furniture were obtained but no cash was paid at the time. As a result, the **Supplies, Furniture,** and **Accounts Payable** (an amount owed to others) accounts are all impacted.

   - *Step 2:* The company now has more supplies and furniture. It also owes more money than it did before the transaction. All three accounts have **increased**.

- *Step 3:* Each account is impacted by a different amount. Supplies increases by **$500**, Furniture increases by **$1,000**, and because the total amount is owed, Accounts Payable increases by **$1,500**.

Assets	=	Liabilities	+	Owner's Equity
$500		$1,500		$0
+ $1,000				
$1,500				

4. On its first day of business, Nathan's Donut School earns $850. For now, the company accepts only cash payments.

   - *Step 1:* The company receives cash in exchange for services and therefore has earned revenue. The **Cash** and **Service Revenue** accounts are impacted.

   - *Step 2:* The company now has more cash and has earned more revenue. Both accounts have **increased**.

   - *Step 3:* As $850 was both earned and received for these services, both accounts increased by **$850**.

Assets	=	Liabilities	+	Owner's Equity
$850		$0		$850

5. The company pays off the $1,500 that was owed from the purchase of supplies and furniture. This represents a cash payment on account.

   - *Step 1:* Cash has been paid out and an amount owed to others has been paid off, so **Cash** and **Accounts Payable** are impacted.

   - *Step 2:* The company now has less cash and owes less money than it did before. Both accounts have **decreased**.

   - *Step 3:* Since $1,500 was paid out to reduce the liability, both accounts are reduced by **$1,500**.

Assets	=	Liabilities	+	Owner's Equity
-$1,500		-$1,500		$0

TIP! Over time you won't need to work through each step independently, as practice will improve your ability to quickly analyze a transaction. Your speed will also increase once you memorize whether each account is an asset, liability, or owner's equity account.

Recording Transactions

View the video "Recording Transactions."

The benefit of recording transactions is that a company can maintain a running balance of the value in each account, allowing the company to review its financial position at any point in time. To calculate account balances, you combine the impact of every transaction. Organization is key. Creating a chart in which all active accounts are listed as column headings across the top and transactions are listed below as rows is an effective way to stay organized when calculating account balances.

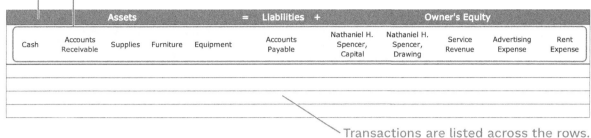

The accounting equation

Active company accounts, organized by account type (asset, liability, owner's equity)

Assets					=	Liabilities	+	Owner's Equity					
Cash	Accounts Receivable	Supplies	Furniture	Equipment		Accounts Payable		Nathaniel H. Spencer, Capital	Nathaniel H. Spencer, Drawing	Service Revenue	Advertising Expense	Rent Expense

Transactions are listed across the rows.

When listing transactions, accounts are displayed within each section of the accounting equation.

Ask Yourself 1-5: Recording transactions allows a company to maintain a running balance of the value in each account. True or false?

CASE IN POINT 1-4

In this example, we will record transactions and calculate the ending balances for each account.

1. Nathaniel invests $35,000 to open Nathan's Donut School (Transaction #1).

Assets					=	Liabilities	+	Owner's Equity				
Cash	Accounts Receivable	Supplies	Furniture	Equipment		Accounts Payable		Nathaniel H. Spencer, Capital	Nathaniel H. Spencer, Drawing	Service Revenue	Advertising Expense	Rent Expense
$ 35,000								$ 35,000				

2. Nathan's Donut School pays $20,000 for baking equipment (Transaction #2).

Assets					=	Liabilities	+	Owner's Equity				
Cash	Accounts Receivable	Supplies	Furniture	Equipment		Accounts Payable		Nathaniel H. Spencer, Capital	Nathaniel H. Spencer, Drawing	Service Revenue	Advertising Expense	Rent Expense
$ (20,000)				$ 20,000								

Parentheses around an amount indicate a negative number.

3. The company purchases $500 of supplies and $1,000 of furniture from Office Space on account (Transaction #3).

Assets					=	Liabilities	+	Owner's Equity				
Cash	Accounts Receivable	Supplies	Furniture	Equipment		Accounts Payable		Nathaniel H. Spencer, Capital	Nathaniel H. Spencer, Drawing	Service Revenue	Advertising Expense	Rent Expense
		$ 500	$ 1,000			$ 1,500						

The result of this transaction is that the company has more supplies, more furniture, and more accounts payable than it did before. All amounts are positive because each account is increasing.

4. Nathan's Donut School opens for business and earns $850 cash on its first day (Transaction #4).

Assets					=	Liabilities	+	Owner's Equity				
Cash	Accounts Receivable	Supplies	Furniture	Equipment		Accounts Payable		Nathaniel H. Spencer, Capital	Nathaniel H. Spencer, Drawing	Service Revenue	Advertising Expense	Rent Expense
$ 850										$ 850		

5. The company pays off the $1,500 owed from the purchase of supplies and furniture (Transaction #5).

Assets					=	Liabilities	+	Owner's Equity				
Cash	Accounts Receivable	Supplies	Furniture	Equipment		Accounts Payable		Nathaniel H. Spencer, Capital	Nathaniel H. Spencer, Drawing	Service Revenue	Advertising Expense	Rent Expense
$ (1,500)						$ (1,500)						

6. On its second day of operations, Nathan's Donut School earns $2,500 on account from SportCo. (Transaction #6).

Assets					=	Liabilities	+	Owner's Equity				
Cash	Accounts Receivable	Supplies	Furniture	Equipment		Accounts Payable		Nathaniel H. Spencer, Capital	Nathaniel H. Spencer, Drawing	Service Revenue	Advertising Expense	Rent Expense
	$ 2,500									$ 2,500		

Companies typically earn revenue throughout the month, and Nathan's Donut School is no exception. However, for simplicity, this is the only revenue transaction we'll examine for the current month of operations.

7. The company purchases advertising in local newspapers for $250 (Transaction #7).

Assets					=	Liabilities	+	Owner's Equity				
Cash	Accounts Receivable	Supplies	Furniture	Equipment		Accounts Payable		Nathaniel H. Spencer, Capital	Nathaniel H. Spencer, Drawing	Service Revenue	Advertising Expense	Rent Expense
$ (250)											$ (250)	

Expenses and withdrawals reduce owner's equity because they result in fewer assets to which the owner can lay claim. As a result, increases in expense and withdrawal accounts are expressed as negative amounts.

8. The company receives $300 on account as partial payment for previously earned revenue (Transaction #8).

Assets					=	Liabilities	+	Owner's Equity				
Cash	Accounts Receivable	Supplies	Furniture	Equipment		Accounts Payable		Nathaniel H. Spencer, Capital	Nathaniel H. Spencer, Drawing	Service Revenue	Advertising Expense	Rent Expense
$ 300	$ (300)											

SportCo. owes Nathan's Donut School $2,500 (Transaction #6), and a portion of that is being paid here. Regardless of the amount paid, this transaction type always increases Cash and decreases Accounts Receivable.

9. Nathan's Donut School pays rent of $1,700 for the month (Transaction #9).

Assets					=	Liabilities	+	Owner's Equity				
Cash	Accounts Receivable	Supplies	Furniture	Equipment		Accounts Payable		Nathaniel H. Spencer, Capital	Nathaniel H. Spencer, Drawing	Service Revenue	Advertising Expense	Rent Expense
$ (1,700)												$ (1,700)

10. Nathaniel withdraws $400 from the business for personal use (Transaction #10).

	Assets				=	Liabilities	+	Owner's Equity				
Cash	Accounts Receivable	Supplies	Furniture	Equipment		Accounts Payable		Nathaniel H. Spencer, Capital	Nathaniel H. Spencer, Drawing	Service Revenue	Advertising Expense	Rent Expense
$ (400)									$ (400)			

11. Using the above transactions, we can determine the ending balances for each account:

	Assets					=	Liabilities	+	Owner's Equity				
	Cash	Accounts Receivable	Supplies	Furniture	Equipment		Accounts Payable		Nathaniel H. Spencer, Capital	Nathaniel H. Spencer, Drawing	Service Revenue	Advertising Expense	Rent Expense
Transaction #1	$ 35,000								$ 35,000				
Transaction #2	$ (20,000)				$ 20,000								
Transaction #3			$ 500	$ 1,000			$ 1,500						
Transaction #4	$ 850										$ 850		
Transaction #5	$ (1,500)						$ (1,500)						
Transaction #6		$ 2,500									$ 2,500		
Transaction #7	$ (250)											$ (250)	
Transaction #8	$ 300	$ (300)											
Transaction #9	$ (1,700)												$ (1,700)
Transaction #10	$ (400)									$ (400)			
Ending Balance	$ 12,300	$ 2,200	$ 500	$ 1,000	$ 20,000		$ -		$ 35,000	$ (400)	$ 3,350	$ (250)	$ (1,700)
	$ 36,000					=	**$0**	+	**$ 36,000**				

Notice that the accounting equation has remained in balance.

👀 A CLOSER LOOK

How Would a Company Handle the Sale of a Product?

Nathan's Donut School is a culinary school that provides a service (baking lessons), but it doesn't sell products. When recording transactions for a company that does sell products, two sets of accounts are used because the company must both remove the merchandise inventory from its books *and* add the revenue earned to its books. Therefore, not only do the Revenue and Cash accounts (or Accounts Receivable, if the customer has not yet paid) increase, but Cost of Goods Sold also increases (accounts for the money the seller originally paid for the item) and Merchandise Inventory decreases (the seller now has less inventory). See Chapter 9 for a detailed discussion of the Merchandise Inventory account.

NOTE! Cost of Goods Sold (COGS) is an expense account that represents the original cost to a business for inventory it plans to sell. This isn't the sales price a business charges the customer, which is typically more than the original cost.

Self-Assessment

Now it's time for you to check your knowledge of the key concepts and skills introduced in this chapter.

1. Accounting provides information for employees within a business but not for those outside of a business.   *True   False* ·

2. Assets represent amounts owed to entities outside of the business.   *True   False* .

3. Notes Payable is a liability account.   , *True   False*

4. Accounts Payable is an asset account.   *True   False* ·

5. The Nathaniel H. Spencer, Capital account represents amounts withdrawn from a business by the owner. REPRESENTS OWNER SHARE OF EQUITY   ✗ · *True   False*

6. With double-entry bookkeeping, at least two accounts are impacted by every transaction.   · *True   False*

7. All transactions must involve at least three accounts.   *True   False* ⸰

8. The sale of services to a customer on account increases the Service Revenue and the Accounts Receivable accounts.   · *True   False*

9. The accounting equation must be in balance after every transaction.   · *True   False*

10. Recording transactions allows a company to maintain a running balance for each account.   · *True   False*

11. What is the accounting equation?   A = L + E

12. Which account is NOT an owner's equity account?
    A. Rent Expense
    B. John Doe, Capital
    C. Service Revenue
    · D. Supplies

13. Identify the action that is NOT a transaction.
    · A. Renaming a business
    B. Purchasing office furniture for cash
    C. Selling goods to a customer
    D. The owner investing cash into a business

14. What two accounts are impacted when a business purchases pens and pencils on account?
    A. Furniture and Cash
    · B. Supplies and Accounts Payable
    C. Cash and Supplies
    D. Accounts Receivable and Accounts Payable

15. What is something a bookkeeper is NOT typically responsible for, per the U.S. Bureau of Labor Statistics?

   A. Analyzing quarterly results

   B. Recording financial transactions

   C. Updating statements

   D. Checking financial records for accuracy

16. What is confidentiality?

   A. Having high moral standards

   B. The prevention of unauthorized access to a company's financials

   C. Ensuring that important information, such as payroll data, is not disclosed without proper authority

   D. The ability to achieve maximum productivity with little effort or waste

17. Identify the asset account.

   A. Buildings

   B. Mortgage Payable

   C. Telephone Expense

   D. John Doe, Drawing

18. Which of these is NOT a liability account?

   A. Loans Payable

   B. Taxes Payable

   C. Interest Payable

   D. Prepaid Insurance

19. Which of these is NOT an equity account?

   A. Common Stock

   B. Unearned Revenue

   C. Additional Paid in Capital

   D. Preferred Stock

20. What account represents the portion of common stock a company has repurchased and that is therefore not presently in the hands of investors?

   A. Treasury Stock

   B. Accounts Receivable

   C. Retained Earnings

   D. Accounts Payable

Putting It Together

Now it's time to move away from Nathan's Donut School as we see how the points and concepts introduced in the chapter affect another company, Amber's Lacrosse Emporium. Just as with the Case in Point examples, these sections are for review and study. You will try your hand at working through the concepts in the Practice Set sections.

PIT 1-1 RECORD THE TRANSACTIONS

Amber's Lacrosse Emporium offers sporting goods for many sports, with an emphasis on lacrosse, and is owned and operated by Amber Stein. In this example, we will record transactions that took place during the first month of operations.

1. Amber invests $75,000 to open Amber's Lacrosse Emporium (Transaction #1).

| Assets | | | | | | = Liabilities + | Owner's Equity | | | | | | | | |
Cash	Accounts Receivable	Supplies	Merchandise Inventory	Furniture	Equipment	Accounts Payable	A. Stein, Capital	A. Stein, Drawing	Sales Revenue	COGS	Ad Expense	Rent Expense	Wages Expense	Phone Expense	Utilities Expense
$ 75,000							$ 75,000								

2. Amber's Lacrosse Emporium pays $15,000 for sporting goods inventory (Transaction #2).

| Assets | | | | | | = Liabilities + | Owner's Equity | | | | | | | | |
Cash	Accounts Receivable	Supplies	Merchandise Inventory	Furniture	Equipment	Accounts Payable	A. Stein, Capital	A. Stein, Drawing	Sales Revenue	COGS	Ad Expense	Rent Expense	Wages Expense	Phone Expense	Utilities Expense
$ (15,000)			$ 15,000												

3. The company purchases display equipment for $12,000 in cash (Transaction #3).

| Assets | | | | | | = Liabilities + | Owner's Equity | | | | | | | | |
Cash	Accounts Receivable	Supplies	Merchandise Inventory	Furniture	Equipment	Accounts Payable	A. Stein, Capital	A. Stein, Drawing	Sales Revenue	COGS	Ad Expense	Rent Expense	Wages Expense	Phone Expense	Utilities Expense
$ (12,000)					$ 12,000										

4. Amber pays rent on the company's retail location of $1,500 (Transaction #4).

| Assets | | | | | | = Liabilities + | Owner's Equity | | | | | | | | |
Cash	Accounts Receivable	Supplies	Merchandise Inventory	Furniture	Equipment	Accounts Payable	A. Stein, Capital	A. Stein, Drawing	Sales Revenue	COGS	Ad Expense	Rent Expense	Wages Expense	Phone Expense	Utilities Expense
$ (1,500)												$ (1,500)			

5. The company purchases $750 of supplies and $2,000 of furniture on account (Transaction #5).

| Assets | | | | | | = Liabilities + | Owner's Equity | | | | | | | | |
Cash	Accounts Receivable	Supplies	Merchandise Inventory	Furniture	Equipment	Accounts Payable	A. Stein, Capital	A. Stein, Drawing	Sales Revenue	COGS	Ad Expense	Rent Expense	Wages Expense	Phone Expense	Utilities Expense
		$ 750		$ 2,000		$ 2,750									

6. On its first day of business, Amber's Lacrosse Emporium sells $2,400 of sporting goods for cash. The cost of the goods sold is $1,350 (Transaction #6).

| Assets | | | | | | = Liabilities + | Owner's Equity | | | | | | | | |
Cash	Accounts Receivable	Supplies	Merchandise Inventory	Furniture	Equipment	Accounts Payable	A. Stein, Capital	A. Stein, Drawing	Sales Revenue	COGS	Ad Expense	Rent Expense	Wages Expense	Phone Expense	Utilities Expense
$ 2,400									$ 2,400						
			$ (1,350)							$ (1,350)					

Remember that transactions involving inventory impact two sets of accounts. The first pair of accounts impacted (Cash, Sales Revenue) recognizes the revenue earned, while the second pair of accounts impacted (Merchandise Inventory, Cost of Goods Sold) recognizes the expense incurred in order to sell these goods.

7. The company pays the $2,750 owed for the supplies and furniture (Transaction #7).

	Assets					=	Liabilities	+			Owner's Equity						
Cash	Accounts Receivable	Supplies	Merchandise Inventory	Furniture	Equipment		Accounts Payable		A. Stein, Capital	A. Stein, Drawing	Sales Revenue	COGS	Ad Expense	Rent Expense	Wages Expense	Phone Expense	Utilities Expense
$ (2,750)							$ (2,750)										

8. On its second day of operations, the company sells $1,450 of sporting goods for cash, plus another $3,000 of sporting goods to a local school district on account. The cost of goods sold is $2,100 (Transaction #8).

	Assets					=	Liabilities	+			Owner's Equity						
Cash	Accounts Receivable	Supplies	Merchandise Inventory	Furniture	Equipment		Accounts Payable		A. Stein, Capital	A. Stein, Drawing	Sales Revenue	COGS	Ad Expense	Rent Expense	Wages Expense	Phone Expense	Utilities Expense
$ 1,450	$ 3,000										$ 4,450						
			$ (2,100)									$ (2,100)					

9. The company purchases advertising in local newspapers for $600 (Transaction #9).

	Assets					=	Liabilities	+			Owner's Equity						
Cash	Accounts Receivable	Supplies	Merchandise Inventory	Furniture	Equipment		Accounts Payable		A. Stein, Capital	A. Stein, Drawing	Sales Revenue	COGS	Ad Expense	Rent Expense	Wages Expense	Phone Expense	Utilities Expense
$ (600)													$ (600)				

10. The company receives $2,100 in partial payment for the sale to the school district on account within transaction #8 (Transaction #10).

	Assets					=	Liabilities	+			Owner's Equity						
Cash	Accounts Receivable	Supplies	Merchandise Inventory	Furniture	Equipment		Accounts Payable		A. Stein, Capital	A. Stein, Drawing	Sales Revenue	COGS	Ad Expense	Rent Expense	Wages Expense	Phone Expense	Utilities Expense
$ 2,100	$ (2,100)																

11. Amber's Lacrosse Emporium pays wages of $1,600 to its employees (Transaction #11).

	Assets					=	Liabilities	+			Owner's Equity						
Cash	Accounts Receivable	Supplies	Merchandise Inventory	Furniture	Equipment		Accounts Payable		A. Stein, Capital	A. Stein, Drawing	Sales Revenue	COGS	Ad Expense	Rent Expense	Wages Expense	Phone Expense	Utilities Expense
$ (1,600)															$ (1,600)		

12. The company pays its telephone bill of $135 (Transaction #12).

	Assets					=	Liabilities	+			Owner's Equity						
Cash	Accounts Receivable	Supplies	Merchandise Inventory	Furniture	Equipment		Accounts Payable		A. Stein, Capital	A. Stein, Drawing	Sales Revenue	COGS	Ad Expense	Rent Expense	Wages Expense	Phone Expense	Utilities Expense
$ (135)																$ (135)	

13. The company pays $200 for monthly utilities (Transaction #13).

	Assets					=	Liabilities	+			Owner's Equity						
Cash	Accounts Receivable	Supplies	Merchandise Inventory	Furniture	Equipment		Accounts Payable		A. Stein, Capital	A. Stein, Drawing	Sales Revenue	COGS	Ad Expense	Rent Expense	Wages Expense	Phone Expense	Utilities Expense
$ (200)																	$ (200)

14. Amber's Lacrosse Emporium buys an additional $2,000 of sporting equipment inventory on account (Transaction #14).

	Assets					=	Liabilities	+			Owner's Equity						
Cash	Accounts Receivable	Supplies	Merchandise Inventory	Furniture	Equipment		Accounts Payable		A. Stein, Capital	A. Stein, Drawing	Sales Revenue	COGS	Ad Expense	Rent Expense	Wages Expense	Phone Expense	Utilities Expense
			$ 2,000				$ 2,000										

15. Amber withdraws $600 from the business (Transaction #15).

	Assets					=	Liabilities	+			Owner's Equity						
Cash	Accounts Receivable	Supplies	Merchandise Inventory	Furniture	Equipment		Accounts Payable		A. Stein, Capital	A. Stein, Drawing	Sales Revenue	COGS	Ad Expense	Rent Expense	Wages Expense	Phone Expense	Utilities Expense
$ (600)										$ (600)							

16. The ending balance for each account is determined using the amounts from each transaction:

	Assets						= Liabilities +	Owner's Equity								
	Cash	Accounts Receivable	Supplies	Merchandise Inventory	Furniture	Equipment	Accounts Payable	A. Stein, Capital	A. Stein, Drawing	Sales Revenue	COGS	Ad Expense	Rent Expense	Wages Expense	Phone Expense	Utilities Expense
Transaction #1	$ 75,000							$ 75,000								
Transaction #2	$ (15,000)			$ 15,000												
Transaction #3	$ (12,000)					$ 12,000										
Transaction #4	$ (1,500)												$ (1,500)			
Transaction #5			$ 750		$ 2,000		$ 2,750									
Transaction #6	$ 2,400									$ 2,400						
Transaction #6				$ (1,350)							$ (1,350)					
Transaction #7	$ (2,750)						$ (2,750)									
Transaction #8	$ 1,450	$ 3,000								$ 4,450						
Transaction #8				$ (2,100)							$ (2,100)					
Transaction #9	$ (600)											$ (600)				
Transaction #10	$ 2,100	$ (2,100)														
Transaction #11	$ (1,600)													$ (1,600)		
Transaction #12	$ (135)														$ (135)	
Transaction #13	$ (200)															$ (200)
Transaction #14				$ 2,000			$ 2,000									
Transaction #15	$ (600)								$ (600)							
Ending Balance	$ 46,565	$ 900	$ 750	$ 13,550	$ 2,000	$ 12,000	$ 2,000	$ 75,000	$ (600)	$ 6,850	$(3,450)	$ (600)	$(1,500)	$(1,600)	$ (135)	$ (200)
	$ 75,765						= $ 2,000 +	$ 73,765								

Practice Set A

Now it's time to get busy! In the Practice Set sections, you will use your new skills to complete a series of exercises. If you have not yet downloaded the resources for this course (boostyourskills.lablearning.com), do so now, as you will need starting files for certain exercises.

PSA 1-1 USE THE ACCOUNTING EQUATION

Determine the missing amounts.

1. Assets: $15,750. Liabilities: $6,250. Owner's Equity: $X. $15,750 = 6,250 + X = 9,500$
2. Assets: $158,000. Liabilities: $X. Owner's Equity: $102,000. $158,000 = X + 102,000 = 56,000$
3. Assets: $X. Liabilities: $2,500. Owner's Equity: $5,000. $X = 2,500 + 5,000 = 7,500$

PSA 1-2 DETERMINE ENDING ACCOUNTING EQUATION BALANCES

Determine the ending balances for assets, liabilities, and owner's equity. Remember to keep the accounting equation in balance.

1. **Beginning of year:**   Assets: $27,000   Liabilities: $19,000
   During the year: Assets: ↑ by $2,000   Liabilities: ↓ by $4,000

   Ending balances: ___29,000___ = ___15,000___ + ___14,000___

2. **Beginning of year:**   Liabilities: $5,500   Owner's Equity: $10,000
   During the year: Assets: ↓ by $1,500   Owner's Equity: ↓ by $950

   Ending balances: ___14,000___ = ___4,950___ + ___9,050___

3. **Beginning of year:**   Assets: $59,000   Owner's Equity: $41,000
   During the year: Liabilities: ↑ by $6,500   Owner's Equity: ↓ by $2,250

   Ending balances: ___63,250___ = ___24,500___ + ___38,750___

PSA 1-3 ADVANCED ACCOUNTING EQUATION WORK

125 500
52,500
3,000

For each scenario, examine two years of activity to determine the first year beginning balances for each accounting equation element.

1. Find the Year 1 beginning balances.
   - Assets: ___157,500___
   - Liabilities: ___60,000___
   - Owner's Equity: ___97,500___

End of Year 2	Assets: $138,500	Liabilities: $49,000
During Year 2	Assets: ↓ by $12,000	Liabilities: ↓ by $3,500
During Year 1	Liabilities: ↓ by $7,500	Owner's Equity: ↑ by $500

EY2 126,500
BY2 52,500
BY2 73,000
B42 73,000

48,800
+ 7,500
41,500

52,500
7,500
41,500

49,000
3,500
52,500

138,500 = 49,000
49,000
98,500
98,500

98,500
147,500

138,500
12,000
150,500

150,500
52,500
98,000

2. Find the Year 1 beginning balances.
   - Assets: _____86,700_____
   - Liabilities: _____23,100_____
   - Owner's Equity: _____63,600_____

End of Year 2	Liabilities: $21,000	Owner's Equity: $68,000
During Year 2	Assets: ↑ by $4,500	Owner's Equity: ↓ by $900
During Year 1	Assets: ↓ by $2,200	Liabilities: ↓ by $7,500

3. Find the Year 1 beginning balances.
   - Assets: _____3,300_____
   - Liabilities: _____700_____
   - Owner's Equity: _____2600_____

End of Year 2	Assets: $6,600	Owner's Equity: $2,700
During Year 2	Liabilities: ↑ by $1,900	Owner's Equity: ↑ by $300
During Year 1	Assets: ↑ by $1,100	Owner's Equity: ↓ by $200

PSA 1-4 IDENTIFY THE ACCOUNT TYPE

Determine whether each account is an asset, liability, or owner's equity account.

	Asset	Liability	Owner's Equity
Cash	✓		
Molly W. Virginia, Capital			✓
Rent Expense		✓	
Sales Revenue			✓
Notes Receivable	✓		
Supplies Expense		✓	
Furniture	✓		

PSA 1-5 MATCH ACCOUNT DEFINITIONS

Match the accounts to their descriptions.

_____ Accounts Payable

_____ Accounts Receivable

_____ Cash

_____ Molly W. Virginia, Capital

_____ Molly W. Virginia, Drawing

_____ Notes Receivable

_____ Rent Expense

_____ Rent Revenue

A. Cost incurred for renting an asset from another party

B. Owner's withdrawal of assets in a period (month, year)

C. Monies owed in the short term from another company

D. Total monies held by a business

E. Monies owed to another company

F. Monies earned from rental of an asset to another party

G. Portion of assets to which the business owner can lay claim

H. Monies owed from another company; interest bearing and associated with a formal, signed document

PSA 1-6 DETERMINE THE IMPACT ON ACCOUNTS

Determine the accounts impacted by each transaction and by how much each increases or decreases.

1. William Martin invests $150,000 to open his new company.

   Account: ___ASSETS 150,000___ ↑ or ↓ $ ___CASH 150000___

   Account: ___EQUITY 150,000___ ↑ or ↓ $ ___EQUITY 15000___

2. The company purchased a building for $65,000 cash, and furniture for $12,000 cash.

   Account: _____ ↑ or ↓ $ ___6___

   Account: _____ ↑ or ↓ $ _____

   Account: _____ ↑ or ↓ $ _____

3. The company earned revenue of $2,500 for services rendered. It is paid $1,500 now and is owed the remaining $1,000.

   Account: _____ ↑ or ↓ $ _____

   Account: _____ ↑ or ↓ $ _____

   Account: _____ ↑ or ↓ $ _____

4. The company purchased $4,500 of equipment on account.

   Account: _____ ↑ or ↓ $ _____

   Account: _____ ↑ or ↓ $ _____

5. The company paid $2,100 of the $4,500 due for the equipment.

Account: _____ ↑ or ↓ $ _____

Account: _____ ↑ or ↓ $ _____

6. The company paid $250 for telephone expenses.

Account: _____ ↑ or ↓ $ _____

Account: _____ ↑ or ↓ $ _____

7. The company paid $825 for weekly employee salaries.

Account: _____ ↑ or ↓ $ _____

Account: _____ ↑ or ↓ $ _____

8. The company is paid the remaining $1,000 owed from the previously rendered services.

Account: _____ ↑ or ↓ $ _____

Account: _____ ↑ or ↓ $ _____

9. The company purchased $600 of supplies on account.

Account: _____ ↑ or ↓ $ _____

Account: _____ ↑ or ↓ $ _____

10. William Martin withdrew $13,000 from the company for his own personal use.

Account: _____ ↑ or ↓ $ _____

Account: _____ ↑ or ↓ $ _____

PSA 1-7 RECORD TRANSACTIONS

Record the transactions and calculate the ending balances for each account.

Starting file: Use the Transactions Listing template file for this exercise. You'll use the templates more than once, so always save a copy of the template file with the exercise number as the filename. This keeps your files organized and retains a clean starting template for the next time you need it. (Remember, the exercise files are available for download at: boostyourskills.lablearning.com)

- Martin Johnson invests $425,000 to open his new appliance repair business.
- The company pays $150,000 for land and $70,000 for a building.
- Martin repairs appliances for three customers. Two of these paid cash totaling $825, while the third customer was billed $300 but has not yet paid.
- The company purchases radio advertisements for $3,000 cash.
- The company purchases a car for $23,000 by taking out a no-interest automobile loan.
- Martin repairs appliances for two customers, receiving a total of $500 in cash.
- The company makes its first automobile loan payment of $475.
- The company pays $350 for utilities expense.
- The company pays $2,000 for employee salaries.
- Martin withdraws $10,000 from the business.

Practice Set B

PSB 1-1 USE THE ACCOUNTING EQUATION

Determine the missing amounts.

1. Assets: $325,000. Liabilities: $92,000. Owner's Equity $X.
2. Assets: $49,000. Liabilities: $X. Owner's Equity $43,000.
3. Assets: $X. Liabilities: $32,000. Owner's Equity: $197,000.

PSB 1-2 DETERMINE ENDING ACCOUNTING EQUATION BALANCES

Determine the ending balances for assets, liabilities, and owner's equity. Remember to keep the accounting equation in balance.

1. **Beginning of year:**   Assets: $15,000   Liabilities: $4,000
   During the year: Assets: ↓ by $600   Liabilities: ↓ by $1,300

   Ending balances: _____ = _____ + _____

2. **Beginning of year:**   Liabilities: $28,500   Owner's Equity: $50,000
   During the year: Assets: ↓ by $9,200   Owner's Equity: ↑ by $1,350

   Ending balances: _____ = _____ + _____

3. **Beginning of year:**   Assets: $140,000   Owner's Equity: $99,000
   During the year: Liabilities: ↓ by $14,000 Owner's Equity: ↑ by $8,400

   Ending balances: _____ = _____ + _____

PSB 1-3 ADVANCED ACCOUNTING EQUATION WORK

For each scenario, examine two years of activity to determine the first year beginning balances for each accounting equation element.

1. Find the Year 1 beginning balances.

   • Assets: _____

   • Liabilities: _____

   • Owner's Equity: _____

End of Year 2	Assets: $61,000	Liabilities: $13,000
During Year 2	Assets: ↓ by $8,000	Liabilities: ↓ by $800
During Year 1	Liabilities: ↑ by $2,100	Owner's Equity: ↓ by $5,000

2. Find the Year 1 beginning balances.
   - Assets: _____
   - Liabilities: _____
   - Owner's Equity: _____

End of Year 2	Liabilities: $6,000	Owner's Equity: $24,000
During Year 2	Assets: ↓ by $3,200	Owner's Equity: ↑ by $200
During Year 1	Assets: ↑ by $6,300	Liabilities: ↑ by $4,100

3. Find the Year 1 beginning balances.
   - Assets: _____
   - Liabilities: _____
   - Owner's Equity: _____

End of Year 2	Assets: $188,200	Owner's Equity: $155,000
During Year 2	Liabilities: ↓ by $18,400	Owner's Equity: ↓ by $9,200
During Year 1	Assets: ↑ by $5,700	Owner's Equity: ↑ by $9,300

PSB 1-4 IDENTIFY THE ACCOUNT TYPE

Determine whether each account is an asset, liability, or owner's equity account.

	Asset	Liability	Owner's Equity
Wages Expenses			
Interest Revenue			
Land			
Loan Payable			
Samuel Collins, Drawing			
Utilities Expense			
Supplies			

PSB 1-5 DISTINGUISH BETWEEN DIFFERENT ACCOUNTS

Match the accounts with their descriptions.

_____ Accounts Payable

_____ Interest Expense

_____ John Doe, Drawing

_____ Utilities Expense

_____ Loans Payable

_____ Loans Receivable

_____ Notes Payable

_____ Rent Expense

_____ Telephone Expense

_____ Interest Revenue

A. Loans owed from another company

B. Cost incurred for renting an asset from another party

C. Interest earned by a company

D. Owner's withdrawal of assets in a period (month, year)

E. Costs incurred for the use of telephone service

F. Interest incurred on an amount owed by a company

G. Loans owed to another company

H. Monies owed to another company; interest bearing, associated with a formal, signed document

I. Monies owed in the short term to another company

J. Costs incurred for utilities such as electricity and water

PSB 1-6 DETERMINE THE IMPACT ON ACCOUNTS

Determine the accounts impacted by each transaction and by how much each increases or decreases.

1. Maximillian Smith invests $70,000 to open his new company.

   Account: _____ ↑ or ↓ $ _____
   Account: _____ ↑ or ↓ $ _____

2. The company purchased a truck for $32,000 cash.

   Account: _____ ↑ or ↓ $ _____
   Account: _____ ↑ or ↓ $ _____

3. Prior to performing any services, the company paid cash to purchase $2,400 of insurance for the first year of operations.

   Account: _____ ↑ or ↓ $ _____
   Account: _____ ↑ or ↓ $ _____

   Insurance purchased in advance of its use is an asset (it is valuable to a company) and is referred to as prepaid insurance.

4. Maximillian performed $1,100 of services and was paid in full.

   Account: _____ ↑ or ↓ $ _____
   Account: _____ ↑ or ↓ $ _____

5. The company paid $825 for office expenses.

   Account: _____ ↑ or ↓ $ _____
   Account: _____ ↑ or ↓ $ _____

6. Maximillian performed $1,400 of services. The customer paid for half of the services and owes the remainder.

Account: _____ ↑ or ↓ $ _____

Account: _____ ↑ or ↓ $ _____

Account: _____ ↑ or ↓ $ _____

7. The company paid $425 for employee wages.

Account: _____ ↑ or ↓ $ _____

Account: _____ ↑ or ↓ $ _____

8. The company received $300 of the amount owed for previously performed services.

Account: _____ ↑ or ↓ $ _____

Account: _____ ↑ or ↓ $ _____

9. The company purchased $2,200 of equipment on account.

Account: _____ ↑ or ↓ $ _____

Account: _____ ↑ or ↓ $ _____

10. Maximillian withdrew $1,000 from the company.

Account: _____ ↑ or ↓ $ _____

Account: _____ ↑ or ↓ $ _____

PSB 1-7 RECORD TRANSACTIONS

Record the transactions and calculate the ending balances for each account.

Starting file: Use the Transactions Listing template file.

- Katherine Johnson invests $200,000 to open her new antique shop.
- The company pays $35,000 for merchandise inventory.
- The company purchases supplies on account for $650.
- On its first day of operations, the company sells $1,850 of merchandise for cash. The cost of the merchandise sold is $775.
- The company pays off the full amount owed for the previously purchased supplies.
- The company pays $110 for telephone expense.
- On its second day of operations, the company sells $2,300 of merchandise for cash. The cost of the merchandise sold is $1,115.
- The company sells $6,200 of merchandise to a local business on account. The cost of the merchandise sold is $4,000.
- The company pays $1,250 for employee wages.
- Katherine withdraws $5,500 from the business.

2 The Accounting Cycle

For accounting information to be meaningful, it must be expressed over periods of time. For example, learning that a company earned $10,000 is not meaningful unless you know the period of time over which the revenue was generated. Following the series of steps collectively referred to as the accounting cycle ensures that all financial information is accurate. In this chapter, we introduce every step of the accounting cycle. As we progress through the course, we'll delve deeper into each.

LEARNING OBJECTIVES

▸ Explain the concept of posting journal entries

▸ Identify the purpose of a trial balance

▸ Distinguish between adjusting entries and closing entries

▸ Discuss the four primary financial statements

Project: Completing the First Month at Nathan's Donut School

You've been helping Nathaniel H. Spencer with the accounting for Nathan's Donut School over the past month. Nathaniel is excited about how many students have taken his culinary classes but doesn't know if the company has made any money during its first month of operations. He'd like to know how well his new business is performing and asks you to summarize the company's performance.

You recognize that gauging the company's performance involves more than examining individual transactions. You decide to spend some time reviewing the accounting cycle, which encompasses all these activities and includes completing all necessary postings, a trial balance, adjusting entries, closing entries, and four different financial statements.

NOTE! This chapter gives a broad overview of the accounting cycle. Don't be intimidated by all the details! In subsequent chapters, each stage will be broken down individually.

Step 1: Analyze Business Transactions

☁ **View the video "The Accounting Cycle."**

The first step in the accounting cycle is to analyze business transactions. The goal is to determine which accounts have been impacted, whether they have increased or decreased, and by what amount for each.

The accounting cycle contains seven stages and is typically completed monthly.

To properly analyze business transactions, a company must examine a variety of source documents. A **source document** provides information regarding one or more transactions and can take on many different forms. Here we discuss some of the most common source documents:

- An **invoice** is a bill for goods or services that summarizes the amounts owed from one party to another. When a company receives an invoice from an outside party, the invoice is analyzed to determine the accounts impacted and the amounts by which they have changed. Similarly, when an invoice is prepared by a company, it uses the information within the invoice when it records the associated sale or service.

- A **check** is a source document that provides information regarding payment that is received from a customer or made to a supplier.

- A **bank statement** is typically sent to a company by the bank for each bank account every month. The statement outlines all activity during the month and can include certain activities (such as the levying of bank fees) of which the company was not previously aware.

- A **purchase order** is prepared by the purchasing company and sent to the seller to indicate a desire to purchase items. The seller then uses the purchase order to prepare the goods for sale and as a source document for determining the accounts impacted by the sale.

- A **sales order** is prepared by the seller upon receipt of a purchase order. If requested, it can be furnished to the purchasing company, though it's primarily used as an internal document that verifies the seller's intent to accept the terms of the purchase order. Various departments, such as the shipping department and the billing department, use sales orders to complete key elements of the sale.

A **recurring entry** is an entry that's recorded in the same manner every accounting period. A recurring entry is initially recorded based on a single source document. When recorded again in a subsequent period, no additional source documents are typically required.

Ask Yourself 2-1: Which of these is NOT a source document?
- **A.** Recurring entry
- **B.** Check
- **C.** Sales order
- **D.** Invoice

CASE IN POINT 2-1

In this example, we will examine source documents that may impact a business. Source documents provide the information necessary to analyze a transaction, so it's important to understand their use.

1. What are three benefits of the source documents noted (invoice, check, bank statement, purchase order, sales order) not yet mentioned?

   Among the additional benefits of these source documents are that they provide evidence of transactions that can be used if a dispute arises. They also allow for convenient communication between a buyer and seller, particularly when source documents are sent electronically. Lastly, they can be saved and referred to as needed later.

2. Bank statements provide a great deal of information and serve as excellent source documents. Aside from bank fees, what information is conveyed via a bank statement?

   A bank statement is likely the first place a company learns of credit card fees that have been assessed. A bank error could also be identified on a bank statement. Additionally, bank statements indicate interest earned on the account and checks that have cleared a checking account, among other things.

3. The source documents noted are only a few of the many that can be used. What are some other source documents?

   Deposit slip: Verifies the date and amount of a deposit

   Receipt: Triggers the recording of a transaction in which goods are purchased

   Employee time card: Records wages earned by employees

Step 2: Record Journal Entries

After a transaction is analyzed, it's expressed as a journal entry. In the last chapter, you expressed the impact of a transaction by listing it within a chart structured around the accounting equation. Although this method works, it's not so much used in practice because the summary would be too large. Instead, journal entries are used (and are examined in detail in Chapter 3). As you'll see, journal entries provide a more concise method for expressing transactions.

3/1	Cash	35,000	
	Nathaniel H. Spencer, Capital		35,000
	Investment by owner		

Example journal entry

Generally Accepted Accounting Principles

Generally Accepted Accounting Principles (GAAP) are the rules used by public companies in the United States to prepare, present, and report financial statements. The standards must be followed when recording journal entries.

The **cost principle** dictates that every asset must be recorded at the amount paid for the item. If a business purchases office furniture for $750 but believes it is worth $1,100, it still must be recorded for the $750 cost.

The **time-period principle** dictates that accounting activity may be expressed over a specific period of time. To understand the benefit of this approach, imagine if revenue for the Disney Corporation were provided to investors from the time the corporation began (1923). This wouldn't provide useful information, because the revenue would have been earned over a century, whereas providing revenue over only the past year would give a far better picture of the company's recent performance.

> **TIP!** Financial information is most commonly conveyed over a year, quarter, or month.

The **revenue principle** dictates that revenue be recorded in the period in which it is earned. For example, if Nathan's Donut School caters the holiday party for a local business this year but is not paid until next year, the revenue must still be recorded this year.

The **matching principle** dictates that expenses be recorded in the same period as the revenue they generated, regardless of when cash is paid to satisfy these expenses. For example, if Nathan buys ingredients and supplies for the holiday party donuts, this expense must be recorded this year, even if he pays for the supplies next year.

Ask Yourself 2-2: Which principle dictates when expenses are recorded?
- **A.** Cost principle
- **B.** Time-period principle
- **C.** Revenue principle
- **D.** Matching principle

CASE IN POINT 2-2

In this example, we will answer a series of questions by applying the accounting principles just discussed.

1. Nathan purchases a piece of equipment at an auction for $12,000 that would cost $16,000 elsewhere. What amount does he use when recording the cost of the equipment and why?

   Per the cost principle, the equipment is recorded at the purchase price of $12,000. Actual market value is not taken into consideration when an asset is recorded on a company's books.

2. Near the end of last year, a moving company completed a cross-country move and charged the customer $6,500. The customer paid in January of this year. In what year does the moving company record the revenue?

   The revenue principle tells us that because the revenue was earned last year, it must be recorded last year. The year the money is received has no bearing on when the revenue is recorded.

3. A company is preparing to discuss its recent performance with a group of investors. What period of time should be used when conveying revenue information?

   We know from the time-period principle that accounting information must be expressed for periods of time. The company should use the period it believes will be most useful in making financial decisions, whether it is by month, quarter, or year.

4. On December 29 of last year, a company received a $125 telephone bill for services provided in November and December. The company pays the bill on January 8 of this year. In what year should the company record the telephone expense?

   Per the matching principle, because the expense was incurred in and helped to generate revenue last year, it must be recorded last year.

Step 3: Post Journal Entries

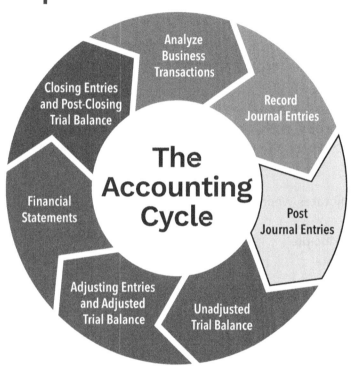

After all journal entries are recorded, the total account balances are determined. In the previous chapter we did this by adding together all amounts within each column. In practice, the method called **posting** is used to calculate these balances. With posting, each amount within a given journal entry is copied to a running total (called a T-account or T-chart) for its respective account. Once all amounts have been posted, the total balance for each account can be determined.

Cash			
$	35,000	$	20,000
$	850	$	1,500
$	300	$	250
		$	1,700
		$	400
$	12,300		

The **monetary unit principle** dictates that these balances can be used to express the performance of the company. Performance is expressed using account balances (shown in U.S. dollars) as of a given date, instead of writing lengthy descriptions for each activity.

> **TIP!** Companies outside of the United States can comply with the monetary unit principle by expressing financial information in the applicable local currency.

The **full disclosure principle** indicates that a public company (one for which shares of stock can be purchased by any outside investor) must disclose all pertinent information regarding the company's activity. This includes the company's financial performance and is why account balances must be accurately calculated at this stage of the accounting cycle.

Ask Yourself 2-3: The monetary unit principle dictates that a public company must disclose all pertinent information regarding the company's activity. True or false?

CASE IN POINT 2-3

In this example, we will continue our examination of vital accounting principles.

1. As he's summarizing the school's first year of operations, Nathaniel is writing a sentence or two to describe the activity and the accounts impacted. What do you tell him?

   According to the monetary unit principle, accounting activity is expressed in monetary terms. Describing the transactions is not enough; entries must be journalized and posted to quantify each account balance. This allows companies to be examined on an apples-to-apples (reasonably comparable) basis.

2. A company owner purchases a truck for $14,000. He's concerned that if he records the purchase in his accounting records, investors will look unfavorably on the company's current cash balance, so he decides to not record the transaction. Is this permissible? Why or why not?

   The full disclosure principle dictates that all activity for a company must be recorded. Failing to do so would result in financial documents that give an incomplete picture of the company's performance. The approach is not permissible; it could lead to legal action against the company.

   The cost principle is also violated in this instance, as the item is not being recorded at its original cost.

3. A company is being sued by a competitor for copyright infringement and will likely lose the lawsuit. Does the company have to disclose information about the lawsuit, per the full disclosure principle?

   Yes, the full disclosure principle tells us that all pertinent activity, including legal proceedings in which the company is unlikely to prevail, must be disclosed. No transactions are recorded in this instance, as the lawsuit is pending, but a note in which the likely resolution of the lawsuit is discussed should be included in the company's annual report.

Step 4: Unadjusted Trial Balance

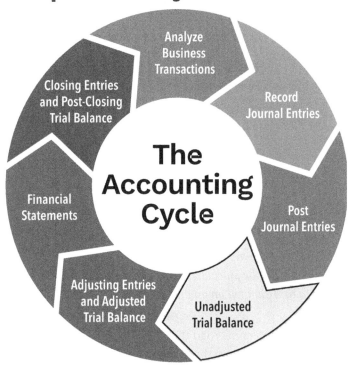

After posting is complete, an unadjusted trial balance is prepared. This financial report summarizes all account balances in one location and ensures all account balances have been correctly calculated. The incorrect calculation of an account balance can happen for various reasons, including:

- An amount was incorrectly copied from a source document.
- A transaction was recorded using the wrong account.
- Digits were transposed (such as $250 instead of $520).
- A transaction was omitted.
- A single transaction was recorded multiple times.

Even one instance of any of these errors can have a devastating impact on a company. And while an unadjusted trial balance can help you identify many errors, it won't necessarily uncover all mistakes.

> **WARNING!** Take care when recording transactions, as accuracy counts. And don't rely on your unadjusted trial balance to subsequently correct all errors.

Ask Yourself 2-4: Which of these is an example of a digit transposition?
- **A.** Recording $100 instead of $1,000
- **B.** Recording $860 instead of $680
- **C.** Recording $230 instead of $360
- **D.** Recording $740 instead of $370

Public companies are required to release an annual report summarizing the company's activity. Investors refer to annual reports when making investment decisions, so their accuracy is vital. In this example, we'll consider how a recording error could impact a company's books.

1. Errors are never desirable, and in relation to a company's accounting records, even a small error can be catastrophic. Consider why this is true and identify two ways in which an error could negatively impact a company.

   Companies make business decisions based on their financial position. If an error leads to the misstatement of an account balance, a poor business decision could result. An error could also lead an investor to believe the company is more or even less desirable as an investment than it is.

Step 5: Adjusting Entries and Adjusted Trial Balance

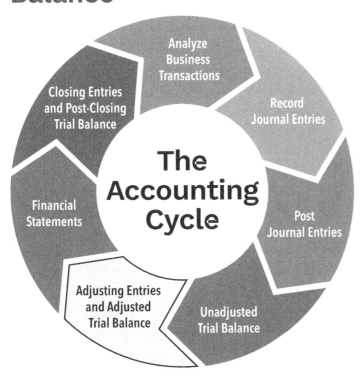

With certain types of transactions there's no obvious trigger that leads to the recording of a journal entry. A good example relates to the expense incurred when office supplies are used. It's not practical to record, say, every instance in which a pencil or a paper clip is used. However, when supplies are depleted and need to be replaced, supplies expense is incurred. We need a method to record this activity.

For such transactions, a company waits until the end of the period and then records an adjusting journal entry for each. Doing so ensures that the transactions are properly reflected on the books. After the adjusting journal entries have been recorded and posted, an adjusted trial balance is prepared. It's similar to the unadjusted trial balance, except that it includes the adjusting entries.

The reason most companies record adjusting journal entries is because they use the **accrual basis of accounting**. Under this method, revenue is recorded when it's earned and expenses are recorded when they're incurred, regardless of when cash changes hands. This is in keeping with the revenue and matching principles and is compliant with GAAP. If these companies were only required to record revenue and expense transactions when cash changes hands, the exchange of cash would trigger the recording of all these transactions and no adjusting entries would be required.

Some smaller companies find themselves in this exact circumstance because they can use the **cash basis of accounting**. Under this method, transactions are only recorded when cash changes hands, regardless of whether revenue has been earned or expenses incurred. As a result, these companies do not record any adjusting journal entries.

> **Ask Yourself 2-5:** A company just earned revenue but has not yet been paid, but it recorded the revenue on the books. What accounting method does the company use?
>
> **A.** Accrual basis
>
> **B.** Cash basis

CASE IN POINT 2-5

In this example, we'll examine four independent circumstances and determine whether each company is using the accrual or the cash basis of accounting.

1. CompuReady Corp. prepares two adjusting journal entries at the end of its first month of operations. Both entries record revenue earned but for which an invoice has not yet been sent.

   Since the invoice hasn't yet been sent, payment cannot have been received from the customer. An adjusting entry is being recorded prior to the receipt of cash, which means the accrual basis of accounting *is being used.*

2. InfoTech Inc. has experienced cash flow problems over the past few months. The company discussed this circumstance with its landlord, who agreed to accept the May rent at the end of June. InfoTech Inc. does not record an adjusting entry at the end of May to record rent expense, as it plans to record the expense when the payment is made.

   InfoTech Inc. does not record the expense when it is incurred but instead waits until payment is made. The cash basis of accounting *is being used.*

3. Legal Assistance Company performs services for a client in February. The company receives payment in March and at that time records a journal entry to account for the cash received and the revenue earned.

   The revenue earned by Legal Assistance Company was recorded after it was earned (when the cash was received). This approach is consistent with the cash basis of accounting.

4. Sewing Masters Inc. has been in business for more than two decades. It's dealt with many of the same companies for most of that time and is often permitted to pay for expenses after they are incurred. In October, the company incurs utilities expense and telephone expense, records journal entries for each, and does not make payment until November.

   The utilities and telephone expenses are recorded prior to payment being made. This is done when a company uses the accrual basis of accounting.

Step 6: Financial Statements

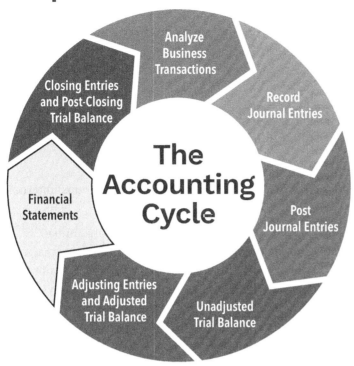

After the adjusting entries are recorded, four financial statements are prepared: the income statement, the statement of owner's equity, the balance sheet, and the statement of cash flows. These statements convey the performance of a company. Such information is valuable to external parties (loan officers, potential investors, etc.), just as it is to company owners themselves in making business decisions. Let's look at the details of these financial statements.

The **income statement** displays ending balances for all revenue and expense accounts. The final figure displayed is **net income**, which can be calculated by subtracting total expenses from total revenue. Essentially, the higher the net income, the better the performance of the company. (The term *net income* is used when revenue exceeds expenses. When expenses exceed revenue, the term *net loss* applies.)

The **statement of owner's equity** is a reconciliation that starts with the beginning owner's equity balance, displays all activity related to owner's equity, and concludes with the ending owner's equity balance. This statement effectively summarizes the activity related to owner's equity for a specific period. Among those items that can impact the owner's equity balance are net income or loss, an additional investment by the owner, and owner withdrawals. The net income or loss in this reconciliation is taken from the income statement. For this reason, the income statement is completed before the statement of owner's equity.

The **balance sheet** displays all asset, liability, and owner's equity account balances and shows that the accounting equation is in balance at the end of the period. The ending owner's equity balance in the balance sheet is taken from the statement of owner's equity, which means the statement of owner's equity is completed before the balance sheet.

> **NOTE!** All revenue and expense accounts are listed on the income statement, so there's no need to include them on the balance sheet.

The **statement of cash flows** summarizes the activities that led to the ending cash balance. As cash is the most important asset on a company's books, it's important to keep a close eye on where it comes from and how it is used. The statement of cash flows organizes transactions related to cash into one of three categories, based on the activity associated with the transaction. The statement concludes by displaying the beginning cash balance, the increase or decrease during the period, and the ending cash balance.

👀 A CLOSER LOOK

Who Uses the Financial Statements?

Many parties may use a company's financial statements, and these parties fall into two groups: internal users and external users.

Internal users work within the company, such as finance professionals (who may prepare annual budgets based on them), marketing professionals (who may gauge the success of marketing campaigns on the results within them), and internal auditors (who will examine the data within them to confirm its accuracy). **External users** work outside the company and may be potential investors (who review the statements to determine if the company would be a good investment), governmental agencies (who examine them to ensure that the company has complied with GAAP and all applicable laws), and potential lenders (who try to ensure that a potential loan could be repaid by reviewing them). Because so many different individuals rely on the financial statements, ensuring their accuracy is critical.

Ask Yourself 2-6: What financial statement displays all asset, liability, and owner's equity account balances?

    A. Income statement

    B. Statement of owner's equity

    C. Balance sheet

    D. Statement of cash flows

CASE IN POINT 2-6

In this example, we will identify on which financial statements certain accounts appear. As you'll see, some accounts appear on more than one statement.

1. Accounts Receivable

   This is an asset account and therefore appears on the balance sheet.

2. John Doe, Capital

   As this is an owner's equity account, it appears on the statement of owner's equity. *The ending John Doe, Capital balance also appears on the* balance sheet.

3. Rent Expense

   All expense and revenue accounts appear on the income statement.

4. Cash

   Cash is an asset account, so it appears on the balance sheet.

5. John Doe, Drawing

   We know that the statement of owner's equity *is a reconciliation that shows all activity related to owner's equity. Withdrawals reduce owner's equity, so this account appears on the reconciliation.*

6. Equipment

   Equipment is another asset account and therefore appears on the balance sheet.

7. Service Revenue

   The income statement *displays all revenue and expenses, including service revenue.*

8. Depreciation Expense

   All expenses, regardless of type, appear on the income statement.

Step 7: Closing Entries and the Post-Closing Trial Balance

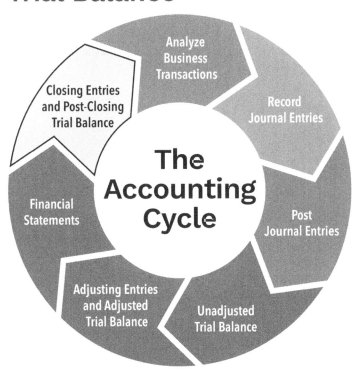

The final stage of the accounting cycle is the preparation of closing journal entries. Closing entries are designed to remove account balances from **temporary accounts**. Temporary accounts include all revenue, expense, and withdrawal accounts. These balances are ultimately transferred to the capital accounts. The closing process ensures that account balances provide pertinent information and that the impact of revenue, expenses, and withdrawals is reflected within the owner's capital accounts. An important result of the closing process is that the balances of the temporary accounts are reset to zero prior to the beginning of the next period.

Recall the example of the Disney Corporation. To understand the company's current position, would it be more beneficial to review total revenue and expenses for the last 100 years or just those for the most recent year? The most recent financial information will give you a far better understanding of the company's current position and its likelihood of being a good investment. That's why it makes sense to close all temporary accounts at the end of each period. When you do, the balances in the accounts revert to zero for the beginning of the subsequent period and you can use the running balance during that period to gauge only current-period activity.

Accounts not closed at the end of a period (asset, liability, and capital accounts) are referred to as **permanent accounts**. For these accounts, the ending balance for one year becomes the beginning balance for the next year. These permanent accounts are then included within the third trial balance that is prepared during the period, the post-closing trial balance.

| **TIP!**   The only accounts that appear on the balance sheet are permanent accounts.

Ask Yourself 2-7:   The ending balance in a temporary account for one year becomes the beginning balance for the next year. True or false?

CASE IN POINT 2-7

In this example, we will determine whether each account is a temporary or permanent account.

1. Furniture

   This is an asset account for which a running balance that extends from one period to the next is beneficial. As a result, this is a permanent account.

2. Sales Revenue

   All revenue accounts are temporary accounts.

3. Utilities Expense

   All expense accounts are temporary accounts.

4. Accounts Payable

   This is a liability account and therefore is a permanent account.

5. Salaries Expense

   All expense accounts are temporary accounts.

6. John Doe, Drawing

   Similar to revenue and expense accounts, all withdrawal accounts are temporary accounts.

7. John Doe, Capital

   This is an owner's equity account and therefore is a permanent account.

8. Cash

   This is an asset account and therefore is a permanent account.

Self-Assessment

Now it's time for you to check your knowledge of the key concepts and skills introduced in this chapter.

1. Bank statements are typically provided to bank account holders monthly. *True False*

2. The first stage of the accounting cycle is to analyze business transactions. *True False*

3. Complying with GAAP is optional when recording journal entries. *True False*

4. The revenue principle dictates that revenue must be recorded in the same period the cash payment is received. *True False*

5. As part of the accounting cycle, three trial balances are completed. *True False*

6. You prepare the unadjusted trial balance before posting journal entries. *True False*

7. A benefit of the unadjusted trial balance is that it identifies all errors made during the period. *True False*

8. Adjusting entries are associated with the accrual basis of accounting. *True False*

9. The final figure on the income statement is net income (or net loss). *True False*

10. The balance sheet is a reconciliation that displays all activity related to owner's equity. *True False*

11. What is NOT considered a source document?
    A. A transaction
    B. A check
    C. A bank statement
    D. A deposit slip

12. What's the first step of the accounting cycle?
    A. Record the journal entries
    B. Prepare the unadjusted trial balance
    C. Analyze the transactions
    D. Create the financial statements

13. Which principle requires expenses are recorded in the same period the revenue is generated?
    A. Time-period principle
    B. Cost principle
    C. Matching principle
    D. Full-disclosure principle

14. Which of these is NOT a financial statement?
    A. A balance sheet
    B. A statement of owner's equity
    C. A statement of cash flows
    D. A post-closing trial balance

15. Which statement describes a sales order?

    A. It's sent by the bank to the company and outlines all activity during the month.

    B. It provides information regarding a payment received from a customer or made to a supplier.

    C. Prepared by the purchasing company, it indicates a desire to purchase items from a seller.

    D. Prepared by a seller upon receipt of a purchase order, it verifies the seller's intent to accept the terms of the purchase order.

16. What is a recurring entry?

    A. An infrequent entry

    B. A type of entry that's recorded differently every accounting period

    C. One that is recorded in the same manner every accounting period

    D. An entry that requires a new source document each time it's recorded

17. Which principle dictates that accounting activity may be expressed over a specific period?

    A. Cost principle

    B. Time-period principle

    C. Full disclosure principle

    D. Matching principle

18. What's something the unadjusted trial balance CANNOT do?

    A. Help confirm account balances are correctly calculated

    B. Summarize account balances in one location

    C. Identify all potential errors

    D. Locate transposition errors (such as $123 instead of $132)

19. Under the accrual basis of accounting, _____ is recorded when earned and expenses are recorded when _____.

20. Which account would appear on a balance sheet?

    A. Sales Revenue

    B. Equipment

    C. Utilities Expense

    D. Service Revenue

Putting It Together

PIT 2-1 EXAMINE THE ACCOUNTING CYCLE

In this example, we'll identify the reason Amber's Lacrosse Emporium benefits from undertaking each stage of the accounting cycle.

1. Analyze Business Transactions

   This stage allows Amber's Lacrosse Emporium to view its business performance as a series of individual activities. By viewing its performance in this manner, Amber's Lacrosse Emporium is able to subsequently quantify and record these activities.

2. Record Journal Entries

   This stage allows Amber's Lacrosse Emporium to express its business transactions in a standardized manner. Not only does this allow the company to compare apples to apples when considering various transactions, but it also ensures its activities will be expressed in the same manner as other businesses' activities.

3. Post Journal Entries

   This stage allows Amber's Lacrosse Emporium to view its business performance on an account-by-account basis. Completion of this stage allows for subsequent comparisons to be made between the current period performance of Amber's Lacrosse Emporium and a competitor's performance. Comparisons can also be made to the company's own prior periods.

4. Unadjusted Trial Balance

   This stage for Amber's Lacrosse Emporium facilitates the comparison of account balances by summarizing them in one location.

5. Adjusting Entries and Adjusted Trial Balance

   The purpose of this stage is to account for all transactions of Amber's Lacrosse Emporium that occurred during the period, including those for which there was no overt trigger. These transactions must be recorded in order to ensure that the company's records are entirely accurate. This results in the subsequent development of accurate financial statements.

6. Financial Statements

   This stage conveys individual account balances in the most useful format. Business decisions for Amber's Lacrosse Emporium can be made based on the information conveyed within the results of this stage.

7. Closing Entries and Post-Closing Trial Balance

   This stage ensures that the balance within all temporary accounts for Amber's Lacrosse Emporium is reduced to zero prior to the beginning of the subsequent period. This stage is beneficial because it results in revenue, expense, and withdrawal accounts only displaying the current period's activity at any given time.

Practice Set A

PSA 2-1 EXAMINE THE ACCOUNTING CYCLE

Organize the seven stages of the accounting cycle in the proper order. Memorization of the accounting cycle will be beneficial as you proceed through the rest of this course. Try to complete this exercise without referring to the chapter discussion.

_____ Prepare the financial statements

_____ Post the journal entries

_____ Record the journal entries

_____ Record adjusting journal entries and prepare the adjusted trial balance

_____ Analyze the business transactions

_____ Complete the closing entries and the post-closing trial balance

_____ Prepare the unadjusted trial balance

PSA 2-2 IDENTIFY ACCOUNTING PRINCIPLES

Connect each accounting principle to its best match.

Time-period principle   Record revenue in the period it is earned.

Monetary unit principle   Report accounting activity over a standard period of time.

Revenue principle   Record expenses in the same period as the revenue they generate.

Matching principle   Express accounting activity in dollars or another unit of currency.

PSA 2-3 REVIEW ACCOUNT PLACEMENT WITHIN FINANCIAL STATEMENTS

Indicate whether each account is temporary or permanent and which financial statement it appears on.

	Account Type		Financial Statement		
Wages Payable	Temporary	Permanent	Income statement	Statement of owner's equity	Balance sheet
Supplies	Temporary	Permanent	Income statement	Statement of owner's equity	Balance sheet
Insurance Expense	Temporary	Permanent	Income statement	Statement of owner's equity	Balance sheet
John Doe, Drawing	Temporary	Permanent	Income statement	Statement of owner's equity	Balance sheet
Interest Revenue	Temporary	Permanent	Income statement	Statement of owner's equity	Balance sheet

PSA 2-4 CONSIDER THE PURPOSE OF FINANCIAL STATEMENTS

Match the financial statements to the primary reason for completing each.

Income statement   To show assets equal liabilities plus owner's equity at period end

Statement of owner's equity   To illustrate the sources and uses of cash during a period

Balance sheet   To determine the net income or loss for a period

Statement of cash flows   To reconcile beginning and ending owner's capital account balances over a period

Practice Set B

PSB 2-1 EXAMINE THE ACCOUNTING CYCLE

Arrange the descriptions of the seven stages of the accounting cycle into the proper order.

_____ Complete the four financial statements to convey company performance.

_____ Transfer journal entry information to the ledger to determine account balances.

_____ Record any accounting activity prior to year end for which there was no trigger to record it earlier.

_____ Convey accounting information such that temporary account balances are reset to $0.

_____ Determine the accounts impacted, if they increased or decreased, and by how much.

_____ Summarize account balances and confirm that debit balances equal credit balances.

_____ Express the company's accounting activity in a manner that can be interpreted universally.

PSB 2-2 IDENTIFY ACCOUNTING PRINCIPLES

Connect each accounting principle to its best match.

Cost principle

Matching principle

Full disclosure principle

Time-period principle

Record expenses in the same period as the revenue they generate.

Report accounting activity over a standard period of time.

Record purchased assets at the actual cost to the business.

Convey all activity that could meaningfully impact potential investors.

PSB 2-3 REVIEW ACCOUNT PLACEMENT WITHIN FINANCIAL STATEMENTS

Indicate whether each account is temporary or permanent and which financial statement it appears on. (Hint: One account appears on more than one statement.)

	Account Type		Financial Statement		
Office Expense	Temporary	Permanent	Income statement	Statement of owner's equity	Balance sheet
Rent Revenue	Temporary	Permanent	Income statement	Statement of owner's equity	Balance sheet
Accounts Receivable	Temporary	Permanent	Income statement	Statement of owner's equity	Balance sheet
John Doe, Capital	Temporary	Permanent	Income statement	Statement of owner's equity	Balance sheet
Land	Temporary	Permanent	Income statement	Statement of owner's equity	Balance sheet

PSB 2-4 CONSIDER THE PURPOSE OF FINANCIAL STATEMENTS

Match each financial statement to the best description of its concluding figure and the information conveyed within it.

Income statement

Statement of owner's equity

Balance sheet

Statement of cash flows

Ending owner's capital account; portion of assets an owner can claim as of the end of a period

Ending cash balance and how the company arrived at this balance

Net income or loss; expresses the performance of a business over a period of time

Total assets and total liabilities plus owner's equity; shows a balanced accounting equation at the end of a period

3 Journal Entries and T-Accounts

Efficiency is one of the most important skills an accountant can learn. Consider our process thus far, which involves listing the impact of transactions on individual rows. This is certainly an effective recording method, but it's not very efficient. As an alternative, companies will record journal entries and then post the components of those entries to a ledger. In this chapter, you will learn about debits and credits, and how these impact the transaction-recording process.

LEARNING OBJECTIVES

▸ Distinguish between debits and credits

▸ Work with T-accounts

▸ Journalize a transaction

▸ Post a transaction

▸ Use a special journal and a subsidiary ledger

Project: Recording the First Month's Transactions

Now that you've given Nathaniel an understanding of the entire accounting cycle, you both agree that a more efficient method of recording transactions would be beneficial. He asks you to provide a formal listing of all transactions related to Nathan's Donut School for the first month of operations. You already have a listing, but it's relatively informal. You start by examining the role of debits and credits. You then learn how T-accounts can be used to visually convey the impact of a transaction. After practicing recording several journal entries, you finish by reviewing special journals and subsidiary ledgers, which are used to summarize account details for specific companies with which Nathan's Donut School does business.

The Accounting Cycle

In this chapter, we'll cover two stages of the accounting cycle—steps 2 and 3—as we see how using journal entries is an efficient method for recording journal entries.

3/1	Cash	35,000	
	Nathaniel H. Spencer, Capital		35,000
	Investment by owner		
3/2	Equipment	20,000	
	Cash		20,000
	Purchase of equipment for cash		
3/4	Supplies	500	
	Furniture	1,000	
	Accounts Payable		1,500
	Purchase of supplies and equipment on account		

Debits and Credits

🔊 **View the video "Debits and Credits."**

The method for recording transactions you practiced in the first chapter, although effective, is not used by most businesses. A more efficient process is to record a **journal entry** for each transaction.

3/1	Cash	35,000	
	Nathaniel H. Spencer, Capital		35,000
	Investment by owner		

A journal entry lists the accounts impacted and the amount by which each account has changed.

Per transaction, a journal entry must contain at least one debited account and one credited account, and remember that debits must equal credits. In the example above, it's easy to see which accounts are impacted (Cash and Nathaniel H. Spencer, Capital). Can you also tell whether each account increased or decreased?

You can by looking at whether a **debit** or **credit** is being booked. We know that Cash is being debited because it's listed at the top. We also know that Nathaniel H. Spencer, Capital is being credited because it's listed at the bottom of the journal entry (after the debit) and is indented.

When a journal entry contains multiple debits, each is listed on an individual row at the top. Similarly, multiple credits are listed individually after the debits, each indented once.

You may be wondering how to determine the impact of a debit or credit on an individual account. It's a matter of memorizing some rules. For example, when a transaction results in an asset increasing, you would convey this by debiting the asset. Conversely, to convey that an asset decreases, you would credit the asset. Review and challenge yourself to memorize the following table. It summarizes the impact of a debit and credit on each type of account.

> **TIP!** While it may initially seem daunting, take the time to memorize the table as soon as possible. It'll make the upcoming work much easier.

IMPACT OF DEBITS AND CREDITS ON ACCOUNT TYPES

Account Type	Debit	Credit
Asset	↑ Increase	↓ Decrease
Liability	↓ Decrease	↑ Increase
Capital	↓ Decrease	↑ Increase
Withdrawal	↑ Increase	↓ Decrease
Revenue	↓ Decrease	↑ Increase
Expense	↑ Increase	↓ Decrease

Evaluating a Transaction—Enhanced!

Remember the three-step process for analyzing transactions? It consists of determining which accounts are impacted, by how much, and whether each increases or decreases. Now that you understand a bit about debits and credits, we can enhance that process:

1. Determine which accounts are impacted.
2. Determine whether the balance in each account increases or decreases.
3. Determine by how much each account is debited or credited based on whether the account is an asset, liability, capital, withdrawal, revenue, or expense account.

Ask Yourself 3-1: When recording a journal entry for the purchase of supplies, do I indent the debit or the credit?

    A. Debit

    B. Credit

⚆⚆ A CLOSER LOOK

Where Have I Seen "Debit" and "Credit" Before?

Many beginning accounting students are confused by the terms *debit* and *credit,* possibly due to how these terms are used in a common banking context. A *debit* card, for example, is used to spend money in your account. A bank error in your favor would *credit* your account. The impact rules we just looked at seem to work backward from this. You might be asking yourself why the rules dictate that a credit *decreases* the Cash account (an asset), while a credit to your personal bank account *increases* the balance.

It's all about perspective. For example, when you receive a credit in your account from the bank, your balance certainly increases. The bank's cash balance also decreases, and recall that a credit decreases an asset. The easiest way to overcome any potential confusion is to view these terms as entirely new; don't even think about how you've used them previously. In other words, don't search for reasons why a debit or credit has the impact indicated in the table. Just memorize the rules.

A good analogy relates to traffic signals. Think about why we proceed at a green light and stop at a red light. Is there some deep philosophical reason? No, it's just how the system works. Debits and credits operate in much the same way. The rules apply simply because it's how accounting functions.

CASE IN POINT 3-1

In this example, we'll record journal entries for multiple transactions for Nathan's Donut School.

1. On March 1, Nathaniel invests $35,000 to open Nathan's Donut School.

3/1	Cash	35,000	
	Nathaniel H. Spencer, Capital		35,000
	Investment by owner		

   The date is displayed to the left of the first debited account, and a brief explanation in italics is added below the final credited account.

2. On March 2, Nathan's Donut School pays $20,000 for baking equipment.

3/2	Equipment	20,000	
	Cash		20,000
	Purchase of equipment for cash		

   The credit to Cash indicates that the account has decreased, which is why the associated $20,000 is not displayed as a negative amount. All figures in journal entries are displayed as positive amounts.

3. On March 4, the company purchases $500 of supplies and $1,000 of furniture from Office Place on account.

3/4	Supplies	500	
	Furniture	1,000	
	Accounts Payable		1,500
	Purchase of supplies and furniture on account		

This journal entry contains multiple debits. Journal entries with more than one debit are referred to as compound journal entries.

*The previous two transactions included the purchase of a **fixed asset**, which is an asset expected to be held for more than 12 months. If a fixed asset is sold instead of purchased, the fixed asset is credited (to reduce its balance) and Cash (if cash is received) or Accounts Receivable (if payment will be made later) is debited. In either case, when a fixed asset is sold there's no impact on the accounting equation because assets increase (Cash or Accounts Receivable) and decrease (fixed asset account) by the same amount.*

4. On March 7, Nathan's Donut School opens for business and earns $850 cash.

3/7	Cash	850	
	Service Revenue		850
	Cooking classes provided for cash		

All $850 in earnings increase the cash balance, which is why Cash is debited here.

Because Nathan's Donut School provides a service to its customers, it uses the Service Revenue account to record its revenue. Other types of revenue, such as interest or royalties, are recorded in the same manner. When these types of revenue are earned, their respective accounts (Interest Revenue, Royalty Revenue) are increased via a credit, thereby increasing total equity in the accounting equation.

5. On March 12, the company pays off the $1,500 that was owed from the purchase of supplies and furniture.

3/12	Accounts Payable	1,500	
	Cash		1,500
	Payment of accounts payable		

In this transaction, cash was paid to satisfy an account payable. The payment of other types of liabilities is recorded similarly. For example, if a company pays off a loan it will debit Loans Payable, and if it repays the principle owed on a bond it will debit Bonds Payable. Any payment of an amount owed results in a debit to the associated liability account, which thereby reduces total liabilities within the accounting equation.

6. On March 13, Nathan's Donut School earns $2,500 on account from SportCo.

3/13	Accounts Receivable	2,500	
	Service Revenue		2,500
	Cooking classes provided on account		

7. On March 18, the company purchases advertising in local newspapers for $250.

3/18	Advertising Expense	250	
	Cash		250
	Payment of advertising expenses		

8. On March 21, the company receives $300 on account in partial payment from SportCo (3/13 transaction).

3/21	Cash	300	
	Accounts Receivable		300
	Receipt of cash owed from prior sale		

The revenue for these cooking classes was recorded on March 13, when it was earned. Now that partial payment is being received, the Accounts Receivable account (amount owed to Nathan's Donut School) is reduced (credited).

9. On March 30, Nathan's Donut School pays rent of $1,700 for the current month.

3/30	Rent Expense	1,700	
	Cash		1,700
	Payment of rent expense		

10. On March 31, Nathaniel withdraws $400 from the business for his personal use.

3/31	Nathaniel H. Spencer, Drawing	400	
	Cash		400
	Withdrawal of cash by owner		

T-Accounts

🎬 **View the video "T-Accounts."**

As we've been discussing debits and credits, you may have noticed there's been no mention of how to determine final balances for each account. After booking journal entries, the next process is posting, which is necessary to calculate these balances. Posting transfers amounts in a journal entry to each account's respective **T-account**, which is a visual representation of the activity in a single account.

In a T-account, enter the account name on the top, account debits on the left side, and account credits on the right side. A debit in a journal entry will always be transferred to the debit (left) side of the appropriate T-account, while a credit will always be transferred to the credit (right) side of the appropriate T-account.

Account Name	
Debit side	Credit side

Debit and credit rules dictate that T-accounts operate as shown here:

			Owner's Equity					
	Assets			**Capital**			**Withdrawals**	
Debit		Credit	Debit		Credit	Debit		Credit
+		–	–		+	+		–
	Liabilities			**Revenue**			**Expenses**	
Debit		Credit	Debit		Credit	Debit		Credit
–		+	–		+	+		–

A T-account holds all activity within a single account for a given period. This allows for an easy way to calculate the ending balance for an account in one convenient location.

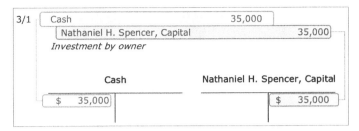

The posting process copies amounts from journal entries to the individual T-accounts.

To determine the ending balance for an account, first add all amounts on the debit side and then add all amounts on the credit side. Lastly, subtract the smaller amount from the larger amount and place the resulting figure on the side with the larger amount.

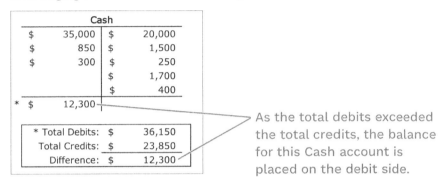

As the total debits exceeded the total credits, the balance for this Cash account is placed on the debit side.

We typically expect to see account balances on the account's **normal balance** side. This is the side on which the account increases. In the case of the Cash account in this example, since cash is an asset, and assets increase on the debit side, this is where the balance usually lies. Therefore, the normal balance side is the debit side.

Ask Yourself 3-2: The right side of the T-account is the debit side. True or false?

Do Companies Really Use T-Accounts?

Although helpful, T-accounts are not used as part of the formal accounting process. Instead, companies commonly use the **balance column format**. This format conveys the same information as a T-account but in a more streamlined manner that shows more information.

Cash				
Date	Explanation	Debit	Credit	Balance
3/1		$ 35,000		$ 35,000
3/2			$ 20,000	$ 15,000
3/7		$ 850		$ 15,850
3/12			$ 1,500	$ 14,350
3/18			$ 250	$ 14,100
3/21		$ 300		$ 14,400
3/30			$ 1,700	$ 12,700
3/31			$ 400	$ 12,300

Here we use the balance column format to calculate the same balance as in the previous T-account.

There are two reasons to use T-accounts when explaining the posting process. First, students typically find it easier to understand how to complete postings and the impact posting has on an account by examining the T-account. Second, companies today use computerized accounting systems that automatically calculate ending balances without the user needing to manually complete the posting process, so students are unlikely to manually use the balance column format in a professional setting.

CASE IN POINT 3-2

In this example, we'll post the transactions we journalized to the T-accounts in Case in Point 3-1.

1. On March 1, Nathaniel invests $35,000 to open Nathan's Donut School.

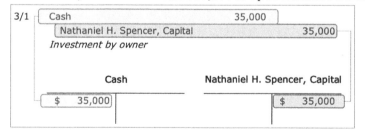

The journal entry was created in Case in Point 3-1. To post the two amounts in the journal entry, we first create T-accounts for the impacted accounts (Cash and Nathaniel H. Spencer, Capital). We then post, or transfer, the amounts from the journal entry to the T-accounts. We move all debits in the journal entry to the left (debit) side and all credits to the right (credit) side of the corresponding T-accounts.

2. On March 2, Nathan's Donut School pays $20,000 for baking equipment.

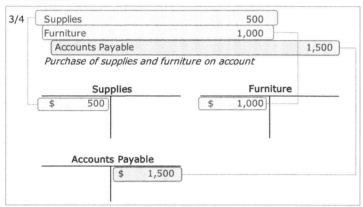

Remember, the $35,000 debit to Cash was established in the March 1 transaction.

3. On March 4, the company purchases $500 of supplies and $1,000 of furniture from Office Place on account.

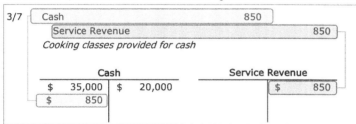

4. On March 7, Nathan's Donut School opens for business and earns $850 cash.

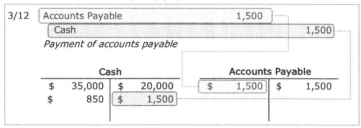

5. On March 12, the company pays off the $1,500 owed from the purchase of supplies and furniture.

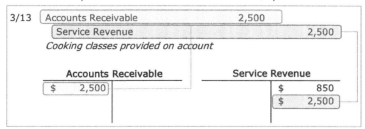

When the debt is paid in this journal entry, neither the Supplies nor the Furniture accounts are impacted.

6. On March 13, Nathan's Donut School earns $2,500 on account from SportCo.

7. On March 18, the company purchases advertising in local newspapers for $250.

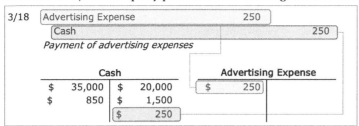

8. On March 21, the company receives $300 on account in partial payment from SportCo (3/13 transaction).

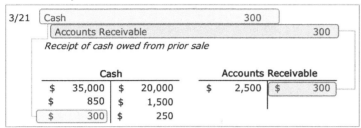

9. On March 30, Nathan's Donut School pays rent of $1,700 for the month.

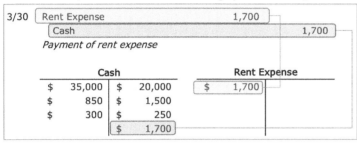

10. On March 31, Nathaniel withdraws $400 from the business for his personal use.

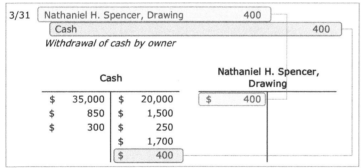

11. Based on the above transactions, here are the ending balances for each account:

Cash		Accounts Receivable		Supplies		Furniture	
$ 35,000	$ 20,000	$ 2,500	$ 300	$ 500		$ 1,000	
$ 850	$ 1,500						
$ 300	$ 250						
	$ 1,700						
	$ 400						
$ 12,300		$ 2,200		$ 500		$ 1,000	

Equipment		Accounts Payable		Nathaniel H. Spencer, Capital		Nathaniel H. Spencer, Drawing	
$ 20,000		$ 1,500	$ 1,500		$ 35,000	$ 400	
$ 20,000			$ -		$ 35,000	$ 400	

Service Revenue		Advertising Expense		Rent Expense	
	$ 850	$ 250		$ 1,700	
	$ 2,500				
	$ 3,350	$ 250		$ 1,700	

To determine ending balances, for every T-account, calculate the total for each side, subtract the smaller amount from the larger one, and place the result on the side with the larger amount. For example, to determine the ending Cash balance, first add all amounts on the debit side ($36,150) and then add all amounts on the credit side ($23,850). Subtract the smaller amount from the larger to arrive at the ending balance: $36,150 – $23,850 = $12,300

The balance is recorded on the debit side of the T-account, as this side has a larger amount.

General and Special Journals

Based on the type of transaction, you may need to book (or record) an entry on a journal that displays all transactions of that specific type. This is helpful for reviewing business activity, and a company can tailor a **special journal** to their own specific needs.

JOURNAL TYPES AND ACTIVITY	
Special Journal	**Displays Transactions...**
Cash receipts journal	in which cash is received
Cash payments journal	in which cash is paid out
Revenue journal	in which revenue is earned on account (accounts receivable)
Purchases journal	in which purchases are made on account (accounts payable)
General journal	that don't fit in the preceding journals

Because each special journal is designed to contain the same type of information, they each can take on a more streamlined appearance. As you review the following examples, you'll notice the abbreviations Cr. (credit) and Dr. (debit). These are common abbreviations used in accounting.

> **NOTE!** The general journal displays entries in the standard manner you learned earlier in the chapter, so there's no example here.

		Cash Receipts Journal			
Date	Account Credited	Accounts Receivable Cr.	Service Revenue Cr.	Other Accounts Cr.	Cash Dr.
3/21	SportCo	300			300

This journal for cash receipts displays the partial payment received from SportCo. Commonly credited accounts (Accounts Receivable and Service Revenue here) have a designated column. Any amounts credited to other accounts are recorded in the Other Accounts Cr. column.

		Cash Payments Journal			
Date	Account Debited	Other Accounts Dr.	Accounts Payable Dr.	Supplies Dr.	Cash Cr.
3/2	Equipment	20,000			20,000

This cash payments journal shows the purchase of equipment with cash.

	Revenue Journal	
Date	Account Debited	Accounts Receivable Dr. & Service Revenue Cr.
3/13	SportCo	2,500

This revenue journal shows revenue earned from SportCo on account.

		Purchases Journal			
Date	Account Credited	Merchandise Inventory Dr.	Supplies Dr.	Account Debited	Other Accounts Dr.
3/4	Office Place		500	Furniture	1,000

This purchases journal shows the purchase of supplies and furniture from Office Place on account.

Ask Yourself 3-3: Which journal records the purchase of equipment for cash?
A. Cash receipts journal
B. Cash payments journal
C. Revenue journal
D. Purchases journal

CASE IN POINT 3-3

In this example, we will identify which special journal each transaction should be recorded in.

1. Purchase of equipment for cash.

   Because cash was paid to make this purchase, the transaction would be recorded in a cash payments journal.

2. A service is provided to a client, who pays in full.

   Cash was received in this transaction, so it would be recorded in a cash receipts journal.

3. A sale is made to a customer on account.

   In this transaction, revenue was earned, but the customer did not yet pay. This type of transaction is recorded in a revenue journal.

4. A withdrawal of cash is made by the owner.

   As cash is being paid to the owner, this transaction is recorded in a cash payments journal.

5. An expense is recorded for the portion of prepaid insurance that has been used up at the end of the month.

   This transaction does not fit in any of the four specialized journals and therefore is recorded in a general journal.

6. Purchase of supplies on account.

   In this transaction, a purchase was made but no cash was paid out. This type of transaction is recorded in a purchases journal.

7. Purchase of office furniture for which seller agrees to accept payment later.

   This circumstance is identical to buying office furniture "on account." When we make a purchase on account, the transaction is recorded in a purchases journal.

8. Cash is received from a customer as a down payment, prior to any services being provided.

   Although the revenue has not yet been earned, the cash was received, and therefore the transaction is recorded in a cash receipts journal.

9. Services are provided to a client, who is given 30 days to remit payment.

   In this transaction, revenue was earned but payment was not received. This type of transaction is recorded in a revenue journal.

10. You realize that you incorrectly increased the Rent Expense account instead of Utilities Expense on a past journal entry. You record a new journal entry to correct the error.

    There is no special journal in which this transaction would fit, so the correction is recorded in a general journal.

General and Subsidiary Ledgers

View the video "General and Subsidiary Ledgers."

Just as journal entries are entered in different journals, T-accounts are contained within ledgers. Most T-accounts are found in the **general ledger**. There are two other ledgers that play a prominent role in recording transactions:

- **Accounts receivable subsidiary ledger**
  - Contains an individual accounts receivable T-account for each company that purchases goods or services on account from a business
  - Associated with the revenue and cash receipts journals

- **Accounts payable subsidiary ledger**
  - Contains an individual accounts payable T-account for each company from which a business purchases goods or services on account
  - Associated with the purchases and cash payments journals

The general ledger contains a **control account** for accounts receivable and accounts payable that displays the total balance across the entire business. The subsidiary ledgers hold multiple versions of each of these T-accounts in which details related to specific outside companies can be examined.

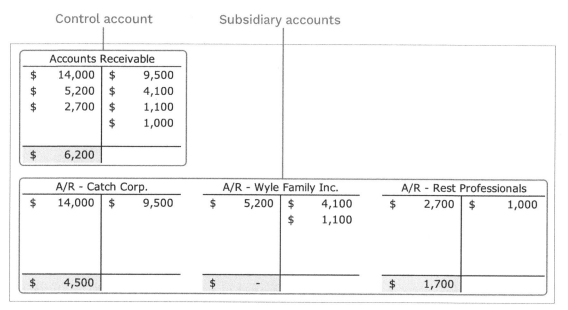

The subsidiary ledger account balances, when added together, equal the total within the general ledger control account ($4,500 + $0 + $1,700 = $6,200).

Ask Yourself 3-4: Control accounts are found in the general ledger. True or false?

CASE IN POINT 3-4

In this example, we will record a journal entry for each transaction and post to the general ledger and accounts payable subsidiary ledger. We'll then determine all applicable accounts payable balances.

1. On Sept. 2, furniture is purchased for $4,350 from Hickory Company on account.

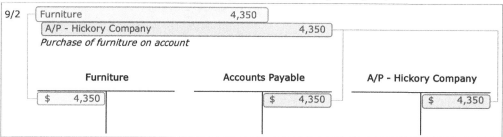

As the furniture is purchased on account, this journal entry debits Furniture and credits A/P - Hickory Company for $4,350. The amount is posted to the general ledger accounts (Furniture, Accounts Payable) and the applicable subsidiary ledger account, which in this instance is A/P - Hickory Company.

2. On Sept. 8, office equipment is purchased for $7,700 from Offices Direct on account.

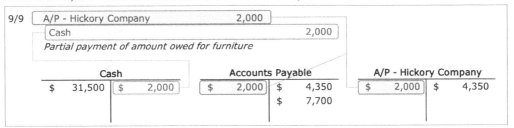

3. On Sept. 9, $2,000 is paid in partial payment for the furniture (9/2 transaction). Prior to this transaction, the Cash account had a balance of $31,500.

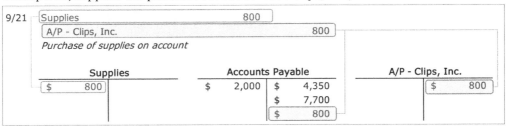

4. On Sept. 21, supplies are purchased for $800 from Clips, Inc., on account.

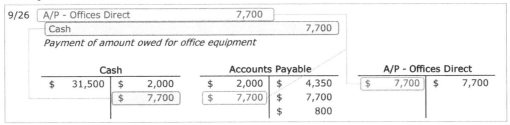

5. On Sept. 26, the entire amount owed to Offices Direct for the office equipment is paid.

9/26	A/P - Offices Direct		7,700		
	Cash			7,700	
	Payment of amount owed for office equipment				

Cash			Accounts Payable			A/P - Offices Direct		
$ 31,500	$ 2,000		$ 2,000	$ 4,350		$ 7,700	$ 7,700	
	$ 7,700		$ 7,700	$ 7,700				
				$ 800				

6. Here are the ending balances for the Accounts Payable control account and its three subsidiary accounts:

Accounts Payable	
$ 2,000	$ 4,350
$ 7,700	$ 7,700
	$ 800
	$ 3,150

A/P - Hickory Company		A/P - Offices Direct		A/P - Clips, Inc.	
$ 2,000	$ 4,350	$ 7,700	$ 7,700		$ 800
$ 2,350		$ -			$ 800

Of course, the sum of the subsidiary accounts ($2,350 + $0 + $800) equals the total in the control account ($3,150).

Self-Assessment

Now it's time for you to check your knowledge of the key concepts and skills introduced in this chapter.

1. An increase to an asset account is conveyed by crediting the account. *True False*

2. Every journal entry must contain at least one debit and one credit. *True False*

3. The right side of a T-account is the credit side. *True False*

4. T-accounts display all activity over a period for a single account. *True False*

5. The debit side of every T-account is the normal balance side. *True False*

6. Journal entries in which cash is paid are recorded in the purchases journal. *True False*

7. When using special journals, there's no need to record transactions in the general journal. *True False*

8. The abbreviation for debit is Dr. *True False*

9. Control accounts are contained within subsidiary ledgers. *True False*

10. The accounts payable subsidiary ledger contains individual T-accounts for each company from which a business has made purchases on account. *True False*

11. A credit increases liability, capital, and _____ accounts.

12. For which account is the debit side the normal balance side?
    A. Accounts Payable
    B. John Doe, Capital
    C. Sales Revenue
    D. Land

13. Which of these is NOT a special journal?
    A. Cash payments journal
    B. Revenue journal
    C. Expenses journal
    D. Purchases journal

14. Which of these is a commonly used ledger?
    A. Expenses ledger
    B. Accounts receivable subsidiary ledger
    C. Purchases ledger
    D. Normal ledger

15. What is a fixed asset?
    A. An asset for which the balance does not change from one period to the next
    B. An asset expected to be held for more than 12 months
    C. An asset on which the company has incurred repair and maintenance expense
    D. An asset the company no longer owns

16. You credited the Royalty Revenue account. What's the impact?

   A. Assets are decreased.

   B. Liabilities are decreased.

   C. Liabilities are increased.

   D. Equity is increased.

17. You paid the monthly rent expense. What's the impact?

   A. The Rent Expense account is credited.

   B. The Accounts Receivable account is debited.

   C. The Cash account is credited.

   D. The Accounts Payable account is credited.

18. Samuel Williams invests cash in the business he owns. Which account is credited?

   A. Service Revenue

   B. Samuel Williams, Drawing

   C. Samuel Williams, Capital

   D. Cash

19. Where is the credit in this journal entry?

20. What is posting?

   A. Transferring the amounts in each journal entry to each account's respective T-account

   B. Transferring the amounts in each account's respective T-account to each journal entry

   C. Transferring the amounts in each account's respective T-account to the appropriate financial statements

   D. Transferring the amounts in each journal entry to the appropriate financial statements

Putting It Together

PIT 3-1 RECORD JOURNAL ENTRIES AND POST TRANSACTIONS

In this example, we'll record journal entries and complete all postings for transactions that took place during the first month of operations for Amber's Lacrosse Emporium.

1. On May 1, Amber invests $75,000 to open Amber's Lacrosse Emporium.

5/1	Cash	75,000	
	Amber Stein, Capital		75,000
	Investment by owner		

Cash			Amber Stein, Capital	
$ 75,000				$ 75,000

2. On May 2, Amber's Lacrosse Emporium pays $15,000 for sporting goods inventory.

5/2	Merchandise Inventory	15,000	
	Cash		15,000
	Puchase of inventory for cash		

Cash		Merchandise Inventory	
$ 75,000	$ 15,000	$ 15,000	

3. On May 4, the company purchases display equipment for $12,000 in cash.

5/4	Equipment	12,000	
	Cash		12,000
	Purchase of equipment for cash		

Cash		Equipment	
$ 75,000	$ 15,000	$ 12,000	
	$ 12,000		

4. On May 5, Amber pays $1,500 of rent on the company's retail location.

5/5	Rent Expense	1,500	
	Cash		1,500
	Payment of rent expense		

Cash		Rent Expense	
$ 75,000	$ 15,000	$ 1,500	
	$ 12,000		
	$ 1,500		

5. On May 8, the company purchases $750 of supplies and $2,000 of furniture on account.

5/8	Supplies	750	
	Furniture	2,000	
	Accounts Payable		2,750
	Purchase of supplies and furniture on account		

Supplies			Furniture		
$ 750			$ 2,000		

Accounts Payable		
	$ 2,750	

6. On May 11, Amber's Lacrosse Emporium opens for business and sells $2,400 of sporting goods for cash. The cost of the goods sold is $1,350.

5/11	Cash	2,400	
	Sales Revenue		2,400
	Sale of sporting goods for cash		

5/11	Cost of Goods Sold	1,350	
	Merchandise Inventory		1,350
	Reduction of inventory associated with above sale		

Cash			Sales Revenue		
$ 75,000	$ 15,000			$ 2,400	
$ 2,400	$ 12,000				
	$ 1,500				

Cost of Goods Sold			Merchandise Inventory		
$ 1,350			$ 15,000	$ 1,350	

7. Also on May 11, the company pays the $2,750 owed from the 5/8 purchase of supplies and furniture.

5/11	Accounts Payable	2,750	
	Cash		2,750
	Payment of accounts payable		

Cash			Accounts Payable		
$ 75,000	$ 15,000		$ 2,750	$ 2,750	
$ 2,400	$ 12,000				
	$ 1,500				
	$ 2,750				

8. On May 12, Amber's Lacrosse Emporium sells $1,450 of sporting goods for cash and another $3,000 on account to a local school district. The cost of all goods sold is $2,100.

5/12	Cash	1,450	
	Accounts Receivable	3,000	
	Sales Revenue		4,450
	Partial payment made on sale of sporting goods		
5/12	Cost of Goods Sold	2,100	
	Merchandise Inventory		2,100
	Reduction of inventory associated with above sale		

Cash				Accounts Receivable			Merchandise Inventory		
$ 75,000	$ 15,000			$ 3,000			$ 15,000	$ 1,350	
$ 2,400	$ 12,000							$ 2,100	
$ 1,450	$ 1,500								
	$ 2,750								

Sales Revenue			Cost of Goods Sold	
	$ 2,400		$ 1,350	
	$ 4,450		$ 2,100	

9. On May 14, the company purchases advertising in local newspapers for $600.

5/14	Advertising Expense	600	
	Cash		600
	Payment of advertising expense		

Cash			Advertising Expense	
$ 75,000	$ 15,000		$ 600	
$ 2,400	$ 12,000			
$ 1,450	$ 1,500			
	$ 2,750			
	$ 600			

10. On May 18, the company receives $2,100 in partial payment for the sporting goods previously sold to the local school district on account.

5/18	Cash	2,100	
	Accounts Receivable		2,100
	Receipt of cash owed from prior sale		

Cash			Accounts Receivable	
$ 75,000	$ 15,000		$ 3,000	$ 2,100
$ 2,400	$ 12,000			
$ 1,450	$ 1,500			
$ 2,100	$ 2,750			
	$ 600			

11. On May 22, Amber's Lacrosse Emporium pays $1,600 in wages to its employees.

5/22	Wages Expense	1,600	
	Cash		1,600
	Payment of wages expense		

Cash			Wages Expene	
$ 75,000	$ 15,000		$ 1,600	
$ 2,400	$ 12,000			
$ 1,450	$ 1,500			
$ 2,100	$ 2,750			
	$ 600			
	$ 1,600			

12. On May 25, the company pays its telephone bill of $135.

5/25	Telephone Expense	135	
	Cash		135
	Payment of telephone expense		

Cash					Telephone Expense		
$	75,000	$	15,000	$	135		
$	2,400	$	12,000				
$	1,450	$	1,500				
$	2,100	$	2,750				
		$	600				
		$	1,600				
		$	135				

13. On May 27, the company pays $200 for monthly utilities.

5/27	Utilities Expense	200	
	Cash		200
	Payment of utilities expense		

Cash					Utilities Expense		
$	75,000	$	15,000	$	200		
$	2,400	$	12,000				
$	1,450	$	1,500				
$	2,100	$	2,750				
		$	600				
		$	1,600				
		$	135				
		$	200				

14. On May 28, Amber's Lacrosse Emporium buys an additional $2,000 of sporting equipment inventory on account.

5/28	Merchandise Inventory	2,000	
	Accounts Payable		2,000
	Purchase of inventory on account		

Merchandise Inventory					Accounts Payable		
$	15,000	$	1,350	$	2,750	$	2,750
$	2,000	$	2,100			$	2,000

15. On May 31, Amber withdraws $600 from the business.

5/31	Amber Stein, Drawing	600	
	Cash		600
	Withdrawal of cash by owner		

Cash					Amber Stein, Drawing		
$	75,000	$	15,000	$	600		
$	2,400	$	12,000				
$	1,450	$	1,500				
$	2,100	$	2,750				
		$	600				
		$	1,600				
		$	135				
		$	200				
		$	600				

16. Based on the above transactions, here are the ending balances for each account:

Cash			
$	75,000	$	15,000
$	2,400	$	12,000
$	1,450	$	1,500
$	2,100	$	2,750
		$	600
		$	1,600
		$	135
		$	200
		$	600
$	**46,565**		

Accounts Receivable			
$	3,000	$	2,100
$	**900**		

Supplies			
$	750		
$	**750**		

Merchandise Inventory			
$	15,000	$	1,350
$	2,000	$	2,100
$	**13(500)**		

Furniture			
$	2,000		
$	**2,000**		

Equipment			
$	12,000		
$	**12,000**		

Accounts Payable			
$	2,750	$	2,750
		$	2,000
		$	**2,000**

Amber Stein, Capital			
		$	75,000
		$	**75,000**

Amber Stein, Drawing			
$	600		
$	**600**		

Sales Revenue			
		$	2,400
		$	4,450
		$	**6,850**

Cost of Goods Sold			
$	1,350		
$	2,100		
$	**3,450**		

Advertising Expense			
$	600		
$	**600**		

Rent Expense			
$	1,500		
$	**1,500**		

Wages Expense			
$	1,600		
$	**1,600**		

Telephone Expense			
$	135		
$	**135**		

Utilities Expense			
$	200		
$	**200**		

Practice Set A

PSA 3-1 DETERMINE THE NORMAL BALANCE

Indicate whether the normal balance for each account is the debit or credit side of the T-account. Remember that the normal balance side is the one that increases.

	Debit Side	Credit Side
Accounts Payable		
Sales Revenue		
Furniture		
Advertising Expense		
Cash		
Notes Receivable		
John Doe, Drawing		
Utilities Expense		
Supplies		
Cost of Goods Sold		

PSA 3-2 CALCULATE ENDING BALANCES

Calculate the ending balance for each T-account.

1.

Cash

$ 25,400	$ 3,100
$ 3,250	$ 1,550
$ 4,500	$ 4,120
	$ 800

2.

Accounts Receivable

$ 19,500	$ 4,500
$ 2,500	$ 3,000
$ 4,500	$ 550
	$ 2,000

3.

Accounts Payable

$ 750	$ 1,550
$ 1,200	$ 1,200
$ 400	

4.

Supplies

$ 1,250	$ 325
$ 400	$ 205
	$ 240

PSA 3-3 RECORD JOURNAL ENTRIES

Record journal entries for each transaction. While it's customary to include explanations in journal entries, for the purposes of this exercise you can omit them.

Starting file: Use the Journal Entries template.

1. Aug. 1: Martin Johnson invests $425,000 to open his new appliance repair business.
2. Aug. 3: The company pays $150,000 for land and $70,000 for a building.
3. Aug. 5: Martin repairs appliances for three customers. Two customers pay cash totaling $825; the third is billed $300 and is yet to pay.
4. Aug. 8: The company purchases radio advertisements for $3,000.
5. Aug. 11: The company purchases a car for $23,000 by taking out an automobile loan.
6. Aug. 15: Martin repairs appliances for two customers, receiving a total of $500 in cash.
7. Aug. 20: The company makes its first automobile loan payment of $475.
8. Aug. 21: The company pays $350 for utilities expense.
9. Aug. 27: The company pays $2,000 for employee salaries.
10. Aug. 31: Martin withdraws $10,000 from the business.

PSA 3-4 POST TO T-ACCOUNTS

Post all ten journal entries from PSA 3-3 to the appropriate T-accounts and determine the ending balance of each account.

Starting file: Use the T-Accounts template.

PSA 3-5 RECORD JOURNAL ENTRIES AND POST TO T-ACCOUNTS

Record journal entries for each transaction (omit explanations) and post all journal entries to the appropriate T-accounts. Then, determine the ending balance for each account.

Starting files: Use the Journal Entries and T-Accounts templates.

1. Oct. 1: Willy Baker invests $150,000 to open his new furniture refinishing business.
2. Oct. 2: The company purchases $18,000 of equipment on account.
3. Oct. 8: The company pays employee wages of $1,100.
4. Oct. 10: Willy refinishes furniture for two customers, receiving $2,200 cash in full payment for the work.
5. Oct. 11: The company purchases supplies for $500.
6. Oct. 14: Willy refinishes furniture for a customer, who agrees to pay the $750 bill within two weeks.
7. Oct. 17: The company pays $425 for telephone expense.
8. Oct. 21: The company receives $200 in partial payment for the bill from the Oct. 14 services.
9. Oct. 25: Willy withdraws $430 from the business.
10. Oct. 29: The company pays $825 in monthly rent.

PSA 3-6 INTERPRET JOURNAL ENTRIES WITHIN SPECIAL JOURNALS

Rewrite the journal entries shown below in special journals as standard journal entries (debits displayed on top, credits displayed at bottom). Each special journal contains two journal entries.

Starting file: Use the Journal Entries template.

1.

		Cash Receipts Journal			
Date	Account Credited	Accounts Receivable Cr.	Service Revenue Cr.	Other Accounts Cr.	Cash Dr.
4/5			1,450		1,450
4/12	CMS, Inc.	2,200			2,200

2.

		Cash Payments Journal			
Date	Account Debited	Other Accounts Dr.	Accounts Payable Dr.	Supplies Dr.	Cash Cr.
4/8				650	650
4/22	Furniture	2,250			2,250

3.

	Revenue Journal	
Date	Account Debited	Accounts Receivable Dr. & Service Revenue Cr.
4/14	AllNight	2,400
4/19	RobbinsCo	785

4.

		Purchases Journal			
Date	Account Credited	Merchandise Inventory Dr.	Supplies Dr.	Account Debited	Other Accounts Dr.
4/9	Fulto, Corp.	6,850			
4/30	BEED, Inc.			Equipment	4,850

PSA 3-7 RECORD AND POST ACCOUNTS RECEIVABLE JOURNAL ENTRIES

Record the journal entry for each transaction and post to the general ledger accounts receivable account and the accounts receivable subsidiary ledger accounts. Finally, determine the ending balances for all accounts receivable balances (the control account and each subsidiary account).

Starting files: Use the Journal Entries and T-Accounts templates.

1. Feb. 4: PaleTech Company is billed $3,000 for services performed on account.
2. Feb. 5: Fernandez Corp. is billed $4,900 for services performed on account.
3. Feb. 14: Fernandez Corp. pays the entire $4,900 that is owed from the Feb. 5 invoice (bill).
4. Feb. 23: MoonSite Corporation is billed $2,500 for services provided on account.
5. Feb. 24: MoonSite Corporation pays $1,000 in partial payment of the Feb. 23 invoice.

Practice Set B

PSB 3-1 DETERMINE THE NORMAL BALANCE

Indicate whether the normal balance for each account is the debit or credit side of the T-account. Remember that the normal balance side is the one that increases.

	Debit Side	Credit Side
Equipment		
John Doe, Capital		
Rent Expense		
Merchandise Inventory		
Accounts Receivable		
Notes Payable		
Land		
Insurance Expense		
Buildings		
Service Revenue		

PSB 3-2 CALCULATE ENDING BALANCES

Calculate the ending balance for each T-account.

1.

John Doe, Capital	
$ 12,500	$ 84,000
	$ 27,000

2.

Furniture	
$ 27,500	$ 3,150
$ 14,000	$ 4,875

3.

Notes Receivable	
$ 12,000	$ 3,275
$ 6,500	$ 7,000
$ 7,000	$ 3,200
	$ 2,000

4.

Merchandise Inventory	
$ 15,000	$ 2,450
$ 9,500	$ 1,380
$ 9,500	$ 3,850
	$ 1,925

PSB 3-3 RECORD JOURNAL ENTRIES

Record journal entries for each transaction. While it's customary to include explanations in journal entries, for the purposes of this exercise you can omit them.

Starting file: Use the Journal Entries template.

1. Jul. 1: Katherine Johnson invests $200,000 to open her new antique shop.
2. Jul. 4: The company pays $35,000 for merchandise inventory.
3. Jul. 6: The company purchases supplies on account for $650.
4. Jul. 7: On its first day of operations, the company sells $1,850 of merchandise for cash. The cost of that merchandise is $775.
5. Jul. 14: The company pays off the full amount owed for the previously purchased supplies.
6. Jul. 16: The company pays $110 for telephone expense.
7. Jul. 19: The company sells $2,300 of merchandise for cash. The cost of the merchandise sold is $1,115.
8. Jul. 22: The company sells $6,200 of merchandise to a local business on account. The merchandise cost is $4,000.
9. Jul. 23: The company pays $1,250 for employee wages.
10. Jul. 31: Katherine withdraws $5,500 from the business.

PSB 3-4 POST TO T-ACCOUNTS

Post all ten journal entries from PSB 3-3 to the appropriate T-accounts and determine the ending balances of each account.

Starting file: Use the T-Accounts template.

PSB 3-5 RECORD JOURNAL ENTRIES AND POST TO T-ACCOUNTS

Record journal entries for each transaction (omit explanations) and post all journal entries to the appropriate T-accounts. Then, determine the ending balances of each account.

Starting files: Use the Journal Entries and T-Accounts templates.

1. Nov. 1: Bernard Oliver invests $325,000 to open his new gardening tool boutique.
2. Nov. 5: The company pays $57,000 for merchandise inventory.
3. Nov. 8: On its first day of operations, the company sells $3,475 of merchandise on account. The cost of the merchandise sold is $1,900.
4. Nov. 13: The company pays $84 for utilities.
5. Nov. 15: The company pays $925 for supplies.
6. Nov. 17: The company receives $3,000 in partial payment for the goods sold on Nov. 8.
7. Nov. 20: The company purchases furniture for $2,000 on account.
8. Nov. 23: The company sells $4,800 of merchandise for cash. The cost of the merchandise sold is $3,100.
9. Nov. 28: The company receives interest earned on its bank account of $45.
10. Nov. 29: Bernard withdraws $24,500 from the business.

PSB 3-6 INTERPRET JOURNAL ENTRIES WITHIN SPECIAL JOURNALS

Rewrite the journal entries shown below in special journals as standard journal entries (debits displayed on top, credits displayed at bottom). Each special journal contains two journal entries.

Starting file: Use the Journal Entries template.

1.

		Cash Receipts Journal			
Date	Account Credited	Accounts Receivable Cr.	Service Revenue Cr.	Other Accounts Cr.	Cash Dr.
11/15	Interest Revenue			125	125
11/29			800		800

2.

		Cash Payments Journal			
Date	Account Debited	Other Accounts Dr.	Accounts Payable Dr.	Supplies Dr.	Cash Cr.
11/4	Buildings	65,000			65,000
11/17	BHV, Corp.		2,750		2,750

3.

	Revenue Journal
Date	Account Debited	Accounts Receivable Dr. & Service Revenue Cr.
11/10	DGY, Co.	1,770
11/24	HIT, Inc.	1,350

4.

		Purchases Journal			
Date	Account Credited	Merchandise Inventory Dr.	Supplies Dr.	Account Debited	Other Accounts Dr.
11/23	HomeCo.		1,500		
11/24	Smith Inc.	4,000			

PSB 3-7 RECORD AND POST ACCOUNTS RECEIVABLE JOURNAL ENTRIES

Record the journal entry for each transaction and post to the general ledger accounts receivable account and the accounts receivable subsidiary ledger accounts. Then determine the ending balances for all accounts receivable accounts (the control and all subsidiary accounts).

Starting files: Use the Journal Entries and T-Accounts templates.

1. Dec. 1: RNI Incorporated is billed $18,500 for services performed on account.
2. Dec. 12: Aerial USA is billed $23,200 for services performed on account.
3. Dec. 16: RNI Incorporated pays $10,000 in partial payment of the Dec. 1 invoice (bill).
4. Dec. 19: TableMakers Cooperative is billed $9,700 for services provided on account.
5. Dec. 29: Aerial USA pays the entire $23,200 that is owed from the Dec. 12 invoice.

4 Adjusting Entries

After recording and posting journal entries, the company summarizes the information so it can be reviewed and interpreted. In addition, since certain journal entries are not recorded during the period, they must be recorded now to ensure the accuracy of financial records. In this chapter, you will learn how a trial balance summarizes information and why completing adjusting entries is a critical step in the accounting cycle.

LEARNING OBJECTIVES

▸ Format and complete a trial balance

▸ Record adjusting entries

▸ Calculate depreciation using the straight-line method

▸ Calculate depreciation using the double-declining balance method

Project: Adjusting the Books at the End of the First Month of Operations

As you review the journal entries for the first month of operations of Nathan's Donut School, you realize that certain activities have not been accounted for. For example, the company used some of the supplies purchased on March 4, but you haven't yet recorded a journal entry to account for this. You also realize that certain assets will lose value as they are used. How do you account for this?

You first review the format of the unadjusted trial balance, which summarizes ending account balances, and then examine different types of adjusting entries and record the necessary ones for the first month. You also examine the purpose behind recording depreciation and the multiple ways in which it can be calculated. To finish up, you complete the adjusted trial balance to display the new account balances.

The Accounting Cycle

In this chapter, we'll cover the next two stages of the accounting cycle—steps 4 and 5—as we examine how recording the adjusting entries affects the trial balance.

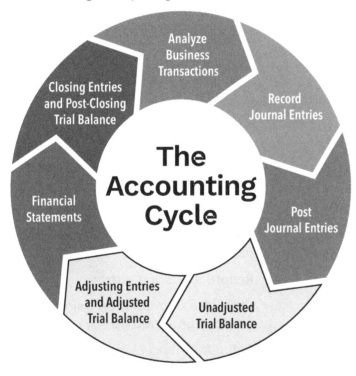

Nathan's Donut School Unadjusted Trial Balance March 31, 2027				Nathan's Donut School Adjusted Trial Balance March 31, 2027		
	Debit	Credit			Debit	Credit
Cash	$ 12,300		Cash		$ 12,300	
Accounts Receivable	2,200		Accounts Receivable		2,350	
Supplies	500		Supplies		185	
Furniture	1,000		Furniture		1,000	
Equipment	20,000		Equipment		20,000	
Accounts Payable		$ -	Accounts Payable			$ -
Nathaniel H. Spencer, Capital		35,000	Wages Payable			750
Nathaniel H. Spencer, Drawing	400		Nathaniel H. Spencer, Capital			35,000
Service Revenue		3,350	Nathaniel H. Spencer, Drawing		400	
Rent Expense	1,700		Service Revenue			3,500
Advertising Expense	250		Rent Expense		1,700	
			Wages Expense		750	
			Supplies Expense		315	
			Advertising Expense		250	
	$ 38,350	$ 38,350			$ 39,250	$ 39,250

A trial balance is completed before and after the recording of adjusting entries.

Trial Balances

After all posting has been completed, the account balances are scattered throughout the different T-accounts. The next step in the accounting cycle is to summarize these balances within the **trial balance**. The trial balance lists all accounts along with their debit or credit balances as of a specific date. An additional benefit of the trial balance is that it offers the opportunity to confirm that the debit balances equal the credit balances.

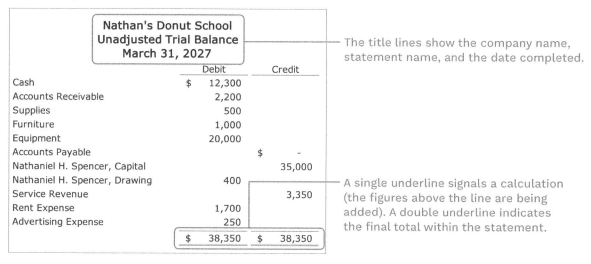

The title lines show the company name, statement name, and the date completed.

A single underline signals a calculation (the figures above the line are being added). A double underline indicates the final total within the statement.

The trial balance displays all account balances and sums the debit and credit columns.

Note that this is the *unadjusted* trial balance. As we work through the accounting cycle, we will complete a total of three trial balances:

- **Unadjusted trial balance**: Completed before adjusting entries
- **Adjusted trial balance**: Completed after adjusting entries
- **Post-closing trial balance**: Completed after closing entries

Each trial balance summarizes accounts and verifies they're in balance. Accounts should be listed in the following order:

TRIAL BALANCE—ORDER OF ACCOUNTS
1. Asset
2. Liability
3. Capital
4. Withdrawal
5. Revenue
6. Expense

Ask Yourself 4-1: What figure is shown in a trial balance?
A. Total liabilities
B. Total expenses
C. Total credits
D. Total assets

CASE IN POINT 4-1

In this example, we'll use the current account balances from Nathan's Donut School to complete the unadjusted trial balance.

Cash				Accounts Receivable				Supplies				Furniture		
$	35,000	$	20,000	$	2,500	$	300	$	500			$	1,000	
$	850	$	1,500											
$	300	$	250											
		$	1,700											
		$	400											
$	12,300			$	2,200			$	500			$	1,000	

Equipment		Accounts Payable				Nathaniel H. Spencer, Capital				Nathaniel H. Spencer, Drawing	
$	20,000	$	1,500	$	1,500			$	35,000	$	400
$	20,000			$	-			$	35,000	$	400

Service Revenue				Advertising Expense				Rent Expense		
		$	850	$	250			$	1,700	
		$	2,500							
		$	3,350	$	250			$	1,700	

Nathan's Donut School
Unadjusted Trial Balance
March 31, 2027

		Debit	Credit
Assets	Cash	$ 12,300	
	Accounts Receivable	2,200	
	Supplies	500	
	Furniture	1,000	
	Equipment	20,000	
Liability	Accounts Payable		$ -
Capital	Nathaniel H. Spencer, Capital		35,000
Withdrawal	Nathaniel H. Spencer, Drawing	400	
Revenue	Service Revenue		3,350
Expenses	Rent Expense	1,700	
	Advertising Expense	250	
		$ 38,350	$ 38,350

Adjusting and Reversing Entries

During a given period, such as the first month of operations for Nathan's Donut School we've been examining, certain business activities are not recorded. This occurs when there is no "trigger" that signals a journal entry should be recorded for that activity. For example, when a sale is made, this triggers a journal entry to record the sale. Or, when a company pays for an item previously purchased, this payment triggers a journal entry. However, when, say, a paper clip or staple is used, no journal entry is booked to record the reduction in supplies even though they have been used. It would be impractical to record an entry for every office supply used during a period. Instead, the company waits until the end of the period and then records an **adjusting entry**.

ADJUSTING JOURNAL ENTRIES: TYPES	
Journal Entry Type	**Definition**
Deferred expense	Expenses paid for in advance and subsequently incurred
Deferred revenue	Cash received in advance of revenue being earned
Accrued expense	Expenses incurred prior to being paid off
Accrued revenue	Revenue earned prior to the receipt of cash
Depreciation	Estimated loss in value that an asset experiences over time

While depreciation will be discussed later in this chapter, the other four types of adjusting entries are addressed here.

Deferred Expenses

View the video "Deferred Expenses and Revenue."

A deferred expense is one incurred after payment is made. For example, when Nathaniel purchases supplies, they are initially recorded as an asset (debit to the Supplies account). Over time, as the company uses its supplies, it incurs supplies expense. This expense was *deferred* until this point of use, which is after the purchase was made.

At the end of the period, the company records an adjusting entry to account for the total supplies expense incurred during that period. This is done by comparing the value of the physical supplies on hand at the end of the period against the amount originally purchased. The difference represents the dollar amount of supplies used. For example, if $600 in supplies are purchased in September and the physical count reveals $150 worth remaining on September 30, the supplies expense incurred during the period is $450 ($600 − $150).

9/30	Supplies Expense	450	
	Supplies		450
	Adjusting entry to record supplies expense		

Another common example of a deferred expense is for insurance expense. When insurance is purchased in advance of its use (to cover the next 12 months, for example), it is recorded as an asset: prepaid insurance. At the end of the period, an adjusting entry is recorded in which insurance expense is booked based on the amount of time that has passed. For example, if twelve months of insurance is purchased for $1,200 on February 1, the adjusting entry on February 28 would record $100 of insurance expense ($1,200 ÷ 12 months).

2/28	Insurance Expense	100	
	Prepaid Insurance		100
	Adjusting entry to record insurance expense		

As $100 of the prepaid insurance is used every month, this same adjusting journal entry is recorded at the end of each of the twelve months over which the insurance policy is in place.

> **TIP!** Remember, the purpose of an adjusting entry for deferred expenses is to account for the previously unrecorded expense incurred during the period. This also reduces the associated asset balance to its correct level.

Because an expense account is debited (increased) when the adjusting entry for a deferred expense is recorded, these entries increase total expenses for the period. This means they also reduce the overall net income on the income statement because higher expenses lead to a lower net income. This lower net income results in a lower balance in the owner's capital account on the balance sheet than would otherwise exist (as you'll see in Chapter 5 when we discuss closing entries). And finally, because an asset account is credited (reduced) when the adjusting entry for a deferred expense is recorded, these entries also reduce total assets on the balance sheet.

Deferred Revenue

Sometimes customers pay prior to services being rendered or received. A good example relates to professional sports teams. Season tickets are purchased prior to the completion of the games. When the team receives this money, it is not yet earned. The revenue is *deferred* until the team plays the games. Therefore, when the money is received, the team credits their Unearned Revenue account. This is a liability account because the team owes entertainment to the customer, the value of which is equal to the amount paid.

Another common example is when a customer pays for a service, such as the painting of a house, in advance. If the customer pays $1,000 on August 12, prior to the work being performed, the painting company would record the following journal entry crediting the Unearned Revenue account:

8/12	Cash	1,000	
	Unearned Revenue		1,000
	Receipt of cash prior to rendering of service		

This is not an adjusting entry. On August 31, if $800 of the $1,000 in services has been provided to date, then the following adjusting entry would be made:

8/31	Unearned Revenue	800	
	Service Revenue		800
	Adjusting entry for completion of services		

Because a revenue account is credited (increased) when the adjusting entry for deferred revenue is recorded, these entries increase total revenue for the period. They also increase the overall net income (more revenue means a higher net income) on the income statement. Adjusting entries for deferred revenue impact the owner's capital account but in a different way from how deferred expenses do. In this case, the higher net income results in a higher balance in the owner's capital account on the balance sheet. And, because a liability account is debited (reduced), these entries also reduce total liabilities on the balance sheet.

Accrued Expenses

 **View the video "Accrued Expenses and Revenue."**

Certain expenses are incurred prior to when they are paid off. We refer to these as *accrued* expenses. A good example of accrued expenses is wages paid to employees. Wages are typically paid on a weekly or biweekly basis, so unless today is payday, at any given time employees will have worked (and the company will have incurred wages expense) prior to cash being paid to them. As an example, imagine that your employees are paid on Friday, July 28; they don't work on the weekend; and they collectively earn $1,100 on Monday, July 31 (the last day of the period). Your adjusting journal entry to account for the accrued expenses would look like this:

7/31	Wages Expense	1,100	
	Wages Payable		1,100
	Adjusting entry for employee wages owed		

Here we credit Wages Payable because the company owes the $1,100 to employees.

Because an expense account is debited (increased) when the adjusting entry for an accrued expense is recorded, these entries increase total expenses for the period. As with deferred expenses, they reduce overall net income on the income statement (higher expenses lead to a lower net income).

Again, as with deferred expenses, this lower net income then results in a lower balance within the owner's capital account on the balance sheet. And because a liability account is credited (increased) in this case, these entries also increase total liabilities on the balance sheet.

Accrued Revenue

Just as expenses can accumulate prior to being paid off, revenue can accumulate prior to cash being received in exchange for it. This revenue is referred to as *accrued* revenue. For example, if as of December 31 your company earns $2,400 for services rendered and has not yet been paid, you would make an adjusting journal entry like this:

12/31	Accounts Receivable	2,400	
	Service Revenue		2,400
	Adjusting entry for revenue earned in advance of payment		

Here we debit Accounts Receivable because $2,400 is owed to the company.

A revenue account is credited (increased) when an adjusting entry for accrued revenue is recorded, so these entries increase total revenue for the period. They also increase the overall net income on the income statement, as higher revenue leads to a higher net income. As with deferred revenue, this higher net income means a higher balance in the owner's capital account on the balance sheet than would otherwise exist. Additionally, because an asset account is debited (increased) when an adjusting entry for accrued revenue is recorded, these entries also increase total assets on the balance sheet.

ADJUSTING JOURNAL ENTRIES: IMPACT ON ACCOUNTS						
	Total Revenue	Total Expenses	Net Income	Owner's Capital	Total Assets	Total Liabilities
Deferred Expenses	n/a	↑	↓	↓	↓	n/a
Deferred Revenue	↑	n/a	↑	↑	n/a	↓
Accrued Expenses	n/a	↑	↓	↓	n/a	↑
Accrued Revenue	↑	n/a	↑	↑	↑	n/a

Ask Yourself 4-2a: Which of these is a type of adjusting entry?

    A. Deferred equity

    B. Deferred asset

    C. Accrued withdrawal

    D. Accrued expense

◉◉ A CLOSER LOOK

Are Adjusting Entries Really Necessary?

Many students ask why they should bother recording adjusting entries since, in most cases, they'll be taken care of eventually. For example, why should we record accrued wage expense when payday will come around in a few days and we'll record the journal entry then?

The answer is simple: To ensure that, at the end of a period, our books are completely accurate. All activity that occurred during the period must be reflected within the account balances. Many people rely on a company's financial statements to make important financial decisions, so the balances that comprise these financial statements must account for everything that has happened to a company. This is why we must be certain to record all adjusting journal entries prior to the end of a period.

Reversing Entries

One additional step that companies may complete is the recording of **reversing entries**. These optional journal entries can simplify the recording process for certain items related to adjusting entries. Companies often record reversing entries for accrued expenses and accrued revenue. As the name suggests, reversing entries reverse (or negate the effect of) adjusting entries. Reversing entries are recorded on the first day of the period following the recording of the associated adjusting entry.

To understand the benefit of reversing entries, let's look at an example. Earlier we examined an adjusting entry for wages earned by employees—an accrued expense. Here's how the adjusting entry recorded on the final day of the period looked:

7/31	Wages Expense	1,100	
	Wages Payable		1,100
	Adjusting entry for employee wages owed		

In this example, employees are paid every Friday, and July 31 was a Monday, so the $1,100 earned on Monday, 7/31, was entered in the adjusting entry. If we opted not to record a reversing entry, then when payday arrived on Friday, 8/4, the journal entry would look like this:

8/4	Wages Expense	4,400	
	Wages Payable	1,100	
	Cash		5,500
	Payment of employee wages		

Typically, it would only be necessary to debit (increase) the Wages Expense account and credit (decrease) Cash on payday. However, because the final day of the period was included within this week, the adjusting entry placed $1,100 of wages payable onto the books. This payable must be removed when employees receive their paychecks on 8/4 (it's no longer owed at that point), resulting in the more complicated journal entry. Reversing entries eliminate this circumstance. So, by recording the reversing entry, it appears on the books on August 1 like this:

8/1	Wages Payable	1,100	
	Wages Expense		1,100
	Revising entry for employee wages owed		

The subsequent journal entry recorded on August 4 will be a standard journal entry recorded on payday:

8/4	Wages Expense	5,500	
	Cash		5,500
	Payment of employee wages		

Because Wages Payable was debited (reduced) by $1,100 in the 8/1 reversing entry, there's no need to include it in the 8/4 journal entry; the $1,100 balance put on the books on 7/31 was removed with the reversing entry. Therefore, we don't need a unique journal entry on 8/4 and instead can record the standard journal entry as shown.

Did you notice that the entry debits Wages Expense for the full $5,500 incurred during the week, not just the $4,400 incurred the current period (8/1–8/4)? When the reversing entry is used, this approach results in the correct amount of Wages Expense being reported on the books. Let's look at the T-account:

Wages Expense			
7/31	$ 1,100		
		$ 1,100	8/1
8/4	$ 5,500		
	$ 5,500		

The credit to Wages Expense in the 8/1 reversing entry eliminates the debit to the same account in the 7/31 adjusting entry. So, when Wages Expense is debited for $5,500 on 8/4, $5,500 is debited to this account. Of this amount, $1,100 (debited on 7/31) will appear on July's income statement, and the remaining $4,400 ($5,500 debited on 8/4 minus $1,100 credited on 8/1) will appear on August's statement.

A similar circumstance exists for accrued revenue. The adjusting entry for accrued revenue examined earlier accounted for $2,400 of services earned but not yet paid. If the company does not record a reversing entry, then the $2,400 debit to Accounts Receivable in this adjusting entry must be removed from the books when payment is received. However, if a reversing entry is recorded in which Service Revenue is debited and Accounts Receivable is credited, then when payment is received the typical journal entry (debit Cash, credit Service Revenue) can be recorded.

Ask Yourself 4-2b: Reversing entries are recorded on the first day of a period. True or false?

CASE IN POINT 4-2

In these examples, we will record adjusting journal entries for Nathan's Donut School. The first month of operations ended on Wednesday, March 31.

1. Nathan's Donut School is hosting an intensive, five-day workshop. It costs $250 and begins on Monday, March 29. Payment is due that Friday.

3/31	Accounts Receivable	150	
	Service Revenue		150
	Adjusting entry for revenue earned in advance of payment		

*The company earns $50 per day ($250 ÷ 5 days). Since the period ended on a Wednesday, three days' worth of revenue has been earned ($50 * 3 days), which is why $150 is used in this entry.*

2. Employees of Nathan's Donut School earn a total of $1,250 for a five-day workweek. They are paid on Friday each week.

3/31	Wages Expense	750	
	Wages Payable		750
	Adjusting entry for employee wages owed		

*Employees earn $250 per day ($1,250 ÷ 5 days). After the last day of the period, the employees have worked three days, which means they have earned $750 ($250 * 3 days) thus far.*

3. On March 4, Nathan's Donut School purchased $500 of supplies. On March 31, a physical examination reveals that $185 of supplies remains.

3/31	Supplies Expense	315	
	Supplies		315
	Adjusting entry to record supplies expense		

This entry is to account for supplies that have been used up. If the company began with $500 of supplies and has $185 remaining at the end of the period, the difference of $315 ($500 – $185) is the supplies expense incurred during the period.

4. During its second month of operations, Nathan's Donut School begins a five-day children's cooking course. It begins on Tuesday, April 27, and ends on Saturday, May 1. Full payment of $550 is due on April 22.

4/30	Unearned Revenue	440	
	Service Revenue		440
	Adjusting entry for completion of services		

*Recall that Cash is debited and Unearned Revenue (a liability) is credited when cash is received in advance of services being performed. That's why we debit Unearned Revenue, reducing it, after a portion of the services has been provided. As of April 30, Nathan's Donut School had earned $440 ($550 ÷ 5 days = $110 per day, $110 * 4 days earned = $440).*

Depreciation

 View the video "Depreciation."

Over time, most fixed assets lose value. A fixed asset (also called a *long-term asset* or *plant asset*, as they are expected to be held for more than 12 months) is one that cannot be easily converted to cash. This contrasts with a **short-term asset** (or *current asset*), such as supplies or inventory, which is expected to be held for less than 12 months and can more easily be used or converted to cash if necessary.

All fixed assets, with the notable exception of land, are subject to depreciation due to the loss in value they experience. Depreciation expense represents an estimate of the loss in value an asset experiences over time. Think about an office table that is purchased for $250. Could a company resell this table for the same amount after five years of consistent use? Very likely not. Since this depreciation process consistently occurs, businesses must be certain to account for it over time. There are two primary ways calculate depreciation: the straight-line method and the double-declining balance method.

| **WARNING!** | Depreciation estimates an asset's loss in value. There's no guarantee an asset could be sold for its current **book value** (Cost – Accumulated Depreciation) at any given point in time. |

Ask Yourself 4-3a: What's another name for a current asset?

    A. Long-term asset

    B. Fixed asset

    C. Short-term asset

    D. Plant asset

Straight-Line Depreciation

Under the straight-line method of depreciation, a company records the same amount of depreciation for each year of the asset's **useful life** (number of years the company expects to use the asset), which is estimated based on experience. For the straight-line method, the **salvage value** (or residual value) also must be estimated. This represents the amount the company expects to receive for the asset at the time of disposal, which is when the company sells or discards the item.

$$\frac{\text{Cost} - \text{Salvage Value}}{\text{Useful Life}} = \text{Annual Depreciation}$$

Straight-line depreciation calculation

Double-Declining Balance Depreciation

The double-declining balance method is also referred to as an *accelerated depreciation method* because it results in more depreciation during the early years of an asset's useful life than in the later years. While not as common as the straight-line method, it is regularly used.

To calculate depreciation using this method:

1. **Determine the straight-line rate** by dividing the number of periods for which you're calculating depreciation (it's always 1) by the useful life. For example, if Nathaniel bought a donut fryer with a useful life of five years, the straight-line rate would be 20% (1 ÷ 5). Alternatively, you can divide 100% by the useful life.

2. **Determine the first year's depreciation** by multiplying the cost of the asset by twice the straight-line rate, hence the name *double*-declining balance. Other "declining balances," such as triple-declining balance or 1.5-declining balance, can be used. It's a matter of preference, but the employer must be consistent with the chosen rate.

	Beginning Book Value	Double-Declining Rate	Depreciation Expense	Accumulated Depreciation	Ending Book Value
Year #1	$2,500	40%	$1,000	$1,000	$1,500

This is the double-declining balance depreciation for year 1 of Nathaniel's donut fryer.

3. In subsequent years, the same calculation is used, except that the current book value (Cost – Accumulated Depreciation) replaces the cost. Let's look at the depreciation of the donut fryer over its useful life of five years and a salvage value of $250:

	Beginning Book Value	Double-Declining Rate	Depreciation Expense	Accumulated Depreciation	Ending Book Value
Year #1	$2,500	40%	$1,000	$1,000	$1,500
Year #2	$1,500	40%	$600	$1,600	$900
Year #3	$900	40%	$360	$1,960	$540
Year #4	$540	40%	$216	$2,176	$324
Year #5	$324	40%	*$74	$2,250	$250

* $324 (Y5 Beginning Book Value) - $250 (Salvage Value) = $74 (Y5 Depreciation)

Up to this point, the salvage value has not impacted the calculation. Under the double-declining balance method, salvage value is not factored until near the end of the useful life. As each year's depreciation is calculated, check that the book value of the asset has not dropped below the salvage value. If it does, as in Year #5 above, disregard the calculation for that year and substitute an amount that brings the book value down to the salvage value—but not below it.

> **Ask Yourself 4-3b:** A company records the same amount of depreciation each year under the double-declining balance method. True or false?

Are There Other Depreciation Methods?

While straight-line depreciation and double-declining balance depreciation are the two most common methods, others can be used. The *units of production* method, for example, works well for an asset that can be used for a finite number of hours or that can produce a finite number of units. Under this method, you first determine the depreciation rate as (Cost – Salvage Value) ÷ Total Units, where Total Units represents the useful life in terms of total hours of use or total units produced. Multiply this rate by the number of actual hours (or units) for each year to determine the depreciation for those years.

#1	$\dfrac{\text{Cost} - \text{Salvage Value}}{\text{Total Units}}$	=	Depreciation Rate

#2	Depreciation Rate * Annual Units Produced	=	Annual Depreciation

Units of production depreciation calculation (two steps)

The *sum of the years' digits* method is an accelerated depreciation method. Under this method, the digits of each year within the useful life are added and then used to calculate annual depreciation. In the first year, useful life is divided by the sum of all digits and then multiplied by the formula (Cost – Salvage Value). For an asset with a five-year useful life, the sum of the years' digits would be 5 + 4 + 3 + 2 + 1 = 15; therefore, the fraction multiplied by the formula (Cost – Salvage Value) would be 5/15. For each subsequent year, the numerator of the fraction is reduced by 1 (the year #2 fraction would be 4/15, for year #3 the fraction would be 3/15, etc.).

Cost – Salvage Value	*	$\dfrac{\text{Remaining Useful Life (Yrs)}}{\text{Sum of the Years' Digits}}$	=	Annual Depreciation

Sum of the years' digits depreciation calculation

One final method of note is the *Modified Accelerated Cost Recovery System (MACRS),* which assigns useful lives and depreciation rates to specific classes of assets. Unlike the other depreciation methods discussed in this chapter, MACRS is not acceptable under GAAP. MACRS is the only method acceptable for tax purposes, though, so depreciation reported on a corporate tax return is calculated using this method.

Recording the Depreciation Adjusting Entry

Once depreciation has been calculated at the end of a period, a journal entry for the depreciation is recorded. This example shows the journal entry for when $260 of depreciation is calculated:

9/30	Depreciation Expense	260	
	Accumulated Depreciation		260
	Adjusting entry for depreciation expense		

This adjusting entry is designed to increase Depreciation Expense and increase Accumulated Depreciation. As opposed to being an asset, liability, or owner's equity account, Accumulated Depreciation is a **contra-asset account**. This type of account is designed to offset the balance of its associated asset account, and it operates in an opposite manner from assets. Because it's associated with an asset account, this contra-asset account appears within the asset section of the balance sheet.

IMPACT OF DEBITS AND CREDITS ON ACCOUNT TYPES		
Account Type	Debit	Credit
Asset	↑	↓
Contra-Asset	↓	↑

Depreciation expense is a type of deferred expense because the fixed asset is first purchased and then the depreciation expense related to that asset is recorded over time. As with other deferred expenses, the adjusting entry for depreciation expense increases total expenses, reduces overall net income on the income statement, reduces the owner's capital account balance, and reduces total assets on the balance sheet.

Accumulated Depreciation is not the only contra-asset account for which an adjusting journal entry can be made. Allowance for Doubtful Accounts (also called Allowance for Uncollectible Accounts) is a contra-asset account that represents the portion of accounts receivable believed to be uncollectible and, therefore, it offsets the Accounts Receivable account balance. Some companies choose solely to remove specific accounts receivables from the books when bad debts are identified; others estimate their bad debts at year end and record an associated adjusting journal entry. As with the adjusting journal entry for depreciation, this entry debits an expense account (Uncollectible Accounts Expense) and credits a contra-asset account (Allowance for Doubtful Accounts), thereby increasing both account balances.

Ask Yourself 4-3c: The balance in a contra-asset account increases via a credit. True or false?

CASE IN POINT 4-3

In this example, we'll calculate the first two years of depreciation for a piece of equipment using the straight-line and the double-declining balance methods. We'll also create the associated adjusting journal entries for the first two years.

Equipment cost: $20,000   Salvage value: $2,000   Useful life: 5 years

1. We begin by calculating the depreciation expense for each of the first two years using the straight-line method and recording the journal entries:

$$\frac{\$20,000 - \$2,000}{5} = \$3,600$$

Depreciation Expense	3,600	
Accumulated Depreciation		3,600
Adjusting entry for Y1 depreciation expense		

Depreciation Expense	3,600	
Accumulated Depreciation		3,600
Adjusting entry for Y2 depreciation expense		

2. Now let's calculate the depreciation expense for each of the first two years using the double-declining balance method and then record the journal entries:

	Beginning Book Value	Double-Declining Rate	Depreciation Expense	Accumulated Depreciation	Ending Book Value
Year #1	$20,000	40%	$8,000	$8,000	$12,000
Year #2	$12,000	40%	$4,800	$12,800	$7,200

Depreciation Expense	8,000	
Accumulated Depreciation		8,000
Adjusting entry for Y1 depreciation expense		
Depreciation Expense	4,800	
Accumulated Depreciation		4,800
Adjusting entry for Y2 depreciation expense		

Adjusted Trial Balance

After the adjusting entries are journalized, it's time to complete a second trial balance, called the adjusted trial balance. Similar to the unadjusted trial balance, the purpose at this stage is to summarize all account balances and ensure that the debit balances equal the credit balances. Unlike the balances in the unadjusted trial balance, those in the adjusted trial balance will have been altered by the adjusting entries. Keep in mind that while debits and credits must be equal, the total amount is a meaningless figure.

WARNING! Don't try to locate the total debit or credit figures elsewhere within the accounting records; you won't find them. Just ensure they are equal.

Ask Yourself 4-4: At the end of a period, what is completed first?
A. Adjusted trial balance
B. Unadjusted trial balance

In this example, we will complete the adjusted trial balance for Nathan's Donut School. This includes accounting for the adjusting entries previously recorded for the first month of operations.

Cash			
$	35,000	$	20,000
$	850	$	1,500
$	300	$	250
		$	1,700
		$	400
$	**12,300**		

Accounts Receivable			
$	2,500	$	300
$	150		
$	**2,350**		

Supplies			
$	500	$	315
$	**185**		

Furniture			
$	1,000		
$	**1,000**		

Equipment			
$	20,000		
$	**20,000**		

Accounts Payable			
$	1,500	$	1,500
		$	**-**

Wages Payable			
		$	750
		$	**750**

Nathaniel H. Spencer, Capital			
		$	35,000
		$	**35,000**

Nathaniel H. Spencer, Drawing			
$	400		
$	**400**		

Service Revenue			
		$	850
		$	2,500
		$	150
		$	**3,500**

Advertising Expense			
$	250		
$	**250**		

Rent Expense			
$	1,700		
$	**1,700**		

Supplies Expense			
$	315		
$	**315**		

Wages Expense			
$	750		
$	**750**		

Nathan's Donut School
Adjusted Trial Balance
March 31, 2027

	Debit	Credit
Cash	$ 12,300	
Accounts Receivable	2,350	
Supplies	185	
Furniture	1,000	
Equipment	20,000	
Accounts Payable		$ -
Wages Payable		750
Nathaniel H. Spencer, Capital		35,000
Nathaniel H. Spencer, Drawing	400	
Service Revenue		3,500
Rent Expense	1,700	
Wages Expense	750	
Supplies Expense	315	
Advertising Expense	250	
	$ 39,250	$ 39,250

Self-Assessment

Now it's time for you to check your knowledge of the key concepts and skills introduced in this chapter.

1. The sum of all debit balances must equal the sum of all credit balances, even in a trial balance.   *True False*

2. In the trial balance, debit balances are listed before credit balances.   *True False*

3. Adjusting entries record transactions accidentally omitted during the period.   *True False*

4. With a deferred expense, cash is paid prior to incurring the expense.   *True False*

5. Accrued revenue is revenue for which the company has been paid but which has not yet been earned.   *True False*

6. Fixed Asset Book Value = Cost – Accumulated Depreciation   *True False*

7. A short-term asset is expected to be held for fewer than 24 months.   *True False*

8. Depreciation is a precise measurement of the loss in value experienced by an asset over time.   *True False*

9. Under the straight-line depreciation method, depreciation expense is the same for every full year of the asset's useful life.   *True False*

10. The salvage value of an asset is disregarded with the double-declining balance method when determining depreciation expense.   *True False*

11. What shows after withdrawals on a trial balance?
    A. Revenue
    B. Liabilities
    C. Assets
    D. Capital

12. Which of these is NOT an adjusting entry?
    A. Accrued expenses
    B. Depreciation
    C. Withdrawals
    D. Deferred revenue

13. When are adjusting entries completed?
    A. After preparing the adjusted trial balance
    B. Before posting journal entries
    C. After generating financial statements
    D. After preparing the unadjusted trial balance

14. What type of account is Accumulated Depreciation?

    A. Expense

    B. Contra-revenue

    C. Contra-asset

    D. Liability

15. What is the impact of an adjusting entry for deferred expenses?

    A. A reduction in total expenses

    B. An increase in net income

    C. A reduction in the owner's capital account balance

    D. An increase in total assets

16. What is the impact of an adjusting entry for accrued revenue?

    A. A reduction in total revenue

    B. A reduction in net income

    C. A reduction in the owner's capital account balance

    D. An increase in total assets

17. Which statement regarding reversing entries is inaccurate?

    A. They are required.

    B. They are typically recorded for accrued revenue and accrued expenses.

    C. They're recorded on the first day of the period after the recording of the associated adjusting entry.

    D. They negate the effect of adjusting entries.

18. Within which category of adjusting entries does depreciation expense belong?

    A. Deferred expenses

    B. Deferred revenue

    C. Accrued expenses

    D. Accrued revenue

19. The adjusting entry for wages expense falls within the _____ category.

20. Jacobson Company records an adjusting entry that debits Wages Expense and credits Wages Payable. What is a component of the reversing entry?

    A. Debit to Cash

    B. Debit to Wages Payable

    C. Debit to Wages Expense

    D. Debit to Accounts Receivable

Putting It Together

PIT 4-1 RECORD THE ADJUSTING JOURNAL ENTRIES

In this example, we'll complete the unadjusted trial balance, the adjusting entry process, and the adjusted trial balance at the end of the first month of operations for Amber's Lacrosse Emporium.

Here are the account balances prior to the adjusting entries:

Cash			
$	75,000	$	15,000
$	2,400	$	12,000
$	1,450	$	1,500
$	2,100	$	2,750
		$	600
		$	1,600
		$	135
		$	200
		$	600
$	46,565		

Accounts Receivable			
$	3,000	$	2,100
$	900		

Supplies			
$	750		
$	750		

Merchandise Inventory			
$	15,080	$	1,350
$	2,000	$	2,100
$	13(580)		

Furniture		
$	2,000	
$	2,000	

Equipment		
$	12,000	
$	12,000	

Accounts Payable			
$	2,750	$	2,750
		$	2,000
		$	2,000

Amber Stein, Capital		
		$ 75,000
		$ 75,000

Amber Stein, Drawing		
$	600	
$	600	

Sales Revenue			
		$	2,400
		$	4,450
		$	6,850

Cost of Goods Sold		
$	1,350	
$	2,100	
$	3,450	

Advertising Expense		
$	600	
$	600	

Rent Expense		
$	1,500	
$	1,500	

Wages Expense		
$	1,600	
$	1,600	

Telephone Expense		
$	135	
$	135	

Utilities Expense		
$	200	
$	200	

1. We use the account balances to complete the unadjusted trial balance.

Amber's Lacrosse Emporium
Unadjusted Trial Balance
May 31, 2027

	Debit	Credit
Cash	$ 46,565	
Accounts Receivable	900	
Supplies	750	
Merchandise Inventory	13,550	
Furniture	2,000	
Equipment	12,000	
Accounts Payable		$ 2,000
Amber Stein, Capital		75,000
Amber Stein, Drawing	600	
Sales Revenue		6,850
Cost of Goods Sold	3,450	
Wages Expense	1,600	
Rent Expense	1,500	
Advertising Expense	600	
Utilities Expense	200	
Telephone Expense	135	
	$ 83,850	$ 83,850

2. A physical count of the supplies on May 31 indicates that $275 of supplies remain at the end of the month.

5/31	Supplies Expense	475	
	Supplies		475
	Adjusting entry to record supplies expense		

3. Employees for Amber's Lacrosse Emporium earned wages totaling $850 for working Monday, May 30 and Tuesday, May 31. They will be paid on Friday, June 3.

5/31	Wages Expense	850	
	Wages Payable		850
	Adjusting entry for employee wages owed		

4. Amber's Lacrosse Emporium now hosts sports-related activities, and a local lacrosse league will soon hold a series of events at the store. Full payment is due after the completion of all events. As of May 31, Amber's Lacrosse Emporium has charged $1,450 for completed events.

5/31	Accounts Receivable	1,450	
	Service Revenue		1,450
	Adjusting entry for revenue earned in advance of payment		

5. During its second month of operations, Amber's Lacrosse Emporium receives $820 in advance of holding two events ($410 per event) at the store. As of June 30, one of the two events was held.

6/30	Unearned Revenue	410	
	Service Revenue		410
	Adjusting entry for completion of services		

6. The equipment purchased has a four-year useful life and a salvage value of $600. Amber's Lacrosse Emporium uses the straight-line method to calculate depreciation.

Remember that Amber's Lacrosse Emporium has completed only one month of operations. Here we are calculating monthly depreciation; useful life in months is expressed in the calculation.

$$\frac{\$12{,}000 - \$600}{48} = \$237.50$$

5/31	Depreciation Expense	237.50	
	Accumulated Depreciation - Equipment		237.50
	Adjusting entry for first month's depreciation expense		

Notice that the depreciation account name includes the word "Equipment." A separate accumulated depreciation account is created for each depreciable asset on a company's books.

7. The furniture that was purchased has a six-year useful life and a salvage value of $200. Again, we use the straight-line method to calculate depreciation.

$$\frac{\$2{,}000 - \$200}{72} = \$25$$

5/31	Depreciation Expense	25	
	Accumulated Depreciation - Furniture		25
	Adjusting entry for first month's depreciation expense		

8. Using these adjusting entries, we can complete the adjusted trial balance.

Keep in mind that one entry occurred during the second month of operations and so does not impact this trial balance. Notice that dollars and cents are displayed. There was no need to display cents in the unadjusted trial balance because all balances were in whole dollar amounts.

Amber's Lacrosse Emporium
Adjusted Trial Balance
May 31, 2027

	Debit	Credit
Cash	$ 46,565.00	
Accounts Receivable	2,350.00	
Supplies	275.00	
Merchandise Inventory	13,550.00	
Furniture	2,000.00	
Accum. Depreciation - Furniture		$ 25.00
Equipment	12,000.00	
Accum. Depreciation - Equipment		237.50
Accounts Payable		2,000.00
Wages Payable		850.00
Amber Stein, Capital		75,000.00
Amber Stein, Drawing	600.00	
Sales Revenue		6,850.00
Service Revenue		1,450.00
Cost of Goods Sold	3,450.00	
Wages Expense	2,450.00	
Rent Expense	1,500.00	
Advertising Expense	600.00	
Supplies Expense	475.00	
Depreciation Expense	262.50	
Utilities Expense	200.00	
Telephone Expense	135.00	
	$ 86,412.50	$ 86,412.50

To confirm your calculated amounts, you may want to post the adjusting entries to the T-accounts on scrap paper prior to completing the adjusted trial balance.

Practice Set A

PSA 4-1 PREPARE THE UNADJUSTED TRIAL BALANCE

Prepare an unadjusted trial balance for Spot Cleaners as of October 31, 2027.

Starting file: Use the Trial Balance template.

Account Name	Balance
Cash	$2,400
Accounts Receivable	$900
Prepaid Insurance	$325
Equipment	$1,900
Accounts Payable	$675
Service Revenue	$1,850
Rent Expense	$700
Salaries Expense	$350
Tom Wilson, Drawing	$200
Tom Wilson, Capital	$4,250

PSA 4-2 CORRECT AN UNADJUSTED TRIAL BALANCE

Prepare a corrected version of this unadjusted trial balance. All accounts ended the period with a normal balance. (Hint: There are nine errors to correct.)

Starting file: Use the Trial Balance template.

Bookworm Central, Inc.
Unadjusted Trial Balance
December 31, 2027

	Debit	Credit
Cash	$ 35,700	
Accounts Receivable		$ 2,120
Supplies	475	
Automobile	9,450	
Equipment		7,200
Accounts Payable	3,450	
Salaries Payable		1,200
Service Revenue		11,000
Advertising Expense	200	
Rent Expense	950	
Supplies Expense		625
Greta Frank, Drawing		400
Greta Frank, Capital		41,470
	$ 50,225	$ 64,015

PSA 4-3 DETERMINE THE ACCOUNT BALANCE AND COMPLETE THE UNADJUSTED TRIAL BALANCE

The following information relates to Magenta Company as of March 31, 2027. Use the T-accounts to determine the ending balance for each account and then complete an unadjusted trial balance based on those balances.

Starting file: Use the Trial Balance template.

Cash				Accounts Receivable			Supplies		Accounts Payable		
$ 20,000	$ 1,250		$ 1,750	$ 1,000		$ 1,250		$ 100	$ 400
$ 1,000	$ 350					$ 400		$ 150	
	$ 200								
	$ 100								
	$ 150								

Vincent Guzman, Capital		Service Revenue		Telephone Expense		Utilities Expense	
	$ 20,000		$ 1,750	$ 350		$ 200	

PSA 4-4 RECORD ADJUSTING ENTRIES

Record the necessary adjusting entries. Today is January 31.

Starting file: Use the Journal Entries template.

1. On January 4, an insurance policy covering the next twelve months was purchased for $2,400.

2. On January 17, a customer paid $4,500 in advance of services being provided. As of today, $1,800 of the services have not been earned.

3. Employees work a five-day workweek, earn total wages of $2,400 each week, and are paid for each week's work on Friday. January 31 falls on a Thursday this year.

4. The company performed services totaling $3,900 this month, and as of today, customers have not yet been billed.

PSA 4-5 IDENTIFY ADJUSTING ENTRIES

Record the adjusting journal entries that led to the account balances shown here for September 30. Heads up! One account was impacted by two different adjusting entries.

Starting file: Use the Journal Entries template.

Account Name	Unadjusted Trial Balance	Adjusted Trial Balance
Accounts Receivable	$820	$1,245
Prepaid Insurance	$1,900	$1,275
Wages Payable	$0	$1,500
Unearned Revenue	$4,600	$1,100
Wages Expense	$7,100	$8,600
Insurance Expense	$0	$625
Service Revenue	$7,700	$11,625

PSA 4-6 DESCRIBE THE ADJUSTING ENTRY

Identify the category for each adjusting journal entry.

Deferred expenses	Accrued expenses
Deferred revenue	Accrued revenue

1.

1/31	Insurance Expense	800	
	Prepaid Insurance		800

_____

2.

1/31	Salaries Expense	1,800	
	Salaries Payable		1,800

_____

3.

1/31	Accounts Receivable	2,850	
	Service Revenue		2,850

_____

4.

1/31	Unearned Revenue	675	
	Service Revenue		675

_____

PSA 4-7 RECORD REVERSING ENTRIES

Review these adjusting entries (they should look familiar). Determine which one needs a reversing entry and then record it.

Starting file: Use the Journal Entries template.

1/31	Insurance Expense	800	
	Prepaid Insurance		800
1/31	Salaries Expense	1,800	
	Salaries Payable		1,800
1/31	Accounts Receivable	2,850	
	Service Revenue		2,850
1/31	Unearned Revenue	675	
	Service Revenue		675

PSA 4-8 CALCULATE DEPRECIATION USING THE STRAIGHT-LINE METHOD

Calculate annual depreciation for a piece of equipment using the straight-line method and record the adjusting journal entry. The equipment costs $65,000, has a useful life of ten years, and has a salvage value of $7,000.

Starting file: Use the Journal Entries template.

PSA 4-9 CALCULATE DEPRECIATION USING THE DOUBLE-DECLINING BALANCE METHOD

Now calculate depreciation for the same piece of equipment using the double-declining balance method. Complete the calculation for the first two years of the asset's life and record the adjusting journal entry for each.

Starting file: Use the Journal Entries template.

- Equipment cost: $65,000
- Useful life: 10 years
- Salvage value: $7,000

PSA 4-10 CALCULATE DEPRECIATION USING TWO METHODS

Calculate depreciation on a piece of machinery for the first two years of its useful life, using both the straight-line and double-declining balance methods. The machinery cost $47,000, has a useful life of eight years, and has a salvage value of $3,000.

Starting file: Use the Journal Entries template.

Using the account balances and adjusting entries shown here, prepare the adjusted trial balance for Spot Cleaners as of October 31, 2027.

Starting file: Use the Trial Balance template.

Account Name	Balance
Cash	$2,400
Accounts Receivable	$900
Prepaid Insurance	$325
Equipment	$1,900
Accounts Payable	$675
Service Revenue	$1,850
Rent Expense	$700
Salaries Expense	$350
Tom Wilson, Drawing	$200
Tom Wilson, Capital	$4,250

10/31	Insurance Expense	75	
	Prepaid Insurance		75
	Adjusting entry to record insurance expense		
10/31	Depreciation Expense	50	
	Accum. Depreciation - Equipment		50
	Adjusting entry for depreciation expense		
10/31	Accounts Receivable	200	
	Service Revenue		200
	Adjusting entry for revenue earned in advance of payment		
10/31	Salaries Expense	1,350	
	Salaries Payable		1,350
	Adjusting entry for employee salaries owed		

Practice Set B

PSB 4-1 PREPARE THE UNADJUSTED TRIAL BALANCE

Prepare the unadjusted trial balance for Willow Branch, Inc., as of April 30, 2027.

Starting file: Use the Trial Balance template.

Account Name	Balance
Cash	$51,000
Accounts Receivable	$6,450
Supplies	$1,895
Furniture	$16,700
Accounts Payable	$8,200
Wages Payable	$1,750
Service Revenue	$11,200
Telephone Expense	$425
Utilities Expense	$360
Tom Wilson, Capital	$55,680

PSB 4-2 CORRECT AN UNADJUSTED TRIAL BALANCE

Prepare a corrected version of this unadjusted trial balance. All accounts ended the period with a normal balance. (Hint: There are eight errors to correct.)

Starting file: Use the Trial Balance template.

Fish Mongers, Corp.
October 31, 2027
Unadjusted Trial Balance

	Debit	Credit
Cash	$ 24,000	
Accounts Receivable	4,200	
Supplies		$ 1,000
Furniture	3,000	
Accounts Payable		7,500
Wages Payable		2,000
Sales Revenue		6,500
Interest Revenue	250	
Advertising Expense	550	
Telephone Expense	260	
Truck		9,000
Joey Irrizary, Drawing	750	
Joey Irrizary, Capital	26,510	
	$ 59,520	$ 26,000

PSB 4-3 DETERMINE THE ACCOUNT BALANCE AND COMPLETE THE UNADJUSTED TRIAL BALANCE

The following information relates to Aquamarine Company as of July 31, 2027. Use the T-accounts to determine the ending balance for each account and then complete an unadjusted trial balance based on those balances.

Starting file: Use the Trial Balance template.

Cash				Accounts Receivable				Equipment			Accounts Payable		
$	47,500	$	8,500	$	3,800	$	1,800	$	8,500		$	875	$	2,500
$	1,800	$	900	$	4,000	$	1,500	$	2,500				
$	1,500	$	3,800										
		$	875										
		$	1,000										

Juanita Morales, Capital			Juanita Morales, Drawing			Sales Revenue			Rent Expense		
	$	47,500	$	3,800			$	3,800	$	900	
			$	1,000			$	4,000			

PSB 4-4 RECORD ADJUSTING ENTRIES

Record the necessary adjusting entries. Today is June 30.

Starting file: Use the Journal Entries template.

1. Prior to June 30, the Supplies account had a $900 balance. A physical count today indicates that $625 of supplies remain.

2. On June 9, a customer pays $7,000 in advance of services being provided. As of today, $4,500 of services have been performed.

3. Employees work a seven-day workweek, earn total wages of $4,200 each week, and are paid for each week's work on Sunday. June 30 falls on a Wednesday this year.

4. The company performed services totaling $12,200 this month, and as of today, customers have not yet been billed.

PSB 4-5 IDENTIFY ADJUSTING ENTRIES

Record the adjusting journal entries that led to the account balances shown here for June 30. Heads Up! One account was impacted by two different adjusting entries.

Starting file: Use the Journal Entries template.

Account Name	Unadjusted Trial Balance	Adjusted Trial Balance
Accounts Receivable	$3,200	$4,750
Supplies	$1,000	$625
Salaries Payable	$0	$800
Unearned Revenue	$2,000	$500
Salaries Expense	$3,700	$4,500
Supplies Expense	$0	$375
Service Revenue	$9,200	$12,250

PSB 4-6 DESCRIBE THE ADJUSTING ENTRY

Identify the category for each adjusting journal entry.

Deferred expenses	Accrued expenses
Deferred revenue	Accrued revenue

1.
7/31	Wage Expense	450	
	Wages Payable		450

_____

2.
7/31	Unearned Revenue	2,700	
	Service Revenue		2,700

_____

3.
7/31	Supplies Expense	525	
	Supplies		525

_____

4.
7/31	Accounts Receivable	1,400	
	Service Revenue		1,400

_____

PSB 4-7 RECORD REVERSING ENTRIES

Review these adjusting entries (they should look familiar). Determine which one(s) need a reversing entry and then record it(/them).

Starting file: Use the Journal Entries template.

7/31	Wage Expense	450	
	Wages Payable		450
7/31	Unearned Revenue	2,700	
	Service Revenue		2,700
7/31	Supplies Expense	525	
	Supplies		525
7/31	Accounts Receivable	1,400	
	Service Revenue		1,400

PSB 4-8 CALCULATE DEPRECIATION USING THE STRAIGHT-LINE METHOD

Calculate annual depreciation for a piece of furniture using the straight-line method and then record the adjusting journal entry. The furniture cost $22,000, has a useful life of five years, and has a salvage value of $2,000.

Starting file: Use the Journal Entries template.

PSB 4-9 CALCULATE DEPRECIATION USING THE DOUBLE-DECLINING BALANCE METHOD

Now calculate depreciation for the same item of furniture using the double-declining balance method. Complete this calculation for the first two years of the asset's life and then record the adjusting journal entry for each.

Starting file: Use the Journal Entries template.

- Equipment cost: $22,000
- Useful life: 5 years
- Salvage value: $2,000

PSB 4-10 CALCULATE DEPRECIATION USING TWO METHODS

Calculate depreciation on a truck for the first two years of its useful life, using both the straight-line and double-declining balance methods. The truck cost $28,000, has a useful life of six years, and has a salvage value of $1,000.

Starting file: Use the Journal Entries template.

PSB 4-11 PREPARE THE ADJUSTED TRIAL BALANCE

Using the account balances and adjusting entries shown here, prepare the adjusted trial balance for Willow Branch, Inc., as of April 30, 2027.

Starting file: Use the Trial Balance template.

Account Name	Balance
Cash	$51,000
Accounts Receivable	$6,450
Supplies	$1,895
Furniture	$16,700
Accounts Payable	$8,200
Wages Payable	$1,750
Service Revenue	$11,200
Telephone Expense	$425
Utilities Expense	$360
Tom Wilson, Capital	$55,680

4/30	Supplies Expense	725	
	Supplies		725
	Adjusting entry to record supplies expense		
4/30	Depreciation Expense	100	
	Accum. Depreciation - Furniture		100
	Adjusting entry for depreciation expense		
4/30	Accounts Receivable	1,800	
	Service Revenue		1,800
	Adjusting entry for revenue earned in advance of payment		
4/30	Wages Expense	800	
	Wages Payable		800
	Adjusting entry for employee wages owed		

5 Financial Statements and Closing Entries

Once the adjusting entries have been recorded, a company is ready to prepare its financial statements. Each financial statement summarizes a different set of information, and all are invaluable when analyzing a company's performance. After completion of the financial statements, the company's books are closed. This closing process ensures that all accounts are ready to be used in the next period. In this chapter, you will learn about each of the four financial statements. You will also examine the closing process through a review of the four closing entries and will complete the post-closing trial balance.

LEARNING OBJECTIVES

▸ Prepare an income statement

▸ Prepare a statement of owner's equity

▸ Prepare a balance sheet

▸ Identify the sections of a statement of cash flows

▸ Record closing entries

Project: Closing the Books for Nathan's Donut School

Having completed the adjusting journal entries, you're certain that all activity related to the first month of Nathan's Donut School has been properly recorded. You also know there's more to be done! Nathaniel has asked you to provide financial summaries of his company's performance, so what exactly should you give him?

You decide to first examine the four financial statements, each of which provides different insights into the performance of Nathan's Donut School. As you consider how you'll approach the second month of operations, you research the closing entry process, which prepares the company's books for the next month.

The Accounting Cycle

The final two stages—steps 6 and 7—of the accounting cycle are examined in this chapter. As part of closing the books for a period, the income statement and balance sheet, as shown here, are two very useful financial statements:

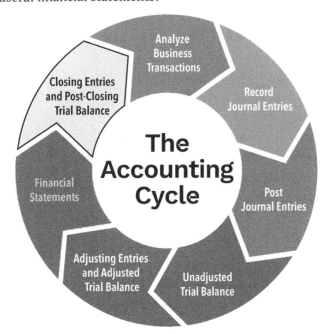

Nathan's Donut School Income Statement For the Month Ended March 31, 2027		
Revenues:		
Service Revenue		$ 3,500
Expenses:		
Rent Expense	$ 1,700	
Wages Expense	750	
Supplies Expense	315	
Advertising Expense	250	
Total Expenses		3,015
Net Income		$ 485

Nathan's Donut School Balance Sheet March 31, 2027		
Assets:		
Cash	$ 12,300	
Accounts Receivable	2,350	
Supplies	185	
Furniture	1,000	
Equipment	20,000	
Total Assets		$ 35,835
Liabilities:		
Accounts Payable	-	
Wages Payable	750	
Owner's Equity:		
Nathaniel H. Spencer, Capital	35,085	
Total Liabilities & Owner's Equity		$ 35,835

Income Statement

View the video "Income Statement."

Most companies are for-profit, meaning they're in business to earn more money than they spend to run the business. Notable exceptions include public universities and charitable organizations, which operate to provide a benefit to specific individuals. It's vital for all companies, whether for profit or not for profit, to closely monitor revenue and expenses. A company can determine whether it has earned a profit by examining its net income.

Net Income = Revenue − Expenses

One way to work the calculation is to add up the necessary figures from the adjusted trial balance. Alternatively, you can display all revenue and expenses in the income statement. It's the first financial statement a company completes, and the final figure shows the net income for the period being examined.

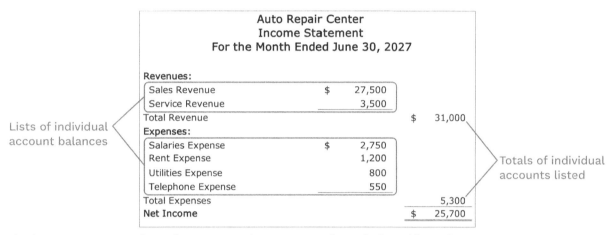

Lists of individual account balances

Totals of individual accounts listed

Auto Repair Center
Income Statement
For the Month Ended June 30, 2027

Revenues:			
Sales Revenue	$	27,500	
Service Revenue		3,500	
Total Revenue			$ 31,000
Expenses:			
Salaries Expense	$	2,750	
Rent Expense		1,200	
Utilities Expense		800	
Telephone Expense		550	
Total Expenses			5,300
Net Income			$ 25,700

The income statement lists all revenue and expenses and concludes with net income.

TIP! Both revenue and expense accounts are listed from largest to smallest within the income statement.

Most financial statements display multiple columns, where account balances are typically on the left and the sum or difference of these figures is on the right. Displaying individual revenue amounts in a different column than the total revenue ensures that the total amounts line up throughout the statement and can be easily added or subtracted.

You may have noticed the "for the month ended" phrase in the header of the example income statement above. The income statement displays activity over the course of a period, so the header reflects that.

NOTE! Use phrases that accurately capture the period considered in the statement (e.g., "for the year ended" or "for the period ended").

Ask Yourself 5-1: When total expenses exceed total revenue, the company has a net loss. True or false?

In this example, we will prepare the income statement for the first month of operations of Nathan's Donut School.

You've already calculated the balances for each account; you did that when you prepared the adjusted trial balance. You will use those balances to complete the income statement. Don't forget to include a three-line header—it's a required element.

Nathan's Donut School
Adjusted Trial Balance
March 31, 2027

	Debit	Credit
Cash	$ 12,300	
Accounts Receivable	2,350	
Supplies	185	
Furniture	1,000	
Equipment	20,000	
Accounts Payable		$ -
Wages Payable		750
Nathaniel H. Spencer, Capital		35,000
Nathaniel H. Spencer, Drawing	400	
Service Revenue		3,500
Rent Expense	1,700	
Wages Expense	750	
Supplies Expense	315	
Advertising Expense	250	
	$ 39,250	$ 39,250

Nathan's Donut School
Income Statement
For the Month Ended March 31, 2027

Revenues:		
Service Revenue		$ 3,500
Expenses:		
Rent Expense	$ 1,700	
Wages Expense	750	
Supplies Expense	315	
Advertising Expense	250	
Total Expenses		3,015
Net Income		$ 485

A standard practice is to list expenses from largest to smallest, as shown here.

Statement of Owner's Equity

 View the video "Statement of Owner's Equity."

Equity represents the portion of assets to which the business owner can lay claim, so naturally it's important for the owner to be able to trace associated business transactions. The statement of owner's equity is often referred to as a reconciliation because it displays the activity within the equity accounts. It shows how transactions during the period resulted in the change from the beginning to ending balance for the period. Similar to on the income statement, all balances in the statement of owner's equity have already been calculated. The task here is to simply organize them in the correct manner for this statement. Another similarity to the income statement is in how the date line header refers to the period being considered.

Auto Repair Center Statement of Owner's Equity For the Month Ended June 30, 2027		
Pawel Krawiec, Capital, June 1		$ 225,000
Add: Net Income	$ 25,700	
Investment	5,000	
	30,700	
Less: Pawel Krawiec, Drawing	5,000	
Increase in Owner's Equity		25,700
Pawel Krawiec, Capital, June 30		$ 250,700

The statement of owner's equity illustrates how the ending owner's equity balance is calculated.

A critical figure in the statement of owner's equity is net income, which is calculated on the income statement. For this reason, the statement of owner's equity is always the second financial statement prepared.

Ask Yourself 5-2: What shows in both the income statement and the statement of owner's equity?

    A. Total revenue

    B. The owner's drawing account

    C. Total liabilities

    D. Net income or loss

CASE IN POINT 5-2

In this example, we will prepare the statement of owner's equity for the first month of operations of Nathan's Donut School.

Nathan's Donut School experienced net income of $485 during the first month of operations, which you determined in the income statement. This amount shows under the Add section in the statement of owner's equity because it's net income. If Nathan's Donut School had instead experienced a net loss (expenses exceed revenue), then the amount would be placed in the Less section and subtracted on the statement. This is because a net loss reduces the portion of assets to which the owner can lay claim, and therefore reduces total owner's equity.

Nathan's Donut School Statement of Owner's Equity For the Month Ended March 31, 2027		
Nathaniel H. Spencer, Capital, March 1		$ -
Add: Net Income	$ 485	
Investment	35,000	
	35,485	
Less: Nathaniel H. Spencer, Drawing	400	
Increase in Owner's Equity		35,085
Nathaniel H. Spencer, Capital, March 31		$ 35,085

Balance Sheet

☁ **View the video "Balance Sheet."**

The balance sheet proves the accounting equation remains in balance at the end of the period; it is, essentially, an expanded display of the accounting equation. This report displays all asset, liability, and equity account balances that haven't been listed in an earlier financial statement.

> **NOTE!** Revenue, expense, and withdrawal account balances are accounted for in either the income statement or the statement of owner's equity and are not repeated on the balance sheet. (This would throw the accounting equation out of balance.)

A key figure in the balance sheet is the balance in the ending Owner's Equity account. Since this balance is calculated in the statement of owner's equity, that report must be completed before the balance sheet can be prepared.

Unlike the income statement and the statement of owner's equity, the balance sheet is a "snapshot" that displays account balances as of a single point in time. This is why the header shows the date the statement is prepared, typically the last day of the period.

Auto Repair Center Balance Sheet June 30, 2027		
Assets:		
Cash	$ 175,000	
Accounts Receivable	31,800	
Merchandise Inventory	7,500	
Buildings	22,000	
Land	35,700	
Total Assets		$ 272,000
Liabilities:		
Accounts Payable	21,300	
Owner's Equity:		
Pawel Krawiec, Capital	250,700	
Total Liabilities & Owner's Equity		$ 272,000

> **TIP!** Assets are listed in order of liquidity, with the accounts that are most easily convertible to cash listed at the top. Liabilities are ordered based on whether they are short-term or long-term, with short-term liabilities at the top.

The balance sheet can be configured in two ways:

- Displaying all asset balances at the top and all liability and owner's equity balances at the bottom
- Displaying assets on the left and liabilities and owner's equity on the right

With either configuration, the goal is to illustrate that total assets are equal to total liabilities plus owner's equity.

The balance sheet example here is a basic version that excludes account categories. A **classified balance sheet** categorizes asset and liability accounts by type and can include subtotals. We've already seen that asset accounts can be considered current assets (held ≤ 12 months) or long-term assets (held $\geq$ 12 months). Liability accounts can also be categorized as **current liabilities** (satisfied within 12 months) or **long-term liabilities** (expected to remain on the books for more than 12 months).

Current Liabilities – Examples	Long-Term Liabilities – Examples
• Credit Cards Payable • Sales Tax Payable • Short-Term Debt (e.g., a line of credit)	Long-term portions of: • Mortgages Payable • Loans Payable • Bonds Payable

Ask Yourself 5-3: In the balance sheet, what always equals total assets?

    A. Total liabilities

    B. Total owner's equity

    C. Accounts payable

    D. Total liabilities and owner's equity

CASE IN POINT 5-3

In this example, we'll prepare a balance sheet for the first month of operations of Nathan's Donut School.

Remember the assets and liabilities were calculated previously. They're shown on the adjusted trial balance (CIP 5-1). The other key figure here is the owner's equity, which we just determined.

Nathan's Donut School
Balance Sheet
March 31, 2027

Assets:		
Cash	$ 12,300	
Accounts Receivable	2,350	
Supplies	185	
Furniture	1,000	
Equipment	20,000	
Total Assets		$ 35,835
Liabilities:		
Accounts Payable	-	
Wages Payable	750	
Owner's Equity:		
Nathaniel H. Spencer, Capital	35,085	
Total Liabilities & Owner's Equity		$ 35,835

Just like the accounting equation, the balance sheet must always be in balance (assets = liabilities + owner's equity). If it's not, you must review each account balance to determine where the error lies. In this case:

Assets	=	Liabilities	+	Owner's Equity
$35,835		**$750**		**$35,085**

Statement of Cash Flows

Cash is the most important asset on any company's books, so keeping a close eye on the factors that led to the current cash balance is vital. The fourth financial statement, the statement of cash flows, is devoted to displaying all activity related to the cash account. Although the completion of the statement of cash flows is beyond the scope of this course, you will find it very helpful to understand the different sections within the statement.

- The Operating Activities section at the top shows all cash-related activity for the standard revenue-generating operations of the company. Basically, any receipt or use of cash associated with the daily running of the business is included here.

- The Investing Activities section is next. It displays any cash spent on long-term (fixed) assets or cash received from the sale of such assets.

- The final section is Financing Activities, and it shows cash-related activity associated with stocks, bonds, withdrawals, and long-term liabilities (amounts owed for longer than one year). Any cash received from these activities, or paid out for these activities, is included in this section.

Auto Repair Center Statement of Cash Flows For the Month Ended June 30, 2027			
Operating Activities:			
Cash Received from Customers			$ 34,800
Cash Paid for Merchandise Inventory	$	25,200	
Cash Paid for Salaries Expense		3,000	
Cash Paid for General & Admin Exp.		2,840	31,040
Net Cash Flow from Operating Activities			$ 3,760
Investing Activities			
Cash Received for Sale of Equipment			12,100
Cash Paid for Buildings		5,000	
Cash Paid for Land		9,000	14,000
Net Cash Flow Used By Investing Activities			$ (1,900)
Financing Activities			
Cash Paid for Withdrawals			5,000
Net Cash Flow Used By Financing Activities			$ (5,000)
Decrease in Cash Balance			(3,140)
Beginning Cash Balance			178,140
Ending Cash Balance			$ 175,000

The statement of cash flows provides a detailed view of activity in the Cash account.

Remember, the statement of cash flows includes only those activities in which *cash* changed hands. If, for instance, furniture is purchased on account, this transaction would not be included in the statement because it did not involve the Cash account.

Ask Yourself 5-4: Both the beginning and ending cash balances appear on the statement of cash flows. True or false?

In these examples, we will determine for each item within which section of the statement of cash flows it belongs.

1. Purchase of a truck with cash.

   A truck is a fixed asset. The purchase or sale of a fixed asset is displayed in the Investing Activities *section.*

2. Sale of bonds for cash.

   Any transaction involving bonds in which cash changes hands is displayed in the Financing Activities *section.*

3. Withdrawal of cash by the owner.

   Initially, you might put this in the Operating Activities section—after all, it involves the use of cash—but owner withdrawals are not a typical part of a company's ongoing operations. Like cash transactions involving stocks and bonds, owner withdrawals are part of the Financing Activities *section.*

4. Payment of telephone expense.

   Bill payment is part of ongoing operations, so this item goes in the Operating Activities *section.*

5. Receipt of cash from a customer.

   Similar to a typical expense, cash received from a customer in exchange for goods or services is displayed in the Operating Activities *section.*

6. Sale of equipment for cash.

   Equipment is another fixed asset, like the truck. This item belongs in the Investing Activities *section.*

Closing Entries

All accounts can be categorized as *temporary* or *permanent*. A temporary account is closed (zeroed out) at the end of each period. Temporary accounts are the revenue, expense, and withdrawal accounts. All other accounts are permanent, meaning their account balances are carried over from one period to the next. For these accounts, the ending balance for one period becomes the beginning balance for the next period.

The closing entry process for all temporary accounts involves recording four journal entries in a specific order:

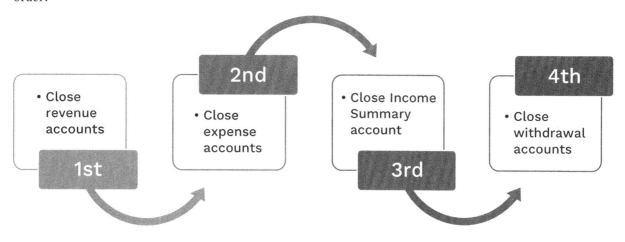

The third closing entry is for the Income Summary account, which is a holding account used to facilitate the closing entry process. It always has a zero balance at the end of the closing process.

6/30	Sales Revenue	27,500	
	Service Revenue	3,500	
	Income Summary		31,000
	Closing entry to close revenue accounts		
6/30	Income Summary	5,300	
	Salaries Expense		2,750
	Rent Expense		1,200
	Utilities Expense		800
	Telephone Expense		550
	Closing entry to close expense accounts		
6/30	Income Summary	25,700	
	Pawel Krawiec, Capital		25,700
	Closing entry to close Income Summary account		
6/30	Pawel Krawiec, Capital	5,000	
	Pawel Krawiec, Drawing		5,000
	Closing entry to close withdrawal accounts		

Example journal entries in the proper order for closing temporary accounts

In the example, notice that the revenue accounts are properly debited in the first closing entry. This is necessary because revenue accounts have a normal credit balance. A debit serves to offset this credit balance and to therefore reduce the revenue account balance to zero (close the account). Similarly, as expense and withdrawal accounts have a normal debit balance, these accounts are credited here to reduce their balances to zero.

When revenue exceeds expenses (leading to net income, as in the example), the Income Summary account has a credit balance after the second closing entry. So, to close the Income Summary account in the third closing entry, a debit to the account is required. If expenses exceed revenue (net loss), then the circumstance is reversed; Income Summary is credited in the third closing entry.

Ask Yourself 5-5: How many closing entries are made at the end of a period?

CASE IN POINT 5-5

In this example, we'll record the four closing entries for the first month of operations of Nathan's Donut School.

You've already determined the balances of the temporary accounts (as well as the Capital account) after the adjusting entries.

Nathaniel H. Spencer, Capital		Nathaniel H. Spencer, Drawing		Service Revenue		Advertising Expense	
	$ 35,000	$ 400			$ 850	$ 250	
					$ 2,500		
					$ 150		
	$ 35,000	$ 400			$ 3,500	$ 250	

Rent Expense		Supplies Expense		Wages Expense	
$ 1,700		$ 315		$ 750	
$ 1,700		$ 315		$ 750	

We close the revenue and expense accounts in the first two journal entries. To determine the amount for the third closing journal entry, we create an Income Summary T-account after the second entry is complete. Then we can see that Income Summary has a credit balance, which means we debit that account to offset the $485 credit balance.

3/31	Service Revenue	3,500	
	Income Summary		3,500
	Closing entry to close revenue accounts		

	Income Summary	
$ 3,015		$ 3,500

3/31	Income Summary	3,015	
	Rent Expense		1,700
	Wages Expense		750
	Supplies Expense		315
	Advertising Expense		250
	Closing entry to close expense accounts		

$ 485

3/31	Income Summary	485	
	Nathaniel H. Spencer, Capital		485
	Closing entry to close Income Summary account		

3/31	Nathaniel H. Spencer, Capital	400	
	Nathaniel H. Spencer, Drawing		400
	Closing entry to close withdrawal accounts		

Post-Closing Trial Balance

The final step in the accounting cycle is to complete the post-closing trial balance. It's similar to the unadjusted trial balance and the adjusted trial balance except the post-closing trial balance includes only the permanent accounts because the temporary accounts have already been closed. Therefore, the post-closing trial balance is the shortest of the three trial balances.

Auto Repair Center Post-Closing Trial Balance June 30, 2027		
	Debit	Credit
Cash	$ 175,000	
Accounts Receivable	31,800	
Merchandise Inventory	7,500	
Buildings	22,000	
Land	35,700	
Accounts Payable		$ 21,300
Pawel Krawiec, Capital		250,700
	$ 272,000	$ 272,000

NOTE! As with other trial balances, the post-closing trial balance must show equal totals for debits and credits.

The ending balance of the capital account was determined when the statement of owner's equity was completed. That ending balance is used in the post-closing trial balance. This is another distinction between the post-closing trial balance and the trial balances completed earlier that did not contain this ending capital balance.

Ask Yourself 5-6: Which account would NOT appear in a post-closing trial balance?
A. Service Revenue
B. Cash
C. Accounts Receivable
D. Accounts Payable

CASE IN POINT 5-6

In this example, we will complete the post-closing trial balance for Nathan's Donut School.

You'll notice that the balance in the Nathaniel H. Spencer, Capital account is higher now ($35,085) than on the adjusted trial balance ($35,000). This is the result of the recording of the closing journal entries.

Nathan's Donut School
Post-Closing Trial Balance
March 31, 2027

	Debit	Credit
Cash	$ 12,300	
Accounts Receivable	2,350	
Supplies	185	
Furniture	1,000	
Equipment	20,000	
Accounts Payable		$ -
Wages Payable		750
Nathaniel H. Spencer, Capital		35,085
	$ 35,835	$ 35,835

Remember, the post-closing trial balance shows the ending balances for all permanent accounts. They become the beginning balances for the next period.

Self-Assessment

Now it's time for you to check your knowledge of the key concepts and skills introduced in this chapter.

1. The income statement lists expenses above revenue. *True   False*

2. The date line in the header of the income statement includes a phrase that describes the period considered in the statement. *True   False*

3. The statement of owner's equity is often referred to as a reconciliation of the beginning and ending capital accounts. *True   False*

4. The statement of owner's equity displays balances as of a single date, not activity over a period. *True   False*

5. The balance sheet can either be designed to display assets on top (liabilities and owner's equity at bottom) or with assets at left (liabilities and owner's equity at right). *True   False*

6. Within the balance sheet total assets must equal total liabilities. *True   False*

7. The statement of cash flows shows all cash-related activity for a period. *True   False*

8. The statement of cash flows shows the beginning and ending balances for the Cash account. *True   False*

9. Only the temporary accounts are closed as part of the closing entry process. *True   False*

10. There are five closing journal entries. *True   False*

11. Which financial statement is completed first?

    A. Balance sheet

    B. Statement of cash flows

    C. Income statement

    D. Statement of owner's equity

12. What is included on both the income statement and the statement of owner's equity?

    A. Net income/loss

    B. Amount in the capital account

    C. Sales revenue

    D. Amount in the drawing account

13. What equation is proven in the balance sheet?

14. Which is NOT a section of the statement of cash flows?

    A. Operating Activities

    B. Investing Activities

    C. Financing Activities

    D. Borrowing Activities

15. Which is a current liability?

    A. One placed on the books in a journal entry during the past month

    B. One expected to be satisfied (paid) within 12 months

    C. One expected to remain on the books longer than a year

    D. One that was satisfied (paid) during the past month

16. Which of these, unless otherwise specified, is NOT a long-term liability account?

    A. Mortgages Payable

    B. Loans Payable

    C. Bonds Payable

    D. Credit Cards Payable

17. Identify the FALSE statement regarding the classified balance sheet.

    A. It categorizes asset and liability accounts based on type.

    B. It does not include subtotals.

    C. It considers assets, both current and long-term.

    D. It considers current and long-term liabilities.

18. What shows on the second line of the three-line balance sheet header?

    A. The words "Balance Sheet"

    B. The name of the company

    C. A phrase such as "For the Month Ended" followed by the date

    D. The date only

19. What is displayed on the final line of the statement of cash flows?

    A. Beginning Cash balance

    B. Ending Cash balance

    C. Increase (or decrease) in the Cash account balance

    D. The total cash received

20. What account is closed as part of the closing entry process?

    A. Cash

    B. Accounts Payable

    C. John Doe, Capital

    D. Service Revenue

Putting It Together

PIT 5-1 COMPLETE THE ACCOUNTING CYCLE

In this example, we will complete the income statement, statement of owner's equity, balance sheet, closing journal entries, and post-closing trial balance for the first month of operations of Amber's Lacrosse Emporium. This process is sometimes referred to as "closing the books" for a period.

The account balances prior to the completion of the financial statements are shown in the adjusted trial balance here:

Amber's Lacrosse Emporium
Adjusted Trial Balance
May 31, 2027

	Debit	Credit
Cash	$ 46,565.00	
Accounts Receivable	2,350.00	
Supplies	275.00	
Merchandise Inventory	13,550.00	
Furniture	2,000.00	
Accum. Depreciation - Furniture		$ 25.00
Equipment	12,000.00	
Accum. Depreciation - Equipment		237.50
Accounts Payable		2,000.00
Wages Payable		850.00
Amber Stein, Capital		75,000.00
Amber Stein, Drawing	600.00	
Sales Revenue		6,850.00
Service Revenue		1,450.00
Cost of Goods Sold	3,450.00	
Wages Expense	2,450.00	
Rent Expense	1,500.00	
Advertising Expense	600.00	
Supplies Expense	475.00	
Depreciation Expense	262.50	
Utilities Expense	200.00	
Telephone Expense	135.00	
	$ 86,412.50	$ 86,412.50

1. We first use the adjusted trial balance figures as we complete the income statement.

Amber's Lacrosse Emporium Income Statement For the Month Ended May 31, 2027		
Revenues:		
Sales Revenue	$ 6,850.00	
Service Revenue	1,450.00	
Total Revenue		$ 8,300.00
Expenses:		
Cost of Goods Sold	3,450.00	
Wages Expense	2,450.00	
Rent Expense	1,500.00	
Advertising Expense	600.00	
Supplies Expense	475.00	
Depreciation Expense	262.50	
Utilities Expense	200.00	
Telephone Expense	135.00	
Total Expenses		9,072.50
Net Loss		$ (772.50)

The company incurred greater expenses during its first month of operations than revenue earned; in other words, it spent more than it made. As a result, the final figure shows as a net loss instead of net income.

2. Next, we use the capital account figure from the adjusted trial balance and the net loss from the income statement to complete the statement of owner's equity.

Amber's Lacrosse Emporium Statement of Owner's Equity For the Month Ended May 31, 2027		
Amber Stein, Capital, May 1		$ -
Add: Investment	$ 75,000.00	
Less: Net Loss	772.50	
Amber Stein, Drawing	600.00	
Increase in Owner's Equity		73,627.50
Amber Stein, Capital, May 31		$ 73,627.50

Unlike net income, net loss is subtracted on the statement of owner's equity.

3. To complete the balance sheet, we use account balances from the adjusted trial balance as well as the owner's equity just determined.

Amber's Lacrosse Emporium
Balance Sheet
May 31, 2027

Assets:		
Cash		$ 46,565.00
Accounts Receivable		2,350.00
Supplies		275.00
Merchandise Inventory		13,550.00
Furniture	$ 2,000.00	
Accum. Dep. - Furniture	25.00	1,975.00
Equipment	12,000.00	
Accum. Dep. - Equipment	237.50	11,762.50
Total Assets		$ 76,477.50
Liabilities:		
Accounts Payable		2,000.00
Wages Payable		850.00
Owner's Equity:		
Amber Stein, Capital		73,627.50
Total Liabilities & Owner's Equity		$ 76,477.50

The Furniture and Equipment accounts are associated with accumulated depreciation. When this is included on the balance sheet, it's listed directly beneath the asset account, and both amounts are displayed in the left column. The net book value (Cost – Accumulated Depreciation) is then calculated and displayed to the right.

4. Next, we record the four closing entries necessary to close the temporary accounts.

5/31	Sales Revenue	6,850.00	
	Service Revenue	1,450.00	
	Income Summary		8,300.00
	Closing entry to close revenue accounts		
5/31	Income Summary	9,072.50	
	Cost of Goods Sold		3,450.00
	Wages Expense		2,450.00
	Rent Expense		1,500.00
	Advertising Expense		600.00
	Supplies Expense		475.00
	Depreciation Expense		262.50
	Utilities Expense		200.00
	Telephone Expense		135.00
	Closing entry to close expense accounts		
5/31	Amber Stein, Capital	772.50	
	Income Summary		772.50
	Closing entry to close Income Summary account		
5/31	Amber Stein, Capital	600.00	
	Amber Stein, Drawing		600.00
	Closing entry to close withdrawal accounts		

Recall that Amber's Lacrosse Emporium experienced a net loss; the Income Summary account shows a debit balance of $772.50 after the second closing entry. That's why here in the third closing entry the Income Summary account is credited by that amount—to close it.

5. Lastly, we prepare the post-closing trial balance.

Notice accumulated depreciation accounts on their own lines with the balances appearing in the credit column.

Amber's Lacrosse Emporium Post-Closing Trial Balance May 31, 2027	Debit	Credit
Cash	$ 46,565.00	
Accounts Receivable	2,350.00	
Supplies	275.00	
Merchandise Inventory	13,550.00	
Furniture	2,000.00	
Accum. Dep. - Furniture		$ 25.00
Equipment	12,000.00	
Accum. Dep. - Equipment		237.50
Accounts Payable		2,000.00
Wages Payable		850.00
Amber Stein, Capital		73,627.50
	$ 76,740.00	$ 76,740.00

Practice Set A

PSA 5-1 DETERMINE THE PURPOSE OF EACH FINANCIAL STATEMENT

Match each financial statement with the information it conveys.

_____ Income statement

_____ Statement of owner's equity

_____ Balance sheet

_____ Statement of cash flows

A. Accounting equation in balance at the end of a period

B. Reconciliation of beginning and ending owner's equity

C. Uses and sources of cash for a period

D. Net income/loss over a period

PSA 5-2 PREPARE AN INCOME STATEMENT

Prepare the income statement for the first month of operations of Max Energy, Inc., as of July 31, 2027.

Starting file: Use the Income Statement template.

	Debit	Credit
Max Energy, Inc.		
Adjusted Trial Balance		
July 31, 2027		
Cash	$ 212,000	
Accounts Receivable	24,500	
Supplies	1,575	
Prepaid Insurance	2,300	
Equipment	18,000	
Accum. Dep. - Equipment		$ 150
Truck	24,000	
Accum. Dep. - Truck		400
Land	65,000	
Accounts Payable		37,500
Notes Payable		11,000
Max Granger, Capital		271,685
Max Granger, Drawing	1,000	
Service Revenue		35,500
Interest Revenue		125
Wages Expense	3,200	
Advertising Expense	1,450	
Automobile Expense	975	
Telephone Expense	885	
Depreciation Expense	550	
Supplies Expense	425	
Utilities Expense	400	
Insurance Expense	100	
	$ 356,360	$ 356,360

Notice that the Land account doesn't have an associated accumulated depreciation account. Although land is a fixed asset, it's never depreciated. You will continue to use this adjusted trial balance as you complete the remaining financial statements for Max Energy, Inc.

PSA 5-3 PREPARE A STATEMENT OF OWNER'S EQUITY

Prepare the statement of owner's equity for the first month of operations of Max Energy, Inc.

Starting file: Use the Statement of Owner's Equity template.

PSA 5-4 PREPARE A BALANCE SHEET

Prepare the balance sheet for the first month of operations of Max Energy, Inc.

Starting file: Use the Balance Sheet template.

PSA 5-5 RECORD CLOSING ENTRIES

Prepare the closing journal entries for the first month of operations of Max Energy, Inc., and then complete the post-closing trial balance.

Starting files: Use the Journal Entries and Trial Balance templates.

PSA 5-6 PREPARE AN INCOME STATEMENT

Prepare the income statement for the first month of operations of Munchkin Snacks, Corp., as of September 30, 2027.

Starting file: Use the Income Statement template.

Heads up! Not all these account balances are needed for the income statement, but you may need them as you complete the remaining financial statements in the following exercises.

Accounts Payable	$8,750	Merchandise Inventory	$3,000
Telephone Expense	$700	Sales Revenue	$7,500
Accounts Receivable	$5,400	Joe Munch, Drawing	$575
Utilities Expense	$825	Cash	$42,000
Office Expense	$225	Rent Expense	$2,200
Equipment	$8,200	Depreciation Expense	$100
Joe Munch, Capital	$46,875	Accum. Dep. – Equip	$100

PSA 5-7 PREPARE A STATEMENT OF OWNER'S EQUITY

Prepare the statement of owner's equity for the first month of operations of Munchkin Snacks, Corp.

Starting file: Use the Statement of Owner's Equity template.

PSA 5-8 PREPARE A BALANCE SHEET

Prepare the balance sheet for the first month of operations of Munchkin Snacks, Corp.

Starting file: Use the Balance Sheet template.

PSA 5-9 COMPLETE THE CLOSING ENTRY PROCESS

Prepare the closing journal entries for the first month of operations of Munchkin Snacks, Corp., and then complete the post-closing trial balance.

Starting files: Use the Journal Entries and Trial Balance templates.

Practice Set B

PSB 5-1 IDENTIFY THE BENEFITS OF CLOSING THE BOOKS

Identify the statements that accurately convey why the closing process is necessary and how it facilitates the assessment of a company's performance.

_____ The closing process ensures all permanent accounts begin each period with a $0 balance.

_____ The closing process ensures all temporary account balances relate solely to the current period.

_____ Completion of the closing entry process ensures that the owner's capital account is impacted by the net income or loss during the period.

_____ Completion of the closing entry process ensures that the owner's capital account is impacted by the owner's withdrawals during the period.

_____ Completion of the closing entry process ensures that the owner's capital account is impacted by the fixed asset purchases made during the period.

PSB 5-2 PREPARE AN INCOME STATEMENT

Prepare the income statement for the first month of operations of Crime Investigators as of October 31, 2027.

Starting file: Use the Income Statement template.

Crime Investigators
Adjusted Trial Balance
October 31, 2027

	Debit	Credit
Cash	$ 27,000	
Accounts Receivable	4,000	
Supplies	1,000	
Equipment	10,000	
Accum. Dep. - Equipment		$ 150
Accounts Payable		6,200
Salaries Payable		400
Melina Giles, Capital		32,190
Melina Giles, Drawing	1,100	
Service Revenue		8,500
Salaries Expense	1,800	
Supplies Expense	1,000	
Telephone Expense	500	
Utilities Expense	490	
Advertising Expense	400	
Depreciation Expense	150	
	$ 47,440	$ 47,440

Refer to this adjusted trial balance as needed in the remaining exercises dealing with Crime Investigators.

PSB 5-3 PREPARE A STATEMENT OF OWNER'S EQUITY

Prepare the statement of owner's equity for the first month of operations of Crime Investigators.

Starting file: Use the Statement of Owner's Equity template.

PSB 5-4 PREPARE A BALANCE SHEET

Prepare the balance sheet for the first month of operations of Crime Investigators.
Starting file: Use the Balance Sheet template.

PSB 5-5 RECORD CLOSING ENTRIES

Prepare the closing journal entries for the first month of operations of Crime Investigators and then complete the post-closing trial balance.
Starting files: Use the Journal Entries and Trial Balance templates.

PSB 5-6 PREPARE AN INCOME STATEMENT

Prepare the income statement for the first month of operations of Dollar Bill Enterprises as of April 30, 2027. Not all the accounts showing are part of the income statement, but you will need them as you complete the closing process for the company.
Starting file: Use the Income Statement template.

Land	$10,000	Prepaid Insurance	$2,000
Cash	$8,750	Bill Samuels, Capital	$23,875
Rent Expense	$1,200	Salaries Expense	$950
Service Revenue	$3,200	Accounts Receivable	$700
Bill Samuels, Drawing	$800	Interest Revenue	$65
Insurance Expense	$90	Auto Expense	$650
Supplies Expense	$500	Supplies	$1,500

PSB 5-7 PREPARE A STATEMENT OF OWNER'S EQUITY

Prepare the statement of owner's equity for the first month of operations of Dollar Bill Enterprises.
Starting file: Use the Statement of Owner's Equity template.

PSB 5-8 PREPARE A BALANCE SHEET

Prepare the balance sheet for the first month of operations of Dollar Bill Enterprises.
Starting file: Use the Balance Sheet template.

PSB 5-9 COMPLETE THE CLOSING ENTRY PROCESS

Prepare the closing journal entries for the first month of operations of Dollar Bill Enterprises and then complete the post-closing trial balance.
Starting files: Use the Journal Entries and Trial Balance templates.

6 Computerized Systems, Cash, and Payroll

In this chapter, we continue our discussion of cash and payroll. They're both addressed in the accounting cycle, but due to their complexity, they warrant additional consideration. Cash must be monitored closely to ensure it hasn't been stolen or lost, and calculating payroll involves figuring not only the gross pay owed, but also the amounts to be withheld from each paycheck. Employers also must pay payroll taxes along with these withheld amounts. Computerized accounting systems can greatly improve the efficiency of the recording process, so we will look at these, too. You'll also examine internal control procedures for cash, bank reconciliations, and journal entries for petty cash.

LEARNING OBJECTIVES

▸ Describe appropriate internal control procedures

▸ Prepare a bank reconciliation

▸ Calculate employer and employee payroll taxes

▸ Record journal entries for payroll

▸ Describe a computerized accounting system

Project: Monitoring Cash and Calculating Payroll for Nathan's Donut School

Now that you've completed the entire accounting cycle, you want to examine certain topics in further detail. Nathaniel wants to be assured that all cash is properly accounted for and being monitored closely. He also asks how payroll taxes for Nathan's Donut School are calculated. And, he's considering purchasing a computerized accounting system and needs your help with this decision.

You begin by considering methods for monitoring cash and internal control procedures to safeguard it. You also examine petty cash journal entries and bank reconciliations. You then examine the calculations for payroll. You know that both the employee and the employer pay payroll taxes and that separate journal entries are used for each. You look closely at each type of tax so you can fully explain them to Nathaniel. You then research the benefits and drawbacks of computerized accounting systems.

Safeguarding Cash

The statement of cash flows is an overview of all cash-related activity for a period. Because it deals with activities only in which cash has changed hands, it's an essential statement for any business, but it's completed at the *end* of a period. How can you ensure that cash is being safeguarded on an ongoing basis *during* the period? One way is through the proper application of internal control procedures.

Using Internal Controls

An organization can use **internal control procedures** to ensure cash is properly safeguarded. These procedures include the following:

- **Maintaining physical safeguards:** Cash registers should be accessible only by authorized employees and should be routinely emptied. Cash should be deposited in the bank daily, and any cash kept at the location of business should be maintained in a lockbox or otherwise secured.

- **Segregation of duties:** Cash-related recordkeeping duties should be performed by an employee who does not physically handle cash. This ensures that the same person cannot both steal money and alter accounting records to hide the theft.

- **Transaction authorization:** Cash-related transactions (such as bank withdrawals and cash returns) exceeding a predetermined amount should be authorized by a manager or owner to ensure they are properly reviewed prior to completion.

- **Record retention:** Cash-related supporting materials, including check stubs, bank statements, and voided checks, should be retained for at least seven years. This ensures that transactions can be properly reviewed if questions regarding their validity are raised.

> **Ask Yourself 6-1:** Internal controls help ensure cash is safeguarded during a period. True or false?

In these examples, we'll consider four independent circumstances and identify which internal control procedure could have prevented each.

1. Express Assistance Corp. has a current cash balance of $24,000. A recently hired junior employee completes the purchase of $22,000 of furniture and delivers a check to the seller. Upon learning of this, the owner is frustrated that such a large portion of the company's cash was spent in this manner.

   The internal control procedure of transaction authorization would have prevented this. If the owner had required all employees to obtain his authorization for large cash-related transactions, he would have been able to stop the transaction from happening.

2. Electronic World, Inc., sells large electronic equipment. One evening, after the store has closed and all employees have gone home, a robbery occurs. The next day the manager confirms that two days' worth of sales, totaling $23,500, was stolen from the cash register.

   Maintaining physical safeguards would have prevented the loss of this large amount of cash. Had the cash register been emptied regularly and the money deposited into the bank each day, only a small amount of cash would have been left in the register and then lost in the robbery.

3. Wallpaper House is a seller and installer of unique wallpaper. The company's new accountant conducted a thorough review of prior financial statements and tax returns and believes a significant amount of cash is missing. No further investigation can be performed because no additional records are available for review.

   Record retention would have allowed for a more thorough investigation in this situation. This investigation, which would have examined documents such as check stubs and payment vouchers with itemized payment details, could have uncovered when the cash went missing and who was responsible.

4. Old World Cabinetry is a small company with six employees. Dmitry was recently hired to handle billing and payments. He creates a fake bill from a vendor, cuts a check to cash to pay, and then deposits the money into his personal bank account.

   This theft could have been avoided through the segregation of duties. The employee who manages billing and payments should not have the authority to write checks. If another employee had been in charge of writing checks, Dmitry couldn't have stolen the cash.

◎◎ A CLOSER LOOK

Do Internal Controls Prevent All Theft?

Effective internal controls can prevent a great deal of theft and accidental loss of assets, but it's almost impossible for a company to prevent *all* theft. For example, the segregation of duties control ensures that no single individual can manipulate the accounting records to hide a theft, but what if two people work together to steal cash? This is **collusion**, and it's much more difficult for a company to prevent.

One way to combat collusion is through audits. An **internal audit** involves having company employees in a different department from those handling cash review a random sampling of transactions. Supporting documentation is examined to confirm the transactions were accurately recorded. Although collusion can still occur when internal auditors are involved, it's far more difficult.

An **external audit** involves the same process but is completed by an outside organization. Public corporations are required to undergo external audits annually so the audit firm can sign off on the accuracy of publicly issued financial statements, but any company can hire an external audit firm. As external auditors do not work for the company being examined, the possibility of collusion is significantly diminished compared to an internal audit when they are involved.

Petty Cash

🎬 **View the video "Recording Petty Cash."**

The proper recording of **petty cash** is another element that helps to safeguard a company's cash. Many companies maintain a lockbox, often overseen by an administrative assistant, containing a small amount of cash used for incidental purchases, such as for the purchase of stamps, the delivery of packages, or miscellaneous expenses (pizza for all employees, for example).

11/5	Petty Cash	500	
	Cash		500
	Establishment of a petty cash fund		

When cash is first set aside for company incidentals, a petty cash fund is established through the recording of a journal entry.

In this example, there is $500 in petty cash. Over the next few weeks, the company spends $220 of this on postage expense, $145 on supplies, and $85 on miscellaneous expenses. Another journal entry is recorded when the fund is replenished.

11/18	Postage Expense	220	
	Supplies Expense	145	
	Miscellaneous Expense	85	
	Cash		450
	Replenishment of the petty cash fund		

Notice that the Petty Cash account is not included in this journal entry. It's only used when the fund is first established or the amount within the fund is altered. In this example, imagine that, over time, the company decides more money is necessary in the petty cash fund. Here's how the journal entry reflecting this increase would look:

1/20	Petty Cash	100	
	Cash		100
	Increase of the petty cash fund		

Ask Yourself 6-2: Petty cash is a liability account. True or false?

In these examples, we will record journal entries for Nathan's Donut School to establish, replenish, and increase the total value of the petty cash fund during the company's second month of operations.

1. On April 2, Nathan's Donut School decides to keep some cash on hand at the front desk and establishes a petty cash fund containing $250.

4/2	Petty Cash	250	
	Cash		250
	Establishment of a petty cash fund		

2. As of April 19, Nathan's Donut School spent $85 of petty cash on postage, $45 on supplies, and $110 on miscellaneous expenses.

4/19	Postage Expense	85	
	Supplies Expense	45	
	Miscellaneous Expense	110	
	Cash		240
	Replenishment of the petty cash fund		

3. On May 5, Nathan's Donut School increases its petty cash fund by $100, as it expects more petty cash purchases in the future.

5/5	Petty Cash	100	
	Cash		100
	Increase of the petty cash fund		

Account Reconciliations

For certain accounts, there will be times when the account balances in the general ledger don't agree with the account balances in supporting documentation for an understandable or predictable reason. For example, it's not uncommon for a monthly bank statement to display a Cash balance that differs from the general ledger. Similarly, there can be discrepancies in the Accounts Payable balance in the general ledger to summary printouts of all payables owed to vendors. One way a company can confirm that no error, theft, or fraud has occurred is to reconcile certain accounts. A reconciliation is an examination of two sets of records regarding the balance in the same account. The goal is to either confirm that the two sets of records match or to determine why they differ and how to resolve the discrepancy.

Many accounts can be reconciled, with the most common being Cash. Other accounts frequently reconciled include Accounts Receivable, Prepaid Expenses (such as Supplies and Prepaid Insurance), Inventory, Fixed Assets (such as Machinery and/or Equipment), Accounts Payable, and Loans Payable. While the format of the reconciliations differs from one account to another, the goal is always the same: to identify the reconciling items that lead to the two different balances and to ensure that once they are considered, the two adjusted balances are equal.

The source documentation used to verify amounts in reconciliations also differs from one reconciliation to the next. Whereas reconciliation of the Cash account will rely heavily on a bank statement, Accounts Payable reconciliations involve vendor statements and Accounts Receivable reconciliations involve credit memos. Fixed asset schedules (for Machinery and/or Equipment) and amortization tables (for Loans Payable) are a few other source documents that can prove vital when completing reconciliations.

Preparing a Bank Reconciliation

☁ **View the video "Bank Reconciliation."**

Companies receive a monthly statement for each of their bank accounts, but certain business activities are not apparent to the bank. At the same time, there are activities that the bank knows about and the company does not. As a result, the balance displayed on the bank statement often differs from the cash balance within the general ledger. Another key component of maintaining close controls over cash is ensuring that the company can account for these differences.

A **bank reconciliation** displays all items that account for the differences between the bank balance and the general ledger (or book) balance.

Azzara Theme Park Guides						
Bank Reconciliation						
January 31, 2027						
Bank Statement Balance		$ 26,500	Book Balance			$ 27,200
Add:			Add:			
Deposits in Transit		1,250	Note Receivable	$	400	
		27,750	Error Recording Check #2174		220	620
						27,820
Deduct:			Deduct:			
Outstanding Checks: #2156	$ 650		NSF Check		1,800	
#2162	1,225	1,875	Bank Charges		145	1,945
Adjusted Bank Balance		**$ 25,875**	**Adjusted Book Balance**			**$ 25,875**

On a bank reconciliation, the bank side is on the left and the book side is on the right. Here we see how outstanding checks, fees and charges, and other items have led to the bank and book balances not matching. Once all reconciling items are accounted for, each side of the reconciliation shows the same balance ($25,875).

You may be wondering how you'll know on which side of the bank reconciliation to place a reconciling item and whether to add or deduct the amount. To determine this, ask yourself two questions:

1. Who was unaware of the reconciling item during the period?
   Put the item on the side that didn't know about it.

2. Did the reconciling item increase or decrease the cash balance?
   This tells you whether to add or deduct the amount from its designated side.

Ask Yourself 6-3a: In a bank reconciliation, the adjusted book balance must equal the bank statement balance. True or false?

How to Evaluate a Reconciling Item

Certain reconciling items appear in most bank reconciliations. These include the following:

- A **deposit in transit** is one made so late in the month that the bank was unable to process it for that month. These deposits will appear on the next month's bank statement, but the company is aware of the deposit this month and therefore includes it in the cash balance. The company knows about them, but the bank doesn't, so deposits in transit go on the bank side. They're added (not deducted) because they increase the amount of cash.

- **Outstanding checks** are checks that haven't yet been cashed by the payees. Because they haven't been cashed, the bank is unaware of them. Outstanding checks are deducted from the bank side because they reduce the cash balance.

- In some instances, a **note receivable** (like an accounts receivable but more formal and can include interest) is paid directly into a company's bank account. The company is unaware that cash has been deposited during the month, so notes receivables are added to the book side.

- An **NSF check**, also referred to as an *insufficient funds* or a *nonsufficient funds check,* is a check that has been rejected by the bank because the payer doesn't have enough money in its account to cover it. When a check "bounces" like this, the bank reduces the balance of the company's account by the amount of the check, but the company is unaware of this. As the reversal of the deposited check decreases the cash balance, it is deducted from the book side.

- **Bank charges** can be levied by a bank for reasons such as low balances or the receipt of NSF checks. Just as the company is not initially aware of the bounced check, it is similarly unaware of the associated charge until the bank statement is available. Bank charges are deducted from the book side.

Each item we just looked at always appears in the same location of the bank reconciliation. Look again at the example reconciliation for Azzara Theme Park Guides shown earlier. The NSF check and bank charge are deducted on the book side. This makes sense because the bank would have known first that the check was returned and would then have charged the company a fee. The company would never charge itself a fee, and then subsequently let the bank know!

Errors are the only reconciling items that can be listed on either side of the bank reconciliation. For example, imagine you deposit a $2,000 check into your account, but the bank records it as $200. The error results in too little cash in your account. Your records are correct, but the bank's records aren't, so the $1,800 ($2,000 – $200) is added to the bank side. Now consider a situation in which you write a check for $2,000 but record it in your ledger as $200. This time the error is on your side because you didn't deduct enough from your records, so the $1,800 is subtracted from the book side.

> **NOTE!** Always place a reconciling error on the side (bank or book) where the mistake was made.

Ask Yourself 6-3b: What's the name for a check that hasn't yet been cashed by the payee?

    A. Deposit in transit

    B. Outstanding check

    C. NSF check

    D. Insufficient funds check

In this example, we'll complete a bank reconciliation at the end of the second month of operations of Nathan's Donut School.

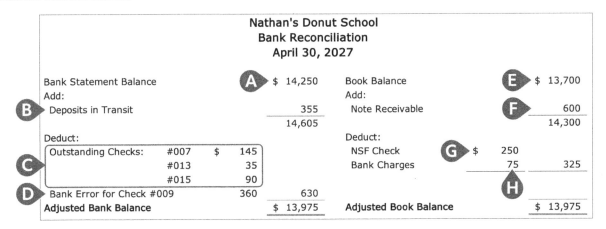

Nathan's Donut School
Bank Reconciliation
April 30, 2027

Bank Statement Balance	**A**	$ 14,250		Book Balance	**E**	$ 13,700
Add:				Add:		
B Deposits in Transit		355		Note Receivable	**F**	600
		14,605				14,300
Deduct:				Deduct:		
Outstanding Checks: #007 $ 145				NSF Check	**G** $	250
C #013 35				Bank Charges		75	325
#015 90					**H**	
D Bank Error for Check #009 360		630				
Adjusted Bank Balance		$ 13,975		**Adjusted Book Balance**		$ 13,975

A. The bank statement displays an ending cash balance of $14,250.

B. Deposits in transit totaled $355.

C. There were three outstanding checks at month end: #007 ($145), #013 ($35), and #015 ($90).

D. The bank made a transposition error and recorded check #009 as $370 instead of the correct $730.

E. The general ledger displays an ending cash account balance of $13,700.

F. The bank collected a note receivable of $600 from Speed Inc. on behalf of the company.

G. A check written by HHO Corp. for $250 was rejected by the bank for insufficient funds.

H. Bank charges for the month totaled $75.

In this example, the bank made an error that resulted in the cash balance being too high. Therefore, the amount of the error was subtracted from the bank side to arrive at the adjusted bank balance. All other reconciling items appear in the same locations within every bank reconciliation.

At the bottom of the reconciliation, we see the two adjusted balances match ($13,975).

Bank Reconciliation Journal Entries

Every transaction must be recorded in journal entry form, including items within a bank reconciliation. Certain of these items are recorded prior to month end, such as deposits in transit and outstanding checks. Remember, all reconciling items on the bank side of the reconciliation are items the bank was unaware of and the company knew about. The company booked the journal entries to account for these items prior to month end but did not do the same for those on the book side because it was unaware of them until now. After completing the bank reconciliation, the next step is to record journal entries for the items that have not yet been recorded.

Ask Yourself 6-4: After completing the bank reconciliation for the current period, where is the information for the journal entries found?

A. On the bank side of the reconciliation

B. On the book side of the reconciliation

In this example, we'll record the journal entries from the book side of the bank reconciliation for Nathan's Donut School.

1.

4/30	Cash	600	
	Notes Receivable - Speed Inc.		600
	Satisfaction of note receivable from Speed Inc.		

The Cash account is impacted by every journal entry that derives from the bank reconciliation. In this instance, the bank collected cash for Nathan's Donut School, so the Cash account is increased (debited).

2.

4/30	Bank Charges	75	
	Cash		75
	Bank charges incurred in April		

These journal entries are recorded in the same manner as standard journal entries recorded during the period. In this instance, bank charges represent a standard expense of doing business.

3.
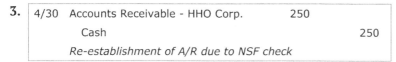

4/30	Accounts Receivable - HHO Corp.	250	
	Cash		250
	Re-establishment of A/R due to NSF check		

This amount was removed from the Nathan's Donut School books when the check was received. Now the company is aware that the check bounced and cash was not ultimately received, so this journal entry is recorded to re-establish the receivable.

Instead of recording the last two journal entries separately, they could have been recorded together in a **compound journal entry** *because each entry is crediting the same account (Cash). Here's how it would look:*

4/30	Bank Charges	75	
	Accounts Receivable - HHO Corp.	250	
	Cash		325
	Monthly bank charges and A/R resulting from NSF check		

Payroll Calculations and Journal Entries

Similar to cash, payroll is an area that is monitored closely by most companies. As you will see, journal entries for payroll are typically more extensive than the basic example you reviewed in prior chapters.

Employee Withholdings

Gross pay for an employee represents the total amount earned for a pay period. The employee's actual payroll check, though, is far less. It includes only the **net pay**, which is gross pay minus withholding amounts. For example, **Social Security tax**, also referred to as FICA (Federal Insurance Contributions Act) tax, is withheld from the employee's pay and remitted to the Internal Revenue Service (IRS) of the federal government. This tax funds the Old Age, Survivors, and Disability Insurance (OASDI) program and since 1990 has been calculated as 6.2% of gross pay. As of 2022, Social Security tax is calculated on only the first $147,000 of an employee's yearly gross pay.

NOTE! The cap on Social Security tax, which is referred to as the wage base, changes almost every year.

Another FICA tax withheld from gross pay and remitted to the IRS is **Medicare tax**. It funds the Hospital Insurance (HI) program. Since 1994 there has been no limit on the amount of Medicare tax an employee can pay, and since 1986 it has been calculated as 1.45% of gross pay.

Federal income tax is one of many taxes designed to fund the general operations of the federal government. It's calculated as a percentage of gross pay and increases as total gross pay increases. The percentage to withhold is determined by examining IRS tax rate tables. Most states also require that **state income tax** be withheld from gross pay. These taxes, used to fund the operations of the state government, are determined using the state's tax rate table.

Employees can also elect to have amounts automatically withheld from their gross pay. These **voluntary deductions** include retirement contributions, insurance premiums, and union dues, among others.

All these withholdings from employee gross pay are immediately owed to the associated organizations. As such, each is credited in the payroll journal entry as a liability.

8/1	Wages Expense	XXXX	
	Social Security Tax Payable		XXXX
	Medicare Tax Payable		XXXX
	Federal Income Tax Payable		XXXX
	State Income Tax Payable		XXXX
	Retirement Fund Tax Payable		XXXX
	Cash		XXXX
	Weekly wages earned by employees		

As shown here, the Wages Expense (could also be Salaries Expense) account is debited for the gross pay amount, while the Cash account is credited for the net pay amount.

> **Ask Yourself 6-5a:** Gross pay for an employee represents the total amount earned for the period. True or false?

Employer Payroll Taxes

Employers are responsible for remitting two sets of taxes. That means that in addition to those taxes that are withheld from an employee's paycheck, employers also pay taxes out of their own pockets. Some of these are the same as those withheld from employee pay, such as for Social Security or Medicare tax. For example, the employer must match the Social Security tax withheld from an employee's pay and remit those funds to the IRS. The employer's tax is calculated as 6.2% of gross pay and as of 2022 has the same $147,000 threshold as the employee's requirement. Similarly, the employer matches the Medicare taxes that are withheld from an employee's pay, again at 1.45% of gross pay.

Certain payroll taxes are levied on the employer only:

- **Federal unemployment tax**, or FUTA (Federal Unemployment Tax Act) tax, is used to pay unemployment benefits to qualified individuals. It's calculated as 6% of the first $7,000 of an employee's gross pay in a year but can be reduced by up to 5.4% (for a FUTA tax rate as low as 0.6%) based on the timely payment of the employer's SUTA tax.

- **State unemployment tax**, or SUTA (State Unemployment Tax Act) tax, also funds unemployment benefits. The tax rates vary from state to state (as do gross pay thresholds), and SUTA taxes paid offset a portion of the FUTA tax owed.

Like employee withholdings, employer payroll taxes are owed as soon as the employee earns the pay, so the amounts are credited to liability accounts in the associated journal entry. The corresponding debit is to the Payroll Tax Expense account, which is a standard expense account, for all employer payroll taxes.

Ask Yourself 6-5b: Which tax is both an employee and an employer payroll tax?

    A. Social Security tax

    B. Federal income tax

    C. State income tax

    D. Federal unemployment tax

CASE IN POINT 6-5

In this example, we will record two journal entries to account for all withholdings and employer payroll taxes for Nathan's Donut School during the first week of its second month of operations. To date, no single employee has reached the Social Security, FUTA, or SUTA tax threshold.

1. Gross pay (wages) for all employees was $4,000. Federal income tax withholding totaled $421, state income tax withholding totaled $157, and retirement fund contributions withheld totaled $40. Here's the April 9 (payday) journal entry to account for all employee withholdings and the cash paid to employees:

4/9	Wages Expense	4,000	
	Social Security Tax Payable		248
	Medicare Tax Payable		58
	Federal Income Tax Payable		421
	State Income Tax Payable		157
	Retirement Fund Tax Payable		40
	Cash		3,076
	Weekly wages earned by employees		

Social Security and Medicare tax amounts are calculated by multiplying the applicable percentages by the $4,000 gross pay. The $3,076 credit to Cash represents net pay for the period and is calculated as gross pay less all payable amounts.

2. Applicable SUTA and FUTA tax rates for Nathaniel's employees are 5.4% and 0.6%, respectively. This information is used to record the journal entry to account for all employer payroll taxes on April 9.

4/9	Payroll Tax Expense	546	
	Social Security Tax Payable		248
	Medicare Tax Payable		58
	SUTA Tax Payable		216
	FUTA Tax Payable		24
	Weekly payroll taxes owed		

SUTA and FUTA tax payable amounts are also calculated by multiplying the applicable percentages by the $4,000 gross pay. Remember, taxes in this second journal entry are paid out of the employer's pocket, not withheld from employee pay.

Payroll Tax Forms

Companies must be familiar with many payroll forms. Some are filed by the employer with various governmental entities; others are completed by employees or independent contractors and submitted to the employer. In this section we'll look at **Form W-4**, **Form W-2**, **Form W-9**, and **Form 1099-NEC**. While we'll overview each form, note that the completion of payroll tax forms is beyond the scope of this course.

Form W-4

One of the first steps taken by a new employee is the completion of Form W-4 (Employee's Withholding Certificate). This form provides the employer with the information necessary to calculate federal and state income tax withholding. The employer retains the form on file. When an employee's circumstances changes, they may submit a new Form W-4.

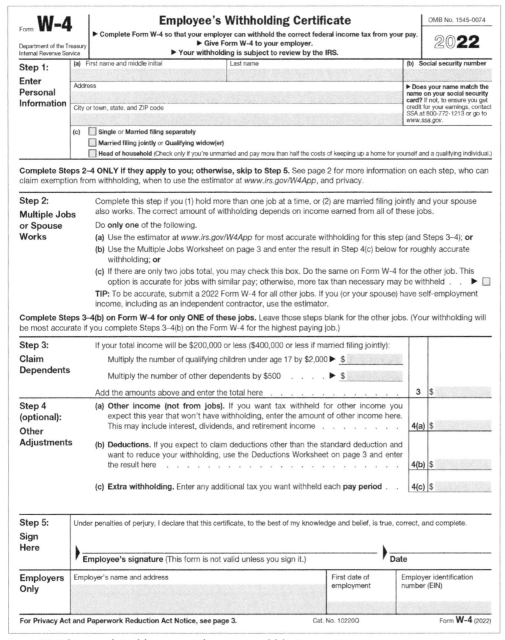

Form W-4 is completed by an employee upon hiring.

Form W-2

Form W-2 displays annual earnings and withholding information. The employer provides three copies of the form to each employee by January 31 of the following year: Copy B (filed with employee's federal tax return), Copy C (for the employee's records), and Copy 2 (filed with employee's state, city, or local tax return). The employer submits Copy A of this form to the Social Security Administration.

22222	a Employee's social security number		
	OMB No. 1545-0008		
b Employer identification number (EIN)		1 Wages, tips, other compensation	2 Federal income tax withheld
c Employer's name, address, and ZIP code		3 Social security wages	4 Social security tax withheld
		5 Medicare wages and tips	6 Medicare tax withheld
		7 Social security tips	8 Allocated tips
d Control number		9	10 Dependent care benefits
e Employee's first name and initial Last name Suff.		11 Nonqualified plans	12a
		13 Statutory employee Retirement plan Third-party sick pay	12b
		14 Other	12c
			12d
f Employee's address and ZIP code			

15 State Employer's state ID number	16 State wages, tips, etc.	17 State income tax	18 Local wages, tips, etc.	19 Local income tax	20 Locality name

Form **W-2** Wage and Tax Statement   **2022**   Department of the Treasury—Internal Revenue Service
Copy 1—For State, City, or Local Tax Department

Form W-2 summarizes earnings and withholding information for a single employee.

Form W-9

To report compensation for an independent contractor to the federal government and to provide that contractor with their compensation information at year end, the employer needs the individual's Social Security or Employer Identification Number. Form W-9 is the Request for Taxpayer Identification

Number and Certification form. It's completed by the independent contractor and provided to the employer, who retains it on file.

Form W-9 primarily contains the independent contractor's demographic information.

Form 1099-NEC

Form 1099-NEC displays total annual earnings for the independent contractor (referred to as nonemployee compensation). The employer provides the independent contractor with a copy of Form 1099-NEC and remits another copy to the IRS by January 31 of the following year.

Only nonemployee compensation exceeding $600 is reported on Form 1099-NEC.

Computerized Accounting Systems

Many companies use a computerized accounting system to help automate work and minimize errors. There are many programs available, such as QuickBooks Online, that can support even the smallest of companies. Among the most important benefits of using computerized accounting programs are noted here:

- *Efficiency*: Many elements of the accounting cycle, such as the preparation of trial balances, are automated within a computerized accounting system, saving the user a great deal of time.

- *Accuracy*: Because of its level of automation, a computerized accounting system highlights errors far more quickly than can be done by a human.

- *Backup capability*: We know that record retention is an important internal control. Digital backup copies of all accounting information are easily created from a computerized accounting system. Doing the same with a pen-and-paper system would be far more time consuming.

- *Cost*: Although these systems can range from relatively inexpensive to very costly, their use can reduce the number of required accounting personnel and, in some instances, can offset the initial cost of the computerized system.

Although they are excellent tools, computerized accounting systems do have certain drawbacks. Among these are the initial purchase price (which can significantly exceed associated savings), the time spent training employees, and the electronic safeguards necessary to prevent the unauthorized access of data.

Implementation

While computerized accounting systems aim to complete the accounting cycle in the same manner as manual systems, the process of entering transactions differs from system to system. Consider the concept of double-entry bookkeeping. With some computerized systems the user enters the debited and credited accounts in the electronic transaction (general) journal; with others the user inputs transaction details only and then the system determines the accounts to include with the journal entry.

Craig's Design and Landscaping Services
Journal
July 1-20, 2027

DATE	TRANSACTION TYPE	NUM	NAME	MEMO/DESCRIPTION	ACCOUNT	DEBIT	CREDIT
07/06/2027	Credit Card Expense		Squeaky Kleen Car Wash		Mastercard		$19.99
					Automobile	$19.99	
						$19.99	$19.99
07/08/2027	Credit Card Credit			Monthly Payment	Mastercard	$900.00	
					Checking		$900.00
						$900.00	$900.00
07/19/2027	Credit Card Expense				Mastercard		$34.00
					Automobile	$34.00	
						$34.00	$34.00
TOTAL						$953.99	$953.99

A transaction journal generated in QuickBooks Online

Similar to a manually created journal, this QuickBooks Online transaction journal displays the accounts affected and by how much (in this instance, three transactions are shown, the first of which is a $19.99 expense incurred at Squeaky Kleen Car Wash). What's different is that the user doesn't have to complete the posting process manually; it's accomplished automatically. The updated ledgers are accessible at any time, typically by running a report through the system.

Craig's Design and Landscaping Services

General Ledger
July 1-20, 2027

DATE	TRANSACTION TYPE	NUM	NAME	MEMO/DESCRIPTION	SPLIT	AMOUNT	BALANCE
Total for Labor							
Total for Landscaping Services with sub-accounts							
▾ Pest Control Services							
Beginning Balance							110.00
Total for Pest Control Services							
▾ Sales of Product Income							
Beginning Balance							912.75
Total for Sales of Product Income							
▾ Services							
Beginning Balance							503.55
Total for Services							
▾ Cost of Goods Sold							
Beginning Balance							405.00
Total for Cost of Goods Sold							
▾ Advertising							
Beginning Balance							74.86
Total for Advertising							
▾ Automobile							
Beginning Balance							59.97
7/06/2027	Credit Card Expense		Squeaky Kleen Car Wash	Mastercard		19.99	79.96
7/19/2027	Credit Card Expense			Mastercard		34.00	113.96
Total for Automobile						**$34.00**	
▾ Fuel							
Beginning Balance							349.41
Total for Fuel							
Total for Automobile with sub-accounts						**$34.00**	
▾ Equipment Rental							
Beginning Balance							112.00

A general ledger report automatically populated by QuickBooks Online

This general ledger for Craig's Design and Landscaping Services displays all debits and credits for several accounts. Note that the $19.99 expense at Squeaky Kleen Car Wash shown earlier within the journal is reflected here in the ledger and increases the balance of the Automobile account.

Ask Yourself 6-6: Why is using a computerized accounting program helpful?

A. Increased efficiency

B. Increased accuracy

C. Backup capability

D. All of these

CASE IN POINT 6-6

In these examples, we will explore how a computerized accounting system is more effective than a manual system for completing each task.

1. Task: Posting journal entries

   When using a manual accounting system, you make individual postings to the general and subsidiary ledgers. This process can be time consuming and is prone to errors. When you book an entry using a computerized accounting system, postings are made automatically and account balances are updated. As long as the journal entries are entered correctly, there's no risk of posting incorrect amounts or accounts.

2. Task: Generating financial statements

   In addition to the benefit of reports being automatically generated within a computerized accounting system, they're also more easily distributed to outside parties (via email, the cloud, etc.) than paper copies.

3. Task: Performing financial analyses

   Analyzing financial records involves comparing account balances for the current period and examining differences between an account's balances over different periods. Many accounting systems can automatically perform and display certain of these analyses. It's also easy to do multiperiod comparisons by generating custom financial statements that display the relevant periods. Performing similar analyses manually is a far more time-consuming process.

Self-Assessment

Now it's time for you to check your knowledge of the key concepts and skills introduced in this chapter.

1. A good internal control over cash is to retain all cash-related supporting materials for at least five years. *True   False*

2. Transaction authorization ensures that employees who record cash-related transactions do not physically handle cash. *True   False*

3. The Petty Cash account increases when petty cash is replenished. *True   False*

4. The petty cash fund can be increased (or decreased) to suit a company's changing needs for incidental cash. *True   False*

5. A bank reconciliation begins with equal bank and company balances. *True   False*

6. An outstanding check is one that the payee has not yet deposited. *True   False*

7. NSF stands for *non-sufficient funds*. *True   False*

8. Journal entries must be recorded for all reconciling items on the bank side of the bank reconciliation. *True   False*

9. The amount of an employee's paycheck is their gross pay. *True   False*

10. State unemployment tax is withheld from an employee's pay. *True   False*

11. What is NOT an internal control procedure?
    - A. Maintaining physical safeguards
    - B. Posting journal entries
    - C. Segregation of duties
    - D. Record retention

12. What would NOT be an appropriate use of petty cash?
    - A. Purchase of copier paper
    - B. Payment of lunch delivery
    - C. Purchase of stamps
    - D. Withdrawal by the owner

13. Which of these would be a reconciling item on the bank side of a bank reconciliation?
    - A. Outstanding checks
    - B. NSF check
    - C. Bank service charges
    - D. Customer payment of a note receivable

14. What tax is both withheld from an employee's pay and matched by the employer?
    - A. Federal unemployment tax
    - B. Federal income tax
    - C. State income tax
    - D. Medicare tax

15. Which source document is used in a bank reconciliation?

    A. Trial balance

    B. Amortization tables

    C. Bank statement

    D. Credit memos

16. Which statement regarding a reconciliation is inaccurate?

    A. A wide variety of accounts can be reconciled.

    B. The format of a reconciliation is the same for all accounts.

    C. A goal of a reconciliation is to identify reconciling items.

    D. Ultimately the two adjusted balances in a reconciliation should be equal.

17. Which form is referred to as the Employee's Withholding Certificate?

    A. Form W-4

    B. Form W-2

    C. Form W-9

    D. Form 1099-NEC

18. Which form reports annual earnings to an independent contractor?

    A. Form W-4

    B. Form W-2

    C. Form W-9

    D. Form 1099-NEC

19. Which form is prepared by an independent contractor and then provided to the employer?

    A. Form W-4

    B. Form W-2

    C. Form W-9

    D. Form 1099-NEC

20. Which form reports annual earnings to an employee?

    A. Form W-4

    B. Form W-2

    C. Form W-9

    D. Form 1099-NEC

Putting It Together

PIT 6-1 EXAMINE CASH AND PAYROLL FOR AMBER'S LACROSSE EMPORIUM

In these examples, we'll look at how Amber's Lacrosse Emporium records petty cash journal entries, completes a bank reconciliation, and records payroll-related journal entries.

1. On June 3, Amber's Lacrosse Emporium records this journal entry to establish a petty cash fund of $1,000.

6/3	Petty Cash	1,000	
	Cash		1,000
	Establishment of a petty cash fund		

2. On June 26, the company records a journal entry to replenish the petty cash fund. Expenses paid from petty cash include postage expense of $135, delivery expense of $370, office expenses of $220, and miscellaneous expenses of $110.

6/26	Postage Expense	135	
	Delivery Expense	370	
	Office Expense	220	
	Miscellaneous Expense	110	
	Cash		835
	Replenishment of the petty cash fund		

3. On September 14, Amber decides to increase the petty cash fund from $1,000 to $1,300.

9/14	Petty Cash	300	
	Cash		300
	Increase of the petty cash fund		

4. Using this information, Amber completes a bank reconciliation for the month of June:

   - June 30 bank statement balance: $33,100
   - June 1 general ledger cash balance: $29,650; during the month, total cash payments were $9,400 and total cash receipts were $10,850.
   - Bank charges: $305
   - Outstanding checks: #021 for $550, #033 for $25, and #038 for $300
   - Deposits in transit: $250
   - Deposited check for $400 from Paws Up Co. was rejected by the bank for nonsufficient funds.
   - A note receivable for $950 from TireHouse was collected by the bank.
   - Amber recorded a $1,400 check from QFT Co. in full payment of its accounts receivable as a $270 receipt.

```
                           Amber's Lacrosse Emporium
                              Bank Reconciliation
                                 June 30, 2027

Bank Statement Balance                $ 33,100    Book Balance                              $ 31,100
Add:                                               Add:
  Deposits in Transit                      250       Note Receivable            $    950
                                        33,350       Error Recording QFT Payment     1,130       2,080
                                                                                              33,180
Deduct:                                            Deduct:
  Outstanding Checks:  #021   $   550                 NSF Check                      400
                       #033       25                  Bank Charges                   305        705
                       #038      300       875
Adjusted Bank Balance                  $ 32,475    Adjusted Book Balance                     $ 32,475
```

The book balance of $31,100 is determined by adding the monthly cash receipts and beginning cash balance and then subtracting the monthly cash payments: ($10,850 + $29,650) − $9,400.

5. Amber records two compound journal entries to account for the items in the bank reconciliation that were previously unrecorded.

```
6/30   Cash                                    2,080
           Notes Receivable - TireHouse                     950
           Accounts Receivable - QFT Co.                  1,130
       Satisfaction of note receivable, correction of A/R error

6/30   Bank Charges                              305
       Accounts Receivable - Paws Up Co.         400
           Cash                                             705
       Monthly bank charges, A/R resulting from NSF check
```

In the first journal entry, the Cash account is debited; in the second, its credited.

6. A journal entry for June 10 (payday) records the cash wages paid and withholding amounts owed on behalf of employees. For the week, gross pay totaled $6,500, federal income tax withholding totaled $628, state income tax withholding totaled $238, and life insurance premiums withheld (they're subject to FICA tax) totaled $115. To date, no single employee has reached the Social Security, FUTA, or SUTA tax threshold.

```
6/10   Wages Expense                       6,500.00
           Social Security Tax Payable                  403.00
           Medicare Tax Payable                          94.25
           Federal Income Tax Payable                   628.00
           State Income Tax Payable                     238.00
           Life Insurance Premium Payable               115.00
           Cash                                       5,021.75
       Weekly wages earned by employees
```

7. Another journal entry for June 10 records the payroll tax expense owed. Applicable SUTA and FUTA tax rates for employees are 5.4% and 0.6%, respectively.

```
6/10   Payroll Tax Expense                   887.25
           Social Security Tax Payable                  403.00
           Medicare Tax Payable                          94.25
           SUTA Tax Payable                             351.00
           FUTA Tax Payable                              39.00
       Weekly payroll taxes owed
```

Practice Set A

PSA 6-1 CONSIDER INTERNAL CONTROL PROCEDURES

Match each internal control procedure to the step that best describes how it might be employed.

Maintaining physical safeguards

Segregation of duties

Transaction authorization

Record retention

Require the signature of multiple executives for transactions over a predetermined dollar level.

Recordkeepers should have no prior association with employees handling cash; cash handlers should sign documents indicating they will do so in an appropriate manner.

Keeping documentation more than seven years is appropriate; take care when determining which documents (physical or electronic) should be kept longer.

Facilities where cash is maintained should have properly working locks on all doors and a security system should be installed.

PSA 6-2 RECORD PETTY CASH JOURNAL ENTRIES

Record the petty cash journal entries for Hound Sports Enterprises.

Starting file: Use the Journal Entries template.

- February 22, Hound Sports Enterprises establishes a petty cash fund of $1,500.
- March 1, the company replenishes the petty cash fund for these expenses:
  - Delivery Expense: $435
  - Supplies Expense: $150
  - Entertainment Expense: $200
  - Miscellaneous Expense: $85
- March 15, the company decides to reduce petty cash from $1,500 to $1,000.

Recording a reduction of a petty cash fund is similar to recording an increase; just remember to reverse the debit and credit.

PSA 6-3 PREPARE A BANK RECONCILIATION

Prepare a bank reconciliation for the month of September for Stepping Stone Corp.

Starting file: Use the Bank Reconciliation template.

- Ending bank statement balance: $8,200
- General ledger ending cash balance: $9,450
- Outstanding checks as of September 30: #547 for $95, #624 for $180, and #627 for $230
- The company's September 24 deposit of $2,000 was recorded by the bank as a $200 deposit.

- The deposited check for $875 from TreeCo. was rejected by the bank for nonsufficient funds.
- Total deposits in transit as of September 30: $350
- The bank collected a $1,400 note receivable from WRM Inc. for Stepping Stone Corp.
- Bank charges: $130

PSA 6-4 RECORD BANK RECONCILIATION–RELATED JOURNAL ENTRIES

Having completed Stepping Stone's September bank reconciliation, record a journal entry for the reconciling items that need one.

Starting file: Use the Journal Entries template.

PSA 6-5 CALCULATE PAYROLL TAXES

Calculate the payroll taxes for BrewHaus Restaurant for the current week.

- Gross wages earned: $3,200
- SUTA tax rate: 5.4%
- FUTA tax rate: 0.6%

No single employee to date has reached the Social Security, FUTA, or SUTA tax threshold.

1. Social Security tax withheld from employee pay: $ _____
2. Medicare tax withheld from employee pay: $ _____
3. SUTA tax owed by BrewHaus Restaurant: $ _____
4. FUTA tax owed by Brewhaus Restaurant: $ _____

PSA 6-6 RECORD PAYROLL JOURNAL ENTRIES

Record the two necessary payroll-related journal entries for Frank's Fuel Corp: one for employee withholdings and one for employer payroll taxes.

Starting file: Use the Journal Entries template.

For the current week:

- Gross salaries: $1,200
- Federal income tax withheld: $114
- State income tax withheld: $44
- The applicable SUTA and FUTA tax rates are 5.4% and 0.6%, respectively.
- No single employee has, to date, reached the threshold for Social Security, FUTA, or SUTA tax.
- Union dues withheld: $55

Practice Set B

PSB 6-1 CONSIDER INTERNAL CONTROL PROCEDURES

Consider what you have learned about internal control procedures and recognize they can also be used to safeguard non-cash assets. Match each procedure with a non-cash asset that could be safeguarded using it.

Maintaining physical safeguards

Segregation of duties

Transaction authorization

Record retention

Maintain and examine documentation for long-term assets like equipment and automobiles to ensure associated transactions (e.g., for depreciation) are properly calculated and recorded.

Inventory should be monitored and recorded by different employees, ensuring those authorized to have access to inventory are unable to steal it.

Similar to cash, inventory is a frequent target for thieves. These types of safeguards can ensure that unauthorized individuals do not have access to inventory.

Long-term assets like equipment and automobiles should not be discarded or sold below market price without approval to prevent outside parties from obtaining them at a particularly low price or for free.

PSB 6-2 RECORD PETTY CASH JOURNAL ENTRIES

Record the petty cash journal entries for Legal Advisors Corp.

Starting file: Use the Journal Entries template.

- April 8, Legal Advisors Corp. establishes a petty cash fund of $750.
- April 29, the company replenishes the petty cash fund for these expenses:
  - Postage Expense: $85
  - Office Expense: $220
  - Transportation Expense: $165
  - Miscellaneous Expense: $185
- May 13, the company decides to increase the petty cash fund from $750 to $950.

PSB 6-3 PREPARE A BANK RECONCILIATION

Prepare a bank reconciliation for the month of December for Salsa Ingredients Co.

Starting file: Use the Bank Reconciliation template.

- Ending bank statement balance: $17,825
- General ledger ending cash balance: $14,200
- The bank collected a $4,050 note receivable from Bad Break Corp. for Salsa Ingredients Co.
- Bank charges: $45
- Outstanding checks as of December 31: #825 for $325, #904 for $100, and #905 for $720

- Total deposits in transit as of December 31: $125
- Deposited check for $1,300 from Holiday Specialties was rejected by the bank due to non-sufficient funds.
- Check received from OJD Inc. for $450 in full payment of its accounts receivable was erroneously recorded by Salsa Ingredients Co. as a $550 payment.

PSB 6-4 RECORD BANK RECONCILIATION–RELATED JOURNAL ENTRIES

Having completed Salsa Ingredients Co.'s December bank reconciliation, record a journal entry for the reconciling items that need one.

Starting file: Use the Journal Entries template.

PSB 6-5 CALCULATE PAYROLL TAXES

Calculate the payroll taxes for BCS Investigators for the current week.

- Gross wages earned: $8,350
- SUTA tax rate: 5.4%
- FUTA tax rate: 0.6%

No single employee to date has reached the Social Security, FUTA, or SUTA tax threshold.

1. Social Security tax matched and paid by BCS Investigators: $ _____
2. Medicare tax matched and paid by BCS Investigators: $ _____
3. SUTA tax owed to IRS: $ _____
4. FUTA tax owed to IRS: $ _____

PSB 6-6 RECORD PAYROLL JOURNAL ENTRIES

Record the two necessary payroll-related journal entries for Betsy's Interior Decorators, one for employee withholdings and one for employer payroll taxes.

Starting file: Use the Journal Entries template.

For the current week:

- Gross salaries: $2,500
- Federal income tax withheld: $260
- State income tax withheld: $101
- The applicable SUTA and FUTA tax rates are 5.4% and 0.6%, respectively.
- No single employee has, to date, reached the threshold for Social Security, FUTA, or SUTA tax.
- Life insurance premiums withheld: $80

7 Financial Statement Analysis

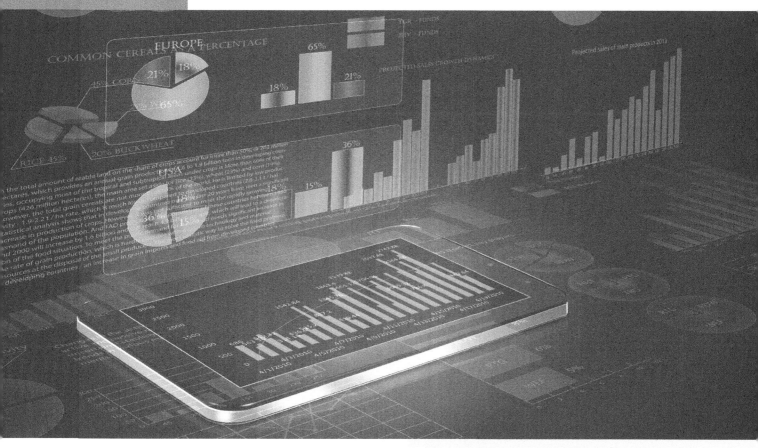

A company uses all the journal entries recorded and financial statements prepared to analyze its financial health. Any number of analysis methods can be used, and all rely on complete and accurate data. The completion of the accounting cycle ensures that accurate financial information is generated. In this chapter, you will examine methods to analyze financial statements. You will also look at relationships between accounts that can provide further insight into an organization's performance.

LEARNING OBJECTIVES

▸ Complete a horizontal analysis

▸ Complete a vertical analysis

▸ Prepare common-size financial statements

▸ Calculate various financial ratios

Project: Performing Financial Statement Analysis for Nathan's Donut School

Over the course of the first few months of operations, Nathaniel has been very pleased with how well you've monitored and recorded the activity of Nathan's Donut School. He'd like to use your accounting records to analyze his company's performance and asks for your help. He wants to understand not only how well the company performed during this time, but also what it can do to improve going forward.

Your first step is to examine the financial statements and compare ending balances from different months. You then make similar comparisons between individual account balances of Nathan's Donut School for a single month. You realize that the size of a competitor can make apples-to-apples (or donut-to-donut!) comparisons difficult, so to combat this you learn how to create common-size financial statements. Lastly, you examine different types of ratios, each of which can provide information about a different aspect of the company's performance.

Completing a Horizontal Analysis

View the video "Horizontal Analysis."

An important element of running any business is to analyze its performance to identify potential improvements. This typically consists of making comparisons between the company's account balances for the most recent period and a useful **benchmark**. The most common benchmarks are noted here:

- **Prior performance:** Comparisons to prior periods allow you to identify trends.
- **Competitor's balances:** Market fluctuations can make financial results appear more/less impressive at different times. Comparisons to competitors facing the same market conditions can provide useful context for the financial results.
- **Industry standards:** A single financial figure can be viewed very differently, depending on the industry of the business. Comparing results to established industry standards provides a clearer view of a company's performance.

One way to compare a company's performance to any of these benchmarks is through a **horizontal analysis**. A horizontal analysis is typically performed on the income statement and/or balance sheet. It involves comparing account balances to determine the dollar and percentage differences between them.

Wileson Legal Advisors Comparative Income Statement For the Years Ended June 30, 2026 and June 30, 2027				
	2027	2026	Dollar Change	Percent Change
Revenues:				
Sales Revenue	$ 48,750	$ 39,000	$ 9,750	25.00%
Interest Revenue	1,350	1,425	(75)	-5.26%
Total Revenue	50,100	40,425	9,675	23.93%
Expenses:				
Rent Expense	14,250	14,250	-	0.00%
Insurance Expense	8,750	7,200	1,550	21.53%
Depreciation Exp. - Truck	3,550	3,550	-	0.00%
Utilities Expense	1,875	1,220	655	53.69%
Supplies Expense	1,530	1,620	(90)	-5.56%
Telephone Expense	1,300	740	560	75.68%
Miscellaneous Expense	475	500	(25)	-5.00%
Total Expenses	31,730	29,080	2,650	9.11%
Net Income	$ 18,370	$ 11,345	$ 7,025	61.92%

This horizontal analysis examines account balances within a company's income statement for two consecutive years.

In the example income statement here, the dollar changes are calculated by subtracting the base (earlier) year figure from the comparison (later) year figure.

The percent change is calculated as:

Percent Change = Dollar Change ÷ Base Year

These account changes can provide a good deal of information regarding a company's performance. In the example, the increase in insurance expense (which is greater than any other expense increase) could indicate that excess insurance coverage is being utilized. A thorough analysis would provide more information.

WARNING! No single piece of analysis can provide a full picture of how well a company has performed. A thorough analysis includes the examination of a variety of data.

Account changes identified in a horizontal analysis can be compared to changes from competitors or industry averages to learn even more about a company's performance.

Ask Yourself 7-1: When completing a horizontal analysis, what is the dollar change divided by?
A. Base year
B. Later year

CASE IN POINT 7-1

In this example, we'll review a horizontal analysis that compares the first two months of operations of Nathan's Donut School.

To complete the horizontal analysis, we use income statements for the two months.

Nathan's Donut School Income Statement For the Month Ended March 31, 2027			
Revenues:			
Service Revenue		$	3,500
Expenses:			
Rent Expense	$	1,700	
Wages Expense		750	
Supplies Expense		315	
Advertising Expense		250	
Total Expenses			3,015
Net Income		$	485

Nathan's Donut School Income Statement For the Month Ended April 30, 2027			
Revenues:			
Service Revenue		$	5,950
Expenses:			
Rent Expense	$	1,700	
Wages Expense		1,100	
Advertising Expense		980	
Supplies Expense		775	
Total Expenses			4,555
Net Income		$	1,395

Any time period (month, quarter, year) can be used in a horizontal analysis. Just be sure the two periods are consecutive.

Nathan's Donut School Comparative Income Statement For the Months Ended March 31, 2027 and April 30, 2027							Percent Change
		April		March		Dollar Change	
Revenues:							
Service Revenue	$	5,950	$	3,500	$	2,450	70.00%
Expenses:							
Rent Expense		1,700		1,700		-	0.00%
Wages Expense		1,100		750		350	46.67%
Advertising Expense		980		250		730	292.00%
Supplies Expense		775		315		460	146.03%
Total Expenses		4,555		3,015		1,540	51.08%
Net Income	$	1,395	$	485	$	910	187.63%

Net income increased by a greater percentage (187.63%) than service revenue (70%), indicating that Nathan's Donut School operated more efficiently in April and required a smaller increase in expenses to generate the increased revenue. That said, two areas of concern are the advertising and supplies expenses. Although the dollar values are relatively low, the significant increase in both expenses could be problematic if it continues. Nathan's Donut School should pay close attention to these expenses.

Budgeted figures, which are estimates of future company performance, may be compared with actual results in a similar manner to that shown within the horizontal analysis here. This allows management to identify areas in which the company over- and underperformed expectations.

Completing a Vertical Analysis

View the video "Vertical Analysis."

Similar to a horizontal analysis, a **vertical analysis** is typically performed on the income statement or balance sheet. Unlike a horizontal analysis, in which account balances for two periods are compared, a vertical analysis compares account balances within the same period. When used in conjunction with a horizontal analysis, a vertical analysis can provide a more complete picture of a business's performance.

Bird Watchers Co.
Balance Sheet
September 30, 2027

	Dollar Amount	Percentage
Assets:		
Cash	$ 58,000	55.37%
Accounts Receivable	13,000	12.41%
Supplies	4,250	4.06%
Furniture	8,000	7.64%
Building	21,500	20.53%
Total Assets	$ 104,750	100.00%
Liabilities:		
Accounts Payable	24,000	22.91%
Owner's Equity:		
Mike Schilling, Capital	80,750	77.09%
Total Liabilities & Owner's Equity	$ 104,750	100.00%

A vertical analysis has been performed on this balance sheet.

The percentages are calculated by dividing the respective balance by the base figure in the balance sheet. The base figure, for which the percentage will always be 100%, is the total assets (or total liabilities and owner's equity, which equals total assets).

Account Percentage = Account Balance ÷ Base Figure

55.37%   58,000   104,750

This is in the balance sheet. When a vertical analysis is performed on an income statement, the base figure is the total revenue.

Ask Yourself 7-2: When completing a vertical analysis on a balance sheet, you can use either total assets or total liabilities and owner's equity as the base figure. True or false?

Common-Size Financial Statements

You can compare the percentages within a vertical analysis to any of the discussed benchmarks to see if any is unusually large or small with a **common-size financial statement**. A common-size financial statement may exclude the actual financial data, in which case it would display only the percentages yielded from a vertical analysis.

Bird Watchers Co. Common-Size Balance Sheet September 30, 2026 and September 30, 2027				
	2027 Dollar Amount	2026 Dollar Amount	2027 Percentage	2026 Percentage
Assets:				
Cash	$ 52,500	$ 58,000	51.78%	55.37%
Accounts Receivable	14,000	13,000	13.81%	12.41%
Supplies	2,000	4,250	1.97%	4.06%
Furniture	11,400	8,000	11.24%	7.64%
Building	21,500	21,500	21.20%	20.53%
Total Assets	$ 101,400	$ 104,750	100.00%	100.00%
Liabilities:				
Accounts Payable	31,000	24,000	30.57%	22.91%
Owner's Equity:				
Mike Schilling, Capital	70,400	80,750	69.43%	77.09%
Total Liabilities & Owner's Equity	$ 101,400	$ 104,750	100.00%	100.00%

This common-size balance sheet compares two years of data for a single company.

Comparisons of different-sized companies can be difficult, as total account balances can be widely different. For example, all account balances for a national restaurant chain will be far larger than the corresponding balances for a small, regional restaurant. You can overcome this using common-size percentages, as the percent calculations create apples-to-apples comparisons in the income statement and balance sheet.

> **TIP!** Common-size financial statements can display more than two sets of data. For example, three years of account balances can be displayed beside one another.

CASE IN POINT 7-2

In these examples, we will again use the income statements for the first two months of operations of Nathan's Donut School as we complete two vertical analyses. We'll also create a common-size income statement to compare data from these months.

Nathan's Donut School Income Statement For the Month Ended March 31, 2027		
Revenues:		
Service Revenue		$ 3,500
Expenses:		
Rent Expense	$ 1,700	
Wages Expense	750	
Supplies Expense	315	
Advertising Expense	250	
Total Expenses		3,015
Net Income		$ 485

Nathan's Donut School Income Statement For the Month Ended April 30, 2027		
Revenues:		
Service Revenue		$ 5,950
Expenses:		
Rent Expense	$ 1,700	
Wages Expense	1,100	
Advertising Expense	980	
Supplies Expense	775	
Total Expenses		4,555
Net Income		$ 1,395

1. First, we complete a vertical analysis of the income statement for the first month of operations.

Nathan's Donut School
Income Statement
For the Month Ended March 31, 2027

	Dollar Amount	Percentage
Revenues:		
Service Revenue	$ 3,500	100.00%
Expenses:		
Rent Expense	1,700	48.57%
Wages Expense	750	21.43%
Supplies Expense	315	9.00%
Advertising Expense	250	7.14%
Total Expenses	3,015	86.14%
Net Income	$ 485	13.86%

Total revenue is the starting point for the vertical analysis; it's the base figure for which 100% is designated. In this instance, as there is only one revenue account, the Service Revenue amount is the total revenue. All other account percentages are displayed as a portion of total revenue.

2. Now we do the same for the second month of operations.

Nathan's Donut School
Income Statement
For the Month Ended April 30, 2027

	Dollar Amount	Percentage
Revenues:		
Service Revenue	$ 5,950	100.00%
Expenses:		
Rent Expense	1,700	28.57%
Wages Expense	1,100	18.49%
Advertising Expense	980	16.47%
Supplies Expense	775	13.03%
Total Expenses	4,555	76.55%
Net Income	$ 1,395	23.45%

Now that two sets of percentages have been calculated, the first two months of operations can be compared.

3. Here's the common-size income statement for the first two months of operations of Nathan's Donut School:

Nathan's Donut School
Common-Size Income Statement
For the Months Ended March 31, 2027 and April 30, 2027

	April Dollar Amount	March Dollar Amount	April Percentage	March Percentage
Revenues:				
Service Revenue	$ 5,950	$ 3,500	100.00%	100.00%
Expenses:				
Rent Expense	1,700	1,700	28.57%	48.57%
Wages Expense	1,100	750	18.49%	21.43%
Advertising Expense	980	250	16.47%	7.14%
Supplies Expense	775	315	13.03%	9.00%
Total Expenses	4,555	3,015	76.55%	86.14%
Net Income	$ 1,395	$ 485	23.45%	13.86%

When analyzing a common-size financial statement, a good rule of thumb is to first examine the bottom-line figure and determine why it changed. Here the bottom-line figure shows the net income, which has significantly increased as a percent of revenue. Of course, the increase in revenue contributed to this higher net income; if expenses had increased at the same rate, then net income as a percent of revenue would have remained steady. Because expenses did not increase by the same magnitude (they now represent 76.55% of revenue versus 86.14% in March), the company is in a better financial position in April.

Liquidity Ratios

👐 **View the video "Liquidity Ratios."**

Horizontal and vertical analyses provide a good deal of information on a company's performance and how it can improve. This picture can be enhanced through the use of **ratio analysis**, which examines relationships between account balances. Studying these relationships can provide further evidence of a company's current level of success and its prospects.

Different ratios provide information about different elements of a company. **Liquidity ratios** indicate how quickly a company can convert assets to cash. Maintaining adequate cash, or being able to access it quickly, allows a company to react to business opportunities as they arise. It also ensures that a business can meet its short-term obligations (amounts owed in the near future). Two of the most widely used liquidity ratios are the current ratio and the quick ratio.

Current Ratio

Current assets are those assets that can be easily converted to cash or used up within the next twelve months. Similarly, current liabilities are liabilities owed within the next twelve months. By comparing current assets to current liabilities, the **current ratio** indicates how well positioned a company is to pay off what it owes in the next twelve months. The higher the ratio, the more current assets are available to make these payments and, therefore, the better the company is positioned.

Current Ratio = Current Assets ÷ Current Liabilities

Quick Ratio

The **quick ratio** (also called the acid-test ratio) provides a similar measurement as the current ratio but takes a more stringent approach in terms of the assets included in the calculation. Instead of including all current assets, the quick ratio includes only the most liquid assets (those that can most easily be converted to cash). By excluding current assets such as merchandise inventory and supplies, this ratio focuses more heavily on a company's ability to spend cash quickly. Similar to the current ratio, a higher quick ratio indicates that a company is better positioned to meet its short-term obligations.

$$\text{Quick Ratio} = \frac{\text{Cash + Short-Term Investments + A/R}}{\text{Current Liabilities}}$$

Ratio results must be compared to a prior period, competitors, and/or industry averages to yield useful information. In a bubble, a ratio result is not an indicator of a company's performance. It can't be because it's just a number; you have to compare that number to another figure in order to make a judgment on it.

> **WARNING!** Don't use a ratio result as an indication of a company's performance. Compare that ratio result to a corresponding figure from a prior period or other metric to gauge performance.

Ask Yourself 7-3: What is used in a current ratio but excluded from a quick ratio?
- **A.** Accounts receivable
- **B.** Cash
- **C.** Merchandise inventory
- **D.** Short-term investments

In this example, we will calculate liquidity ratios for the first two months of operations of Nathan's Donut School and analyze our results.

We use the balance sheets to calculate the ratios.

Nathan's Donut School Balance Sheet March 31, 2027		
Assets:		
Cash	$	12,300
Accounts Receivable		2,350
Supplies		185
Furniture		1,000
Equipment		20,000
Total Assets		$ 35,835
Liabilities:		
Accounts Payable		-
Wages Payable		750
Owner's Equity:		
Nathaniel H. Spencer, Capital		35,085
Total Liabilities & Owner's Equity		$ 35,835

Nathan's Donut School Balance Sheet April 30, 2027		
Assets:		
Cash	$	8,750
Accounts Receivable		3,250
Supplies		275
Furniture		1,000
Equipment		20,000
Total Assets		$ 33,275
Liabilities:		
Accounts Payable		150
Wages Payable		600
Unearned Revenue		440
Owner's Equity:		
Nathaniel H. Spencer, Capital		32,085
Total Liabilities & Owner's Equity		$ 33,275

1. We begin by calculating the current ratio and quick ratio for the first month of operations.

    For the current ratio, the $14,835 numerator is calculated by adding the Cash, Accounts Receivable, and Supplies account balances. All other figures are shown directly in the March balance sheet.

$$\frac{\$14,835}{\$750} = 19.78 \text{ to } 1$$

    In this example, only a small Supplies balance was removed from the current asset total to arrive at the numerator for the quick ratio (referred to as the quick assets). Because this difference is so small, the current ratio and quick ratio results are very similar.

$$\frac{\$12,300 + \$0 + \$2,350}{\$750} = 19.53 \text{ to } 1$$

2. Now we calculate the current ratio and quick ratio for the second month of operations of Nathan's Donut School.

    Similar to the March ratios, the $12,275 in the current ratio is calculated by adding the Cash, Accounts Receivable, and Supplies account balances, though this time from the April balance sheet. The $1,190 in both ratios is calculated by adding the Accounts Payable, Wages Payable, and Unearned Revenue account balances from the April balance sheet.

$$\frac{\$12,275}{\$1,190} = 10.32 \text{ to } 1$$

$$\frac{\$8,750 + \$0 + \$3,250}{\$1,190} = 10.08 \text{ to } 1$$

    Now that we've calculated two sets of ratios, we can compare them to determine if Nathan's Donut School's liquidity position has improved or deteriorated during the first two months of operations.

3. What can we conclude from the ratios?

Both ratios have decreased significantly from March to April, indicating that Nathan's Donut School's ability to pay its short-term debt has declined. However, the April ratios indicate that short-term assets exceed current liabilities by approximately 10 to 1, so despite the decreased liquidity, the company should still have no trouble meeting its financial obligations.

Keep in mind that ratios should not be examined independent of other types of analyses. And while these ratios suggest that Nathan's Donut School can meet all financial obligations, they may be below that of competitors and/or industry averages. To determine if this ratio is favorable or unfavorable for this type of business, Nathaniel would need to perform more analyses.

Solvency Ratios

Whereas liquidity ratios gauge a company's ability to meet short-term obligations, **solvency ratios** gauge a company's ability to meet long-term obligations. An organization can raise funds for operations by either borrowing cash (liability) or selling an ownership stake in the business (equity). Solvency ratios measure the extent to which each of these methods is used and the balance between them. Leaning too heavily on either can be viewed negatively. Why? Because while a business doesn't want to incur more debt than it can pay off over the long term, it also wants to avoid selling too many ownership stakes such that the value of each owner's share is diluted.

$$\text{Debt Ratio} = \text{Total Liabilities} \div \text{Total Assets}$$

$$\text{Equity Ratio} = \text{Total Equity} \div \text{Total Assets}$$

$$\text{Debt-to-Equity Ratio} = \text{Total Liabilities} \div \text{Total Equity}$$

Unlike liquidity ratios, which focus only on current assets and liabilities, solvency ratios are calculated using total figures. The **debt ratio** expresses the portion of assets generated through liabilities, while the **equity ratio** expresses the portion generated through equity. As you may guess, the **debt-to-equity ratio** expresses the balance between liabilities and equity. When liabilities exceed equity, this ratio will be greater than 1; the reverse leads to a ratio less than 1.

> **TIP!** Although a favorable debt-to-equity ratio differs from one industry to another, a general rule of thumb is that a particularly high or low ratio is concerning.

Ask Yourself 7-4: What is NOT a solvency ratio?
- **A.** Debt ratio
- **B.** Equity ratio
- **C.** Debt-to-equity ratio
- **D.** Dividend yield

In this example, we will calculate solvency ratios for the first month of operations of Nathan's Donut School and analyze our results.

Nathan's Donut School
Balance Sheet
March 31, 2027

Assets:		
Cash	$ 12,300	
Accounts Receivable	2,350	
Supplies	185	
Furniture	1,000	
Equipment	20,000	
Total Assets		$ 35,835
Liabilities:		
Accounts Payable	-	
Wages Payable	750	
Owner's Equity:		
Nathaniel H. Spencer, Capital	35,085	
Total Liabilities & Owner's Equity		$ 35,835

1. To begin, using figures from the March balance sheet, we calculate the debt ratio, equity ratio, and debt-to-equity ratio for the school's first month of operations.

Debt Ratio $750 ÷ $35,835 = 2.09%

Equity Ratio $35,085 ÷ $35,835 = 97.91%

Debt to Equity $750 ÷ $35,085 = 0.02

2. Imagine that 0.40 is the industry average for the debt-to-equity ratio. What could we conclude about Nathan's Donut School after its first month of operations?

It's clear that the school has obtained the vast majority of its assets through equity instead of liabilities. That's why the debt ratio is so low and the equity ratio is so close to 100%. The result is that the debt-to-equity ratio is very small, and this is confirmed by comparing it to the industry average.

While it's good that Nathan's Donut School doesn't owe a great deal to creditors compared to its competitors, keep in mind that at times it can be beneficial to borrow funds. For example, if the company is presented with an expansion opportunity that can lead to significantly increased revenue, it may be worth borrowing the funds and paying the associated interest to be able to take advantage of the opportunity. One key to effectively running a business is finding the appropriate balance between debt and equity.

Profitability Ratios

Another group of ratios, referred to as **profitability ratios**, provide insight into a company's ability to effectively generate income. Among the most commonly used profitability ratios are those that calculate profit margin and return on assets.

Profit Margin = Net Income ÷ Revenue

Return on Assets = Net Income ÷ Avg. Total Assets

The **profit margin** ratio indicates the percentage of revenue that a company converts to net income. Companies want as high a profit margin as possible because it means the company is efficiently generating net income. **Return on assets** illustrates a company's ability to use assets to generate net income. This calculation uses the average (avg.) total assets, which is half the sum of beginning and ending total assets. Just as with profit margin, the higher the return on assets the better.

$$\text{Avg. Total Assets} = \frac{(\text{Beginning Total Assets} + \text{Ending Total Assets})}{2}$$

Ask Yourself 7-5: To calculate the profit margin, net income is divided by what?

A. Revenue

B. Investments

C. Total assets

D. Cash

👓 A CLOSER LOOK

Can Other Ratios Be Used for Evaluation?

We've looked at just a few of the many ratios used to analyze business performance. Other popular ratios include a*ccounts receivable turnover* and *inventory turnover* (which gauge company efficiency), *times interest earned* (a solvency ratio), and *gross margin ratio* (a profitability ratio).

Some ratios only apply to corporations. For example, the **basic earnings per share (EPS)** is a profitability ratio used to gauge a corporation's performance. It indicates how much a company has earned for each share of stock it has outstanding (that is, held by an investor). The higher the EPS, the better the company is performing and the more attractive it appears as an investment.

$$\text{Basic EPS} = \frac{\text{Net Income} - \text{Preferred Dividends}}{\text{Weighted Avg. Common Shares Outstanding}}$$

Two other ratios investors use to gauge how attractive a company is as an investment are the price-earnings ratio (P/E ratio) and the dividend yield. The P/E ratio compares the market price of the stock (what an investor would pay for each share) to the EPS. A high EPS in comparison to the market price per share could indicate a bargain price for an investor.

$$\text{P/E Ratio} = \frac{\text{Market Price per Share}}{\text{Earnings per Share}}$$

The dividend yield indicates how much an investor receives in dividends (distributions of corporate earnings to investors) in comparison to the market price. A high dividend yield indicates that investors receive a healthy dividend for their investment, which can make the company's stock appear attractive to new investors.

$$\text{Dividend Yield} = \frac{\text{Cash Dividends per Share}}{\text{Market Price per Share}}$$

In this example, we'll calculate profitability ratios for the first two months of operations of Nathan's Donut School and then analyze the results.

Here are the balances we need to calculate the ratios:

	March 2027	April 2027
Revenue	$3,500	$5,950
Net Income	$485	$1,395
Avg. Total Assets	$35,835	$34,555

1. First, we calculate the profit margin and return on assets for the first month of operations.

   March was the first month of operations. We're using the ending total asset balance for the month ($35,835) because averaging that with the beginning balance of $0 would provide a skewed result.

   Profit Margin $485 ÷ $3,500 = 13.86%
   Return on Assets $485 ÷ $35,835 = 1.35%

2. And now we calculate the same ratios for the school's second month of operations.

   Profit Margin $1,395 ÷ $5,950 = 23.45%
   Return on Assets $1,395 ÷ $34,555 = 4.04%

3. What can you conclude from the calculated ratios?

   Both the profit margin and return on assets increased from March to April. These increases were significant in both instances, indicating that the company is now doing a better job of converting revenue to net income and using assets to generate net income. Ideally, Nathan's Donut School would like to see a trend of improved profitability ratios in future months.

Self-Assessment

Now it's time for you to check your knowledge of the key concepts and skills introduced in this chapter.

1. A horizontal analysis can compare financial figures across time.   *True   False*

2. Horizontal analyses are performed on income statements but not balance sheets.   *True   False*

3. A vertical analysis examines account balances over multiple periods.   *True   False*

4. The base figure in a vertical analysis using the balance sheet is total assets.   *True   False*

5. Common-size financial statements allow for comparisons between businesses of different sizes.   *True   False*

6. Ratio analysis examines relationships between specific account balances.   *True   False*

7. The quick ratio is an example of a liquidity ratio.   *True   False*

8. Solvency ratios indicate to what extent a company has balanced debt and equity.   *True   False*

9. A company can raise funds by either borrowing cash or selling an ownership stake in the business.   *True   False*

10. Profit margin is defined as net income divided by expenses.   *True   False*

11. What is NOT a good benchmark to use with a horizontal analysis?
    A. Balances of companies in different industries
    B. Prior performance
    C. Competitor balances
    D. Industry standards

12. What does a liquidity ratio do?
    A. Gauges a company's ability to meet long-term obligations
    B. Provides insight into a company's ability to effectively generate income
    C. Indicates how quickly a company can convert assets to cash
    D. Compares account balances across time

13. Which of these is a profitability ratio?
    A. Current ratio
    B. Debt ratio
    C. Equity ratio
    D. Return on assets

14. Which of these is a solvency ratio?
    A. Quick ratio
    B. Debt-to-equity ratio
    C. Profit margin
    D. Return on assets

15. What ratio indicates the percentage of revenue a company converts to net income?

    A. Quick ratio

    B. Equity ratio

    C. Basic EPS

    D. Profit margin

16. What ratio indicates how well positioned a company is to pay off its debts in the next 12 months?

    A. Current ratio

    B. Debt ratio

    C. Return on assets

    D. Dividend yield

17. Debt ratio = _____   ____   _____

18. Current ratio = _____   ____   _____

19. Return on assets = _____   ____   _____

20. PE ratio = _____   ____   _____

Putting It Together

PIT 7-1 ANALYZE FINANCIAL STATEMENTS

In this example, we'll perform a variety of financial statement analyses, including a horizontal analysis, a vertical analysis, a common-size financial statement, and a series of financial ratios. We will show how to draw conclusions from our work as we complete these analyses.

1. To complete a horizontal analysis of the balance sheet, we first prepare the June 30 balance sheet:

<table>
<tr><td colspan="4" align="center">Amber's Lacrosse Emporium
Balance Sheet
June 30, 2027</td></tr>
<tr><td>**Assets:**</td><td></td><td></td><td></td></tr>
<tr><td>Cash</td><td></td><td>$ 38,500.00</td><td></td></tr>
<tr><td>Accounts Receivable</td><td></td><td>4,200.00</td><td></td></tr>
<tr><td>Supplies</td><td></td><td>750.00</td><td></td></tr>
<tr><td>Merchandise Inventory</td><td></td><td>11,225.00</td><td></td></tr>
<tr><td>Furniture</td><td>$ 2,000.00</td><td></td><td></td></tr>
<tr><td>Accum. Dep. - Furniture</td><td>50.00</td><td>1,950.00</td><td></td></tr>
<tr><td>Equipment</td><td>12,000.00</td><td></td><td></td></tr>
<tr><td>Accum. Dep. - Equipment</td><td>475.00</td><td>11,525.00</td><td></td></tr>
<tr><td>**Total Assets**</td><td></td><td></td><td>$ 68,150.00</td></tr>
<tr><td>**Liabilities:**</td><td></td><td></td><td></td></tr>
<tr><td>Accounts Payable</td><td></td><td>7,250.00</td><td></td></tr>
<tr><td>Wages Payable</td><td></td><td>975.00</td><td></td></tr>
<tr><td>**Owner's Equity:**</td><td></td><td></td><td></td></tr>
<tr><td>Amber Stein, Capital</td><td></td><td>59,925.00</td><td></td></tr>
<tr><td>**Total Liabilities & Owner's Equity**</td><td></td><td></td><td>$ 68,150.00</td></tr>
</table>

We use this statement, along with the May 31 balance sheet we already created, to prepare a horizontal analysis.

<table>
<tr><td colspan="5" align="center">Amber's Lacrosse Emporium
Comparative Balance Sheet
May 31, 2027 and June 30, 2027</td></tr>
<tr><td></td><td>June</td><td>May</td><td>Dollar Change</td><td>Percent Change</td></tr>
<tr><td>**Assets:**</td><td></td><td></td><td></td><td></td></tr>
<tr><td>Cash</td><td>$ 38,500.00</td><td>$ 46,565.00</td><td>$ (8,065.00)</td><td>-17.32%</td></tr>
<tr><td>Accounts Receivable</td><td>4,200.00</td><td>2,350.00</td><td>1,850.00</td><td>78.72%</td></tr>
<tr><td>Supplies</td><td>750.00</td><td>275.00</td><td>475.00</td><td>172.73%</td></tr>
<tr><td>Merchandise Inventory</td><td>11,225.00</td><td>13,550.00</td><td>(2,325.00)</td><td>-17.16%</td></tr>
<tr><td>Furniture</td><td>2,000.00</td><td>2,000.00</td><td>-</td><td>0.00%</td></tr>
<tr><td>Accum. Dep. - Furniture</td><td>50.00</td><td>25.00</td><td>25.00</td><td>100.00%</td></tr>
<tr><td>Equipment</td><td>12,000.00</td><td>12,000.00</td><td>-</td><td>0.00%</td></tr>
<tr><td>Accum. Dep. - Equipment</td><td>475.00</td><td>237.50</td><td>237.50</td><td>100.00%</td></tr>
<tr><td>**Total Assets**</td><td>$ 68,150.00</td><td>$ 76,477.50</td><td>$ (8,327.50)</td><td>-10.89%</td></tr>
<tr><td>**Liabilities:**</td><td></td><td></td><td></td><td></td></tr>
<tr><td>Accounts Payable</td><td>7,250.00</td><td>2,000.00</td><td>5,250.00</td><td>262.50%</td></tr>
<tr><td>Wages Payable</td><td>975.00</td><td>850.00</td><td>125.00</td><td>14.71%</td></tr>
<tr><td>**Owner's Equity:**</td><td></td><td></td><td></td><td></td></tr>
<tr><td>Amber Stein, Capital</td><td>59,925.00</td><td>73,627.50</td><td>(13,702.50)</td><td>-18.61%</td></tr>
<tr><td>**Total Liabilities & Owner's Equity**</td><td>$ 68,150.00</td><td>$ 76,477.50</td><td>$ (8,327.50)</td><td>-10.89%</td></tr>
</table>

Review the numbers carefully and remember that accumulated depreciation amounts are subtracted when calculating total assets.

Look at the bottom-line figures in the balance sheet where total assets (and, therefore, also total liabilities and owner's equity) have declined by almost 11%. To determine what this decline indicates, we need to look at the individual accounts.

Two asset accounts, Cash and Merchandise Inventory, have decreased by approximately 17%. The reduction in cash is somewhat concerning, although if the company has used cash to generate higher revenue, the reduction would be reasonable. The increased accounts payable and reduced owner's capital are also concerning. But again, if the increase in amounts owed allows the company to generate more revenue, then it's acceptable. The reduction in Amber Stein, Capital likely resulted from either the company experiencing a net loss or Amber withdrawing funds. Further examination of the other financial statements would provide more clarity.

2. To complete a vertical analysis of the income statement, we begin by preparing the June 30 income statement:

Amber's Lacrosse Emporium
Income Statement
For the Month Ended June 30, 2027

Revenues:		
Sales Revenue	$ 5,900.00	
Service Revenue	350.00	
Total Revenue		$ 6,250.00
Expenses:		
Cost of Goods Sold	3,620.00	
Advertising Expense	3,575.00	
Wages Expense	2,700.00	
Rent Expense	1,500.00	
Supplies Expense	700.00	
Utilities Expense	450.00	
Depreciation Expense	262.50	
Telephone Expense	125.00	
Total Expenses		12,932.50
Net Loss		$ (6,682.50)

We then use that and the May 31 statement for the vertical analysis.

Amber's Lacrosse Emporium
Income Statement
For the Month Ended May 31, 2027

	Dollar Amount	Percentage
Revenues:		
Sales Revenue	$ 6,850.00	82.53%
Service Revenue	1,450.00	17.47%
Total Revenue	8,300.00	100.00%
Expenses:		
Cost of Goods Sold	3,450.00	41.57%
Wages Expense	2,450.00	29.52%
Rent Expense	1,500.00	18.07%
Advertising Expense	600.00	7.23%
Supplies Expense	475.00	5.72%
Depreciation Expense	262.50	3.16%
Utilities Expense	200.00	2.41%
Telephone Expense	135.00	1.63%
Total Expenses	9,072.50	109.31%
Net Loss	$ (772.50)	-9.31%

Amber's Lacrosse Emporium
Income Statement
For the Month Ended June 30, 2027

	Dollar Amount	Percentage
Revenues:		
Sales Revenue	$ 5,900.00	94.40%
Service Revenue	350.00	5.60%
Total Revenue	6,250.00	100.00%
Expenses:		
Cost of Goods Sold	3,620.00	57.92%
Advertising Expense	3,575.00	57.20%
Wages Expense	2,700.00	43.20%
Rent Expense	1,500.00	24.00%
Supplies Expense	700.00	11.20%
Utilities Expense	450.00	7.20%
Depreciation Expense	262.50	4.20%
Telephone Expense	125.00	2.00%
Total Expenses	12,932.50	206.92%
Net Loss	$ (6,682.50)	-106.92%

Over time, you'll find that you won't need to complete vertical analyses to prepare a common-size financial statement. As you become more comfortable with the process, you'll be able to jump directly to completing the common-size financial statement.

3. And now let's look at the common-size income statement for the months of May and June:

Amber's Lacrosse Emporium
Common-Size Income Statement
For the Months Ended May 31, 2027 and June 30, 2027

	June Dollar Amount	May Dollar Amount	June Percentage	May Percentage
Revenues:				
Sales Revenue	$ 5,900.00	$ 6,850.00	94.40%	82.53%
Service Revenue	350.00	1,450.00	5.60%	17.47%
Total Revenue	6,250.00	8,300.00	100.00%	100.00%
Expenses:				
Cost of Goods Sold	3,620.00	3,450.00	57.92%	41.57%
Wages Expense	2,700.00	2,450.00	43.20%	29.52%
Rent Expense	1,500.00	1,500.00	24.00%	18.07%
Advertising Expense	3,575.00	600.00	57.20%	7.23%
Supplies Expense	700.00	475.00	11.20%	5.72%
Depreciation Expense	262.50	262.50	4.20%	3.16%
Utilities Expense	450.00	200.00	7.20%	2.41%
Telephone Expense	125.00	135.00	2.00%	1.63%
Total Expenses	12,932.50	9,072.50	206.92%	109.31%
Net Loss	$ (6,682.50)	$ (772.50)	-106.92%	-9.31%

Heads up! Did you notice that expenses in the two individual income statements were listed in a different order? Remember that expenses are listed from largest to smallest. Pay attention when completing a common-size income statement so you don't mix up balances.

Looking first at net loss, it's clear the company's performance declined from May to June, as the loss for June represents a significantly larger percentage of total revenue than it did in May. Now looking at individual expenses, one of the most prominent changes is in advertising expenses. Amber's Lacrosse Emporium likely kicked off a large marketing campaign in June, and while this explains some of the increase in net loss, the fact remains that the company must start to convert the money spent on expenses into a profit (net income). If the company experiences a few more months similar to June, it will quickly run into cash-flow problems.

One other item to note: We now have more information regarding the decrease in owner's equity that we saw on the comparative balance sheet. That decrease was approximately $13,700, and we now know that about $6,700 of that was attributable to the net loss. The only other common reduction to a capital account results from an owner withdrawal, so the remaining $7,000 is likely that. This is potentially concerning, as the company could run into cash-flow problems if Amber continues to withdraw cash while it is losing money (experiencing a net loss).

Now we'll switch gears and complete financial ratios for the company.

4. Using the June balance sheet, we can calculate the current and quick ratios:

Current ratio:

$$\text{Current Assets } \$54{,}675 \div \text{Current Liabilities } \$8{,}225 = 6.65 \text{ to } 1$$

Quick ratio:

$$\frac{\text{(Cash + Short-Term Liabilities + A/R)}\ (\$38{,}500 + \$0 + \$4{,}200)}{\text{Current Liabilities } \$8{,}225} = 5.19 \text{ to } 1$$

The ratio results indicate that current assets exceed current liabilities by more than 6.5 times, while quick assets exceed current liabilities by approximately 5 times. Presently, the company is able to repay its short-term debts. To determine if these ratios indicate that the company is performing well, you'd need to compare these results to those of competitors and industry averages.

5. We also use the June balance sheet to calculate ratios related to debt and equity:

Debt ratio:

$$\text{Total Liabilities } \$8{,}225 \div \text{Total Assets } \$68{,}150 = 12.07\%$$

Equity ratio:

$$\text{Total Equity } \$59{,}925 \div \text{Total Assets } \$68{,}150 = 87.93\%$$

Debt-to-equity ratio:

$$\text{Total Liabilities } \$8{,}225 \div \text{Total Equity } \$59{,}925 = 0.14$$

These ratios indicate that equity is significantly greater than debt. Remember, there are benefits and drawbacks to using debt (liabilities) or equity. A company must determine the proper balance between the two. Here, results should be compared to those of competitors and industry averages to determine whether the balance for Amber's Lacrosse Emporium is appropriate.

6. To complete our analysis, we'll use the June balance sheet and income statement as we calculate profit and return on investment:

Profit margin:

$$\textbf{Net Income} \atop \textbf{\$(6,682.50)} \quad \div \quad {\textbf{Revenue} \atop \textbf{\$6,250}} \quad = \quad \textbf{-106.92\%}$$

Return on assets:

$$\textbf{Net Income} \atop \textbf{\$(6,682.50)} \quad \div \quad {\textbf{Avg. Total Assets} \atop \textbf{\$72,313.75}} \quad = \quad \textbf{-9.24\%}$$

These profitability ratios are very concerning. Not only are they negative, a result of the company experiencing a net loss instead of income, but they are relatively large. This means that the net loss was large in comparison to both total revenue and average total assets. In fact, the net loss exceeded total revenue, indicating that expenses were more than twice as large as revenue for the month. This circumstance must be corrected for the company to have enough money to continue operating.

Practice Set A

You will refer to these statements as you complete Practice Set A for this chapter:

Rhythmic Dance Studio
Income Statement
For the Year Ended December 31, 2026

Revenues:		
Service Revenue		$ 194,000
Expenses:		
Salaries Expense	$ 82,400	
Rent Expense	32,275	
Supplies Expense	8,370	
Telephone Expense	7,000	
Utilities Expense	6,200	
Depreciation Expense	4,200	
Postage Expense	2,700	
Miscellaneous Expense	8,500	
Total Expenses		151,645
Net Income		$ 42,355

Rhythmic Dance Studio
Balance Sheet
December 31, 2026

Assets:			
Cash		$ 41,000	
Accounts Receivable		8,250	
Supplies		24,975	
Furniture	$ 12,500		
Accum. Dep. - Furniture	2,200	10,300	
Equipment	26,500		
Accum. Dep. - Equipment	14,750	11,750	
Total Assets			$ 96,275
Liabilities:			
Accounts Payable		52,500	
Salaries Payable		4,150	
Owner's Equity:			
Lucia Manning, Capital		39,625	
Total Liabilities & Owner's Equity			$ 96,275

Rhythmic Dance Studio
Income Statement
For the Year Ended December 31, 2027

Revenues:		
Service Revenue		$ 261,500
Expenses:		
Salaries Expense	$ 101,450	
Rent Expense	32,275	
Supplies Expense	13,500	
Telephone Expense	9,150	
Depreciation Expense	6,300	
Utilities Expense	5,850	
Postage Expense	4,000	
Miscellaneous Expense	17,200	
Total Expenses		189,725
Net Income		$ 71,775

Rhythmic Dance Studio
Balance Sheet
December 31, 2027

Assets:			
Cash		$ 62,500	
Accounts Receivable		11,200	
Supplies		24,140	
Furniture	$ 12,500		
Accum. Dep. - Furniture	4,350	8,150	
Equipment	38,000		
Accum. Dep. - Equipment	18,900	19,100	
Total Assets			$ 125,090
Liabilities:			
Accounts Payable		50,300	
Salaries Payable		5,650	
Owner's Equity:			
Lucia Manning, Capital		69,140	
Total Liabilities & Owner's Equity			$ 125,090

▍PSA 7-1 PREPARE HORIZONTAL ANALYSES

Use the financial statements for Rhythmic Dance Studio to complete one horizontal analysis based on income statement balances and another based on balance sheet balances. (Hint: Use amounts from two statements to create each horizontal analysis.)

Starting files: Use the Horizontal Analysis Balance Sheet and Horizontal Analysis Income Statement templates.

PSA 7-2 PREPARE VERTICAL ANALYSES

Use the financial statements for Rhythmic Dance Studio to complete four vertical analyses, one each based on the:

- 2026 income statement
- 2027 income statement
- 2026 balance sheet
- 2027 balance sheet

Starting files: Use the Vertical Analysis Balance Sheet and Vertical Analysis Income Statement templates.

PSA 7-3 PREPARE COMMON-SIZE FINANCIAL STATEMENTS

Now use your vertical analyses to compare accounts balances for 2026 and 2027. Prepare both a common-size income statement and a common-size balance sheet.

Starting files: Use the Common-Size Income Statement and Common-Size Balance Sheet templates.

PSA 7-4 CALCULATE LIQUIDITY RATIOS

Use the financial statements for Rhythmic Dance Studio to calculate liquidity ratios.

1. Current ratio for 2026: _____
2. Current ratio for 2027: _____
3. Quick ratio for 2026: _____
4. Quick ratio for 2027: _____

PSA 7-5 CALCULATE SOLVENCY RATIOS

Use the financial statements for Rhythmic Dance Studio to calculate solvency ratios.

1. Debt ratio for 2026: _____
2. Debt ratio for 2027: _____
3. Equity ratio for 2026: _____
4. Equity ratio for 2027: _____
5. Debt-to-equity ratio for 2026: _____
6. Debt-to-equity ratio for 2027: _____

PSA 7-6 CALCULATE PROFITABILITY RATIOS

Use the financial statements for Rhythmic Dance Studio to calculate profitability ratios.

1. Profit margin for 2026: _____
2. Profit margin for 2027: _____
3. Return on assets for 2026 (use 2026 total assets as the average total assets): _____
4. Return on assets for 2027: _____

Practice Set B

You will refer to these statements as you complete Practice Set B for this chapter:

Photography Professionals
Income Statement
For the Year Ended December 31, 2026

Revenues:		
Service Revenue		$ 108,500
Expenses:		
Salaries Expense	$ 61,500	
Photo Supplies Expense	14,750	
Advertising Expense	11,350	
Telephone Expense	1,740	
Depreciation Expense	1,400	
Postage Expense	925	
Office Supplies Expense	625	
Miscellaneous Expense	370	
Total Expenses		92,660
Net Income		$ 15,840

Photography Professionals
Balance Sheet
December 31, 2026

Assets:			
Cash		$ 8,450	
Accounts Receivable		13,500	
Photo Supplies		3,150	
Office Supplies		170	
Photo Equipment	$ 6,950		
Accum. Dep. - Photo Equip.	5,270	1,680	
Truck	21,500		
Accum. Dep. - Truck	11,000	10,500	
Total Assets			$ 37,450
Liabilities:			
Accounts Payable		12,350	
Salaries Payable		1,350	
Owner's Equity:			
Lucia Manning, Capital		23,750	
Total Liabilities & Owner's Equity			$ 37,450

Photography Professionals
Income Statement
For the Year Ended December 31, 2027

Revenues:		
Service Revenue		$ 88,500
Expenses:		
Salaries Expense	$ 59,000	
Photo Supplies Expense	16,200	
Advertising Expense	6,800	
Telephone Expense	1,600	
Depreciation Expense	1,400	
Postage Expense	1,125	
Office Supplies Expense	500	
Miscellaneous Expense	440	
Total Expenses		87,065
Net Income		$ 1,435

Photography Professionals
Balance Sheet
December 31, 2027

Assets:			
Cash		$ 12,100	
Accounts Receivable		3,250	
Photo Supplies		5,750	
Office Supplies		425	
Photo Equipment	$ 6,950		
Accum. Dep. - Photo Equip.	5,670	1,280	
Truck	21,500		
Accum. Dep. - Truck	12,000	9,500	
Total Assets			$ 32,305
Liabilities:			
Accounts Payable		5,805	
Salaries Payable		300	
Owner's Equity:			
Lucia Manning, Capital		26,200	
Total Liabilities & Owner's Equity			$ 32,305

▌PSB 7-1 PREPARE HORIZONTAL ANALYSES

Use the financial statements for Photography Professionals to complete one horizontal analysis based on income statement balances and another based on balance sheet balances. (Hint: Use amounts from two statements to create each horizontal analysis.)

Starting files: Use the Horizontal Analysis Balance Sheet and Horizontal Analysis Income Statement templates.

PSB 7-2 PREPARE VERTICAL ANALYSES

Use the financial statements for Photography Professionals to complete four vertical analyses, one each for the:

- 2026 income statement
- 2027 income statement
- 2026 balance sheet
- 2027 balance sheet

Starting files: Use the Vertical Analysis Balance Sheet and Vertical Analysis Income Statement templates.

PSB 7-3 PREPARE COMMON-SIZE FINANCIAL STATEMENTS

Now use your vertical analyses to compare account balances for 2026 and 2027. Prepare both a common-size income statement and a common-size balance sheet.

Starting files: Use the Common-Size Income Statement and Common-Size Balance Sheet templates.

PSB 7-4 CALCULATE LIQUIDITY RATIOS

Use the financial statements for Photography Professionals to calculate liquidity ratios.

1. Current ratio for 2026: _____
2. Current ratio for 2027: _____
3. Quick ratio for 2026: _____
4. Quick ratio for 2027: _____

PSB 7-5 CALCULATE SOLVENCY RATIOS

Use the financial statements for Photography Professionals to calculate solvency ratios.

1. Debt ratio for 2026: _____
2. Debt ratio for 2027: _____
3. Equity ratio for 2026: _____
4. Equity ratio for 2027: _____
5. Debt-to-equity ratio for 2026: _____
6. Debt-to-equity ratio for 2027: _____

PSB 7-6 CALCULATE PROFITABILITY RATIOS

Use the financial statements for Photography Professionals to calculate profitability ratios.

1. Profit margin for 2026: _____
2. Profit margin for 2027: _____
3. Return on assets for 2026 (use 2026 total assets as the average total assets): _____
4. Return on assets for 2027: _____

8 Comprehensive Project

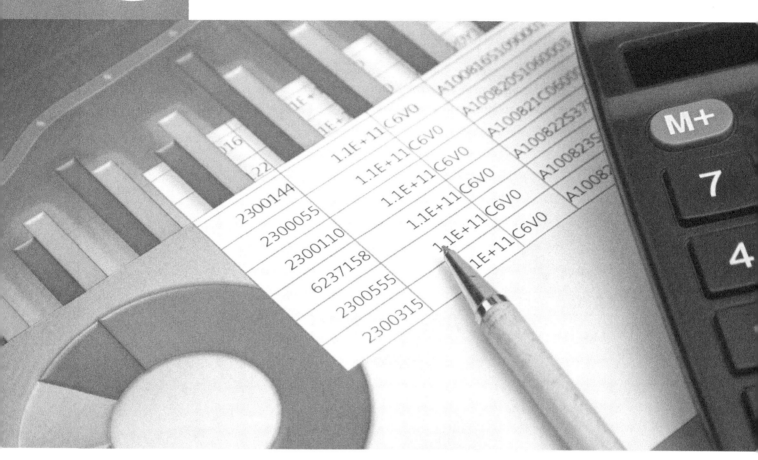

Now that you have examined the individual aspects of the accounting cycle, you're ready to put everything together and practice your new skills. In this project chapter, you will complete the accounting cycle for the first month of operations for a company. You will then analyze the financial results from these two bi-weekly pay periods.

Project: Completing the Accounting Cycle for Mother Molly's Childcare

Nathaniel has been raving to his friends about the excellent job you've done managing the financial records for Nathan's Donut School. One of his closest friends, Molly Fabrizio, is about to begin operating her new daycare business and babysitting service named Mother Molly's Childcare. Because of how highly Nathaniel has spoken of you, Molly asks you to assist with her business as well. She'd like you to complete all accounting work for the first month of operations, teaching her as you do so she can take over after the first month.

Your first step is to let Molly in on the plan: You'll complete the accounting cycle for the first month of operations and will then analyze the results. And since you know you'll be teaching Molly how to perform the accounting functions, you take care to complete all work correctly. Refer to the earlier chapters, if necessary, as you work through the accounting cycle.

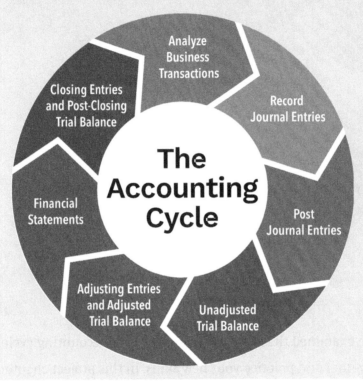

One-Month Project

Perform the following actions to complete the accounting cycle for the first month of operations at Mother Molly's Childcare.

You will work with all the template files for this project. Be sure to save your work and keep your files organized.

1. Record journal entries for each of the transactions in the May Transactions table that follows.

2. Post all journal entries to T-accounts for each account the company uses.

3. Prepare the unadjusted trial balance.

4. Record adjusting journal entries for these items:

   - A physical count of supplies on May 31 indicates that supplies worth $625 remain in the supply cabinet.

   - $750 of the unearned revenue received on May 22 has been earned as of May 31.

   - As of May 31, the company has provided $850 of services for which it has not yet billed the client and which were not previously recorded.

   - As of May 31, employees have worked for one day and earned wages of $200. They will not receive paychecks until the following month.

5. Post the adjusting journal entries.

6. Prepare the adjusted trial balance.

7. Prepare the income statement.

8. Prepare the statement of owner's equity.

9. Prepare the balance sheet.

10. Record the closing entries.

11. Post the closing entries.

12. Prepare the post-closing trial balance.

13. Prepare a vertical analysis for the income statement and for the balance sheet.

14. Calculate the liquidity ratios (current ratio, quick ratio).

15. Calculate the solvency ratios (debt ratio, equity ratio, debt-to-equity ratio).

16. Calculate the profitability ratios (profit margin, return on assets ratios).

MAY TRANSACTIONS (2027)	
Date	**Transaction Details**
May 1	Molly invested $50,000 to open Mother Molly's Childcare.
May 2	Spent $11,000 on furniture for use in the childcare facility.
	Purchased $1,450 of supplies from a local office supply store on account.
May 8	Established a petty cash fund containing $400.
May 12	Purchased $350 of children's snacks on account. Mother Molly's Childcare treats this as a Miscellaneous Expense.
May 13	Purchased advertising in a local newspaper for $505 cash.
May 15	Paid employees. Gross wages for the first half of the month: $3,000. Federal income tax withholding: $337. State income tax withholding: $130. Life insurance premiums withheld: $65. Applicable SUTA and FUTA tax rates for employees: 5.4% and 0.6%, respectively. To date, no single employee has reached the Social Security, FUTA, or SUTA tax thresholds.
May 15	The company determined that revenue for the first half of the month totaled $7,350. Of this, $4,000 was paid in cash; the remainder is owed.
May 17	Paid $800 of the amount owed from the May 2 purchase of supplies.
May 19	Received $1,200 of the amount owed from the revenue recorded on May 15.
May 22	Received $2,000 cash from a customer paying for the next two months of childcare services in advance.
May 23	Life insurance premiums withheld on May 15 are remitted to the insurance company.
May 24	The company replenished its petty cash fund, from which $305 had been spent ($157 of supplies + $83 of postage + $65 of miscellaneous expense).
May 25	Received $1,325 of the amount owed from the revenue recorded on May 15.
May 29	Paid $1,620 cash for monthly rent.
May 30	Paid $220 cash for the telephone bill.
May 30	Paid $315 cash for the utility (electric) bill.
May 31	The company determined that revenue for the second half of the month totaled $9,200. Of this, $7,600 was paid in cash; the remainder is owed.
May 31	Molly Fabrizio withdrew $4,000 cash for personal use.
May 31	Paid employees. Gross wages for the second half of the month: $3,500. Federal income tax withholding: $389. State income tax withholding: $156. Life insurance premiums withheld: $70. Applicable SUTA and FUTA tax rates for employees: 5.4% and 0.6%, respectively. To date, no single employee has reached the Social Security, FUTA, or SUTA tax thresholds.

9 Merchandise Inventory

Up to this point we have focused primarily on service businesses, but many businesses don't provide services to clients and instead sell products to customers, while many others do both. In this chapter, you will learn how to record transactions involving the purchase and sale of merchandise inventory.

LEARNING OBJECTIVES

▸ Record journal entries for merchandise inventory

▸ Apply valuation methods to merchandise inventory

▸ Adjust merchandise inventory

▸ Analyze the Cost of Goods Sold account and gross margin

Project: Expanding Nathan's Donut School

Over the first calendar year of operations, Nathan's Donut School has been very successful, with student enrollment steadily increasing from one month to the next and the school's reputation continuing to strengthen. Nathaniel has decided, as of December 1, to expand the business. In addition to offering a variety of baking classes, a small corner of the facility will be reserved for the sale of select products such as baking tools, instructional videos, and recipe books.

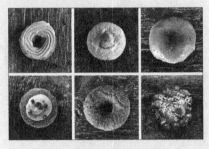

Nathaniel continues to be pleased with your performance and asks for your help as he expands Nathan's Donut School. To ensure the company's financial statements continue to be accurate, you must now become familiar with journal entries and calculations related to merchandise inventory, including the new expense, Cost of Goods Sold.

The Merchandise Inventory Account

 **View the video "Merchandise Inventory Account."**

The **Merchandise Inventory** account is an asset account that represents the cost of goods a business intends to sell. Retail stores like Target, Home Depot, and countless others purchase merchandise inventory and then sell it at a higher price to you, the customer. These businesses have Merchandise Inventory accounts. All retail businesses record journal entries both for the purchase of merchandise inventory and for its sale to customers.

Let's first examine the purchase of merchandise inventory. The Merchandise Inventory account is another current asset, so the purchase is recorded similarly to that for assets such as supplies. Here we see a journal entry showing the purchase of merchandise inventory for $2,400 in cash on December 2:

12/2	Merchandise Inventory	2,400	
	Cash		2,400
	Purchase of merchandise inventory for cash		

This journal entry results in no change to total assets because as the balance in one asset account (Merchandise Inventory) increases, the balance in another asset account (Cash) decreases by the same amount. What would be different if the same merchandise inventory were purchased on account?

12/2	Merchandise Inventory	2,400	
	Accounts Payable		2,400
	Purchase of merchandise inventory on account		

When merchandise inventory is purchased on account, the liability account Accounts Payable increases.

Now we see total assets increase (because Merchandise Inventory is increased) as well as total liabilities (Accounts Payable is increased). When merchandise inventory is purchased on account, a subsequent journal entry is recorded when payment is made. Here's the resulting journal entry if full payment is made on December 19:

12/19	Accounts Payable	2,400	
	Cash		2,400
	Payment for merchandise inventory purchased on account		

This payment reduces both total assets (Cash is reduced) and total liabilities (Accounts Payable is reduced).

Now that the business has purchased merchandise inventory, it can sell it within its retail location for a higher amount. Let's assume that on December 22 the business sells 25% of the merchandise inventory for $1,000 on account. The cost of the goods sold is $600 ($2,400 * 25%). This example is unique in that this single transaction (the sale of merchandise inventory) results in the recording of two journal entries. The first records the amount owed to the seller (increasing total assets by debiting Accounts Receivable) and the revenue earned from the sale (increasing total owner's equity by crediting Sales Revenue).

12/22	Accounts Receivable	1,000	
	Sales Revenue		1,000
	Sale of merchandise inventory on account		

Note that Sales Revenue is increased via a credit here. In previous chapters, we used Service Revenue in similar transactions. Now that we're dealing with the sale of merchandise, we use Sales Revenue.

TIP! If the sale is made for cash, the Cash account would be debited here instead of Accounts Receivable.

The second journal entry records the expense incurred, which is equal to the purchase price of the merchandise inventory and the reduction in the Merchandise Inventory asset account that results from the sale.

12/22	Cost of Goods Sold	600	
	Merchandise Inventory		600
	Sale of merchandise inventory on account		

Here we see a new expense account, **Cost of Goods Sold** (also known as *Cost of Merchandise Sold*). When merchandise inventory is first purchased, it's considered an asset; we saw this in the December 2 transaction. When it's subsequently sold, the cost of the inventory is transferred to Cost of Goods Sold from Merchandise Inventory, which is reduced in this journal entry, leading to a reduction in total assets. Since Cost of Goods Sold is an expense account, it's increased via a debit, which leads to a reduction in total owner's equity.

Did you notice the difference in the amounts recorded in these two journal entries? The first journal entry, which reflects the cash received and revenue earned, was recorded for the $1,000 sales price; the second journal entry reflects the cost of the goods that have been sold and so was recorded for the $600 cost.

If the customer then pays for the merchandise inventory on December 29, the journal entry will be recorded as follows. This journal entry has no impact on the accounting equation because one asset increases (Cash) by the same amount another asset decreases (Accounts Receivable).

12/29	Cash	1,000	
	Accounts Receivable		1,000
	Payment for sale of merchandise inventory on account		

Ask Yourself 9-1: Merchandise Inventory is a current asset account. True or false?

👀 A CLOSER LOOK

Do All Companies Take This Approach to Recording Merchandise Inventory Journal Entries?

The approach Nathan's Donut School is using here is referred to as the **perpetual inventory system**. When using this system, Cost of Goods Sold is debited and Merchandise Inventory is credited on the date of the sale, which means both accounts have up-to-date balances at all times. In other words, these account balances are *perpetually* updated.

Using the **periodic inventory system**, a company waits to record Cost of Goods Sold and changes in Merchandise Inventory until the end of the period. So, when merchandise inventory is purchased, the company debits the Purchases account (an expense account, so it's increased via a debit), not the Merchandise Inventory account.

> **NOTE!** The perpetual inventory system is typically used by businesses with computerized systems capable of recording journal entries in real time. The periodic inventory system is suited for businesses that would not derive a significant benefit from such real-time accounting.

When a sale is subsequently made, the company records the revenue earned just as is done for the perpetual inventory system but does not record a journal entry for the cost of the goods. Both Cost of Goods Sold and Merchandise Inventory are updated as part of an adjusting journal entry at the end of the period. See Case in Point 9-3 for more information on these adjusting journal entries.

CASE IN POINT 9-1

In this example, we'll examine the initial journal entries recorded by Nathan's Donut School as it expands into the sale of merchandise inventory.

1. On December 1, Nathan's Donut School purchases $5,000 of merchandise inventory on account.

12/1	Merchandise Inventory	5,000	
	Accounts Payable		5,000
	Purchase of merchandise inventory on account		

   As a result of this asset purchase, the Merchandise Inventory account is debited (increased) and Accounts Payable is credited (increased).

2. On December 4, Nathan's Donut School sells merchandise inventory on account for $2,000. The cost of the goods sold is $900.

12/4	Accounts Receivable	2,000	
	Sales Revenue		2,000
	Sale of merchandise inventory on account		
12/4	Cost of Goods Sold	900	
	Merchandise Inventory		900
	Sale of merchandise inventory on account		

   Here we see the two journal entries that result from the sale of goods. Note how the sales price of $2,000 is used in the first journal entry while the $900 cost of the goods is used in the second.

3. On December 6, Nathan's Donut School pays in full for the merchandise inventory purchased on December 1.

12/6	Accounts Payable	5,000	
	Cash		5,000
	Paid for merchandise inventory on account		

Here Accounts Payable is debited (reduced) and Cash is credited (reduced) to record the payment of $5,000 owed from the merchandise inventory purchase on December 1.

4. On December 11, Nathan's Donut School receives payment in full for the sale made on December 4.

12/11	Cash	2,000	
	Accounts Receivable		2,000
	Payment for sale of merchandise inventory on account		

In this journal entry, the Cash account is debited (increased) to account for the receipt of cash and Accounts Receivable is credited (reduced) to indicate the $2,000 owed to Nathan's Donut School from the sale on December 4 has now been paid in full.

Determining the Value of Merchandise Inventory

View the video "Determining the Value of Merchandise Inventory."

Having now seen how merchandise inventory journal entries are recorded, you're ready to consider how the cost of goods sold for a given sale is determined. Ideally, a business would track all inventory and the associated costs such that when goods are sold, it can identify the exact cost of the goods purchased by the customer. For most products, this isn't a practical approach. Instead of tracking the exact cost of goods sold, most businesses use valuation methods to both determine the cost of the goods recorded when a sale is made and to determine the balance in the Merchandise Inventory account at any given time.

There are three valuation methods:

- **FIFO method** (first in, first out)
- **LIFO method** (last in, first out)
- **Average cost method** (aka *weighted average method*)

To examine these three methods, let's look at an example. Electronic Works is a corporation based in Cherry Hill, NJ. The business sells a variety of electronics, primarily for commercial use. For its best-selling microwave, Model H-211, the company began March with 100 units in its warehouse, each of which cost Electronic Works $40. On March 5 the company purchases an additional 160 units for $42/unit, on March 13 it sells 190 units for $95/unit, and on March 17 it purchases 80 more units for $43/unit. This activity is summarized in the following table:

Date	Purchases			Sales			Merchandise Inventory Balance		
	Quantity	Unit Cost	Total	Quantity	Unit Cost	Total	Quantity	Unit Cost	Total
3/1							100	$ 40	$ 4,000
3/5	160	$ 42	$ 6,720						
3/13				190					
3/17	80	$ 43	$ 3,440						

Notice there's no cost listed for the 190 units sold on 3/13. The $95 per unit sales price is not considered here because the goal is to determine the *cost* of the goods, not the sales price. The three estimation methods are used to determine the cost of the goods sold (in this case, from the sale on 3/13) and the ending inventory balance (the cost of the goods remaining in the warehouse at the end of the period).

FIFO Method (First In, First Out)

Under the FIFO method, a company assumes that the first inventory to enter the warehouse is also the first inventory to leave it. When a sale is made, the company uses the cost of the oldest inventory to determine the cost of goods sold for that sale. In the Electronic Works example, the oldest inventory is the units at the top of the table (3/1 beginning inventory) but while 190 units were sold, there were only 100 units in that beginning inventory. So, we first assume that all 100 units from the beginning inventory are included within the 190 units sold. To account for the remaining 90 units under FIFO, we move to the next row down in the table and assume the remaining 90 units are derived from the 160 units purchased on 3/5.

The cost of goods sold for the 3/13 sale is calculated under FIFO as:

100 units x $40/unit = $4,000   **$4,000**

90 units x $42/unit = $3,780   **+ $3,780**

                                               $7,780

We begin by multiplying the 100 units from the beginning inventory by their cost of $40 each to calculate a total cost for these units of $4,000. We then multiply 90 units from the 3/5 purchase by their $42 per unit cost to calculate $3,780 for those units. Lastly, we add the two calculated amounts to determine that the total cost of goods sold is $7,780.

Now we can expand our table:

Date	Purchases			Sales			Merchandise Inventory Balance		
	Quantity	Unit Cost	Total	Quantity	Unit Cost	Total	Quantity	Unit Cost	Total
3/1							100	$ 40	$ 4,000
3/5	160	$ 42	$ 6,720				100	$ 40	$ 4,000
							160	$ 42	$ 6,720
3/13				100	$ 40	$ 4,000	70	$ 42	$ 2,940
				90	$ 42	$ 3,780			
3/17	80	$ 43	$ 3,440				70	$ 42	$ 2,940
							80	$ 43	$ 3,440

As you examine the table, first look at the sale of 190 units made on 3/13. Within the Sales columns, we've now broken up the sale into two rows, with the first row listing the 100 units sold from the beginning inventory and the second listing the 90 units sold from the 3/5 purchase.

Also notice that the Merchandise Inventory balances are being updated after each transaction. On 3/5, 160 units were purchased at a cost of $42/unit. This is included in the Purchases columns and Merchandise Inventory Balance columns, where a second row shows the new merchandise inventory. Updating the Merchandise Inventory Balance columns helps calculate the cost of goods sold. On 3/13, when the 190 units are sold, we can refer to the most recent figures in the Merchandise Inventory Balance columns to see the cost of the units that have been sold.

The Merchandise Inventory Balance columns on 3/13 contain 70 units at a cost of $42/unit. These are the remaining units from the 3/5 purchase (160 – 90 = 70). When the 80 units are purchased for

$43 each on 3/17, the new inventory is added as a second row in the Merchandise Inventory Balance columns.

The $6,380 balance in the Merchandise Inventory account on 3/17 can be determined by reviewing the figures within the Merchandise Inventory Balance columns:

70 units x $42/unit = $2,940   **$2,940**
80 units x $43/unit = $3,440   **+ $3,440**
                                      $6,380

LIFO Method (Last In, First Out)

The LIFO method is, essentially, the reverse of FIFO. Under LIFO, a company assumes the most recent inventory to enter the warehouse is the first inventory to leave the warehouse. So, when a sale is made, the company uses the cost of the newest inventory to determine the cost of goods sold for that sale.

Once again using the Electronic Works example, instead of starting with the beginning inventory, we begin with the most recently purchased inventory on 3/5. Of the 190 units sold on 3/13, we can use 160 units from the 3/5 purchase, so under LIFO, we move to the next row up in the table and assume the remaining 30 units sold come from the 100 units in the beginning inventory.

The cost of goods sold for the 3/13 sale is calculated under LIFO as:

160 units x $42/unit = $6,720   **$6,720**
30 units x $40/unit = $1,200   **+ $1,200**
                                      $7,920

In this situation, our table would appear as follows:

Date	Purchases			Sales			Merchandise Inventory Balance		
	Quantity	Unit Cost	Total	Quantity	Unit Cost	Total	Quantity	Unit Cost	Total
3/1							100	$ 40	$ 4,000
3/5	160	$ 42	$ 6,720				100	$ 40	$ 4,000
							160	$ 42	$ 6,720
3/13				160	$ 42	$ 6,720	70	$ 40	$ 2,800
				30	$ 40	$ 1,200			
3/17	80	$ 43	$ 3,440				70	$ 40	$ 2,800
							80	$ 43	$ 3,440

As you can see on the 3/17 row, just as the cost of goods sold under LIFO is different from that calculated using FIFO, so is the Merchandise Inventory balance. Under LIFO, the $6,240 merchandise inventory balance on 3/17 is calculated as follows:

70 units x $40/unit = $2,800   **$2,800**
80 units x $43/unit = $3,440   **+ $3,440**
                                      $6,240

While the cost of goods sold under FIFO ($7,780) is less than that under LIFO ($7,920), the Merchandise Inventory balance as of 3/17 under FIFO ($6,380) is greater than that under LIFO ($6,240). In a period of inflation (rising prices) as with Electronic Works here, the cost of goods sold will be greater under LIFO, while the Merchandise Inventory balance will be greater under FIFO.

TIP! Don't lose sight of the fact that these are estimation methods under which certain assumptions are made. The FIFO and LIFO methods don't require that the *actual* flow of goods follows these patterns.

Ask Yourself 9-2: In the FIFO and LIFO acronyms, what does the *FO* stand for?

    A. Final off

    B. First one

    C. Final on

    D. First out

Average Cost Method

As the name suggests, the **average cost method** uses the average cost for every unit in the warehouse to calculate the cost of goods sold and the Merchandise Inventory balance. To determine Electronic Works' cost of goods sold on 3/13, we first divide the total cost of all merchandise in the warehouse by the total number of units in the warehouse. Recall that after the purchase of goods on 3/5 the balance in the Merchandise Inventory account is calculated as:

$$\begin{array}{ll} \underline{} 100 \text{ units x } \$40/\text{unit} = & \$4,000 \text{ (beginning inventory)} \\ \underline{+ \ 160} \text{ units x } \$42/\text{unit} = & \underline{+ \ \$6,720} \text{ (3/5 purchase)} \\ 260 \text{ units} & \$10,720 \end{array}$$

To determine the average cost per unit, divide the $10,720 total inventory cost by the 260 units in the warehouse to arrive at $41.23 (rounded). When 190 units are sold on 3/13, use this average cost to calculate the cost of goods sold of $7,834 (rounded).

Date	Purchases			Sales			Merchandise Inventory Balance		
	Quantity	Unit Cost	Total	Quantity	Unit Cost	Total	Quantity	Unit Cost	Total
3/1							100	$ 40.00	$ 4,000
3/5	160	$ 42.00	$ 6,720				260	$ 41.23	$ 10,720
3/13				190	$ 41.23	$ 7,834	70	$ 41.23	$ 2,886
3/17	80	$ 43.00	$ 3,440				150	$ 42.17	$ 6,326

With the average cost method, the average cost per unit is recalculated after each purchase. That's why the new average cost of $42.17 (rounded) per unit is calculated after 80 units are purchased on 3/17. The $6,326 (rounded) merchandise inventory balance as of 3/17 is calculated by multiplying 150 units by the $42.17 (rounded) average cost per unit.

NOTE! As seen in this example, amounts calculated for cost of goods sold and the Merchandise Inventory Balance under the average cost method fall between those calculated using FIFO and LIFO.

Are Inventory Valuation Methods the Same Under the Periodic Inventory System?

Yes, sort of. The calculations for the FIFO, LIFO, and average cost methods are the same for the perpetual and the periodic inventory systems, but there is a difference in the frequency of the calculations.

A perpetual inventory system involves making calculations after each sale or purchase (for average cost) during the period. Under a periodic inventory system, the cost of goods sold calculations are done just once, at the end of the accounting period. This involves reviewing all beginning inventory and purchase rows in the table for the entire period without considering when the sales were made. Therefore, when using the FIFO and LIFO methods in a periodic inventory system, a company examines many more rows to calculate the cost of goods sold than would exist at the time of any single sale (when calculating the cost of goods sold under a perpetual system).

The periodic inventory system is far simpler than the perpetual inventory system, as it requires only one set of calculations at the end of the period, instead of calculations after every individual sale.

CASE IN POINT 9-2

In this example, we'll calculate the cost of goods sold and the resulting Merchandise Inventory balance for the sale of 150 spatulas under three methods (FIFO, LIFO, average cost) on 8/5.

Prior to the sale, you recorded this cost information:

Date	Purchases			Sales			Merchandise Inventory Balance		
	Quantity	Unit Cost	Total	Quantity	Unit Cost	Total	Quantity	Unit Cost	Total
8/1							80	$ 24	$ 1,920
8/3	130	$ 25	$ 3,250				80	$ 24	$ 1,920
							130	$ 25	$ 3,250

1. First, we calculate the cost of goods sold under the FIFO method.

   Beginning at the top with the earliest merchandise inventory balance amounts (8/1), work down to identify all units sold. In this case, all 80 units from the beginning inventory and 70 units from the 8/3 purchase represent the 150 units sold on 8/5. The cost of goods sold is calculated as:

   80 units x $24/unit = $1,920 $1,920
   70 units x $25/unit = $1,750   + $1,750
   ** $3,670**

   The remaining merchandise inventory is the 60 units left over from the 8/3 purchase (130 – 70). We multiply these 60 units by their $25 cost to determine the Merchandise Inventory balance after the sale on 8/5 of $1,500.

2. Now let's see how things change using the LIFO method.

   Similar to with FIFO, we consider both the beginning inventory and the 8/3 purchase, but where FIFO begins at the top of the list, this time we begin at the bottom of the list and work up to identify units sold under LIFO. That means all 130 units from the 8/3 purchase and 20 units from the beginning inventory represent the units sold. The cost of goods sold is calculated as:

   130 units x $25/unit = $3,250 $3,250
   20 units x $24/unit = $ 480   + $ 480
   $3,730

   This time we calculate the remaining 60 units as 80 units in the beginning inventory minus 20 units sold on 8/5, and we calculate the Merchandise Inventory balance after the sale on 8/5 as 60 units multiplied by $24 each for $1,440.

3. And finally, let's calculate the cost of goods sold using the average cost method.

   We first calculate the average cost per unit. The total cost of inventory in the warehouse after the 8/3 purchase is $5,170 ($1,920 beginning inventory cost + $3,250 purchased on 8/3). The total number of units in the warehouse is 210 (80 beginning inventory units + 130 units purchased on 8/3). When we divide the total cost by the total units in the warehouse, we arrive at an average cost per unit of $24.62 (rounded). We then multiply this average cost per unit by the number of units sold to calculate the cost of goods sold as $3,693 (rounded).

   $5,170 ÷ 210 total units = $24.62 (rounded)
   $24.62 * 150 units sold = $3,693 (rounded)

   The Merchandise Inventory balance can similarly be calculated by multiplying the $24.62 (rounded) average cost per unit by the 60 remaining units (210 total units – 150 units sold) for $1,477 (rounded).

Adjusting Merchandise Inventory

🔊 View the video "Adjusting Merchandise Inventory."

As part of a company's internal controls at the end of a period, a physical count of all merchandise inventory is performed. As the name suggests, a physical count requires that one or more individuals count the units of inventory as of the end of the period. A company using the perpetual inventory system is updating the Cost of Goods Sold and Merchandise Inventory account balances throughout the period so, in theory, the balance in Merchandise Inventory should match the cost of the units counted at the end of the period. If so, then no adjusting journal entry is necessary. This doesn't usually happen, though. Often the cost of the units counted at period end does not match the Merchandise Inventory account balance, whether due to theft, breakage, recording error, or other reason. In this case, an adjusting entry is recorded.

Consider a company with a Merchandise Inventory balance of $126,000 at the end of the period. If the physical count on 12/31 indicates that only $125,200 of merchandise inventory is actually in the warehouse, then an adjusting journal entry must be recorded to reduce the balance of Merchandise Inventory and increase the balance of Cost of Goods Sold by the $800 difference ($126,000 −$125,200):

12/31	Cost of Goods Sold	800	
	Merchandise Inventory		800
	Adjusting entry for merchandise inventory		

Now imagine the physical count on 12/31 indicates that $126,500 of merchandise inventory is in the warehouse. In this case, the Merchandise Inventory balance is increased and the Cost of Goods Sold balance is decreased as follows:

12/31	Merchandise Inventory	500	
	Cost of Goods Sold		500
	Adjusting entry for merchandise inventory		

Ask Yourself 9-3: Adjusting entries for merchandise inventory are rarely needed. True or false?

◉◉ A CLOSER LOOK

Are Adjusting Entries Necessary with the Periodic Inventory System?

Yes. The periodic inventory system doesn't record entries impacting the Cost of Goods Sold or Merchandise Inventory accounts during the period, so adjusting entries must be recorded for these accounts at period end. To begin with, the balance within the Purchases account is transferred to Merchandise Inventory by debiting (increasing) Merchandise Inventory and crediting (reducing) Purchases:

12/31	Merchandise Inventory	XXX	
	Purchases		XXX
	Adjusting entry to increase merchandise inventory		

This increases the Merchandise Inventory account by the total purchases of goods made during the period. The company must then reduce the Merchandise Inventory account (via a credit) and increase the Cost of Goods Sold account (via a debit) by the total cost of the goods sold during the period:

12/31	Cost of Goods Sold	XXX	
	Merchandise Inventory		XXX
	Adjusting entry to decrease merchandise inventory		

The amount used in this adjusting entry is based on the physical count of inventory that takes place at the end of the period.

CASE IN POINT 9-3

In this example, we'll examine two independent circumstances and record the required adjusting journal entries for each.

1. Stepstool Corp. has a Merchandise Inventory balance of $362,000, but the physical inventory count indicates that there's $359,500 of merchandise inventory in the warehouse at year end.

12/31	Cost of Goods Sold	2,500	
	Merchandise Inventory		2,500
	Adjusting entry for merchandise inventory		

The physical count shows less merchandise inventory than the account balance, so the Merchandise Inventory account is reduced by the difference of $2,500. The Cost of Goods Sold account increases by the same amount.

2. Unofficial Inc. has a Merchandise Inventory balance of $61,000, and the physical inventory count indicates that there is $61,700 of merchandise inventory in the warehouse at year end.

12/31	Merchandise Inventory	700	
	Cost of Goods Sold		700
	Adjusting entry for merchandise inventory		

This time the physical count shows there's more merchandise inventory in the warehouse than is reflected in the Merchandise Inventory account balance. This adjusting entry therefore increases the Merchandise Inventory account and decreases the Cost of Goods Sold account by the $700 difference.

Analyzing Cost of Goods Sold and Gross Profit

As we've seen in this chapter, companies that sell inventory must account for many elements that don't impact a service business. One implication of this is that additional measures must be taken to evaluate the performance of these companies. Two ratios that help with this are the **cost of goods sold ratio** and the **gross margin ratio**. Similar to ratios for profit margin and return on assets, these ratios are profitability ratios.

> **TIP!** Recall that profitability ratios provide insight into a company's ability to effectively generate income.

Cost of Goods Sold Ratio = Cost of Goods Sold ÷ Total Sales
Gross Margin Ratio = Gross Margin ÷ Total Sales

The cost of goods sold ratio indicates the portion of total sales that are required for the cost of goods sold. Companies seek to keep this ratio as low as possible, as doing so indicates that the cost of goods sold (an expense) is being minimized.

Gross margin (or *gross profit*) represents the difference between total sales and the cost of goods sold. Gross margin is distinct from net income in that it doesn't consider operating expenses (telephone, utilities, rent, etc.). The **gross margin ratio** (or *gross profit ratio*), therefore, indicates the portion of total sales that covers all other expenses that are not the cost of goods sold. A high gross margin ratio means a company has funds remaining to cover all other expenses and contribute to net income.

Ask Yourself 9-4: What type of ratio is the gross margin ratio?
  - **A.** Liquidity ratio
  - **B.** Profitability ratio

CASE IN POINT 9-4

In this example, we will calculate merchandise-related profitability ratios for two months of operations for Backyard Brothers Company and analyze the results.

We'll use these balances to calculate the ratios:

	September 2027	October 2027
Cost of Goods Sold	$83,000	$87,400
Total Sales	$204,000	$203,800

1. Let's begin by calculating the cost of goods sold and gross margin ratios for September.

$$\text{Cost of Goods Sold Ratio} \quad \frac{\$83,000}{\$204,000} = 40.69\%$$

$$\text{Gross Margin Ratio} \quad \frac{\$204,000 - \$83,000}{\$204,000} = 59.31\%$$

2. Next, we'll calculate the cost of goods sold and gross margin ratios for October.

$$\text{Cost of Goods Sold Ratio} \quad \frac{\$87,400}{\$203,800} = 42.89\%$$

$$\text{Gross Margin Ratio} \quad \frac{\$203,800 - \$87,400}{\$203,800} = 57.11\%$$

3. What can we conclude from these ratios?

   While the cost of goods sold ratio increased from September to October, the gross margin ratio decreased. This indicates that the company is increasing its cost of goods sold expense relative to total sales. While this isn't uncommon over time, the higher cost of goods sold ratio and lower gross margin ratio could be cause for concern if this is the beginning of a trend that continues in subsequent months.

Self-Assessment

Now it's time for you to check your knowledge of the key concepts and skills introduced in this chapter.

1. Merchandise Inventory is an asset account.   *True   False*

2. The journal entry recorded when merchandise inventory is purchased includes a credit to the Merchandise Inventory account.   *True   False*

3. Under the perpetual inventory system, the Merchandise Inventory balance is updated solely at the end of the period.   *True   False*

4. FIFO stands for first-in, first-out.   *True   False*

5. Under the average cost method, both the cost of goods sold and the merchandise inventory balance will fall between those calculated using the FIFO and LIFO methods.   *True   False*

6. The frequency of calculations under the LIFO method is the same, regardless of the inventory system used (perpetual or periodic).   *True   False*

7. The physical inventory count for a company using the perpetual inventory system shows that the cost of the merchandise inventory in the warehouse is lower than the Merchandise Inventory account balance. The adjusting journal entry will indicate a credit to the Cost of Goods Sold account.   *True   False*

8. The physical inventory count for a company using the perpetual inventory system shows that the cost of the merchandise inventory in the warehouse is higher than the Merchandise Inventory account balance. In this case, no adjusting journal entry is necessary.   *True   False*

9. The gross margin ratio is a merchandise-related profitability ratio.   *True   False*

10. Companies want to increase their gross margin ratio.   *True   False*

11. Cost of Goods Sold is a(n) _____ account.

12. You sold merchandise inventory on account to your best customer for $3,600. The merchandise inventory cost you $2,100. What do you include in the journal entry you record?

    A. A debit to Accounts Receivable for $2,100.

    B. A credit to Sales Revenue for $3,600.

    C. A debit to Cost of Goods Sold for $3,600.

    D. A debit to Merchandise Inventory for $2,100.

13. When a business sells merchandise inventory for cash, how many journal entries are typically recorded on the date of the sale? _____

14. What account is credited in the journal entry recorded by the seller when a business remits payment for merchandise inventory purchased two weeks ago?

    A. Merchandise Inventory

    B. Accounts Receivable

    C. Accounts Payable

    D. Cash

15. What statement about inventory valuation methods is accurate?

    A. They track the exact cost of all units sold.

    B. You use average cost amounts with all of them.

    C. There are two inventory valuation methods from which a business can choose.

    D. They determine the Cost of Goods Sold and Merchandise Inventory account balances.

16. Under LIFO, what units are assumed to have been sold first?

    A. The most expensive

    B. The oldest

    C. The least expensive

    D. The most recently obtained

17. What usually happens during a period of inflation?

    A. Cost of goods sold is higher under FIFO.

    B. Total expenses are lower under LIFO.

    C. Merchandise inventory is higher under FIFO.

    D. Total assets are higher under LIFO.

18. Average cost per unit (using the average cost inventory valuation method) =

    A. Total cost of all merchandise ÷ total number of units available for sale

    B. Total number of units available for sale ÷ total cost of all merchandise

    C. Total sales price of all merchandise ÷ total number of units sold

    D. Total number of units sold ÷ total sales price of all merchandise

19. Gross Margin = _____   _____   _____

20. Cost of Goods Sold Ratio = _____   _____   _____

Putting It Together

PIT 9-1 RECORD THE TRANSACTIONS

Amber's Lacrosse Emporium continues to perform well as it enters its third month of operations. In this example, we'll record the July transactions.

1. On July 2, Amber purchases $2,700 of merchandise inventory on account.

7/2	Merchandise Inventory	2,700	
	Accounts Payable		2,700
	Purchase of merchandise inventory on account		

2. On July 4, Amber pays $1,600 cash for merchandise inventory.

7/4	Merchandise Inventory	1,600	
	Cash		1,600
	Purchase of merchandise inventory for cash		

3. On July 5, Amber sells merchandise inventory for $4,800 cash. The cost of the goods sold was $2,200.

7/5	Cash	4,800	
	Sales Revenue		4,800
	Sale of merchandise inventory for cash		
7/5	Cost of Goods Sold	2,200	
	Merchandise Inventory		2,200
	Sale of merchandise inventory for cash		

4. On July 6, Amber remits $2,700 in full payment for the merchandise inventory purchased on 7/2.

7/6	Accounts Payable	2,700	
	Cash		2,700
	Payment for merchandise inventory purchased on account		

5. On July 8, Amber sells merchandise inventory on account for $3,100. The cost of the goods sold was $1,400.

7/8	Accounts Receivable	3,100	
	Sales Revenue		3,100
	Sale of merchandise inventory on account		
7/8	Cost of Goods Sold	1,400	
	Merchandise Inventory		1,400
	Sale of merchandise inventory on account		

6. On July 14, Amber receives $3,100 in full payment for the merchandise inventory sold on 7/8.

7/14	Cash	3,100	
	Accounts Receivable		3,100
	Payment for sale of merchandise inventory on account		

7. A few months later, Amber is reviewing the company's accounting policies and wonders if she's been assigning proper valuations to her merchandise inventory. She decides to examine select transactions during September and to compare the calculation of the cost of goods sold and merchandise inventory using the FIFO, LIFO, and average cost methods.

Here are the transactions Amber examines:

Date	Purchases			Sales			Merchandise Inventory Balance		
	Quantity	Unit Cost	Total	Quantity	Unit Cost	Total	Quantity	Unit Cost	Total
9/1							65	$ 31	$ 2,015
9/4	80	$ 33	$ 2,640						
9/10				100					
9/13	60	$ 35	$ 2,100						

We begin by using the FIFO method to calculate the cost of goods sold on 9/10 and the merchandise inventory balance after the 9/13 purchase.

65 units x $31/unit = $2,015　　　　**$2,015**
35 units x $33/unit = $1,155　　　　**+ $ 1,155**
　　　　　　　　　　　　　　　　　　$3,170

Date	Purchases			Sales			Merchandise Inventory Balance		
	Quantity	Unit Cost	Total	Quantity	Unit Cost	Total	Quantity	Unit Cost	Total
9/1							65	$ 31	$ 2,015
9/4	80	$ 33	$ 2,640				65	$ 31	$ 2,015
							80	$ 33	$ 2,640
9/10				65	$ 31	$ 2,015	45	$ 33	$ 1,485
				35	$ 33	$ 1,155			
9/13	60	$ 35	$ 2,100				45	$ 33	$ 1,485
							60	$ 35	$ 2,100

Now it's clear that the cost of goods sold for the 9/10 transaction is $3,170 ($2,015 + $1,155). By adding the Merchandise Inventory Balance column amounts for 9/13, Amber can also see that the merchandise inventory balance on 9/13 is $3,585 ($1,485 + $2,100).

8. Next, we'll calculate the cost of goods sold and merchandise inventory using the LIFO method.

80 units x $33/unit = $2,640 $2,640
20 units x $31/unit = $620   + $ 620
                                        $3,260

Date	Purchases			Sales			Merchandise Inventory Balance		
	Quantity	Unit Cost	Total	Quantity	Unit Cost	Total	Quantity	Unit Cost	Total
9/1							65	$ 31	$ 2,015
9/4	80	$ 33	$ 2,640				65	$ 31	$ 2,015
							80	$ 33	$ 2,640
9/10				80	$ 33	$ 2,640	45	$ 31	$ 1,395
				20	$ 31	$ 620			
9/13	60	$ 35	$ 2,100				45	$ 31	$ 1,395
							60	$ 35	$ 2,100

Using the LIFO method, Amber has now calculated the cost of goods sold as $3,260 and a merchandise inventory balance of $3,495 ($1,395 + $2,100).

9. Now, use the Average Cost Method to calculate the Cost of Goods Sold and the Merchandise Inventory account balances on these dates.

65 units x $31/unit = $2,015 **(beginning inventory)**
+ 80 units x $33/unit =   + $2,640 **(9/4 purchase)**
145 units $4,655

Amber may use these figures to calculate an average cost per unit as of the 9/4 purchase of $32.10 (rounded) by dividing $4,655 by 145 units. This average cost per unit may then be used to create the following table:

Date	Purchases			Sales			Merchandise Inventory Balance		
	Quantity	Unit Cost	Total	Quantity	Unit Cost	Total	Quantity	Unit Cost	Total
9/1							65	$ 31.00	$ 2,015
9/4	80	$ 33.00	$ 2,640				145	$ 32.10	$ 4,655
9/10				100	$ 32.10	$ 3,210	45	$ 32.10	$ 1,445
9/13	60	$ 35.00	$ 2,100				105	$ 33.76	$ 3,545

Under the average cost method, the cost of goods sold is $3,210 (rounded) and the merchandise inventory balance as of 9/13 is $3,545 (rounded). Notice that the average cost per unit was $32.10 (rounded) after the 9/4 purchase and was updated to $33.76 (rounded) after the 9/13 purchase (reflecting the cost of the units purchased on that date). Having calculated this data, there's now sufficient information to consider the optimal inventory valuation method for Amber's Lacrosse Emporium.

10. Moving on, the company performs a physical count of inventory at the end of every month. Usually, the cost of the units counted equals the merchandise inventory balance, but at the end of October, this was not the case. The Merchandise Inventory account balance was $16,200 and the physical inventory count indicated $16,100 of goods in the warehouse.

Record the adjusting journal entry at the end of October for the discrepancy between the account balance and the physical inventory count.

10/31	Cost of Goods Sold	100	
	Merchandise Inventory		100
	Adjusting entry for merchandise inventory		

At the end of November, the company once again has a discrepancy between the Merchandise Inventory account balance and the results of the physical inventory count. This time, the account balance shows $15,300, while the physical inventory count indicates $15,600 of goods in the warehouse.

11. Record the adjusting journal entry at the end of November for this discrepancy.

11/30	Merchandise Inventory	300	
	Cost of Goods Sold		300
	Adjusting entry for merchandise inventory		

Over time, Amber wonders whether it would be beneficial to examine the cost of goods sold and the gross margin more closely. To that end, she gathers the following information for November and December:

	November	December
Cost of Goods Sold	$4,100	$4,500
Total Sales	$8,000	$8,600

12. Here we calculate the cost of goods sold and gross margin ratios for November and December.

November:

$$\text{Cost of Goods Sold Ratio} \quad \frac{\$4,100}{\$8,000} = 51.25\%$$

$$\text{Gross Margin Ratio} \quad \frac{\$8,000 - \$4,100}{\$8,000} = 48.75\%$$

December:

$$\text{Cost of Goods Sold Ratio} \quad \frac{\$4,500}{\$8,600} = 52.33\%$$

$$\text{Gross Margin Ratio} \quad \frac{\$8,600 - \$4,500}{\$8,600} = 47.67\%$$

13. How would you explain the ratio results to Amber?

The change in these ratios from November to December is not positive; the cost of goods sold ratio has increased, and the gross margin ratio has decreased. Continuing to monitor these ratios in the upcoming months to uncover whether a concerning pattern is emerging is an important step that should be taken.

Practice Set A

PSA 9-1 RECORD JOURNAL ENTRIES (PURCHASE TRANSACTIONS)

For each transaction, record the necessary journal entry assuming the company uses the perpetual inventory system.

Starting file: Use the Journal Entries template.

1. On July 3, the company purchases merchandise inventory on account for $3,000.
2. On July 8, the company pays $2,200 cash for merchandise inventory.
3. On July 15, the company remits full payment of $3,000 for the merchandise inventory purchased on 7/3.

PSA 9-2 RECORD JOURNAL ENTRIES (SALES TRANSACTIONS)

For each transaction, record the necessary journal entries assuming the company uses the perpetual inventory system.

Starting file: Use the Journal Entries template.

1. On November 2, the company sells merchandise inventory for $7,000 cash. The cost of the merchandise inventory was $2,700.
2. On November 8, the company sells $5,000 of merchandise inventory on account. The cost of the merchandise inventory was $2,300.
3. On November 11, the company receives $5,000 in full payment of the merchandise inventory sold on 11/8.

PSA 9-3 RECORD JOURNAL ENTRIES (PURCHASES AND SALES)

For each transaction, record the necessary journal entries assuming the company uses the perpetual inventory system.

Starting file: Use the Journal Entries template.

1. On February 1, the company pays $8,400 cash for merchandise inventory.
2. On February 2, the company sells $6,100 of merchandise inventory on account. The cost of the merchandise inventory was $3,000.
3. On February 6, the company purchases merchandise inventory on account for $7,800.
4. On February 7, the company sells merchandise inventory for $2,900 cash. The cost of the merchandise inventory was $1,300.
5. On February 19, the company receives $6,100 in full payment of the merchandise inventory sold on 2/2.
6. On February 24, the company remits full payment of $7,800 for the merchandise inventory purchased on 2/6.

PSA 9-4 DETERMINE THE COST OF GOODS SOLD AND THE MERCHANDISE INVENTORY BALANCE

Metalworks Inc. sells office furniture to corporate customers. The company uses the perpetual inventory system and keeps careful records. The August purchases and sales of merchandise inventory are summarized here (note that the sales price on 8/10 and 8/26 was $195 per unit).

Date	Purchases			Sales			Merchandise Inventory Balance		
	Quantity	Unit Cost	Total	Quantity	Unit Cost	Total	Quantity	Unit Cost	Total
8/1							45	$ 82	$ 3,690
8/4	60	$ 83	$ 4,980						
8/10				80					
8/20	110	$ 85	$ 9,350						
8/26				55					

Calculate the total cost of goods sold for the month (hint: 8/10 cost of goods sold + 8/26 cost of goods sold) and the Merchandise Inventory balance at the end of the month using three methods:

1. FIFO
2. LIFO
3. Average cost

PSA 9-5 RECORD ADJUSTING ENTRIES FOR MERCHANDISE INVENTORY

Record the necessary journal entry for the following independent circumstances. These companies use the perpetual inventory system.

Starting file: Use the Journal Entries template.

1. On December 31, the Merchandise Inventory account has a balance of $43,000. The physical inventory count indicates $44,100 of merchandise inventory in the warehouse.
2. On December 31, the Merchandise Inventory account has a balance of $163,000. The physical inventory count indicates $162,800 of merchandise inventory in the warehouse.

PSA 9-6 CALCULATE MERCHANDISE-RELATED PROFITABILITY RATIOS

Calculate the April and May cost of goods sold and gross margin ratios for Anthem Corp.

	April 2027	May 2027
Cost of Goods Sold	$163,600	$169,400
Total Sales	$352,000	$354,900

(Hint: For each month you are calculating two ratios.)

Practice Set B

PSB 9-1 RECORD JOURNAL ENTRIES (PURCHASE TRANSACTIONS)

For each transaction, record the necessary journal entry assuming the company uses the perpetual inventory system.

Starting file: Use the Journal Entries template.

1. On October 11, the company purchases merchandise inventory on account for $900.
2. On October 17, the company pays $1,400 cash for merchandise inventory.
3. On October 28, the company remits full payment of $900 for the merchandise inventory purchased on 10/11.

PSB 9-2 RECORD JOURNAL ENTRIES (SALES TRANSACTIONS)

For each transaction, record the necessary journal entries assuming the company uses the perpetual inventory system.

Starting file: Use the Journal Entries template.

1. On January 19, the company sells merchandise inventory for $1,600 cash. The cost of the merchandise inventory was $600.
2. On January 20, the company sells $3,300 of merchandise inventory on account. The cost of the merchandise inventory was $1,400.
3. On January 25, the company receives $3,300 in full payment of the merchandise inventory sold on 1/20.

PSB 9-3 RECORD JOURNAL ENTRIES (PURCHASES AND SALES)

For each transaction, record the necessary journal entries assuming the company uses the perpetual inventory system.

Starting file: Use the Journal Entries template.

1. On March 3, the company pays $5,000 cash for merchandise inventory.
2. On March 8, the company sells $4,400 of merchandise inventory on account. The cost of the merchandise inventory was $2,300.
3. On March 12, the company purchases merchandise inventory on account for $6,200.
4. On March 13, the company sells merchandise inventory for $9,100 cash. The cost of the merchandise inventory was $4,000.
5. On March 16, the company receives $4,400 in full payment of the merchandise inventory sold on 3/8.
6. On March 31, the company remits full payment of $6,200 for the merchandise inventory purchased on 3/12.

PSB 9-4 DETERMINE THE COST OF GOODS SOLD AND THE MERCHANDISE INVENTORY BALANCE

Lightning Corp. sells fishing equipment to corporate customers. The company uses the perpetual inventory system and keeps careful records. The June purchases and sales of merchandise inventory are summarized here (note that the sales price on 6/10 and 6/28 was $44 per unit).

Date	Purchases			Sales			Merchandise Inventory Balance		
	Quantity	Unit Cost	Total	Quantity	Unit Cost	Total	Quantity	Unit Cost	Total
6/1							90	$ 16	$ 1,440
6/9	70	$ 18	$ 1,260						
6/10				100					
6/12	85	$ 19	$ 1,615						
6/28				95					

Calculate the total cost of goods sold for the month (hint: 6/10 cost of goods sold + 6/28 cost of goods sold) and the Merchandise Inventory balance at the end of the month using three methods:

1. FIFO

2. LIFO

3. Average cost

PSB 9-5 RECORD ADJUSTING ENTRIES FOR MERCHANDISE INVENTORY

Record the necessary journal entry for the following independent circumstances. These companies use the perpetual inventory system.

Starting file: Use the Journal Entries template.

1. On December 31, the Merchandise Inventory account has a balance of $26,200. The physical inventory count indicates $25,900 of merchandise inventory in the warehouse.

2. On December 31, the Merchandise Inventory account has a balance of $492,000. The physical inventory count indicates $494,300 of merchandise inventory in the warehouse.

PSB 9-6 CALCULATE MERCHANDISE-RELATED PROFITABILITY RATIOS

Calculate the July and August cost of goods sold and gross margin ratios for Reverberate Company.

	July 2027	**August 2027**
Cost of Goods Sold	$70,200	$67,500
Total Sales	$147,900	$146,100

(Hint: For each month you are calculating two ratios.)

A The Intuit Certified Bookkeeping Professional Exam and This Text

The Intuit Certified Bookkeeping Professional certification can be an important credential for those in accounting and bookkeeping roles. To obtain certification, you must pass a comprehensive exam that focuses on bookkeeping topics. This appendix includes a table that shows you where each of the exam objectives is covered in this course.

Exam Objectives

You can use this table as you prepare for the Intuit Certified Bookkeeping Professional exam. For each exam objective (left column) you can see a reference to the most prominent sections in your learning solution text that deal with that objective (right column). Be sure to also check out the information presented by Certiport, the company that delivers the certification, at: **certiport .pearsonvue.com/Certifications/Intuit**

OBJECTIVE			SECTION TO REVIEW
1	**Accounting Basics**		
1.1	Define accounting and the concepts underlying accounting measurement		
	1.1.1	Explain the ethical responsibilities of bookkeepers	Accounting and Bookkeeping Defined (Ch. 1)
	1.1.2	Explain the accounting equation	The Accounting Equation (Ch. 1)
	1.1.3	Describe the purpose and content of balance sheets, statements of equity, income statements, and statements of cash flows	Income Statement, Statement of Owner's Equity, Balance Sheet, Statement of Cash Flows (Ch. 5)
1.2	Summarize the double-entry accounting method		
	1.2.1	Define double-entry accounting terms	Evaluating Transactions (Ch. 1)
	1.2.2	Explain how double-entry accounting works in accounting software	Computerized Accounting Systems (Ch. 6)
	1.2.3	Demonstrate an understanding of T-accounts	T-Accounts (Ch. 3)
	1.2.4	Read and interpret the transaction journal and general ledger in accounting software	Debits and Credits, General and Special Journals (Ch. 3); Computerized Accounting Systems (Ch. 6)
1.3	Describe the fundamental concepts of the accounting cycle		
	1.3.1	Demonstrate an understanding of the accounting cycle	Chapter 2 (entire)
	1.3.2	Summarize the adjusting process	Adjusting and Reversing Entries (Ch. 4)
	1.3.3	Describe the entries related to the adjusting process	Adjusting and Reversing Entries, Depreciation (Ch. 4)
	1.3.4	Explain the impact of posting adjusting journal entries on net income, the balance sheet, and equity	Adjusting and Reversing Entries (Ch. 4)
1.4	Summarize accounting principles		
	1.4.1	Explain the key assumptions of financial accounting, reporting, and measurement-triggering transaction events	Generally Accepted Accounting Principles, Step 3: Post Journal Entries (Ch. 2)
	1.4.2	Determine whether to record transactions as revenue or expense	Generally Accepted Accounting Principles (Ch. 2); Chapter 3 (entire)
	1.4.3	Compare and contrast accrual accounting and cash-basis accounting	Step 5: Adjusting Entries and Adjusted Trial Balance (Ch. 2)

OBJECTIVE	SECTION TO REVIEW
2 **Accounting for Assets and Sales Transactions**	
2.1 Summarize assets and sales transactions	
2.1.1 Define assets and identify natural account balance	The Accounting Equation (Ch. 1); T-Accounts (Ch. 3)
2.1.2 Differentiate between current and long-term assets	Case in Point 3-1 (Ch. 3); Balance Sheet (Ch. 5)
2.1.3 Identify the financial statements on which assets appear	Balance Sheet, Statement of Cash Flows (Ch. 5)
2.1.4 Explain accounting for sales, accounts receivable, and cash receipts	Chapter 3 (entire); General and Special Journals (Ch. 3)
2.1.5 Identify other notes receivable and uncollectible accounts	Case in Point 1-2 (Ch. 1); Recording the Depreciation Adjusting Entry (Ch. 4)
2.2 Describe the importance of merchandise inventory	
2.2.1 Identify and define merchandise inventory	The Merchandise Inventory Account (Ch. 9)
2.2.2 Apply inventory valuation methods	Determining the Value of Merchandise Inventory (Ch. 9)
2.2.3 Describe when and how to adjust inventory balance	Adjusting Merchandise Inventory (Ch. 9)
2.3 Define depreciation concepts and terminology	
2.3.1 Describe principles relating to service life and depreciation	Depreciation (Ch. 4)
2.3.2 Identify how depreciation expense is reported on income statements	Recording the Depreciation Adjusting Entry (Ch. 4)
2.4 Describe the effect of asset and sales transactions on the accounting equation	
2.4.1 Describe the effect of sales transactions on the accounting equation	Case in Point 1-3, Case in Point 1-4 (Ch. 1)
2.4.2 Describe the effect of merchandise inventory on the accounting equation	PIT 1-1 Record the Transactions (Ch. 1)
2.4.3 Describe the effect of common property and equipment entries on the accounting equation	Case in Point 1-3, Case in Point 1-4 (Ch. 1)
2.4.4 Describe the effect of other asset transactions on the accounting equation	Case in Point 1-3, Case in Point 1-4 (Ch. 1)

OBJECTIVE	SECTION TO REVIEW
3 Accounting for Liabilities, Equity, and Purchase Transactions	
3.1 Summarize liabilities and purchase transactions	
3.1.1 Define liabilities and identify natural account balance	The Accounting Equation (Ch. 1); T-Accounts (Ch. 3)
3.1.2 Differentiate between current and long-term liabilities	Balance Sheet (Ch. 5)
3.1.3 Identify the financial statements on which liabilities appear	Balance Sheet (Ch. 5)
3.1.4 Explain accounting for purchases, accounts payable, and cash payments	Chapter 3 (entire); General and Special Journals (Ch. 3)
3.1.5 Identify other liabilities	Balance Sheet (Ch. 5)
3.2 Describe basic payroll transactions	
3.2.1 Define basic payroll accounting terms	Payroll Calculations and Journal Entries (Ch. 6)
3.2.2 Explain accounting for payroll	Payroll Calculations and Journal Entries (Ch. 6)
3.2.3 Explain payroll tax forms	Payroll Tax Forms (Ch. 6)
3.3 Compare and contrast different types of equity	
3.3.1 Identify types of equity accounts	Account Names and Descriptions (Ch. 1)
3.3.2 Explain the connection between equity and income statements	Statement of Owner's Equity (Ch. 5)
3.4 Describe the effect of liability, equity, and purchase transactions on the accounting equation	
3.4.1 Describe the effect of purchase transactions on the accounting equation	Chapter 3 (entire); General and Special Journals (Ch. 3)
3.4.2 Describe the effect of payroll transactions on the accounting equation	Payroll Calculations and Journal Entries, Case in Point 6-5 (Ch. 6)
3.4.3 Describe the effect of equity transactions on the accounting equation	Chapter 3 (entire); General and Special Journals (Ch. 3)
3.4.4 Describe the effect of other liability transactions on the accounting equation	Chapter 3 (entire); General and Special Journals (Ch. 3)

OBJECTIVE		SECTION TO REVIEW
4	**Reconciliation and Financial Statements**	
4.1	Describe the purpose and process of account reconciliations	
	4.1.1 Define reconciliation concepts	Account Reconciliations (Ch. 6)
	4.1.2 Identify accounts that are typically reconciled	Account Reconciliations (Ch. 6)
	4.1.3 Identify reconciliation source documentation types	Account Reconciliations (Ch. 6)
4.2	Describe the process of bank reconciliations	
	4.2.1 Prepare for a bank reconciliation	Account Reconciliations (Ch. 6)
	4.2.2 Reconcile bank accounts	Account Reconciliations (Ch. 6)
	4.2.3 Explain bank reconciling items	Account Reconciliations (Ch. 6)
4.3	Describe basic financial statement analytical methods	
	4.3.1 Read and comprehend balance sheets	Completing a Horizontal Analysis, Completing a Vertical Analysis (Ch. 7)
	4.3.2 Read and comprehend comparative income statements	Completing a Horizontal Analysis, Completing a Vertical Analysis (Ch. 7)
	4.3.3 Read and comprehend budget vs. actual reports	Case in Point 7-1 (Ch. 7)
	4.3.4 Analyze cost of goods sold and comparative revenue	Analyzing Cost of Goods Sold and Gross Profit (Ch. 9)
	4.3.5 Compare month-over-month income statements to identify potential issues	Completing a Horizontal Analysis (Ch. 7)

Answer Keys

Ask Yourself Questions

Item	Answer	Feedback
1-1	True	The accounting cycle is completed at the end of each fiscal period and begins again at the start of the next fiscal period.
1-2	C	Assets are items of value, such as land, supplies, and equipment. Liabilities represent amounts owed to entities outside of the business, such as outstanding loans.
1-3	D	Owner's equity accounts include revenue, expense, capital, and drawing (withdrawal) accounts. All of these are owner's equity accounts.
1-4	False	The Financial Accounting Standards Board (FASB) establishes and maintains the Generally Accepted Accounting Principles (GAAP), not the other way around.
1-5	True	It's a primary reason recording transactions is so important. These running balances allow the company to review its financial position at any point.
2-1	A	A recurring entry is an entry that's recorded in the same manner every accounting period. While it's initially based on a single source document, it's not a source document itself.
2-2	D	The matching principle dictates that expenses be recorded in the same period as the revenue they generated, regardless of when the cash is paid to satisfy these expenses.
2-3	False	This is a description of the full disclosure principle. The monetary unit principle dictates that account balances can be used to express the performance of a company (shown in U.S. dollars).
2-4	B	A digit transposition occurs when two digits within a figure are erroneously reversed.
2-5	A	As the company is recording revenue when earned and not waiting to record revenue until the cash is received, it is using the accrual basis of accounting.
2-6	C	The balance sheet shows that the accounting equation is in balance at the end of a period, so it displays all asset, liability, and owner's equity balances.
2-7	False	This is a description of a permanent account, not a temporary account. The balance within a temporary account is removed through the recording of closing entries at the end of the period. These temporary accounts begin each period with a $0 balance.
3-1	B	Debits are entered at the top of a journal entry and are not indented. Credits are entered below debits and are indented.
3-2	False	The left side of a T-account is the debit side. The right side of a T-account is the credit side.
3-3	B	Transactions in which cash is paid, such as for the purchase of equipment, are recorded in the cash payments journal. The purchases journal is used for transactions in which purchases are made on account.
3-4	True	The general ledger contains control accounts while the subsidiary ledger contains subsidiary accounts.

Item	Answer	Feedback
4-1	C	The trial balance displays both total debits and total credits.
4-2a	D	Types of adjusting journal entries include deferred expense, deferred revenue, accrued expense, and accrued revenue.
4-2b	True	Reversing entries are recorded on the first day of the period following the recording of the associated adjusting entry.
4-3a	C	Short-term assets, also called *current assets*, are expected to be held for less than 12 months. Fixed assets, also called *plant assets* or *long-term assets,* are expected to be held for more than 12 months.
4-3b	False	A company records the same amount of depreciation each year when using the straight-line method. Under the double-declining balance method, more depreciation is recorded in the early years than in the later years.
4-3c	True	A contra-asset account works in an opposite manner from a standard asset account; it increases on the credit side and decreases on the debit side.
4-4	B	The unadjusted trial balance is completed first, as the adjusted trial balance must be completed after the adjusting entries have been recorded.
5-1	True	Net income occurs when revenue exceeds expenses, while a net loss occurs when expenses exceed revenue.
5-2	D	The final figure within the income statement, either Net Income or Net Loss, is added to (Net Income) or subtracted from (Net Loss) the beginning owner's capital account within the statement of owner's equity.
5-3	D	The balance sheet illustrates that the accounting equation (assets = liabilities + owner's equity) is in balance.
5-4	True	The statement of cash flows shows the activity that led to the change in the cash balance and, therefore, includes the beginning and ending cash balances.
5-5	4	The four closing entries close 1) revenue accounts, 2) expense accounts, 3) income summary, and 4) withdrawal accounts, respectively.
5-6	A	Temporary accounts, including revenue, expense, and withdrawal accounts, are closed prior to the completion of the post-closing trial balance and therefore do not appear on the post-closing trial balance.
6-1	True	Internal controls such as maintaining physical safeguards, segregation of duties, transaction authorization, and record retention all help ensure that cash is being safeguarded continually throughout a period.
6-2	False	Petty cash is an item of value and is therefore an asset account.
6-3a	False	The adjusted book balance must equal the adjusted bank balance within a bank reconciliation. The bank statement balance is the starting point for the bank side of the reconciliation.
6-3b	B	An outstanding check hasn't been cashed, so it's deducted from the bank side.
6-4	B	Journal entries must be recorded for the items of which the company was unaware during the period. Therefore, journal entries are required for items on the book side of the reconciliation.
6-5a	True	Gross pay represents total earnings. Net pay is calculated as gross pay minus withholding amounts.
6-5b	A	Social Security (and Medicare) taxes are employee and employer taxes, federal and state income taxes are employee taxes, and federal unemployment tax is an employer tax.
6-6	D	Benefits of using computerized accounting programs include efficiency, accuracy, backup capability, and cost.

Item	Answer	Feedback
7-1	A	A horizontal analysis conveys percent change from the base year, so the dollar change is divided by the base year amount.
7-2	True	Total assets and total liabilities and owner's equity are equal, which means they're interchangeable as the base figure in a vertical analysis on a balance sheet.
7-3	C	The quick ratio excludes certain current assets such as merchandise inventory and supplies from the numerator of the calculation.
7-4	D	Unlike the debt, equity, and debt-to-equity ratios, the dividend yield is not considered to be a solvency ratio.
7-5	A	Profit Margin = Net Income ÷ Revenue
9-1	True	Merchandise Inventory is expected to be used within 12 months, so it's considered a current asset account.
9-2	D	FIFO stands for *first in, first out*. LIFO stands for *last in, first out*.
9-3	False	Due to theft, breakage, recording error, or another reason, the physical count of merchandise inventory usually differs from what is indicated in the books. Adjusting entries account for this difference.
9-4	B	The gross margin ratio, like the cost of goods sold ratio, provides insight into a company's ability to effectively generate income. It is a profitability ratio.

Self-Assessment Quizzes

Chapter 1: Evaluating Transactions

Item	Answer	Section to Review
1	False	Accounting and Bookkeeping Defined
2	False	The Accounting Equation
3	True	Account Names and Descriptions
4	False	Account Names and Descriptions
5	False	Account Names and Descriptions
6	True	Evaluating Transactions
7	False	Evaluating Transactions
8	True	Case in Point 1-4, step #6
9	True	Case in Point 1-3
10	True	Recording Transactions
11	Assets = Liabilities + Owner's Equity	The Accounting Equation
12	D	Account Names and Descriptions
13	A	Evaluating Transactions
14	B	Case in Point 1-4, step #3
15	A	Accounting and Bookkeeping Defined
16	C	Accounting and Bookkeeping Defined
17	A	Account Names and Descriptions
18	D	Account Names and Descriptions
19	B	Account Names and Descriptions
20	A	Account Names and Descriptions

Chapter 2: The Accounting Cycle

Item	Answer	Section to Review
1	True	Step 1: Analyze Business Transactions
2	True	Step 1: Analyze Business Transactions
3	False	Generally Accepted Accounting Principles
4	False	Generally Accepted Accounting Principles
5	True	Step 7: Closing Entries and the Post-Closing Trial Balance
6	False	Step 4: Unadjusted Trial Balance
7	False	Step 4: Unadjusted Trial Balance
8	True	Step 5: Adjusting Entries and Adjusted Trial Balance
9	True	Step 6: Financial Statements
10	False	Step 6: Financial Statements
11	A	Step 1: Analyze Business Transactions
12	C	Step 1: Analyze Business Transactions
13	C	Generally Accepted Accounting Principles
14	D	Step 6: Financial Statements
15	D	Step 1: Analyze Business Transactions
16	C	Step 1: Analyze Business Transactions
17	B	Generally Accepted Accounting Principles
18	C	Step 4: Unadjusted Trial Balance
19	revenue; incurred	Step 5: Adjusting Entries and Adjusted Trial Balance
20	B	Step 6: Financial Statements

Chapter 3: Journal Entries and T-Accounts

Item	Answer	Section to Review
1	False	Debits and Credits
2	True	Debits and Credits
3	True	T-Accounts
4	True	T-Accounts
5	False	T-Accounts
6	False	General and Special Journals
7	False	General and Special Journals
8	True	General and Special Journals
9	False	General and Subsidiary Ledgers
10	True	General and Subsidiary Ledgers
11	revenue	Debits and Credits
12	D	T-Accounts
13	C	General and Special Journals
14	B	General and Subsidiary Ledgers
15	B	Case in Point 3-1, step #3
16	D	Case in Point 3-1, step #4
17	C	Debits and Credits
18	C	Debits and Credits
19	C	Debits and Credits
20	A	T-Accounts

Chapter 4: Adjusting Entries

Item	Answer	Section to Review
1	True	Trial Balances
2	False	Trial Balances
3	False	Adjusting and Reversing Entries
4	True	Deferred Expenses
5	False	Accrued Revenue
6	True	Depreciation
7	False	Depreciation
8	False	Depreciation
9	True	Straight-Line Depreciation
10	False	Double-Declining Balance Depreciation
11	A	Trial Balances
12	C	Adjusting and Reversing Entries
13	D	Trial Balances
14	C	Recording the Depreciation Adjusting Entry
15	C	Deferred Expenses
16	D	Accrued Revenue
17	A	Reversing Entries
18	A	Deferred Expenses
19	accrued expenses	Accrued Expenses
20	B	Reversing Entries

Chapter 5: Financial Statements and Closing Entries

Item	Answer	Section to Review
1	False	Income Statement
2	True	Income Statement
3	True	Statement of Owner's Equity
4	False	Statement of Owner's Equity
5	True	Balance Sheet
6	False	Balance Sheet
7	True	Statement of Cash Flows
8	True	Statement of Cash Flows
9	True	Closing Entries
10	False	Closing Entries
11	C	Income Statement
12	A	Statement of Owner's Equity
13	Assets = Liabilities + Owner's Equity	Balance Sheet
14	D	Statement of Cash Flows
15	B	Balance Sheet
16	D	Balance Sheet
17	B	Balance Sheet
18	A	Balance Sheet
19	B	Statement of Cash Flows
20	D	Closing Entries

Chapter 6: Computerized Systems, Cash, and Payroll

Item	Answer	Section to Review
1	False	Using Internal Controls
2	False	Using Internal Controls
3	False	Petty Cash
4	True	Petty Cash
5	False	Preparing a Bank Reconciliation
6	True	How to Evaluate a Reconciling Item
7	True	How to Evaluate a Reconciling Item
8	False	Reconciling Journal Entries
9	False	Employee Withholdings
10	False	Employer Payroll Taxes
11	B	Using Internal Controls
12	D	Petty Cash
13	A	How to Evaluate a Reconciling Item
14	D	Employer Payroll Taxes
15	C	Preparing a Bank Reconciliation
16	B	Preparing a Bank Reconciliation
17	A	Form W-4
18	D	Form 1099-NEC
19	C	Form W-9
20	B	Form W-2

Chapter 7: Financial Statement Analysis

Item	Answer	Section to Review
1	True	Completing a Horizontal Analysis
2	False	Completing a Horizontal Analysis
3	False	Completing a Vertical Analysis
4	True	Completing a Vertical Analysis
5	True	Common-Size Financial Statements
6	True	Liquidity Ratios
7	True	Quick Ratio
8	True	Solvency Ratios
9	True	Solvency Ratios
10	False	Profitability Ratios
11	A	Completing a Horizontal Analysis
12	C	Liquidity Ratios
13	D	Profitability Ratios
14	B	Solvency Ratios
15	D	Profitability Ratios
16	A	Current Ratio
17	Total Liabilities ÷ Total Assets	Solvency Ratios
18	Current Assets ÷ Current Liabilities	Current Ratio
19	Net Income ÷ Average Total Assets	Profitability Ratios
20	Market Price per Share ÷ Earnings per Share	Profitability Ratios (A Closer Look)

Chapter 9: Merchandise Inventory

Item	Answer	Section to Review
1	True	The Merchandise Inventory Account
2	False	The Merchandise Inventory Account
3	False	The Merchandise Inventory Account (A Closer Look)
4	True	FIFO Method (First In, First Out)
5	True	Average Cost Method
6	False	LIFO Method (Last In, First Out)
7	False	The Merchandise Inventory Account (A Closer Look)
8	False	The Merchandise Inventory Account (A Closer Look)
9	True	Analyzing Cost of Goods Sold and Gross Profit
10	True	Analyzing Cost of Goods Sold and Gross Profit
11	expense	The Merchandise Inventory Account
12	B	The Merchandise Inventory Account
13	2	The Merchandise Inventory Account
14	B	The Merchandise Inventory Account
15	D	Determining the Value of Merchandise Inventory
16	D	LIFO Method (Last In, First Out)
17	C	LIFO Method (Last In, First Out)
18	A	Average Cost Method
19	Sales – Cost of Goods Sold	Analyzing Cost of Goods Sold and Gross Profit
20	Cost of Goods Sold ÷ Total Sales	Analyzing Cost of Goods Sold and Gross Profit

Glossary

accounting equation A basic principle of accounting that states that a company's total assets must equal the sum of its liabilities and owner's equity (Assets = Liabilities + Owner's Equity)

accounting A system that provides a way individual business events, and the cumulative impact of those events, can be expressed

accounts payable subsidiary ledger Where the T-accounts for the Accounts Payable subsidiary account are maintained; there's a T-account for each company from which the business purchases goods or services on account

accounts receivable subsidiary ledger Where the T-accounts for the Accounts Receivable subsidiary accounts are maintained; there's a T-account for each company that purchases goods or services on account

accrual basis A method of accounting under which revenue is recorded when earned and expenses are recorded when incurred regardless of when cash changes hands

Additional Paid in Capital An account that represents the ownership interest in a corporation that exceeds the portion comprising Common Stock or Preferred Stock

adjusted trial balance The second of three trial balances a company completes during a period (after recording adjusting entries and prior to recording closing entries); step 5 in the accounting cycle

adjusting entry Records activity for which there was no previous trigger indicating that it should have already been recorded; part of the adjusting entry process

assets Items of value within a business; can be cash, accounts receivable, supplies and equipment, or land; part of the accounting equation (Assets = Liabilities + Owner's Equity)

average cost method An inventory valuation method that uses the average cost of all goods in the warehouse to determine the cost of goods sold and the Merchandise Inventory account balance; also called the *weighted average method*

balance column format A way to display the posting process in a table format with columns for the date, a transaction explanation, debit amount, credit amount, and the running balance; an alternative to using T-accounts

balance sheet One of the main financial statements used to evaluate a business; shows that the accounting equation is in balance by displaying asset, liability, and owner's equity balances

bank charges Any charges levied by the bank for a variety of services

bank reconciliation A process through which the differences between the cash balances within the bank statement and those in the general ledger are reviewed for accuracy

bank statement A source document that outlines a business's banking activity for a single month

basic earnings per share ("EPS") A profitability ratio used by corporations that shows the earnings per share of stock outstanding; calculated as (Net Income − Preferred Dividends) ÷ Weighted Average Common Shares Outstanding

benchmark An amount that can be compared against a company's current period results to gauge its performance; common benchmarks include prior performance, competitor's balances, and industry standards

book value The cost of an asset minus accumulated depreciation

bookkeeper An accounting professional who records a business's financial transactions, updates statements, and checks financial records for accuracy and completeness

cash basis A method of accounting in which revenue and expenses are only recorded when cash changes hands

cash payments journal A special journal that records entries in which cash is paid out

cash receipts journal A special journal that records entries in which cash is received

check A source document that provides information regarding payment that is received from a customer or made to a supplier

classified balance sheet A balance sheet that categorizes asset and liability accounts by type

collusion A type of theft in which multiple employees work together to conceal their actions

common-size financial statement A financial statement in which percentages are displayed, thus allowing for comparisons of the financial performance of different-sized companies; usually performed on the income statement and balance sheet

Common Stock An account that represents the ownership interest in a corporation

compound journal entry A journal entry that contains multiple debits and/or credits

confidentiality The act of keeping or being kept private; confidentiality in bookkeepers is key, as they have access to sensitive and private information about a business

contra-asset account A type of account that offsets the balance of its associated asset account; Accumulated Depreciation is an example of a contra-asset account

control account A general ledger account that summarizes the balances in its subsidiary accounts

corporation A business that issues shares of stock to its owners; can be public or private

Cost of Goods Sold An expense account that represents the cost of the merchandise inventory sold during the period; also known as *Cost of Merchandise Sold*

cost of goods sold ratio A profitability ratio that indicates the portion of total sales that remain after the cost of goods sold has been considered; calculated as Cost of Goods Sold ÷ Total Sales

cost principle A generally accepted accounting principle; dictates that every asset must be recorded at the amount paid for the item

credit The right side of a T-account and the bottom (indented) account(s) in a journal entry

current liabilities Those liabilities the company expects to pay off within 12 months; a short-term debt such as a line of credit is a current liability

current ratio A type of liquidity ratio; calculated as Current Assets ÷ Current Liabilities

debit The left side of a T-account and the top (not indented) account(s) in a journal entry

debt ratio A solvency ratio that expresses the portion of assets generated through liabilities; calculated as Total Liabilities ÷ Total Assets

debt-to-equity ratio A solvency ratio that expresses the balance between liabilities and equity; calculated as Total Liabilities ÷ Total Equity

deposit in transit A deposit made on one of the last days of a period and that the bank does not process prior to the end of the month

dividend yield A profitability ratio that shows dividends received compared to market price; calculated as Cash Dividends per Share ÷ Market Price per Share

double-entry bookkeeping A method of accounting in which every transaction is recorded using at least two accounts; must include at least a debit to one account and a credit to one account

equity ratio A solvency ratio that expresses the portion of assets generated through equity; calculated as Total Equity ÷ Total Assets

external audit A process through which an outside organization reviews a random sampling of transactions for accuracy

external users Individuals outside of a company who use financial statements to evaluate the performance of the company

federal income tax A tax withheld from employee pay to fund the general operations of the federal government; increases as total gross pay increases

federal unemployment tax A tax an employer pays to the federal government to provide unemployment benefits to qualified individuals

FIFO method An inventory valuation method that assumes the earliest units purchased are the first ones sold; first in, first out

Financial Accounting Standards Board (FASB) The organization that establishes accounting standards (including GAAP) in the United States

fixed asset An asset expected to be held for at least 12 months; examples of fixed assets include machinery, equipment, land, and buildings; also called a *plant asset*

Form W-2 The Wage and Tax Statement form; annual tax form showing earnings and withholding information for the year

Form W-4 The Employee's Withholding Certificate form; provides information for calculating federal and state withholding

Form W-9 The Request for Taxpayer Identification Number and Certification form; completed by an independent contractor and submitted to the employer

Form 1099-NEC The Nonemployee Compensation form; annual tax form showing the yearly earnings for an independent contractor

full disclosure principle A generally accepted accounting principle; dictates that a public company must disclose all pertinent information regarding its activities

general journal A journal that records entries that are not recorded in the special journals for cash receipts, cash payments, revenue, or purchases

general ledger The location where T-account balances, including those for the Accounts Receivable and Accounts Payable control accounts, are maintained

Generally Accepted Accounting Principles (GAAP) Principles that dictate the manner in which businesses in the United States account for their activity

gross margin The difference between total sales and the cost of goods sold; also referred to as *gross profit*

gross margin ratio A profitability ratio that indicates the portion of total sales available to cover expenses other than the cost of goods sold; calculated as Gross Margin ÷ Total Sales; also referred to as the *gross profit ratio*

gross pay The total amount earned by an employee before taxes and other deductions are withheld; see also *net pay*

horizontal analysis Comparison of account balances across time to determine dollar and percentage differences; commonly performed on the income statement and balance sheet

income statement One of the main financial statements used to evaluate a business; displays the balances for all revenue and expenses accounts, as well as the net income

integrity The quality of having high moral principles; it is a key responsibility of bookkeepers, as they must act in accordance with both applicable professional standards and all applicable laws

internal audit A process through which company employees review a random sampling of transactions for accuracy

internal control procedures The procedures a company can undertake to ensure that cash is properly safeguarded; includes procedures for maintaining physical safeguards, segregating duties, transaction authorization, and record retention

internal users Company employees who use financial statements to improve the performance of the company

invoice A bill for goods or services that summarizes amounts owed from one party to another; a type of source document

journal entry A method for recording transactions that lists the accounts impacted and by how much

LIFO method An inventory valuation method that assumes the most recent units purchased are the first ones sold; last in, first out

liabilities Anything owed by the business, such as loans or accounts payable; part of the accounting equation (Assets = Liabilities + Owner's Equity)

liquidity ratios Types of ratios that indicate how quickly a company can convert assets to cash; common liquidity ratios include the current ratio and quick ratio

long-term liabilities Those liabilities the company expects to hold longer than 12 months; a mortgage is an example of a long-term liability

matching principle A generally accepted accounting principle; dictates that expenses must be recorded in the same period as the revenue they generate

Medicare tax A tax withheld from employee pay to fund the Hospital Insurance program; since 1986, it's been calculated as 1.45% of gross pay

Merchandise Inventory An asset account that represents the cost of goods a business intends to sell

monetary unit principle A generally accepted accounting principle; dictates that account balances can be used to express the performance of a company

net income Revenue minus expenses

net pay The amount received by an employee after taxes and other deductions are withheld; see also *gross pay*

normal balance The side of a T-account on which an account increases; for asset, withdrawal, and expense accounts, the debit (left) side is the normal balance side; for liability, capital, and revenue accounts, the credit (right) side is the normal balance side

note receivable An amount owed to a company that must not only be repaid, but for which interest is also owed

NSF check A nonsufficient funds check; a deposited check that subsequently bounces

outstanding check A check that has been written but not yet cashed

owner's equity The portion of the assets not owed to an entity outside of the business, and therefore to which the owner can lay claim; part of the accounting equation (Assets = Liabilities + Owner's Equity)

partnership A business owned by two or more individuals

periodic inventory system An approach to recording inventory transactions in which the Cost of Goods Sold and Merchandise Inventory accounts are only updated once, at year end; contrasts with the perpetual inventory system

permanent accounts The accounts that remain open at the end of a period; in these accounts, the ending balance from one period becomes the beginning balance for the next period

perpetual inventory system An approach to recording inventory transactions as they happen such that balances in the Cost of Goods Sold and Merchandise Inventory accounts are always current and up to date; contrasts with the periodic inventory system

petty cash A small amount of cash on hand for the business; easily accessible and used for incidental purchases

post-closing trial balance The third and final trial balance a company completes during a period (after recording closing entries); step 7 in the accounting cycle

posting The process of transferring amounts within journal entries to the corresponding T-accounts

Preferred Stock Account that represents a class of ownership interest in a corporation; includes benefits beyond those of common shareholders

price-earnings (P/E) ratio A profitability ratio that compares stock market price to the earnings per share; calculated as Market Price per Share ÷ Earnings per Share

profit margin A profitability ratio that determines the percentage of revenue that is converted to net income; calculated as Net Income ÷ Revenue

profitability ratios Types of ratios that analyze a company's ability to effectively generate income; include the profit margin and return on assets ratios

purchase order A source document prepared by the purchasing company and sent to the seller to indicate a desire to purchase items

purchases journal A special journal that records entries in which purchases are made on account

quick ratio A type of liquidity ratio; calculated as (Cash + Short-Term Investments + A/R) ÷ Current Liabilities; also called the *acid test ratio*

ratio analysis The examination of the relationships between account balances

reconciliation An examination of two sets of records to confirm agreement and, where there is difference, to determine which set of records is in error

recurring entry A journal entry that is recorded in the same manner for every accounting period

Retained Earnings The portion of corporate earnings not distributed to owners and therefore retained for future investment

return on assets A profitability ratio that determines a company's ability to use assets for net income generation; calculated as Net Income ÷ Average Total Assets

revenue journal A special journal that records entries in which revenue is earned on account

revenue principle A generally accepted accounting principle; dictates that revenue must be recorded in the same period it's earned

reversing entry An optional journal entry that can be used to simplify the recording process for certain items related to adjusting entries

sales order Primarily used as an internal document that verifies the seller's intent to accept the terms of the purchase order

salvage value The amount a company expects to receive for an asset at the time of disposal; also referred to as *residual value*

security For bookkeepers, this refers to keeping corporate information protected from those who should not have access to it

short-term asset An asset expected to be held for fewer than 12 months; also called a *current asset*; examples include cash, inventory, and prepaid insurance or rent

Social Security tax A tax withheld from employee pay to fund the Old Age, Survivors, and Disability Insurance program; also called *FICA (Federal Insurance Contributions Act) tax*

sole proprietorship A business owned by one individual

solvency ratios Types of ratios that gauge a company's ability to meet long-term obligations; include the debt ratio, equity ratio, and debt-to-equity ratio

source document Any document that provides information regarding one or more transactions

special journal A journal designed to record one specific type of business activity; examples of special journals include those for cash receipts, cash payments, revenue, and purchases

state income tax A tax withheld from employee pay to fund the general operations of the state government; the state's tax rate table determines the amount withheld

state unemployment tax A tax an employer pays to the state government to provide unemployment benefits to qualified individuals; rates vary by state

statement of cash flows One of the main financial statements used to evaluate a business; financial statement that displays a summary of all activities that led to the ending cash balance

statement of owner's equity One of the main financial statements used to evaluate a business; reconciles beginning owner's equity with ending owner's equity by displaying net income/loss, owner investments, and owner withdrawals

T-account A visual representation of the activity in a single account; also called a *T-chart*

temporary accounts The accounts that are closed at the end of a period (revenue, expense, and withdrawal accounts)

time-period principle A generally accepted accounting principle; dictates that accounting activity may be expressed over specific periods of time

transaction A single business event

Treasury Stock The portion of common stock that the company has repurchased and is therefore not presently in the hands of investors

trial balance Lists all accounts and displays their respective debit or credit balances as of a specific date; three trial balances are completed as part of the accounting cycle for a period

unadjusted trial balance The first of three trial balances a company completes during a period (prior to recording adjusting entries); step 4 of the accounting cycle

useful life The number of years a company expects to use an asset

vertical analysis Comparison of different account balances within the same period; commonly performed on the income statement and balance sheet; often used in conjunction with a horizontal analysis

voluntary deductions Any amount an employee elects to have withheld from pay; can be used for a variety of reasons such as retirement contributions, insurance premiums, and union dues

Index

Made in the USA
Las Vegas, NV
30 April 2025

21525714R00136

Bourdillon's Spinal Manipulation

Bourdillon's Spinal Manipulation

SIXTH EDITION

EDWARD R. ISAACS, MD, FAAN

Associate Professor of Neurology, Virginia Commonwealth University School of Medicine, Richmond; Clinical Associate Professor of Neurology and Osteopathic Manipulative Medicine, Michigan State University College of Osteopathic Medicine, East Lansing

MARK R. BOOKHOUT, MS, PT

Clinical Associate Professor of Physical Medicine and Rehabilitation and Osteopathic Manipulative Medicine, Michigan State University College of Osteopathic Medicine, East Lansing; President, Physical Therapy Orthopaedic Specialists, Inc., Minneapolis

BUTTERWORTH
HEINEMANN

Boston • Oxford • Auckland • Johannesburg • Melbourne • New Dehli

Copyright © 2002 by Butterworth–Heinemann

 A member of the Reed Elsevier group

All rights reserved.

No part of this publication may be reproduced, stored in a retrieval system, or transmitted in any form or by any means, electronic, mechanical, photocopying, recording, or otherwise, without the prior written permission of the publisher.

Every effort has been made to ensure that the drug dosage schedules within this text are accurate and conform to standards accepted at time of publication. However, as treatment recommendations vary in the light of continuing research and clinical experience, the reader is advised to verify drug dosage schedules herein with information found on product information sheets. This is especially true in cases of new or infrequently used drugs.

Recognizing the importance of preserving what has been written, Butterworth–Heinemann prints its books on acid-free paper whenever possible.

Library of Congress Cataloging-in-Publication Data
Isaacs, Edward R., 1943-
    Bourdillon's spinal manipulation / Edward R. Isaacs, Mark R. Bookhout.—6th ed.
        p. ; cm.
    Rev. ed. of: Spinal manipulation / J.F. Bourdillon, E.A. Day, M.R. Bookhout. 5th ed. 1992.
    Includes bibliographical references and index.
    ISBN 0-7506-7239-0
    1. Spinal adjustment. I. Title: Spinal manipulation. II. Bookhout, M.R. III. Bourdillon,
J.F. Spinal manipulation. IV. Title
    [DNLM: 1. Back Pain—therapy. 2. Manipulation, Spinal—methods. 3. Osteopathic
Medicine—methods. WB 940 I73b 2001]
    RZ399.S7 B6 2001
    615.5'03—dc21
                                                                    00-067476

British Library Cataloguing-in-Publication Data
A catalogue record for this book is available from the British Library.

The publisher offers special discounts on bulk orders of this book.
For information, please contact:
Manager of Special Sales
Butterworth–Heinemann
225 Wildwood Avenue
Woburn, MA 01801-2041
Tel: 781-904-2500
Fax: 781-904-2620

For information on all Butterworth–Heinemann publications available, contact our World Wide Web home page at: http://www.bh.com

10 9 8 7 6 5 4 3 2 1

Printed in the United States of America

In memory of John F. Bourdillon, FRCS, FRCSC

Contents

Preface to the Sixth Edition

Dr. John F. Bourdillon was my friend. He and Dr. Philip Greenman instructed the first tutorial in manual medicine that I attended in November 1984. My classmates included five other neurologists and a mix of other physicians and physical therapists from across the country who were interested in new or different approaches in the diagnosis and management of patients with musculoskeletal disorders. I was fortunate in being able to quickly incorporate these techniques into my medical neurology practice and to have the opportunity to continue taking additional tutorials offered by the Department of Continuing Medical Education of the College of Osteopathic Medicine at Michigan State University in East Lansing, Michigan. By 1988, I had completed most of the available courses, at least once, and was accepted as one of the instructors for the course in basic principles and for the course in muscle energy techniques. Dr. Bourdillon also taught at these courses, which were 5 days long and offered at least four times per year. It was during these years, from 1988 until his death in 1992, that our friendship grew. We became colleagues, teaching together, teaching each other, disagreeing and agreeing, and always learning more about musculoskeletal medicine. He was always kind, approachable, polite, and unassuming, despite his wealth of knowledge as an orthopedic surgeon and a renowned expert in the field of manual medicine. John was immediately loved and respected by his students, a feeling shared by all of us who knew him. He practiced manual medicine in Vancouver, British Columbia, and continued to practice during his last year when he moved back to Great Britain with his wife after his health began to fail. He believed that the best teachers were those who continued to be in active clinical practices and that he would continue to teach and practice as long as he was "meant to." I watched him write and read over many portions of the fifth edition of this book. He was always ready to improve the text with new ideas and upgraded techniques. It was especially like him to ask Mark Bookhout, PT, to write two new chapters on exercise. When these concepts were appropriately applied to patients with specific dysfunctions or recurrent problems, long-lasting successful outcomes became easier to obtain. The wisdom of these applications proved to be a key element in helping Dr. Philip Greenman to overcome his chronic back problems, allowing him to delay his retirement from active clinical practice and to continue teaching while directing the continuing medical education program of the Michigan State University College of Osteopathic Medicine.

It has been an honor to have had the opportunity to revise and edit the sixth edition of *Spinal Manipulation* and work with my colleague, Mark Bookhout, as co-author. We hope that this new edition is presented in the spirit and with the wisdom so freely shared by John Bourdillon.

This sixth edition has been updated with newer concepts and ideas about the musculoskeletal system and manual medicine that have evolved since publication of the fifth edition. Many of our techniques have been clarified and are shared along with many useful clinical observations that are the result of active outpatient practices.

E.R.I.

Preface to the First Edition

So many people have helped me in my efforts to produce this book that it would be impossible to mention them all.

I must gratefully acknowledge the permission given by the *British Medical Journal* for the extracts from a 1910 Editorial; from H.K. Lewis & Company Limited to quote from Timbrell Fisher's *Treatment by Manipulation*; from the J.B. Lippincott Company for permission to quote from an article by Dr. Horace Gray in the *International Clinics*, and from the Editors of *Brain* and the *Anatomical Record* for permission to reproduce the dermatone charts in the papers by Sir Henry Head and by Drs. Keegan and Garrett respectively.

It is invidious to thank individuals but I must express my gratitude for the cheerful and untiring help which I have received from the British Columbia Medical Library Service and from the Staff of the Records Department of the Gloucestershire Royal Hospital.

I cannot leave out my secretary who has typed, typed, and retyped every word that is here written, nor indeed, my wife who has in turn typed, criticized, encouraged and proofread. Finally it would be very discourteous not to mention both my long suffering model and her husband who took the photographs.

I have endeavored to shed light on the mystery that surrounds manipulation, to explain how to do it in terms that I hope will be easy enough to understand, to produce a working hypothesis as a basis for argument and a guide for research, and to show some of the reasons why I believe that it is essential that Medicine should incorporate this teaching into its structure.

J.F.B.
Vancouver, British Columbia
1970

Acknowledgments

I am deeply grateful to my loving wife, Sandy, for her patience, understanding, and tolerance while I spent most of my spare time preparing this manuscript. Her support for this work was especially meaningful because she had the opportunity to know and love John Bourdillon as much as the authors did. I would also like to thank my daughter, Jessica, my daughter-in-law, Christine, my son-in-law, Darren, and my son, Jonathan, for allowing me to use them as models for the many photographs that were taken by my son Robert. This indeed was a family endeavor.

E.R.I.

To my wife, Marla, and my children, Yaicha and Mariah, whom I hope understand that as much as I love my work, they will always take precedence in my heart.

I would also like to acknowledge several people without whose help I would not have been in a position to write this book. First and foremost, I am truly indebted to Dr. John Bourdillon, who originally asked me to contribute to the fifth edition of this book in 1991. It was so untimely that his death came just 2 short weeks after the fifth edition was published. Second, I am indebted to the teaching faculty at the College of Osteopathic Medicine at Michigan State University, who have accepted me as a peer in their teaching faculty and have supported me as a colleague, teacher, and clinician. I am especially thankful for my friendship with my mentor, Philip Greenman, DO, who, along with Fred Mitchell, Jr., DO, Paul Kimberly, DO, Ed Stiles, DO, Robert Ward, DO, Barbara Briner, DO, and Allen Jacobs, DO, taught me all I could comprehend.

My list of acknowledgments would be incomplete if I did not give my utmost thanks to Carl Steele, DO, PT, who, as the first physical therapist to attend the continuing medical education courses offered through the College of Osteopathic Medicine at Michigan State, blazed the way for future therapists. I have Carl to personally thank for his patience in teaching me many of the techniques presented in this book. I hope this book accurately reflects the teaching of my colleagues.

M.R.B.

1

Introduction

In this chapter, to save words and make meanings clear, the initials *MD* are used when referring to the orthodox medical profession and its practitioners in general, in spite of the fact that, in the United Kingdom, MD is a higher degree.

The art of manipulation of the spine is a very old one. It has been practiced over the centuries and was known to Hippocrates and the physicians of ancient Rome. Bonesetters have existed for as long as there are records, and in many countries, including England, they still exist. In the library of the Royal College of Surgeons in London is a book dated 1656, which is a revision done by Robert Turner of a work by an Augustinian monk, Friar Moulton, entitled *The Compleat Bone Setter*.

In 1745, the surgeons separated from the old City of London Company of Barbers and Surgeons and formed a new company that in the early nineteenth century became the Royal College of Surgeons of England. Before this time it is probable that the bonesetters were regarded as the orthopedic surgeons of their day, but for reasons that are unknown they became less and less respected as the art of medicine and surgery gradually became more scientific.

The art of bone setting appears often to have been passed from father to son, and there is some evidence to suggest that a hereditary trait is of some value. Certainly it is accepted that, even now, some learn the art of manipulation much more easily than others. This art has not at any time been supported by "adequate" scientific investigation, but the experience of patients previously handled by bonesetters shows that these practitioners were sometimes surprisingly skillful. Despite their almost total lack of knowledge of structural anatomy, physiology, or pathology, bonesetters

must have possessed an intuitive knowledge about dysfunctions within the musculoskeletal system.

At a time when bonesetters were well known in England, there is evidence of rejection of their work. The celebrated John Hunter was quoted by Timbrell Fisher[1] as having said

> Nothing can promote contracture of a joint so much as motion before the disease is removed. . . . When all inflammation has gone off and healing has begun, a little motion frequently repeated is necessary to prevent healing taking place with the parts fixed in one position.

This concept, unfortunately, was interpreted by Hunter's successors in such a way that they felt justified in allowing adhesions to form in a joint and relying on their ability afterward to mobilize them. Immobilization is still accepted as being of the greatest value in infective arthritis. The concept was extended to joints stiffened by injury, and it is now well known that in such patients early movement of the injured joint is a much more reliable method of restoring function.

It must be remembered that, at the time, there were no x-rays, tuberculosis was common in England, and diagnosis presented serious difficulties. The standard of orthodox treatment for joint disease was far from satisfactory, and many patients ultimately required joint excision or amputation. At the same time, the fear of litigation against bonesetters was almost nonexistent, and there can be no doubt that some patients were injured by forcible manipulation of infected joints.

The famous British surgeon Sir James Paget[2] was one of the few physicians of his day who appreciated the value of manipulative therapy, and in a lecture published in the *British Medical Journal*, he gave the following advice:

> Learn then, to imitate what is good and avoid what is bad in the practice of bone setters. . . . Too long rest is, I believe, by far the most frequent cause of delayed recovery of injured joints, and not only to injured joints, but to those that are kept at rest because parts near them have been injured.

The medical profession of the time paid little heed to Paget's advice. Hugh Owen Thomas taught that an overdose of rest was impossible—an idea that appears to have taken hold at a time when Thomas had a bitter quarrel with his father, who, like his father, was a bonesetter. He is quoted by Timbrell Fisher[1] as having written a letter in reply to Paget's lecture, in which he said

> For many years after the commencement of my experience in surgery I had the opportunity of observing the practice of those who had acquired a good reputation for skill as successful manipulators. . . . I cannot find suitable cases on which I would perform the deception known as passive motion.

Later, however, his own sufferings led Thomas to visit one of the most celebrated bonesetters of the nineteenth century. The following passage in another letter, quoted by Timbrell Fisher,[1] reflects the change of heart produced by Thomas's personal experience:

> In my own case, after submitting to Mr. Hutton's manipulation, I was instantly relieved of that pain, tension and coldness in the joint that I had suffered for six years and was able to walk. . . . Professional men accounted for the manifest change in my condition on one hypothesis or another, whilst all affected to smile at my ignorance and delusion. . . . I had been lame and in pain and could now walk and was at ease . . . and had the whole College of Surgeons clearly demonstrated to their entire satisfaction that I could not possibly have been benefited by Mr. Hutton's treatment, my opinion would not have been in the smallest degree shaken by it.

Since as long ago as 1871, there have been those within the medical profession who have tried to understand and use the skills of bonesetters like Hutton. Peter Hood attended Hutton through a long illness without charge because Hutton himself was in the habit of treating the poor without charge. In a gesture of gratitude, Hutton offered to demonstrate his skills as a bonesetter to Peter Hood, who declined the offer; however, his son, Wharton Hood, accepted the offer instead.

Wharton Hood[3] witnessed and published a description of the treatment and relief of two patients by Hutton, and he described what he learned from Hutton. Wharton Hood reported that Hutton described himself as having a plain education and being "entirely destitute of anatomical knowledge." Hutton was fully convinced that he was putting something back in place, and the sound of the bone setting, followed by relief, made his patients feel that he was correct. Wharton Hood suggested that rupture of adhesions was more likely to be the true effect of Hutton's treatment. He described, in some detail and with illustrations, the type of manipulation Hutton used on limb joints. Hood answered a letter from one Mr. Prall describing a fatal complication from treatment by a bonesetter, yet urged his colleagues in the medical profession to incorporate the study and use of these skills for the benefit of their patients. Hood concluded reasonably "that professional discrimination must be exercised in the selection of cases."[3]

The advent of routine radiography, research into the anatomy of the intervertebral joint and of the disc, and operative findings have not demonstrated that there is literally a bone out of place. The orthodox medical profession has, therefore, found itself unable to understand the manipulator's claims.

It is easy to forget that, only a few generations ago, the art of medicine, including the large majority of medical and surgical treatments, was based on the results of practical experience rather than on controlled, analytical, scientific observation. However, under the right conditions such anecdotal observations, when sound, can eventually be proven correct. In an editorial, M. Menken[4] calls for papers describing the anecdotal experiences of qualified neurologists:

> For most physicians, the goal of improved performance in practice, as measured by the clinical outcomes of patients, is the principal objective of all self-directed learning. . . . We seem to have forgotten that what counts in medical care cannot always be counted, nor does everything that we count, count. . . . As an educational tool, the anecdotal method assumes that the practising physician who is roughly right is preferable to one who is precisely wrong.

Many medical and surgical remedies, such as carotid endarterectomy as a means to prevent stroke, have been used for many years based on the clinical wisdom of physicians who believed that such an intervention was necessary and without being subjected to scientific scrutiny. In 1991, carotid endarterectomy was finally subjected to a randomized prospective study,[5] which confirmed the clinical wisdom of those physicians. Because medicine is in many ways still an art, there are many patients for whom the truly scientific approach has nothing constructive to offer but who respond to unproved treatments, even if their response and resolve that they have been helped are not completely understood. The inability to prove that someone has been in some way helped should not in any way imply that the patient's complaints were unfounded and not real or that the results were simply a "placebo response." It is interesting to look back to one's early days as a physician and realize how, with experience and increasing knowledge, many of the patients who were branded as neurotics or worse had genuine treatable organic conditions that one failed to recognize.

For many years, the attitude of the medical profession toward manipulation was skeptical, and spinal manipulation often was dismissed from consideration as a bona fide method of treatment. The reasons are not difficult to understand, given that the spinal joint is situated deep beneath powerful muscles, and it does not seem possible to detect joint dysfunctions by palpation alone. The observation and confirmation of these physical findings remain limited to those with abilities to manipulate the spine. It is a skill that comes with training and perseverance, but, as with any other skill demanding manual dexterity, some people find it more difficult than others. Since the symptoms of a spinal joint dysfunction can be surprisingly diverse[6] and often manifest at some distance from the spine, some spinal manipulators have claimed to be able to cure all types of diseases. Such ideas, which are obviously unacceptable to the medical profession, have instigated publications to refute such claims and, thereby, generalize that there are no benefits from manipulation.[7] As a consequence, the alienation generated by over-promoting the value of manipulation has adversely affected a reasonable consideration of its benefits, even when appropriately applied.

Since the end of the nineteenth century, two major schools of manipulative therapy have developed, and their practitioners are spread through many parts of the world. In spite of this development, there are still large numbers of practicing "natural" manipulators—successors to the old bonesetters—and some of them may still be found without basic scientific training.

From time to time, the voices of highly respected and competent doctors of medicine have been raised in favor of manipulative treatment, but after World War II, the number of such medical manipulators was small, and they generally were spurned by their colleagues. As a medical student at Oxford University, John F. Bourdillon was encouraged to attend a special meeting of the Osler

Society addressed by a famous physician of the time, who, it seems apparent in retrospect, attempted to prejudice listeners against manipulators and their art. Later, when training at St. Thomas's Hospital in London, where manipulative treatment was practiced by James Mennell in the physiotherapy department, and intending to enter the field of orthopedic surgery, Bourdillon was strongly advised by the orthopedic surgeons to avoid any contact with Mennell's department. Even within his own hospital, he (and later his successor, James Cyriax) was considered almost an outcast. After more than forty years of manipulative practice since World War II, Bourdillon still found that the attitudes of large sections of the medical profession still showed prejudice. This attitude has changed. There is increasing interest from those who specialize in physical medicine and rehabilitation and in sports medicine in the United States. Continued interest and contributions from Europe, Australia, and New Zealand add to an expanding appreciation of manipulative medicine, along with an increasing assimilation of doctors of osteopathy into allopathic medical practices and a trend to seek the assistance of these physicians to provide manipulative treatments to appropriate patients.

OSTEOPATHY

The two modern manipulative disciplines—osteopathy and chiropractic—are probably derived in part from the bonesetters, in spite of some claims that they were started *ab initio* by their respective founders. The first of these, osteopathy, was started by Andrew Taylor Still (1828–1917). Although there has been some doubt about his training, he was registered as a medical practitioner in Missouri. Northup[8] says that Still entered the Kansas City College of Physicians and Surgeons but, with the advent of the Civil War, dropped out to enlist. The rest of his training appears to have been at his physician father's side by preceptorship, a method common in the United States at that time. Hildreth[9] reproduces copies of two certificates: one of registration as a physician in Adair County in 1883 and the other dated 1893, stating that Still was on the roll of physicians and surgeons in Macon County as early as 1874.

Gevitz[10] agrees that Still's training was largely at his father's side and from books on anatomy, physiology, and materia medica and goes on to say that much of the medical treatment of the time was brutal and often ineffective, which made Still very dissatisfied. This dissatisfaction was increased when the best efforts of a fellow practitioner failed to save three of Still's family members, who were dying of cerebrospinal meningitis.

It is interesting to note that there was a well-known family of bonesetters in that part of the United States at the time, and it is recorded that Still's ideas began to crystallize after he saw a woman with shoulder problems and mobilized her spine and rib joints. She came back, relieved of her symptoms, and later returned to tell him that the "asthma" from which she had long suffered was also gone. Downing[11] recorded that Still's interest in manual therapy started from a personal experience. Still is said to have obtained relief from a severe headache by lying on the ground with his head supported by a rope hung from a tree. The rope was under his upper neck, evidently close to the point where direct pressure on muscle is described in Chapter 6 as a means of relaxing the tense neck muscles as a partial treatment for headache.

Unfortunately, Still appears to have antagonized the medical profession of his day, which did little to further the acceptance of manipulative treatment. He was nonetheless able to attract a large number of patients from considerable distances, encouraging the development of many small hotels and lodgings and the crossing of north-south and east-west railroad lines in Kirksville, Missouri. It was in this environment that Still created the American School of Osteopathy in 1892. The school is now the Kirksville College of Osteopathic Medicine, and, in addition to learning the basic skills and uses of manipulative techniques, its students, like those in other American colleges of osteopathy, receive a full "orthodox" medical education.

In the United States, doctors of osteopathy (DOs) trained in American schools are equally licensed with MDs and often practice in the same hospitals and share medical practices with MDs. Indeed, DOs are to be found in all branches of medicine, but many do not continue to use or develop their manipulative skills. The consequence of this assimilation into allopathic medicine is a progressive erosion of osteopathic principles.[12] In other countries, the term *osteopath* is used by a variety of practitioners, of whom many (e.g., graduates of the British School of Osteopathy) are not fully trained physicians. They are trained in anatomy and manual techniques.

CHIROPRACTIC

The second manipulative discipline is the Chiropractic School, which was started in 1895 in Davenport, Iowa, by D. D. Palmer, a "self-educated erstwhile grocer."[13]

The origin of chiropractic study is said to date from an incident in which Palmer manipulated the thoracic vertebrae of a porter, curing him of the deafness from which he had suffered for some years.

The fact that Palmer claims to have manipulated a specific vertebra indicates at least a modicum of knowledge and experience of manipulative treatment. The incident is considered to be the starting point of chiropractic health care, but it is clear that Palmer must have been working on his ideas for some years before. It seems likely that he actually learned techniques from some other person, either an osteopath or a bonesetter. It is said that Palmer was at one time in Kirksville, but it is not known to what extent he might have been exposed to Still or his ideas.

Unlike osteopaths, chiropractors are not fully qualified physicians, and some relatively modern books on chiropractics contain passages that are completely unacceptable to the medical profession, MDs, or DOs. In spite of this, the availability of chiropractic treatments has spread far and wide, not only in North America, but also in Europe and most other parts of the world. The continued existence and spread of chiropractic health care is evidence that chiropractors are giving relief to a reasonable proportion of those who seek their help. It is a pity that at the present time, there exist several different "schools" (in the sense of methods and teachings) of chiropractics with widely varying treatments. This division is sad, both for the profession itself (Matthew 12:25: "A house divided against itself cannot stand") and for patients, in particular for those who move to a different area and wish to continue receiving the same kind of therapy.

Following successful litigation from opponents, the American Medical Association was forced to modify its position that it was "unethical" for a doctor of medicine to refer patients to a chiropractor (*Chiropractic Coop. Assoc. v AMA*, 867 F2d 270, 275 [6th Cir 1989]). Accordingly, it is now ethical for a physician to associate professionally with and refer patients to a chiropractor if that physician believes that such a referral would be in the interest of the patient. In 1987 and 1993, chiropractors sued and won the right to be reimbursed from various health insurance programs and carriers. With any opposition silenced, chiropractors have been able to promote their skills and foster their legitimate place among licensed health care providers. Although significant philosophical differences may remain,[14] there is at least the opportunity now for meaningful dialogue and debate that can result in improved patient care. Unfortunately, in many states there are also intense lobbying efforts directed toward placing chiropractics as the only legitimate or primary form of manipulative therapy. Doing so would only further segregate the chiropractor from all others interested and skilled in manual therapy techniques. With an inherent philosophy of free trade and competitive drive for successful, cost-effective treatments, restrictions mandated by changes in state laws against qualified health care providers seem both counter-productive and contrary to the best interests of our patients.

PHYSICAL THERAPY

No overview of the development of manual medicine would be complete without recognizing the important contributions of physical therapists in the United States, Australia, and New Zealand. Skilled physical therapists have been invaluable as part of a team of health professionals providing special knowledge and abilities that can enable the delivery of an effective rehabilitation process, especially for patients with musculoskeletal dysfunctions. Their understanding of biomechanics and the continued development of effective manual therapies, appropriate exercise, and self-treatment programs enable increasing numbers of patients to recover more rapidly and maintain the benefits of their treatment.

Schools of physical therapy remain closely allied with medical and osteopathic teaching institutions, often sharing the same faculty and textbooks. The origins of this profession began in Europe and developed in the United States in response to the needs for rehabilitation of the wounded soldiers injured during the conflicts of World War I and later for those afflicted with polio. The development of formal training in physical therapy[15] is attributed to the work and devotion of Margurite Sanderson and Mary McMillan. The evolution of physical therapy began with the 1917 development of the Division of Special Hospitals and Physical Reconstruction by the Surgeon General's Office, which also appointed Sanderson, neurologist Frank B. Granger, and two orthopedic surgeons, Elliott G. Brackett and Joel E. Goldthwait. McMillan was the first professional physical therapist in the United States and first president of the American Physical Therapy Association. Since then, many have contributed to the knowledge and skills currently enjoyed by physical therapists around the world. One of the authors (M. B.) has been instrumental in this regard. Significant advances in the treatment of musculoskeletal dysfunctions are attributed to the collective works of Stanley Paris,[16] R. A. McKenzie,[17] Geoffrey Maitland,[18] Freddie Kaltenborn,[19] and, more recently, David Butler,[20] along with many others.

PROGRESS

In 1910, Alexander Bryce wrote about osteopathy in the *British Medical Journal.*[21] His paper, which serves as an example of the broad-mindedness that was often lacking in the medical profession, includes the following excerpts:

> The treatment of disease by physical methods has in recent years received a large share of attention. . . . At all times interested in such methods of treatment, my attention was . . . forcibly directed to this system in particular by the remarkable improvement of several of my patients, and at once took steps to inform myself as to the good and bad points of such a potent method of treatment.
>
> I learnt that in America, there were over 5,000 practitioners of the art of osteopathy. . . . I subsequently visited America to see the treatment in the land of its birth. . . . I was cordially welcomed not only at the schools but also at the dispensaries, and took every opportunity of conversing with the patients as to any benefit received, as well as comparing the methods of various practitioners.
>
> I came to the conclusion that there must be some virtue in a method, which has such vitality as to spread over the continent. . . . I was hardly surprised at this, as my own experience in its practice had at least disclosed the fact that it was of striking benefit in selected cases.

An editorial[22] about Bryce's paper appearing in the same issue of the *British Medical Journal* reads

> In the sphere of medicine there is a vast area of "undeveloped land," which Mr. Lloyd George has somehow failed to include in his budget. It comprises many methods of treatment which are scarcely taught at all in the schools, which find no place in textbooks and which consequently the "superior person" passes with gown uplifted to avoid a touch that is deemed pollution. The superior person is, as has more than once been pointed out, one of the greatest obstacles to progress.
>
> Not to go so far back as Harvey, who was denounced by the leaders of the profession in his day as a circulator or quack, we need only recall how the open-air treatment of consumption was ridiculed when the idea was first put forward by Bebbington . . . famous physicians refused to listen to Pasteur because he was not a medical man; Lister was scoffed at; the laryngoscope was sneered at as a physiological toy; the early ovariotomists were threatened by colleagues with the coroner's court; electricity was looked upon with suspicion; massage, within our own memory, was looked upon as an unclean thing. But even now the vast

field of physiotherapy is largely left to laymen for exploitation.

Rational medicine should take as its motto Molière's saying "Je prends mon bien ou je le trouve"; whatever can be used in this warfare against disease belongs to it of right. . . . Now Dr. Bryce has witnessed the mysteries of osteopathy and tells us what he saw in a paper published in this week's issue. . . . The results recorded by him are of themselves sufficient to justify us in calling attention to the method.

In an address to the Pacific Interurban Clinical Club in 1938, Horace Gray[23] quoted Sir Robert Jones, nephew of Hugh Owen Thomas, as saying

. . . forcible manipulation is a branch of surgery that from time immemorial has been neglected by our profession, and as a direct consequence, much of it has fallen into the hands of the unqualified practitioner. Let there be no mistake, this has seriously undermined the public confidence, which has on occasion amounted to open hostility. If we honestly face the facts, this should cause us no surprise. No excuse will avail when a stiff joint, which has been treated for many months by various surgeons and practitioners without effect, rapidly regains its mobility and function at the hands of an irregular practitioner. We should be self-critical and ask why we missed such an opportunity ourselves. Pointing out mistakes made by the unqualified does not solve the problem; the question at issue is their success. Reputations are not made in any walk of life simply by failures. Failures are common to us all and it is a far wiser and more dignified attitude on our part to improve our armamentarium than dwell upon the mistakes made by others.

In Great Britain in the early 1930s, there was a move on the behalf of osteopaths to obtain licensing, but the 1935 report of a House of Lords Select Committee appointed for the purpose showed such grave deficiencies in the practice of some of the so-called osteopaths that the move was dropped. Since then, British schools of osteopathy have trained large numbers of students who now practice in the field of manual medicine and are established all over the country. Their position in Britain is similar to that of chiropractors both in the United States and elsewhere. There is still no full licensure as physicians in the United Kingdom, even for American-trained DOs. The unethical practices that were a major part of the problem in 1935 have since been dealt with by the profession.

Much of the published research regarding musculoskeletal disorders has been devoted to surgical interven-

tion, especially in patients with back pain, even though the percentage of back pain patients with surgical lesions is less than 10%. Since the 1970s, an ever-increasing contribution from allopathic and osteopathic physicians, physical therapists, chiropractors, and basic research scientists has increased our knowledge about the biomechanics of the spine.

Several attempts have been made by each group to produce a controlled study[24-26] comparing treatment by manipulation with other methods. The difficulty has proved to be greater than expected, in particular because of the following reasons:

1. The nature of the treatment is such that it is almost impossible to make the study double blind.
2. There are a variety of different, specific dysfunctions, each of which requires a precise diagnosis followed by an appropriate, well-defined treatment.[27]
3. There is a wide range of talent and ability between different practitioners, making any comparison difficult and limiting the possibility of incorporating the suggested treatments based on outcome studies from various authors.

In time, these difficulties will be overcome, but in the meantime, those with personal experience either as a patient or as a practitioner will have no doubt about the possibilities of good manual therapy.

THE CHALLENGE

The challenge remains.

The sick person comes to a health care provider for help, not for the random application of a theory that may not be flawless. It is crucial that the differences between the branches of the profession be healed. This will be difficult because practitioners of any of the three branches under consideration will lose part of their "heritage." One problem is the feeling among some groups that their territory is being invaded and that they stand to lose patients and political influence. Each discipline has thought that its treatment was best, failing to recognize that something better may be available.

The DOs also have had the experience in California when, as a result of accepting MD degrees, they ceased to be "visible" in the sense that patients wanting manual treatment (or an osteopath's treatment for other reasons) were unable to identify them. To do nothing more than to give all DOs MD degrees would not be a satisfactory answer. All medical students should be exposed to methods of manual treatment as undergraduates, and there should be a specialty for practitioners who are experts in manual medicine. In the meantime, there is room for much closer cooperation between MDs and DOs and between both of them and chiropractors. Physical therapists have much to offer, but they are constrained by prescriptions often written by those with less knowledge about manual treatment, severe financial limitations by third-party payers, and the lack of funding for continued education, which is vital if skills are to be advanced.

The greatest challenges facing those who wish to incorporate additional or advanced skills in manual therapy are the increasing cost of education, the decreasing reimbursement provided to the practitioner by third-party carriers, and the suppressing constraints of "managed care" in all of its variations. The excesses of the past practices of providing continued and, at times, unnecessary treatments have caused severe restrictions for all who wish to provide manual therapies. It is now necessary to show that with proper, skilled, and appropriate treatment, manual therapy can prove to be a most cost-effective means of treating musculoskeletal complaints. This can be true for both the cost of health care and the cost of lost wages and productivity for those who have these dysfunctions.

VALUE OF MANIPULATIVE MEDICINE

Probably the greatest contribution from manipulative medicine is the evolution of a diagnostic framework defining the various dysfunctions that affect the musculoskeletal system. Despite comprehensive reviews describing the effectiveness of treatments for back pain, back pain is only a symptom of musculoskeletal dysfunctions, and without a proper diagnosis a more basic question remains: What are the causes of back pain, and how can they be differentiated?

Many authors have arrived by similar means at similar conclusions and have developed theories of their own. These theories and our own and the reasons for them are discussed in this text, but for the moment, manipulative techniques can be thought of as a means of getting muscle to let go and putting a stiffened joint through a range of movement rather than anything more complicated.

Stiffness of the involved joints can best be demonstrated clinically by the dynamics of a physical examination rather than by standard radiological imaging.

Clinical demonstration depends on appreciation of abnormalities of movement of spinal joints and tension differences in the soft tissues around them. These are not easily felt by untrained fingers, which may make the demonstration unconvincing to a newcomer to the field.

Some people have tissues through which abnormalities are easy to feel, but there are those whose subcutaneous tissues are dense and apparently fibrous. Severe obesity also causes increased difficulty. For the skeptical beginner, it may be important to find a model or patient with the thin type of soft tissue until his or her palpatory skill is better developed.

Soft tissue changes are various but one of the most important is hypertonus in muscle. It was suggested in earlier editions that muscle changes were the fundamental cause of problems. The present feeling is that muscle changes are important manifestations of more fundamental changes occurring partly in the central nervous system and partly in other soft tissues, including the fascial investment of the muscles. From a treatment perspective, it is reasonable to start with the concept that hypertonic muscles are a primary source of symptoms.

Thrusting techniques are not new. They have been used in some form for at least 100 years, and other nonthrusting techniques have been used much longer. One of the earliest British books describing similar techniques was published in 1934 by Thomas Marlin.[28] He was in charge of what later became the physiotherapy department at University College Hospital in London and had been to the United States to learn osteopathic techniques. He records that, following one of his demonstrations, a colleague told him that similar techniques had been practiced in England 40 years before. How slowly we learn!

Before proceeding, it must be emphasized that what is being described is not a new system of medicine. Manual treatment does not stand alone, and it should only be given in the context of total patient care, even if much of the care is more directly the responsibility of another practitioner. One of the advantages of the system in which patients are only seen by specialists in consultation with or on referral by the primary physician is that the practitioner of manual medicine has the opportunity to obtain a history from another physician in addition to that given by the patient. The goal of the manipulator should be to restore function; if, at the same time, pain is relieved, then it is likely that the treated dysfunction also caused a painful condition. If pain does not subside, then one must remain open-minded to the possibilities that a dysfunction located elsewhere in the musculoskeletal system may be at fault or that the problem lies outside the musculoskeletal system.

REFERENCES

1. Timbrell Fisher AG. Treatment by Manipulation (5th ed). London: Lewis, 1948.

2. Paget J. Cases that bone setters cure. Brit Med 1867; 1:1–4.
3. Hood W. On so-called "bone-setting," its nature and results. Lancet 1871;Apr 1:336–338, 372–374, 441–443, 499–501.
4. Menken M. The practice of neurology. Arch Neurol 1990;47:1173.
5. North American Symptomatic Carotid Endarterectomy Study Group. Beneficial effect in symptomatic patients with high-grade stenosis. N Engl J Med 1991;325:445–507.
6. Lewit K. Manipulative Therapy in Rehabilitation of the Locomotor System (2nd ed). Oxford: Butterworth–Heinemann, 1991.
7. Balon J, Aker PD, Crowther ER, et al. A comparison of active and simulated chiropractic manipulation as an adjunctive treatment for childhood asthma. N Engl J Med 1998;339:1013–1020.
8. Northup GW. Osteopathic Medicine. An American Reformation. Chicago: American Osteopathic Association, 1936.
9. Hildreth AG. The Lengthening Shadow of Dr. Andrew Taylor Still. Macon, MO: Hildreth, 1938.
10. Gevitz N. The D.O.s, Osteopathic Medicine in America. Baltimore: Johns Hopkins University Press, 1982.
11. Downing CH. Osteopathic Principles in Disease. San Francisco: Orozco, 1925.
12. Guglielmo WJ. Are D.O.s losing their unique identity? Med Econ 1998;75:200–214.
13. Homewood AE. The Neurodynamics of Vertebral Subluxation. Publisher not cited, 1972.
14. Shekelle PG. What role for chiropractic in health care? N Engl J Med 1998;339:1074–1075.
15. Vogel EA. The beginning of "modern physiotherapy." Phys Ther 1976;56:15–21.
16. Paris SA. Spinal manipulative therapy. Clin Orthop 1983;179:55–61.
17. McKenzie RA. The Lumbar Spine, Mechanical Diagnosis and Therapy. Waikenae, New Zealand: Spinal Publications Ltd, 1981.
18. Maitland GD. Spinal Manipulation (2nd ed). London: Butterworth, 1977.
19. Karltenborn FM. Manuelle Therapie der Extremitätengelenke. Oslo: Olaf Norlis Bokhandel, 1976.
20. Butler D. Mobilisation of the Nervous System. Melbourne: Churchill Livingstone, 1991.
21. Bryce A. Remarks on mechano-therapy in disease: with special reference to osteopathy. BMJ 1910;2:581–584.
22. Editorial. "Undeveloped land" of medicine. BMJ 1910;2:638–639.
23. Gray H. Sacro-iliac joint pain. Int Clin 1938;2:54–96.
24. Shekelle PG. Spinal update: spinal manipulation. Spine 1994;19:858–861.
25. Curtis P. Spinal Manipulation: Does It Work? In R Deyo (ed). Spine: State of the Art Reviews. Philadelphia: Hanley & Belfus, 1987;2:31–44.
26. Brunarski DJ. Clinical trials of spinal manipulation: a critical appraisal and review of the literature. J Manipulative Physiol Ther 1984;4:243–249.
27. Kimberly PE. Formulating a prescription for osteopathic manipulative treatment. J Am Osteopath Assoc 1980;79:506–513.
28. Marlin T. Manipulative Treatment. London: Edward Arnold, 1934.

2

Anatomy and Biomechanics

In their training, practitioners acquire a basic working knowledge of the anatomy of the spinal column and pelvis. The objectives of this chapter are to refresh the reader's memory on points that he or she may have forgotten, to go into detail about specific anatomical landmarks that we use to assist in diagnosing somatic dysfunction, and to present evidence to show that some standard anatomical beliefs should be changed in the light of recent research. In trying to understand the reasons for the success of manual therapy, it is of the utmost importance to have as clear as possible a picture of the structure and normal function of the joint concerned. If one wishes to use manual treatment, the need is even greater.

It is from the clinical experience of countless manipulators that patients obtain relief from certain symptoms after manipulation of not only spinal joints themselves, but also the joints of the pelvis (including the pubic symphysis) and the joints between the ribs and vertebrae. The fact that symptoms can be caused by dysfunction of a rib joint is not well recognized by medical doctors (MDs), but clinical experience suggests that rib cage dysfunctions are important sources of chest wall and arm pain. Early recognition of these dysfunctions might both hasten relief for the sufferer and reduce the need for costly cardiac investigations.

In regard to the low back, the classic paper of Mixter and Barr[1] stimulated the interest of the medical profession in the structure and pathology of the intervertebral disc. Unfortunately, after Mixter and Barr's discovery, attention was turned away from other sources of low back pain, and manipulation became a less attractive tool in the medical armamentarium. Since then, many papers have been published and much research work has been carried out regarding the intervertebral disc. Armstrong[2] gives an excellent review of the work done before Mixter

and Barr. There is a summary of more recent research on the low back with a comprehensive list of references in Bogduk and Twomey's *Clinical Anatomy of the Lumbar Spine*[3] and, more recently, in *Movement, Stability and Low Back Pain: The Essential Role of the Pelvis*, edited by Vleeming et al.[4] Those who plan to work in this field would be well advised to read these works.

ANATOMY OF THE PELVIS

The pelvis is a three-part bony ring with two diarthrodial joints posteriorly, the sacroiliac (SI) joints, and a so-called symphysis anteriorly. The term *so-called* is used because there is often a synovial cavity, and there is an upward and downward gliding movement, albeit of a small excursion. The upward glide of the pubis on the side of weightbearing during one-legged standing is illustrated and reproduced (Figure 2-1), with permission, from Kapandji.[5]

The paired innominate bones are regarded by many as lower limb bones rather than belonging to the trunk. Their function is greatly influenced by the muscles of the hip and thigh. Each innominate is formed by the fusion of three bones: the ilium anteriorly, the ischium posteriorly, and the pubis inferiorly. In examining the pelvis, we need to find the anterior and posterior superior iliac spines (ASIS and PSIS), the ischial tuberosities, and the superior ramus and tubercles of the pubes.

The midline sacrum is formed by the fusion of five vertebral elements (sometimes six) and may show incomplete fusion at one or more levels. The sacrum is broad at its base and narrows to its apex postero-inferiorly. On either side of the apex is the *inferior lateral angle* (ILA), which is, developmentally, the transverse process (TP) of

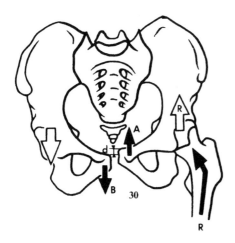

FIGURE 2-1

"Vertical" shear of pubic symphysis. Arrows indicate (A) left pubis riding up, (B) right pubis dragged down, (R) right side. (d = difference in the resulting height or position of the two pubic bones.) (Reproduced from IA Kapandji. The Physiology of the Joints [Vol 3]. London: Churchill Livingstone, 1974;70.)

S5. The shape of the ILA is quite variable: There may be an obvious angle, or it may be rounded, which can make it more difficult to identify, especially because it is buried within dense ligamentous structures (Figure 2-2).

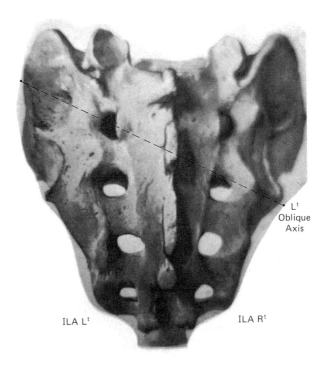

FIGURE 2-2

Posterior view of sacrum to show the left oblique "axis" and the inferior lateral angles (ILA). (L^t = left; R^t = right.)

SACROILIAC JOINT

The SI joints have an irregular articular surface with a marked variation in the details of their shape between different subjects and even between the two joints in the same patient. This may be part of the reason for the variations in pelvic dysfunctions seen in the patient population. Fryette[6] describes three main types of sacral shape. The first (type A) has the most typical shape, with the upper segments having a wider transverse measurement dorsally than on the ventral surface. The second (type B) has a wider ventral than dorsal transverse measurement of the first sacral segment, and the third (type C) has the articular surface sloping down and in on one side and down and out on the other (Figure 2-3). Fryette found that a sacrum that is wider on the dorsum is usually associated with coronal facing facets (thoracic type) at the L5-S1 joint, whereas a sacrum that is wider on the ventral aspect tends to have sagittal facing facets (lumbar type). In the type C sacrum, the facet on the side with the "down and in" slope (the type A slope) is likely to be coronal, and the facet on the side with the type B slope tends to be sagittal. Below the second segment, the ventral surface is typically wider than the dorsum. The typical shape of the upper and lower seg-

ments is what would be expected on mechanical grounds as giving the best resistance to the tendency of the superincumbent body weight to force the sacrum into the anterior nutated position (with the sacral base anterior and caudad and the apex superior and craniad).

In 10–15% of SI joints, the bevel change from upper to lower segments is absent, resulting in a flattened articulation between the sacrum and the ilium. Such an articulation would reduce the capacity for proper form closure, as described by Vleeming,[7] thereby having greater potential for traumatic shearing of the innominate on the sacrum. The usual sacral auricular surface is concave from antero-inferior to postero-superior, whereas the surface of the ilium is convex (Figure 2-4A). That shape prevents rotation of the ilia about an axis along the length of the sacrum. A less common shape appears when the concavity is on the ilial side (Figure 2-4B), which would permit a horizontal rotation to occur about an abnormal longitudinal sacral axis, and the subsequent, but rare, in-flare and out-flare movements of the innominates become possible. In a study of the anatomy of 40 SI joints from embryonic life to the eighth decade, Bowen and Cassidy[8] found that, at all ages studied, the sacral articular cartilage was hyaline, but the cartilage on the ilium was similar to fibrocartilage.

FIGURE 2-3

Diagram of types of sacral shape in transverse section. (A) Fryette type A. (B) Fryette type B. (C) Fryette type C.

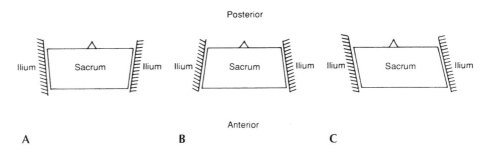

A   B   C

More recently, however, Bernard and Cassidy[9] found the ilial cartilage to be made of type II collagen, typical of hyaline. The sacral cartilage is approximately three times as thick as that on the ilium, and Bernard and Cassidy[9] noted relatively early degenerative changes more marked on the ilial side. They describe a joint capsule with an inner synovial layer and an outer layer of dense fibrous tissue.

The body weight is transmitted from the sacrum to the innominates almost entirely by the SI ligaments. These are quite thin and weak anteriorly but very strong posteriorly, and the sacrum is, in effect, slung from the iliac portion of the innominates by these ligaments. The short posterior SI ligaments are oriented transversely and form the major support for the sacrum, and, along with the joint contour, limit the range of motion. The more superficial long dorsal ligament is more vertical and blends inferiorly with the sacrotuberous ligament, which, through the ischial tuberosity, is in line with, and indeed may be regarded as a continuation of, the tendon of the long head of the biceps femoris.[10] Typically, the body's center of gravity falls anterior to the center of rotation of the SI joint and, therefore, tends to rotate the sacrum into anterior nutation about a transverse axis. This motion is resisted primarily by the sacrotuberous ligaments. In lower animals and many mammals, parts of the biceps femoris and semitendinosus originate from the sacrum with a cutaneous nerve separating the two.[11] Perhaps its phylogenetic history helps account for the importance of that ligament in certain pelvic dysfunctions.

In spite of the development of anatomical thought since 1950, there remains in the mind of many physicians the idea that the SI joint is neither mobile nor likely to be a source of symptoms. Accordingly, it may be worth mentioning the blank disbelief in the mind of one of the authors (John F. Bourdillon) in 1953 at the first suggestion that symptoms could arise from the SI joint! The anatomical evidence shows that the SI joint is a mobile diarthrodial joint, and, according to Brooke,[12] ". . . the old description of fibrous or a bony ankylosis was a description of a pathological change." Brooke, working on laboratory specimens, located the center of motion for the SI joint in the short posterior SI ligament and emphasized that the movement had both rotatory and gliding components. Weisl[13] used live subjects with the pelvis restrained in a special apparatus and then had radiographs taken of various positions of the trunk and lower limbs. He reported the following:

> In a minority of subjects, the sacral displacement was such that the sacral line remained parallel to its position at rest. Angular displacement occurred much more frequently and it was possible to locate an axis of rotation. It was situated approximately 10 cm below the promontory in the normal subjects, both recumbent and standing, and was placed a little higher in puerperal women. Contrary to the belief of previous authors, the site of this axis was variable in a majority of subjects, either the axis moved more than 5 cm following various changes of posture, or angular and parallel movement occurred in the same subject . . .

> The position of this axis of rotation differed from that described by earlier authors who based their opinions only on the examination of the sacroiliac joint surfaces . . .

In 1936, Pitkin and Pheasant[14] described referred pain to the gluteal and sacral regions and to the lower extremities

FIGURE 2-4

Concave-convex relationship at the sacroiliac joint. (A) Typical. (B) Unusual, thought to be required for flare dysfunction.

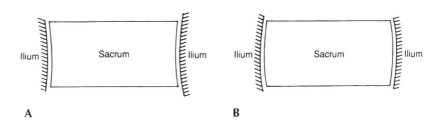

A   B

originating in the SI and lumbosacral joints and their accessory ligaments and coined the term *sacrarthrogenic telalgia*. They drew the following conclusions:

1. SI mobility can be demonstrated in vivo by measuring the movements of the ilia.
2. In a standing position, all motions of the trunk, with the exception of flexion and extension, are normally associated with unpaired antagonistic movements of the ilia about a transverse axis that passes through the center of the pubic symphysis.
3. Rotation and lateral bending of the sacrum do not normally occur alone, but as correlated motions that are coincidental to antagonistic movements of the ilia.
4. The syndrome sacrarthrogenic telalgia is not the result of irritation or compression of trunks of peripheranerves, but more a result from abnormal ligamentous tension associated with altered SI mobility.

The differences in the conclusions of Brooke and Weisl are striking, and the probability is that both are at least partially correct. Consideration of the mechanics of the SI joint—in particular, the interosseous portion of the posterior ligament—suggests that any rotatory motion not centered in that area must be very small. Also, irregularities in the auricular surface itself must restrict gliding motion or rotation about an antero-inferior axis, especially when weightbearing compresses the joint.[15] It seems certain that there are both rotatory and gliding movements; therefore, there cannot be any fixed axis, and it may be that when certain restrictions are imposed, the axis appears to be where Weisl found it. There is no doubt that the innominate must be able to move one or the other about an axis through or near the pubic symphysis. Is this perhaps the motion recorded by Weisl?

MOTION OF THE JOINTS OF THE PELVIS

The function of the joints of the pelvic ring has been the subject of much research and argument. It is clear, however, that there is no longer any doubt that SI joints are mobile, diarthrodial joints[16] subject to dysfunctions like other such joints in the axial skeleton. Motion analysis of forward walking indicates that counter rotation of the innominates[9] constitutes an important part of the normal walking cycle.[17] However, rotation of the innominates can only happen if the pubic symphysis is able to rotate about its transverse axis, a movement that can be lost if there is a fixed dysfunction of the symphysis. Also, as one of the

innominates rotates anteriorly, the sacrum is forced to rotate toward it with a side-bending motion toward the other side. In response to the side bending of the sacrum and therefore the unlevelling of the sacral base, the lumbar spine, if it is freely mobile, will side bend and rotate in the opposite direction of the sacrum as an adaptation to sacral base unlevelling. Anything that interferes with the ability of the pelvis to perform any of these movements will render the walking cycle abnormal. For this reason, dysfunctions of the pelvis are of primary importance when treating patients with back and leg pain, even if the complaint is higher up the back. Other movements of the pelvic joints are discussed later, and when any of these movements is restricted, the walking cycle will be affected.

Movements of the Pubic Symphysis

In addition to rotational movement at the pubic symphysis about a transverse axis, there can be a vertical shearing motion (see Figure 2-1). In previous editions, this shearing movement of the pubic symphysis was described as abnormal. That description is probably incorrect. Kapandji[5] describes a shearing through the symphysis on one-legged standing as abnormal, but it seems that shearing can occur in normal joints if one-legged standing is prolonged.[18,19] The shearing is actually parallel to the anatomical plane of the symphysis and not truly vertical. It is produced by the innominate on the weightbearing side riding up, while that on the opposite side is dragged down by the weight of the lower limb. If the symphysis remains mobile, correction will occur spontaneously upon standing on the other leg or on prolonged two-legged standing.

Movements of the Innominates on the Sacrum (Iliosacral)

Normally, during forward bending, both innominates will symmetrically rotate posteriorly, and during backward bending, they will symmetrically rotate anteriorly around a horizontal axis just inferior to S2. Counter rotation of the innominates on the sacrum is described as part of the normal walking cycle. The innominate on one side rotates posteriorly until heel-strike and then anteriorly until the leg is in position for toe-off. The opposite innominate rotates in a counter direction (i.e., while one innominate rotates posteriorly, the other rotates anteriorly).

Movements of the Sacrum between the Innominates (Sacroiliac)

The best-studied movement of the sacrum is now commonly known as *nutation*,[20] or *nodding*, which may be anterior or posterior, sometimes called *inferior* and *superior nutation* or *nutation* and *counternutation*. The reason for these descriptors is that the older terms of *sacral flexion* and *extension* are confusing, because they are used in the opposite sense in the context of craniosacral treatment.

Motion of the sacrum between the ilia is now well described.[4,21] Increased tension along the long dorsal ligament of the SI joint occurs with posterior nutation of the sacral base during forward bending. Backward bending causes anterior nutation of the sacral base and reduces tension in this ligament, but it increases tension in the sacrotuberous ligament and the hamstring muscle group.[22]

Motion of the SI joint is probably a consequence of altering ligamentous tension responding to changes in muscle tone or "force closure" from a variety of sources.[23] Its stability is inherently dependent on the shape of the SI joint surfaces (form closure).[23] Normally, there is a resultant "locking" mechanism,[16] which provides the stability necessary for normal motion. Clinically, when sacral dysfunctions are seen, there is an imbalance of tension and tone between the muscles and ligaments responsible for force closure, which can also lock the sacrum and prevent normal function.[11,24] Aside from the direct action from the pyriformis and gluteus maximus that attach to the sacrum, sacral motion is in a sense "co-dependent . . . it wants to please 'everyone' above, and below" (Stiles E. G., personal communication, 1996). When acting unilaterally, the piriformis can externally rotate the femur and assist in force closure of the SI joint.[25] Because of its sacral origin, the piriformis also seems capable of anteriorly tilting and rotating the sacrum to the opposite side, which may be assisted by the ipsilateral gluteus maximus. The contralateral latissimus dorsi can also assist the gluteus maximus through the thoraco-lumbar fascia[26] to nutate the sacrum anteriorly and extend the lumbosacral junction. The long head of the biceps femoris attaches to the sacrotuberous ligament and tends to tilt the sacrum backward and rotate the sacrum to the same side, whereas the longissimus and multifidus are so positioned from above that they can pull the base superiorly and posteriorly directly through attachments to the dorsal ligaments.[22]

1. *Anterior nutation* is the movement anteriorly and inferiorly of the sacral base with respect to the innominates. It involves rotation of the sacrum about a horizontal transverse axis located at the level of S2 and a translation of the sacrum caudally along the auricular surface of the innominate. This movement makes the sacral base less prominent from behind but makes the inferior lateral angle (the TP of S5) more prominent. Anterior nutation is the normal reaction of the sacrum to extension of the lumbar spine and also occurs during exhalation.

2. *Posterior nutation* is the movement of the sacral base superiorly and posteriorly about the same hypothetical axis with translation of the sacrum cranially along the auricular surface. The sacral base becomes prominent posteriorly, and the inferior lateral angle is less prominent. Posterior nutation is the reaction of the sacrum to lumbar flexion and also occurs during inhalation.

3. *Sacral torsion* is defined as the motion of the sacrum around a hypothetical oblique axis that begins at the upper pole of one of the SI joints and ends at the lower pole of the opposite SI joint. The axis is named by its origin at the upper pole as viewed from behind (see Figure 2-2). With any torsional movement, there is a coupled side bending of the sacrum to the opposite side, which is a consequence of the slanted position of the sacrum relative to L5 above. *Anterior* or *forward torsion* is the sacral movement that accompanies the counter rotation of the innominates in normal walking.[27] The axis of rotation originates on the side of the weightbearing leg. For example, at left mid-stance, the sacrum rotates forward about an axis beginning at the left superior pole and ending at the right inferior pole, resulting in anterior nutation of the right sacral base. The anterior surface of the sacrum is now facing (rotated) toward the left. Both the left base and inferior lateral angle remain in place and appear posterior to those on the right. This torsional movement can then be described as an anterior torsion to the left on the left oblique axis (left on left). Similarly, when weight is borne only by the right leg, at midstance, the torsional motion is then observed as an anterior torsion to the right on the right oblique axis (right on right).

When standing, the center of motion of the hip joint is anterior to the vertical axis through the apparent center of motion of the SI joint. Because of this, when the weight of the body is borne on the left leg at mid-stance, and the right innominate falls away, weight-bearing force from below closes the left SI joint. The right sacral base nutates anteriorly, and the sacrum rotates to the left, while L5 side bends to the left and rotates to the right. The complexities and interactions associated with the walking cycle as it relates to normal lumbar and pelvic motions are still not fully understood, but using current knowledge and clinical observation, Greenman[17] proposes this "theoretical model . . . to describe all the movements found within the pelvic girdle and the potential dysfunctions therein."

4. *Posterior* or *backward torsion* is a physiological movement that also occurs across the oblique axis but can only occur when the lumbar spine is flexed and then

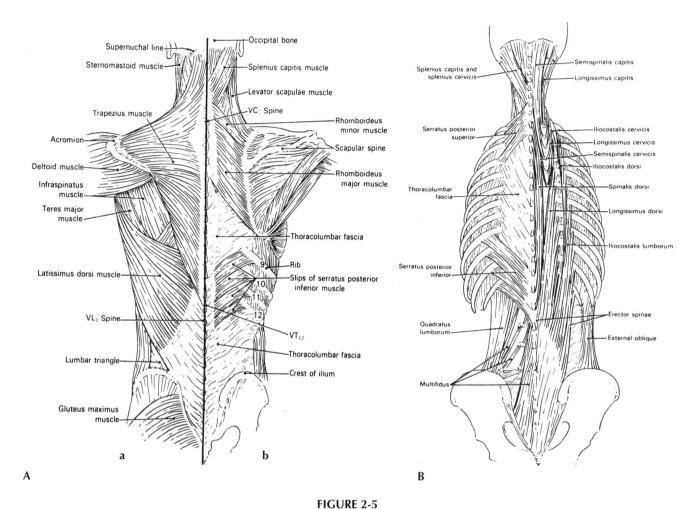

FIGURE 2-5

(A) Superficial (a) and intermediate (b) muscles connecting the back and upper limb. (B) Deep muscles of the back. (Reproduced from RF Becker, JW Wilson, JA Gehweiler. The Anatomical Basis of Medical Practice. Baltimore: Williams & Wilkins, 1971.)

rotates and side bends to one side. When the spine flexes enough to reach the lumbosacral junction, the sacrum posteriorly nutates around its transverse axis. If the flexed lumbar spine is then taken into left side bending, then non-neutral coupling of lumbar rotation to the left will also occur. The sacrum responds to the lumbar non-neutral mechanics by rotating to the right across the left oblique axis, resulting in posterior nutation of the right sacral base (i.e., a right on left posterior sacral torsion). If the patient forward bends, then side bends and rotates to the right, the sacrum will rotate to the left across the right oblique axis, resulting in posterior nutation of the left sacral base (i.e., a left on right posterior sacral torsion). It is in this position of spinal flexion with rotation that not only is the lumbar spine at risk of injury, but the SI joint is also particularly vulnerable. If L5 is deeply positioned between the ilia, then the lum-

bosacral junction may appear to be between L4 and L5, with L5 moving with S1.

ANATOMY OF THE LUMBAR AND THORACIC SPINE

Muscles

To find dysfunctions, it is essential that the operator be familiar with the anatomy of the posterior spinal muscles (Figure 2-5). From the clinical perspective, the back muscles are usually described as forming four layers: first, the trapezius and latissimus dorsi; second, the rhomboids and the levator scapulae; third, the spinalis, longissimus, and iliocostalis; and fourth, the deep, short layer of multifidus, rotatores, interspinales, and intertransversarii.

The muscles of the upper back are arranged in three main groups.[27] The superficial group comprises the muscles connecting the shoulder girdle to the trunk. These are in two layers: trapezius and latissimus dorsi superficially, and deeper, the rhomboids and levator scapulae. These muscles have all migrated caudally and are innervated by nerves from cervical segments. From the clinical point of view, these two layers are separate and can be distinguished by palpation because of the different fiber orientation. In the lumbar spine, the superficial layer is still latissimus dorsi, but in this region it is largely tendinous.

The second layer is the serratus posterior superior and inferior, which are small muscles of respiration that are difficult to feel. Fortunately, they are of little significance, except in the interaction between the thoracic spine and the ribs and shoulders.

The third layer includes the muscles that are collectively known as the *erector spinae*, or *sacro-spinalis*. These are of great importance clinically and consist of three long muscles:

1. Medially, the spinalis, which is relatively small and may not be easy to feel because it is very close to the spinous processes.

2. Laterally, the iliocostalis is attached to the angles of the ribs and is important in the diagnosis and treatment of structural rib dysfunctions.

3. Intermediate, the longissimus, which is the muscle that produces the long bulge visible under the skin of many patients, centered approximately 2.5 cm (1 in.) lateral to the midline. Often known as the *medial gutter*, it is separated from the spinalis by the medial intermuscular septum that can be felt as a longitudinal depression $1/2$ to 1 cm ($1/4$ to $1/2$ in.) lateral to the midline. There is a similar intermuscular septum lateral to the longissimus, the lateral gutter, separating it from the third muscle in this layer, the iliocostalis.

The intermuscular septa are less well defined in the lumbar region, but along the thoracic spine they are convenient routes for deep palpation in the area because it is easier to feel through the septum than through muscle. This is especially so if there is a spasm in the fourth layer muscle, as may happen in the early stages after injury. These deep muscles include (1) the multifidus, which, according to Gray,[28] cross over from one to three joints; (2) the rotatores, which are only found in the thoracic region and only cross one joint; (3) the intertransversarii, which are divided into medial and lateral groups with different innervation; and (4) the interspinales. Both the intertransversarii and interspinales only cross one joint. Except for the lateral intertransversarii, these latter two groups are innervated by the dorsal rami of the spinal nerves. The anterior primary divisions innervate the lateral intertransversarii, and their action is thought to be lateral bending with a tendency to produce forward flexion.

In a paper presented to, and later published by, the North American Academy of Musculoskeletal Medicine (now merged with the American Academy of Orthopedic Medicine) in 1991, Willard[25] explained the concepts integrating the anatomy of these posterior muscles with spinal function. He showed that the multifidus is roughly confined to the lumbar region and consists of small bipinnate muscles, the parts of which are not equal in length, some crossing only one joint and others two or three joints. The deepest fibers are interesting in that they have tendons caudally ending as far down as the sacrotuberous ligament. The multifidus group is conical in shape, narrowing from below, but near the thoracolumbar junction the group is replaced by the semispinalis superficially and the rotatores deeply. The semispinales are wider and cross several joints. The rotatores are more transverse and cross only one joint. In the cervical spine, at least, there is a higher concentration of muscle spindles in the rotatores than has been found in other muscles, and the extrafusal portions are weak with relatively few contractile fibers.

Clinically, the deep short muscles are of great importance in diagnosis and in assessing the result of treatment, because the presence of hypertonicity in them is one of the tissue texture changes that best indicate the level of spinal dysfunction. The rotatores, the intertransversarii, and the multifidus are all small muscles, but they appear to be very important in any spinal joint dysfunction. It has been suggested that these muscles function as "spindles" for the larger, more superficial muscles rather than as prime movers or restrictors.[3] Because of their small size, they are difficult to palpate; because their ability to generate a forceful contraction is limited, it is important not to expect them to provide powerful muscular resistance during a technique that requires their voluntary contraction.

One study conducted in 1994 found that the multifidus are inhibited usually at a single segmental level in both acute and subacute low back pain patients.[29] More important, the multifidus does not spontaneously recover after the relief of low back pain, and inhibition of the multifidus may further predispose the patient to recurrent low back pain. This situation may be remedied by specific exercises for multifidus retraining.[30]

Lumbar Bones and Joints

In the lumbar spine, the facet orientation is variable. This is known as *facet tropism* and increases the incidence of asymmetrical motion, especially the degree of rotation at a lumbar vertebral segment. According to Bogduk and Twomey,[3] at birth the facets face forward and backward so that the joints are coronal. With growth, the facets tend to rotate, and the joints may become fully sagittal, but more commonly they are curved either in a C shape facing posteromedially or in a J shape with the short limb projecting medially from the anterior end. Facets that are strictly sagittal provide little stability against forward displacement of the superior vertebra. Those that are curved provide better stability in the sagittal plane, and both restrict rotation. Facets that are coronal provide excellent stability in the sagittal plane but allow free rotation, hypothetically placing an additional strain on the disc annulus. At the L5-S1 joint, and sometimes at L4-5, the facets may be coronal and therefore allow more rotation. It is not unusual to find coronal-facing facets on one side and sagittal-facing facets on the other. In 1991, Guntzburg and others[31] reported that rotation is less when the spine is flexed than when it is in neutral and that the amplitude of rotation is not influenced by articular tropism. For a description of how rotation takes place and the strains involved even within the 3 degrees permitted, see Bogduk and Twomey.[3] Cossette et al.[32] plotted instantaneous centers of rotation and found that the centers were anterior to the zygapophyseal joints and that they tended to move toward the side to which rotation was forced. Farfan and Sullivan[33] observed that rotatory injuries to the lumbar region are likely to damage the disc annulus, especially when there is asymmetry of the zygapophyseal joints. Yet the degree of asymmetry does not appear to correlate with the degree of axial torque.[34] This issue is still in debate.[35,36] As a result of his research, Farfan[37] postulated that disc degeneration is the result of torsional strains rather than compression injuries.

In view of these findings, it seems strange that several of the classic techniques for treating lumbar joint dysfunction use rotation as the corrective movement, whether it is introduced externally by the operator or intrinsically by the patient. These techniques have proved to be satisfactory for countless patients, but sometimes they may be contraindicated. Other techniques not using rotation as the corrective force are emphasized in this text.

Atypical segmentation is often seen at the lumbosacral junction, and, if there is asymmetrical sacralization of L5 and facet tropism at L4-5 with a coronal facet on the side with the larger TP, it is relatively common to find an L4-5 disc protrusion on that side.[38] There will also be varying influence of the iliolumbar ligaments in different individuals, depending on how deeply situated L5 is within the pelvis.[39]

Functionally, the lumbar spine can be thought of as beginning at T11 or even T10. Although the morphology of the joints is not the same as in the lumbar region, from the point of view of the types of symptoms produced, T11 and T12 appear more related to the lumbar spine than to dysfunctions higher up.[40] Treatment of the T11-12 and T12-L1 joints is commonly needed in patients with low back and leg pain, or even in those with leg pain alone, and dysfunctions of the eleventh and twelfth ribs can often be found in patients whose pain is entirely in the lower back. It is important to recognize that a full structural examination is necessary before the operator can be satisfied that pain at one level is not a manifestation of a dysfunction at another level.

Thoracic Spinal Bones and Joints

The length of the TPs is not the same as one moves up and down the spine. Seen from behind, the TPs form two "diamonds," of which the lower is widest at L3 and then narrows rapidly so that the shortest TPs are usually at T12. From there up, the length increases slowly up to T1. It is relatively easy to feel the TPs in the upper thoracic region but very difficult at T12 (Figure 2-6A).

The spinous processes of the thoracic vertebrae tend to slope downward and backward, although the spinous process of T1 is horizontal and T2 and T3 have only a small slope. The "rule of threes" describes the relative positions of the tips of the spinous processes with the corresponding TPs. The tips of the spinous processes of T4 through T6 are found one-half of a vertebral level below the corresponding TPs, whereas those of T7 through T9 are a full vertebral level lower. This trend reverses in the lower thoracic spine so that the spinous processes of T10 through T12 are again at the same level as that of the TPs. This is only an approximation. There is a gradual increase in the slope of the spinous processes down to T7 or sometimes T6 and then a gradual decrease (Figure 2-6B). For clinical purposes, it is enough to remember that the tip of the spinous process of T7 is level with the TPs of T8 and that both above and below this segment the tip of a spinous process is closer to its corresponding TPs.

In the thoracic spine, the superior facets of the lower vertebrae face posteriorly and superiorly. This would permit a free range of rotation were it not for the rib cage.

Anatomy of the Ribs

The first rib is almost flat and has an inner and an outer margin. The inner margin is part of the boundary of the thoracic inlet (outlet), and any dysfunction of the first rib is an important aspect of syndromes arising in this area.[41,42] The anterior end of the first costal cartilage can be found immediately inferior to the medial end of the clavicle. The lateral shaft can be palpated laterally in the anterior triangle of the neck, but care is needed to avoid the neurovascular bundle. The first rib does not have a rib angle, which makes it atypical.

The second rib is also described as atypical, largely because of its relation to the sternum with which it articulates at the angle of Louis. This junction between the manubrium and the body of the sternum is mobile at least into the early teens and retains some flexibility for much longer; therefore, it is involved in the mechanics of the thoracic cage. The second rib can also be involved in the thoracic outlet syndrome when the space between it and the clavicle is narrowed with entrapment of the neurovascular bundle to the upper extremity.

Like the typical ribs (third through ninth), the second has a head with two separate articular facets—one for the first thoracic vertebra and one for the second. It has a tubercle on which is the facet of the costotransverse joint, a curved shaft and a costal cartilage that articulate with the sternum at the junction of the manubrium and the body (the angle of Louis). By this attachment, the second rib influences movement of the sternum. There is disagreement between anatomists as to the presence or absence of an angle in this rib (Figure 2-7).

The typical ribs have a sharp lower and a rounded superior border posteriorly. They are attached at both ends and normally move together.

Ribs 11 and 12 have no anterior attachment and move in a manner somewhat different from those above. The motion is described as being like that of calipers, opening on inhalation and closing on exhalation, along with some craniad and caudad movement.

Normal rib motion is usually dependent on normal motion between adjacent thoracic vertebrae.

Costovertebral and Costotransverse Joints

The first through tenth ribs are linked to each other posteriorly and to the sternum anteriorly, which stabilizes the thoracic spine and prevents the degree of rotation that would be permitted by the configuration of the thoracic zygapophyseal joints alone. The eleventh and twelfth ribs have no firm anterior attachment.

In addition to the intervertebral joints, there are costovertebral and costotransverse joints that guide normal rib motion. On the body of T1 is a single facet for the head of the first rib. At the lower margin of the upper eight thoracic vertebrae, and sometimes at T9, is a demifacet for the upper aspect of the head of the rib from the next level below. The vertebrae from T2 to

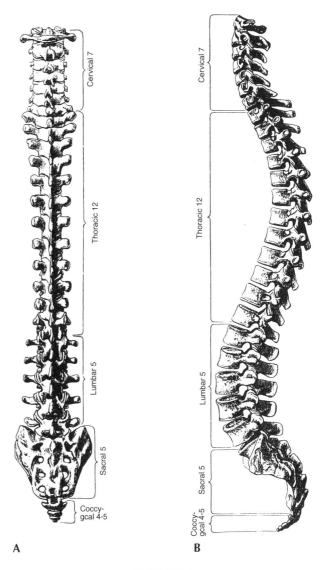

FIGURE 2-6

(A) Posterior view of spinal column to show variation in length of transverse processes. (B) Side view of spinal column to show spinal process slope. (Reproduced from DJ Cunningham, GJ Jgeorge John Romanes. Cunningham's Textbook of Anatomy [12th ed]. London: Oxford University Press, 1981.)

T10 also have a demifacet that articulates on their upper vertebral margin to the lower demifacet of the corresponding rib head. If T9 has no demifacet at its lower vertebral margin, then there will be a single full facet for the whole of the rib head at T10. The TPs of thoracic vertebrae T1 through T10 have articular facets for their corresponding ribs to form the costotransverse joints (Figure 2-8). The second rib articulates with the bottom of the body of T1, the top of the body of T2, and the TP

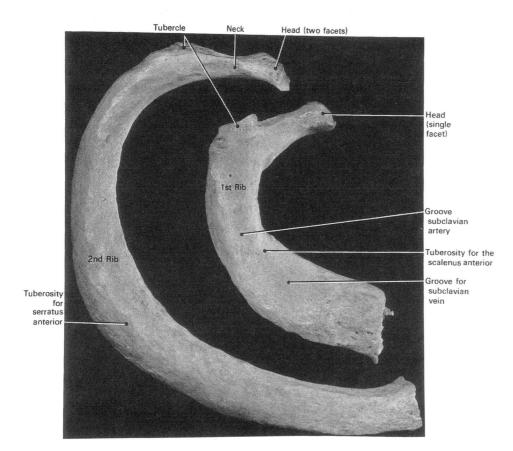

FIGURE 2-7
Ribs 1 and 2. (Reproduced from RF Becker, JW Wilson, JA Gehweiler. The Anatomical Basis of Medical Practice. Baltimore: Williams & Wilkins, 1971.)

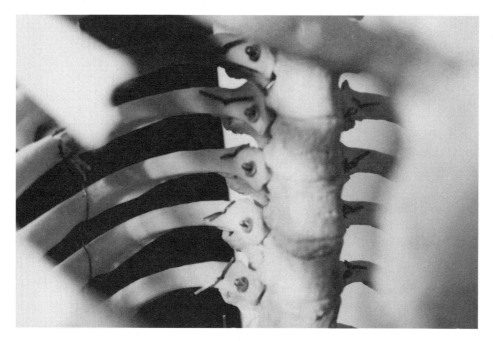

FIGURE 2-8
Anterior view of individual rib articulations between adjacent vertebrae.

FIGURE 2-9

(A) Rib motion diagram to show pump-and bucket-handle motion. (Reproduced from RF Becker, JW Wilson, JA Geh-weiler. The Anatomical Basis of Medical Practice. Baltimore: Williams & Wilkins, 1971.) (B) Change in axis of rib motion, upper y, and lower x. Arrow x—x' indicates the axis of respiratory motion of the upper ribs and arrow y—y' indicates the axis of respiratory motion of the lower ribs, which depends on the angle between the transverse process and the vertebral body. (a = anterior motion of rib with inhalation—demonstrates the pump-handle component of rib motion; INF. = inferior; l = lateral motion of rib with inhalation—demonstrates the bucket-handle component of rib motion; SUP. = superior.) (Reproduced from IA Kapandji. The Physiology of the Joints [Vol 3]. London: Churchill Livingstone, 1974;139.)

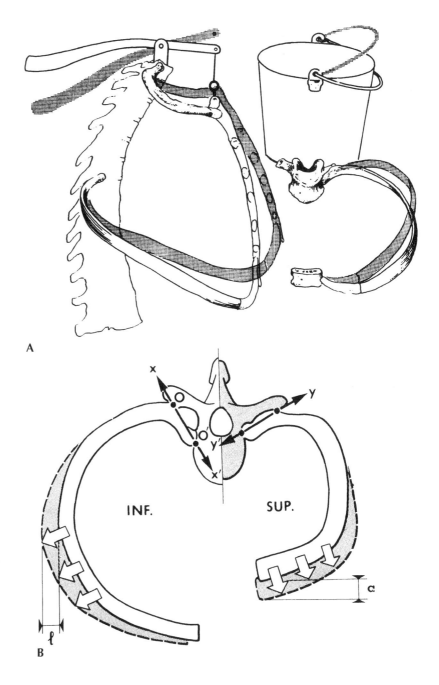

of T2; the third rib articulates with the bottom of T2, the top of the body of T3, and the TP of T3; and so on.

Rib Motion

Respiratory rib movement is both up and down and in and out; the proportion of each changes as the rib number increases. The direction of the combined motion is determined by the orientation of the line joining the costotransverse to the costovertebral joints, which serves as the axis of motion. This orientation gradually changes from T1, where it is more coronal, to T12, where it is closer to the sagittal plane. The corresponding rib motion is therefore nearly sagittal in the upper ribs and more nearly coronal in the lower ribs. The former is known as *pump-handle motion* (from nineteenth-century kitchen hand pumps), whereas the latter is known as *bucket-handle motion*. In some ways, this latter term is unfortunate, because bucket handles have fixed attachments at both ends, whereas the rib does not. There is always an element of pump-handle motion and bucket-handle motion in all ribs (Figure 2-9A and B).

Restriction of rib motion may occur either in inhalation or in exhalation and may need treatment. It may be

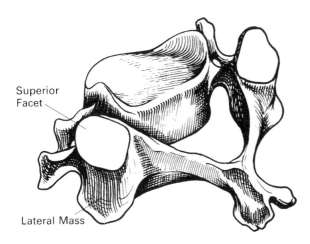

FIGURE 2-10
Typical cervical vertebra showing facet facing and "lateral mass" or interarticular pillar. (Reproduced from IA Kapandji. The Physiology of the Joints [Vol 3]. London: Churchill Livingstone, 1974;193.)

necessary to treat specifically the pump or bucket handle element of the restriction, but it is of greater importance to treat the correct phase of respiration.

The ribs also move in response to movement of the thoracic spine and can therefore be considered as extensions of the TPs. During flexion of the thoracic spine, the ribs move anteriorly and superiorly and also internally rotate and can be described as a rib torsion. Likewise, during thoracic spinal extension, the ribs move posteriorly and inferiorly and externally rotate. Palpation of the rib angles with flexion and extension of the thoracic spine can therefore assist the operator in examining the thoracic spine for any motion restrictions detected by asymmetrical movement of the ribs. Rotation of the thoracic spine imparts a twist or torsion to the ribs such that, with spinal rotation to the right, the posterior aspect of the ribs externally rotate (torsion) on the right, while the ribs on the left internally rotate (torsion). Consequently, rib motion is adversely affected by non-neutral vertebral dysfunctions, which not only affect the rib to which the vertebra is directly attached at the costotransverse joint, but also can result in a twisting or torsional change imparted through the costovertebral joint to the rib immediately below it.

ANATOMY OF THE CERVICAL SPINE

The vertebrae in the neck are different in many respects from those lower down. The upper two form a two-joint complex with the occiput, and there is a striking difference in structure between them and the typical cervical verte-

brae from the lower half of C2 down to C7. In some skeletons, the C7-T1 joint is more cervical than thoracic in type. The complex of joints between the skull and C2 consists of the occipitoatlantal and atlantoaxial joints—each have their own motion characteristics but have complementary function between them, allowing motion in all directions.

Facet Orientation

The zygapophyseal joints of the typical vertebrae are set at an angle of approximately 45 degrees to the horizontal, with the superior facet facing posteriorly and superiorly (Figure 2-10). They are weightbearing at all times and only have coupled movement of side bending and rotation to the same side. The various types of spinal motions are described under Physiological Movements of the Spine, later in this chapter.

The facets of the C1-2 joint may appear flat or concave in the skeleton (Figure 2-11), but in life, when covered with cartilage, they are both convex.[43] This leads to a small amount of vertical to caudal translation of C1 on C2 when the head is turned to either side (Figure 2-12). This elegant mechanism allows the ligaments, which hold the odontoid process in place, to remain tight even when the head is rotated fully to one side. The main movement at this joint is rotation, but there is also a small range of flexion and extension.

The facets of the occipitoatlantal joint are set at an angle of approximately 60 degrees to each other, being closer together at their anterior ends than at their posterior ends (Figure 2-13). The superior facets of C1 are concave from side to side and from front to back; the facets on the occipital bone are correspondingly convex. The plane of the facets is nearly horizontal in the anatomical position, and, unlike all other joints in the spine, flexion of the skull causes the superior (occipital) facet to slide backwards on the inferior (C1) (Figure 2-14). The shape of the facets and the angle between them cause the joint to "bind" in extension by the impingement of the wider, more posterior part of the occipital facets on the narrow anterior part of the C1 facets. The same kind of bind does not appear to happen at the extreme of flexion. The main occipitoatlantal movements are flexion and extension, but there is a small amount of side bending and rotation to the opposite side. Kapandji[44] gives 3 degrees of side bending to the occipitoatlantal joint and an even smaller amount of rotation to the opposite side.

Transverse Processes and Articular Pillars

The TPs of C2 and of the typical cervical vertebrae are small, placed anteriorly, and in close relation to the seg-

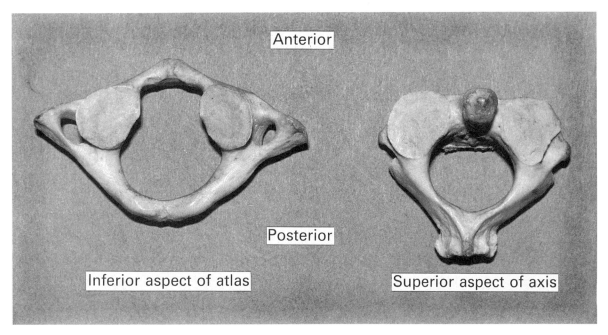

FIGURE 2-11
Left: *Inferior aspect of C2.* Right: *Superior aspect of C1.*

mental nerves and vessels. They are often very tender and are unsuitable as points for palpation. Fortunately, the typical vertebrae have large interarticular pillars or "lateral masses" (see Figure 2-10), which are convenient for the cervical evaluation and treatment techniques to be described in Chapter 11. It is important to recognize that the articular pillars are some distance in front of and lateral to the spinous processes.

Spinous Processes

With the exception of C7, the spinous processes of the cervical vertebrae are usually bifid, often with one side longer than the other, and for this reason they are not reliable indicators of the midline. There is no spinous process at C1, only a small posterior tubercle that is very difficult to feel. The spinous process of C2 is long and easily felt, but the remaining vertebrae down to C7 are covered by the nuchal ligament and may not be easy to feel accurately. The spinous process of C2 may be used as a landmark in the upper neck and that of C7 at the lower end. The spinous process of C7 is often, but not always, the most prominent. When there is doubt about which spinous process is C7, one method of ascertaining its location is described in Chapter 3 in the section Segmental Definition.

FIGURE 2-12

Mechanism of vertical translation at C1-2. (e = the degree of vertical translation downward associated with either left or right rotational movements; L = left; R = right; Rot. = rotation.) (Reproduced from IA Kapandji. The Physiology of the Joints [Vol 3]. London: Churchill Livingstone, 1974;179.)

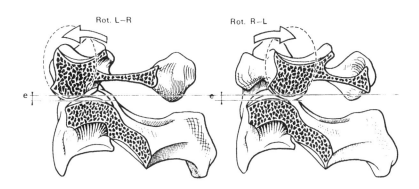

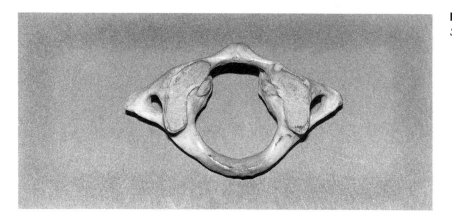

FIGURE 2-13
Shape of superior facets C1.

INTERVERTEBRAL DISC

The intervertebral disc consists of three components: a vertebral end plate that articulates with the vertebra above and the one below, a nucleus pulposus, and the surrounding annulus fibrosis. The vertebral end plates are sometimes considered part of the vertebral body and are composed of cartilage. They are surrounded on all sides by the ring apophyses of the vertebrae so that they cover the nucleus completely but cover only part of the annulus. The layer next to the bone is hyaline cartilage, but the layer next to the nucleus is fibrous. The fibers of the inner layers of the annulus turn centrally when they reach the end plate and continue across to the other side so that they completely surround the nucleus.

The nucleus is a remnant of the notochord and is semi-fluid with a few cartilage cells and irregular collagen fibrils.[3,45] The annulus consists of 10 to 20 lamellae. The fibers in each lamella are parallel to each other, with directional changes in alternate lamellae so that the fibers of one are set at an angle of approximately 130 to 140 degrees to each other, the third having the same orientation as the first. The fibers of the outer lamellae are inserted into bone in the area of the ring apophysis. The thickness of individual laminal layers increases with age, and the posterolateral layers of the annulus have been found to contain more incomplete layers and less symmetry than in other locations.[46]

Buckwalter[47] has reviewed the questions of how the disc gets its nutrition and how it regenerates. It is known that there is no major arterial supply to the disc except to the outermost layers of the annulus. Diffusion is thought to be the most important method for the delivery of nutrients and oxygen and for the removal of waste. The theory that normal intrasegmental motion aids diffusion by squeezing out fluid, which then is regained by osmotic imbibition, is an attractive one.[48,49] Colloidal proteoglycans within a collagen matrix attract

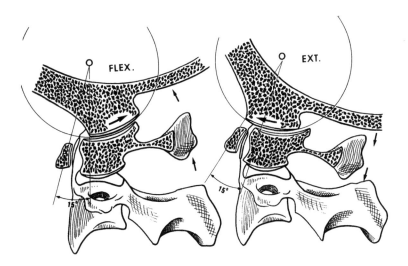

FIGURE 2-14
Flexion and extension at occipitoatlantal joint. (EXT. = extension; FLEX. = flexion.) (Reproduced from IA Kapandji. The Physiology of the Joints [Vol 3]. London: Churchill Livingstone, 1974;177.)

and hold fluids with an inherent imbibition pressure. In the intervertebral disc, this tendency is balanced by the action of hydraulic pressure trying to squeeze out fluid from the disc substance. When the disc imbibes fluid, its size increases, the fibers of the fibrocartilaginous annulus become taut, and, even if there is neither superincumbent weight nor muscle action, the imbibition process reaches a point of equilibrium. This is because of the hydrostatic pressure exerted on the disc substance by the end plates of the vertebral bodies above and below and the fibrocartilage of the annulus around the sides. That the process of imbibition could continue if the disc were not contained is shown by the fact that when a horizontal section is made through a normal disc and the cut surface is then immersed in saline, the nuclear material swells and rises above the level of the surrounding annulus. When the patient sits down or bends forward, the hydrostatic pressure increases on the disc nucleus (Nachemson and Morris[50]), and it is probable that this increased pressure squeezes fluid out through the foramina in the vertebral end plate into the cancellous bone of the vertebral body. The rich blood supply of this bone is well equipped to remove metabolites and supply nutrients to the tissue fluid. When the posture is changed to one in which the hydraulic pressure is lower, a fresh supply of fluid-containing nutrients is sucked back into the disc by the imbibition pressure.

If this is a correct explanation of the process of disc nutrition, it is but a small step to assume that the function of this imbibition pump is dependent on the mobility of the intervertebral joint at that level. When one considers the structure of the intervertebral joint as a whole and the pressure to which the discs are subjected, it is probably unreasonable to say that the loss of movement would be so complete as to prevent the pump from working at all. On the other hand, it seems certain that the efficiency of such a pump would be interfered with by stiffness to the degree that a loss of vertebral movement is detectable on x-ray examination with standing flexion and extension films. T2-weighted magnetic resonance images (MRI) at the L4-5 and L5-S1 levels often show reduced signal intensity, indicating reduced water content or other biochemical alterations[51] that hypothetically occur secondarily to alterations in the nutritional process. These MRI changes seen in the hydration of the disc seem to correlate well with abnormal discograms.[52] The suggestion that the loss of nutrition is partial rather than absolute could be part of the explanation of the delay so often observed between the original injury and the appearance of any sign of a true disc protrusion.[53]

RANGE OF MOTION IN SPINAL JOINTS

Before one can be expected to determine whether a joint is restricted in its motion, knowledge of the expected range is needed. The variation between one person and another is wide, even if one does not include those who, for reasons of profession, hobby, or genetic makeup (e.g., dancers, acrobats, and those with Marfan-like syndromes), have a wider range of motion in their joints than do most people.

Lumbar

Troup[54] used statistical analysis to show that using the radiographic measurement of range of motion by successive superimpositions of individual vertebral outlines was significantly superior to other methods. Radiographic measurement was originally described by Begg and Falconer[55] and was used for the cervical spine by Penning (Table 2-1).

Troup's figures are based on patients needing radiography for clinical purposes. His models all had lumbar symptoms, and it is interesting to see from the tables that his patients had significantly less sagittal plane motion at L4-5 and L5-S1 when compared to the supposedly asymptomatic subjects tested by Froning and Frohman.[56]

Troup's and Froning and Frohman's results are reproduced in Tables 2-2 and 2-3. It is remarkable to note from Froning and Frohman[56] that there is very little loss of motion with advancing age in those who are apparently normal. A somewhat unexpected finding from Troup's figures is that there appears to be a reduction in the range of motion between L1 and L2 when the subject fully extends compared to when the subject assumes the erect, non-extended posture.

TABLE 2-1

Range of Sagittal Motion in the Cervical Spine

Joint	Range in Degrees	Average
CO-1	6–30	—
C1-2	3–35	—
C2-3	5–16	12.5
C3-4	13–26	18
C4-5	15–29	20
C5-6	16–29	21.5
C6-7	6–26	15.5
C7-T1	4–12	8

Source: Reproduced with permission from L Penning. Functional Pathology of the Cervical Spine. Amsterdam: Excerpta Medica, 1968.

TABLE 2-2
Range in Degrees of Sagittal Motion in the Lumbar Spine

	Full Flexion to Extension		Full Flexion to Erect Position	
Joint	*Mean*	*SD*	*Mean*	*SD*
L1-2	7.5	2.3	8.6	1.7
L2-3	10.5	3.4	10.3	3.6
L3-4	11.5	2.8	11.2	2.5
L4-5	12.9	4	12	3.9
L5-S1	11	3.9	9	6.4

SD = standard deviation.
Source: Reproduced with permission from JD Troup. Ph.D. thesis. London: London University, 1968.

Pearcy et al.[57] and Pearcy and Tibrewal[58] have recorded radiographic analysis of motion in apparently normal males. Their results show a remarkable uniformity in the overall range of flexion-extension of approximately 14 degrees (16 at L4-5), but the proportion of flexion to extension varied from 1 degree of extension and 13 degrees of flexion at L3-4 to 5 degrees of extension and only 9 degrees of flexion at L1-2 and L5-S1. The mean figures for rotation were 2 degrees at L1-2, L2-3, and L5-S1 and 3 degrees at L3-4 and L4-5.

In these tests, the rotation was accompanied by lateral bending that was always to the opposite side at L1-2, L2-3, and L3-4 but varied at L4-5, whereas some individuals, possibly with dysfunctional segments, showed rotation to the same side. If side bending occurred during rotation at L5-S1, it was always coupled to the same side as the rotation.

In results in patients with abnormal spines, Froning and Frohman[56] also found that there was a significant increase in the range of neighboring joints adjacent to those showing restriction. Jirout[59] confirmed this.

More important, when viewed cineradiographically, the dynamic motion of the lumbar spine occurs in a stepwise fashion, with flexion beginning at L3-4, followed by L4-5 and L5-S1. The range of motion available between each segment would suggest that, in vivo, the "neutral range" is greater than measured in vitro. Furthermore, in the standing position, motion from neutral to extension occurs primarily at L5-S1.[60]

Thoracic

The anatomy and biomechanics of the thoracic spine have been reviewed by Cropper[61] and include the the in vitro motion analysis described by White and Panjabi's[62] and Lee's[63] clinical observations. In general, thoracic mobility is less than in the neck or the lumbar spine because of the ribs and the effect of the rib attachments on the sternum.[64] Based on these observations, the coupled motion characteristics, which are described later, depend on whether side bending or rotation is introduced first.

There is a limited range of rotation at the lower end of the thoracic spine,[57] especially at T10-11, T11-12, and T12-L1, and there is a striking change in the morphology of this region between the typical thoracic facets and the lumbar type. Davis[65] describes the transitional joint at which most change occurs like a mortise joint that locks in place and further noted that, although this transitional joint is most commonly the T11-12, it may be either T12-L1 or, less commonly, T10-11.

Cervical

Many investigators have examined the range of motion in the cervical joints. One of the difficulties in doing so is that the person must be exposed to radiation for reasons other than clinical requirements. Penning[66] reviewed figures given by several authors (including himself) and describes his method of drawing lines on x-ray films taken of different positions and

TABLE 2-3
Range in Degrees of Sagittal Motion in the Lumbar Spine

Number of Cases	Ages (yrs)	L5-S1	L4-L5	L3-L4	L2-L3	L1-L2
5	20–29	18	17	14	14	13
11	30–39	17	16	14	10	9
8	40–49	16	16	13	10	8
5	50–59	16	15	12	11	7
1	60–70	16	14	10	10	6
	Average	17	16	13	11	9

Source: Reproduced with permission from EC Froning, B Frohman. Motion of the lumbar spine after laminectomy and spine fusion. J Bone Joint Surg 1968;50A:897–918.

superimposed on each other. His figures are reproduced in Table 2-1, and his results are similar to those of others. There is an abrupt change in mobility between C5-6 and C7-T1, as shown in Table 2-1, but the major part of the change is between C5-6 and C6-7. Penning points out that there is difficulty in assessing the range of flexion at the occipitoatlantal joint. A lateral film must be taken with the head flexed on the neck and avoiding full neck flexion, because in full neck flexion, the chin contacts the sternum and causes the occipitoatlantal to extend.

PHYSIOLOGICAL MOVEMENTS OF THE SPINE

Motion between Adjacent Vertebrae

The position and motion of a vertebral body are always described in relation to the adjacent vertebral body immediately below it. *Rotation* is defined as the direction of movement of the anterior surface of the vertebral body. If, for example, a vertebral body rotates to the left, then its left TP will be more posterior than that of the vertebra below it. The interaction between these two vertebrae defines a *vertebral segment*. Movement of the upper vertebral body in relation to the one below it is described as occurring along three possible axes of motion. The motion along each axis is a combination of rotation and translation. Rotation occurs around the axis and translation, a linear movement, occurs parallel to the axis. Movements along these axes are as follows:

1. Flexion or extension occurs as a combination of rotation of the vertebral body forward or backward around a horizontal axis and translatory motion that occurs parallel to the anterior-posterior axis (i.e., with flexion, the superior vertebra translates anteriorly, and with extension, it translates posteriorly) (Figure 2-15).
2. Rotation occurs to the left or right around a vertical axis with a corresponding translatory glide in a caudal direction, parallel to the vertical axis, narrowing the space between vertebrae with rotation and separating with derotation (Figure 2-16).
3. Side bending occurs with a rotational motion to the right or left around an anterior-posterior axis along with a translatory gliding motion, parallel to the transverse plane. For example, with left side bending, the superior vertebra translates to the left, and with right side bending, it translates to the right (Figure 2-17).

Movement of the superior vertebra in relation to the inferior vertebra results in a change in the position of

NEUTRAL POSITION

**FLEXION
FACETS OPEN**

A

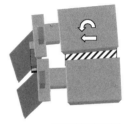

**EXTENSION
FACETS CLOSE**

B

FIGURE 2-15
(A) Flexion of superior vertebra on inferior vertebra, by combined anterior rotation and translation, and facets open. (B) Extension of superior vertebra on inferior vertebra by combined posterior rotation and translation, and facets close. Curved arrows indicate the rotational movements and straight arrows indicate the translatory movements of the vertebral body.

the inferior facet of the superior vertebra relative to the superior facet of the inferior vertebra:

1. During flexion, the inferior facets of the superior vertebra glide anteriorly and superiorly over the superior facets of the inferior vertebra, and the zygapophyseal joints "open" (see Figure 2-15A).
2. During extension, the inferior facets of the superior vertebra glide posteriorly and inferiorly over the superior facets of the inferior vertebra, and the zygapophyseal joints "close" (see Figure 2-15B).
3. During left side bending, the left zygapophyseal joint closes and the right zygapophyseal joint opens (see Figure 2-17B).
4. During right side bending, the right zygapophyseal joint closes and the left zygapophyseal joint opens (see Figure 2-17A).
5. There is a free range of motion available at each zygapophyseal joint between opening and closing in which the ligamentous tension and facet opposition are minimal. This range of motion denotes the "neutral zone."

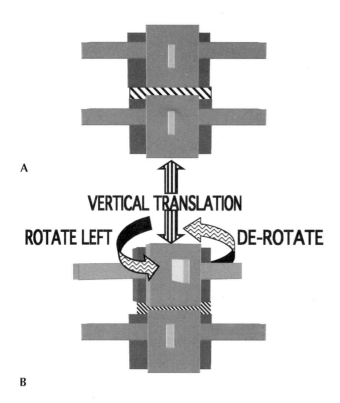

FIGURE 2-16
(A) Neutral position between superior and inferior vertebra. (B) Vertical downward translatory motion when the superior vertebra rotates left in relation to inferior vertebra. With de-rotation back to (A), there is an upward vertical translatory motion. Arrows indicate the vertical translation bringing the two vertebrae closer together with left or right rotation and returning to their original positions with de-rotation.

Coupling of Rotation and Side Bending

The first recorded observation of the coupling of rotation and side bending in the spine was by Lovett[67] while he analyzed scoliosis. He found that, when an intact spine was side bent from the neutral or flexed position, the vertebrae rotated to the side opposite the side bend, as if trying to escape from under a load. If the spine was in extension when side bent, the bodies rotated toward the same side as the side bending. In looking for an explanation, Lovett found that, if a column of vertebral bodies were separated from its posterior elements, during side bending the bodies would rotate toward the side of the convexity of the side bend. He found, however, that the column of posterior elements always rotated toward the same side as the side bending. Lovett further recorded his observation that, in extension, the facets were in close apposition but that this did not occur in flexion. He concluded that, in extension, the facets "con-

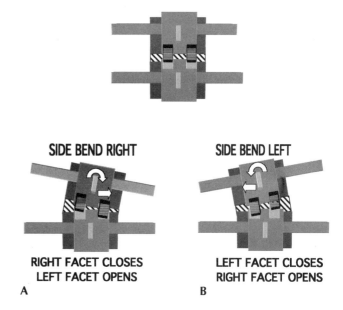

FIGURE 2-17
(A) Superior vertebra side bends to the right in relation to the inferior vertebra as a combination of right lateral rotation and translation to the right. With this motion, the right facet closes and the left facet opens. (B) Superior vertebra side bends to the left in relation to the inferior vertebra as a combination of left lateral rotation and translation to the left. With this motion, the left facet closes and the right facet opens. Curved arrows indicate the rotational movements and straight arrows indicate the translatory movements of the vertebral body.

trol" the movement; in flexion, the vertebral bodies were not constrained in that manner.

Kapandji[68] describes automatic rotation of the intact vertebral column but does not mention the changes that occur if the spine is flexed or extended.

Fryette[6] confirms Lovett's observations but shows that Lovett had not tested the movement in the hyper-flexed position. He found that, near the limit of flexion, the coupling pattern again follows the facet pattern due to ligamentous tension and the rotation that occurs toward the same side as the side bending. He proposed two concepts, which he termed "laws," of spinal motion arising from these observations, and, for completeness, a third law was later added. These concepts are widely accepted, but there has been a recent change of opinion about the application of these laws to the lumbar spine.

Fryette's concepts are as follows:

I. With the spine in easy normal (neutral), the facets are "idling" and not engaged and rotation is always coupled to the opposite direction of side bending (toward the convexity) (Figure 2-18*A*).

II. In extension and in nearly full flexion, when the zygapophyseal joints between two vertebrae are engaged either by contact (closed) or by ligamentous tension (open), the rotation between them is coupled to the same direction of side bending (toward the concavity) (Figure 2-18*B*).

III. If movement is introduced into a spinal segment in any plane, the range of motion in the other two planes will be reduced.

The coupled motion described by the first concept throughout the thoracic and lumbar spine was initially discussed by Lovett.[69] It also appears that the lumbar spine cannot rotate as an isolated motion without an associated coupled side bending.[70,71]

Clinically, the second concept appears to occur only one segment at a time between two adjacent vertebrae. The neutral range for flexion and extension will vary between segments with an expanded range for extension in the lumbar spine due to the lordosis and an expanded range for flexion in the thoracic spine below the apex of the kyphosis. With increasing flexion and extension, there is a "rippling" effect between vertebrae so that only the segment at the apex of the curve for flexion or extension has escaped the neutral zone, and non-neutral mechanics are demonstrable at the apex of the side bending (see Figure 2-18*B*). As the flexion or extension motion increases along the spine, the apex of the curve moves, and the segment, which was non-neutral, again becomes neutral; the new apex for flexion or extension and side bending behaves with non-neutral mechanics. This observation has recently been supported by an analysis of the firing pattern of the paraspinal muscles by myoelectric recordings during flexion and extension of the lumbar spine.[72] In the thoracic spine, because of the anatomy of the zygapophyseal joints and the effect of the rib cage, segmental non-neutral coupling mechanics can be achieved only if rotation is introduced first; if side bending occurs first, rotation is coupled to the opposite side.[62]

When the spine is flexed forward and side bending of the spine is introduced, one can often observe adaptive neutral mechanics with side bending and rotation coupled in the opposite direction both above and below the apex of spinal flexion (the non-neutral segment) (see Figure 2-18*B*).

One of the points of clinical significance arising from these observations is that in moving from flexion to extension or vice versa, the apex of motion is in danger of a strain or sprain, which can result in this segment remaining fixed in the non-neutral position.

In the cervical spine, the picture is different. The second concept always applies to the typical cervical

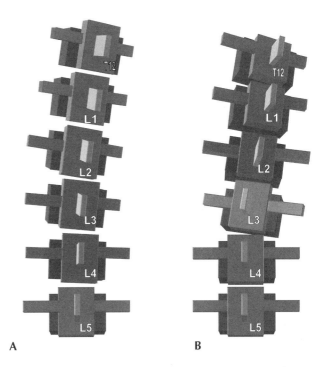

FIGURE 2-18

(A) When the spine is in the neutral position and the intervertebral facets are in the mid range of motion, side bending is coupled with rotation in the opposite direction. In this example, all of the lumbar vertebrae are side bent to the right and rotated to the left. (B) When the spine is flexed or extended beyond the neutral range, side bending is coupled with rotation in the same direction. For example, with lumbar flexion and right side bending, only the facet joints at the apex of the forward bending and side bending curve between L3 and L4 have moved beyond the neutral range. The facet joints between the upper vertebrae L1, L2, and T12 remain within their neutral ranges, so when the lumbar spine side bends to the right, these segments follow the side-bending curve and may continue to demonstrate neutral coupling behavior by rotating to the left.

joints. Consequently, there is no "neutral" zone, and all coupled motion from C2 to C7 is to the same side. At the atlantoaxial joint, the motion is almost all rotatory, and the concepts do not apply. At the occipitoatlantal joint, the facets are set at such an angle to each other that what little side bend there is must always be accompanied by an even smaller amount of rotation to the opposite side. This should not be confused with the "free" neutral (concept I) motion found in the spine in the thoracic and lumbar regions.

Concept III is important for both examination and treatment. During the examination, if the patient inadvertently slumps, the remaining range of motion is limited, because some of the available movement is reduced by the slumped posture. This is of particular importance when motion in the thoracic spine is examined in the sitting position. Nearly all patients tend to slump, and, if they are allowed to, the overall range may be so reduced that specific segmental restrictions are not detected. The instruction must be to "sit up tall" or some similar instruction. The third concept is also useful when positioning a patient to localize treatment to a precise level. Because movement in one direction reduces motion in all other directions, introducing flexion or extension to a segmental level limits the available range left for side bending and rotation. Also, restoration of a restricted movement in one plane of motion increases the motion available in the other directions as well. The details of this application are given in the descriptions of the various techniques.

NATURE OF THE RESTRICTION

There has been extensive research into the detailed anatomy of the facet joints, some of which was referred to in previous editions.[73-77] The precise cause, or probable causes, of joint restriction remains complex and open to debate. That there is palpable tissue texture change at the level of any dysfunction in the spine indicates that the soft tissues are closely involved in whatever is the cause. The disappearance of symptoms and tissue texture changes that sometimes immediately follows restoration of joint motion suggests that soft tissues—including skin, muscle, tendon, ligament, fascia, joint capsule, vascular, and neural elements—are involved in maintenance of a dysfunction. For example, when in the course of a treatment a muscle lengthens after postisometric relaxation, sometimes the joint suddenly lets go with a palpable (and often audible) movement. The concept of the interplay between soft tissue and joint function then is more apparent.

The most consistent findings with joint dysfunction are restriction of motion, asymmetry of position, and tissue texture changes, usually including hypertonus in muscle and other soft tissues. In some areas, tissue changes may be difficult to feel, especially in the pelvis. In other areas, positional bony asymmetry may be so common that it is of little value. Because no one has found a convincing mechanical basis for joint restriction that can be instantly relieved by treatment, the question comes back to soft tissues. The immediate nature of the release that often happens in treatment might be likened to the release of a locked knee and thought to be due to entrapment of a damaged intra-articular meniscoid, but

research to confirm the theory is lacking. This immediate release strongly suggests that there is no structural change in the muscle or other soft tissues. The most likely answer appears to be a change in the efferent bias, by which the central nervous system controls muscle tone[78] (see Chapter 6).

TYPES OF SPINAL JOINT DYSFUNCTION

According to the first two of Fryette's concepts, two different types of dysfunctions may occur in the spine. Type I (neutral) dysfunctions occur when three or more segments are held in a curve and rotated opposite of the concavity or side-bent position. The dysfunction often occurs as an adaptive response when neutral mechanics are operative, and it is maintained by restrictors that are multisegmental. This dysfunction is maximally evident in the neutral position and improves, but does not resolve, with either flexion or extension of the spine through this region. The persistence of a physiological neutral mechanical response is now a pathophysiological dysfunction. Many neutral dysfunctions resolve, apparently spontaneously when the cause requiring this compensatory curve is removed. For this reason, they are secondary in priority for treatment.

The second and more important type of dysfunction is based on a persistence of type II (non-neutral) mechanics and thereby classified as a non-neutral dysfunction. These dysfunctions are nearly always traumatic in origin and occur at a segment between two vertebrae when one vertebra is either flexed or extended in relation to the adjacent vertebra below it. Clinically, the superior vertebra may remain flexed with a demonstrable restriction for extension, or remain extended, with a demonstrable restriction for flexion. If the traumatic event occurs while the superior vertebra is also side bent and rotated to the same side, then the restriction to extension or flexion is unilateral, restricting the range of motion of only one facet joint between these two vertebrae (Figure 2-19). These dysfunctions are frequently tender and pain-provoking. When either flexion or extension of the spine is introduced during the examination process, the appearance of the vertebrae above the non-neutral dysfunction should follow the position of the superior vertebra of the dysfunctional segment. For example, if L3 is rotated and side bent right in relation to L4 when the spine is flexed, then all the vertebrae above L3 should appear rotated and side bent to the right to the same degree. This is true only if there

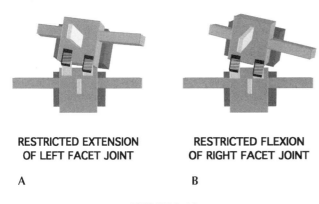

RESTRICTED EXTENSION OF LEFT FACET JOINT

A

RESTRICTED FLEXION OF RIGHT FACET JOINT

B

FIGURE 2-19

(A) An example of a non-neutral dysfunction with the superior vertebra unable to extend at the left facet in relation to the one below and becoming side-bent right and rotated right when extension is introduced. (B) An example of a non-neutral dysfunction with the superior vertebra unable to flex at the right facet in relation to the one below and becoming side-bent right and rotated right when flexion is introduced.

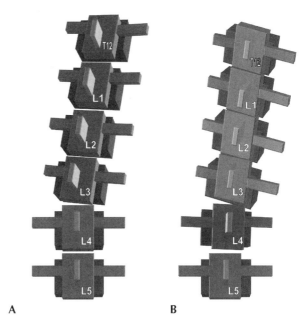

A   **B**

FIGURE 2-20

Diagrams showing the response of the superior vertebrae above a non-neutral dysfunction at L3-4, (A) when the spine is flexed, and (B) when the spine is extended.

are no other restrictions for flexion in the segments above L3. The appearance of the spine is very much like a stepladder that has been rotated and tilted to one side at the base; the top of the ladder is rotated and tilted to the same degree as the bottom of the ladder (Figure 2-20). This positional appearance of the vertebrae is much different from the neutral adaptive response seen when the spine is in the neutral position (prone, sitting, or standing) and is free to rotate and side bend to adapt to any unlevelling of the spine from below. It must be remembered that when the spine is flexed or extended in the sagittal plane, the movement occurs through the symmetrical opening and closing of the facet joints, provided that motion is equally available on both the right and left sides. Therefore, any rotation of the TPs seen in either flexion or extension of the spine represents the inability of the facet joints to open or close symmetrically and indicates that dysfunctional mechanics are probably operative somewhere in the spine or pelvis.

In most instances, non-neutral dysfunctions are single (in a directional sense) within any joint, but sometimes one finds that both flexion and extension are limited in the same joint or that the joint may have restriction on both sides. These individual dysfunctions need individual treatment, but they may occur as multiple dysfunctions stacked one on another. This makes a precise diagnosis more difficult. However, it is emphasized that the position of a vertebra is always assessed with refer-

ence to the one below it, with the comparison seeking to answer this diagnostic question: Is the vertebra above in the same position or in a different position than the one below it? If there is a difference between these two vertebrae, it is the position of the superior vertebra that is diagnostically relevant.

Although both neutral (type I) and non-neutral (type II) dysfunctions can occur in the thoracic and lumbar regions, the picture in the cervical spine is not the same. In typical cervical joints, there is only non-neutral (type II) motion, and therefore all dysfunctions are of the non-neutral variety. At the atlantoaxial joint, the dysfunction is in rotation only, and at the occipitoatlantal joint, there is a small amount of rotation in the opposite direction to the side bending. The occipitoatlantal joint, however, is unique, and its mechanics are not the same as in the thoracic and lumbar neutral (type I) group.

INNERVATION OF THE INTERVERTEBRAL JOINTS

Pedersen et al.[79] and Wyke[80,81] have described the innervation of the intervertebral joints. Wyke's findings are essentially similar to Pedersen's, but he describes the innervation as follows:

1. Branches of the posterior primary rami supplying the zygapophyseal joints, the periosteum and the related fasciae of the surfaces of the vertebral bodies and their arches, the interspinous ligaments, and the blood vessels
2. Pain afferents in the sinuvertebral nerves having endings in the posterior longitudinal and flaval ligaments, the dura mater and the surrounding fatty tissue, the epidural veins, and the periosteum of the spinal canal
3. A plexus of nerve fibers surrounding the paravertebral venous system

Wyke reports that receptors supplied by these nerves are found in the same area as those supplied by the sinuvertebral nerve. All the pain afferent fibers are small and either thinly or not at all myelinated.

Wyke makes many interesting observations, which later were supported in a comprehensive review by Willard,[82] showing that nociceptor afferent innervation of dermatomes is not unisegmental. The sinuvertebral nerves have branches that extend over at least four segments and may cross the midline. The innervation in the lumbar region may have contributions from branches from three to five dorsal nerve roots. No joint in the lumbar region has monosegmental innervation.

AUTONOMIC NERVOUS SYSTEM

Knowledge of the anatomy of the autonomic nervous system is important in manual medicine partly because of the frequent involvement of spinal musculature as a secondary effect of visceral disease (viscero-somatic reflexes).

Barnes[83] concluded that it is unlikely that pain actually travels in sympathetic afferent fibers—an assertion made on the following grounds:

1. No sensory change of any kind has ever been demonstrated in a sympathectomized limb.
2. In cord lesions, in which the cord is damaged below the lowest sympathetic outflow, the sympathetic innervation of the lower limbs is intact, but there is a total insensibility of the area supplied by somatic nerves arising in segments below the damage.
3. A low spinal anesthetic relieves the pain of causalgia before there is any effect on the sympathetic fibers.

The concepts regarding "reflex sympathetic dystrophy" have been challenged and have resulted in a reclassification of regional pain syndromes.[84] Focal somatic representations of spinal dysfunctions include increased sweating and coolness of the overlying tissues. This certainly must reflect increased sympathetic activity as a participant of a segmentally localized and altered efferent response to these dysfunctions and, as such, is not a cause but a consequence of this situation.

Table 2-4, based on Mitchell's[85] findings, summarizes his description of the anatomy of the sympathetic system. He states that the afferent pain fibers from the cervix uteri, the base of the bladder, the prostate, and the rectum are carried in the pelvic splanchnic nerves with cell bodies located in the dorsal root ganglia of the second, third, and fourth sacral nerves.

TABLE 2-4
Sympathetic Innervation of More Important Structures

Structure	Location of Pre-Ganglionic Cells	Chief Efferent Pathways
Eyes	T1-2	Internal carotid plexus to ciliary nerves or along vessels
Vessels of head	T1-2 (and 3)	Vascular plexuses
Upper limbs	T2(3) to T6(7)	Rami communicates to roots of brachial plexus
Heart	T1-4(5)	Cardiac sympathetic nerves to cardiac plexus
Stomach	T6-9(10)	Via celiac plexus
Kidneys	T12(11) to L1(2)	Via celiac plexus
Bladder and uterus	T12(11) to L1(2)	Lumbar splanchnic nerves
Lower limbs	T11(10) to L2	Rami communicates to lumbar and sacral nerves

Source: Adapted from G Mitchell. The Anatomy of the Autonomic Nervous System. Edinburgh, UK: Livingstone, 1963.

The diagram of the autonomic nervous system (Figure 2-21) shows how the various parts of the body are innervated. It is included because it shows the fundamental difference between the innervation of the soma and that of the organ systems. The internal organs have innervation from both parts of the autonomic system, but the soma only receive sympathetic fibers, even for the skin viscera.

The sympathetic chain ganglia, which contain many cell stations for that part of the autonomic system, are in close anatomical relation to the sides of vertebral bodies and the costovertebral joints. This introduces the possibility that any edema or inflammatory reaction around those joints could affect the function of the ganglia.

SENSORY DISTRIBUTION OF THE SPINAL NERVE ROOTS

It has been known since 1893 that the distribution of sensory fibers to the skin from the various spinal nerve roots does not correspond to the distribution of any of the cutaneous nerves, except over the trunk, where the correspondence is fair. Head[86] observed the distribution of the cutaneous hyperalgesia and the vesicles in cases of herpes zoster. His results allowed him to draw a map showing the distribution of the various spinal nerves to the skin, and he also drew a chart of the points at which the sensation appeared to be maximal from each nerve. His charts were reproduced in the fourth and earlier editions. In 1893, Sherrington,[87] working with experimental nerve sectioning in the rhesus monkey, drew a similar chart. There was some difference in the lumbar and sacral nerves, possibly because the rhesus monkey has a different configuration of the lumbar spine. Sherrington found significant overlap of neighboring areas, whereas Head's were discrete. Both Head's and Sherrington's results appeared to show a gap in innervation of some of the nerves in the proximal part of the limbs. The concept (the loop theory) that the growing limb bud drew away all the fibers to the periphery has not been confirmed by subsequent researchers, but the general distribution is considered to be very similar to that described by Head and Sherrington.

Keegan and Garrett,[88] using data from patients with sensory nerve damage from disc protrusion, showed a similar chart, although it differed in some details (Figure 2-22). They were also able to demonstrate a fainter overlap distribution, often extending 2.5–5.0 cm (1–2 in.) on either side of the main distribution.

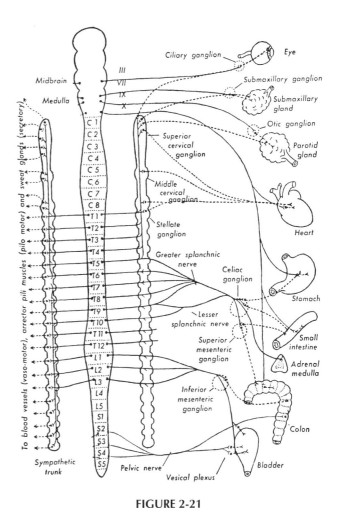

FIGURE 2-21

Autonomic nervous system. (Adapted from RC Truex, MB Carpenter. Human Neuroanatomy. Baltimore: Williams & Wilkins, 1969.)

This may well explain the difference between Head's and Sherrington's charts. Sutherland[89] provided a chart for the anterior distribution that is similar to Keegan's and Garrett's. He does not show a posterior chart, but he does say that the dorsal root of T12 "descends through muscle to pierce the lumbo-dorsal fascia . . . to innervate the skin of the buttock as far down as the greater trochanter." This is shown by Head, but not by Keegan. Clinically, there appears to be evidence that the T11 dorsal ramus also has a distribution in the buttock.

Although it may be helpful to recognize the distribution of sensory fibers from each level, it must be remembered that referred pain does not always follow anatomical nerve pathways.

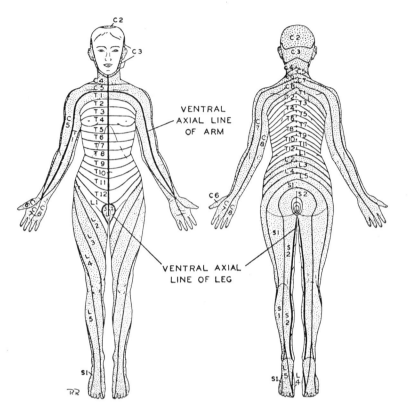

FIGURE 2-22
Dermatome chart of the human body. (Reproduced from JJ Keegan, FD Garrett. Segmental sensory nerve distribution. Anat Rec 1948;102:409–437.)

REFERENCES

1. Mixter WJ, Barr JS. Rupture of the intervertebral disc. N Engl J Med 1934;211:210–215.

2. Armstrong JR. Lumbar Disc Lesions (3rd ed). London: Livingstone, 1965.

3. Bogduk N, Twomey L. Clinical Anatomy of the Lumbar Spine. London: Churchill Livingstone, 1987.

4. Vleeming A, Mooney V, Snijders CJ, Dorman T, Stoekart R (eds). Movement, Stability and Low Back Pain: The Essential Role of the Pelvis. New York: Churchill Livingstone, 1997.

5. Kapandji IA. The Physiology of the Joints (Vol 3). London: Churchill Livingstone, 1974;70.

6. Fryette HH. The Principles of Osteopathic Technique. Carmel, CA: Academy of Applied Osteopathy, 1954.

7. Vleeming A, Stoeckart R, Volkers ACW, Snijders CJ. Relation between form and function in the sacro-iliac joint, part I. Clinical anatomical aspects. Spine 1990;15:130–132.

8. Bowen V, Cassidy JD. Macroscopic and microscopic anatomy of the sacroiliac joint until the eighth decade. Spine 1981;6:620–628.

9. Bernard TN, Cassidy JD. The Sacroiliac Syndrome: Pathophysiology, Diagnosis, and Management. In: JW Frymoyer (ed). The Adult Spine, Principles and Practice. New York: Raven Press, 1991;2107–2130.

10. Vleeming A, Stoeckart R, Snijders CJ. The sacrotuberous ligament: a conceptual approach to its dynamic role in stabilizing the sacroiliac joint. Clin Biomech 1989;4:201–203.

11. Midttun M, Midttun A, Bojsen-Møller F. The N. Cutaneous Perforans S2-S3 [Abstract]. In: Laboratory for Functional Anatomy. Copenhagen: University of Copenhagen Activity Report, 1989.

12. Brooke R. The sacro-iliac joint. J Anat 1934;58:299–305.

13. Weisl H. Movement of the sacroiliac joint. Acta Anat 1955;23:80–91.

14. Pitkin HC, Pheasant HC. Sacrarthrogenic telalgia. J Bone Joint Surg 1936;18:111–133, 365–374.

15. Vleeming A, Snijders CJ, Stoeckart R, Mens JMA. A New Light on Low Back Pain: The Self-Locking Mechanism of the Sacroiliac Joints and Its Implications for Sitting, Standing and Walking. In: A Vleeming, et al. (eds). Second Interdisciplinary World Congress on Low Back Pain: The Integrated Function of the Lumbar Spine and Sacroiliac Joints. November 9–11,1995; San Diego, CA.

16. Vleeming A, Stoeckart R, Snijders CJ, van Wingerden J-P, Dijkstra PF. The sacroiliac joint, anatomical, biomechanical and radiological aspects. J Man Med 1990;5:100–102.

17. Greenman PE. Clinical Aspects of the Sacroiliac Joint in Walking. In: A Vleeming, V Mooney, CJ Snijders, T Dorman, R Stoeckart (eds). Movement, Stability and Low Back Pain: The Essential Role of the Pelvis. New York: Churchill Livingstone, 1997;235–242.

18. Chamberlain WE. The symphysis pubis in the roentgen

examination of the sacroiliac joint. Am J Roentgenol 1930;24:621.

19. Dihlmann W. Diagnostic Radiology of the Sacroiliac Joint. Chicago: Yearbook Medical Publishers, 1980.

20. Kapandji IA. The Physiology of the Joints (Vol 3). London: Churchill Livingstone, 1974;64.

21. Mitchell FL. The balanced pelvis and its relationship to reflexes. Yearbook, Amer Acad Appl Osteop 1948;48: 146–151.

22. Vleeming A, van Wingerden JP, Snijders CJ, Stoeckart R, Stijnen T. Load application to the sacrotuberous ligament: influences on sacroiliac joint mechanics. Clin Biomech 1989;4:204–209.

23. Levin SM. A Different Approach to the Mechanics of the Human Pelvis: Tensegrity. In: A Vleeming, V Mooney, CJ Snijders, T Dorman, R Stoeckart (eds). Movement, Stability and Low Back Pain: The Essential Role of the Pelvis. New York: Churchill Livingstone, 1997;157–167.

24. Pool-Goudzward AL, Vleeming A, Stoeckart R, Snijders CJ, Mens JMA. Insufficient lumbopelvic stability: a clinical, anatomical and biomechanical approach to 'a-specific' low back pain. Man Ther 1998;3(1):12–20.

25. Willard FA. The Muscular, Ligamentous and Neural Structure of the Low Back and Its Relation to Back Pain. In: A Vleeming, V Mooney, CJ Snijders, T Dorman, R Stoeckart (eds). Movement, Stability and Low Back Pain: The Essential Role of the Pelvis. New York: Churchill Livingstone, 1997;3–35.

26. Mooney V, Pozos R, Vleeming A, Gulick J, Swenski D. Coupled Motion of Contralateral Latissimus Dorsi and Gluteus Maximus: Its Role in Sacroiliac Stabilization. In: A Vleeming, V Mooney, CJ Snijders, T Dorman, R Stoeckart (eds). Movement, Stability and Low Back Pain: The Essential Role of the Pelvis. New York: Churchill Livingstone, 1997;115–122.

27. Grant's Method of Anatomy (7th ed). Baltimore: Williams & Wilkins, 1965.

28. Gray's Anatomy (22nd English ed). London: Longmans Green, 1930;460.

29. Hides JA, Stokes MJ, Saide M, Jull GA. Evidence of lumbar multifidus muscle wasting ipsilateral to symptoms in patients with acute/subacute low back pain. Spine 1994;19:165–172.

30. Hides JA, Richardson CA, Jull GA. Multifidus muscle recovery is not automatic after resolution of acute first episode low back pain. Spine 1996;21:2763–2769.

31. Guntzburg R, Hutton. W, Fraser R. Axial rotation of the lumbar spine and the effect of flexion. Spine 1991;16:22–28.

32. Cossette JW, Farfan HF, Robertson GH, Wells RV. The instantaneous center of rotation of the third lumbar intervertebral joint. J Biomech 1971;4:149–153.

33. Farfan H, Sullivan JD. The relation of facet orientation to intervertebral disc failure. Can J Surg 1967;10:179–185.

34. Ahmed AM, Duncan NA. The effect of facet geometry on the axial torque-rotation response of lumbar motion segments. Spine 1990;15:391–401.

35. Vanharanta H, Floyd T, Ohnmeiss DD, Hochschuler SH, Guyer RD. The relationship of facet tropism to degenerative disc disease. Spine 1993;18:1000–1005.

36. Ishihara H, Matsui H, Osada R, Oshima H, Tsuji H. Facet joint asymmetry as a radiologic feature of lumbar intervertebral disc herniation in children and adolescents. Spine 1997;22:2001–2004.

37. Farfan HF. The effects of torsion on the lumbar intervertebral joints. J Bone Joint Surg 1970;52a:468–497.

38. Farfan HF, Sullivan JD. The relation of facet orientation to intervertebral disc failure. Can J Surg 1967;10:179–185.

39. Ravin T. Visualization of Pelvic Biomechanical Dysfunction. In: A Vleeming, V Mooney, CJ Snijders, T Dorman, R Stoeckart (eds). Movement, Stability and Low Back Pain: The Essential Role of the Pelvis. New York: Churchill Livingstone, 1997;372.

40. Maigne R. Sur L'origine Dorsale de la Plupart des Douleurs Lombaires Basses. In: K Lewit, G Gutmann (eds). Functional Pathology of the Motor System. Rehabilitácia 1975;(suppl 10–11):72–75.

41. Lee R, Farquharson T, Domleo S. Subluxation and locking of the first rib: a cause of thoracic outlet syndrome. Aust Assoc Manual Med Bull 6(2):50–51.

42. Lindgen K-A, Leino E. Subluxation of the first rib: a possible thoracic outlet syndrome mechanism. Arch Phys Med Rehabil 1988;68:692–695.

43. Kapandji IA. The Physiology of the Joints (Vol 3). London: Churchill Livingstone, 1974;174.

44. Kapandji IA. The Physiology of the Joints (Vol 3). London: Churchill Livingstone, 1974;184.

45. Taylor JR. The development and adult structure of lumbar intervertebral discs. J Man Med 1990;5:43–47.

46. Marchand F, Ahmed AM. Investigation of the laminate structure of the lumbar disc annulus fibrosus. Spine 1990;15:402–410.

47. Buckwalter JA. Aging and degeneration of the human intervertebral disc. Spine 1995;20:1307–1314.

48. Hendry NGC. The hydration of the nucleus pulposus. J Bone Joint Surg 1958;40B:132–144.

49. Sylven B. On the biology of the nucleus pulposus. Acta Orthop Scand 1951;20:275–279.

50. Nachemson A, Morris JH. In vivo measurements of intradiscal pressure. J Bone Joint Surg 1964;46a:1077–1092.

51. Boos N, Boesch C. Imaging corner: quantitative magnetic resonance imaging of the lumbar spine: potential for investigations of water content and biochemical composition. Spine 1995;20:2358–2366.

52. Guyer RD, Ohnmeiss DD. Lumbar discography. Position statement from the North American Spine Society Diagnostic and Therapeutic Committee. Spine 1995;20:2048–2059.

53. Saal JA. Natural history and non-operative treatment of lumbar disc herniation. Spine 1996;21(24 suppl):2S–9S.

54. Troup JD. PhD thesis. London: London University, 1968.

55. Begg C, Falconer MA. Plain radiography in intraspinal protrusions of intervertebral discs. J Bone Joint Surg 1949;36:225.

56. Froning EC, Frohman B. Motion of the lumbar spine

after laminectomy and spine fusion. J Bone Joint Surg 1968;50A:897–918.

57. Pearcy MJ, Portek I, Shepherd J. Three dimensional x-ray analysis of normal movement in the lumbar spine. Spine 1984;9:294–297.

58. Pearcy MJ, Tibrewal SB. Axial rotation and lateral bending in the normal lumbar spine. Spine 1984;9:582–587.

59. Jirout J. Studies in the dynamics of the spine. Excerpta Acta Radiol 1955;46.

60. Kanayama M, Abumi K, Tadano S, Ukai T. Phase lag of the intersegmental motion in flexion-extension of the lumbar and lumbosacral spine. Spine 1996;20:1416–1422.

61. Cropper JR. Regional Anatomy and Biomechanics. In: TA Flynn (ed). The Thoracic Spine and Rib Cage: Musculoskeletal Evaluation and Treatment. Boston: Butterworth-Heinemann, 1996;3–29.

62. White AA, Panjabi MM. Clinical Biomechanics of the Spine. Philadelphia: Lippincott, 1990.

63. Lee D. Biomechanics of the thorax: a clinical model of in vivo function. J Man Manip Ther 1993;1:13–21.

64. Andriacchi T, Schultz A, Belytschko T, et al. A model for studies of mechanical interactions between the human spine and rib cage. J Biomech 1974;7:497–507.

65. Davis PR. The thoraco-lumbar mortice joint. J Anat 1935;89:370–371.

66. Penning L. Functional Pathology of the Cervical Spine. Amsterdam: Excerpta Medica, 1968.

67. Lovett RW. The mechanics of lateral curvature of the spine. Boston M.S.J., 1900;142:622–627.

68. Kapandji IA. The Physiology of the Joints (Vol 3). London: Churchill Livingstone, 1974;42.

69. Lovett RW. The study of the mechanics of the spine. Am J Anat 1902;2:457–462.

70. Stoddard A. Manual of Osteopathic Technique. London: Hutchinson Medical Publications, 1962;73.

71. McFadden KD, Taylor JR. Axial rotation in the lumbar spine and gaping of the zygapophyseal joints. Spine 1990;15:295–299.

72. Kaigle AM, Wessberg P, Hannsson TH. Muscular and kinemantic behavior of the lumbar spine during flexion-extension. J Spinal Disord 1998;11:163–174.

73. Schmincke A, Santo E. Zur normalen und pathologischen Anatomie der Halswirbelsaule. Zbl Path 1932;55:369–372.

74. Santo E. Zur Entwicklungsgeschichte und Histologie der Zwischenscheiben in den kleinen Gelenken. Z Anat Entwicklungsgesch 1935;104:623–634.

75. Tondury G. Beitrag zur Kentniss der kleinen Wirbelgelenke. Z Anat Entwicklungsgesch 1940;110:568–575.

76. Dorr WM. Uber die Anatomie der Wirbelgelenke. Arch Orthop Unfall-Chir 1958;50:222–234.

77. Lewin T, Moffett B, Viidik A. The morphology of the lumbar synovial intervertebral joints. Acta Morphol Neerlando-Scand 1961;4:299–319.

78. Davidoff RA. Skeletal muscle tone and the misunderstood stretch reflex. Neurology 1992;42:951–963.

79. Pedersen HE, Blunk GFJ, Gardner E. Anatomy of lumbosacral posterior rami. J Bone Joint Surg 1956;38A:377–391.

80. Wyke B. The neurological basis of thoracic spinal pain. Rheumatol Phys Med 1970;10:356–366.

81. Wyke B. The Neurology of Low Back Pain. In: M Jayson (ed). The Lumbar Spine and Back Pain (2nd ed). London: Pitman Medical, 1980;265–339.

82. Willard FA. The Muscular, Ligamentous and Neural Structure of the Low Back and Its Relation to Back Pain. In: A Vleeming, V Mooney, CJ Snijders, T Dorman, R Stoeckart (eds). Movement, Stability and Low Back Pain: The Essential Role of the Pelvis. New York: Churchill Livingstone, 1997;22–28.

83. Barnes R. Causalgia in Peripheral Nerve Injuries. In: MRC Special Reports, Series 282. London: HMSO, 1954.

84. Ochoa J. Afferent and Sympathetic Roles in Chronic "Neuropathic" Pains: Confessions on Misconceptions. In: JM Besson, G Guilbaud (eds). Lesions of Primary Afferent Fibers as a Tool for the Study of Clinical Pain. New York: Excerpta Medica, 1991;25–43.

85. Mitchell G. The Anatomy of the Autonomic Nervous System. Edinburgh: Livingstone, 1963.

86. Head H. Disturbances of sensation with special reference to the pain of visceral disease. Brain 1893;16:1–33, 339–480.

87. Sherrington CS. Experiments in the examination of the peripheral distribution of the fibers of the posterior roots of some spinal nerves. Philos Trans R Soc Lond B Biol Sci 1893;B184:641–763; B190:45–187.

88. Keegan JJ, Garrett FD. Segmental sensory nerve distribution. Anat Rec 1948;102:409–437.

89. Sutherland S. Nerves and Nerve Injuries. London: Churchill Livingstone, 1978.

3

Examination: General Considerations

TERMINOLOGY AND NOMENCLATURE

There is a troubling diversity of names for many of the dysfunctions of the pelvic ring. Members of the osteopathic profession have worked out the details that are presented, but even among them there are differences.

The distinction of *sacroiliac* (SI) from *iliosacral* is based on the clinical observation that dysfunctions of the sacrum as it moves between the ilia need different treatment than do dysfunctions in the motion of one innominate on the sacrum. To diagnose SI dysfunction, comparisons are made in regard to the symmetry or asymmetry of motion and position of the sacral base and ILA from one side to the other. To diagnose iliosacral dysfunction, motion and positional tests compare one innominate to the other.

The need for a revision of nomenclature is illustrated by the fact that one sacral position often is referred to in one context as *flexion* and in another context as *extension*. Unfortunately, there are still a number of different names in use for some of the dysfunctions, and for these the original terminology is given in brackets, while the newer terms are used in preference.

To avoid any misunderstanding, the following terms are defined:

1. *Flexion* is used to mean forward tilting of the superior surface of the vertebra.

2. *Extension* means backward tilting of the same surface.

3. *Rotation* of both vertebrae and the sacrum is named according to the side to which the anterior surface faces.

4. *Side bending* is named according to the side to which the superior surface of the vertebra tilts.

5. *Translation* is used to describe motion in a plane, most often referring to the horizontal (transverse) plane with respect to the body in the anatomical position. An anterior-posterior horizontal translatory movement accompanies flexion-extension. Similarly, lateral translation in the horizontal plane accompanies side bending. However, with rotational motion, the accompanying translation is in the vertical plane.

The use of translation to localize sagittal or coronal plane overturning motion is mentioned in many technique descriptions. Figure 3-1 illustrates side bending to the left by lateral rotation (overturning) of the spine from above and moving down to the third vertebra and compares this position to side bending left created by translating the fourth vertebra from left to right under the third vertebra.

6. *Motion of a vertebra*, or of the skull, is described in reference to the structure immediately below. For instance, if L4 is said to be flexed and side bent to the right, the joint involved is that between L4 and L5.

7. *Neutral* refers to the midrange of the available flexion-extension movement between vertebrae. In a neutral range, there is minimal ligamentous tension or facet opposition within the zygapophyseal joint. In most zygapophyseal joints, this neutral zone has a fairly wide range before flexion or extension influences the joint. While still in the neutral range, lumbar and thoracic spinal motion are coupled in a specific way so that side bending in one direction is accompanied by rotation in the opposite direction. Historically, this is also known as *Fryette's type I* motion.

8. *Non-neutral* refers to the range closer to the end of flexion or extension when there is either increased ligamentous tension or facet opposition within the zygapophyseal joints and therefore a decrease in joint

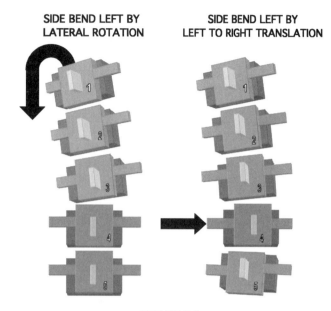

FIGURE 3-1
Side bending to the left by lateral rotation of the spine from above down to the third vertebra over the fourth vertebra compared to side bending to the left by translating the fourth vertebra from left to the right to achieve side bending between the third and fourth vertebra. The curved arrow indicates a rotational movement and the straight arrow denotes a lateral translatory movement.

play. Any additional motion results in movement of the next adjacent vertebrae. When the spine is in its nonneutral range, coupled motion occurs in a specific way, with side bending and rotation in the same direction. Historically, this is also identified as *Fryette's type II* motion.

9. *TP(s)* is used as an abbreviation for the transverse process(es) of the vertebrae.

10. *TrP(s)* refers to myofascial trigger point(s), as defined by Dr. Janet Travell and which are characteristic findings in her description of myofascial pain syndromes (MPS).

11. *TeP* refers to the tender point(s) found in muscle and described in the fibromyalgia syndrome (FMS).

12. *Sulcus* is used for the interval between the medial aspect of the posterior superior iliac spine (PSIS) and the lamina of the first sacral vertebra (sacral base), unless otherwise specifically stated.

13. *Caudad* is of Latin derivation, is in general use, and needs no explanation.

14. *Craniad* is the corresponding term of Latin parentage for the opposite direction. This is used rather than *cephalad*, which means the same but is of Greek derivation.

15. *Nutation* literally means *nodding* and *anterior nutation* is used to describe the forward motion of the sacral base; *posterior nutation* is the backward motion of the sacral base.

16. *Innominate bone* is a long-established term that refers to the hemipelvic structure resulting from the fusion of the ischium, ilium, and pubis.

SOMATIC DYSFUNCTION

Somatic dysfunction was coined by the osteopathic profession and is now widely used for what has had many names in the past: "spinal joint lesions," "an osteopathic lesion," "chiropractic subluxation," and so on. It is also known as the "manipulable lesion." The term has the advantage that it emphasizes the concept of a dysfunction rather than anatomical pathology. This concept, in a broader form, can be conveyed by the term *joint dysfunction* if that is preferred. In Europe, *joint blockage* is the most common term, which also suggests the absence of pathological abnormal anatomy. However, both *joint blockage* and *joint dysfunction* could imply that the fault is primarily of a mechanical nature in the joint—a concept still widely debated. In the United States, *somatic dysfunction* is used as a diagnostic term referenced by a national coding system that fulfills a requirement for management reimbursement by osteopathic manipulative treatment. The term is defined as "Impaired or altered function of related components of the somatic (the body framework) system; Skeletal, arthrodial, and myofascial structure; and the related vascular, lymphatic and neural elements."[1] The all-inclusive nature of the definition is important in reminding us that the human body is a whole, not simply a number of separate systems. Although each separate organ system may need its own specific treatment, the patient is not well until the systems all work together in harmony. Of these systems, the musculoskeletal is the largest, consumes by far the most energy, and is the system through which we communicate and express ourselves. It is strange that the musculoskeletal system has been neglected by orthodox medicine.

The characteristic signs of a somatic dysfunction for which treatment by manipulation may be appropriate are the following:

1. Asymmetry of position
2. Restriction of motion
3. Tissue texture change, primarily hypertonus in muscle

Because it is not possible for a patient to produce asymmetry at will, restrict motion voluntarily at only one spinal joint, or cause tissues to tighten at one individual level, these signs are truly objective. The subjective sign of tenderness may also be useful, but it should not be forgotten that the points to which pain is referred may be as tender as the points of origin of the referred pain. Tenderness is more helpful to the operator as a confirmation of objective findings at the same level. It is also helpful to the patient when, for instance, the point of origin of a referred pain is found in an area about which the patient is not complaining. If it were not for tenderness, some patients might regard the treatment of such primary areas as meddlesome.

In teaching, the acronym *ART* (*a*symmetry, *r*estriction of motion, and *t*issue texture change) is often used (some use *TART*, *t*enderness *ART*). These serve as a reminder of the signs of somatic dysfunction.

Asymmetry is common in the axial skeleton, and structural asymmetry must be distinguished from asymmetry due to dysfunction. This is especially true of the pelvis. Recall that no two SI joints are alike, even in the same patient. Asymmetry of structural origin can be distinguished from asymmetry due to dysfunction by the fact that, although a dysfunctional joint always has some restriction of motion, with structural asymmetry the joint has normal mobility when passively tested.

Restriction of motion is often a consequence of joint injury. This happens in spinal as well as peripheral joints and, if untreated, may be persistent. Stiff joints are not necessarily painful, but in the event of further injury or strain, they may easily become so. In the spine, there are other factors that can cause silent dysfunctional joints to become painful, and it seems that increased muscle tension, even from emotional stress, is one of these factors. Stiff joints around which there is no detectable tissue texture change are probably not often the immediate cause of symptoms, but treatment may be important in the management of the patient. This is because restrictive segmental motion at any spinal level tends to cause appropriate postural adaptations at other levels that may also become dysfunctional.

In the presence of an old injury with degenerative changes that have altered the anatomy, it may be impossible to restore normal range of motion. For the relief of symptoms, however, it is usually enough to restore some motion and, as much as possible, correct the asymmetry. If this is done, the tissue texture abnormality will usually lessen. In this context, it is important to address asymmetry of muscle length and strength, as well as joint motion, to maintain restored function (see Chapter 14).

It is appropriate, at this point, to emphasize that manipulative treatment is not dealing with disloca-

tions; there is not "a little bone out of place," nor is it designed to reduce a "slipped disc." Some of the pelvic and rib dysfunctions do involve unphysiological movements and can therefore be described as subluxations, but, in the large majority of dysfunctional spinal joints, the problem is a loss of mobility for normal range of motion.

There are a number of different tissue texture changes, some or all of which may be present at a dysfunctional level. One of the most important of these is a localized hypertonicity in muscle at that joint. This is most significantly found in the fourth (deepest) layer muscles close to the laminae and transverse processes (TPs). The fourth layer muscles are quite small; they can only be felt when they are hypertonic; and, of importance when using muscle energy treatment, the force that they can generate is also small. There are other palpable changes that can be helpful in localizing the dysfunction, and some of these appear to be due to altered tone in the autonomic nervous system, including

1. Localized skin changes, such as "skin drag," probably due to increased water content in the epidermis
2. Changes in the skin and subcutaneous tissues leading to a positive skin-rolling test (loss of ability to roll skin between the examiners fingers and thumb due to a localized increased stiffness or tension in skin and subcutaneous structures; see Scanning Examination)
3. Actual edema, which may be superficial or deep
4. Circulatory changes in which the area may have a different temperature and color when compared to neighboring skin; it is common to find a "red reaction" after touching the area

A red skin reaction can be of diagnostic value as an indication of altered sympathetic activity at that level. If the operator slides the index and middle fingers down the spine from above while using an even, moderately firm pressure, a red reaction at any level strongly suggests a local dysfunction.

In patients who have abnormal tension in the skin-rolling test, a "pop" is sometimes produced by lifting the skin and subcutaneous tissues off the deeper layers at the dysfunctional level, which suggests that there may be actual adhesions.

Tenderness can be from deep or superficial tissues. Skin that gives a positive rolling test is usually tender, and hypertonic muscle is almost always so. As men-

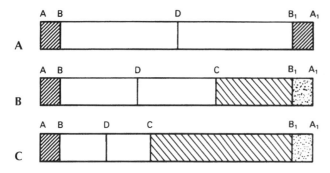

FIGURE 3-2

The barrier concept. (A) Represents a normal joint. The range of physiological movement is represented as the distance between B *and* B₁*. The total possible movement is that between* A *and* A₁*. The ranges* A *to* B *and* A₁ *to* B₁ *are the passive ranges at either end.* D *represents the point of maximum ease. (B) A joint with a minor motion restriction. (C) A joint with major motion restriction. In both (B) and (C), the available active range is from* B *to* C*, and the total range from* A *to* C*. Note the change in location of* D*, the point of maximum ease.*

tioned previously, tenderness is also found at the point to which pain is referred, and it is most important that the point of origin and the reference point are not confused. Treatment of the reference point may reduce the pain for a short time, but unless the point of origin is also treated, there is unlikely to be any lasting relief.

PALPATORY SKILL

One of the difficulties people have in understanding and applying techniques of manual medicine is that both diagnosis and treatment require a degree of palpatory skill that is different from, and in some ways greater than, that used in other branches of medicine. The difficulty can be likened to an untrained person trying to read the dots of Braille writing. To those who have not practiced, doing so seems impossible, but, as is known, the skill can be learned.

In addition to its variation in thickness, subcutaneous tissue varies in its density from one person to another. Some patients have tissue through which it is easy to feel. There are others in whom the tissue is dense and through which it is difficult to feel, even when not very thick. Practice helps, but the skill takes time and perseverance to develop. An important point is that palpatory pressure should be as light as possible. Excess pressure reduces proprioceptor sensitivity.

Palpation is used to find asymmetry of position or structure, changes in tissue texture, and range and quality

of motion. Rough or irregular movement may signify a dysfunction, even in the presence of full range in the plane being examined (there will often be restriction in one of the other planes of motion). There is also a difference in the "end feel," the sensation perceived as the end of the range of motion of a joint is approached or reached. This will differ between one patient and another depending on the cause of the motion restriction. In selecting a treatment approach, it is helpful to distinguish between differences in the end feel of joints with restricted or abnormal movement to select the technique that is most likely to succeed (see End Feel).

BARRIER CONCEPT

The point beyond which a joint will not move is referred to as the *barrier*. There is no joint in the body in which motion is unlimited; all joints have barriers. A normal joint moves through a certain range of active motion. Beyond the end of what the muscles can do actively, there is a small additional passive range. The limit of active motion is called the *physiological barrier*, and the limit of passive motion is the *anatomical barrier*. If the anatomical barrier is exceeded, there will be disruption of tissue and either subluxation, dislocation, or fracture at the joint.

In manual medicine, we are particularly interested in what is called the *restrictive barrier*; in some texts it is called *pathological*, but in manual medicine we are concerned with dysfunctions rather than pathology. A truly pathological barrier is unlikely to be caused by something that would respond to manual treatment. A restrictive barrier is abnormal and may be due to a variety of causes.

Restrictions may be major or minor; the barriers for these are illustrated diagrammatically (adapted from Kimberly[2]; Figure 3-2). In a normal joint, motion between the physiological barriers is free and should be smooth. As passive motion is introduced at the end of the active range, tension increases steadily but slowly, and then much more rapidly, until motion ceases as the barrier is reached. This end point in the range of normal motion may be described as having an elastic quality, depending on the resiliency of the muscles and fascia.[1]

In Figure 3-2, the barrier is shown as existing in one plane, but in the spine the joints are all multiplanar. For successful treatment, these barriers must be found for each direction of motion. For descriptive purposes, the three cardinal planes of the body in the anatomical position are used; however, it must be noted that the barrier is not strictly a point but rather a continuum. The precise position of the barrier in any plane depends in part on whether the movement first introduced was in that plane or in one of the others.

The operator's ability to sense the position of the barrier is of great importance in treatment. Before using either a muscle energy or a thrusting technique, it is most important to take the joint up to, but only just up to, the restrictive barrier in all three planes of flexion-extension (sagittal), side bending (coronal), and rotation (horizontal). After the initial treatment, any residual barrier(s) must be identified, and the patient must be repositioned again in all three planes by movement just up to the beginning of this new barrier. If, during the positioning, movement is taken beyond the restrictive barrier, localization is lost and the procedure is likely to fail. This is the most common fault of those starting to use manual treatment.

In medical-legal work, the barrier assumes importance because it is objective evidence that can be found and demonstrated if necessary, and after treatment can be shown to have been removed. The ability of the expert witness to indicate where the barrier is or was enhances the validity of the more subjective, associated complaints of stiffness or pain.

END FEEL

There are different palpatory sensations or "end feels" that occur at or near the restrictive barrier and correspond to a variety of different causes for that restriction. The most important causes and their end feels are the following:

- Edema is associated with an end feel that is "boggy."
- Myofascial shortening causes a similar elastic springlike restriction found at both ends of the range. It is this that athletes try to remove via their warm-up routines and is relatively common with advancing age or after a period of rest, especially after arising from a night's sleep.
- Hypertonic muscle is identified by an asymmetrical and reduced range of motion associated with an early, gradual increasing resistance with a residual springlike sensation at the end of the remaining free range of motion.
- Fibrosis usually occurs in the more chronic restrictions with a very rapid build-up in tension occurring close to the limiting barrier, but there still is some elasticity that is a bit firmer than that felt from hypertonic muscle.
- When there are bony changes, such as hypertrophy of bone at articulations or altered bony anatomy due to disease or developmental quirks, the result is a sudden,

hard, non-elastic end feel with an abrupt stop short of the normal range.
- Pain causes a sudden, jerky, and at times inconsistent ratcheting sensation, often before any increasing tension is felt. This guarding behavior is also variable, so that the barrier caused by pain is not consistent in location and is often accompanied by either a verbal or at least a facial expression of discomfort. It is important to see the patient's face or have an open dialogue while examining or treating. At times, the end feel is empty when the patient expresses severe pain, but no resistance is palpable to the examiner.
- Hypermobility is difficult to appreciate by palpation. There is very little resistance until close to the end (the anatomical or bony barrier) when the tension builds rapidly to a sense of hardness and there is a detectable, overall increase in range.

The importance of the end feel is that it gives some indication of what is likely to be the most efficient and effective treatment. For instance, joints with edematous barriers are better treated by gentler techniques, such as mobilization after an isometric muscle contraction (described later as a *muscle energy technique*), rather than by applying a quick, direct mobilizing force described by the thrusting or impulse techniques. Fibrosis, on the other hand, is probably best treated by a thrusting technique. Myofascial shortening may need exercises with gentle but steady stretching and will probably respond better to muscle energy than to thrusting treatment.

Hypermobility is one of the few real contraindications to manipulation, certainly to thrusting, because it may signify a damaged or disrupted joint, but only at that level. More often, these joints move more easily and over a greater range as *an adaptation to a hypomobile joint nearby*. Indeed, the *hyper*mobile joint is frequently the cause of the painful symptoms, because the innervating nociceptors that are sensitive to changes in tissue tension can now be more easily physically distorted by this increased joint movement.

POINT OF EASE

In every joint there is a point of maximum ease, which is the point from which movement in any direction increases the tension in the surrounding soft tissues. In a normal joint, it is usually near the midpoint of the range. When there is a restrictive barrier, the point of ease moves, usually toward the midpoint of the remaining free range. When there is a major restriction in one direction, the point of ease moves or is found closer to the physio-

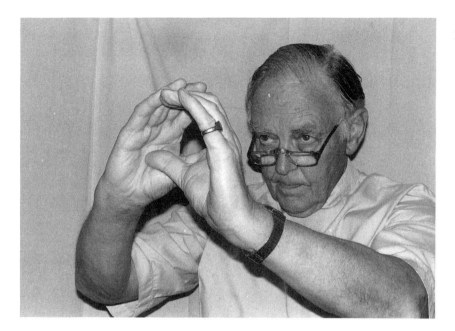

FIGURE 3-3
Method of finding one's dominant eye.

logical barrier in the opposite direction or toward the normal end. As with the barrier, the point of ease exists in each plane of motion; in this case, it also exists around each axis. Finding this remaining unrestricted region of equal tissue tensions is of great importance when using techniques that do not directly engage the barrier. Once the position in which all the tissues around the joint are the most relaxed is found, that position is held long enough to reduce the postural feedback mechanisms that encourage the persistence of the barrier. There are a number of variations of these techniques identified by such terms as *indirect, functional, strain-counterstrain,* and *myofascial.* The term *loose-packed* is used for a joint that has been positioned at the point of maximum ease in its available planes of motion. The converse is *close-packed,* as when a joint is positioned so that there is maximum articular congruency, maximum ligamentous tension, and reduced joint play motion available in any direction.

PHYSICAL EXAMINATION OF THE MUSCULOSKELETAL SYSTEM

Dominant Eye

The differences that have to be appreciated when one is examining for minor changes of level, rotation, et cetera, are small enough that it is essential that one's dominant eye is located equidistant from the two sides for anatomical landmarks to be compared. In other words, the dominant eye should be over or directly behind the midline of the patient being examined. The use of one eye to observe asymmetries permits a more accurate, simultaneous observation, rather than looking back and forth and making any comparison rely on the memory of what was just previously seen.

The dominant eye is found most easily by making a circle with the index finger and thumb of one hand or between the index fingers and thumbs of both hands (Figure 3-3). The hands are held out in front at arm's length, and, with both eyes open, a specific object is sighted through the hole. Without moving the hands, the left eye is closed. If the object remains visible through the hole, the right is the dominant eye. If the object is no longer seen in the hole, the left is the dominant eye. This finding can be confirmed by performing this exercise again with the right eye closed. The dominant eye is fixed in most people, but there are those in whom it may change from time to time. Those who tend to switch dominance from one eye to the other are advised to shut one eye when examining a patient. If the dominant eye is opposite the dominant hand, there will be greater difficulty in observing asymmetry that visually corresponds to what is palpated. In such situations, the student is advised to trust the information received by palpation in deference to the visual.

Proprioceptors

For many operators who are blessed with ipsilateral eye and hand dominance, there are times when visual observations are not possible. For example, in patients with even moderately long hair, examination of the cervicothoracic junction in extension is obscured unless something is done about the hair. With practice, it is not difficult to assess relative position and motion by means of the proprioceptors in one's hands. The practice required is no more than taking the trouble to notice what the proprioceptors feel when one examines a patient in the ordinary way. With this ability to feel as well as see, the operator will find that the perception of asymmetry is easier than when using vision alone, even when it is not obscured. Developing the skills required for accurate palpation is no easy task! There is a definite learning curve for this skill, which requires repetition and the ability to learn from one's own mistakes. The hands have exquisitely sensitive touch receptors directly connected to the most sophisticated computer on earth, the human brain, and when used together, the examiner can become a most remarkable diagnostic instrument.

Consider the hands as listening devices: Moving them about or applying too much pressure causes "static." The palpating hand must be gently applied, as if caressing the tissues. Any hand movement should be slow and only to reposition to a new area or to help the examiner assume a more relaxed posture; do not try to "feel more." Attention must be focused on what is being palpated. Avoid distractions, such as conversation with the patient or others or anything else that can interrupt the focus of attention, at least until this focus can easily be called upon. Palpation is a nonverbal skill. There are words to describe what we think we feel. What is needed is the ability to appreciate what is felt as a nonverbal feeling. Our dominant cerebral hemispheres only interfere with this process, and in the beginning they try to verbalize these sensations in thought. There may be very negative thoughts, which logically tell you what you can and cannot feel. This, too, is a distraction. As a learning tool, Betty Edwards[3] appreciated these concepts in her art instruction book, *Drawing from the Right Side of the Brain*, in an effort to enhance nonverbal skills. Most of us have drawing skills that do not develop beyond the age of 12 years, the time when cerebral dominance is established. Drawing something upside down, for example, confuses the dominant influence, and the replication is much more accurate. Ignoring the "logic" and persevering with repeated attempts to accurately palpate eventually seems to convince the dominant hemisphere to "leave you alone."

With increasing palpatory skills, cognitive skills also improve. As the mechanics of normal and abnormal spinal motion become more obvious, they become eas-

ier to relearn and apply toward an accurate physical diagnosis. With repetition, one begins to visualize spinal motion, including which facet is restricted and in which direction. As these concepts develop into three-dimensional images, there is a gradual shift toward describing what is in the "mind's eye" instead of verbalizing the learned descriptions of spinal mechanics and comparing the verbal with the nonverbal skills. It is a process that never stops developing and improving with use.

MUSCULOSKELETAL SYSTEM

To make a structural diagnosis, it is necessary to examine the appropriate joint and the associated segmental muscles. In the same way, to perform a treatment properly, it may be necessary to treat each abnormal segment. Constraints of time and consideration of the patient's general condition may make a less thorough treatment necessary on some occasions. Considerations of time when in practice make it essential to have some means by which abnormal segments can be located rapidly for detailed examination. It would take far too long to put every joint through the full examination procedure. This is the reason the screening tests are used to identify abnormal regions and, where appropriate, scan to pinpoint the actual segment.

The examination should not be restricted to the axial skeleton and pelvis. A short lower limb will have a marked effect on both the pelvis and spine as they adapt to keep the eyes and vestibular mechanisms level. This applies no less to those with a congenital leg-length difference than to those whose legs are of unequal length from injury or disease. Lack of symmetry of length, strength, or both, and resting tone of the lower limb muscles may be very important in the maintenance of an axial joint dysfunction. Although the effect is less striking, the upper limbs can also affect the spine, especially if their mobility or strength is not symmetrical.

The structural examination can then be divided into

1. Overall screen
2. Scan of areas indicated by the screen
3. Segmental definition

When the examination is complete, it should be possible to say which joints need treatment, where the barrier is in all three planes, and what type of treatment is advisable. It will be seen that, to save time and patient movement, some

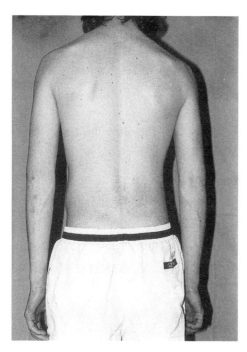

FIGURE 3-4
Asymmetry of the gap between the elbow and the trunk.

of the tests done during the overall screen really are part of the scan or even of the segmental definition.

OVERALL SCREENING EXAMINATION

The overall screening examination is done walking, standing with and without movement, sitting, supine, and prone. The whole examination should be complete in a few minutes.

1. Walking

The examination is best done from the front, back, and at least one side. Attention is directed to any gross abnormality of gait rather than a formal gait analysis, such as limping with an asymmetry of stride, loss of foot motion by altered heel and toe strike, loss of pelvic tilting as the side of weightbearing alternates, reduced or altered swing of the arms, and rotation of the shoulder girdle. In addition, notation is made of any loss of the smooth, side-bending curve of the thoracic and lumbar spine or a loss of the associated counter rotation of the shoulders and pelvis to the opposite sides. This is also an ideal time to ask the patient to walk on toes, heels, and in tandem and if possible to hop on one foot and then the other as means

to screen for any loss of coordination, balance, and strength of the lower extremities.

2. Standing, Static

1. From in front, observe the placement of the feet, the general posture, the relative shoulder height, any tilting of the head, and any rotation of the face.

2. From the side, observe for any flattening or exaggeration of the spinal curves; look for the "plumb line" (is the head "poked" forward)?

3. From behind, observe the relative levels of the gluteal folds, the height of the scapulae and the shoulders, any tilting of the head, and any difference in the gap between the elbow and the trunk on the two sides as indicators of scoliosis, lateral shift, or asymmetry of muscle tension in the feet, legs, or thighs (Figure 3-4). It is important to remember that in the lumbar spine, scoliosis may not be seen if one looks at the spinous processes because, with the vertebrae rotating toward the convexity of the scoliotic curve, the spinous processes may be in a straight line, even though the bodies are not. Fullness on one side produced by the rotation of the TPs is easier to see.

At this time, it becomes important that the patient stands evenly on both legs with the heels approximately 15 cm (6 in.) apart. The operator sits or kneels to view from behind with eyes roughly at the level of the patient's pelvis. An easy way to have the feet at the correct separation is for the operator to put one foot between the patient's heels, having the patient bring both feet as close together as the operator's shoe will permit (Figure 3-5).

Palpating over the most superior portion of the iliac crests, the height of each iliac crest is observed simultaneously and compared (Figure 3-6). Note that the right innominate is slightly anteriorly rotated while the left innominate is usually rotated posteriorly so that the top of each iliac crest requires an appropriate anterior placement of the operator's right hand and posterior placement of the left hand. After palpating the iliac crests, following them posteriorly helps find the posterior superior iliac spines (PSISs). To judge the height of the PSISs, the thumbs are placed underneath the ledge formed by each spine (Figure 3-7).

3. Standing with Motion

Standing Forward Flexion Test
In a clinical situation, it saves time if the standing forward flexion test (FFT) is performed at this stage, because the examiner's thumbs are already in the proper

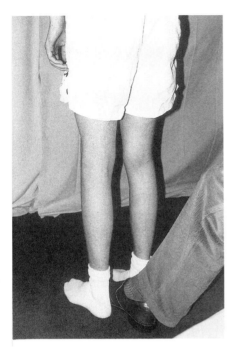

FIGURE 3-5
The operator's foot as a gauge for the patient's foot position.

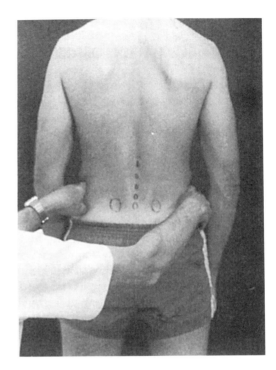

FIGURE 3-6
Examination for the heights of the iliac crests, standing.

position under each PSIS. It is actually a scanning test (rather than a screening test) for loss of normal motion in the pelvic mechanism, and although it does not indicate which type of dysfunction is present, it does give an indication of the abnormal side.

1. The operator's thumbs remain *under* the ledge of each PSIS while the operator still sights with the dominant eye behind the midline of the patient (Figure 3-8).

2. The patient is then asked to bend forward as far as possible without bending the knees. The operator observes whether the motion of the PSIS on the two sides is symmetrical, being sure to maintain the thumb contact by moving along with the spine (Figure 3-9).

If one side rises superiorly or goes forward (anteriorly) more than the other, the test is positive. *The side that moves first or farthest is usually the restricted side*, because the ilium is recruited sooner with the sacrum when there is a loss of normal motion between the ilium and the sacrum at the SI joint.

While observing the motion of the PSIS on each side from behind, the smoothness of the curve of the lumbar and thoracic spine in flexion can be noted.

Stork or One-Legged Standing Test

After the standing forward flexion test, the operator and the patient are already positioned for the stork or

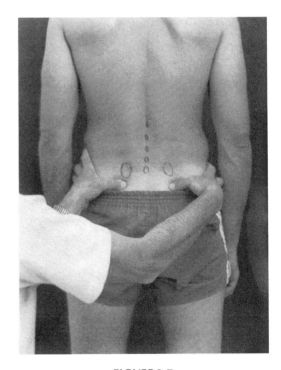

FIGURE 3-7
Examination for the height of the posterior superior iliac spine, standing.

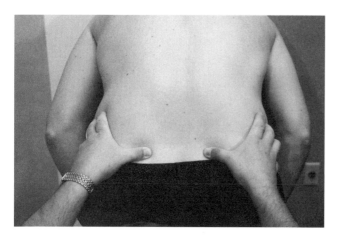

FIGURE 3-8
Palpation under inferior ledges of posterior inferior iliac spines.

FIGURE 3-10
The L-shaped right sacroiliac joint has an upper and a lower pole. Motion along the upper pole allows the sacral base to nutate anteriorly and posteriorly. Motion along the lower pole allows for a craniad-caudad motion.

one-legged standing test, which also is a scanning test that identifies restricted motion in the SI joint without identifying the actual dysfunction. This test is performed in two stages. The first test assesses motion of the upper pole of the SI joint, and the second test is a means of assessing the motion at the lower pole (Figure 3-10). The patient stands with feet 6 in. apart and close enough to a table or other object so that, if necessary, a loss of balance can be minimized by fingertip contact. The operator sits or kneels behind the patient to get his or her eyes close to the level of the patient's PSISs. For both tests, the patient is asked to raise one

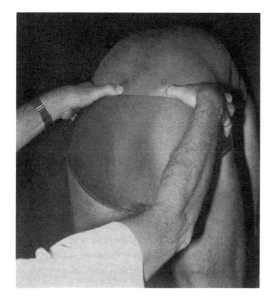

FIGURE 3-9
The standing forward bending test.

knee on one side and then on the other. The knee on the side being tested must be lifted at least as high as the hip joint (or 90 degrees of hip flexion) for the test to be reliable.

To test the motion of the upper pole (the superior portion of the SI joint), the operator places one thumb on *the most posterior part* of the patient's PSIS on that side, while the other thumb contacts the midline of the upper part of the sacrum, preferably a part of the median sacral ridge (Figure 3-11A). Normally, the PSIS should be seen to drop inferiorly and move laterally by 90 degrees of hip flexion (Figure 3-11B). The test is considered abnormal when the PSIS does not drop, or if it moves superiorly[4] (Figure 3-11C).

To test the motion of the lower pole (inferior portion of the SI joint), the operator places one thumb on the ilium in the region of the posterior inferior iliac spine (PIIS or ischial tuberosity) and the other thumb on the lowest part of the median sacral ridge (Figure 3-12A). Normal motion with 90 degrees of hip flexion on the ipsilateral side should be associated with the PSIS moving laterally and inferiorly (Figure 3-12B). The test is considered abnormal if the PIIS does not drop or if it moves superiorly[3] (Figure 3-12C).

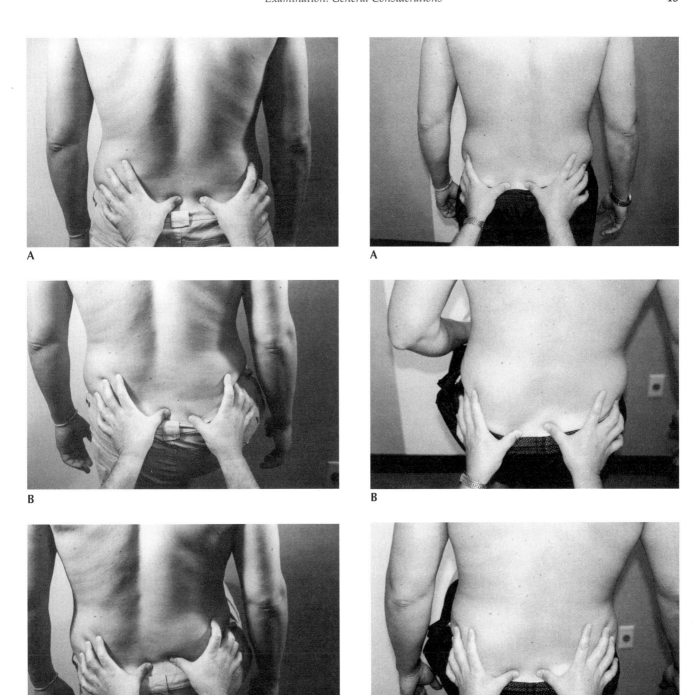

FIGURE 3-11

Stork test, right upper pole. (A) Thumbs positioned at start of test, left thumb on spine of S1 and right thumb on posterior superior iliac spine with patient standing on both legs. (B) Negative test. Right thumb drops below left thumb and moves laterally when right hip is flexed. (C) Positive test. Right thumb moves upward or does not drop below left thumb.

FIGURE 3-12

Stork test, left lower pole. (A) Thumbs positioned at start of test, left thumb on posterior inferior iliac spine and right thumb over spine of S4 with patient standing on both legs. (B) Negative test. Left thumb moves laterally and down compared to right thumb when left hip is flexed. (C) Positive test. Left thumb does not move when left hip is flexed.

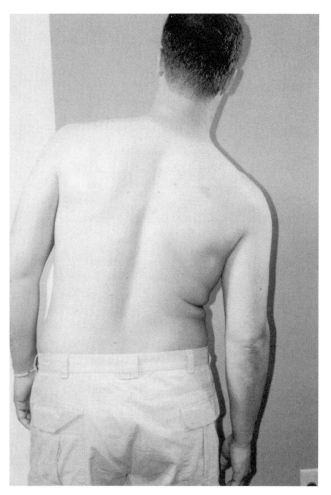
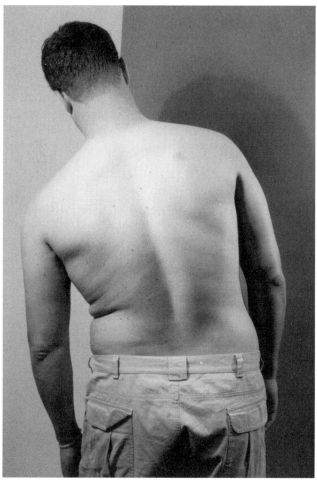

A   B

FIGURE 3-13
Standing side bend test with patient avoiding lumbar flexion. **(A)** *Side bend to right.* **(B)** *Side bend to left.*

Lumbar Mobility

Lumbar flexion has already been viewed during the standing forward flexion test. As the patient returns to an upright posture, the ability to extend the lumbar spine and de-rotate the pelvis is observed. The patient is then asked to side bend to each side, but the patient should not be allowed to move into lumbar flexion while side bending (Figure 3-13). Attention is directed to observe if there are "flat spots"—segments that do not move with the rest and are indicative of abnormal coupling of the lumbar spine in neutral mechanics. An alternative to side bending is the "hip drop" test, in which the patient allows one knee to flex while keeping the other leg straight (Figure 3-14). The amount of lumbar side bending produced provides information about the ability of L5 to side bend to the opposite side.

Lower Limb Screen

A general test for mobility of the lower limb joints may be done while the patient is still standing by having the patient attempt a full knee bend, keeping the heels flat on the floor (squat test; Figure 3-15).

4. Clinical Estimation of Relative Leg-Length Difference

If there is a suggestion or a concern that there may be a leg-length discrepancy, then this is an ideal time to investigate the possibility, because leg-length inequality is important and often overlooked. Even more common is failure to recognize that estimation of relative leg length is difficult by any clinical test. The standard measurement from the anterior superior spine to the tip of the medial malleolus is

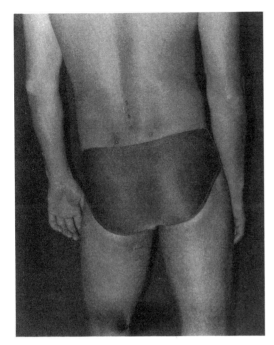

FIGURE 3-14
The hip-drop test. Flexion of the left knee allows the left hip to drop, side bending primarily at L5-S1.

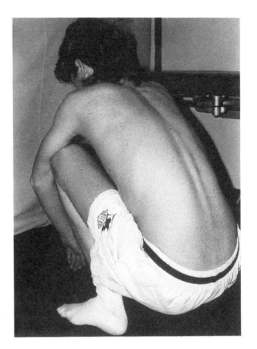

FIGURE 3-15
The squat test.

open to gross errors if the pelvis is twisted, as is common. Measurement from the greater trochanter to the lateral malleolus is incomplete and tends to be inaccurate, especially in the obese. The clinical methods of estimation that are most helpful are as follows:

1. Compare the levels of the PSISs from behind with the patient standing (see Figure 3-7).
    a. Turn the patient around and examine the levels of the anterior superior iliac spines (ASISs), again coming up from below to find the ledge underneath. If the ASIS is high on the same side as the PSIS, the probability is that the leg is long (or the pelvis is asymmetrical).
    b. Keeping the thumbs in position under the PSISs, have the patient sit down on a level seat (Figure 3-16). If the PSISs now become level, the probability is that the legs are unequal because their influence has now been removed. If the PSISs remain unleveled, the likelihood is that the pelvis is twisted with restricted mobility or there is an asymmetry in the anatomy of the pelvis (smaller hemipelvis).
2. Compare the leveling of the sacral base plane by having the patient flex fully. Then sight along the index fingers placed medial to the PSISs on each side (Figure 3-17). The higher side is ipsilateral to the longer leg.

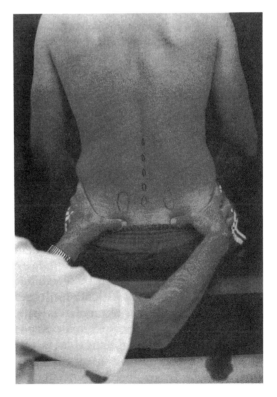

FIGURE 3-16
Finding the ledge under the posterior superior iliac spine, sitting.

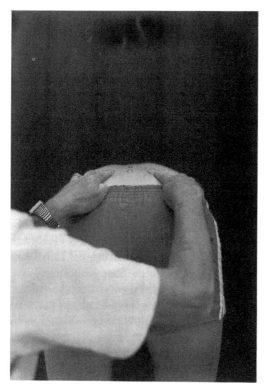

FIGURE 3-17
Examination for unlevelling of the sacral base as a guide to relative leg length.

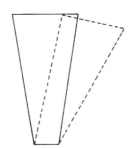 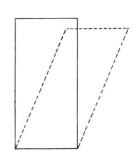

FIGURE 3-18
Diagram to show the possible error in leg-length estimation if the feet are close together. If the feet are too close together, a triangular effect is caused by the difference between the distance between the hips and the distance between the feet, thereby permitting loss of balance and tilting of the pelvis, which allows inaccuracies of measurement. When the feet are placed directly under the hips, the pelvis remains level and the relationship between leg-length asymmetries is more stable.

3. Compare the levels of the gluteal folds from behind with the patient erect.
4. Compare the iliac crest height by placing the index fingers along the crest on each side (see Figure 3-6). Remember that it is easy to include an asymmetrical amount of soft tissue under the fingers in this examination. It is most accurate if the fingers approach the crest by contacting the lateral aspect first and sliding over the top close to the bone. It is then important to palpate over the most superior portion of the iliac crest, because with even slight pelvic rotation, one crest will be more posteriorly located (usually on the left) or more anteriorly positioned (usually on the right).

In all these examinations, it is important to be aware of the possibility of observer error, even in operators with much experience. It is helpful to use proprioception as well as sight when making these height estimations. Accurate measurement requires special x-rays and is described at the end of this chapter.

James Fisk points out that an error can be introduced in these estimations if the patient stands with both feet together.[5] The error will be small unless there is marked unilateral muscle spasm causing the patient to lean to one side. If the feet are together, the leg away from which the patient leans appears longer; if they are separated by the distance between the hip joints, the error is removed (Figure 3-18). As described earlier in preparation for the standing forward flexion test, a useful approximation can be achieved by putting a shoe between the patient's feet (see Figure 3-5).

5. Seated

The patient should be seated, with weight equally distributed on the two sides. If the patient's feet do not reach the floor, they should be supported on a stool and placed parallel to the floor. This position maintains 90 degrees of hip flexion, prevents a loss of balance on forward bending, and prevents unwanted myofascial loading. In the seated position, the spinal motion tests are repeated, this time without the effect of weightbearing on the lower extremities.

Sitting Forward Flexion Test
The sitting forward flexion test is performed in a similar manner to the standing test, except the patient sits with knees apart. The operator finds the ledge under the PSIS on each side with each thumb (see Figure 3-16) and with the dominant eye observes the motion of the PSISs as the patient bends forward between the knees as far as possible. As in the standing test, the side that moves first and the farthest superiorly, anteriorly, or both is the abnormal side. If possible, the operator should sit or kneel so that his or her eyes are approximately at the level of the patient's

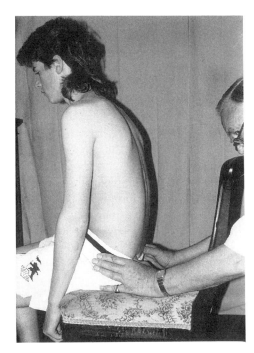

FIGURE 3-19
The sitting forward-flexion test on a chair with a sloping seat.

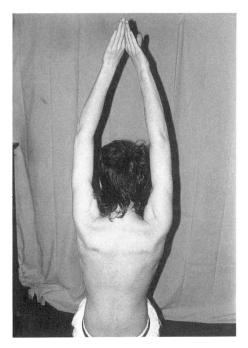

FIGURE 3-20
Screen for upper limb function. Note the loss of abduction of the left shoulder and pronation of the forearm.

PSISs. This test is most conveniently performed with the patient sitting on a stool with both feet on the floor. If the patient sits on the treatment table and the legs cannot reach the floor, there is the probability that the patient will tense the paraspinal extensors to prevent from falling forward. It is therefore necessary to provide some support under the feet, which still maintains the proper degree of hip flexion. If it is necessary to have the patient sit on a chair, the examination should be done with the patient sitting facing forward near the front of the seat while the operator observes from behind the chair back (Figure 3-19). This position is necessary because most chair seats are tilted front to back. If the seat is level, it is easier to perform this test with the patient sitting sideways.

Lumbar and Thoracic Spine
While the patient is in the flexed position during the seated forward bending test, the lumbar and thoracic spine can be sighted from behind, noting any rotation that results in a fullness on one side, any focal areas of flattening, or loss of forward curvature. Spinal motion can then be observed during the return to the neutral position and then into extension, noting any segmental restriction of backward bending. Side bending can then be observed, and restrictions can be noted by a loss of a smooth side-bending curve or by a loss of the associated vertebral rotation toward the convexity of the curve.

It should be emphasized that, when assessing the full range of side bending or rotation, it is important that the patient sits up and does not slump, because slumping adds flexion and reduces the available motion.

Spinal rotation can be screened for range and symmetry. This can be done actively by having the patient rotate the upper trunk as far as possible and passively by the operator performing the movement by gently grasping the patient's shoulders and rotating the trunk first to the right and then to the left.

Cervical and Upper Thoracic Spine
When the patient is still in the sitting position, the active and passive movements of the head and neck can be tested. Passive extension is normally approximately 45 degrees and flexion approximately 90 degrees. Rotation and side bending are also tested, and emphasis is placed on observing any asymmetry of motion rather than range.

Upper Extremities
In a sitting position, an overall evaluation of function of the upper limbs can be made by having the patient fully abduct both arms, placing the backs of both hands together while reaching above the head. If the patient can do this symmetrically, there is no major dysfunction in the shoulders, elbows, wrists, or hands (Figure 3-20).

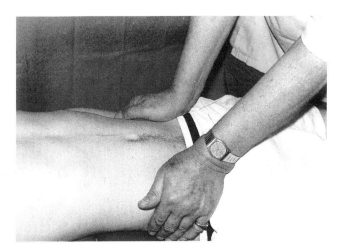

FIGURE 3-21
The supine iliac springing (bounce) test.

6. Supine

Lumbar Spine and Pelvis

With the patient in the supine position, pelvic and lumbar restrictions can be screened by applying light downward (posterior) pressure to the patient's ASIS on each side, maintaining light pressure on one side while pressing more firmly on the other side. When this test is per-

formed on each side, the operator is often able to appreciate the difference in resistance between the two sides (Figure 3-21). This test also detects rotational restrictions of the lumbosacral junction, as might be found with restricted rotation of L5. For example, if L5 is rotated to the left and cannot rotate to the right, there is a resistance to downward pressure over the right ASIS, with freedom to downward springing motion on the left.

Pubic Tubercles

The pubic tubercles are examined to compare their relative craniad or caudad positions and to look for any tissue texture change at the attachment of the inguinal ligaments. To determine the position of the superior surface of the pubic ramus, the operator first places the palm of one hand on the patient's lower abdomen and then slides it caudad until the bottom of the palm contacts the pubic rim (Figure 3-22A). Once the top of the pubic symphysis is identified, the operator places the index fingers of both hands on the most anterior surface of the pubic symphysis and pushes the overlying skin craniad until the fingertips contact the top of the rim. The distal phalangeal joints are then flexed so that the finger pads overlie the superior surface. The fingers then slide laterally over the top of each pubic tubercle, and the relative craniad or caudad position of each tubercle

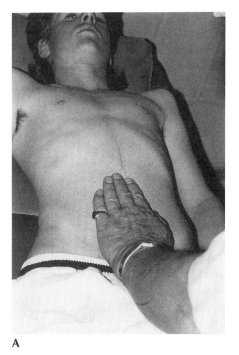 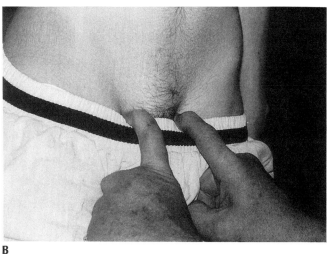

A   B

FIGURE 3-22
(A) Position of the pubes. (B) Fingertips hooked over tubercles of pubes.

is assessed by placing downward (caudad) pressure through the fingertips and sighting over the top of the fingertips with the dominant eye (Figure 3-22*B*).

Functional and Anatomical Leg Length

The position of the medial malleoli with respect to relative superiority is examined in this position and reflects the rotatory position of the innominate bones. The innominates are free to rotate in the supine position because the weight of the body is resting on the sacrum. Anterior rotation of the innominate will make the leg on that side appear longer, and posterior rotation will make it appear shorter. The medial malleoli are palpated by bringing the thumbs upward from the feet until the most inferior edge of the malleolus is contacted. With the legs as close together as possible to the midline, the palpating edges of the thumbs are sighted by the dominant eye and compared monocularly (Figure 3-23).

An anatomically short leg may be detected as well, or it may be masked by pelvic dysfunction, which can make the legs appear equal in length by functionally lengthening or shortening a leg.

Hip Mobility and Hamstring Tone

In the supine position, mobility and strength of the lower limbs may be tested. This is especially indicated if the squat test proved positive. The examination should include an assessment of the range of motion in the joints (especially the hips) and the relative length and strength of the muscles (especially the long muscles of the hip and thigh). By palpating over the contralateral ASIS with the palm of the hand, a craniad rotational

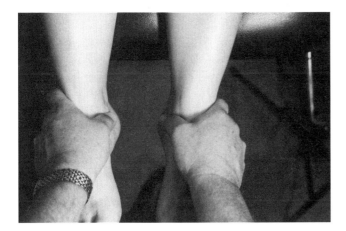

FIGURE 3-23
Examination of medial malleoli with patient supine is done by bringing thumbs up to inferior edge of malleoli and sighting over tops of thumbs from directly above.

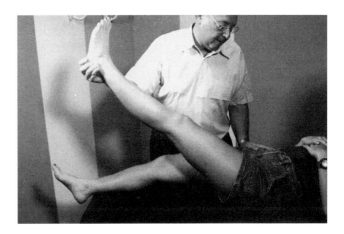

FIGURE 3-24
Hamstring muscle tone is assessed by raising patient's leg while palpating opposite anterior superior iliac spine for motion signaling posterior rotation of pelvis.

motion of the pelvis can be felt while lifting the extended leg when the tension of the hamstring is enough to move the pelvis (Figure 3-24). Other hip restrictions can influence the lumbar spine and pelvis and are described in Chapter 14.

Thoracic Cage

Motion of the thoracic cage is tested in the supine position by using respiration. Asymmetrical mobility of the rib cage noted with respiration is a useful way to detect dysfunctions not only of the ribs, but also of the thoracic intervertebral joint. It is important to evaluate both inhalation and exhalation movement. The examination starts in the upper ribs and proceeds down. The operator's finger contact must be light or the movement of the rib cage may be affected. While standing over the patient, the operator's dominant eye should be directly over the patient's midline so as to observe on which side rib movement stops first. The examination is described in detail in Chapter 10.

7. Prone

Lumbosacral Junction

With the patient lying prone, the operator places the palm of one hand over the lumbosacral junction with fingers pointed craniad. With the elbow straight, the operator applies a downward springing force over the junction (Figure 3-25). If the lumbar lordosis is compromised by a dysfunction, there are resistance and loss of flexibility that restrict lumbosacral extension. When these are found, the spring test is considered positive. If the lumbosacral junction is able to spring forward and back when the downward pressure is applied, the test is negative.

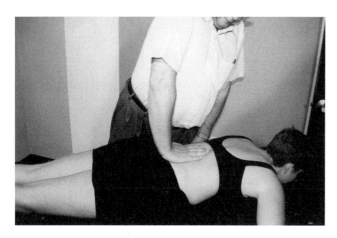

FIGURE 3-25
The lumbosacral spring test is performed by placing the palm over the lumbosacral junction and applying a downward springing force by dropping weight down from the shoulder while keeping the elbow straight.

Lumbar Spine, Thoracic Spine, and Sacrum

Extension restrictions in the thoracic and lumbar spines and sacrum may be screened in the prone and in the prone-propped (modified "sphinx") position. The prone-propped position is accomplished by asking the patient to rise up on both elbows and support the chin in both hands. This allows the spinal extensors to relax (Figure 3-26*A*) and provides a view of segmental spinal extension that may have been more difficult to see when the patient was standing or sitting. The elbows should be close together and almost directly under the chin so that good extension is obtained. It is best if the patient can allow the abdominal muscles to relax. Again, note any spinal rotation that appears or disappears in extension (Figure 3-26*B*); note any kyphotic areas, which fail to reverse and interrupt the backward curvature of the spine.

Lower Extremities

With the patient prone and his or her feet freely hanging off the table, the operator places each thumb on the inferior surface of each medial malleolus. The thumb positions are then sighted by the operator's dominant eye placed directly over and between the malleoli (Figure 3-27). A relative superiority of one of the medial malleoli in the prone position may be the consequence of lumbar scoliosis or the result of adaptive neutral lumbar spinal behavior for an unlevelling of the sacral base as a consequence of SI dysfunction. In the prone position, the innominates are not free to rotate because the weight is being borne on the pubis and the ASIS on each side.

Leg-length discrepancies seen in the prone position can also be the result of an anatomically shortened leg and should be compared to the findings noted previously when estimating leg length in standing and sitting.

SCANNING EXAMINATION

If the screening tests show an abnormality in a region, it may be worth using scanning procedures to narrow further the possible levels that require segmental definition or, in other words, to assist in making a definitive diagnosis.

The most valuable of these scanning tests include examination of soft tissues for texture abnormalities and segmental motion testing. Identification of tissue texture changes is most frequently done with the tips of the index fingers alone or with the tips of the index and middle fingers, because the fingertips are usually thought to be more sensitive to skin, subcutaneous changes, and hypertonus in the deep and superficial muscles; the thumbs are better for depth perception.

Examination for tissue texture changes can be done in many ways, either directly or by a technique known as *skin rolling*. In both the lumbar and thoracic spine, skin rolling is most easily done with the patient prone. To perform the test from below and moving upward, the operator should stand to one side, facing the back of the patient's head. The test may be used either across the midline or parallel to the spine, rolling up on one side and then the other. It is performed by picking up a fold of skin between the index (or index and middle) finger and thumb of each hand. The digits of one hand are moved while those of the other, holding the same skin fold, are still (Figure 3-28). In this way, the skin can be rolled so that the fingers advance up the back and the skin texture is palpated. The movements, which should be smooth, should maintain the lifted roll of skin as it is advanced up the back. The process can be done from above, moving downward, if more convenient.

Normal skin is easily rolled, although the roll varies in thickness between patients. When it is abnormal, the skin feels thicker, does not roll easily, is likely to cause pain provocation, and in some patients even has an appearance similar to peau d'orange. There almost always is tenderness in the restricted area, which gives an indication of the level of the associated spinal dysfunction.

Lumbar

With the patient lying first on one side, then on the other, tissue texture and motion testing can be done at the same time in the lumbar region. The operator uses one hand to examine both for tissue texture on the side away from the table and for motion when the spine is

FIGURE 3-26
(A) The sphinx position. (B) Examination for lumbar rotation in extension.

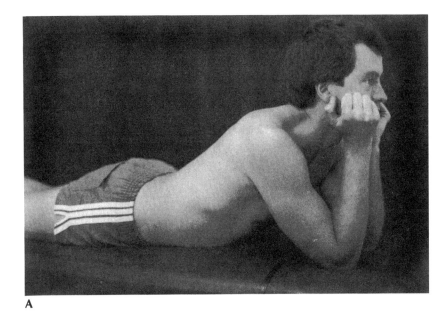

A

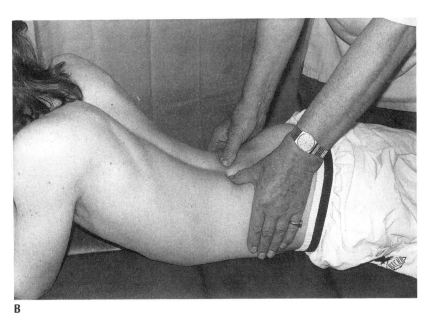

B

gently flexed and extended by the operator's other hand controlling the flexed upper leg. The fingers are best placed so that they can palpate in the "gutter" between the longissimus and spinalis muscle (Figure 3-29*A*). Alternatively, the operator can control the upper leg by supporting it on the operator's abdomen or hip, which allows the freedom to palpate with the second hand (Figure 3-29*B*).

The scanning examination can also be done prone, and the two sides can then be compared for tissue texture abnormalities. In this position, it is also possible to observe positional vertebral asymmetry by palpating the TPs or lamina. Passive mobility testing in the prone and prone-propped positions uses lateral translation with transverse pressures applied to the spinous processes that assess for segmental mobility restrictions for side bending with the spine in extension.

Thoracic

In the thoracic spine, tissue texture examination can be done prone, sitting, or even supine, but it is difficult to perform motion testing at the same time unless the patient is sitting. For the prone examination the fingers

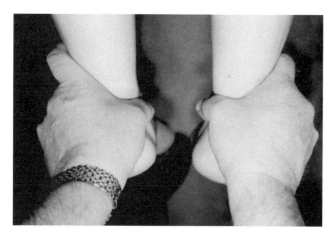

FIGURE 3-27
Examination of medial malleoli with patient prone is done with the operator's thumbs at the inferior edge of the malleoli, sighting over the thumbs from directly above.

are, once again, in the medial gutter. In this region, the tension in the deep structures is often most easily felt by moving the fingertips gently up and down in the gutter. In the sitting position, the fingers can be used in the same manner.

Examination of the upper thoracic region for levels of excess muscle tone in the medial gutter can be done from the front with the patient's head resting against the operator's chest (Figure 3-30). Tissue texture change often can be located very quickly, and the patient is likely to recognize that the operator has found something by the fact

that the area is tender. Examination of the upper thoracic region also helps pinpoint the level of dysfunction, even if it is still necessary to find the precise position of the barrier by other tests. However, female operators may not feel comfortable using this examination technique.

Motion testing of the thoracic intervertebral joints can be done with the patient sitting, using side bending, flexion-extension, or rotation. When examining for motion restrictions, it is essential that the patient sits up "tall" to avoid inadvertent flexion caused by slumping, which reduces the available motion in normal segments. Side bending while slumped will become more restricted in segments that are unable to flex fully and more restricted in extension in segments that are unable to extend fully. For the side-bending examination, the operator stands to one side behind the patient; if on the right, the right forearm and hand are used to control motion (Stiles E. G., personal communication, 1989) (Stiles' grip; Figure 3-31).

The operator's index finger is extended over the patient's left shoulder, the thumb points downward while the other fingers curl over the patient's trapezius, and the forearm rests on the patient's right shoulder. This position gives surprisingly good control of side bending to either side and leaves the operator's left hand free to localize the motion by lateral pressure on the spinous process at each level. If desired, or when in doubt about a finding, the test may be repeated from the other side. For flexion-extension and rotation, the patient sits with fingers laced together behind the neck and elbows held together in front. The operator controls motion through the elbows in either direction,

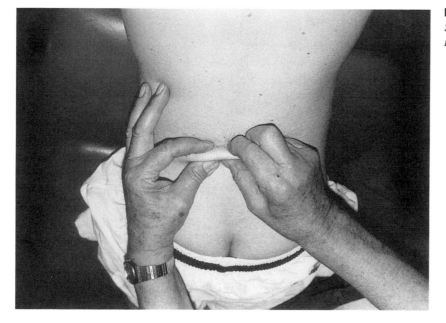

FIGURE 3-28
Skin rolling.(Stiles E. G., personal communication, 1989).

FIGURE 3-29
Scanning the lumbar spine with patient lying on side. (A) Using hand control. (B) Using abdomen to control motion.

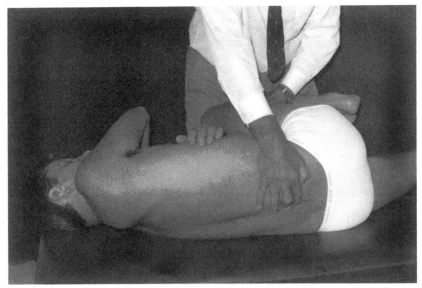

A

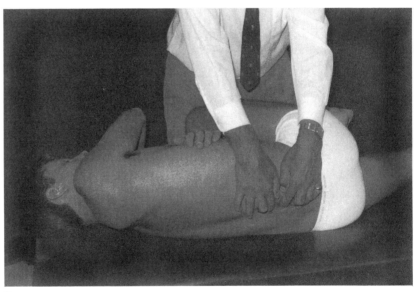

B

while the other hand is free to assess where there is a loss of normal range (Figure 3-32).

Cervical

The scanning examination of the cervical spine is best accomplished by finding the levels of tissue texture change. This can be done easily when the patient is seated, the operator is in front of the patient with the head resting against the operator's chest, and the operator palpates both sides of the cervical muscles at the same time. Simultaneous, bilateral assessment of the soft tissues of the cervical spine can be accomplished while the patient is supine

and the examiner is seated at the head of the table. In this position, the cervical examination also serves conveniently as a start to the segmental definition in this region.

In a clinical setting, all of this examination needs to be completed in a few minutes!

SEGMENTAL DEFINITION

Screening and scanning examinations provide an overview of the musculoskeletal system and detect areas that appear to be dysfunctional enough to require treatment. The degree of influence that these dysfunctions have on

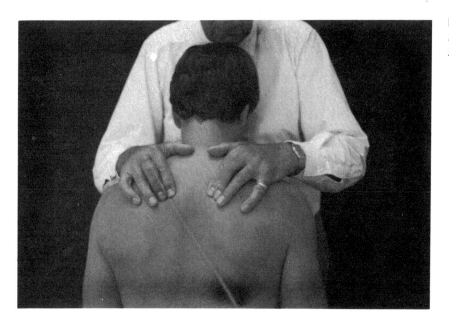

FIGURE 3-30
Sitting test for hypertonus in upper-thoracic, fourth-layer muscles.

the interference of normal function allows for an analysis in planning a more definitive evaluation and treatment sequence. The specific diagnoses of a dysfunction between vertebrae or within the pelvis are detailed in later chapters. Detailed examination of the spine requires the ability to determine the position of an individual vertebra in relation to the one below it, and these adjacent vertebrae define a vertebral motion segment.

The TPs are the most convenient part of the vertebra for determining the position of a vertebra, but they are used more for detecting rotation than side bending. In the thoracic region, the TPs can conveniently be found by using the thumbs or fingers to find the posterior rib shaft via the lateral gutter and then sliding medially along the rib until the tip of the TP is felt as an elevated bony resistance (Figure 3-33). The TP of T12 is almost nonexistent; the TP of L5 is anterior to the ilium and cannot be palpated, so the lamina of L5 is used instead. The TP of L3 is easy to feel, being usually the longest of all TPs, and it is also possible to feel the TPs of L1, L2, and L4. The TP of T12 is the shortest, and failure to recognize this may lead to force being applied to the posterior aspect of the ribs instead of the vertebra. At the lumbosacral junction and at T12, the lamina of the vertebra is usually used in the assessment of rotation instead of the TPs. The lamina is approached through the intermuscular septum between the longissimus and spinalis portions of the erector spinae muscle (the medial gutter). The TP is most easily approached via the septum between the longissimus and the iliocostalis muscles (the lateral gutter).

The spinous processes are often used in the determination of the level of the joint being examined. The most prominent spinous process at the cervicothoracic junction is typically that of T1, but sometimes C7 is even more prominent. The accurate identification of C7 is possible by first locating C6. The operator places his or her index finger on the area of the spine thought to be C6 and then passively extends the patient's neck. In extension, the spinous process of C6 is covered by C5 from above and by C7 from below so that it can no

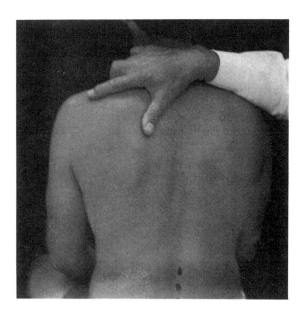

FIGURE 3-31
Stiles' grip for motion testing of the spine.

FIGURE 3-32
Upper-thoracic motion test, sitting.

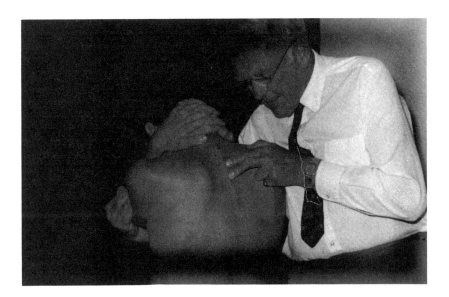

longer be felt. If the spinous process being felt does not disappear on extension, it is not C6. In the cervical spine, the TP is at the same level as the spinous process. The TP of C1 is easily felt just in front of the tip of the mastoid process and is useful as a landmark in the upper neck. This vertebra should be handled with care because of the proximity of the vertebral artery as it arches over the top of the TP on its way posteromedially before perforating the occipitoatlantal membrane. In the thoracic spine, recall that the tip of the spinous process is level with the TPs at T1 through T3, one-half a segment below the TPs at T4 through T6 and a full segment below at the TPs at T7 through T9. The spinous processes then become level again with the TPs at T10 through T12.

Palpation of adjacent spinous processes can be used to determine the range of motion between two vertebrae during both flexion and extension. It is possible to induce these movements selectively between individual vertebrae by gradually increasing flexion or extension, sensing increasing or decreasing tension in the intraspinous ligament, and noting the separation or approximation of the spinous processes. Loss of motion indicates a restriction for flexion or extension, depending on the direction of the passive movement. In the upper thoracic spine, from T1 to T5, motion testing can be accomplished through passive or active extension or flexion movement of the cervical spine and head. The patient should sit erectly to avoid inadvertent slumping, which would induce flexion below the upper thoracic region. The remaining thoracic and lumbar region can be evaluated in this seated position during flexion and extension of the trunk.

Palpation of the TPs is used to monitor both rotation and side-bending movements that may occur between dysfunctional vertebrae during active flexion or extension. With the operator's thumb pads placed over the tips of the TPs, their motion can be followed by maintaining a light bony contact and moving the thumbs along with the TPs. This is most easily done in the upper thoracic spine (T1 through T5). Restrictions are identified by an increase in tension in the adjacent soft tissues, and the occurrence of a rotation of the vertebral body that is felt as a prominence of one of the TPs as it moves or remains in a rotated position. Side-bending restrictions can be found in the thoracic and lumbar spine in the seated position by using translatory move-

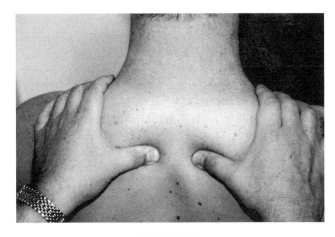

FIGURE 3-33
Palpation of transverse processes approaching from along the rib shaft.

ments with transverse pressures applied to the spinous processes.

The ability to feel these motion restrictions improves with practice, and what at first appears to be a very subtle change becomes increasingly more obvious.

RADIOGRAPHIC ANALYSIS

Films Taken in Standard Positions

Somatic or joint dysfunctions are not usually visualized by ordinary x-rays, which emphasize static anatomy rather than function. These abnormalities, often seen in patients who present with back pain, are commonly the result of injury some years before and may bear little relation to the problem with which the patient presents.

One abnormal finding in standard films that seems to be of unexpected significance is unilateral sacralization of L5 with a "bat wing" TP that joins the sacrum below and possibly the ilium laterally. The lumbosacral junction is then between L4 and L5 and may place this intervertebral disc at more risk.

If reliance is put on x-ray pictures, it is essential that they be of good quality. Poor-quality films are a serious danger. Appearances that can warn the operator to be more careful or not to proceed can be subtle and may well be missed in poor films. Even normal films of good quality are no guarantee that no condition is present that would be better off not manipulated.

Although it is wise for the inexperienced operator to see good films before treating patients with thrusting manipulation, there is reason to consider that the muscle energy and myofascial and indirect treatments are such that if a diagnosis of a somatic dysfunction has been made, it is proper to proceed before seeing films. For the experienced operator with well-trained fingers, the necessity for radiography is much less. Fingers tell much more than x-rays, and in these circumstances it is reasonable to treat a patient without ever having films, as long as recovery is occurring satisfactorily. On the other hand, if films already exist, there is an argument that failure to see them could amount to malpractice. If old films are available, there may be no need to obtain new ones unless the operator wishes to exclude the development of some other pathology.

It is important that any manipulator maintain a high index of suspicion for contraindications. Of these, the most important are hypermobility, osteoporosis, infection, and tumors. These are dealt with in more detail in Chapters 11 and 12.

Demonstration of Altered Mobility

In most spinal joints, loss of mobility and, occasionally, hypermobility can be demonstrated by x-ray, but special projections may be needed. For typical cervical joints, lateral views in flexion and extension provide evidence that is usually sufficient. At the occipitoatlantal joint, a special film is needed to demonstrate flexion. When the head and neck are fully flexed in the usual way, the chin soon comes up against the manubrium; from then on, with continued flexion effort, the occipitoatlantal joint is forced to extend.[6] To see full flexion of the occipitoatlantal joint, a lateral film must be taken with the neck extended and the head fully flexed. For the remaining thoracic and lumbar joints, plain, lateral films in flexion and extension should suffice for simple mobility, but films taken with stressed motion are needed to exclude instability.

A radiologic technique for demonstrating SI motion was devised by Chamberlain in 1932 and might be useful for those who still do not believe![7]

Lordosis

The concept that a deep lordosis is associated with dysfunctional spinal joints is an old one. Hansson et al.[8] tested this hypothesis and showed that there was no difference in the distribution and range of lordosis between three groups of men. The first group was those who had pre-employment films and claimed to have had no back pain at any time. The second group was those who had films during what they claimed to be their first episode of back pain. The third group was chronic back pain patients.

Pope et al.[9] had similar findings regarding lordosis, but they also recorded that "LBP (low-back pain) patients had less flexor and extensor strength and were flexor overpowered, had diminished range of motion for spinal extension and axial rotation and diminished straight leg raising capacity."

Demonstration of Evidence of a Dysfunction

Except when motion loss can be demonstrated, the only evidence of a dysfunction is positional because there is no associated change in bone structure. When there is a major restriction, great enough to distort the neutral position, then an anterior-posterior (AP) projection can sometimes show a loss of normal coupling for side bending and rotation at that level during side bending.[10] This is also evident during physical examination when the standing patient side bends, and the operator observes from behind for a loss of symmetrical side-bending curves.

Degenerative Changes and Spondylosis

Regrettably, spurring on the edges of the vertebral bodies is still sometimes called *osteoarthritis*. Osteoarthritis is a disease of diarthrodial joints, and the term should not be applied to changes on the margins of the disc. It is the opinion of the authors that these degenerative changes represent the adaptation of the body to the absence of a normally resilient disc structure and that they usually occur slowly over many years, nearly always being the result of trauma to the joint. These changes of spondylosis are not a contraindication to treatment by manipulation, and it is worth remembering that the symptoms may arise from another joint. Certainly, any changes that affect the articulatory surfaces alter the available range of motion for that joint, but within that range, dysfunctions can still occur and be relieved.

Torgerson and Dotter[11] at the Lahey Clinic showed that "spondylosis (osteophyte formation) did not appear to have any direct relationship to low back pain, but degenerative disc disease appeared to be a major cause of low back pain." It is possible that their findings would more correctly be interpreted as showing that degenerative disc disease and back pains are closely associated rather than that degenerative discs are necessarily causative. However, it has also been observed by others that there may be x-ray findings of degenerative changes in the lumbar spine[12] and magnetic resonance imaging findings of lumbar disc degeneration with or without herniation in a population of asymptomatic people.[13]

Measuring Leg-Length Difference

For the accurate determination of leg-length difference in a patient with chronic back pain, x-ray examination is essential. There are many ways of doing it, but the method that seems to best address this problem in the patient with low back pain is described in detail by Greenman.[14] The measurement that he prefers is in respect to the sacral baseline, because it takes into account how asymmetry of the pelvis and structural leg-length difference affect the lumbosacral junction. When this film is taken, it is important that the x-ray table is vertical and the patient's feet are approximately 15 cm (6 in.) apart, with the backs of the heels against the tabletop and the knees straight.

The tilt of the sacral base is not easy to measure accurately, and an x-ray film is needed to show comparable parts of the upper margin of S1. The difficulty is finding strictly comparable points on the outline of the surface of S1, as discussed by Irvin,[15] from whose paper Figure

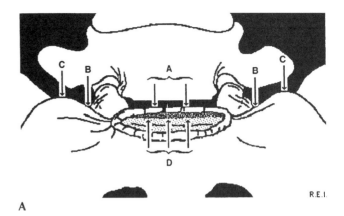

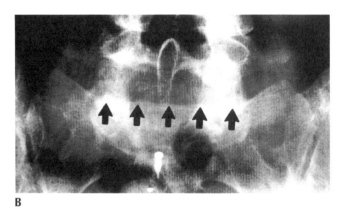

FIGURE 3-34
*Assessment of sacral base plane by x-ray. (**A**) Bony references for delineation of the sacral base. Those used by previous investigators are the most posterior superior margin of the sacral base (A), the lateral junction of the superior articular process with the sacral aspect of the sacral alae (B), the most superior aspect of the sacral alae (C). and the radio-opaque stratum of eburnation used by Irvin (D). (**B**) The radio-opaque stratum of eburnation (arrows) used by Irvin to delineate the weightbearing plane of the sacral base. (Reprinted with permission from RE Irvin. Reduction of lumbar scoliosis by use of a heel lift to level the sacral base. J Am Osteopath Assoc 1991;91:36–44.)*

3-34*A* is reproduced. A line is then drawn across S1 and extended on either side at least as far as the vertical through the weightbearing area of the hip joints. In this way, the difference in effective leg length can be measured by comparing the distance between the lower edge of the film and the point at which the line crosses the vertical through the hip joint on each side (Figure 3-35). This measurement can then be converted directly into a heel lift if required. Correction of leg-length discrepancies by lift therapy are then more correctly designed to level the sacral base as a means of treating a patient with chronic back pain and an anatomically short leg.

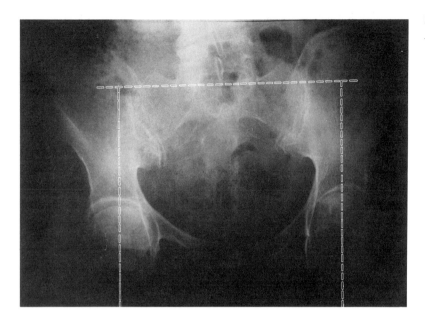

FIGURE 3-35
Method of measuring leg length and sacral base unlevelling by standing pelvis x-ray.

REFERENCES

1. Hospital Adaptation of the International Classification of Disease (2nd ed). Ann Arbor, MI: Commission on Professional and Hospital Activities, 1973.
2. Kimberly PE. Formulating a prescription for osteopathic manipulative treatment. J Am Osteopath Assoc 1980;79: 506–513.
3. Edwards B. Drawing on the Right Side of the Brain. Los Angeles: Jeremy P. Tarcher, Inc., 1989.
4. Kirkaldy-Willis WH. Managing Low Back Pain (2nd ed). New York: Churchill Livingstone, 1988; 137.
5. Fisk JW. Clinical and radiological assessment of leg length. N Z Med J 1975;81:477–480.
6. Penning L. Functional Pathology of the Cervical Spine. Amsterdam: Excerpta Medica, 1968.
7. Chamberlain WE. The x-ray examination of the sacro-iliac joint. Delaware State Med J 1932;4: 195–201.
8. Hansson T, Bigos S, Beecher P, Wortley M. The lumbar lordosis in acute and chronic low back pain. Spine 1985;10:154–155.
9. Pope MH, Bevins T, Wilder DG, Frymoyer JW. The relation between anthropometric, postural, muscular and mobility characteristics of males ages 18-25. Spine 1985;10:644–648.
10. Dupuis PR, Yong-Hink K, Cassidy JD, Kirkaldy-Willis WH. Radiologic diagnosis of degenerative lumbar spinal instability. Spine 1985;10:262–276.
11. Torgerson WR, Dotter WE. Comparative roentgenographic study of the asymptomatic and symptomatic lumbar spine. J Bone and Joint Surg 1976;58A:850–853.
12. Van Tulder MW, Assendelft JJ, Koes BW, Bouter LM. Spinal radiographic findings and nonspecific low back pain. Spine 1997 22:427–434.
13. Jensen MC, Brant-Zawadski MN, Obuchowski N, Modic MT, Malkasian D, Ross JS. Magnetic resonance imaging of the lumbar spine in people without back pain. N Engl J Med 1994;331:69–73.
14. Greenman PE. Lift therapy, use and abuse. J Am Osteopath Assoc 1978;79:238–250.
15. Irvin RE. Reduction of lumbar scoliosis by use of a heel lift to level the sacral base. J Am Osteopath Assoc 1991;91:36–44.

4

Detailed Examination: The Pelvis

FUNCTIONAL ANATOMY AND BIOMECHANICS OF THE PELVIS

A comprehensive review of normal pelvic mechanics and the diagnosis and treatment of pelvic dysfunctions was first presented in 1958 by Fred L. Mitchell and again in 1965.[1] This review provides the basis for what has evolved to our current understanding of this subject.

The complexities of dysfunctions at the sacroiliac (SI) joints seem to defy simple mechanical explanation. Asymmetry of the joint anatomy between the two sides in the same patient is normal. The angle at the lumbosacral junction varies between patients, and the slanted position of the sacrum adds an architectural perception, which accounts for the fact that this one bone always appears to side bend and rotate in opposite directions. Movements of the ilia on the sacrum vary, depending on whether the patient is standing or sitting. In the standing position, the ilia are primarily influenced by the hamstrings, adductors, gluteals, and iliopsoas muscles. In the sitting position, the long thigh muscles are usually inactive, and the influence is more from the anterior abdominal muscles (especially rectus), quadratus lumborum, and erector spinae. In both standing and sitting positions, the sacrum will respond to movement or to changes in the myofascial tensions of the trunk and legs. The standing forward flexion test (FFT) gives a better indication of restriction of motion of the ilium on the sacrum, whereas the sitting FFT gives more information about the motion of the sacrum between the ilia. The pelvis and particularly the length of the legs are influenced by the patient's recumbent position; there are differences depending on whether the patient is lying supine or prone. When the patient is supine, weight is borne largely on the sacrum, and the innominates are free to rotate in response to myo-

fascial imbalances from above and below. When the patient is prone, the innominates are stabilized by the weight resting on the two anterior superior iliac spines (ASISs) and the pubic symphysis so that the sacrum can freely respond to the influence of the lumbar spine (or vice versa).

The absence of readily palpable muscle crossing the SI joint makes the detection of tissue texture abnormalities more difficult than with intervertebral joints. Diagnosis, therefore, depends primarily on asymmetry of position and of motion. Tender areas around the SI joint do not necessarily mean a dysfunction of that joint. The numbers in Figure 4-1 refer to common areas of tenderness: (1) Tenderness over the long dorsal ligament is likely to be connected with an actual SI dysfunction; (2) tenderness is more likely to be caused by trouble at the L5-S1 joint; and (3) tenderness in the origin of the gluteal muscles may be found in association with a dysfunction several joints higher. In common dysfunctions of the pubic symphysis, the insertion of the inguinal ligament at the pubic tubercle on the dysfunctional side is often the site of tissue texture abnormality and tenderness. Asymmetries in the tension of the sacrotuberous ligaments are often associated with an altered spatial relationship between the sacrum and the ilium, and any associated tenderness or pain may be greatest in the ligament in which the tension has been changed (i.e., when tension has been either increased or decreased).

The distinction between iliosacral movement (that of one ilium on the sacrum) and SI movement (that of the sacrum between the ilia) reflects the predominance of dysfunctions that influence the two halves of the same joint differently. At times, it is easier to consider that the sacrum is an atypical lumbar vertebra, especially when considering the influence of the sacrum on these vertebra

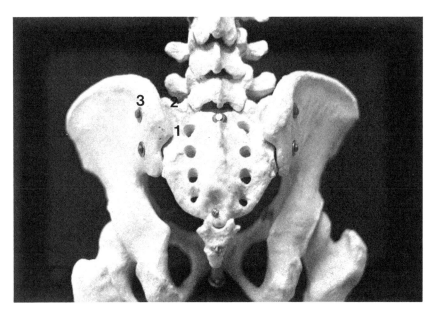

FIGURE 4-1
Posterior view of the pelvic bones. Tenderness over the long dorsal ligament is likely to be connected with an actual sacroiliac dysfunction (1); tenderness is more likely to be caused by trouble at the L5-S1 joint (2); and tenderness in the origin of the gluteal muscles may be found in association with a dysfunction several joints higher (3).

and vice versa. This inter-relationship is further complicated by the high incidence of facet asymmetry (facet tropism), especially at the lumbosacral junction.

Portions of the screening examination described in Chapter 3 have directed attention toward any significant pelvic dysfunction. The first sign to raise suspicion occurs when there is an obvious gait disturbance with altered shifting of weight or a unilateral reduced length of stride. The next sign occurs when there are asymmetries between iliac crest height and trochanteric height, suggesting the possibility of a leg-length discrepancy that could affect pelvic function. The most important indicators of probable pelvic dysfunction are an abnormal stork test and positive standing and seated forward-flexion tests. If these tests are positive, it then becomes necessary for a more detailed examination of the pelvis to formulate an accurate structural diagnosis. Because re-examination is often required, some of the details already covered by the screening examination are reviewed in this chapter.

Palpatory Landmarks and Motion Testing

To determine whether the pelvis is functioning normally or to make a diagnosis of a pelvic dysfunction, the most important landmarks are as follows.

1. Iliac Crests

The iliac crests are assessed against the transverse (horizontal) plane for vertical height (with the patient standing and sitting) and for relative superiority (with the patient both prone and supine). Care must be taken to palpate the apices at the top of both crests, because the apex will

be more anterior and lateral if there is an anterior rotation of the innominate; the apex will be more posterior and medial if the innominate is rotated posteriorly around its transverse axis. Once hand placement is adjusted for this common asymmetry, iliac crest height is determined by sighting with the operator's dominant eye (see Figure 3-3) focused between both crests and at the same level as the palpating hands to see the superior surface of the palpating fingers of both hands at the same time (see Figure 3-6). Comparisons can be made while maintaining hand contact with the patient standing and then sitting.

2. Greater Trochanters

The greater trochanters are assessed for vertical height against the transverse plane and are helpful in distinguishing leg-length differences as opposed to pelvic asymmetries. The most craniad portions of each femoral head are palpated from behind using the corresponding hands and noting any difference in height while sighting with the operator's dominant eye in the midline.

3. Pubic Tubercles

The pubic tubercles are examined with the patient supine to compare their relative craniad or caudad positions and to note any tissue texture change at the attachment of the inguinal ligaments. To determine the position of the superior surface of the pubic ramus, the operator first places the palm of one hand on the patient's lower abdomen and then slides it caudad until the bottom of the palm contacts the pubic rim (see Figure 3-22A). Once the top of the pubic symphysis is identified, the operator places the index fingers of both hands on the most anterior surface of the pubic symphysis and

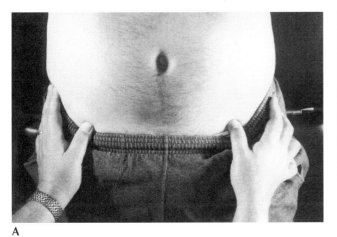

A

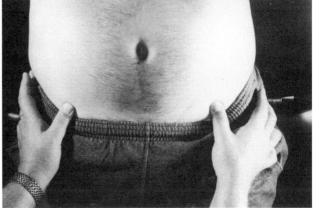

B

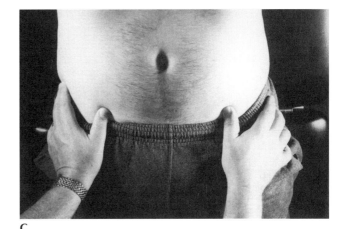

C

FIGURE 4-2
(A) Thumbs positioned for palpation of inferior ledges of anterior superior iliac spines (ASISs). *(B)* Palpation of anterior surfaces of ASISs. *(C)* Medial edges of ASISs.

pushes the overlying skin craniad until the fingertips contact the top of the rim. Then the distal phalangeal joints are flexed so that the finger pads overlie the superior surface. The fingers can then slide laterally over the top of each pubic tubercle (see Figure 3-22B). The relative craniad or caudad differences between the two tubercles are assessed by placing downward (caudad) pressure through the fingertips and sighting over the fingertips with the dominant eye.

4. Anterior Superior Iliac Spines
The ASISs are also assessed with the patient supine and are compared with each other for their relative positions. Usually, the operator uses the thumb pad of each hand and sights with the dominant eye between each ASIS. The inferior ledge of the ASIS (Figure 4-2A) is used to determine whether one ASIS is superior (craniad) or inferior (caudad) in comparison with the other. To compare the anterior and posterior positions, the anterior portion of the spine is

used (Figure 4-2B); the medial aspect is used to compare the medial and lateral positions (Figure 4-2C). It is important to assess for pelvic asymmetries using this landmark before and after treatment of pelvic dysfunctions.

5. Posterior Superior Iliac Spines
The relative positions of the posterior superior iliac spines (PSISs) are used for both static examination and motion testing of the iliosacral and SI interactions. To find the PSIS, it is easiest to follow the iliac crest posteriorly using the thumb pads of each hand (see Figure 3-7). Recall that there is often a lipoma at or near this landmark that can be gently moved out of the way. In the static examination, the inferior ledges of the PSISs (Figure 4-3A) are used to compare their superior and inferior (craniad and caudad) positions by sighting with the dominant eye at the level of the PSISs. The most posterior aspects of the PSISs (Figure 4-3B) are used to detect anterior and posterior asymmetries,

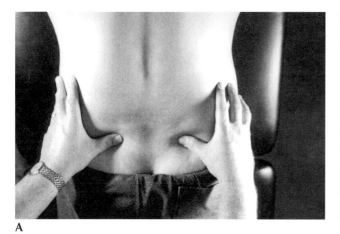

A

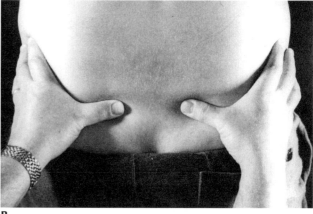

B

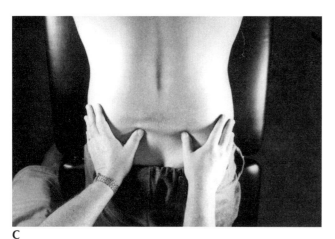

C

FIGURE 4-3
(A) Thumbs positioned for palpation of inferior ledges of the posterior superior iliac spines (PSISs). (B) Palpation of posterior surfaces of PSISs. (C) Medial edges of PSISs.

whereas the medial side is used to assess for medial and lateral asymmetries (Figure 4-3C). To observe asymmetries of motion between the two sides of the pelvis, the inferior ledge of the PSIS is used for both the standing and seated forward-flexion tests. The most poste-

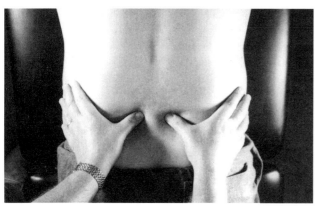

FIGURE 4-4
Thumbs positioned to palpate sacral base.

rior portion of the PSISs is used for the one-legged standing stork tests.

6. Sacral Base

The sacral base is assessed bilaterally for relative posterior or anterior positioning with respect to the coronal plane. Each side of the sacral base is palpated by placing the thumbs on the posterior aspect of the PSISs, rotating the thumbtips 30 degrees caudad, flexing the interphalangeal joint, and letting the tips of the thumbs sink down medial to the PSISs over each base until a bony contact is appreciated (Figure 4-4). Asymmetries may indicate a rotation of the sacrum to the left or right, reflecting the position of the anterior surface of the sacrum or simply the normal structural asymmetries between each SI joint. The base is also used to evaluate sacral mobility by assessing, with passive motion testing, the ability to spring the base anteriorly. Moreover, the sacral base is a monitor for detecting posterior nutational movement when the examiner applies an anterior and supe-

FIGURE 4-5
Method to find the inferior lateral angles.

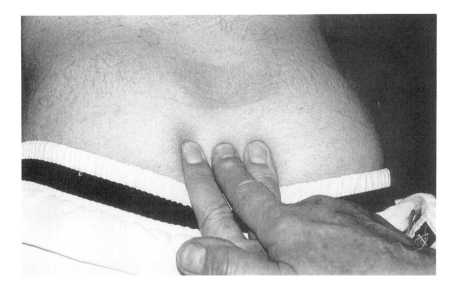

rior force to the ipsilateral or contralateral inferior lateral angle (ILA).

7. Sacral Sulcus

The depth of the sacral sulcus is a measure of the position of the sacral base with respect to the PSIS on each side. The depth of the sulcus is determined by using the same technique as palpating the sacral base, but this time it is the distance between the PSIS and the sacral base that is to be determined. A deep sulcus on one side with a sacral base that is level in the coronal plane indicates a relative posterior rotation of the innominate on that side.

8. Inferior Lateral Angle of the Sacrum on Either Side of the Sacral Apex

The ILA is easier to palpate than the sacral base (see Figure 2-2) and is found by first locating the sacral hiatus and moving a finger's breadth laterally (Figure 4-5). The ILA is actually the transverse process (TP) of S5 and is embedded in dense ligaments. After gentle continuous pressure with the thumbs, a flattened bony surface can be appreciated, which nicely accommodates the thumb pad (Figure 4-6A). Diagnostically, ILAs are compared for their relative posterior position against the coronal plane. They can also be examined for their relative superior or inferior positions by rolling the thumbs under-

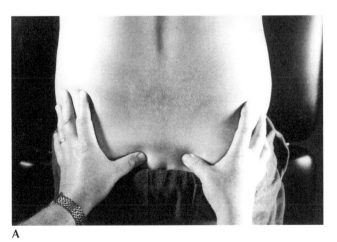

A

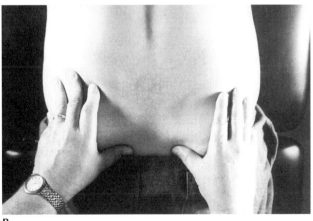

B

FIGURE 4-6
(A) Thumbs positioned to palpate the posterior surface of the inferior lateral angles (ILAs). (B) Thumbs maintain bony contact and are rolled under the inferior ledge of the ILAs.

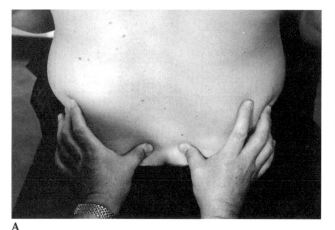

A

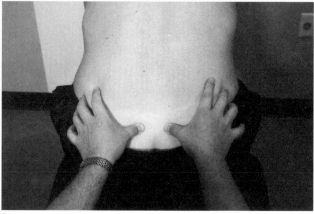

B

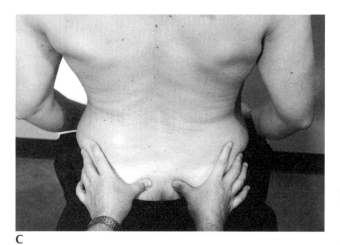

C

FIGURE 4-7
(A) Palpation of inferior lateral angles with patient seated upright neutral, (B) during lumbar flexion, and (C) during lumbar extension.

neath without losing bony contact (Figure 4-6*B*). Typically, the ILAs are palpated first while the patient is seated (Figure 4-7*A*) and can be examined after seated forward flexion (Figure 4-7*B*) and with seated extension (Figure 4-7*C*). Then the ILAs are examined with the patient in the prone-neutral position (see Figure 4-6*A*) and also in the prone-propped position (Figure 4-8). If the ILAs are asymmetrical and do not become symmetrical in flexion, prone-neutral, or prone-propped positions, they must be re-examined for any asymmetry in their superior and inferior positions by palpating the inferior edges (see Figure 4-6*B*) when the patient is seated in flexion, lying prone neutral, and then prone propped. Finally, springing of the ILAs can be used to assess passive mobility for sacral base posterior nutation across the transverse and the oblique axes (Figure 4-9).

9. Ischial Tuberosities
Ischial tuberosities are large rounded pieces of bone, and it is essential to find the most inferior (caudal) part on both. This is assessed in the prone position by first

pressing down with the thumbs into the region of the hamstring attachment and then by rotating the thumbs so that the thumb pads can contact the tuberosities by moving them craniad. The ischial tuberosities are compared for their relative craniad or caudad positions. A difference in height equal to the width of a thumb is considered significant and abnormal (Figure 4-10).

10. Sacrotuberous Ligaments
The sacrotuberous ligaments are found relative to the ischial tuberosities by sliding the thumbs around the medial edge of the tuberosity without losing contact with the bone. The thumbs are advanced craniad deep to the edge of the gluteal muscles and then a little posteriorly. The curved edge of the ligament can be felt and is assessed for relative tightness and tenderness (Figure 4-11).

11. Long Dorsal Sacroiliac Ligament
The long dorsal SI ligament is easily palpable inferior to the PSIS. This ligament functions to restrain posterior nutation of the sacral base.[2] Clinically, this liga-

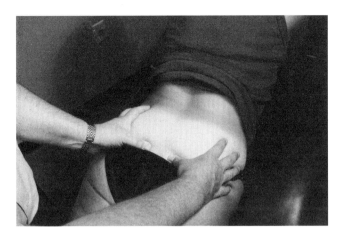

FIGURE 4-8
Palpation of the inferior lateral angles with the patient prone propped and with the operator sighting between the thumbs.

ment feels thickened and swollen and is often reported by the patient as tender when it is palpated in the presence of a posteriorly nutated sacral base. This is often misinterpreted as a tender lipoma, which frequently overlies the long dorsal SI ligament and may be the reason why lipomas are occasionally surgically removed from this area.

12. Medial Malleoli

The operator's thumbs contact the inferior ledges of the medial malleoli. The relative craniad or caudad positions are compared with the patient's ankles off the end of the table in both the supine and prone posi-

tions and are used as measures of functional or anatomical leg-length discrepancies (see Figures 3-23 and 3-27).

MOTION CHARACTERISTICS OF THE PUBIC SYMPHYSIS, SACRUM, AND INNOMINATES AND THE WALKING CYCLE

In this section, normal physiological motion is described. If in the course of normal motion an injury occurs, the injured joint may remain fixed in this position. As a consequence, there is loss of normal motion and the development of a somatic dysfunction.

Pubic Motion

There are two basic physiological movement patterns at the pubic symphysis. The movement patterns are as follows:

1. The motion of the pubic symphysis, which is an essential component of the normal walking cycle, is an antagonistic rotation about an axis that passes roughly transverse through the symphysis. If this motion is lost, the remaining movements of the pelvic bones are altered, and, for this reason, treatment of unlevelling of the pubis is considered the first priority.

2. The second movement is a vertical shear (see Figure 2-1). Research suggests that, like many other move-

FIGURE 4-9
The prone springing test of the inferior lateral angles for sacroiliac mobility.

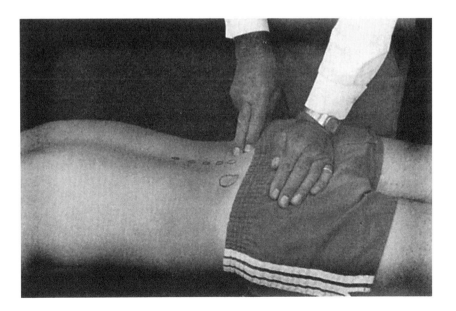

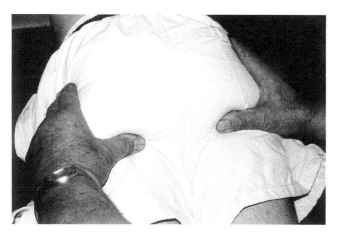

FIGURE 4-10
Test for asymmetry of ischial tuberosity position.

ments in the pelvis, this shear should only be regarded as dysfunctional when the pubis becomes restricted and is held in an asymmetrical position (Figure 4-12). It has been shown that there is often a small amount of vertical shear at the pubis in prolonged ipsilateral one-legged standing.[3]

Sacral Motion

The possible movements of the sacrum are explained in this section.

1. Anterior and Posterior Nutation

Anterior and posterior nutation was formerly called *sacral flexion and extension*. In this movement, the sacrum rotates forward and downward (anterior) or backward and upward (posterior) around a transverse axis and is

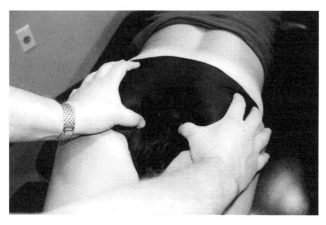

FIGURE 4-11
Palpation of the sacrotuberous ligaments.

accompanied by a translatory movement of the sacrum on the innominate. Owing to the shape of the auricular surface, anterior nutation must be associated with inferior translation of the sacrum, and posterior nutation must be associated with superior translation. There is ongoing discussion about the mechanics of this motion. Kapandji[3] has diagrammatically presented several theories describing normal sacral motion. The nature of the short, deep fibers of the posterior SI ligament appear to make the mechanism ascribed to Farabeuf (Figure 4-13) the most likely theory to describe sacral motion. In that mechanism, the center of motion is considered to be in the area of the short posterior fibers, but because there is translation as well as rotation, the center itself must move as the nutation occurs.

Anterior and posterior nutations are physiological movements and describe the reaction of the sacrum respectively to backward and forward bending of the lumbar spine. When motion is unrestricted, the sacrum always nutates and rotates in the opposite direction of the movement of the lumbar spine.

2. Anterior or Forward Sacral Torsion

Anterior or forward sacral torsion occurs about a line from the superior pole of one SI joint to the inferior pole of the other (see Figure 2-2). This line is known as the *oblique axis* and is named for the side of the superior pole. In anterior torsion, the sacrum rotates forward on one side toward the side of the axis (i.e., the side of the superior pole). It is a physiological movement and is part of the normal cycle of pelvic motion in walking. Sacral rotation in one direction is always coupled with side bending of the sacrum in the opposite direction.

Anterior or forward torsion may be to the left on the left oblique axis, often known as *left on left* (LOL). It may also rotate to the right on the right oblique axis, often known as *right on right* (ROR).

3. Posterior or Backward Sacral Torsion

Posterior or backward sacral torsion occurs when the sacrum rotates backward on one side, opposite the side of the oblique axis around which it moves. It is a physiological movement that occurs in response to nonneutral coupling behavior of the lumbar spine in flexion. It does not occur during the normal walking cycle. For posterior torsion to occur, the lumbar spine must be forward bent far enough to introduce non-neutral lumbar mechanics. Because posterior sacral torsions occur secondarily to the introduction of non-neutral lumbar spine mechanics, they are often considered the "non-neutral" mechanics of the sacrum. For example, if lumbar flexion is introduced first, followed by lumbar side

FIGURE 4-12
X-ray showing unlevelling of pubic symphysis.

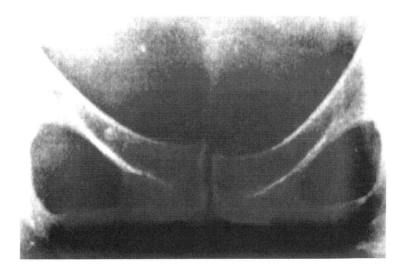

bending to the left, there is an obligatory coupling of side bending and rotation of L5 to the left. The sacrum responds to this coupling by rotating to the right with the right sacral base posteriorly nutating around the left oblique axis. This is discussed in detail in Chapter 12.

Posterior or backward torsion of the sacrum can be to the right on the left oblique axis, also known as *right on left* (ROL), or to the left on the right oblique axis, also known as *left on right* (LOR).

Innominate Motion

In normal walking, the innominates perform an alternating counter rotation about a transverse axis through the pubic symphysis. This movement must involve anterior rotation against the sacrum on one side and posterior rotation on the other side. This innominate motion is a necessary counterpart to the anterior torsional movement of the sacrum.

Walking Cycle

Before walking begins (*in stance*), the legs are parallel, both feet are flat, the sacrum is level, the innominates are in mid-position, and the lumbar spine is not side bent or rotated. With the outset of motion, as one leg is lifted (*mid-stance*), the pelvis drops on the same side, creating side bending in the lumbar spine to the opposite side. The sacrum displays its neutral mechanics, responding to lumbar side bending by rotating toward the lumbar concavity. This sacral rotation occurs around an oblique axis, resulting in an anterior torsional movement. For example, at right mid-stance, the lumbar spine side bends to the right and rotates left, and the sacral base rotates anteriorly on the left around the fixed right oblique axis,

resulting in ROR forward sacral torsion. The reverse occurs at left mid-stance. The innominates rotate reciprocally into anterior and posterior rotation during the gait cycle. At right mid-stance, the right innominate rotates anteriorly, and the left innominate rotates posteriorly until left heel-strike. At left heel-strike, the left innominate is maximally posteriorly rotated, and the right innominate is maximally anteriorly rotated; because both feet are now in contact with the ground, the sacral base is once again level. From left heel-strike to left toe-off, the left innominate reverses its rotation from a posteriorly rotated position to a maximally anteriorly rotated position. The right innominate rotates the opposite way of the left innominate. Innominate rotation is dependent on the ability of the pubic symphysis to rotate around its

FIGURE 4-13
Farabeuf's axis of rotation (arrow) of sacrum. (Reproduced from IA Kapandji. The Physiology of the Joints [Vol 3]. London: Churchill Livingstone, 1974:67.)

horizontal axis during gait. This helps explain why a pubic dysfunction adversely affects the gait cycle and is therefore a key dysfunction that needs treatment to balance the pelvis.[4]

SEQUENCE OF A DETAILED EXAMINATION

It is clear that more than just the pelvis is being examined during these tests. The tests are arranged in this manner because this is how they are usually performed to save time in a clinical situation.

Patient Standing

1. Iliac crest height. If asymmetrical, consider the possibility of an anatomical leg-length discrepancy or incorrect hand placement with the most superior portion of each crest not actually being palpated.

2. Standing forward bending test. If positive, check for pubic symphysis dysfunction and treat this before going on to the next test.

3. Stork test upper pole. If positive, there is a strong indication of an SI dysfunction present in the upper portion of the joint. Normally, the PSIS should begin to drop inferiorly and move laterally after 90 degrees of hip flexion. The test is considered abnormal when the PSIS does not drop or if it moves superiorly.[5]

Stork test lower pole. If positive, there is a strong indication of an SI dysfunction present in the lower portion of the joint. Normally, the posterior inferior iliac spine (PIIS) should begin to drop inferiorly and move laterally after 90 degrees of hip flexion. The test is considered abnormal when the PIIS does not drop or if it moves superiorly.

If the stork test is positive for both poles on the same side, there is a strong indication of an SI dysfunction present in both portions of the joint, and consideration is directed toward the possibility of an innominate shear dysfunction. The diagnosis is described later in this chapter, but if this dysfunction were found, it would need to be treated at this time.

If the stork test is positive for both upper poles or both lower poles, there is a strong indication of an SI dysfunction present on both sides (i.e., a bilateral dysfunction). It is also possible for the stork test to be positive for an upper pole on one side and the lower pole on the other side.

4. Side bending during standing and the hip drop test can be used to assess lumbar, sacral, and innominate function.

When used to evaluate motion at the lumbosacral junction, any loss of free side-bending motion to one side causes the spine to appear straightened, whereas a smooth curve occurs on the side that can side bend. The ability to side bend indicates that there is the ability of the zygapophyseal joint on the convex side to open and of the zygapophyseal joint on the concave side to close. If no restriction is present and the range of motion remains within the neutral range for those joints, the vertebral rotation occurring with side bending is in the opposite direction, demonstrating neutral mechanics of coupled motion. If there is a restriction, then lumbar rotation is in the same direction as the attempted side bend, demonstrating nonneutral mechanics. Side bending then appears to occur primarily between the two vertebrae either at the top or bottom of a straight portion of the lumbar spine.

Palpating both sacral bases is a technique that can be used to assess the sacral response to a lumbar side-bending motion by having the subject reach down toward the knee on one side while avoiding flexion. If not restricted, the sacral base on the side of the lumbar convexity nutates anteriorly, rotating the sacrum toward the lumbar concavity.[6] This is also the case if side bending is created by dropping one hip with the unrestricted sacral base anteriorly nutating on the side of the flexed knee, rotating to face the lumbar concavity as it normally does during the walking cycle.

There is also a coupling motion of the innominates that occurs during lumbar side bending. The innominate normally rotates anteriorly on the side toward which the lumbar spine is side bending and posteriorly on the opposite side. For example, left side bending of the lumbar spine is coupled with anterior rotation of the left innominate and simultaneously posterior rotation of the right innominate. Palpation of the PSISs by the operator's thumbs during active side bending of the lumbar spine to the right and left reveals whether normal coupled innominate rotation freely occurs.

Patient Seated

1. Sitting FFT. The patient should be seated on a flat, level chair or stool with both feet on the floor. The operator palpates with the thumb pads under each PSIS and asks the patient to bend forward with hands clasped behind the neck or with arms extended between (but not resting on) the legs. While sighting between and level to the PSISs, the operator notes if one PSIS moves superiorly and anteriorly in relation to the other. The side that moves further is the abnormal (dysfunctional) side.

2. From the forward-bent position, note any rotation of the lumbar vertebrae. The laminae of L5 are found by placing the thumbs over the patient's PSISs and directing the thumbs 30 degrees upward and medially (Figure 4-14). The TPs are used above that level. Assessment of positional rotation could be done when the patient is standing, but that would put more strain on the spine.

3. While maintaining thumb contact over each ILA (see Figure 4-6*A*), the relative position of each ILA is observed as the patient fully flexes from an upright posture. The ILAs can also be followed from an upright posture to a hyperextended posture by asking the patient to roll the pelvis forward and arch the spine backward (see Figure 4-7). It is important to note whether any asymmetry of the ILAs in the coronal plane disappears, remains the same, or increases as the patient moves from an upright posture to full flexion or hyperextension.

To determine the relative superior or inferior position of the ILAs, the thumbs should slide downward and curl around the lower edge of the ILA while maintaining bone contact (see Figure 4-6*B*). If the ILA on one side is more posterior than the other, it is always more inferior (caudad). If one ILA is more anterior than the other, then it is always more superior (craniad). When there is a unilateral sacral dysfunction (i.e., a unilateral anteriorly or posteriorly nutated sacrum), the asymmetry of the ILAs in a superior or inferior direction is more pronounced than the asymmetry in the anterior or posterior direction. Also, with this type of sacral dysfunction, the ILA asymmetry persists despite changing the patient's position from full spinal extension to full flexion.

Patient Supine

1. Because a significant number of patients have hip abnormalities in addition to or instead of the back problem for which the patient has been referred, it is prudent to examine the hip joint in every patient. One of the most sensitive indicators of abnormality of the hip is a loss of adduction and internal rotation when the hip is flexed to 90 degrees. This indicator can conveniently be tested at this point in the examination. The possibility that any restriction of motion may be due to tight muscle must also not be forgotten. A correlation has been shown between a loss of internal rotation of the hip and low back pain.[7,8]

2. The straight leg-raising test may also be performed at this stage. Hamstring length is determined at the first palpable motion of the opposite ASIS, not the limits of pain-free motion. Care must be taken that the patient is relaxed and not assisting the examiner by lifting the leg being tested, because this action itself creates motion at the ASIS. Several repetitions are often necessary to

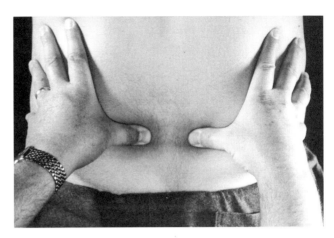

FIGURE 4-14
Thumbs positioned to palpate the lamina of L5.

ensure that resting, relaxed muscle tension is being assessed. Increased hamstring tone on one side is one of the possible causes for a false-positive standing FFT, because the ipsilateral PSIS is held down while the normal side is free to move anteriorly and superiorly.

3. The relative superiority of one pubic ramus in comparison to the other is assessed by palpating symmetrically either over the rami or the pubic tubercles. The tubercle is found approximately 2 cm ($^3/_4$ in.) lateral to the symphysis and is preferred because, being the site of insertion of the inguinal ligament, it is often tender and sometimes swollen when there is a pubic dysfunction (see Figure 3-22*B*). This is often the cause of unexplained inguinal pain, but its major significance is its effect on pelvic mechanics and the walking cycle.

Recall that when there is unlevelling of the pubes, all other diagnostic signs in the pelvis may be unreliable. Therefore, this dysfunction should be treated first, as described in Chapter 7, before continuing with the examination.

4. The relative height of the iliac crest on each side is assessed when the patient is supine by placing one hand on each crest and sighting in the midline between them. Again, care must be taken to ensure that the top of each crest is palpated, because innominate rotations can produce an erroneous asymmetry if hand placement is incorrect. If there is a significant height difference, suspect an innominate shear. There should be even greater concern about the presence of this dysfunction if the iliac crest height appeared level when the patient was standing and if the stork test was positive in both the upper and lower poles on the same side.

If an innominate shear dysfunction is found, it is the next priority in treatment, because it is so disruptive to

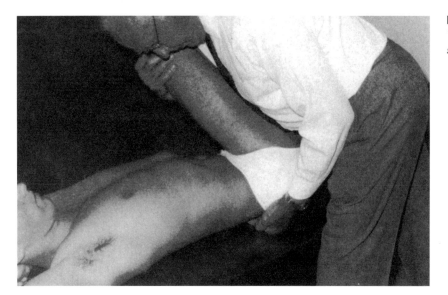

FIGURE 4-15
The supine femoral leverage motion test for sacroiliac mobility.

pelvic mechanics that further diagnostics may be inaccurate, and successful treatment of other dysfunctions may be impossible. Additional examination is needed to confirm the diagnosis and is described later in this chapter. The treatment for innominate shear dysfunctions is described in Chapter 7.

5. At this time in the examination, the relative superiority of the ASIS on each side is determined by the position of the inferior ledges (see Figure 4-2*A*). After treatment of the SI dysfunctions, if the standing FFT remains positive, the relative anteriority and laterality of the ASISs also need to be examined (see Figures 4-2*B* and *C*).

The supine iliac shear test as described in Chapter 3 can be repeated here (see Figure 3-21). While maintaining light downward pressure over one ASIS, the operator presses more firmly on the other side with a springing motion to detect resilience. When this test is performed, the patient is often be able to appreciate the difference in resistance between one side and the other. This test also detects rotational restrictions of the pelvis that might be found with restricted rotation of L5. For example, if L5 is rotated to the left and cannot rotate to the right, there is resistance to downward pressure over the right ASIS and freedom to downward springing motion on the left.

6. An adjunctive test for SI function can also be performed when the patient is in the supine position (Figure 4-15) by first fully flexing the patient's hip and knee closest to the operator. If needed, stability can be increased by dropping the patient's other leg over the table edge. Using one hand, the operator palpates under the buttock until both index and middle fingertips reach the sulcus and the sacral base, allowing palpation of both the sacrum and PSIS at the same time. The operator takes up

the slack in the patient's hip joint by adduction and, using his or her own trunk and free hand, alternately rocks the ilium on the sacrum by adduction and abduction, using the palpating fingers to assess motion.

7. The relative position of the medial malleolus on each side is measured last to assess relative leg length. If the legs are structurally equal in length, then apparent inequality of leg length in the supine position indicates dysfunction related to innominate rotation. Innominate shear dysfunctions also affect leg length in this position and should correspond to the iliac crest asymmetries. Likewise, if there are innominate rotations or shear dysfunctions and the legs appear equal in length in the supine position, then an anatomical leg-length discrepancy should be suspected.

Patient Prone

1. The relative height of the iliac crest on each side is assessed with the same precautions as described for tests with the patient supine. When there is an innominate shear dysfunction, the asymmetry in iliac crest height in the prone position is the same as in the supine position.

2. The relative position of the PSIS on each side is assessed with respect to superiority and anteriority for assessment of innominate rotation (see Figure 4-3). The position of the PSIS should also be compatible with the position of the ipsilateral ASIS for a rotation both superiorly or inferiorly and also medially or laterally. For example, if the right innominate has rotated anteriorly, the right ASIS should be relatively inferior and lateral to the left ASIS, and the right PSIS should be more superior and medial relative to the left

FIGURE 4-16
The two-thumb springing test for sacroiliac mobility.

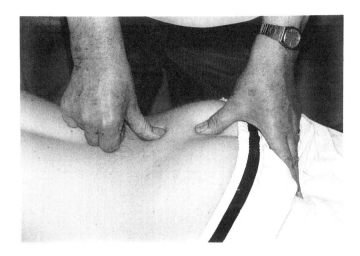

PSIS. The ipsilateral PSIS and ASIS are equally superior or inferior compared to the other side in the presence of an innominate shear dysfunction.

3. Lumbar rotation in the neutral position is assessed positionally. The thumbs are placed over the PSISs and directed craniad 30 degrees and medially to palpate the lamina of L5. In this position, there is usually less tension in the superficial muscles, ligaments, and fascia, making it easier to palpate than when the lumbar spine is flexed. Likewise, it is easier to palpate the TPs of the other lumbar vertebra. Comparisons are made from each side and to the vertebral position immediately below the one being palpated. Comparisons are also made with the lumbar spine extended when the patient is in the prone-propped position.

4. The examination of the sacrum positionally and by motion testing is best done with the patient either in the seated position or in the prone and prone-propped positions.

   a. The position of the sacral base is assessed relative to the coronal plane (see Figure 4-4). Palpation of the position of the sacral base is less reliable than the ILA due to the depth of soft tissues overlying the base.

   b. The relative position of the ILA on each side with respect to posteriority and inferiority is assessed with the patient prone and prone propped for comparison. Remember to allow time for the thumbs to descend through the overlying tissues, especially the sacrotuberous ligamentous attachment (see Figure 4-6).

   c. The sacrum can be motion tested for its ability to "spring" across either the transverse or oblique axes (see Figure 4-9). Using the index and middle finger of one hand placed in the sacral sulcus, the operator

applies a downward springing force with the heel of the other hand over the ILA. If the springing motion can be felt at the sacral base, then posterior sacral nutation is possible. Mobility across the transverse axis is tested when the sacral base ipsilateral to the ILA is palpated. Mobility across the oblique axis is tested when the contralateral sacral base is palpated.

   d. Using two thumbs (Figure 4-16), one on the ILA and the other on the sacral base on the same or the opposite side, springing pressure can be applied from above or below while the other thumb monitors the motion. The mobility for anterior sacral nutation, posterior sacral nutation, or both can be tested across either the transverse or oblique axes.

   e. Using both index fingers and both thumbs, mobility testing of the SI joints can be accomplished from both bases and both ILAs (Figure 4-17). With this four-point contact, it is possible to spring either SI joint in either direction across both the transverse and oblique axes. This hand position is also useful as a means to monitor sacral motion during respiration.

   f. Isolated regions of the SI joint can be assessed by monitoring SI gapping. Both the upper and lower poles of the joint can be assessed, depending on the degree of ipsilateral knee flexion introduced before internally rotating the hip. The palpating fingers are placed in the sacral sulcus to monitor the sacral base and ilium, and the other hand is used to flex the patient's knee and introduce internal rotation by oscillating the leg from the midposition, laterally and back. When the patient's knee is flexed less than 90 degrees and the leg is internally rotated, there should be a gapping motion at the SI joint posteriorly at the lower pole if motion is unrestricted. When the patient's

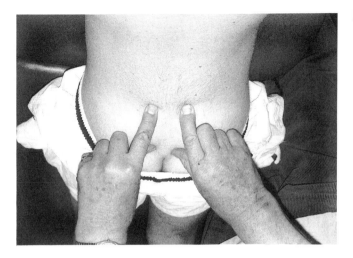

FIGURE 4-17
The four-point springing test.

knee is flexed more than 90 degrees, passive internal rotation causes posterior gapping over the upper pole if motion is unrestricted.

    g. The lumbar spring test is performed by delivering a downward springing force directed anteriorly over the spine of L5 (see Figure 3-25). A normal springing sensation, comparable to pushing down on an inflated ball, indicates that there is a lumbar lordosis and that the sacrum is capable of anterior nutation. The test is considered positive when there is a resistance to springing similar to the sensation of pressing on a hard unyielding surface, as would be the case when the sacrum is posteriorly nutated, L5 is flexed, or both. When the spring test is positive, a normal lumbar lordosis is not present.

5. The relative position of the ischial tuberosities against the transverse plane is determined by pressing downward into the proximal hamstring muscle and then cephalad against the tuberosities (see Figure 4-10). Because the ischial tuberosity is a rounded structure, it is important that symmetrical contact points at the most inferior aspects are compared. This is difficult, and the margin of error is significant enough that there must be at least a thumb's thickness (1 cm) difference between the relative cephalad positions of the two tuberosities before the asymmetry is considered to be significant. Such a difference would be seen in the presence of an innominate shear, but this result should agree with the other clinical findings and not stand as an isolated diagnostic finding.

6. The relative tightness of the sacrotuberous ligament on each side can be determined by palpating the medial edge of each ligament simultaneously. The sacrotuberous ligaments are found by moving the thumbs medially and craniad around the ischial tuberosities, then laterally and diagonally toward the femoral heads (see Figure 4-11). Normal tension should be approximately equal to that of the stretched web of skin that results from maximally spreading the index finger from the thumb.

    Note: The ligament on the side of a superior innominate shear has no tension and may not be felt at all, although the patient notes discomfort. The ligament on the side of an inferior innominate shear is very taut and tender compared to the normal side.

7. The relative position of the medial malleolus on each side is examined last. In the prone position, rotation of the innominates is prevented by the contact of the ASISs and the pubes on the table. Differences in apparent leg length in the prone position are then a function of the capacity of the lumbar spine to side bend and rotate with neutral mechanics as a normal adaptation to a dysfunctional and unlevel sacral base. Therefore, in the presence of a sacral dysfunction, the short leg occurs as a response to the lumbar adaptive side-bending curve. There is a relative increase in the muscular tension on the side of the lumbar concavity, which pulls the leg craniad and makes it appear shorter, while a decrease in tension on the side of the lumbar convexity allows that leg to appear longer. If there is no anatomical leg length discrepancy, and if there is a sacral dysfunction present, there should be a positional difference in the malleoli, provided that the lumbar spine is capable of adapting to the unlevel sacral base. This is an important observation because it indicates whether there are any significant non-neutral dysfunctions in the lumbar spine interfering with the lumbar spine's ability to adapt to the sacral base unlevelling. For example, in the presence of a known sacral dysfunction

that results in the sacrum rotating and facing the right, failure of the right leg to appear shorter in the prone neutral position indicates the continued presence of non-neutral lumbar spine dysfunction(s).

Prone in Hyperextension

The modified "sphinx" or prone-propped position is obtained by having the patient support his or her chin after propping up on the elbows. To maximize extension, the elbows need to be close together and almost directly under the chin. It is essential that the patient allow the abdominal and posterior paraspinal muscles to relax (see Figure 3-26*A*).

Most patients assume a true sphinx position by actively extending the lumbar spine while resting the forearms and hands on the table without supporting the chin. The position of the examiner may not allow direct visualization of the patient's method of extension, and this needs to be checked, especially if the paraspinal muscles are not relaxed.

The following landmarks are assessed to determine whether any asymmetry is increased or decreased in extension compared to the prone position.

1. The relative position of the ILAs, both anterior or posterior and superior or inferior.
2. The operator notes whether there is an asymmetry of the ILAs that disappears, remains the same, or increases with extension of the spine.
3. The sacral base position.
4. The position of the lumbar TPs.

Re-Examine after Treatment

After treatment of all pubic, innominate shear, and SI dysfunctions, there may still be iliosacral dysfunctions. The following tests are recommended to exclude the presence of innominate rotations and the very rare in-flare or out-flare. These tests are also recommended to exclude the possibility of incomplete treatment of any other pelvic dysfunction.

1. Repeat standing FFT and stork tests. If the stork test is still positive, recheck for sacral dysfunctions.
2. Supine, re-examine position of ASIS.
3. Prone, re-examine position of PSIS.

Because a structural diagnosis is a physical diagnosis, it is easy to use the same techniques to re-examine the area of previous treatment, checking for a change in the physical findings commensurate with a return of symmetrical normal motion, which is the goal of treatment. At times, patients indicate a persistence of symptoms, and a repeated, more critical examination is needed to seek out any residual minor restrictions.

DIAGNOSIS OF PELVIC DYSFUNCTIONS

Fourteen different dysfunctions are described in the pelvis,[9] including two for the pubic symphysis (superior and inferior pubic dysfunctions), six for the sacrum (anterior torsions, posterior torsions, unilateral anterior nutation, unilateral posterior nutation, bilateral anterior nutations, and bilateral posterior nutations), and six for the innominates (anterior rotated, posterior rotated, superior shear, inferior shear, in-flare, and out-flare). The diagnostic method presented is that used and taught at the courses in manual medicine offered at Michigan State University College of Osteopathic Medicine and in its present form is due in large part to the expertise and energy of Drs. Philip E. Greenman and Paul E. Kimberly.

Among the following pelvic dysfunctions, the superior and inferior pubic symphysis dysfunctions, innominate shear dysfunctions, unilateral posterior sacral nutations, and posterior sacral torsions are commonly found in a high incidence of patients with chronic low back pain or otherwise identified as those with a "failed back syndrome."[9] When the diagnostic findings are unilateral, they are described on the side where they are most commonly found. In each case, the findings for the other side are found by reversing the side labels.

The pelvic dysfunctions that need to be recognized are as follows:

Pubic Symphysis Dysfunction

Unlevelling at the symphysis may be due to one pubic bone's being superior or to the other's being inferior and is perpetuated by one-legged standing, with imbalances between the abdominals and hip adductors. This dysfunction is very common and important because it prevents the normal rotational movement at the pubis necessary for motion of the pelvis in the walking cycle.

If the pubis shears superiorly and is unable to return to symmetry with the other side, it is named a *superior pubic dysfunction*. If the pubis that is restricted is inferior, it is named an *inferior pubic dysfunction*. Because asymmetry alone does not indicate which side is actually dysfunctional, it is necessary to determine which pubic bone is restricted from moving either inferiorly or superiorly. The first and most important lateralizing

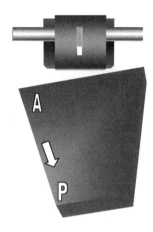

FIGURE 4-18
Diagram of a left unilateral anteriorly nutated sacrum. Arrow indicates the direction that the sacrum has moved. (A = anterior; P = posterior.)

sign for dysfunction of the pubis is a positive standing FFT on that side.

Superior Pubis on the Left

1. The standing FFT is positive on the left because the pubic symphysis dysfunction interferes with normal iliosacral mechanics on the left side.
2. The pubic tubercle and superior ramus are high (superior) on the left side.
3. The left inguinal ligament is tender and may be tense.
4. The left pubis does not move caudally (inferior) on direct motion testing.
5. There is increased tone palpated in the left rectus abdominis.

Inferior Pubis on the Right

1. The standing FFT is positive on the right because the pubic symphysis dysfunction interferes with normal iliosacral mechanics on the right side.
2. The pubic tubercle and superior ramus are low (inferior) on the right side.
3. The right inguinal ligament is tender and may be tense.
4. The right pubis does not move craniad (superior) on direct motion testing.
5. There is increased tone palpated in the right hip adductors.

Sacral Dysfunctions

Editors' note: Personal observations are included that describe as-yet unpublished clinical experience correlating the usefulness of the stork test. Differentiation

between the upper pole (upper SI function) and the lower pole (lower SI function) is described in this chapter. These observations seem to correlate well with the additional diagnostic parameters that define the observed sacral dysfunctions. A positive stork test for the inferior pole may also indicate a tight ipsilateral hip capsule.

Unilateral and Bilateral Sacral Nutational Dysfunctions

When there is restriction of nutational movement, it may be bilateral but is much more commonly seen on one side; therefore, it is correct to prefix the description with *unilateral*. The one-sided restriction is so much more common that, if *bilateral* is not specified, the dysfunction described is assumed to be unilateral.

Unilateral Anterior Nutation of the Sacrum

Unilateral anterior nutation of the sacrum, formally called an *inferior sacral shear* or *unilateral sacral flexion*, is a nonphysiological dysfunction most commonly seen on the left side and often associated with a posterior innominate on that side and a non-neutral dysfunction at L5, which positionally is extended, rotated, and side bent to the left. Such nutation is a rarity on the right side alone. Unilateral anterior nutations are difficult to correct and tend to recur. The mechanism of injury is thought to be due to landing hard on one leg when jumping, as in volleyball or basketball when a force from above, coupled with an extended lumbar spine, drives the sacrum deep into the pelvis on one side. Because no two SI joints are the same from side to side, this dysfunction may also occur secondarily to the failure of the sacral base on one side to return to its neutral position after being anteriorly nutated during hyperextension of the lumbar spine. This dysfunction is usually found in those with chronic low backache and buttock pain that gets worse after standing, usually for twenty minutes or less, and is relieved by sitting.

When there is a unilateral anterior sacral nutation on the left, the main restriction is an inability of the left sacral base to move craniad and nutate posteriorly (Figure 4-18). The sacrum is side bent left and rotated right because the left sacral base has moved inferiorly and anteriorly.

1. The seated FFT and the stork test are positive on the left, but mostly for the lower pole.
2. The ILA of the sacrum is inferior and slightly posterior on the left. With increased lumbar flexion in the sitting position, there is more asymmetry of the ILAs of the sacrum. With increased lumbar extension, the ILA asymmetry improves, *but the ILAs never become totally symmetrical.* (This dysfunction

disrupts the normal anatomy and mechanics so that the sacrum remains side bent to the left.)

3. The left base of the sacrum is more anterior than the right base. (The sacrum is side bent left and rotated right.)

4. There is an inability to spring the left sacral base posteriorly from the left ILA when performing passive mobility testing across the transverse axis.

5. There is an inability to gap the left inferior pole of the SI joint when the left knee is flexed less than 90 degrees and the left femur is internally rotated.

6. The lumbar lordosis is normal or increased, and the lumbosacral spring test is negative.

7. The normal lumbar adaptive scoliosis is convex left when L5 is free to rotate to the left and side bent right at the bottom of the left lumbar convexity. The sacrum is more side bent than rotated, but it is still turned in the same direction as the lumbar concavity (i.e., to the right).

8. When the patient is in the prone-neutral position, the medial malleolus is superior on the right due to shortening of the right leg secondary to the adaptive lumbar response. The anterior surface of the sacrum faces the lumbar concavity and the shortened leg.

Unilateral Posterior Sacral Nutation

Unilateral posterior sacral nutation, formally called a *superior sacral shear* or *unilateral sacral extension*, is a nonphysiological dysfunction most commonly seen on the right side (but rare on the left) and may be associated with an anterior innominate dysfunction on the right side. It is often caused by a strain associated with bending and lifting with hypertonus of the ipsilateral longissimus thoracis. This primarily right-sided dysfunction is easily confused with ROL posterior torsion and, likewise, may cause severe symptoms.

When there is a unilateral posterior sacral nutation on the right, the main restriction is the inability of the right sacral base to move caudally and nutate anteriorly (Figure 4-19). The sacrum is side bent left and rotated right because the right sacral base has moved superiorly (craniad) and posteriorly.

1. The seated FFT is positive on the right, and the stork test is positive for the right upper pole.

2. The ILA of the sacrum is superior and slightly anterior on the right. With increased lumbar extension, there is more asymmetry of the ILAs. With increased lumbar flexion, the ILA asymmetry improves, *but the ILAs never become totally symmetrical*. (The sacrum remains side bent to the left.)

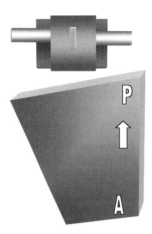

FIGURE 4-19
Diagram of a right unilateral posteriorly nutated sacrum. Arrow indicates the direction that the sacrum has moved. (A = anterior; P = posterior.)

3. The right sacral base is more posterior than the left sacral base. (The sacrum is side bent left and rotated right.)

4. Passive mobility testing of the sacrum in a prone position confirms a restriction for anterior nutational movement of the right sacral base, especially across the transverse axis.

5. There is an inability to gap the right superior pole of the SI joint when the right knee is flexed greater than 90 degrees and the right femur is internally rotated.

6. The lumbar lordosis is reduced, and the spring test is positive.

7. The adaptive lumbar response for a sacrum that is side bent left and rotated right is a left convexity, beginning with L5 rotating left and side bending right when the spine is in prone neutral. The anterior surface of the sacrum is turned to the right, and the adaptive lumbar response is a right side-bent curve.

8. When the patient is prone, the right medial malleolus is superior or craniad. The right-sided lumbar concavity causes the right leg to shorten. The anterior surface of the sacrum faces the shortened leg.

Note: Although rarely seen, a left unilateral anterior sacral nutation can occur in conjunction with a right unilateral posterior sacral nutation on the other side. In this case, the stork test is positive for the left lower pole and right upper pole. The seated FFT is bilaterally positive, which is noted by a more rapid onset of motion of both PSISs at the onset of lumbar flexion. The lumbosacral spring test is positive, and it is not

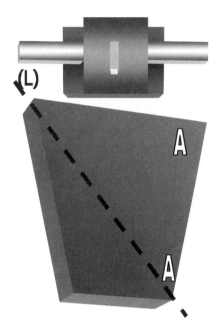

FIGURE 4-20
Diagram of a left on left anterior sacral torsion. Dashes indicate the axis of sacral rotation. (A = anterior; L = left.)

possible to spring the left sacral base posteriorly from the left ILA or the right sacral base anteriorly across the transverse axis. The prone gapping test indicates a loss of ability to gap the left lower pole and the right upper pole. In the prone position, if there is a normal adaptive lumbar response, the right leg appears shorter.

Bilaterally Anteriorly Nutated Sacrum

A *bilaterally anteriorly nutated sacrum*, formally called a *bilaterally flexed sacrum*, although rare, can occur and markedly restricts the patient's ability for forward flexion of the lumbar spine.

1. The seated FFT is bilaterally positive. The stork test is bilaterally positive for both lower poles.
2. The ILAs appear symmetrical but are actually more caudad and posterior than normal and do not change with lumbar flexion or extension.
3. Neither the left nor right sacral base springs posteriorly from the ipsilateral ILA.
4. Neither the left nor the right lower poles of the SI joint gap when either knee is flexed less than 90 degrees and the femur internally rotated.
5. The lumbar lordosis is increased, and the lumbosacral spring test is negative.

6. Because the sacral base is level, the prone leg lengths should be equal.

Bilaterally Posteriorly Nutated Sacrum

A *bilaterally posteriorly nutated sacrum*, formally called a *bilaterally extended sacrum*, prevents normal extension of the lumbar spine. If this dysfunction is present, the patient prefers to sit with arms resting on the legs.

1. The seated FFT is bilaterally positive. The stork test is bilaterally positive for both upper poles.
2. The ILAs appear symmetrical but are actually more craniad and anterior than normal.
3. Neither the left nor the right sacral base springs anteriorly.
4. Neither the left or right upper poles of the SI joint gap when either knee is flexed more than 90 degrees and the femur internally rotated.
5. The lumbar lordosis is diminished, and the spring test is positive.
6. Because the sacral base is level, the prone leg lengths should be equal.

Anterior Torsion of the Sacrum

Anterior torsion of the sacrum about the hypothetical oblique axis, or torsion to the left (anterior surface of the sacrum turning to the left) on the left oblique axis, is far more common than an anterior torsion to the right on the right oblique axis. Anterior torsional movements occur in normal walking; it is only when the motion becomes restricted (i.e., the sacral base cannot return back to neutral) that treatment may be needed. Symptoms are usually minor, but correction of the dysfunction may be important because the function of other joints is compromised. Anterior torsions, we believe, are the result of and are perpetuated by imbalances of the piriformis muscles and hip rotator muscles. Consequently, they respond well to specific exercises that address these imbalances (see Chapter 14).

When there is an anterior or forward sacral torsion to the left on the left oblique axis (LOL), the main restriction is the inability of the right sacral base to move posteriorly during lumbar spinal flexion (Figure 4-20). This dysfunction also prevents the right sacral base from returning back to neutral at mid-stance on the right leg during the walking cycle.

1. The seated FFT and stork test are positive on the right.
2. The left ILA of the sacrum is posterior and slightly inferior compared to the right when the patient is for-

ward bent (sitting test), but the ILAs become symmetrically level when the lumbar spine is extended. The asymmetry of the ILAs becomes more marked with increased lumbar flexion because the right sacral base is unable to nutate posteriorly, whereas the left sacral base does nutate posteriorly; anterior torsion worsens around the left oblique axis. If there is a major restriction, the sacral torsion is present when the patient is in the prone-neutral position. The torsion worsens with increased lumbar flexion and improves with increased lumbar extension.

In the absence of any dysfunction between L5 and the sacral base, L5 follows the sacral base and appears rotated to the left when the lumbar spine is flexed, along with and to the same degree as the sacrum. If there are no intervening flexion restrictions between adjacent vertebrae above L5, these vertebrae, too, are aligned and appear rotated left to the same degree as L5. With increased lumbar flexion and subsequent sacral rotation, the lumbar vertebrae appear increasingly rotated as well. This rotation is neither an adaptation nor a dysfunction, but it simply represents the fact that the rest of the spine has been turned left to follow the left-rotated sacral base. This situation is similar to a stack of blocks: With the bottom block rotated to the left, the stack rotates along with it; the more the bottom block is rotated, the more rotated the upper blocks appear.

3. Both the right sacral base and the right ILA become more anterior, and the left sacral base and left ILA become more posterior with increased lumbar flexion.

4. There is a reduced ability to spring the right sacral base posteriorly from the left ILA when tested across the left oblique axis.

5. The lumbar lordosis is increased, and the spring test is negative.

6. The adaptive lumbar scoliosis in the prone-neutral position for LOL anterior sacral torsion is a convexity to the right. This occurs if L5 and the rest of the lumbar spinal segments are free to rotate to the right and side bend left in response to the left rotation and right side bending of the sacral base. Although the degree of left side bending may be small (limited by the iliolumbar ligaments), it is the relationship of L5 to the sacrum that is most important. This relationship begins the left side bending and right rotation of the rest of the lumbar spine if no additional, major, non-neutral lumbar dysfunctions are present when the patient is in the prone-neutral position. The sacrum is, therefore, rotated to the left, and the adaptive lumbar concavity is also on the left. This is described again in Chapter 12.

7. When the patient is prone, the left medial malleolus is superior or craniad relative to the right medial malle-

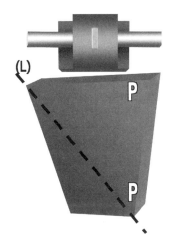

FIGURE 4-21

Diagram of a right on left posterior sacral torsion. Dashes indicate the axis of sacral rotation. (L = left; P = posterior.)

olus. The shorter left leg is produced by the adaptive response of the lumbar spine to the left-rotated and right side-bent sacrum. The anterior surface of the sacrum then faces the shorter leg.

Remember that if you are sure the sacrum is rotated left when the patient is in the prone-neutral position and there is no anatomical leg-length discrepancy, then the left leg should appear shorter than the right leg. If the left leg is not shorter than the right, then the lumbar spine is not demonstrating normal adaptive behavior, and a non-neutral lumbar dysfunction must be present. To correct the sacral torsion, the lumbar spine must be capable of neutral coupling mechanics, and, therefore, any non-neutral lumbar dysfunctions must first be identified and then corrected.

8. The piriformis is usually tight on the right side.

Posterior Sacral Torsions

Posterior sacral torsions also occur about the hypothetical oblique axis. There can be either a posterior sacral torsion to the right on the left axis, or a posterior sacral torsion to the left on the right axis (Figures 4-21 and 4-22). These occur physiologically in response to non-neutral lumbar mechanics operating when the lumbar spine is flexed and side-bent at the same time. Based on our understanding of normal physiological spinal mechanics, if an individual forward bends far enough to engage the lumbosacral junction, the sacral base nutates posteriorly. Then, with the addition of lumbar left side bending enough to engage non-neutral mechanics, the sacral base also side bends to the left, coupled with sacral base rotation to

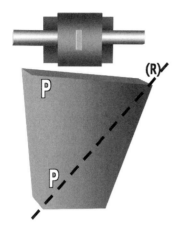

FIGURE 4-22
Diagram of a left on right posterior sacral torsion. Dashes indicate the axis of sacral rotation. (P = posterior; R = right.)

the *right*. The dysfunction occurs when the sacrum "locks" in this position with attempted return to upright standing or with lifting from that position. This is referred to as a *physiological ROL posterior sacral torsion dysfunction*.

A nonphysiological posterior sacral torsion dysfunction has also been described (Steel C., personal communication, 1999). The mechanism of injury is the same in that the lumbar spine is in flexion and the patient moves into left side bending with coupled rotation to the left (non-neutral mechanics). However, in this scenario, when the patient attempts to rotate further left or extend the spine while fully flexed, side bent, and rotated left, the lumbar spine acts as a long lever and forces the sacral base to rotate posteriorly on the *left* side. This is referred to as a *nonphysiological LOR posterior sacral torsion dysfunction*. There is disagreement as to which mechanism of injury for posterior sacral torsions is more common. Factors that determine the strain pattern are probably multiple and are significantly influenced by the unique individual anatomy concerning the shape of the SI joint, the relative position of how deeply situated L5 is between the ilia, and the asymmetry of the zygapophyseal joints at L5-S1. Whether the sacrum rotates posteriorly on the left or right oblique axis probably also depends on the degree of forward flexion mobility and, consequently, the degree of ligamentous and facet opposition lock that can occur at L5-S1 with the addition of side bending and rotation at the time of strain, overload, or injury. Regardless of the mechanism of injury, treatment for the posterior sacral torsion (i.e., ROL or LOR) is the same once the diagnosis is made. Because

non-neutral sacral mechanics occur secondarily to the introduction of non-neutral lumbar mechanics, posterior sacral torsions are always associated with one or more non-neutral lumbar vertebral dysfunctions that are positionally flexed, rotated, and side bent and restrict extension of the lumbar spine. Because posterior sacral torsions are also corrected by using neutral lumbar spine mechanics, non-neutral lumbar dysfunctions must be treated before attempting to treat the sacrum (see Chapter 8).

Unlike anterior torsional dysfunctions, which do not usually interfere with the walking cycle, posterior sacral torsions disrupt the walking cycle, are usually symptomatic, and require treatment. As with anterior torsional dysfunctions, the positional diagnosis of a posterior torsional sacral dysfunction can only be made if sacral motion becomes restricted and limited to this position (i.e., the sacral base is unable to anteriorly nutate on one side around the hypothetical oblique axis). Symptoms are often severe. Patients report the need to try to sleep only on one side, but even this is uncomfortable. Other reported symptoms include morning stiffness; inability to cross one leg over the other; inability to use a broom or a vacuum cleaner; increasing pain while walking; and difficulty in making transitional movements, such as rising from a chair or from a forward-bent position.

When there is a posterior or backward sacral torsion to the right on the left oblique axis (ROL), the main restriction is the inability of the right sacral base to move into anterior nutation with extension of the lumbar spine (see Figure 4-21).

1. The seated FFT is positive on the right, and the stork test is positive at the right upper pole.
2. The right ILA of the sacrum is more posterior and slightly inferior when the patient is sitting in the neutral position or lying in the prone-neutral position. The right ILA becomes level compared to the left ILA when the lumbar spine is forward bent (sitting test) and significantly more posterior than the left ILA with lumbar extension.
3. The right sacral base is posterior compared to the left side when the patient is in the neutral sitting or prone lying position and becomes increasingly posteriorly nutated with lumbar extension. The right sacral base returns to a position level to the left base with increased lumbar flexion.
4. Specific passive mobility testing of the sacrum in prone lying confirms a restriction of anterior nutational movement of the right sacral base, especially across the left oblique axis.

5. There is an inability to gap the right superior pole of the SI joint when the right knee is flexed greater than 90 degrees and the right femur is internally rotated.

6. The lumbar lordosis is absent, and the spring test is positive.

7. The normal adaptive lumbar scoliosis for ROL sacral torsion will be convex left when L5 is still free to rotate left and side bend to the right in relation to the sacral base, which is rotated right and side bent left. Although the degree that L5 rotates to the left and side bends to the right may seem slight, it must be regarded positionally in relationship to the sacral base. The right side bending at L5 begins a right side-bending curve over multiple segments, which also rotate to the left as an adaptive response operating under neutral mechanics to sacral base unlevelling.

With the patient seated, increased lumbar flexion forces the left base of the sacrum to nutate posteriorly, restoring a level sacral base when the left sacral base becomes as posterior as the right. The ILAs also become symmetrical, and the adaptive left lumbar convexity disappears with full lumbar flexion.

With increased lumbar extension, the right sacral base appears further rotated to the right as the left sacral base moves further into anterior nutation. Whenever the position between L5 and S1 exceeds the remaining neutral zone, L5 follows the sacral base, and if L5 is not also dysfunctional it follows the sacral base and appears rotated to the right to the same degree as the sacrum. There is no difference between the positions of L5 in relation to the sacrum, so L5 does not actually rotate in comparison to the sacrum. If there are no additional dysfunctions that limit extension in the rest of the spine, each successive vertebra also appears turned toward the right to the same degree as L5 and the sacrum. However, because of the nature of the mechanics operating at the time of the initial strain (i.e., the lumbar spine is flexed and rotated), a non-neutral dysfunction(s) somewhere in the lumbar spine should be anticipated. Comparisons between individual vertebrae, superior to inferior, identify the non-neutral segment either because it appears level (actually, rotated left) or, in this example, more rotated to the right than the one below it.

8. When the patient is in the prone-neutral position, the right medial malleolus should be superior or craniad compared to the left, assuming that there is no anatomical leg-length discrepancy and that the lumbar spine is capable of an adaptive response to sacral base unlevelling. The anterior surface of the sacrum then faces the shorter leg. If the right leg does not appear shorter than the left leg, the lumbar spine is not demonstrating normal adaptive behavior, and a non-neutral lumbar dys-

function is present. To correct the sacral torsion, the lumbar spine must be capable of neutral coupling mechanics, and, therefore, any non-neutral lumbar dysfunctions must first be identified and then corrected.

Note: An understanding of the ILA's response to lumbar spinal flexion and extension is a valuable key to diagnosing sacral dysfunctions. In sacral torsions, the sacral base and ILA are posterior on the same side, and the ILAs become symmetrical in either full flexion (posterior sacral torsion) or full extension (anterior sacral torsion) of the lumbar spine. In unilateral anterior or posterior nutations, the sacral base and ILA are opposite on the same side (i.e., if the left base is anterior, the left ILA is posterior), and the ILAs never become symmetrical, even with full flexion or extension of the lumbar spine.

Iliosacral Dysfunctions

The primary physiological motion of the innominates involves a rotational movement around a transverse axis just inferior to S2. The innominates rotate posteriorly and anteriorly during forward and backward bending of the spine and counter rotate during gait. Rotational dysfunctions of the innominates begin as physiological movements that become fixed at either end of the range and resist rotation in the opposite direction. These dysfunctions are usually seen in combination with sacral dysfunctions and often occur as a consequence of muscle imbalances in the lower quarter. If they do not resolve with the successful treatment of the sacral dysfunctions, innominate dysfunctions can be a cause for the recurrence of sacral dysfunction, or at least be the source of continued asymmetry in pelvic function. Because both the anterior and posterior innominate dysfunctions are greatly influenced by, and perhaps perpetuated from, muscle imbalances of the lower quarter, a specific home exercise program to balance the length and strength of the lower extremities is often needed to correct and maintain normal and reciprocal innominate rotation (see Chapters 14 and 15).

Anterior Innominate Dysfunctions

Anterior innominate dysfunctions are more common on the right than on the left. After treating the sacral dysfunctions, the diagnostic criteria for an anterior innominate dysfunction on the right are the following:

1. The standing FFT is positive on the right.
2. With the patient supine, the right ASIS is inferior and lateral when compared to the left.

3. The medial malleolus is inferior on the right so that the right leg appears longer than the left in supine lying.

4. With the patient prone, the right PSIS is superior and lateral when compared to the left.

5. The sacral sulcus is shallow on the right.

Posterior Innominate Dysfunctions

Posterior innominate dysfunctions are more common on the left than on the right.

1. The standing FFT is positive on the left.

2. With the patient supine, the left ASIS is superior and medial when compared to the right.

3. The medial malleolus is superior on the left so that the left leg appears shorter than the right in supine lying.

4. In the prone position, the left PSIS is inferior and medial when compared to the right.

5. The sacral sulcus is deeper on the left.

Innominate Shear Dysfunctions

Innominate shear dysfunctions are most disruptive to normal pelvic function.[10] These are true subluxations, which actually change anatomical relationships and are therefore nonphysiological. The potential for such disruptions depends on a flattening of the SI articulation (see Chapter 2) with a loss of the bevel change that is characteristic of most SI joints. It is estimated that this flattening occurs in 15% of all SI joints, and because no two joints have the same configuration (even in the same individual), this dysfunction is overwhelmingly unilateral and always occurs as a consequence of pelvic trauma.

Superior Innominate Shear Dysfunctions

Superior innominate shear dysfunctions are a consequence of a flattened SI joint and an injury when the patient falls and lands on either both ischial tuberosities or just the one on the side of the flattened joint. Pain is immediate, and the patient usually complains of severe coccygeal pain, which is often mistaken for a fractured "tail bone." Another common traumatic event that can cause a superior innominate shear is a motor vehicle accident when there is a rear-end collision. In this case, the force is through the legs, against one of the pedals or the floorboard with a downward force through the sacrum when the spine is abruptly extended. Patients often have pain when sitting on a hard or soft surface, and often these patients can be recognized by the fact that they carry a soft, donut-shaped pillow. The pain is often chronic, and it is common to find this dysfunction among a population with failed back syndrome with symptoms that span several years. Radiographic studies

and magnetic imaging do not usually demonstrate this dysfunction.

Recall that it is important to identify this dysfunction early on in the evaluation of a patient because of its significant influence on pelvic mechanics and diagnostic assessments.

When there is a superior innominate shear dysfunction on the left, the following is diagnostic:

1. The standing FFT is positive on the left, and the stork test is positive for the left upper and lower poles.

2. The left iliac crest is superior relative to the right when the patient is lying prone and supine. The iliac crests are usually symmetrically level when they are examined while the patient is standing.

3. Both the left PSIS and left ASIS are craniad (superior) compared to those on the right.

4. The left ischial tuberosity is craniad (superior) when compared to the right ischial tuberosity by at least a thumb's thickness or 1 cm.

5. The left sacrotuberous ligament is lax, and there may be no palpatory sense of it, whereas the right sacrotuberous ligament is easily identified and of normal tension (equal to skin tension produced between the abducted thumb and the extended index finger).

6. The left medial malleolus is superior or craniad (the left leg appears shortened) to the right medial malleolus when the patient is in both the prone and supine positions. This is not a true leg-length discrepancy and simply reflects the position of the left innominate relative to the sacrum. The difference should be similar to the differences seen in the height of the iliac crests and ischial tuberosities.

Inferior Innominate Shear Dysfunctions

Inferior innominate shear dysfunctions can also occur when there is a flattening of the SI joint but are much less common and require an unusual type of injury to cause them. The injury involves a downward pull of the leg on the side of the flattened SI articulation. Such injuries can occur when a horseback rider falls off the horse and catches a leg in the stirrup, when a skier catches a ski and falls forward, or when an individual catches a shoe and falls forward. One patient reported being struck by a car and thrown over a tow bar, catching one leg on the bar. The clinical presentation is one of severe pain in the pelvic region and the inability to sit. As with the superior innominate shear dysfunctions, imaging studies are usually not helpful. Because simple weight-bearing may correct an inferior innominate shear, this dysfunction is less commonly seen.

For a right inferior innominate shear dysfunction, the following is diagnostic:

1. The standing FFT is positive on the right, and the stork test is positive for both the right upper and lower poles.

2. The right iliac crest is caudad (inferior) when compared to the left while the patient is in the prone and supine position. The iliac crests appear level when the patient is standing.

3. The right pubis is usually inferior (caudad) in comparison to the left.

4. Both the right PSIS and the right ASIS are caudad (inferior) when compared to the left.

5. The right ischial tuberosity is caudad (inferior) in comparison to the left by at least a thumb's width or 1 cm.

6. The right sacrotuberous ligament is obviously taut and tender, whereas the left sacrotuberous ligament still exhibits normal tension.

7. The right medial malleolus appears more caudad or inferior (the right leg appears longer) than the left when the patient is lying in either the prone or supine position.

Innominate In-Flare and Out-Flare Dysfunctions

Innominate in-flare and out-flare dysfunctions are extremely rare and can occur only in those SI articulations that are unusual with the sacral surface convex and the innominate concave (see Chapter 2). They are most commonly misdiagnosed in the presence of innominate rotations because the ASIS moves laterally when the innominate rotates anteriorly, and the ASIS moves medially when the innominate rotates posteriorly. The position of the PSIS also changes with innominate rotation, being medial with posterior rotation and lateral with anterior rotation. True flare dysfunctions only occur when the innominate is capable of rotating around a vertical axis, which is possible only under the previously described anatomical conditions.

When there is an innominate out-flare dysfunction on the right,

1. The standing FFT is positive on the right.

2. The right ASIS is more lateral than the left.

3. The right PSIS is more medially positioned than the left.

4. The right sacral sulcus is narrower than the left.

5. The right and left ASISs and PSISs are level with each other.

When there is an innominate in-flare dysfunction on the left,

1. The standing FFT is positive on the left.

2. The left ASIS is more medially positioned than the right.

3. The left PSIS is more lateral than the right.

4. The left sacral sulcus is wider than the right.

5. The left and right ASISs and PSISs are level with each other.

Clinical Notes, Reminders, and Pearls

In FFTs, the innominate on the restricted side is picked up by the moving sacrum more easily than the innominate on the mobile side due to the loss of joint play between the innominate and sacrum. The more severe the restriction, the sooner the movement begins. The PSIS that moves first or the furthest superiorly, anteriorly, or both is the positive (restricted) side.

The standing FFT is usually viewed as the primary factor that determines which side is the abnormal side for pubic symphysis dysfunction, innominate rotational dysfunctions, and innominate flare dysfunctions, because the observed positional asymmetries alone are indistinguishable. For example, is the left pubis superior or the right pubis inferior? Or, is the right innominate anteriorly rotated or the left posteriorly rotated? Yet, the standing FFT can be falsely positive if, for example, asymmetrical hamstring tightness holds the PSIS back and down on one side, causing an apparent standing FFT that appears positive on the opposite side. Conversely, asymmetrical quadratus lumborum tightness may pull the PSIS upward, causing an apparent positive standing FFT on that side. At times, it is difficult to be sure which is the positive side or whether the test is bilaterally positive. In all instances, additional motion testing can be used by directly attempting to move or spring the suspected dysfunctional side in the direction of the suspected restriction.

The normal adaptation of the lumbar spine in neutral to an unlevelling or tilting of the sacral base is a neutral lumbar curve to bring the superincumbent spine back to a vertical position. This is only possible when there are no major non-neutral lumbar spine dysfunctions of a type that would prevent the adaptation. If non-neutral dysfunctions are present, the leg length observed in the prone position does not appear as anticipated. Sacral nutations often cannot be corrected if L5 is nonadaptive. Sacral torsions are treated by neutral mechanics and, therefore, require the capacity of the lumbar spine (especially at the lumbosacral junction) to be capable of rotating, side bending, and flexing or extending opposite of the sacrum. Therefore, non-neutral lumbar dysfunctions (commonly L5 or higher) need to be treated before the sacrum. It is also important to remember that all dysfunctions are first identified by comparing the position of the superior segment to the one below it. If, with positional testing, the sacrum is rotated left in flexion or extension and L5 appears to be level, then in relation to the sacrum, L5 is actually rotated to the right and is dysfunctional. This is true throughout the lumbar and thoracic spine: A "level" segment palpated above a rotated segment when the spine is either flexed or extended is actually rotated in the opposite direction of the lower one.

Pelvic dysfunctions are commonly multiple, and some patterns are much more common than others. The less common patterns are indications to check that the results of the examination have been correctly interpreted. The less common patterns seem to be associated with more severe symptoms than the common patterns.

The more common patterns include the following:

1. Right inferior pubis, LOL sacral torsion, right anterior innominate
2. Left superior pubis, left unilateral anterior sacral nutation, left posterior innominate
3. Right inferior pubis, ROL posterior sacral torsion, right anterior innominate

Among the less common findings are the following:

1. Right superior pubis
2. Left inferior pubis
3. Unilateral posterior sacral nutation on the left
4. Unilateral anterior sacral nutation on the right

REFERENCES

1. Mitchell FL. Structural pelvic function. Acad Appl Osteopath 1965;II:178–199.
2. Vleeming A, Pool-Goudzwaard AL, Hammudoghlu D, Stoeckart R, Snijders CJ, Mens JMA. The function of the long dorsal sacroiliac ligament: its implication for understanding low back pain. Spine 1996;21:556–562.
3. Kapandji IA. The Physiology of the Joints (Vol 3). London: Churchill Livingstone, 1974:67.
4. Greenman PE. Clinical Aspects of the Sacroiliac Joint in Walking. In A Vleeming, V Mooney, CJ Snijders, T Dorman, R Stoeckart (eds). Movement, Stability and Low Back Pain: The Essential Role of the Pelvis. New York: Churchill Livingstone, 1997:235–242.
5. Kirkaldy-Willis WH. Managing Low Back Pain (2nd ed). New York: Churchill Livingstone, 1988: 137.
6. Stevens A. Side-Bending and Axial Rotation of the Sacrum inside the Pelvic Girdle. In A Vleeming, V Mooney, CJ Snijders, T Dorman (eds). First Interdisciplinary World Congress on Low Back Pain and Its Relation to the Sacroiliac Joint. 5–6 November 1992:209–230, San Diego, CA.
7. Mellin G. Correlations of hip mobility with degrees of back pain and lumbar spinal mobility in chronic low back pain patients. Spine 1990;13:668–670.
8. Ellison JB, Rose SJ, Sarhman SA. Patterns of hip rotation range of motion: a comparison between healthy subject patients with low back pain. Phys Ther 1990;70:537–541.
9. Greenman PE. Principles of Manual Medicine (2nd ed). Baltimore: Williams & Wilkins, 1996:328.
10. Greenman PE. Innominate shear dysfunction in the sacroiliac syndrome. Man Med 1986;2:114–121.

5

Detailed Examination: The Spine

The spinal joints are examined to determine their mobility, the location of any restriction, and the presence or absence of tissue texture abnormalities. Tissue texture changes include hypertonic muscle and tightness of the surrounding fascia and overlying skin, which may be cool and moist in the more chronic conditions and boggy or edematous when acute. At first, students of manual medicine find these tissue texture changes difficult to feel. Like learning to read the dots of Braille, which at first seems impossible, nearly any student can learn to feel tissue texture changes well enough with practice.

To make a fully specific diagnosis, it is necessary to find the precise point in the patient's range of motion at which there is a restriction. The normal motion of all spinal joints is similar to that of a universal joint, except that there are limitations in the range of all three planes of motion (i.e., flexion-extension, right and left side bending, and right and left rotation) that are determined by the particular anatomy peculiar to each of these spinal articulations. When there is a restriction that interferes with normal motion, it interferes in all three planes. For this reason, when motion is abnormally restricted, the barrier must be identified in all three planes of available motion. The identification of the three-dimensional barrier applies to every dysfunctional joint, each of which must be treated as a separate entity.

When performing this examination, it will be found that a position is reached from which no further free movement is possible in that direction; this position represents the barrier. The barrier is not truly a point, because its precise position changes depending on which plane of motion is first introduced and because it represents the sum of all available motion. For exam-

ple, the amount of side bending needed to reach the barrier is different (less) if the positioning starts with the patient slumped (already flexed) rather than sitting erect in the more "neutral" position.

LESION DESCRIPTION AND NOTATION

When dysfunction in a joint is described in records or in a report, the description should be in sufficient enough detail that someone else would know what treatment to give. The level must be specified: By convention, the structure mentioned (vertebra or skull) is the superior component of the joint; thus, L4 would refer to the L4-5 joint, and C1 would refer to the atlantoaxial joint. By this convention, the position or motion characteristics of the superior component are described in relation to the inferior component; thus, the position or restricted motion of L4 in relation to L5 is inferred. *Sacroiliac* is used to signify a dysfunction of the sacrum between the ilia; *iliosacral* is used to signify dysfunction of one ilium on the sacrum.

In this book, as in previous editions, the position of the joint as it is found at examination is used and emphasized by the past tense (e.g., flexed, rotated, and side bent). When restrictions are described, the present tense is used (e.g., restriction of extension, side bending, or rotation). The actual notation consists of capital letters to indicate the position in the three planes, followed by lowercase letters (*rt* or *lt*) to designate *right* or *left*. Thus, *FRSrt* means that the upper component of the motion segment specified is flexed, rotated, and side bent to the right in relation to the lower segment. (The movement restriction notation would be of extension, rotation, and side bending to the left.) This notation is a slight simplification from the original, *FRrtSrt*. The simplification is possible because, if the joint is either *flexed* or *extended*, it must be a non-neutral dysfunction, and, in these dysfunctions, rotation and side bending are always coupled to the same side.

For neutral dysfunctions (type I), the letter *N* may be used and followed by *rt* or *lt* to designate the side of the convexity of the side bent group. In older texts, the longer notation *NRrtSlt* may be found, indicating the same dysfunction. In some texts, the notation *EN* (*easy normal*) may be used instead of the single *N*.

At the occipitoatlantal (OA) joint, there is a small amount of rotation to the side opposite of the side bend. For this reason, the notation is *FRltSrt* or *FRrtSlt* for flexed joints with restriction of extension and *ERltSrt* or *ERrtSlt* for extended joints with restriction of flexion. The side bend is more important than the rotation, and the notation may be shortened to *FSrt* (or *lt*) and *ESlt* (or *rt*). The shorter notation is used in this book.

Terminology that defines the position of the joint is useful because it also defines the restrictors. For example, if a joint is described as being flexed, rotated, and side bent to the right, then the restricting myofascial elements include muscles that can be functionally identified as the flexors, right rotators, and right side benders. Successful treatment depends on the ability to lengthen these specific myofascial elements. However, when reporting the physical findings and treatment, the positional diagnosis often requires some explanation to anyone who receives this report and is unfamiliar with this particular terminology. For this reason, describing the motion restrictions that apply to a particular patient may be better understood by those not familiar with the terminology of a positional, structural diagnosis.

SPINAL MOTION CHARACTERISTICS AND TYPES OF DYSFUNCTION

As stated in Chapter 2, side bending and rotation are coupled movements at all levels in the spine except at C1-2, at which the primary motion is rotation alone. We refer to the coupled motion of side bending and rotation to the opposite sides as *neutral coupling behavior* and side bending and rotation to the same side as *non-neutral coupling behavior*. In the lumbar spinal joints, the coupling of side bending and rotation changes from neutral coupling to non-neutral coupling mechanics during flexion, but this change in coupling

behavior is not normally observed in extension, during which the coupling of side bending and rotation continue to be to the opposite sides. Despite this behavior, dysfunctions can occur in the lumbar spine when it is in the extended position and can present to the examiner as a restriction of coupled motion of side bending and rotation to the same side (i.e., ERSlt or rt). When this coupling happens, non-neutral flexion restrictions are observed. The situation is similar in the thoracic spine for non-neutral behavior during flexion because of the kyphosis, but, more important, it is the restriction imposed by the rib attachments to a fixed sternum that determines coupled motion characteristics. With an intact rib cage, non-neutral coupling behavior in the thoracic spine occurs only if rotation is introduced first; neutral coupling behavior occurs when side bending is introduced first.[1]

In the neutral, "sit-up-tall" position, the joints in both the thoracic and lumbar spines follow Fryette's first concept of spinal motion.[2] Side bending to the right is always accompanied by rotation to the left—a motion defined as *neutral coupling behavior*. The vertebrae can be viewed as sharing the load while maintaining postural balance.

In the flexed position, both the upper thoracic and lumbar joints follow Fryette's second concept and rotate to the same side as the side bending—a motion defined as *non-neutral coupling behavior*. That this behavior happens in the fully flexed spine is certain, but it does not seem to require the limit of full flexion for non-neutral coupling behavior to be operative. On the other hand, there is a fairly wide neutral range in which neutral coupling behavior occurs. It is probable that the precise amount of flexion at which coupled motion characteristics change varies from joint to joint and from patient to patient.

Because motion coupling in the neutral range of the antero-posterior plane follows Fryette's first concept, when dysfunctions occur that keep three or more vertebrae side bent in one direction and rotated in the other, the term *Type I dysfunction* has been used. However, because restricted spinal motion reflects a coupled response defined by neutral mechanics, it is now more commonly described as a *neutral dysfunction*. For the same reason, those dysfunctions occurring in a non-neutral situation have been known as *Type II dysfunctions* because of the association with Fryette's second concept and are now better described as *non-neutral dysfunctions*. This nomenclature applies equally to dysfunctions that have a restriction of flexion or extension.

In the cervical spine, the mechanics are not the same as in the lumbar and thoracic spines. In the typical cervical joints (C2 to T1), there is no neutral zone, probably because the shape and orientation of the articular facets are such that they are always "engaged" and therefore control movement. For this reason, neutral dysfunctions do not occur in these joints. However, non-neutral dysfunctions in flexion and extension do occur. At the atlantoaxial joint, the only movement with a range of more than a few degrees is rotation, so there is a minimal flexion or extension component to dysfunctions at this level.

The OA joint is also unusual. At this joint, the main movement is flexion or extension, but there is enough side bending and just enough rotation for coupled motion. The shape of the articular facets and the alar ligaments determines the coupling behavior, so rotation always occurs to the opposite side of side bending. This motion should not be confused with the neutral coupling mechanics described for the thoracic and lumbar spine, because it is not a neutral mechanism. Treatment of the OA joint always includes a barrier to either flexion or extension.

Facet and Transverse Process Motion

When a vertebra flexes on the one below, as though it were rotating anteriorly around a transverse axis, the inferior facets of the superior vertebra glide upward and forward to a new position determined by the unique facing of the facets at that joint. Therefore, the degree of spinal flexion varies from one region to another. It is important to recognize that in addition to the rotation that occurs with spinal flexion, there is also an associated anterior translation of the superior vertebra on the inferior vertebra along a horizontal plane. This translatory motion results in the superior facet of the inferior vertebra remaining in a relatively posterior position to the inferior facet of the vertebra above (see Figure 2-15*A*). However, when the patient is in the seated position and translation is used as the major component to induce flexion, in order to maintain postural balance, the superior vertebra is translated posteriorly by slumping the patient backward. Therefore, forward bending in sitting involves more anterior rotation around a transverse axis, whereas slumping backward produces more anterior-to-posterior translation in the transverse plane. Creating an apex of flexion between two vertebrae by primarily using translation requires the upper vertebra to glide posteriorly further than the vertebra below (Figure 5-1).

When the superior vertebra extends on the one below, as though it were rotating backward around a transverse axis, the inferior facets of the superior vertebra glide downward and posteriorly to a position that also depends on the unique anatomical shape and orientation of the

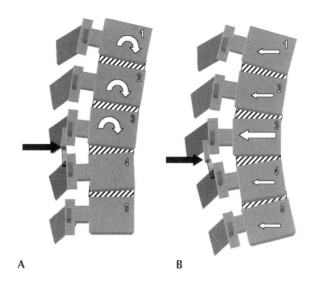

A   **B**

FIGURE 5-1
(A) Flexion accomplished by rotation from above down to the third vertebra on the fourth vertebra. (B) Flexion accomplished by posterior translation of the third or middle vertebra, making this vertebra the apex of the flexion curve. Black arrows indicate the apex of facet joint opening between the third and fourth vertebrae; white arrows indicate the direction of translatory motion of the vertebrae; curved arrows indicate the direction of rotational (overturning) movement of the vertebrae.

facet facings at that joint. Therefore, the degree of spinal extension varies from one region to another. As with flexion, extension is also associated with a translatory motion in the horizontal plane. With extension of the spine, translation of the superior vertebra occurs in a posterior direction. When extension of the spine is accomplished by backward bending from above down, the rotational component predominates, and the inferior facet of the superior vertebra must be able to slide down and behind the superior facet of the inferior vertebra (see Figure 2-15*B*). However, when translation is used as the major component to induce extension and, at the same time, to maintain postural balance, the inferior vertebra is translated anteriorly when the operator asks the patient to sit up tall. By introducing anterior translation from below up, the superior facets of the inferior vertebra glide anteriorly and superiorly and underneath the inferior facets of the vertebra above (Figure 5-2). We believe it is primarily the loss of translation in the horizontal plane that is the major cause of restriction for flexion or extension of the spine.

In most patients, the facets in the thoracic and lumbar regions are difficult to feel. The transverse processes (TPs) are easier to palpate and are used to determine the position of each vertebra with respect to the one below

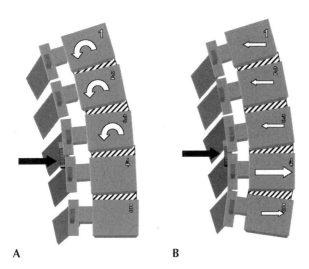

FIGURE 5-2

(A) *Extension accomplished by rotation from above down to the third vertebra on the fourth vertebra with facet closure occurring sequentially.* **(B)** *Extension accomplished by the anterior translation of the fourth vertebra under the third vertebra with localized facet closure from below (L4) up (L3). When translation is used for extension, the vertebrae above the apex must be able to move in the opposite direction. Black arrows indicate the apex of the facet joint closing between the third and fourth vertebrae; white arrows indicate the direction of translatory motion of the vertebrae. Curved white arrows indicate the direction of rotational (overturning) movement of the vertebrae.*

as the spine is flexed and extended. At L5, the lamina is used because the TP cannot be reached (see Figure 4-14).

In the cervical spine, articular pillars that carry the facets above and below are the most important landmarks in the typical joints (C2-7) and can easily be felt. The TPs are small, very tender, and in close relation to both nerves and vessels. For these reasons, TPs are avoided in the cervical spine, although the TP of C1 is a useful landmark.

In summary, interpretation of the findings of the spinal examination depends on these observations (Figure 5-3):

1. On flexion, the facet joints "open" (the inferior facet of the superior vertebra slides up on the superior facet of the inferior vertebra). Similarly, the TPs rise and, because of the obliquity of the joints, move anteriorly as well and become less easy to palpate.

2. On extension, the facets "close" (the inferior facet of the superior vertebra slides down on the superior facet of the inferior vertebra) and the TPs drop, become more posterior, and become easier to palpate.

3. On side bending right, the right facet closes and the left facet opens. The right TP drops and becomes

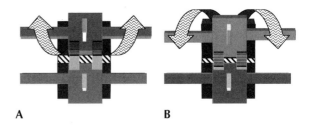

A   **B**

FIGURE 5-3

(A) *Transverse processes (TPs) move away from palpating fingers during flexion.* **(B)** *TPs move toward the palpating fingers during extension.*

more inferior, whereas the left TP raises and becomes more superior (see Figure 2-17*A*).

4. On side bending left, the left facet closes and the right facet opens. The left TP drops and becomes more inferior, whereas the right TP raises and becomes more superior (see Figure 2-17*B*).

It is possible to make a definitive diagnosis either dynamically or statically. In the dynamic method, the operator observes and palpates the motion of the TPs while the patient is moving. In the static method, observations are made in regard to the symmetry or asymmetry of the TPs when the spine is in three different positions: flexed, neutral, and extended. Either method provides the required information; the dynamic method is usually easier in the upper thoracic spine, and the static method is easier in the lower thoracic and lumbar regions. In any of these examinations, sighting with the eyes can be reinforced by the proprioceptors of the operator's hands. It is not very difficult to train oneself to feel position and movement in this way; that ability is useful, for instance, when examining the upper thoracic area in a patient with long hair.

The point in the range of motion at which restriction to flexion or extension begins defines whether there is a major or minor motion barrier present. Major barriers extend beyond the normal physiological neutral zone of motion, so a major motion restriction for flexion begins on the extension side of neutral, and, likewise, a major restriction for extension begins on the flexion side of neutral (Figure 5-4). Minor barriers do not extend into the normal physiological neutral zone, and, therefore, a minor motion restriction for extension is found on the extension side of the neutral zone, and a minor motion restriction for flexion is found on the flexion side of the neutral zone (Figure 5-5). Major motion barriers are suspected during static positional testing when asymmetry of the TPs is already present

FIGURE 5-4

Major barriers for flexion and extension demonstrating the position of the superior transverse processes with increasing motion toward and into the barrier and the positional diagnosis of a major ERS (extended, rotated, side bent) or FRS (flexed, rotated, side bent) dysfunction. Horizontal arrows indicate the barriers. Vertical arrows indicate the direction of motion of the body relative to the examiner standing behind the patient. The upward arrows indicate increasing movement away from the examiner (patient is flexing the spine), whereas the downward arrows indicate increasing movement toward the examiner (patient is extending the spine). (TP = transverse process.)

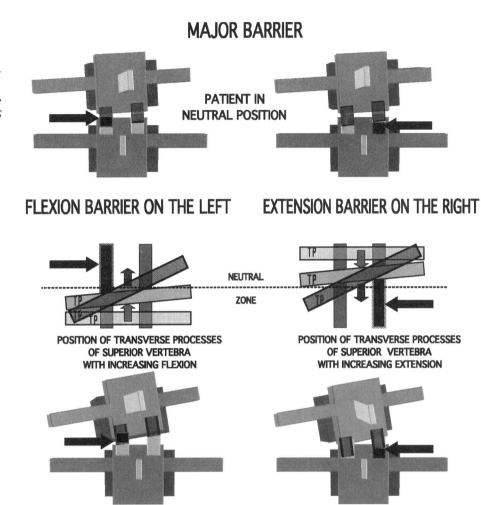

MAJOR BARRIER

PATIENT IN
NEUTRAL POSITION

FLEXION BARRIER ON THE LEFT   **EXTENSION BARRIER ON THE RIGHT**

NEUTRAL

ZONE

POSITION OF TRANSVERSE PROCESSES
OF SUPERIOR VERTEBRA
WITH INCREASING FLEXION

POSITION OF TRANSVERSE PROCESSES
OF SUPERIOR VERTEBRA
WITH INCREASING EXTENSION

ERS LEFT
LEFT FACET
CANNOT OPEN

FRS LEFT
RIGHT FACET
CANNOT CLOSE

when examining the spine with the patient in the neutral position.

The conversion of these physical findings into a positional diagnosis is as follows:

1. If, in extension, the TPs of T4 and T5 are level, but, in flexion, the left TP of T4 becomes more prominent and remains lower (posterior and inferior) than the TP on the right (but the TPs of T5 remain level), then T4 is extended, rotated left, and side bent left in relation to T5. The position of T4 is a consequence of the inability of the left zygapophyseal joint between T4 and T5 to open or glide superiorly and anteriorly. Because the left facet remained closed but the right facet opened with flexion, T4 is side bent to the left. Because the left facet did not open, the left TP remained posterior when compared to

the right one, and, with the coupled rotation of T4 to the left, the left TP became even more prominent than the TP on the right. There is a restrictive barrier for flexion at the left T4-T5 facet joint, and because this joint cannot open, there is a concurrent restriction for right side bending and the coupled right rotation. If the barrier preventing facet opening is somewhere between the fully extended position and the fully flexed position, and the left facet can partially open, the TPs of T4 will remain level during flexion until the barrier for left facet opening is reached. Once the barrier for flexion is reached, the left TP of T4 becomes more prominent with increasing spinal flexion (see Figure 5-5). If the flexion barrier is at or near the normally fully extended position, then the dysfunctional facet remains fully closed, and the asymmetry of the TPs of T4 occurs at the beginning of flexion (see Figure 5-4).

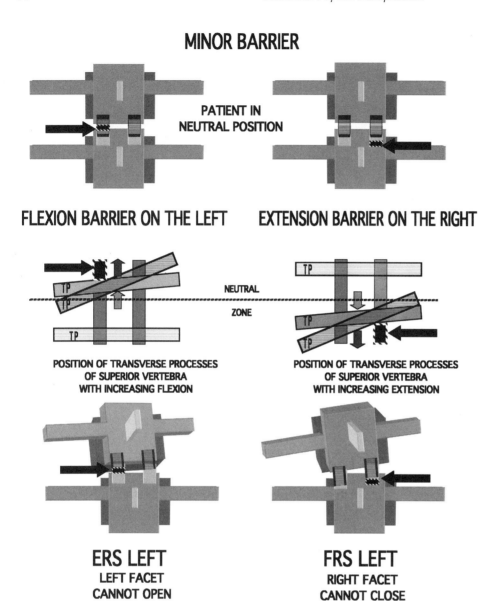

MINOR BARRIER

PATIENT IN
NEUTRAL POSITION

FLEXION BARRIER ON THE LEFT   **EXTENSION BARRIER ON THE RIGHT**

NEUTRAL

ZONE

POSITION OF TRANSVERSE PROCESSES
OF SUPERIOR VERTEBRA
WITH INCREASING FLEXION

POSITION OF TRANSVERSE PROCESSES
OF SUPERIOR VERTEBRA
WITH INCREASING EXTENSION

ERS LEFT
LEFT FACET
CANNOT OPEN

FRS LEFT
RIGHT FACET
CANNOT CLOSE

FIGURE 5-5
Minor barriers for flexion and extension demonstrating the position of the superior transverse processes with increasing motion toward and into the barrier and the positional diagnosis of a minor ERS (extended, rotated, side bent) or FRS (flexed, rotated, side bent) dysfunction. Arrows point at the barriers limiting motion at the zygapophyseal joint. The vertical arrows indicate the direction of motion of the vertebral body relative to the examiner standing behind the patient. The upward arrows indicate increasing movement away from the examiner (patient is flexing the spine), whereas downward arrows indicate increasing movement toward the examiner (patient is extending the spine).

Therefore, the position of T4 in relation to T5 at the barrier is described as extended (left facet is closed), rotated, and side bent left, or ERSlt (see Figures 5-4 and 5-5).

2. If, in flexion, the TPs of T4 and T5 are level, but, in extension, the left TP of T4 becomes more prominent (posterior and inferior) than the TP on the right (but the TPs of T5 remain level), then T4 is flexed, rotated left, and side bent left in relation to T5. The position of T4 is a consequence of the inability of the right zygapophyseal joint between T4 and T5 to close or a consequence of the inability of the superior facet of T5 on the right to glide anteriorly and superiorly under the inferior facet of T4. When the left facet closes with extension but the right facet remains open, T4 side bends to the left. Because the left facet closed, the left TP moves inferi-

orly and posteriorly, and because the right facet remained open, the right TP remains in an anterior and superior position and is less prominent. With the coupled rotation of T4 to the left, the left TP becomes more prominent than the TP on the right. There is a restrictive barrier for extension at the right T4-5 facet joint, and because this joint cannot close, there is a concurrent restriction for right side bending and coupled right rotation. If the barrier preventing facet closure at this joint is somewhere between the fully flexed position and the fully extended position, and the right facet can partially close, the TPs of T4 will remain level during extension until the barrier for right facet closure is reached (see Figure 5-5). Once the barrier for extension is reached, the left TP of T4 becomes more prominent with increas-

FIGURE 5-6

An example of a neutral dysfunction involving T1, T2, and T3 as a spinal curve that is side bent right and rotated left and persists when the spine is flexed and when it is extended. The rotation and side-bending behavior is maximal in the neutral position. If T1, T2, and T3 were demonstrating normal adaptive behavior, the rotation and side bending would only be seen in the neutral position.

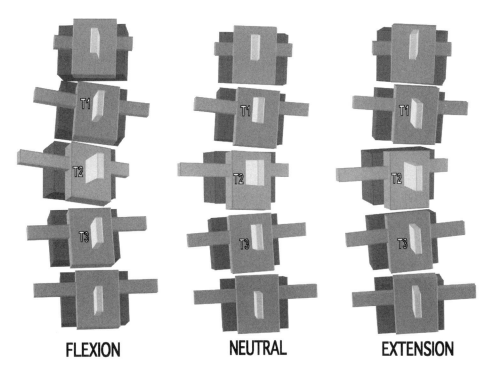

FLEXION　　　**NEUTRAL**　　　**EXTENSION**

ing spinal extension. If the extension barrier is at or near the fully flexed position, then the dysfunctional facet remains fully opened, and the asymmetry of the TPs of T4 occurs at the beginning of extension from the fully flexed position (see Figure 5-4).

Therefore, the position of T4 in relation to T5 at the barrier is described as flexed, rotated, and side bent left, or FRSlt (see Figures 5-4 and 5-5).

Note that the process by which the positional diagnosis is made for both examples is used consistently. Both are recorded as left (for rotation and side bending) despite that, in one example, the left facet joint is dysfunctional and will not open (ERSlt), and in the other example, it is the right facet joint that is not moving properly and will not close (FRSlt).

3. If there is a neutral dysfunction of the group T1 through T3 so that all three are rotated left and side bent to the right, the rotation is greatest at the apex (T2). This asymmetry is present throughout the range of flexion and extension, but it is usually maximal in the neutral position (Figure 5-6). The neutral dysfunctions occur only in groups of three or more contiguous vertebrae, all of which are rotated in the direction opposite the concavity (side bend). The acuteness of the side bend and the differences in the stepwise increasing and decreasing rotation above and below the apex of the curve depend on the number of vertebrae involved and the magnitude of the non-neutral dysfunction that is usually at either the top or bottom or at both ends of the group.

The common notation for such a neutral dysfunction is neutral left (Nlt).

In the absence of a neutral dysfunction, the spine may still demonstrate adaptive neutral mechanics (type I) when examined in the neutral position if a non-neutral dysfunctional segment, ERS or FRS, is of such a magnitude (major barrier) that a neutral coupling adaptive responsive is required. However, when the spine moves out of the neutral position, either by flexion or extention, then the non-dysfunctional vertebral segments above the ERS or FRS will follow the position of the dysfunctional non-neutral segment below them (see Figure 2–20). Therefore, these non-dysfunctional vertebral segments are neither adaptive nor abnormal. In the example of an ERSlt at T4 in the extended position, if there are no other non-neutral dysfunctions, the TPs of T3, T2, and T1 all appear level because the TPs of T4 are also level. With increasing flexion beyond the flexion barrier of T4, the left TP of T4 becomes prominent as T4 rotates and side bends left in relation to T5. The spinal segments above T4 appear to tilt to the left and rotate to the left to the same degree as T4. Although the left TPs of T3, T2, and T1 are more prominent than those on the right, their position is no different than the TP of T4. With increasing extension, the rotation diminishes, and when T4 has extended beyond its flexion barrier, the TPs of T4 become level, as do the TPs of T3, T2, and T1. The vertebral response of T1–T3 in this example does not represent a group dysfunction. In fact, there are also no non-neutral

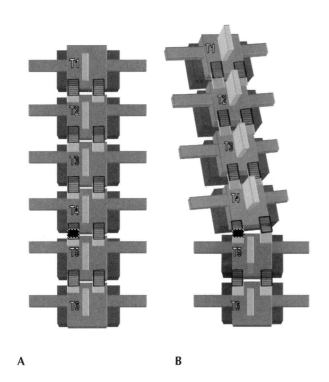

A   B

FIGURE 5-7

An example of how a section of vertebral segments responds above a minor non-neutral dysfunction—in this case, ERSlt (extended, rotated, side bent left) at T4. (A) Neutral position with a minor flexion barrier on left between T4-5. (B) During flexion, the normal segments, T1, T2, and T3, simply follow the position of T4. Because these segments are not positionally different between each other or with T4, there are no other neutral or non-neutral ERS dysfunctions between them.

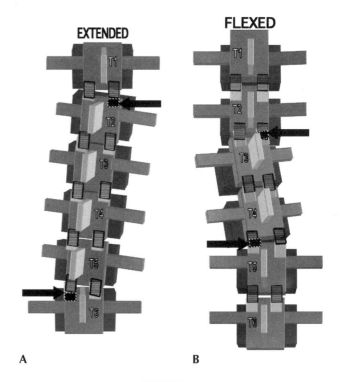

A   B

FIGURE 5-8

When there is more than one non-neutral dysfunction, the positional diagnosis is based on the relationship of the superior vertebra to the one immediately below it. (A) FRSlt (flexed, rotated, side bent left) T1 and FRSrt (flexed, rotated, side bent right) T5. Vertebrae T2, T3, and T4 are normal because there is no difference in their positions relative to the vertebra below. (B) ERSrt T2 (extended, rotated, side bent right) and ERSlt T4 (extended, rotated, side bent left) T4. T1 simply follows T2, T3 follows T4, and both are normal. Arrows indicate the barriers limiting motion at the zygapophyseal joint.

dysfunctions that prevent flexion between T3-4, T2-3, and T1-2 in this example (Figure 5-7). Similarly, if T4 is FRSlt, the TPs of T3, T2, and T1 appear symmetrical with T4 when the upper thoracic spine is flexed and appear left-rotated to the same degree as T4, with increasing extension beyond the extension barrier between T4 and T5.

Certainly, non-neutral dysfunctions can occur in multiple segments. When they occur one on top of the other, they are described as "stacked" non-neutral dysfunctions. The positional diagnosis follows the principle of comparing the superior vertebra to the one immediately below and applies for both stacked and multiple non-neutral dysfunctions. In the example of an FRSrt at T5 with an FRSlt at T1, the TPs of T2, T3, and T4 all appear rotated to the right as far as the rotation of T5 when the spine is extended. However, the TPs of T1 appear level or less right-rotated than T2 when the upper thoracic spine is extended (Figure 5-8A). Likewise, in the example of an

ERSlt at T4 with an ERSrt at T2, the TPs of T3 appear as left-rotated as T4 with the spine in flexion, but the TPs of T2 may actually appear level in flexion. In this example, T2 appears different than T3, and it is relatively rotated to the right compared to T3, when the spine is flexed. This observation occurs because there is restricted facet opening on the right between T2 and T3 (Figure 5-8B).

POSITIONAL DIAGNOSTIC TECHNIQUES OF THE THORACIC AND LUMBAR

Static Examination

Static examination usually begins immediately after the sitting forward flexion test. In patients for whom forward bending while standing is comfortable, the examination can be done standing. For most patients with back trouble, the sitting position is preferable.

Like most examinations, this examination requires a prohibitive amount of time to check each joint in turn all the way up the spine. This is the reason to have the examination process begin with an overall screen to demonstrate which areas need further attention, followed by a scan to pinpoint joints for detailed assessment. The third step, segmental definition, defines the precise position of the barrier at each of the dysfunctional joints identified by the scan. The following description refers to the segmental definition.

Because the TPs are used as the main indicators of vertebral position and segmental definition in these tests, it is important that they can be found with some accuracy. It must be remembered that they vary in length (see Figure 2-6*A*). The longest TPs are usually at L3, and the shortest TPs are at T12. TPs are most easily found by palpating deep in the lateral gutter between the longissimus and iliocostalis muscles. In the thoracic region, the tip of the TP is easily found by palpating in the lateral gutter to find the posterior part of the rib; the rib is then followed medially until a resistance or "bump" is felt; the bump is the tip of the TP. Alternatively, it is possible to palpate medial to the longissimus on the lamina of the lumbar vertebrae or the TPs of the thoracic vertebrae. It is important at that point to lighten one's pressure until the TP can only just be felt, because the lighter the contact, the more one can feel. It is possible to feel through a relaxed longissimus, but this palpation is less accurate, and, when this muscle is hypertonic, it can be impossible to feel the bone.

Any rotation of the lumbar and lower thoracic vertebrae is estimated by finding the relative posteriority of the TPs. It is generally accepted that the thumbs are more sensitive for perception of depth, and they are used in preference for this examination. When there is a major restriction in either flexion or extension, there is asymmetry of the TPs, even in the neutral position. When the restriction is relatively minor, the TPs should be symmetrical in the neutral position.

The most important part of the examination at this stage is the determination of the position of the vertebra by comparing the TPs of the superior vertebra to the TPs of the immediate level below and asking this question: Are these TPs in the same position, or are they in a different position?

Spine Flexed
In the fully flexed position of the lumbar spine, the tightness of the lumbosacral fascia makes the examination more difficult, and, occasionally, it is necessary to examine the

spine in the other two positions and to extrapolate from those results the probable position of the TPs in flexion. At L5, the laminae are palpated, as the TPs are hidden by the ilium. This makes it a little more difficult to determine the position of L5, because the contact is closer to the midline and positional differences between the two sides are less obvious than if the TPs could be used as in the other lumbar and thoracic vertebrae. If the left lamina of L5 is prominent in the prone-neutral position and becomes level with the right lamina when the patient is prone propped, it can be inferred that the left lamina of L5 will be even more prominent with flexion (ERSlt), assuming that the sacrum is level and not dysfunctional. The rotation of L5 is always to be assessed as compared to the position of the sacral base, which is found by moving the thumbs from the most posterior part of the posterior superior iliac spine medially and *caudad* approximately 30 degrees (see Figure 4-4). Because palpation of the sacral base is the least reliable pelvic landmark, it may help to confirm its position by deduction from the relative positions of the inferior lateral angles in flexion, neutral, and extension (as described in Chapter 4).

1. The patient sits with knees apart and feet on the floor or a stool and bends forward as far as possible with arms hanging between the knees. An alternative approach is to have the patient sit slumped and then sit up tall or even arch backward; the operator notes the changes in symmetry of the TPs. This technique is more sensitive for the major restrictions than for the minor restrictions.

2. The thumbs are placed one on either side of the same vertebra to find the tips of the TPs from L4 up. At L5, the laminae are found from the most posterior part of the posterior superior iliac spine, moving the thumbs medially and craniad at an angle of approximately 30 degrees (see Figure 4-14).

3. With moderate pressure equal on the two sides, the depth (posteriority) of the thumbs is noted and compared with the level below.

The specific examination is repeated at each of the levels indicated by the scanning examination up to the mid-thoracic spine.

The observations are described in the order in which they are often done in the routine examination of a patient. The order in which these are performed is not important and can be altered to suit the operator.

Spine Neutral
The easiest way to examine the lumbar spine in the neutral position is with the patient lying prone. For patients

unable to lie prone, the examination can be done sitting, but this is more difficult.

The examination is performed in exactly the same manner as in forward bending, but at L5, palpation is easier because the fascia is no longer tight. Notation is made of any level at which the TPs of a lumbar or lower thoracic vertebra appear rotated in comparison to the level below, paying particular attention to levels indicated by the scanning examination.

Spine Extended

For this examination, the prone position is also easiest, but, in this case, the patient props up on elbows and holds up the chin as high as possible (i.e., with the elbows close together and almost directly below the chin) (see Figure 3-26). This is known as the "sphinx" position, although the analogy is inaccurate. For this position to be useful, it is necessary for patients to relax their back and abdominal muscles. This examination can also be done with the patient sitting and arching backward as much as possible. The examination is done in the same manner as in the other two positions, but it usually proceeds from below up.

Interpretation of Examination Findings

Interpretation of the static examination can be envisioned by the following examples. If

- In the neutral examining position, the TPs of L2 are level or the TP on the left is more posterior and, therefore, easier to feel than the TP of L3,
- In flexion, the relative asymmetry of L2 is exaggerated, but L3 still appears level,
- In extension, the rotational asymmetry of the TPs of L2 disappears.

The inference is that the left facet joint at L2-3 will not open (flex). This indicates a loss of right rotation and the associated right side bending with a loss of flexion. Positionally, the joint is extended, rotated, and side bent left, or ERSlt at L2 (see Figures 5-4 and 5-5).

If, on the other hand,

- In the neutral examining position, the TPs of L2 are level or the TP on the left is more posterior than the TP of L3 (the same scenario as described previously),
- In flexion, the relative rotation disappears (no asymmetry of the TPs of L2),
- In extension, the asymmetry of L2 is exaggerated, the left TP becomes more posterior, but the TPs of L3 remain level.

The inference is that the right facet joint at L2-3 will not close (extend). This indicates a loss of right rotation and right side bending, but, in this case, there is a loss of extension at the L2-3 joint. Positionally, the joint is flexed, rotated, and side bent to the left, or FRSlt (see Figures 5-4 and 5-5).

If

1. In the neutral examining position, the TP of L2 is prominent on the right;
2. The rotation may vary a little but is present in both flexion and extension,
3. There is rotation to the right at L1 and L3 but not at L4.

The inference is that there is a neutral group dysfunction centered at L2 that is side bent left and rotated right, or NRrt (neutral, rotated right or right convexity).

If there is rotational asymmetry that involves three or more vertebrae and does not change on flexion or extension, the possibility of a structural asymmetry or primary scoliosis must also be considered.

If the rotational asymmetry involves less than three vertebrae and does not change with flexion or extension, there may be

1. A fusion, congenital or other (e.g., post traumatic, surgical), or
2. A bilateral dysfunction located at the same vertebral segment; the facet joint on one side is restricted for flexion, and the facet joint on the other side is restricted for extension.

None of these examples can be regarded as a rarity. Asymmetry is common and, in certain areas, the rule rather than the exception. The sacroiliac joint is an example because the auricular surface on one side is rarely, if ever, the same shape as that on the other side, which may, in part, account for the complexity of dysfunctions found in the pelvis.

If a spinal joint has restricted flexion on one side (ERS) and restricted extension on the other side (FRS), the rotation may not change when flexion or extension is introduced to that region of the spine. A bilateral restriction can be distinguished from a structural asymmetry by examining passive mobility for flexion and extension at the interspinous interval. This motion is normal in a joint at which the asymmetry is structural, but it is absent or significantly restricted if there is a bilateral facet joint dysfunction with one facet flexed and the other extended (as described previously).

Intervertebral fusion of any type is apparent on x-rays and, unless complicated by a neighboring joint dysfunction, is not accompanied by tissue texture changes.

Examples of Multiple Non-Neutral Dysfunctions

1. In neutral, L2 rotates left in relation to L3 and rotates further to the left with flexion, but diminishes with extension (major restriction).

2. L1, T12, T11, and up through T1 all appear to rotate as much as L2 in neutral, and the additional rotation at L2 provoked by flexion is matched by all the segments above. There is no difference between the position of L1 and L2 and, therefore, no dysfunction for flexion between them. The same is true for T12-L1, T11-12, and so on up to T1-2.

3. If there is a major restriction for flexion at T6 on the right (ERSrt), then, in neutral and with flexion, T6 will appear to be level when compared to T7, which appears rotated left following the levels below. The level-appearing T6 does not follow T7 and is, therefore, rotated right in comparison to T7 in flexion.

The only dysfunctional segments in this example are L2-3, with L2 rotated to the left (ERSlt), and T6-7, in which T6 is ERSrt but appears to be level in space (i.e., *if* not compared to T7).

Clinically, the same scenario applies for FRS dysfunctions, which, if major, are seen in the neutral examining position. The TP asymmetry worsens with increasing extension of the spine. Normal segments above the dysfunction appear to rotate to the same degree as the dysfunctional segment when in spinal extension. Abnormal or restricted segments appear either more rotated or can appear level if they are actually rotated in the opposite direction. For example, if there is an FRSlt dysfunction at L3 (with extension of the spine, L3 rotates and side bends left in relation to L4), the non-dysfunctional spine above L3 will appear rotated left as much as L3 in extension. If, suddenly, T6 appears to be level in relation to T7, which appears to be rotated left following T8 and all the way down to L3, then T6 is not following the vertebrae below (T7). The inference is then made that T6 is actually rotated right or in the opposite direction of T7 and is therefore dysfunctional. In relation to T7, T6 (although it appears level in space) is actually FRSrt. If, on the other hand, T6 were found to be rotated to the left more than T7 in extension, then the dysfunction would be described as FRSlt.

Bilateral dysfunctions can also occur either extended or flexed, but sometimes, in these cases, there is no rotational asymmetry of the TPs associated with the restriction because both facets are equally restricted. An increase in tension can be felt with intersegmental passive mobility testing, and, depending on the dysfunction, the spinous process of the superior vertebra quickly approaches the one below during attempted extension (if the vertebra is bilaterally flexed), or does not separate from the one below with flexion (if the vertebra is bilaterally extended). Passive mobility testing and palpation of tissue texture changes in the spinal gutter are essential in diagnosing bilateral dysfunctions.

Asymmetrical bilateral non-neutral dysfunctions are probably the norm. For example, if there is a major FRSlt and a minor FRSrt at L5, only the major FRSlt will be observed (the left lamina of L5 is posterior) when the lumbar spine is fully extended. However, after successful treatment of the FRSlt at L5, the FRSrt (the right lamina of L5 is now posterior) will become apparent when the patient is re-examined in full extension (Steele C., personal communication, 1999). This scenario explains why re-examination after treatment is important and why subsequent positional findings can appear different from the initial evaluation.

Dynamic Examination

Dynamic examination is most useful in the upper half of the thoracic spine but can be used lower, if needed. It is normally done with the patient sitting on a stool or with each leg over the side of the examination table. It is important to see that the patient's feet are supported to prevent a loss of balance when forward bending is required.

The examination can be performed actively by having the patient initiate the movement into flexion and extension, or it can be performed passively when the operator does both the moving and the examination. The former is easier for the operator and is used unless the patient finds it difficult to understand or seems unable to follow instructions. The movements for flexion should be done segmentally, curling from above down rather than regionally, which encourages flexion at only one or two segments with the rest of the spine following en bloc. Likewise, the movement for extension should also be done segmentally with the emphasis of movement beginning from the pelvis and lumbar spine and moving upward. When the patient is sitting erect and is asked to push the abdomen forward for anterior translation, extension of the spine occurs from below up.

When using the dynamic method, it is sometimes easier to observe the upward motion of the TP and some-

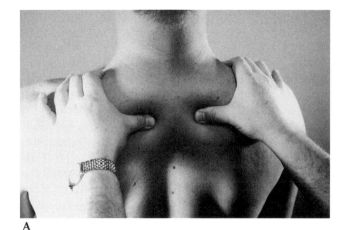

A

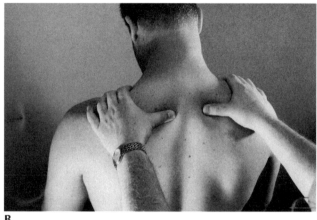

B

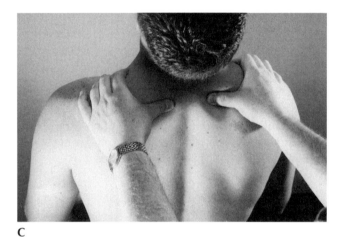

C

FIGURE 5-9
(A) Dynamic examination of upper thoracic spine by locating transverse processes palpating between longissimus and iliocostalis muscles and moving thumbs medially; (B) following transverse processes by maintaining thumb contact when patient flexes neck; and (C) when patient extends neck.

times easier to observe the forward motion, which makes the TP less prominent. These observations provide the same information: If the TP on one side moves superiorly, it is also moving forward, and vice versa. The starting posture is important because any deviation from flexion or extension in the neutral position is reflected in the amount of movement available in the other planes. An easy way to get the patient to assume the neutral position when examining the thoracic spine is to ask the patient to "sit up tall." It is also important to make sure that a barrier between two vertebrae was not already passed in the starting position. For a major restriction of extension, the motion examination must be started from a point at which the joint is free to move from flexion to extension. The same is true for a major restriction of flexion identified from the starting position, at which motion from extension to flexion is initially free. As previously described, to avoid inadvertent flexion of the lumbar and lower thoracic joints when assessing flexion and extension in the upper thoracic spine, the patient is instructed to

extend the spine from below upward by anteriorly tilting the pelvis and pushing the belly forward to maintain postural balance.

Active Examination
It is often helpful to assess for spinal dysfunctions by palpation of the TPs during active flexion or extension of the spine, observing for a progressive increase or decrease in asymmetry of the TPs, because the motion being tested has either encountered a restrictive barrier or is moving away from this barrier.

The operator places his or her thumbs in the fascial plane between the longissimus and iliocostalis muscles and moves them medially along the rib shaft to find the tips of the TPs. With the patient in neutral, the thumbs are placed over the TPs of the vertebra to be tested (Figure 5-9A). The patient is then instructed to bend his or her head (or, for lower down, the head and shoulders) forward, and the relative motion of the TPs is observed (Figure 5-9B). Normally, both TPs (monitored by the thumbs) move anteriorly and superiorly symmetrically with spinal flexion. Abnormal motion is shown by the TP on one side rising superiorly and becoming less easy to feel, whereas the other TP remains low and prominent. The patient is then instructed to tilt the head backward to extend the neck and upper thoracic spine (Figure 5-9C). Normally, both TPs (monitored by thumbs) move posteriorly and inferiorly symmetrically with spinal extension. An abnormality seen this time would be the failure of one TP to descend and become prominent. In the upper thoracic spine, it is often not enough for the patient simply to extend his or her neck, especially in the patient who has an increase in the cervico-thoracic kyphosis. If extension from below is omitted, the asymmetry easily may be missed. The necessary anterior translation from below (extension) can be achieved by having the patient push his or her stomach forward and then bring the head back with the chin tucked in (extension of the neck on the thorax is required, not extension of the head on the neck). The palpatory observations are all made with reference to the next lower vertebra.

Passive Examination for the Upper Thoracic Spine
The operator uses the index and middle fingers of one hand to perform the examination while, with the other hand on the patient's head, flexion and extension of the upper thoracic spine are introduced. The fingertips should be on the tip of each of the TPs of the vertebra being examined or in the interspinous spaces. Forward flexion of the thoracic spine can be examined by rotating the patient's head and working from above down, but localizing to a given segment of the spine is difficult (Figure 5-10A). Localization is better achieved by using posterior translation of the spine working from above down and below up by guiding the patient into a slumped position until the desired segment is at the apex of a forward-bending curve (Figure 5-10B). Extension can also be accomplished by rotating the patient's head and working from above down, but, again, localization is difficult, and a strain may be placed on the cervical spine (Figure 5-10C). Extension in the upper thoracic spine is best accomplished by using anterior translation of the spine from below up by having the patient push his or her stomach forward. At the same time, the patient is instructed to tuck the chin down and allow the operator to translate the neck and upper thoracic spine posteriorly until the desired segment is at the apex of a backward bending curve (Figure 5-10D).

Passive Examination for the Lower Thoracic and Lumbar Spine
At times, it may be difficult to identify a dysfunction based on the position of the TPs because of the overlying tissue tension, muscle bulk, and the size of the TPs, especially at the thoraco-lumbar junction. If this difficulty is encoun-

tered, a structural diagnosis of a flexion or an extension restriction between two adjacent vertebrae may be achieved by using passive, side-to-side translatory motion testing. This technique can be applied when the patient is in the seated position with the feet supported or when the patient is in the prone-neutral or prone-propped position. In the seated position, translatory motion from left to right and from right to left can be applied with the spine in flexion and extension to detect ERS and FRS dysfunctions, respectively. In the prone position, translatory motion from side to side is useful primarily in detecting FRS dysfunctions, especially when they are bilateral and symmetrical and located at the thoraco-lumbar junction.

Passive Motion Testing in the Seated Position
The patient is seated on a chair or stool with both feet on the floor. The operator stands to one side, facing the patient.

1. If standing on the patient's left side, the operator places his or her left hand on top of the patient's left shoulder, and the operator's right thumb pad or fingertip is placed against the left side of the spinous process of the vertebra to be motion tested (Figure 5-11A).

2. With the patient sitting in a neutral position, the operator applies a slight compressive force on the patient's left shoulder, directed downward toward the operator's right thumb or fingertip. Using translation, the operator attempts to create an apex of left side bending of the spine at his or her right thumb or fingertips (see Figure 5-11A).

3. After slumping the patient by using an anterior-to-posterior translation to induce flexion, the lateral translation is repeated, keeping the vertebra to be motion tested at the apex of the flexed spine (Figure 5-11B). If resistance is felt at the spinous process that is being translated, then there is an ERS dysfunction on the right between the vertebra palpated and the one below. The right facet joint below will not open.

4. Lateral translation is repeated after extending the spine by posterior-to-anterior translation as the patient sits up taller and pushes the abdomen forward (Figure 5-11C). The vertebra being motion tested should remain at the apex of the extended spine. If resistance is felt at the spinous process that is being translated, then there is an FRS on the right between the vertebra palpated and the one above. The left facet joint above will not close.

5. Motion testing for lateral translation is repeated in all three positions from the other side. The operator stands on the patient's right side and tests the capacity for the individual vertebra to translate from right to left, resulting in right side bending in the neutral, flexed, and extended positions.

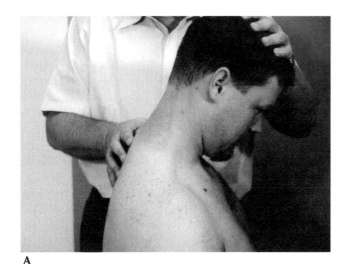

A

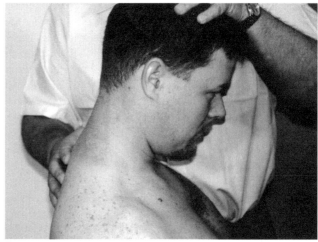

B

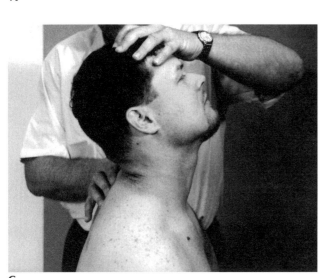

C

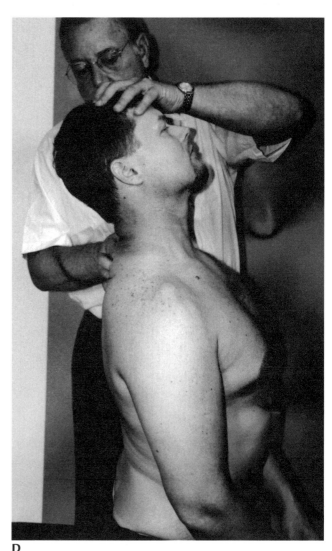

D

FIGURE 5-10
Palpation over spinous processes from one side and placing desired vertebra at the apex of a forward-bending curve by (A) overturning the head or (B) translation in an anterior-to-posterior direction. Placing the desired vertebra at the apex of a backward-bending curve by (C) overturning the head or (D) translation in a posterior-to-anterior direction, working from below up.

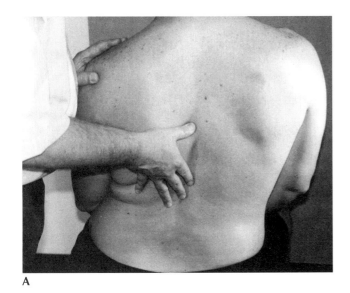

A

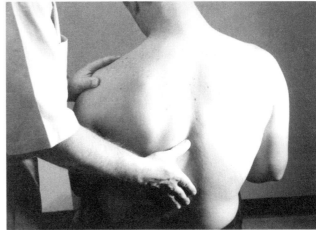

B

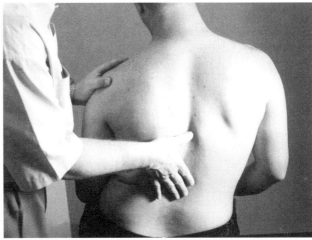

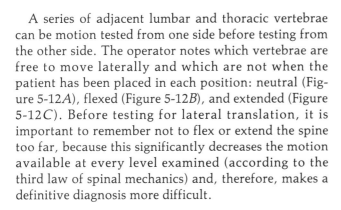

C

FIGURE 5-11
The position of the operator and patient for passive localized translatory movements at a particular thoracic vertebra. While palpating for motion on the medial side of the spinous processes using the thumb or fingertip, the operator depresses and translates the ipsilateral shoulder toward the palpating thumb. **(A)** *With patient in the neutral position.* **(B)** *With patient flexed or slumped.* **(C)** *With patient extended or sitting up tall.*

A series of adjacent lumbar and thoracic vertebrae can be motion tested from one side before testing from the other side. The operator notes which vertebrae are free to move laterally and which are not when the patient has been placed in each position: neutral (Figure 5-12*A*), flexed (Figure 5-12*B*), and extended (Figure 5-12*C*). Before testing for lateral translation, it is important to remember not to flex or extend the spine too far, because this significantly decreases the motion available at every level examined (according to the third law of spinal mechanics) and, therefore, makes a definitive diagnosis more difficult.

Passive Motion Testing in the Prone Position
The patient lies prone, and the operator stands to either side. Motion testing in the prone position is done with

the patient in the prone-neutral and prone-propped (extended) positions. Major restrictions that occur in the flexed position (ERS) can be inferred if the restriction lessens or disappears when the patient moves from the prone-neutral to the prone-propped position.

1. The operator places each thumb against the same spinous process on both sides.
2. While the patient is lying in the prone-neutral position, the operator pushes the spinous process laterally with one thumb and then the other. A springing motion through the thumbs works best, and several adjacent vertebrae can be examined while the patient is in this position.
3. Motion testing for lateral translation is repeated in the same fashion with the patient in the prone-propped position.

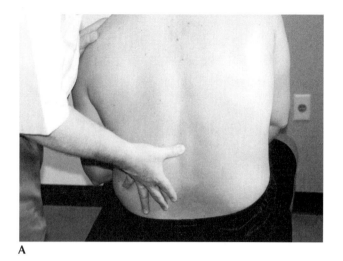

A

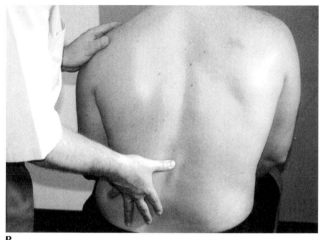

B

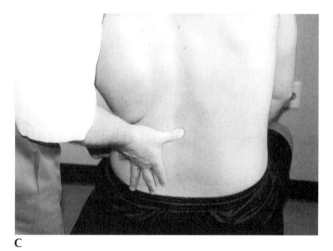

C

FIGURE 5-12
*The position of the operator and the patient for passive localized translatory movements of a particular lumbar vertebra by springing the shoulder down to the medial side of the spinous process of L1 from left to right. **(A)** With patient in the neutral position. **(B)** With patient flexed or slumped. **(C)** With patient extended or sitting up tall.*

4. An alternative method in the prone-propped position is to motion test from one side at a time. A thumb is placed against the spinous process of the inferior vertebra to stabilize it while monitoring motion at the interspinous space above (Figure 5-13*A*). Lateral translation is induced through the shoulders by the operator's other hand pulling the patient's shoulders toward the operator. An assessment of the motion available for lateral translation of the superior vertebra relative to the vertebra below is made through the operator's palpating thumb (Figure 5-13*B*). This palpation is repeated at successive segmental levels, first from one side and then the other.

Interpretation of Thoracic and Lumbar Dysfunctions Using Passive Lateral Translation

During the screening examination, the patient was asked to side bend to either side, and any loss of a smooth side-bending curve was noted. For example, if there is a restriction for left side bending between L2 and L3, a smooth right side-bending curve would be observed. However, an angulation of the spine occurs when left side bending is attempted with a straightening of the spine above L2, along with a reduced range of left side-bending motion. L2 can be viewed as being able to side bend right and *is*, therefore, side bent to the right. Considering facet function, to side bend to the right, the right facet between L2 and L3 must be able to close and the left facet must be able to open. If left side bending is limited, then either the right facet between L2 and L3 cannot fully open or the left facet cannot fully close. If the ability to left side bend improves when the patient slumps (flexes) and worsens when the patient arches backward (extends), L2 *can* flex on L3, and, therefore, the right facet joint at L2-3 can open, but the left facet joint at L2-3 cannot close. If left side bending improves with extension and worsens with flexion, then L2 *can* extend, and, therefore, the left facet joint at L2-3 can

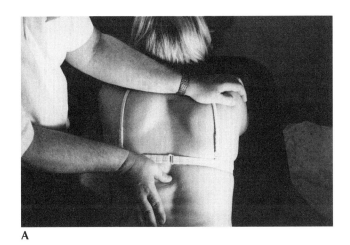
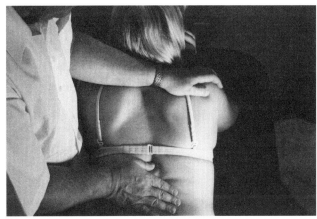

A　　　　　　　　　　　　　　　　　　　　**B**

FIGURE 5-13

Lateral translatory motion testing at the thoraco-lumbar junction when the patient is prone propped. (A) Palpating medial to spinous process. (B) Translating right to left from patient's shoulders.

close, but the right facet joint cannot open. Thus, the screening observation gives the operator a good idea of what will probably be found at L2.

It is helpful to review the interpretation of the examination findings that focus on positional changes of the TPs before discussing the interpretations of the observations made during passive motion testing using lateral translation. The two techniques should complement each other when used interchangeably or as a double check for accuracy.

To review, if the TPs of a vertebra become increasingly asymmetrical during flexion in comparison to the TPs of the vertebra below it, or if they are asymmetrical in the fully flexed position and symmetrical in the extended position, then the vertebra is considered to be ERS to the side of the prominent TP. There is a restrictive barrier that prevents the zygapophyseal joint on the side of the prominent TP from opening completely during flexion. As a consequence, there is also a motion restriction for flexion, rotation, and side bending to the opposite side but no restriction for extension, rotation, and side bending to either side. If, during or after flexion, the left TP has become prominent, it is ERSlt, and if the TP has become prominent on the right, it is ERSrt.

If the TPs of a vertebra become increasingly asymmetrical during extension in comparison to the TPs of the vertebra below it, or if they are asymmetrical in the fully extended position and symmetrical in the flexed position, then the vertebra is considered to be flexed, rotated, and side bent (FRS) to the side of the prominent TP. There is a restrictive barrier that prevents the zyga-

pophyseal joint on the side opposite the prominent TP to close completely during extension. As a consequence, there is also a motion restriction for extension, rotation, and side bending to the opposite side but no restriction for flexion, rotation, and side bending to either side. If, during or after extension, the left TP has become prominent, it is FRSlt, and if the TP has become prominent on the right, it is FRSrt (see Figures 5-4 and 5-5).

Passive lateral translation can be used to motion test for side bending restrictions to determine whether the zygapophyseal joint is able to open or close fully. Recall that if a vertebra side bends to the left, the joint between it and the vertebra below must close on the left side and open on the right side. The mechanics of side bending are a little different when translation is used. If a vertebral body can be laterally translated from left to right but not from right to left, then it is able to side bend to the left in relation to the vertebral body below it, but it cannot side bend to the right. *Positionally, that vertebra is then considered side bent to the left.* The next question, then, is this: Is the side bending restriction to the right caused by the inability of the left zygapophyseal joint to open (ERSlt) or the right zygapophyseal joint to close (FRSlt)?

Recall the example of a restriction between L2 and L3 when, positionally, L2 was ERSlt. In this situation, the left zygapophyseal joint between L2 and L3 cannot open fully. Using lateral translation, the following will be observed:

1. When the spinous process of L2 is contacted, it is felt to move laterally to the right (side bend left) when a left-to-right translatory force is applied and the lumbar spine is either in the neutral, flexed, or extended position. Because

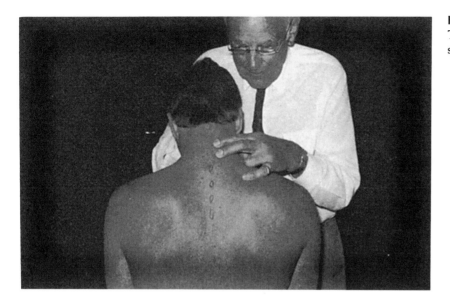

FIGURE 5-14
Testing sagittal mobility in the cervical spine.

the left zygapophyseal joint is closed and the right zygapophyseal joint can open, L2 *is* side bent to the left, and, therefore, there is no restriction for left side bending.

2. When attempting to move the spinous process of L2 laterally from right to left, a resistance is felt when the lumbar spine is flexed. If there is a major restriction, it is also felt in the neutral position.

3. When the lumbar spine is in the extended position, the left zygapophyseal joint is free to move from its fully closed position to the partially opened position up to its flexion barrier. Because side bending to the right in the extended position is determined more by the ability of the right facet joint to close than the ability of the left facet joint to open, L2 freely moves when it is translated laterally from right to left. The range of translation normally is less than in the neutral position, following the third rule of spinal mechanics: Motion in one direction reduces motion in the other two.

If L2 is positionally FRSlt in relation to L3, there is a barrier preventing the right zygapophyseal joint from fully closing between L2 and L3. Because the ability for L2 to side bend to the right in relation to L3 is limited in extension, passive mobility testing in extension reveals a loss in translation of L3 from right to left underneath L2. Therefore, any restriction for right side bending in extension between L2 and L3 will be encountered at L3 when using lateral translation. With this in mind, the following will be observed:

1. When the spinous processes of L2 and L3 are sequentially contacted, each one is felt to move laterally to the right (side bend left) when a left-to-right translatory force is applied and the lumbar spine is either in the neutral,

flexed, or extended position. This movement is observed because L2 *is* able to side bend to the left because the left zygapophyseal joint between L2 and L3 can close and the right zygapophyseal joint *is* open. Assuming that there is no restriction between L3 and L4, L3 is free to translate from left to right in all three positions as well.

2. When the translatory force is applied from right to left to test the capacity for right side bending, a resistance is felt when the spine is extended. Resistance may also be felt in the neutral position, if there is a major restriction for zygapophyseal joint closure on the right. However, the resistance to translation from right to left will be felt at L3 only, because its ability to move laterally to the left depends on the ability of the right zygapophyseal joint between L2 and L3 to close, and it cannot. Assuming that there is no FRSlt dysfunction at L1-2, there is no resistance felt when the spinous process of L2 is translated to the left, even when the lumbar spine is extended.

3. When the lumbar spine is flexed, side bending to the right is possible, and both L2 and L3 can freely translate right to left. The range of translation normally is less than in the neutral position, following the third rule of spinal mechanics.

Cervical

In contrast to the examination of the thoracic and lumbar spine by both positional and motion testing, the cervical spine is examined primarily by passive motion testing alone. Motion of the individual joints in the cervical region can be tested in the sitting position, while the operator monitors with the fingers of one hand and controls the patient's head with the other hand (Figure 5-14). This position is easiest for flexion-extension testing. Most

FIGURE 5-15
Four-finger examination of cervical spine.

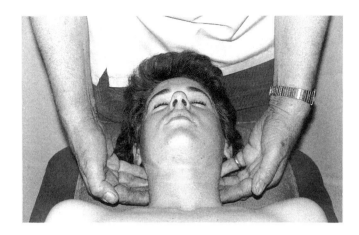

experienced operators prefer to have the patient supine and, in that position, passively motion test typical cervical joints (C2-T1) by translation, which introduces movement from above and below at the same time. *Translation to the left causes side bending to the right and translation anteriorly causes extension, and so on.*

For the atlantoaxial joint, rotation is tested; for the OA joint, the primary test is of forward and backward translation.

Although classified as cervical, the joint between C7 and T1 is often more easily examined by the dynamic method described for the thoracic spine. Sometimes, the joints between C6 and C7 are also more easily examined in this manner.

Typical Cervical Joints

The patient lies supine with his or her head close to the end of the table where the operator can sit, kneel, or stoop. If the patient is unable to lie supine, the examination can be done in the seated position. It is more difficult in the seated position, and it helps if the seat is low or if the operator stands on a stool. The examination is performed separately at each segmental level by alternately pushing on the lateral mass (an articular pillar) of one vertebra, first in one direction (for instance, left to right), then in the other (right to left), to induce lateral translation. The operator attempts to keep the patient's head in the midline and move the head and all the vertebrae above the level being examined en bloc by using the rest of the examiner's fingers and hands. By introducing translation in this way, the operator can specifically determine whether there is a motion restriction between the translated vertebra and the vertebra immediately below it. The dysfunctional levels in the neck are most easily found by palpating for tissue texture change around the joints. For those operators whose fingers have not yet achieved the

required sensitivity, it is necessary to examine each of the six joints in turn.

Examination

1. The patient is supine with the operator seated at the head of the table. The patient must be relaxed, and the operator must be comfortable, as for all motion testing.

2. The spinous process of C2 is easily felt, and the operator's fingertips are placed in order from above down (Figure 5-15): the little finger against the lateral mass of C2 and the ring, middle, and index fingers against the next three vertebrae to C5. By light palpation around the lateral masses, it is usually possible to identify, by tissue texture changes, those levels that require detailed testing. If this identification is uncertain, it is better to test each level in turn. Care must be taken not to press against the ends of the TPs, because these are always tender, and the discomfort may induce unwanted muscle guarding.

3. After the level of a somatic dysfunction has been identified with the four fingers (as described previously), the vertebral segment identified can be evaluated further by inducing lateral translation by gently pushing it sideways, first to one side and then to the other, being careful to avoid side bending of the neck by tilting the head. It is often easier to assess motion if the tips of the index fingers support the vertebra to be translated, and the shafts of the index fingers and additional fingers, if necessary, fully support the vertebrae above the one to be translated (Figure 5-16). Supporting the neck in this fashion, motion is blocked above the vertebra that is being examined and localized so that the operator can test the mobility between the vertebra supported by the index fingers relative to the vertebra immediately below (Figure 5-17).

It is often a good idea to check all levels for motion restrictions, beginning with those levels that are identified by the hypertonic, deep muscles.

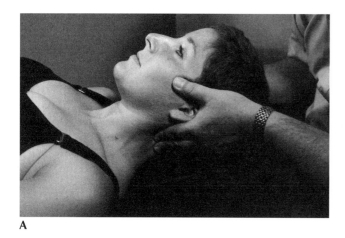

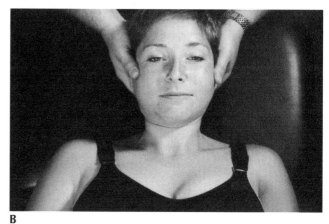

A   B

FIGURE 5-16

Finger positions to support cervical spine from above down to localize translatory movements. (A) Lateral view. (B) View from above.

Interpretation of Cervical Dysfunctions between C2 and T1

To make a diagnosis, the examination of each suspected level of dysfunction must be done in full flexion (Figure 5-18) and full extension (Figure 5-19) to avoid

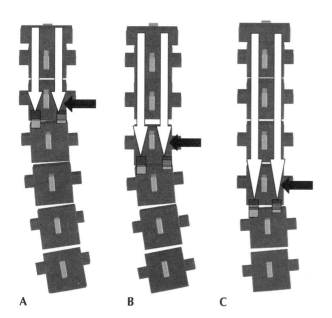

A   B   C

FIGURE 5-17

The lateral translation of the cervical spine from above down by blocking successive segments (white arrows) to localize motion to the level below the blocked segments. (A) C3-4 and below. (B) C4-5 and below. (C) C5-6 and below. Black arrows indicate the level of right-to-left translatory movement.

misdiagnosis of major restrictions. For example, if there is a major FRS dysfunction, there may be freedom of side bending (tested by using lateral translation) only at the fully flexed position. If this spinal level is examined when the head is partially flexed, a restriction may be felt and erroneously interpreted as an ERS dysfunction. Some operators prefer to start testing in the mid-position and then re-test in full flexion and full extension.

If there is a loss of translation to the *right* (left to right), there is a restriction of *left* side bending; the segment can be considered to be side bent *right*. If a loss of translation to the *left* (right to left) is found, there is a restriction of *right* side bending between the vertebra palpated and the vertebra below that level; the segment can be considered to be side bent *left*.

If the restriction of side bending (lateral translation) is more marked in extension and absent in flexion, the segment has a restriction for extension but not for flexion and, therefore, is flexed, or FRS. If the restriction of lateral translation is more significant in flexion and absent in extension, the segment is said to be extended, or ERS.

Therefore, if a segment is found with restriction of translation to the *left* (right to left) most marked in extension, it is said to be FRSlt. In this instance, the restriction indicates that the right facet joint between the superior and inferior vertebrae will not open. The palpated sense of restricted side bending is greatest at the dysfunctional segment when compared to the levels above and below. For example, in extension, if lateral translation from right to left is free at C3, blocked at C4, but free again when translating C5 along with C1 to

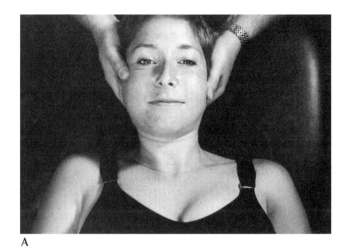
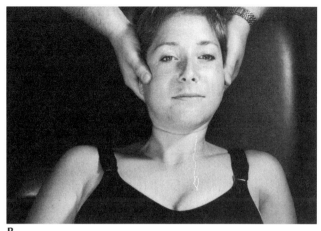

A   B

FIGURE 5-18
*Lateral translation of the flexed cervical spine. (**A**) Left to right. (**B**) Right to left.*

C4 above from right to left, then, by deduction, the dysfunction is located between C4 and C5 (Figure 5-20).

Similarly, if a segment is found with restriction of translation to the *left* (right to left) more marked in flexion, it is positionally described as being ERSlt. This time, however, the restriction indicates that the left facet joint between the superior and inferior vertebrae will not open.

To evaluate the ability of one vertebra to rotate, the motion of the superior vertebra is assessed by stabilizing the inferior vertebra at the articular pillar and passively inducing rotation from above down over the stabilizing finger. Between C2 and T1, rotation is coupled with side bending, and the translatory component is vertical. For example, rotating a vertebral body to the left is associated with left side bending and a compression of the intervertebral disc on the left as well. If there is a restriction for left rotation with flexion (ERSrt), there is also a restriction for left side bending. If there is a restriction for left rotation with extension (FRSrt), there is also a restriction for left side bending. Therefore, rotation for motion testing of a single vertebra can also be used to test the ability of the inferior facet of the superior vertebra either to separate or to approximate the vertebra below.

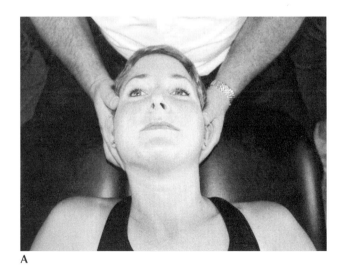
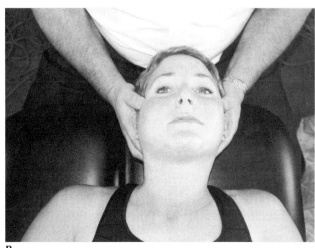

A   B

FIGURE 5-19
*Lateral translation of the extended cervical spine. (**A**) Left to right. (**B**) Right to left.*

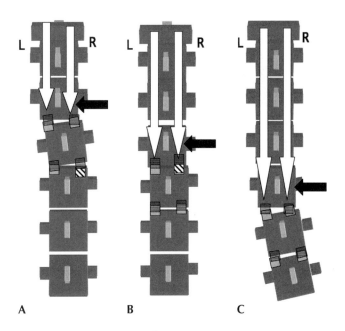

FIGURE 5-20
Examination of the cervical spine with lateral translation. In this example, the cervical spine is extended first, and then individual segments are motion tested with lateral translation. There is an FRSlt (flexed, rotated, side bent left) at C4-5 indicated by a restriction to right-to-left translation. (A) While C2 and C3 are held en bloc, motion is relatively free, and right side bending is possible between C3 and C4. (B) Because the right facet between C4 and C5 cannot close, right-to-left lateral translation is restricted when an attempt is made to translate C2, C3, and C4 en bloc from right to left. (C) There is no restriction for right-to-left lateral translation between C5 and C6 when C2, C3, C4, and C5 are held en bloc and translated together from right to left. Black arrows indicate the level of right-to-left translatory force; white arrows indicate the levels of the cervical spine that are stabilized and moved together en bloc. (L = left; R = right.)

Note: The authors recognize that some operators are taught to describe a lesion in terms of restriction of motion. However, for consistency and clarity, in this text, the shorthand abbreviations FRS and ERS are used only to describe dysfunctions by the position of the restricted vertebrae and are not used interchangeably to describe the restriction of motion.

Occipitoatlantal and Atlantoaxial Joints

The upper cervical complex consists of the OA and the atlantoaxial (C1-2) joints. These joints work together with a wide range of flexion-extension at OA and rotation at C1-2. There are other minor movements that occur in both joints. In the OA joint, there are a few degrees of side bending associated with a small range of rotation to the opposite direction. At the C1-2 joint, there is approximately 5 degrees of side bending,[3] and the biconvex shape of the cartilage-covered facets causes a small range of superior-to-inferior (craniad to caudad) translation.

Examination of the Atlantoaxial Joint

1. The patient is supine, and the operator sits, stands, or kneels at the head of the table.

2. To localize the rotation as much as possible to the C1-2 level, and in accordance with Fryette's third concept of spinal motion, the operator flexes the patient's neck as far as it easily goes. Forced flexion is not required, and it should be emphasized that the flexion is of the neck, not of the head on the neck. The operator uses both hands to hold the occiput and C1 en bloc and palpates the spinous process of C2 with the index finger of each hand.

3. With the patient relaxed, the head is turned passively to one side, then to the other, while monitoring with the index or middle fingers at the C2 level on each side. The movement must be stopped just as C2 begins to move. The normal range is more than 45 degrees to each side, of which probably only 30–35 degrees of movement take place at the C1-2 joint itself.[4] The flexed position must be maintained during the rotation, or movement will occur at other joints and the examination will be inaccurate. The range should be symmetrical to each side (Figure 5-21).

Examination of the Occipitoatlantal Joint

There are two different methods used to examine the OA joint. The first method, which is easier to interpret and is usually the only one required, is by lateral translation in full flexion and in full extension of the OA joint. The second method is useful to confirm a doubtful finding and is by anterior and posterior translation of the skull in 30 degrees of rotation, first to one side and then to the other.

Note: All non-neutral dysfunctions of the typical cervical vertebrae should have been successfully treated before this technique is used.

Side-to-Side Translation

1. The patient is supine and must be relaxed. The operator is at the head of the table, preferably sitting.

2. The operator's hands cradle the patient's head and lift it a short distance off the table. The index fingers are placed so that the operator can monitor motion at the OA joint on each side. Care must be taken not to press on

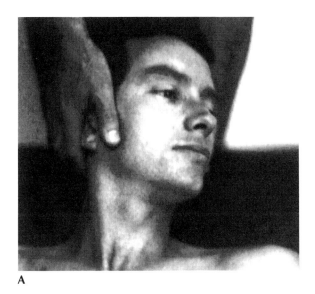
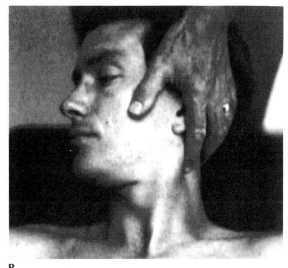

A   B

FIGURE 5-21

Examination of the range of motion for rotation at C1-2 with the cervical spine fully flexed while palpating the spinous process of C2 with the index fingers. (A) Rotation to the left. (B) Rotation to the right.

the posterior OA membrane while palpating the lateral masses of C1.

3. The operator introduces flexion at the OA joint by rotating the skull as if rolling a ball around an imaginary axis through the external auditory meatus. This motion does not need to be taken to the barrier, and extreme flexion is not required. With the patient's head flexed, the operator translates the head to one side, keeping the mid-

line of the head parallel to that of the body. The distance between the midline of the head and the midline of the body is noted, and the head is then translated to the other side. The distance from the midline that the head moves should be symmetrical (Figure 5-22).

4. The skull is then "rolled" into extension around the same axis, and the examination is repeated (Figure 5-23). Extreme extension is not needed, and it is important to

FIGURE 5-22

Examination of motion at the occipitoatlantal joint by translation in flexion. (A) Lateral translation of patient's occiput to the left. (B) Lateral translation of patient's occiput to the right.

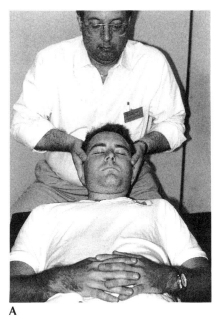
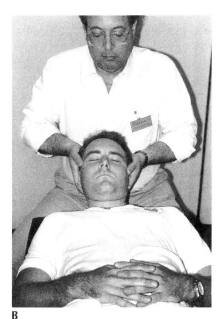

A   B

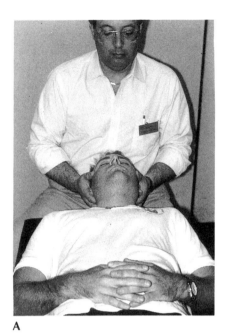 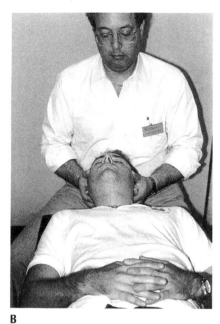

A   B

FIGURE 5-23
Examination of motion at the occipitoatlantal joint by translation in extension. **(A)** *Lateral translation of patient's occiput to the left.* **(B)** *Lateral translation of patient's occiput to the right.*

remember that the position of full extension of the head on the neck combined with rotation places the vertebral artery at risk for injury.

In many patients, there will be a restriction at the OA joint with the same side bending restriction on one side and rotation restriction to the opposite side with both flexion and extension. If this occurs (restricted side bending to the left and restricted rotation to the right when the occiput is either flexed or extended), then there is a bilateral dysfunction with the right OA joint extended (restricted flexion) and the left OA joint flexed (restricted extension).

Antero-Posterior Translation

1. The patient is supine and must be relaxed, and the operator is seated at the head of the table.

2. The operator cradles the patient's head with both hands and, without using the fingertips, lifts it off the table and turns it 30 degrees to the right. This motion aligns the right facets of the occiput and atlas so that they are nearly perpendicular to the table and the facets on the left are horizontal. Motion testing is performed by translating the patient's head with the operator's hands (not the fingertips) upward (anteriorly) and then downward (posteriorly), thus sliding one facet on the other (Figure 5-24). A rotational movement of C1 indicates the beginning of the motion restriction and is palpated by the operator's index fingers that are placed on the lateral masses

of C1 bilaterally. Because anterior–posterior motion can only occur along the right facet (the left is now horizontal), a restriction for anterior glide (extension) will carry C1 anteriorly on the right, forcing it to rotate left into the palpating finger of the operator's left hand. If there is a restriction in the posterior direction (flexion), C1 rotates to the right (into the operator's right index finger) and away from the left.

3. The head is then turned 30 degrees to the left of the mid-position, and the test is repeated on that side. The amount of movement in the anterior–posterior direction should be bilaterally symmetrical; the side with the smaller range is the restricted side.

Interpretation

Interpretation of the standard method is similar to interpretation of the translatory examination of the typical cervical joints.

1. *If* there is restricted lateral translation of the head to the right, there is limitation of left side bending at the OA joint, and the OA joint, therefore, must be side bent right (Srt). This determination is made assuming that the lower cervical joints are mobile.

2. *If* restriction is more marked in the extended position, there is restriction of extension, written as *F* (flexed), *Rlt* (rotated left), *Srt* (side bent right), or *FSrt*. The simpler diagnostic notation emphasizes the side-bending restriction that is critical for normal motion in the OA joint, much like a sliding drawer requires side-to-side

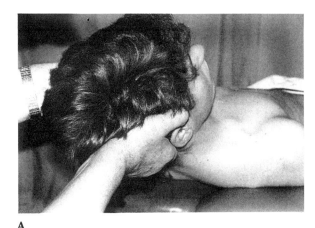

A

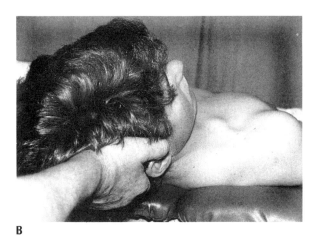

B

FIGURE 5-24
Anterior-posterior translation test for motion at the right facet of the occipitoatlantal joint. **(A)** *Anterior translation.* **(B)** *Posterior translation.*

freedom to glide in and out. Because rotation and side bending are always coupled in opposite directions at the OA joint, identification of the rotational restriction is superfluous.

3. *If* the restriction is more marked in the flexed position, there is restriction of flexion at the OA joint, written as *E* (extended) *RltSrt,* or *ESrt.*

4. *If,* on testing antero-posterior translation of the 30 degree–rotated head, there is restriction of anterior translation on the right, the indication is that the right facet of the occiput will not slide fully forward on the atlas. This indication is actually detected when anterior translation of the occipital condyle causes a left rotation of the atlas palpated by the operator's left index finger. Therefore, there is a restriction of the occiput for exten-

sion and rotation to the left (*not* of flexion, as in upward and forward sliding of intervertebral facets). Because rotation and side bending at the OA joint are always coupled to opposite sides, and the occiput is rotated right, the occiput must also be side bent left. This position corresponds to a restriction of right-to-left translation of the head in the extended position (FRrtSlt, or FSlt).

5. *If* there is restriction of posterior translation of the occiput on the atlas on the right, the head will not fully flex, and as the right occipital condyle reaches the flexion barrier, the atlas translates posteriorly on the right and is detected by the operator's right index finger. Therefore, there is a restriction of the occiput for flexion and rotation to the right. Because rotation and side bending at the OA joint are coupled in the opposite direction, the occiput must also be restricted for side bending to the left. This position corresponds to restriction of translation of the head to the right in the flexed position (ErltSrt, or Esrt).

6. *If* the restriction is on the left side, the inferences are the same but with reversal of the side.

In summary,

1. The structural diagnosis formulated by the observed restriction of the right occipital condyle to glide anteriorly on the atlas is *FSlt.*

2. The structural diagnosis for an observed restriction of the right occipital condyle to glide posteriorly on the atlas is *ESrt.*

3. The structural diagnosis for an observed restriction of the left occipital condyle to glide anteriorly on the atlas is *FSrt.*

4. The structural diagnosis for an observed restriction of the left occipital condyle to glide posteriorly on the atlas is *ESlt.*

REFERENCES

1. Cropper JR. Regional Anatomy and Biomechanics. In TA Flynn (ed). The Thoracic Spine and Rib Cage: Musculoskeletal Evaluation and Treatment. Boston: Butterworth–Heinemann, 1996;3–29.

2. Fryette HH. The Principles of Osteopathic Technique. Carmel, CA: Academy of Applied Osteopathy, 1954.

3. Kapandji IA. The Physiology of the Joints (vol 3). London: Churchill Livingstone, 1974;184.

4. Penning L. Functional Pathology of the Cervical Spine. Amsterdam: Excerpta Medica, 1968.

6

Manipulation

There is disagreement about the breadth of the meaning of the word *manipulation*. In Europe, the term is used almost solely for procedures involving a high-velocity, low-amplitude, thrusting movement. In North America, the term is used in a much wider sense to include any active or passive movement initiated, assisted, or resisted by the operator and includes treatments sometimes listed as articulation; mobilization; isometric and isotonic techniques; and myofascial, functional, indirect, and even craniosacral techniques.

To help clarify this terminology, the International Federation of Manual Medicine, after a workshop at Fischingen in 1983, proposed the term *mobilization with impulse* to be used for what is here called *thrusting*. *Mobilization without impulse* was proposed for the treatments that are here included under the heading *manipulation* but that do not have a component of operator thrusting. These terms are somewhat cumbersome, and, in this edition, the authors use the term *manipulation* in the broad sense defined as *the skillful use of the hands in a therapeutic fashion*.

The phrase *high-velocity, low-amplitude* is thought to have led some practitioners to emphasize the velocity too much, so the simple word *thrust* is becoming the preferred term. It is still important that the thrust is of high velocity, however small the amplitude; if the thrust is done slowly, the muscles will have time to tighten and prevent the movement. In this edition, the term *muscle energy* is used to describe techniques that involve patient participation usually associated with operator resistance. This text includes what, in earlier editions, had been called *isometric*: Many of the techniques described are fully, or in part, isometric, but some techniques use *isotonic*, in addition to or instead of *isometric*, contraction. Some techniques also use respiratory assistance from the patient; in some techniques, the operator may assist as well as resist.

TYPES OF MANIPULATION

Many different techniques have been used to remove or alter the restrictive barrier and its associated tissue texture abnormalities. In the early editions of this book, only high-velocity techniques were described, and of these, some were quite nonspecific. The non- and semi-specific techniques have been omitted from this edition. Instead, this edition focuses on the identification of a restrictive barrier and specific techniques to engage and remove that barrier to normal pain-free motion within the context of restoring overall postural balance and neuromotor control of the musculoskeletal system.

Manipulative techniques may be direct or indirect. *Direct techniques* are those in which the barrier is located and directly addressed. High-velocity and muscle energy treatments are direct techniques. The term *indirect* is used for techniques in which the joint is positioned away from the barrier, usually localizing to the point of maximum ease identified by a palpable decrease in tissue tension. The various functional techniques are all indirect. Combined techniques also exist in which some aspects are direct and some indirect.

A third approach uses what is known as an *exaggeration technique*. In this case, the joint is positioned away from the dysfunctional barrier toward the opposite end of its normal range, and a thrust is applied toward the normal end. In France, Maigne[1] developed his own variety of this method based on his belief that the thrust should only be in the painless direction. There are many disciples of his techniques.

Mobilizing Forces

A variety of forces can be applied to the joint to perform whatever treatment is needed. These forces are broadly classified as *extrinsic* or *intrinsic*. Extrinsic forces are used when the operator does the work, as in thrusting, or when gravity or some mechanical apparatus is used. Intrinsic forces are generated by the patient, whether by pushing or breathing, and also include the natural tendency of the body to self-correct whenever possible. Muscle energy treatment is regarded as using intrinsic force, because the patient generates and is able to control the degree of force used, even if the operator must use an equal and opposite force to produce the desired effect.

Thrusting manipulation using extrinsic force was the standby of manual medicine practitioners since the end of the nineteenth century. It is probable that often these were only semispecific techniques, but they helped patients enough to justify research to improve and refine them. There are many reasons to look for other types of manipulation. First, thrusting manipulation is unsuitable for certain patients, such as those who suffer from osteoporosis, metastatic disease, and rheumatoid arthritis, who may still benefit from other manipulative techniques. Second, thrusting manipulation is not always painless, although the more accurate the localization, the higher the velocity and the less force used, the less uncomfortable this technique will be. Third, thrusting is not entirely without risk and occasional hazards, particularly to the vertebro-basilar circulation. Since 1947, when the first cerebrovascular complication was reported,[2] a significant number of vascular accidents have been reported involving manipulation of the upper cervical spine. It was originally thought that these accidents were due to direct injury to the vertebral arteries by high-velocity manipulation, and, certainly, some of them have happened at the moment of such a treatment. Reported complications[3] suggest that the problem is often one of an intimal tear with development of a dissection and occlusion of the lumen. Yet cases have been recorded in which the arterial occlusion occurred when the patient had merely held the neck in full extension with the head fully rotated to one side. Carotid artery injuries have also been reported.[4]

The first sign of cerebral vascular insufficiency is anxiety. This symptom appears before the onset of nystagmus, and it is recommended that if a patient becomes anxious during the examination or treatment of the neck, the maneuver should immediately be stopped and the situation reassessed before any similar position or technique is again adopted. This problem is discussed in more detail in Chapter 11.

There have also been concerns about the use of spinal manipulation in patients with known lumbar disc herniation and the potential of spinal manipulation causing a cauda equina syndrome. This uncommon complication has been most closely associated with the application of forceful manipulation to the lumbar spine to patients under general anesthesia with the associated loss of spinal muscular and tendinous support.[5,6]

Types of Technique

It was a wise man who said, "If all you have in your toolbox is a hammer, it is funny how many things look like nails." High-velocity thrusting can be used to treat most dysfunctions if necessary. Until the work of Fred Mitchell, Sr., the original proponent of the muscle energy technique, became known, thrusting was all that was available to many practitioners in the field, including John F. Bourdillon. Techniques that allow the patient to gauge the force being applied have obvious advantages in patients who have weakened bones from old age, osteoporosis, or disease. A less forceful alternative treatment is highly desirable in the patient with a very acute condition and in whom thrust manipulation could cause severe pain.

There are a variety of other techniques. The oldest is probably what is now classified as *soft tissue technique* and can be regarded, in part, as an extension of therapeutic massage and articulatory techniques.

Muscle energy technique is a method used most by many practitioners and is widely applicable for the mobilization of any joint in the musculoskeletal system. Because it depends on the active participation of the patient by voluntary effort, there is an inherent safety in this technique, as the patient has some control over the amount of force used.

Myofascial techniques combine aspects of soft tissue, indirect, and even craniosacral techniques and are applicable to situations in which other treatments sometimes fail. Functional or indirect techniques do not put any significant strain on the patient's cardiovascular system, although the very gentle nature of the indirect techniques contrasts strongly with the physical handling of the patient by the operator using the direct myofascial techniques.

Craniosacral techniques address dysfunctions of the joints between the bones of the skull and membranous imbalances of the dural structures. When properly applied, these techniques can benefit patients who have experienced post-traumatic headaches from head injury and patients with temporomandibular joint dysfunctions. These techniques are also applicable for dysfunctions anywhere in the musculoskeletal system because they rely on the body's inherent spontaneous motion and ability to self-correct.

SOFT TISSUE TECHNIQUES

All articular dysfunctions have a soft tissue component, and in some cases, this component may be very important. In many patients, correction of the articular or skeletal component allows the soft tissues to return to normal, but if not, the soft tissue abnormality may bring back a skeletal dysfunction that had been successfully treated. Soft tissue techniques can be applied to the skin, subcutaneous tissues, and deeper structures. These techniques have a range of effects, including muscle and other tissue stretching, relief of edema, increased circulation, and so on. Soft tissue techniques may be used to "tidy up" after a skeletal treatment or as preparation. Having the soft tissues relaxed certainly makes skeletal treatment easier.

Muscles and their associated fascia can be treated with stretching either longitudinally or transversely or with deep pressure. These techniques are perhaps the most commonly used, and they can be very helpful when, for instance, there is superficial muscle tightness associated with an intervertebral dysfunction. Traction can be localized to some extent in the neck with the patient supine. To apply the traction principally at one level, the operator can use his or her fingertips deep in the muscles posterolaterally or on the articular pillars themselves. Side bending with flexion or extension positioning can also be used in the neck and may be combined with traction to add to the specificity of the technique.

In the trunk, a lateral stretch of the paraspinal muscles can be applied from either side. If the operator is on the side to be treated, the medial edge of the muscle mass can be pulled with the fingertips; if the operator is on the opposite side, the muscle mass can be pushed laterally either with the heel of the hand or with the thumb and thenar eminence of one or both hands. This technique requires the application of steady pressure with the fingers or hand on the medial edge of the muscle. The stretch is continued until no further improvement is obtained or until the muscles are normally relaxed. Lateral stretch is also applicable to the cervical region and can be done with the tips of the fingers of one hand while the other hand is used to steady the head and apply a counter force.

Sustained deep pressure can be used to persuade muscles to relax. Initially, the pressure may be quite painful, which does not help the patient to relax while it is being applied, but the results can be rewarding. This form of soft tissue treatment comes very close to some of the myofascial techniques described in the section Myofascial Release Techniques, although myofascial techniques are more demanding in palpatory skill.

Spray and stretch is another method of treating hypertonic muscle. Travell[7] described this originally for the true trigger point. The true trigger point is of great importance and should be considered in any patient who is making less progress than expected. The cold spray and stretching also helps areas of muscle hypertonus that do not fit Travell's definition. Similarly, soft tissue treatments can be used for the true trigger points instead of or in addition to the cold spray. Techniques to address trigger points in the upper and lower body are described in detail by Travell and Simons.[8,9] The cold spray is designed to lightly chill the skin over the hypertonic muscle; this spraying results in relaxation, allowing the muscle to be stretched further. The muscle itself should *not* be chilled; cold muscle tends to shiver with recurrence of the hypertonus.

For the trigger points that do not respond well to spray and stretch and for trigger points that are too acute to allow muscle energy treatment, injection of local anesthetic is a valuable measure. The most important points to remember when using trigger point injections are the following:

1. Use plain, local anesthetic, preferably novocaine with no adrenalin and no steroid.

2. One-half percent or 1% is a strong enough concentration.

3. Care is needed that the actual trigger point is not missed.

4. The muscle should be gently stretched after the injection.

Articulation or Mobilization

The articulatory techniques are direct because they address the restrictive barrier. The techniques are based on the finding that if the joint is moved up to the barrier and the barrier is lightly "teased," there is a tendency for it to give away. The movement is repeated as long as there is a gain in the range of motion. This procedure is painless, as long as the operator does not push into the barrier. Not only is pushing painful, but it also can cause increased hypertonus. It should be remembered that the barrier is not a single point. It is more like a curved plane. The objective is to come up to part of that plane; move along it; and move away again rhythmically, with slow velocity and increasing amplitude of motion.

There are competent manipulators, well skilled in high-velocity and muscle energy treatments, who regularly treat their patients with articulation and report that, often, articulation is all they need to do to restore motion and relieve muscle hypertonus.

Detailed descriptions of articulatory technique can be found in a number of texts.[10,11]

Muscle Energy Techniques

The muscle energy treatment as we know it was the brainchild of the late Fred L. Mitchell, Sr., and it seems likely that his interest in this approach was partly based on work done in the 1950s by another osteopathic physician, T. J. Ruddy, who developed a contract-relax method of treating some of the eye muscle imbalances and other conditions that he saw in his ophthalmologic practice. Mitchell not only worked out the system of treatment, but he also made a detailed study of anatomy (especially of the pelvis), and his description of spinal mechanics and spinal dysfunctions have been further developed by those who learned from him into the classification used in this book. Like so many innovators, when Mitchell first described his ideas, they were not well received. Finally, at about the time he was ready to give up trying, he taught a small group of osteopaths who became enthusiastic disciples, and from three of whom the authors have had the privilege of learning.

Muscle energy treatments are classified as direct techniques because the joint is taken up to the barrier with the intent of moving or removing it. When treating spinal joints, the barrier can be viewed as the cause of a concavity for either multiple segments or individual segments, because the side-bent position between two vertebrae can be considered a small concavity. The goal of the treatment is to stretch the muscles that maintain this concavity. For the techniques to be effective, the barrier must just be engaged in all three planes: flexion-extension, side bending, and rotation. If the barrier has not been reached, the technique is less effective; if the positioning of the restricted joint has been forced into the barrier so that motion is now available only in those joints beyond the restriction, there will be no benefit at all to the treatment. These techniques demand a fair degree of palpatory skill, and beginners almost invariably fail to stop at the barrier, instead passing beyond it and becoming frustrated by the poor result. It is not uncommon, for example, to see that, when treating the cervical spine supine, the trainee operator thinks that he or she still has not reached the barrier when the amount of side bending introduced by the operator has taken the localization into the thoracic region.

The physiological principles on which muscle energy technique rests are based on the ability to alter muscle tone by postisometric relaxation and reciprocal inhibition. The majority of muscle energy procedures are isometric, but some are isotonic. Other forces may assist muscle energy techniques. Two of the most important forces are exhalation, which increases the spinal curves, and inhalation, which reduces these curves. Exhalation also helps relax the tissues and, in this regard, is helpful for high-velocity, low-amplitude thrust techniques.

When using muscle energy techniques, the direction of patient effort is away from the barrier. As stated earlier, the barrier has to be found in all three planes; the patient may push away in any of these planes, but because the operator must prevent this motion from taking place, it is best to use the planes of motion that are easier to resist and control. As a general rule, resisting rotational effort is best avoided, because it is the most difficult motion for the operator to control. The preferred patient effort is usually for side bending, flexion or extension (whichever is appropriate). The operator may ask for the patient's effort to be first in one direction and then another. It is always worth trying a different direction if the first does not produce the desired result.

To make a contraction isometric, movement must be blocked, so that there is no change in the length of the contracting muscle. Prevention of movement in an isometric contraction is achieved by the counter force of the operator, who must warn the patient not to push too forcefully and overpower this counter force. A forceful contraction is not only difficult for the operator to control, but it is also less effective than other techniques. The reason for this is that the muscles to be treated are small and they are capable of generating only a light force. If more force is used, accessory long-lever muscles are activated, and the effect on the primary muscles may be lost.

When treating isometrically, the contraction should be maintained for a finite period (3–5 seconds). After the first period of contraction, the patient is asked to relax, and many patients will do no more than stop pushing. Relaxing and ceasing to push are not the same thing, because a voluntary reduction in muscle tone is required for complete relaxation. It is essential to have the patient relaxed before attempting to move the joint to a new barrier, and this new position must be established before the patient is asked to make the second effort. The instruction "let go" is often effective, or the patient may be asked a second time to relax fully. When relaxation has been secured or palpated by the operator, *and not before*, the joint is taken to the new barrier in all three planes and the contraction repeated. This is done three or more times, until no further motion is gained or the physiological barrier has been reached. It is important at the end of a muscle energy treatment to re-examine the patient to find out if the treatment has been effective. It is unusual to hear any audible release ("pop") with the muscle energy technique.

There are a number of muscle energy techniques in which the treatment is designed to cause movement of the joint during the muscle contraction. Therefore, these techniques are isotonic and not isometric, and when used for treatment of the axial skeleton and pelvis, they are often used in combination with respiratory assistance, operator guiding, and patient positioning to produce the desired effect. The method used is similar to the isometric techniques; the difference is that, when the patient's dysfunctional joint is positioned at the barrier, slightly more force is necessary against the operator's unyielding resistance for the joint to be pulled through the barrier. It is probable that reciprocal inhibition is responsible for the concurrent relaxation of any antagonistic muscles that were important in the establishment of that barrier. After the contraction has continued for 3–5 seconds, as in isometric methods, the patient is asked to relax. When relaxation is complete, the operator takes up the slack, in all three planes, to the new barrier, and the procedure is repeated two or more times, depending on response. The muscle energy techniques described in this book use isotonic and isometric principles.

High-Velocity Thrusting

In manual medicine, the term *high-velocity* is not complete unless followed by the rest of the description, *low-amplitude*. Mennell,[12] in his description of joint play techniques, describes low amplitude as "less than an eighth of an inch at the joint." The use of the lever principle to make this thrusting easier is discussed in the section Localization of Force. Once again, it must be emphasized that we are not reducing a dislocation or subluxation, that there is literally no little bone out of place, and that the objective of the treatment is to restore "maximal pain-free movement of the musculoskeletal system in postural balance."[13]

The belief shared by some patients and operators that if there is no joint noise associated with the manipulative procedure then nothing has happened, is incorrect. The successful treatment of flexed, rotated, and side-bent (FRS) dysfunctions in which the dysfunctional joint is being "closed" is usually silent. Facet-opening thrusts (ERS) are more likely to be accompanied by a pop or other sound. The objective is not simply to gap the joint, which could be noisy, but to restore a normal range of gliding movement by enabling the facets to open (flexion) or close (extension). It is important to remember that there is an anatomical barrier that, by definition, is the final limit of available motion in that joint. A thrust that forces the joint beyond the anatomical barrier causes structural damage. The thrust must be localized to the restrictive barrier; having the patient exhale before the maneuver can induce additional relaxation of the surrounding tissues. Indeed, after proper localization to the three-dimensional barrier, mobilization may occur during the exhalation, even before the thrust is applied. The barrier may be approached in stages, taking up all available movement and laxity of the surrounding tissues in each of the available three planes of motion. The thrust, then, is a continuation of this three-dimensional positioning. Even after proper localization to the barrier, localization is often lost when the operator unconsciously "winds up" or backs off the barrier in preparation for the high-velocity thrusting motion.

The belief that the basic dysfunction being treated is of soft tissue instead of joint or bone raises the question of what a high-velocity treatment achieves. There is no doubt in the minds of the authors that such treatment can be very effective; sometimes, it seems to be the only really effective method. This is particularly true in the more chronic dysfunctions, in which there is myofascial shortening with loss of elasticity of the surrounding connective tissues within the joint capsule. After treatment, there is also a reduction in the muscle tone that was previously palpable in the area of dysfunction so that there seems to be an associated effect on central nervous system reflex mechanisms due to altered mechanoreceptor and proprioceptor input. This reduction in muscle tone may also be palpated after a successful indirect treatment is performed when the joint is positioned at the point of maximum ease (see the section on Functional Techniques).

High-velocity treatment has been performed and often has given the patient relief with scant attention paid to specificity. Indeed, there are operators using techniques that cannot even be described as semispecific. Occasional accidents have occurred, but, omitting the special case of the upper cervical spine, the majority of accidents appears to have occurred because the manipulation was done incorrectly, either because the diagnosis was in error or because the treatment was performed without accurate localization.

There is no total contraindication to treatment by thrusting manipulation, provided that a proper diagnosis has been made and the force and amplitude used are suitable.

Myofascial Release Techniques

Physicians practicing manual techniques find that, even when motion has been restored to the segment, there is often a residual myofascial component that can be relieved by treating the soft tissues. Practitioners have found that release of abnormal soft tissue tensions sometimes results in restoration of symmetry and motion to previously dysfunctional joints that, at first, appeared to need more direct mechanical treatment. Development of the various functional techniques has also given credence to the concept that soft tissue changes are fundamental rather than secondary to the joint changes.

Robert C. Ward[14] developed the myofascial release approach specifically to address the myofascial elements of joint dysfunction. Based on the anatomical and physiological properties of the connective tissue, Ward descried a "tight-loose" phenomenon in soft tissues occurring as the response to imposed asymmetrical loads. These responses are normal and self-correcting unless the tissues are deformed beyond their innate ability to recover. Symptoms arise when the deformation persists, and the tight-loose condition can be palpated in the soft tissues. To treat this condition with his myofascial techniques, Ward addresses the tissues by applying a load with the hands in specific directions and continuously monitors the changes that take place, working against tight areas to produce a release of tension. Ward further encourages the release by using activating techniques, which can further facilitate tone in the soft tissues in response to postural commands from the central nervous system. Ward views myofascial release not only as an integrated system that addresses the musculoskeletal and neurological systems but also as a fundamental approach to the entire function of the body.

Functional Techniques

Functional techniques were developed in the osteopathic profession in the 1940s and 1950s under the guidance of Drs. W. G. Sutherland, H. W. Hoover, W. L. Johnston, and others. With these techniques, the segment being treated is passively moved away from the restrictive barrier and toward the normal physiological barrier at the opposite end of the range of motion. Functional techniques are different from thrusting or muscle energy technique or mobilization by articulation, all of which address the restrictive barrier directly.

Between the restrictive barrier and the opposite physiological barrier, there is a dynamic balance point (DBP), or point of maximum ease described as the point reached when the joint is positioned so that the tensions in the soft tissues are balanced equally on either side. This positioning must be done in all three planes in both translation and rotation and also involves distraction or compression and inhalation or exhalation. If motion in any plane is initiated away from the DBP, the soft tissue tension around the treated segment will rise, and there will be an increased palpatory sense of binding.

Once the dynamic balance point is reached, the operator has three treatment options:

1. *Position and hold.* In this method, the segment being treated is maintained at the DBP for a period of usually 30 to 90 seconds.
2. *Operator active.* In this method, the operator initiates movement along the path of least resistance through the sequential releases of soft tissue tension that occur. An analogy would be that the segment is taken through a maze, while the operator monitors the surrounding soft tissues to continue on the path of least resistance.
3. *Operator passive.* In this method, the operator passively follows the segmental unwinding through sequential releases of the segment being treated to the point of full soft tissue release, at which time the restrictive barrier is no longer detectable and normal motion is restored.

With each of these approaches, the end point should be normal motion of the segment being treated.

Another functional approach is the strain-counterstrain technique of Larry Jones.[15] With this technique, the operator monitors specific tender points while positioning the patient so that the tension at the monitor is at a minimum. The position is then held for 30 to 90 seconds, or until the release is felt at the specific tender point.

Functional techniques are indicated with acute traumatic injuries, chronic and complicated structural patterns, acutely ill patients, and patients with osteoporosis, marked arthritic changes, spinal stenosis, or disc pathology.

While a student at the Kirksville College of Osteopathic Medicine, Kirksville, MO, in the early 1960s, Edward G. Stiles[16] became interested in the unusual approach of George Andrew Laughlin, the great grandson of A. T. Still. Although Laughlin was not a member of the faculty, the success of his methods made him widely known and respected by patients from all over the Midwest. Laughlin had some difficulty putting into words what he was doing, but during three and a half years of observation, Stiles became aware of the effectiveness of functional techniques and became an advocate for their incorporation into manual medicine. Laughlin's techniques were mainly operator passive and operator active techniques. In the acute setting, this type of treatment should be brief, well directed, and repeated daily (or every other day), encouraging restoration of pain-free motion as soon as possible.

Craniosacral Manipulation

The majority of those in the medical profession believe that the skull is an immobile composite of multiple cranial bones that fuse sometime after birth. The concept that the suture lines are articulations that maintain some degree of mobility has not been considered valid despite the fact that there are synovial membranes and that it is relatively easy to disarticulate the skull by expanding it from internal hydrostatic pressure. In 1932, when Sutherland started talking about his ideas in the osteopathic profession, he met with a similar response to this concept of a mobile cranium from his colleagues. In spite of his results with patients and the requests by individual physicians for instruction, it was not until approximately 1940 that Sutherland obtained academic recognition of any kind for his ideas. Since then, such recognition has grown steadily, and many different varieties of cranial treatment are now taught.

When a student at the American School of Osteopathy (now the Kirksville College of Osteopathic Medicine) in 1899, Sutherland's interest in cranial osteopathy had been kindled by study of the disarticulated skull. He could not understand suture anatomy in terms of immobility. After much studying and experimenting on himself and others, Sutherland developed concepts that have become the basis for craniosacral manipulative treatment.[17]

Normal cranial motion can be palpated as a rhythmic expansion and contraction of the transverse diameter of the skull and an associated decrease and increase, respectively, in the vertical diameter. All the bones of the skull take part in the motion, including those of the face, and motion is also transmitted to the sacrum by the dural tube. This transmission is the reason for the name *craniosacral*. The normal rate of oscillation is 8–12 cycles per minute. In some states of disease, especially disease associated with coma, the rate may be

greater or lesser.[18] For descriptive purposes, the movements are named by starting at the sphenobasilar junction, which was regarded by Sutherland as the primary location for this inherently small motion of the skull.

When the sphenobasilar junction flexes, the sphenoid and ethmoid bones rotate in opposite directions about transverse axes. The anterior end of the sphenoid (and the posterior end of the ethmoid) becomes inferior, and the anterior part of the ethmoid becomes superior. The occiput rotates so that the posterior part becomes more inferior; the temporal bones are pushed into what is known as *external rotation*, with the mastoid processes becoming closer together and the squamous portions becoming further apart. At the same time, the temporal bones rotate about a transverse axis so that the tip of the mastoid process moves inferiorly and posteriorly. The resultant widening of the skull at the parietosquamous suture causes the inferior part of the parietal bones to separate and the skull to lose vertical diameter as the angle between the parietal bones at the sagittal suture becomes more obtuse. There are corresponding movements of the remaining skull bones, and even the relationship of the mandible to the temporal surface at the temporomandibular joint is changed. These movements comprise what is called *flexion and external rotation*. The cycle is completed by the reverse movements, which are described as *extension and internal rotation*.

When the occiput moves into flexion, the posterior rim of the foramen magnum becomes inferior with respect to the anterior rim. The tube of dura mater surrounding the spinal cord is attached to the margin of the foramen magnum, and when the occiput is flexed, the anterior aspect of the dura is raised, and the posterior aspect drops. Although it has an attachment to C2, the dura is sufficiently rigid to transmit motion to its inferior attachment at the second sacral vertebra. Flexion of the occiput pulls the anterior aspect of the dura toward the skull, and, for this reason, in craniosacral terminology, flexion of the sacrum is what is termed *posterior nutation* in this text. For practitioners unfamiliar with craniosacral work, sacral flexion is usually taken to mean what is here called *anterior nutation*.

If there is motion in the skull, there must be a driving mechanism, and, in the human skull, there are few mechanisms that have no purpose. Therefore, it is pertinent to consider the nature of the driving mechanism. The most reasonable theory considers the cyclical absorption of cerebrospinal fluid[19-21] that occurs episodically after intracranial pressure reaches the necessary threshold to open the one-way valves of the arachnoid villi and permit the subsequent outflow of spinal fluid into the venous system until the intracranial pressure drops

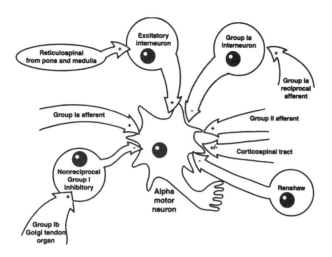

FIGURE 6-1

Diagram of the overview of input to alpha-motoneuron. (+ = excitatory postsynaptic potentials; – = inhibitory postsynaptic potentials.)

low enough to close the valves. As intracranial pressure increases, the skull expands and then decompresses with a reduction in pressure.

To the mechanically minded individual, it is difficult to understand how the relationship of bones like those in the skull can be influenced accurately from outside. We owe the development of these techniques to Sutherland's persistence and experimentation.

No attempt is made in this book to describe specific techniques. Those wishing to study them can find descriptions in Magoun,[17] Upledger,[18] and Hruby.[22] It is strongly recommended that no attempt be made to use these techniques without first taking a recognized course of instruction.

EFFECT OF MANIPULATIVE TECHNIQUES ON THE CENTRAL NERVOUS SYSTEM AND MUSCLE TONE

As a neurologist, the editor (E. R. I.) has tried to understand the interplay between manipulation and the central nervous system. It seemed reasonable to consider the gamma motor system and, in particular, the silent period or reduced type Ia afferent input after muscle spindles were unloaded as important factors in the development of postisometric muscle contraction relaxation. Over time, a concept developed that if the nervous system could be viewed as an advanced computer, then the standard neurological examination was simply testing the "hardware" of that computer. The postural mechanisms and motion characteristics of any musculoskeletal system would reflect the

operations of either an inherent or learned "program." Dysfunctions of the musculoskeletal system then could be viewed as altered programs causing faulty performance that would persist as long as the altered program was in place. Because the nervous system functions mostly as a reflex system that responds to input, information received from altered mechanoreceptors and proprioceptors could perpetuate this program. This scenario is analogous to the computer jargon for "garbage in means garbage out." If there is a way to change input, to get rid of the "garbage," then the computer should be able to be reprogrammed back to a better operating version.

An overview of current understanding of central and peripheral nervous system physiology and the effect on muscle tone was written by R. A. Davidoff.[23] This presentation of basic neuroscience might appear to have little practical value to the neurologist practicing standard neurology. However, the overview has tremendous practical value when one considers manipulation as a means to reprogram the nervous system.

Considering the end point of treatment as a modification of muscle tone, the responsible mechanisms or "hard wiring" must influence the output from the alpha-motoneuron to its muscle fibers. The final common path to the initiation of nerve action potential is the sum of all of the postsynaptic inhibitory and excitatory potentials delivered to the alpha-motoneuron at any given instant (Figure 6-1).

Mechanically Activated Peripheral Sensory Receptors

Muscle Spindles

1. Primary spindle endings on bag_1, bag_2, and chain fibers respond to static stretch and are very sensitive to changes in the rate of stretching, and give rise to group Ia afferents.

2. Secondary spindle endings on bag_2 and chain fibers are primarily affected by slow or prolonged static stretch and give rise to group II afferents.

Muscle spindles are innervated by gamma-motoneurons, and as many as 70% may also be directly innervated by collateral axons from certain alpha-motoneurons called *beta axons* (Figure 6-2). Dynamic fusimotor fibers enhance spindle sensitivity for small, rapid changes in length. Static fusimotor fibers shorten intrafusal muscle fibers, maintaining sensitivity during unloading by contraction of extrafusal fibers. There is independent supra spinal control for the dynamic and static fusimotor systems.

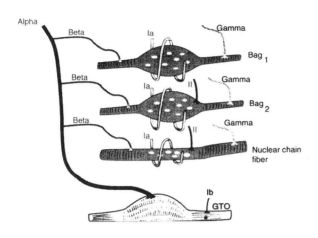

FIGURE 6-2
Diagram of muscle spindles and beta axons. (GTO = Golgi tendon organ.)

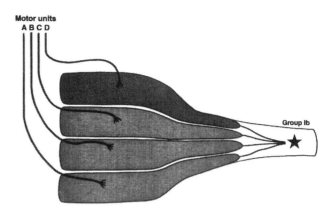

FIGURE 6-3
Diagram of a Golgi tendon organ. (A, B, C, and D = axons from four different motor units.)

There is no significant fusimotor background drive to relaxed muscles.

Golgi Tendon Organs

Golgi tendon organs (GTOs) are receptors that lie in series with muscle fibers and tendons and are located at the myotendinous junction (Figure 6-3). Each GTO is activated by 10–20 extrafusal muscles fibers that are inserted through the tendinous fascicle and represent portions of different motor units. It is difficult to fire a GTO by passive stretch alone, because the force must be generated first through the surrounding connective tissue. However, it may be possible for one muscle fiber contracting in series to fire its GTO. The GTO gives rise to group Ib afferents.

Interneurons

Renshaw Cells

Renshaw cells (Figure 6-4) are excited by recurrent collaterals from alpha-motoneurons and input from complex descending and other afferents. These cells generate inhibitory postsynaptic potentials (IPSPs) to

1. Homonymous and synergistic alpha-motoneurons
2. Gamma-motoneurons
3. Ia inhibitory interneurons
4. Other Renshaw cells

Ia Inhibitory Interneurons

Ia inhibitory interneurons (Figure 6-5) are responsible for reciprocal inhibition to antagonist muscles and their syner-

gistic cohorts and receive excitatory postsynaptic potentials (EPSPs) from Ia afferents from the directly stimulated muscles and their synergists. This interneuron also generates an IPSP in other alpha-motoneurons to muscles that are not antagonists and to other types of interneurons. The Ia interneuron receives additional afferents from

1. High threshold afferents from skin, muscle, and joints
2. Axons from Renshaw cells
3. Descending fibers from vestibular and red nuclei
4. Descending fibers from sensorimotor cortex

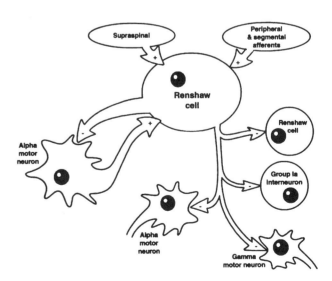

FIGURE 6-4
Diagram of a Renshaw cell. (+ = excitatory postsynaptic potentials; − = inhibitory postsynaptic potentials.)

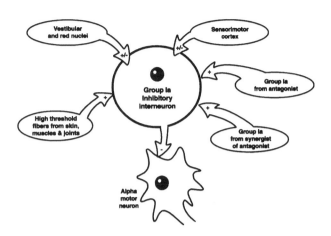

FIGURE 6-5
Diagram of a reciprocal inhibitory Ia interneuron. (+ = excitatory postsynaptic potentials; – = inhibitory postsynaptic potentials.)

Interneurons That Mediate Group I Nonreciprocal Inhibition

Interneurons that mediate group I nonreciprocal inhibition (Figure 6-6) are excited by Ib afferents and, in a parallel fashion, by Ia afferents and receive additional input from

1. Cortico-, rubro-, and reticulospinal tracts
2. Afferents other than group I peripheral afferents

All three types of interneurons receive additional converging afferents from supraspinal systems, so transmission through any interneuron is gated by the summation

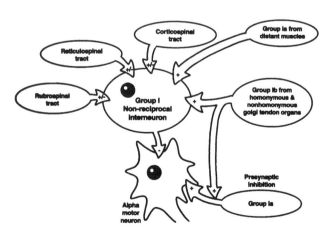

FIGURE 6-6
Diagram of a nonreciprocal inhibitory Ib interneuron. (+ = excitatory postsynaptic potentials; – = inhibitory postsynaptic potentials.)

of IPSPs and EPSP derived from these central and peripheral sources (see Figure 6-1).

Presynaptic Inhibition

Primary afferent depolarization is a means for inhibition that appears to occur between Ib and Ia afferents; thus, a GTO can have an inhibitory effect on a muscle spindle by presynaptic inhibition. There also appears to be a way in which supraspinal effects can be mediated to bias whether muscle spindle or GTO feedback is critical (see Figure 6-6).

Long-Latency Responses

Muscle spindle afferents project to the sensorimotor cortex, causing cortical motoneurons to discharge and generate late muscle responses or possibly programmed patterns of activity triggered by external cues.

Alpha-Motoneurons

The alpha-motoneuron is the final common path that responds to heterogeneous synaptic input from afferent and descending pathways. The force developed by a muscle is determined by the number of alpha-motoneurons recruited and the frequency of the discharge rate from them.

Synaptic contacts include the following:

1. Group Ia afferents. Fifteen percent of input from homonymous muscle may have multiple synapses with their inhibitory interneurons and, along with those Ia afferents from synergistic muscles, generate EPSP.
2. Group II afferents also derive from homonymous muscle and their synergists and synapse with the alpha-motoneuron, generating EPSPs.
3. Descending reticulo-, vestibulo-, rubro-, and corticospinal fibers with extensive excitatory connections. *Reticulospinal fibers from the pons, medulla, and vestibulospinal tracts influence alpha-motoneurons that innervate proximal and axial musculature concerned with the control of posture.*
4. Excitatory and inhibitory interneurons account for the majority of synaptic connections on alpha-motoneurons.

Recruitment of motor units correlates to the size of the alpha-motoneuron. The smaller neurons innervate small motor units with small-diameter fibers that contract slowly and develop small twitch and tetanic tensions that are highly resistant to fatigue. Small alpha-motoneurons discharge at a slow rate but can do so for long periods. By contrast, large alpha-motoneurons innervate large motor units with large muscle fibers that contract rapidly and develop large twitch and tetanic tensions, but the fibers fatigue easily. These neurons are capable of discharging in brief, high-frequency bursts.

In most reflex activities, the alpha-motoneurons discharge in order of increasing size. The smaller, slower, twitch motor units are first excited by initial afferent input so that, as input increases, recruitment of larger units occurs smoothly to equal the level of afferent input.

Postural tone is facilitated by long-latency reflexes (anti-gravity) from the legs and modified by descending vestibulospinal pathways and from proprioceptive responses from the neck, trunk, or both, along with visual inputs and voluntary responses.

Reprogramming the Central Nervous System by Various Manipulative Techniques

Barriers that limit joint motion are, at least in part, due to imbalances in muscle tone across the joint with facilitation of tone in some muscle groups and inhibition of tone in others. Increase in the resting muscle tone results in muscle fiber shortening that, over time, alters the associated intrinsic and extrinsic connective tissues of the muscles, tendons, fascia, and joint capsules. One inherent "program" that takes priority, especially in predatory animals (like humans), is to maintain a posture that preserves a head position that keeps the eyes and ears level. The drive to maintain this posture with the least expenditure of energy encourages the vertebral axis and extremities to accommodate to positional changes or dysfunctions that can perpetuate an unbalanced postural system. Any factor that can change the discharge frequency of the alpha-motoneuron not only affects muscle stiffness at the local barrier, but can also affect adaptations that may have generated other barriers for free motion elsewhere.

In summary, those factors that can reduce the discharge frequency of an alpha-motoneuron include the following:

1. Reflex inhibition by
   a. reciprocal inhibition by muscle spindles
   b. inhibition mediated by GTOs
   c. presynaptic inhibition
   d. Renshaw cell inhibition of alpha- and gamma-motoneurons
2. Postural, long-latency reflexes mediated by the vestibulospinal and rubrospinal pathways, especially to the axial musculature, by considering

a. adaptive postures
b. position of patient during treatment
c. mechanical loads
d. changes in posture after treatment
3. The inhibitory effect of contact with skin and pressure over joints and fascia by either the treating hand or the palpating, monitoring hand
4. Corticospinal effects initiated by voluntary muscle control to assist inadvertently the operator while adding the influence of a patterned, controlled movement
5. Corticospinal effects on learned behaviors and motor responses that may be influenced by the expectations of the patient
6. Controlling level of patient effort to focus on either smaller or larger muscles

These factors may be emphasized or predisposed by various techniques. Muscle energy techniques probably use most of these factors, including (1) unloading of the spindle for postcontraction relaxation; (2) the effects of reciprocal inhibition; (3) inhibition from the GTO and Renshaw cells; and (4) long-latency reflexes from the cortex and brainstem, while emphasizing the changes associated with static stretch of the muscle. Certainly, functional techniques use reflex changes, long-latency responses, and skin and joint contact. Impulse techniques emphasize reflex responses from joint, fascia, and skin, along with dynamic stretch responses from the muscles. Myofascial techniques rely heavily on contact reflexes, long-latency postural reflexes, and segmental reflexes. Counterstrain seems to rely on postural changes and segmental reflexes.

Appropriate exercises after treatment reinforce the proper retraining of weakened muscles by techniques, including disinhibition and proprioceptive neuromuscular facilitation, and by increasing stimulation through postural and corticospinal mechanisms.

LOCALIZATION OF FORCE

To precisely treat a dysfunctional joint, it is necessary to localize the forces that focus the treatment on just that joint and on all of the barriers to motion found within that same joint. Proper localization of force can be illustrated by the model of a garden hose. If a length of hose is twisted from one end, the twist travels along the hose; the greater the twist, the further it reaches down the hose. If, for whatever reason, it is required that the twist go to a certain point and then stop, localization is difficult. On the other hand, if a kink is introduced at the point in the hose before the twist begins, the hose can easily be twisted up to the desired point and no further.

Diagnostic localization to the barriers of motion at a vertebral segment is described in Chapter 5. The method of localization of the manipulative force is an extension of the principles used in diagnosis. For both muscle energy and high-velocity treatments, localization is achieved through positioning the patient. Although there are minor differences between the methods, the position from which a high-velocity treatment is performed is often the same as the position required for muscle energy.

The precise position for localization is determined by palpation; there is no rule of thumb for positioning that will do the job. Palpation can be for motion or tension in the tissues, or both. Most experienced manipulators seem to use a combination of palpation techniques. In some situations, tension is easier to feel; in other situations, motion is easier to feel. For the beginner, the greatest difficulty is in feeling the start of the restrictive barrier. This beginning location can be missed easily and result in localizing to the normal joint above or below the restriction. If force is still localized to the dysfunctional joint but beyond the barrier for motion, there is more discomfort and less success, especially when using the high-velocity technique. It is sound advice to a beginner to stop slightly short of the barrier rather than to go beyond it.

When using thrust (high-velocity, low-amplitude treatment), it is an advantage to be able to control the dysfunctional joint through a long lever. Nature provides only short levers on the vertebrae, of which the transverse and spinous processes are the longest. Long-lever, short-lever, and hybrid techniques are described in this book. Hybrid techniques use a short lever on one side and a long lever on the other. Hybrid and short-lever techniques have the advantage that, at least on the short lever side, the contact is on the actual vertebra to be treated. It might be thought that this advantage would make overall localization unnecessary. However, if the tensions over neighboring joints are adjusted, the treatment will be more successful. It is true that localization through a long lever requires greater care, but if the lever is long, it requires less force to move the joint. Most of the supine thoracic techniques are hybrid, with a long lever for the superior component and a short lever for the inferior component. The "crossed pisiform" is an example of short-lever technique for the thoracic spine, and, as is pointed out later in this text, the crossed pisiform technique can easily be abused.

The principle of operation of a lever is that, with a longer lever, the distance traveled by the force is multi-plied, and the amount of the force is divided by the ratio of the length of the long lever to the length of the short lever. In other words, if the tip of the transverse process is 2.5 cm (1 in.) from the facet joint, and a lever 15 cm (6 in.) long can be constructed, the force that has to be applied at the end of the lever is one-sixth the force needed at the tip of the transverse process, and the distance through which that force has to move is six times as much. This principle can be used to an advantage, because it is difficult to apply a force of sufficient magnitude to overcome the resistance and stop the force before it has moved the bone more than "less than an eighth of an inch at the joint"—the limit imposed by Mennell.[12]

Levers are constructed by a process known as *locking* the spinal (and other) joints. Locking is achieved by positioning the joint so that no further movement is possible in the direction chosen. It should be pointed out that a locked joint is not the same as a joint with a restrictive barrier; the former is what is done to a joint to prevent further motion in one direction, and the latter is what is found by examination. Locking can be produced by taking a joint as far as it will go in any direction (e.g., full flexion). The problem with the locking method is that spinal joints move a little like traffic lights on busy streets. In many places, these "lights" are linked in such a way that long before the first light has finished its green phase, the next light (and probably the third) has turned green. For a joint to move, it must not be locked.

Fryette's third concept of spinal motion tells us that if motion in one plane is introduced in a spinal joint, motion in the other two planes is thereby restricted. By the same principle, locking can be produced by combining motion in more than one plane. If the dysfunction to be treated is flexed, rotated, and side bent (FRS), so that part of the correction is the restoration of extension, the sagittal plane component of the locking, for both the segments above and below the level to be treated should be in extension. Similar considerations apply to the other planes of movement. If there is a neutral group dysfunction (type I), neither flexion nor extension is used and locking is achieved by side bending and rotating to the opposite side.

The objective when introducing either flexion-extension or side bending by translation is to localize the treated vertebra in such a way that it becomes the apex of two curves. This localization produces the required spinal lock by positioning the remaining spinal segments at their physiological barriers from below up and from above down to the dysfunctional joint. Translation of the dysfunctional joint in an anterior–posterior or posterior–anterior direction and a left-to-right or right-to-left direction will bring the dysfunctional joint to its flexion or extension barrier and to its right or left side bending barrier while maintaining a vertical position tangent to these curves. This position allows patients to be comfortably balanced with their shoulders remaining aligned over their hips.

The details of localization are described with the various techniques, but the principle of localization is that the motion is continued only to the point when the tension in the tissues begins to increase at the levels above and below the joint being treated. The point is reached when the vertebra above the dysfunctional motor segment (e.g., L3, if the L4-5 joint is to be treated) can be felt to move. The localization from below would be the sacrum. Alternatively, the movement or tension can be taken just to the point at which the tension reaches the upper component of the motion segment (L4 in the previous example), and the position can then be adjusted by a small reverse movement until that segment is relaxed. The locking from below can, of course, be done in the same manner. Fine tuning will place tension at the barrier. Those differences between the patient and operator positioning to achieve the localization of force before a muscle energy treatment and the positioning needed when a thrust is to be applied as the treatment are described in Chapters 7 through 11.

Reactions to Treatment

Mild reactions to treatment are common, whether the treatment is thrusting, muscle energy, or even indirect. Reactions usually occur in the first 12 hours after treatment but may be delayed (although not commonly) for more than 36 hours. The most common reaction is soreness in the areas treated, and this is more likely in patients whose state is more acute. Other reactions include nausea, dizziness, tachycardia, and diaphoresis, especially when treating the upper thoracic or cervical spine. The reactions that usually follow more extensive treatment for chronic dysfunctions are likely to last more than 24 hours, with muscle soreness being more widespread, either due to the multiple treatment sites or because of the need to readapt to major postural changes. Post-treatment with analgesics and nonsteroidal anti-inflammatory drugs or ice and good hydration with plain water may lessen this temporary discomfort. Patients should be warned to expect these delayed reactions and further assured that such reactions do not signify anything more than the soreness that accompanies muscle pain after initial exercise or unaccustomed physical activity. This assurance can be reinforced at the next follow-up visit. Subsequent treatments are not usually followed by similar reactions.

SUBSEQUENT VISITS

When the patient returns for a follow-up visit, the examination must be repeated to reassess whether the same dysfunction has recurred or whether there are residuals. Some dysfunctions that were not initially appreciated may become obvious. It is not uncommon for recurrent dysfunctions to be consequences of a readaptation to a more fundamental, but asymptomatic, dysfunction elsewhere. Recurrences may also represent the consequence of loss of endurance of previously weakened muscles and the reliance on supporting connective tissues that will deform again to accommodate strain forces. Obtaining additional history about the timing of any recurrent symptoms, especially regarding previous activity and body posture, can give clues to the location of a dysfunction that was not previously diagnosed.

A special example of this recurrence is the patient who has had previous trouble in the same or neighboring area and who comes with symptoms after a fresh injury. Treatment of the recently injured level may make him or her much better, but if the old dysfunctions are not looked for and dealt with, the recent dysfunction is likely to recur quickly. This scenario is not unexpected, because an old, unresolved dysfunction leaves asymmetrical tension that not only predisposes the patient to dysfunctions at other levels, but also tends to make such dysfunctions recur precisely because of the asymmetry. It has been inferred that most patients have multiple dysfunctions. Often, the dysfunction occurs in an old and no longer symptomatic joint that is the basic cause of recurrences. The recurrence of localized pain is usually the patient's primary concern, but the site of pain is often distant from the site of the dysfunction. For example, pain in the buttock and leg is often found with a dysfunction at the thoraco-lumbar junction. Similarly, pain in the neck and arm is frequently associated with an upper thoracic dysfunction. Of equal concern is the identification of dysfunctions that are asymptomatic and without apparent consequence. It is unwise to overtreat. Some dysfunctions are necessary adaptations to problems that cannot easily be found or corrected, or they represent the activities peculiar to that patient. Treatments of any kind are only a means to assist the patient's capacity to heal or to resume his or her particular level of function.

Sometimes, making a precise diagnosis is difficult, even for operators with experience. It is unrealistic to deny that even the seasoned practitioner can occasionally take the wrong view of a problem. If the patient fails to improve with what appears to have been the right treatment, the operator's first objective is to start from the beginning and check the diagnosis. There are times when that the operator has a difficult time properly focusing his or her attention (due to fatigue, stress, or illness). Taking a short break in the schedule or even rescheduling those patients with more difficult problems may be necessary.

If the structural diagnosis fails to uncover a dysfunction that might be the cause of the patient's symptoms, then the source of these symptoms may not originate from the musculoskeletal system. If a structural dysfunction cannot be changed by manipulation of any kind, then it is likely that an underlying pathological condition has not yet been identified.

REFERENCES

1. Maigne R. Diagnostic et Traitment des Douleurs Communes D'origine Rachidienne. Paris: Expansion Scientifique Francaise, 1989.
2. Thomas HR, Berger KE. Cerebellar and spinal injuries of chiropractic manipulation. *JAMA* 1947;133:600–603.
3. Dvorak J, Orelli FV. How dangerous is manipulation of the cervical spine? Case report and results of survey. Man Med 1985;2:1–4.
4. Peters M, Bohl J, Thomke F, et al. Dissection of the internal carotid artery after chiropractic manipulation of the neck. Neurology 1995;45:2284–2286.
5. Dan GD, Saccasan PA. Serious complications of lumbar spinal manipulations. Med J Aust 1983;2:672–673.
6. Haldeman S, Rubinstein SM. Cauda equina syndrome in patients undergoing manipulation of the lumbar spine. Spine 1992;17:1469–1473.
7. Travell J. Myofascial Trigger Points: Clinical View. In JJ Bonica, D Albe-Fessard (eds). Advances in Pain Research and Therapy (vol 1). New York: Raven Press, 1976;919–926.
8. Travell J, Simons DG. Myofascial Pain and Dysfunction: the Trigger Point Manual. The Upper Extremities (vol 1). Baltimore: Williams & Wilkins, 1983.
9. Travell J, Simons DG. Myofascial Pain and Dysfunction: the Trigger Point Manual. The Lower Extremities (vol 2). Baltimore: Williams & Wilkins, 1992.
10. Stoddard A. Manual of Osteopathic Technique (3rd ed). London: Hutchinson, 1980.
11. Maitland GD. Vertebral Manipulation (5th ed). London: Butterworth–Heinemann, 1986.
12. Mennell JM. Joint Pain. Boston: Little, Brown, 1964.
13. Dvorak J, Dvorak V, Schneider W. Manual Medicine 1984. Heidelberg: Springer-Verlag, 1985.
14. Ward RC. Integrated Neuromusculoskeletal and Myofascial Release: an Introduction to Diagnosis and Treatment. In RC Ward, et al. (eds). Foundations for Osteopathic Medicine. Baltimore: Lippincott Williams & Wilkins, 1997; Chap. 62.
15. Jones LH. Strain and Counterstrain. Colorado Springs, CO: American Academy of Osteopathy, 1981.
16. Stiles EG, Shaw HH. Functional Techniques Based Upon the Approach of George Andrew Laughlin, D.O. [course syllabus]. East Lansing, MI: Michigan State University, Continuing Education, 1991.
17. Magoun HI. Osteopathy in the Cranial Field (3rd ed). Produced under the auspices of the Sutherland Cranial Teaching Foundation of The Cranial Academy. Kirksville, MO: The Journal Printing Co, 1990.
18. Upledger JE, Vredevoogd JD. Craniosacral Therapy. Seattle: Eastland Press, 1983.
19. Tripathi RC. The functional morphology of the outflow systems of ocular and cerebrospinal fluids. Exp Eye Res 1977;25(Suppl):65–116.
20. Alksne JF, Lovings ET. Functional ultrastructure of the arachnoid villus. Arch Neurol 1972;27:371–377.
21. Gomez DG, Potts G, Deonarine V, Reilly FF. Effects of pressure gradient changes on the morphology of arachnoid villi and granulations of the monkey. Lab Invest 1973;28:648–657.
22. Hruby RJ. Craniosacral Osteopathic Technique: a Manual (Revised ed). Loxidan Seminars, 1994.
23. Davidoff RA. Skeletal muscle tone and the misunderstood stretch reflex. Neurology 1992;42:951–963.

7

Treatment of Dysfunctions of the Pelvis

When using a biomechanical model for musculoskeletal dysfunctions, it is important to follow a specific sequence for evaluation and treatment. This is especially important when treating dysfunctions of the pelvis. The treatment sequence is based on the general premise that the non-physiological and thus the most disruptive pelvic dysfunctions should be treated first. Also, because lumbar non-neutral dysfunctions can have an influence on the muscles that control and move the pelvis, and because neutral lumbar spinal mechanics are often required to treat certain sacral dysfunctions, another recommended approach is to treat the lumbar spine before the pelvis. If we combine these two philosophies, the recommended treatment sequence is the following:

1. *Dysfunctions of the pubis.* Because the normal operation of the pelvic mechanism depends on free rotation around a transverse axis at the symphysis, pubic dysfunctions will significantly upset the diagnostic criteria and should be treated first.

2. *Innominate (iliac) shear dysfunctions* (superior or inferior). These are nonphysiological dysfunctions that significantly upset the pelvic anatomy and function.

3. *Nonadaptive lumbar dysfunctions.* If nonadaptive lumbar dysfunctions are not treated first, treatment of the pelvis may prove difficult or even impossible. These are non-neutral dysfunctions that prevent the sacrum and the next adjacent lumbar vertebra from moving in opposite directions when the spine is in the neutral position. Freedom of motion for neutral lumbar spinal coupling is necessary for correction of sacroiliac (SI) dysfunctions, especially when the lumbar spine is to be used as a long lever.

4. *SI dysfunctions.* These dysfunctions include those described as anterior and posterior sacral torsions and unilateral sacral nutations (formerly known as *extended or flexed sacra*).

5. *Iliosacral dysfunctions.* In addition to the shear dysfunctions listed above, there are anterior and posterior innominate dysfunctions and the uncommon in- and out-flares.

The treatment techniques described are arranged in the order in which the diagnoses were set out. Where available, both muscle energy and thrusting (high-velocity) treatments are discussed. Only one side, usually the more common one, is described. For dysfunctions that affect the other side, it is only necessary to reverse the side descriptors. It is always a good practice to test again after treatment to see whether the desired result has been achieved. Retesting is always important following any treatment.

1. PUBIS

1.1 Superior Pubis on the Left

Clinically, a superior pubic dysfunction on the left prevents normal rotation of the pubic bones at the pubic symphysis across a transverse axis. It may be asymptomatic, yet it interferes with normal pelvic motion during the walking cycle. Restrictions of motion at the pubic symphysis interfere with normal iliosacral function, as demonstrated by an abnormal standing forward-flexion test (FFT). This dysfunction can also be the source of otherwise unexplained inguinal pain. It can be caused by prolonged one-legged standing or remain as an adaptive dysfunction associated with other pelvic restrictions. It

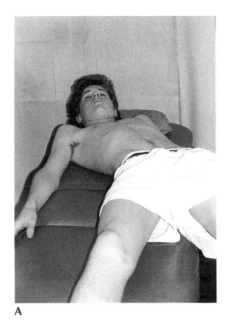
A

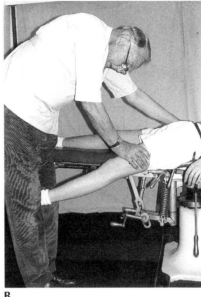
B

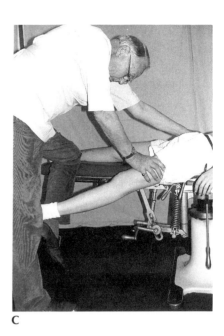
C

FIGURE 7-1

*Treatment for a left superior pubic dysfunction. (**A**) Patient's position on the table with the left posterior superior iliac spine still on the table. (**B**) Patient's leg supported between operator's legs. (**C**) Operator supports patient's leg by hooking one leg under patient's ankle.*

can be maintained by an increase in tone of the left rectus abdominis secondary to thoracic spine non-neutral dysfunctions, especially from T5 to T8.

Diagnostic Points

The standing FFT is positive on the left. The left pubic tubercle is superior (craniad) to the right, and there may be tissue texture change at the insertion of the left inguinal ligament.

1.1.1. Muscle energy technique.

1.1.1.1. The patient is supine, with the pelvis moved to the edge of the table so that the left posterior superior iliac spine (PSIS) is still on the tabletop. For stability, both shoulders should remain on the table (Figure 7-1*A*).

1.1.1.2. The operator stands beside the patient's left leg and takes it off the table, supporting the ankle either between the operator's lower legs or on the back of the left ankle while standing on the right leg with the left knee bent (Figure 7-1*B* and *C*). The patient should be asked to maintain a straight left leg.

1.1.1.3. The operator uses the left hand to press lightly down on the patient's right anterior superior iliac spine (ASIS). This pressure helps to prevent the patient from feeling at risk of falling off the table and also provides a monitor, which moves when the barrier for pubic motion is encountered and is sensed at the beginning of anterior rotation of the right innominate.

1.1.1.4. The operator's right hand is then placed on the front and medial side of the patient's lower left thigh to resist adduction. The patello-femoral joint is sensitive and should be avoided.

1.1.1.5. The operator uses one leg to control the motion by allowing the patient's leg to drop, until motion is felt at the right ASIS. This may need to be repeated a few times, because the patient will tend to flex at the left hip until a sense of security develops to relinquish the weight of the leg to the operator's control. Inadvertent tension in the patient's left leg may cause a shift of the pelvis and give a sense of motion at the ASIS before the actual barrier is encountered.

1.1.1.6. Once the barrier for the left inferior glide at the pubic symphysis is reached, the patient is instructed to try to raise the left thigh up and in against the operator's hand. The pressure should be moderate, because the contraction is isotonic, recruiting the hip adductors to pull the left pubis inferiorly. The contraction is maintained for 3 to 5 seconds.

1.1.1.7. The patient is asked to fully relax so that the operator can sense that there is no patient effort to support the left leg. The operator then allows the patient's leg to either slide down between the operator's legs or the leg is lowered as the operator lowers his or her supporting ankle until the next barrier is sensed at the patient's right ASIS. The next barrier is signaled by an increasing sense of resistance to extension of the patient's left leg and the beginning of movement of the patient's right ASIS. The patient's knee should not be allowed to hang bent.

1.1.1.8. Repeat steps 1.1.1.6 and 1.1.1.7 three or four times or until there is no further gain after relaxation.

1.1.1.9. Retest by palpation of the pubic symphysis with the patient supine and with both legs on the table.

1.2 Inferior Pubis on the Right

Clinically, an inferior pubic symphysis dysfunction on the right also interferes with normal rotational movement through the pubic symphysis and interferes with the walking cycle and iliosacral function. It is a cause for right inguinal pain and is always associated with other pelvic dysfunctions. This dysfunction is maintained by increased tone in the right hip adductors, and decreased tone in the ipsilateral rectus and oblique abdominal muscles.

Diagnostic Points
The standing FFT is positive on the right. The pubic tubercle is inferior on the right and there may be tissue texture change at the insertion of the inguinal ligament.

1.2.1. Muscle energy technique

1.2.1.1. The patient is supine. For operators who find it too difficult to reach over the supine patient, it may be easier to stand on the side to be treated. The instructions for that method are shown in parentheses.

1.2.1.2. The operator stands on the patient's left side at the level of the pelvis and, using the right hand, brings the patient's right hip and knee into full flexion (Figure 7-2*A*).

1.2.1.3. The patient's pelvis is rolled toward the operator, allowing the placement of the left hand under the right buttock so that the ischial tuberosity rests in the palm of the hand (Figure 7-2*B*) or, alternatively, against the left wrist and closed hand, which rests on the table top to support a lever action against the patient's right ischial tuberosity (Figure 7-2*C*).

1.2.1.4. Having rolled the patient back to the supine position, the operator leans over enough to control the patient's knee position with his or her trunk and grips the edge of the table with the right hand to stabilize for the muscular effort that will push against him or her. The hip is adducted and internally rotated to close pack it and the SI joint. The degree of hip flexion is adjusted to the motion barrier of the pubic symphysis that is felt when the flexion motion just begins to move the ilium posteriorly.

1.2.1.5. At the barrier for superior glide at the pubic symphysis, induced through the palm of the left hand or by extension of the left wrist, the instruction is *"gently push* your right foot toward the foot of the table." This patient effort is resisted by an equal counter force and,

as the muscles concerned are powerful, the caution to be gentle is important.

1.2.1.6. After 3 to 5 seconds, ask the patient to stop the effort, relax, and, having waited for complete relaxation, take up the slack in an antero-medial direction toward the pubic symphysis. This procedure is done either by lifting the right ischial tuberosity with the palm of the left hand (see Figure 7-2*B*) or by further extending the left wrist (see Figure 7-2*C*). At the same time, hip flexion should be increased slightly, but only to the point of the new barrier, as described in 1.2.1.4. Remember that the intent of this technique is to treat the pubis and not to posteriorly rotate the innominate.

1.2.1.7. While maintaining tension with the left hand contact, the patient repeats steps 1.2.1.5 and 1.2.1.6 three or four times or until there is no further gain.

1.2.1.8. Retest at the pubic symphysis for any residual somatic dysfunction.

An alternative to this direct technique for correcting a right inferior pubic symphysis dysfunction that is especially useful if the patient is too large for the operator to comfortably treat from the patient's left side is to treat from the patient's right side. From this position, the patient's knee and hip are fully flexed by the operator's left hand, the patient's pelvis is rolled away from the operator, and the palm of the operator's right hand or wrist is placed against the patient's right ischial tuberosity. The operator can then use the left hand to stabilize the patient's right flexed knee while using a superior and medially directed counter pressure with the right hand or wrist against the patient's right ischial tuberosity (Figure 7-2*D*). The degree of hip flexion is adjusted to the motion barrier of the pubic symphysis that is felt when the flexion motion just begins to move the ilium posteriorly. Steps 1.2.1.5, 1.2.1.6, and 1.2.1.7 are followed using the right hand or wrist to lift the patient's right ischial tuberosity and retest as outlined in 1.2.1.8.

1.3 Pubic "Blunderbuss" Technique for Superior or Inferior Dysfunction

---

Diagnostic Points
See 1.1. and 1.2. In both technique 1.3.1 and 1.3.3, the patient often feels a separation occur at the symphysis as a "popping" sensation that may be uncomfortable or, at the least, surprising. Patients should be forewarned of this possibility.

1.3.1 Muscle energy technique: The muscle energy technique uses reciprocal inhibition followed by an isotonic contraction of the hip adductors to balance the pubic sym-

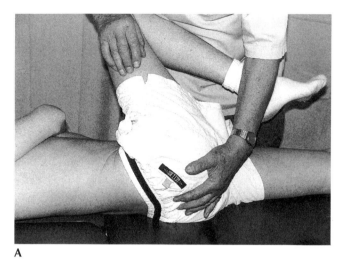

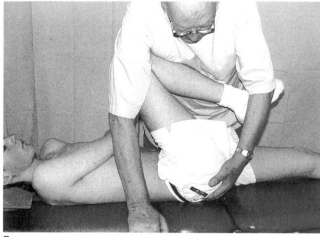

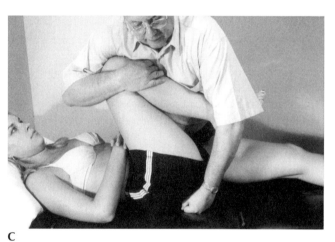

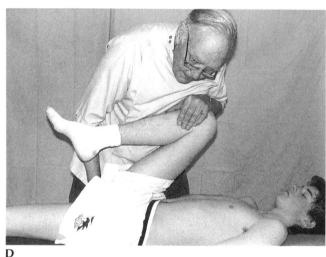

FIGURE 7-2

Treatment of a right inferior pubic dysfunction. (A) Patient's position on the table and placement of the operator's left hand in contact on the ischial tuberosity. (B) Treatment position from the contralateral (patient's left) side. (C) An alternative contact under the ischial tuberosity using the wrist with the hand in a fist to act as a lever and a wedge. (D) Treatment position from the ipsilateral (patient's right) side.

physis. Reciprocal inhibition of the adductors occurs secondarily to an isometric contraction of the hip abductors. This may help to reset and balance the tone in the adductors, which can enhance the success of this technique. When the patient presses the knees together, the adductors contract isotonically; because their action is blocked distally but not proximally, the tension that develops can pull the inferior pubic rami laterally, distracting the joint.

1.3.1.1. The patient is supine with both hips and knees flexed and feet flat on the table.

1.3.1.2. The operator stands to either side of the patient but this time, puts both arms around the flexed knees and holds them tightly (Figure 7-3A).

1.3.1.3. The instruction is "try to separate your knees," which is prevented by the operator.

1.3.1.4. The operator stands to either side and separates the patient's knees by inserting either forearm to keep the knees apart. The dorsiflexed palm of the operator's hand is placed against the medial side of one knee and the back of the elbow against the medial side of the other knee (Figure 7-3B).

1.3.1.5. The patient is then instructed to try to pull the knees together, and the effort is maintained for not less than 3 seconds. If desired, this procedure may be repeated, and if this is done, there is an advantage in sliding the "prop" a short distance proximally to increase the

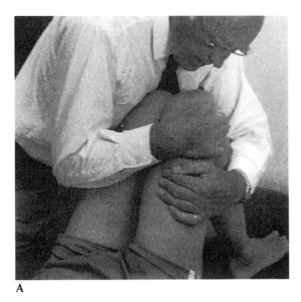
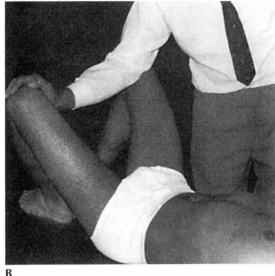

A B

FIGURE 7-3

*Treatment of pubic symphysis dysfunction using "shotgun" technique. (**A**) Reciprocal inhibition of adductors when patient tries to bring knees apart. (**B**) Isotonic contraction of adductors when patient tries to bring knees together.*

abduction in the position of effort. There is no slack to be taken up in this technique.

1.3.1.6. Retest by examining the positions of the superior rami of each pubic bone.

2. INNOMINATE (ILIAC) SHEARS

2.1 Superior Innominate (Iliac) Shear

As described in Chapter 2, no two SI joints are of the same configuration, even in the same patient. Approximately 15% of these joints have no bevel change, which reduces the self-locking capacity for form closure. These relatively flat articular surfaces are inherently unstable and are less capable of resisting a traumatic superior or inferior shearing of the innominate on the sacrum. Because the innominate shear dysfunctions reflect a disruption of the normal anatomy, they are described as nonphysiological dysfunctions.

Clinically, there are two common traumatic events that can cause a superior innominate shear in the susceptible patient. The first event is a fall in which the patient's legs slip out in front, resulting in a direct impact of the ischial tuberosities on a hard surface. This fall commonly occurs on icy steps or ground or on wet or newly waxed floors. Although both tuberosities usually impact, only the side with the flattened articulation shears upward. Pain is immediate,

severe, and usually localized to the coccygeal region, lending support for the misdiagnosis of a fractured "tailbone." Patients may find sitting terribly uncomfortable and use "donut" cushions, especially when sitting on hard surfaces. Very soft seats are equally uncomfortable. The coccygeal pain may persist or spread to the leg, SI joint, and low back. The discomfort becomes worse while walking but subsides after lying down. The second precipitating situation that is commonly encountered is associated with motor vehicle accidents in which the patient's vehicle is struck from behind. At impact, the spinal curves straighten, driving the innominate upward on a fixed sacrum. The history then is one of increasing pain over the next few days, usually affecting the leg and low back more than the coccygeal region. Typically, the painful condition that results in both situations is chronic and not responsive to physical modalities and aggravated by "therapeutic" exercise. Most patients become disheartened by their inability to improve with physical therapy, injection therapy, epidural steroids, and "pain clinics." They are further discouraged by the lack of diagnostic findings by computed tomographic (CT) scans, magnetic resonance imaging (MRI) scans, and electrodiagnostic studies directed to the lumbar spine, pelvis, and leg.

Although the treatment to be described is quite simple and painless, and usually followed by an immediate relief or significant reduction of symptoms, patients should be warned about the consequences of treatment that can cause widespread pain anywhere along the spinal axis and lower extremities. Post-treatment symptoms can occur as a consequence of the necessary readaptations that are required for the resumption of a posture now responsive to equal leg length and a level sacral base. It may be necessary first to treat the non-neutral lumbar and thoracic dysfunctions that are commonly found in association with a superior innominate shear, especially if there is excessive tone in the ipsilateral quadratus lumborum and paraspinal muscles. The stability at this joint will have been further reduced by the prolonged overstretching of the supporting SI ligaments, which may necessitate the use of an SI cinch belt postcorrection.

Described for the Left Side

> *Diagnostic Points*
> The standing FFT is positive on the left. The stork test is positive for both the left upper and lower poles. Iliac crest height appears level while standing but is higher (more craniad) than the right in both the prone and supine positions. Both the ASIS and the PSIS are more craniad on the left when palpated in the supine and prone positions, respectively. The ischial tuberosity is higher on the left by at least a thumb's thickness when compared to the right. The left sacrotuberous ligament is lax and may be tender. The left leg is shorter than the right leg in both the prone and supine positions.

2.1.1. Combined respiratory-thrust technique.

2.1.1.1. The patient is supine, but the same technique can be performed in the prone position, if preferred. The patient's feet should be just over the end of the table.

2.1.1.2. The operator stands at the foot of the table and lifts the patient's left leg off the table, gripping just above the malleoli with both hands, locking the fingers, and crossing the thumbs. At the same time, downward movement of the right leg should be blocked either by pressing against it using the left thigh, or with the help of an assistant who can stand at the operator's side and block the right leg by pressing against the patient's right foot.

2.1.1.3. The operator internally rotates the left leg to close pack the hip joint, moves the leg medially and laterally to find the midrange of free motion to loose pack the SI joint, and then applies traction to the patient's left leg (Figure 7-4).

2.1.1.4. The patient should be asked to inhale and exhale deeply to rock the sacrum between the ilia; during exhalation, the operator increases the traction on the left leg.

2.1.1.5. At the end of the third or fourth exhalation, the patient is instructed to cough, and at that moment the operator adds a moderately sharp and quick distracting tug to the left leg.

2.1.1.6. Retest.

Because of the residual instability of the SI joint due to the laxity of the SI ligaments with this type of dysfunction, there is a tendency for recurrence whenever there is weightbearing on the affected side. Stability can be enhanced by the use of a suitable cinch belt placed below the ASIS anteriorly and the PSIS posteriorly. This belt must be worn whenever the patient is standing or sitting for a 4- to 6-week period after the correction of this dysfunction. It may be necessary to provide two belts, so that one can be worn while bathing or using a shower and always reapplied while supine. It is possible to try one belt and advise the patient to limit weightbearing on the affected side when not wearing the belt while showering or bathing. If two belts are needed, it is best to keep one of them on at all times, until stability has been achieved by the natural shortening of the supporting ligaments while SI joint alignment has been maintained. Walking is a suitable exercise that may enhance this process.

All such cinch belts are uncomfortable and tend to irritate the skin over time. One of the more comfortable varieties is the SI-LOC, which was developed in conjunction with the International Academy of Orthopaedic Medicine and is distributed by Orthopedic Physical Therapy Products (Minneapolis, MN).

2.2 Inferior Innominate (Iliac) Shear

Unlike the superior shear, this dysfunction is inherently stable when reduced and is probably often self-reduced by weightbearing. Again, these shear dysfunctions can occur only in the susceptible SI joint with little or no bevel and are inherently less stable by form closure.

Clinically, the injury occurs when the leg is forcefully distracted, as in the example of a horseback rider who falls off a horse with one leg still caught in the stirrup, or a skier who falls forward with one ski caught behind and a binding that does not release. This injury can also occur when one shoe gets caught while tripping and falling forward. The incidence of these dysfunctions is rare, but when they occur, there

FIGURE 7-4
Treatment of superior innominate shear (upslip).

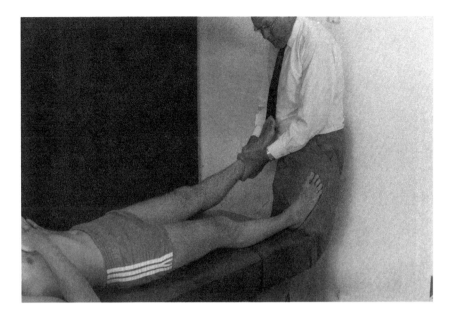

is severe pelvic and leg pain until the dysfunction is corrected. The diagnosis of such dysfunctions may be even less common because of the tendency for self-correction during weightbearing. Treatment rarely needs to be repeated and, because of the immediate restoration of joint stability after reduction, a cinch belt is not needed.

When the patient is of the opposite gender, it is wise to explain carefully the method of treatment; otherwise, the procedure could be thought to be invasive.

Described for the Right Side

> *Diagnostic Points*
> The standing FFT is positive on the right. The stork test is positive for the right upper and lower poles. The iliac crest height appears to be level while standing, but the right iliac crest is lower (more caudad) than the left, both prone and supine. The right PSIS and ASIS are more caudad than those on the left when palpated in the prone and supine positions, respectively. The ischial tuberosity is lower on the right compared to the left by at least a thumb's thickness. The right sacrotuberous ligament is very tight and usually tender. The right leg is longer than the left in both the supine and prone positions.

2.2.1. Mobilization with respiratory assist, side-lying technique.

2.2.1.1. The patient lies on the left side.

2.2.1.2. The operator stands behind the patient's hips and must raise the patient's right lower limb using either his or her right arm, preferably, with the help of an assistant.

2.2.1.3. The operator contacts the patient's right innominate bone with both hands. Both thumbs are medial to the ischial tuberosity. The index and middle fingers of the right hand pass forward to contact the body of the patient's right pubic bone (Figure 7-5A), and the left index and middle fingers are on the medial side of patient's right PSIS (Figure 7-5B). For male patients, it is best to tilt the pelvis forward before contacting the pubic bone, allowing the genitalia to move away first, and then tilt the pelvis back to a perpendicular side-lying position.

2.2.1.4. The patient breathes in and out deeply to rock the sacrum while the operator lifts to distract the innominate toward the ceiling and, with a rocking motion to help free the joint, translates the innominate craniad. A thrust in the craniad direction at the end of the last exhalation may be added but is rarely needed.

2.2.1.5. Retest.

2.2.2. Mobilization with respiratory assist, prone technique.

2.2.2.1. The patient lies prone with the right leg off the table, supported at the knee by the operator's right hand. The operator abducts and adducts the patient's right leg while palpating the SI joint with the left hand to find the

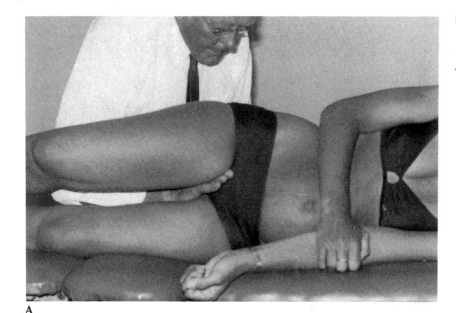

A

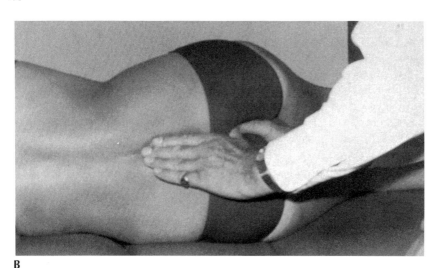

B

FIGURE 7-5
Treatment of inferior innominate shear (downslip). (A) From anterior. (B) From posterior.

loose-packed position. The right SI joint should gap open by the weight of the hanging right leg. The patient should hold the front leg of the table or side of the table with the right hand to help block craniad motion.

2.2.2.2. The operator then places the palm of his or her left hand on the patient's right ischial tuberosity and applies a direct cephalad force from the shoulder through the arm to the ischial tuberosity, rocking it while the patient inhales and exhales deeply. The patient is instructed to push against the right leg of the table with the right hand while the operator provides a distinct counter force in a cephalad direction to guide the innominate superiorly (Figure 7-6).

2.2.2.3. Retest.

3. SACROILIAC DYSFUNCTIONS

3.1 Anterior Sacral Torsion

Described for Anterior Torsion to the Left (Left on Left)

Clinically, this dysfunction may cause little or no pelvic restriction as part of the normal walking cycle, because the major motion loss with this dysfunction is posterior nutation of the right sacral base back to the neutral (level) position, whereas anterior nutation is not affected (see Chapter 4 and Figure 4-20). Because left rotation of the sacrum is coupled with lumbar side bending to the left, the adaptive lumbar curve is convex right when the spine is in neutral. Left on left (LOL) sacral torsions are typically not a cause of low back pain, unless they occur in combination with a flexion restriction of L5 on the right (ERSrt).

> ### Diagnostic Points
> The sitting FFT is positive on the right. The sacral base and the inferior lateral angle (ILA) are posterior on the left in flexion and probably when prone, but they become level in extension. The lumbar spine is in lordosis and the spring test negative. When the lumbar spine can normally adapt to the sacral base unleveling by side bending to the left and rotating to the right in the prone-neutral position, the left leg appears shorter than the right, as measured at the medial malleoli (the sacrum faces the shorter leg).

Two techniques are described. The first is an easier technique, because it is less awkard and difficult for the operator than the second technique, especially if the patient is much larger than the operator. In both techniques, the sacrum is derotated using neutral mechanics so that the sacrum rotates in the opposite direction of L5. It is, therefore, imperative that there be no non-neutral dysfunctions present between L5 and the sacrum for these techniques to work. For this reason, if there is a dysfunction, L5 should be treated first. The first clue that the lumbar spine is unable to properly adapt to the sacral base unleveling comes when examining the leg length in the prone-neutral position. If the sacrum is rotated left in the prone-neutral position (LOL), then the left leg should be short if the lumbar spine is capable of normal adaptation to sacral base unleveling. If, however, the leg lengths are found to be equal or the right leg appears to be short, then there is probably a non-neutral lumbar spine dysfunction interfering with the normal adaptive response. This lumbar adaptive response to sacral base unleveling in the prone (neutral) position also holds true for the other sacral dysfunctions to be described.

3.1.1. The preferred muscle energy technique for an LOL sacral torsion is with the patient lying on the right side.

3.1.1.1. The operator stands in front of the patient. The patient lies on the right side. The hips and shoulders are perpendicular to the table, and the interspinous space at L5, S1 is monitored by the operator's left hand while the right hand flexes and extends the lower extremities to find the neutral range at L5, S1 (Figure 7-7A). In this position, the lumbar spine can be seen to be side bent to the left (Figure 7-7B). The patient's right arm is grasped above the elbow and gently pulled toward the operator so the shoulder can slide forward and initiate left rotation of the spine. At the same time, the lumbar

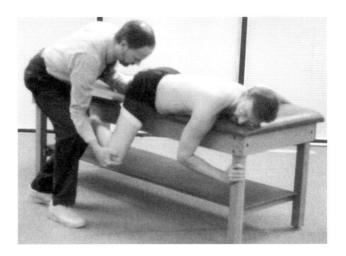

FIGURE 7-6
The correction of an inferior innominate shear dysfunction on the right with the patient in the prone position.

side-bending curve reverses, and now the spine can be seen to be side bent to the right (neutral mechanics) (Figure 7-7C and D).

3.1.1.2. The operator then guides the patient's left shoulder backward, further rotating the spine to the left while monitoring at L5 with the right hand until the left rotation has just started to rotate L5. With the patient's left arm fully extended, the patient can then reach backward and grasp the left edge of the table with the left hand to maintain this position (Figure 7-7E).

3.1.1.3. The operator's right hand is placed around the patient's flexed knees, and the index finger of the left hand monitors the right sacral base (the base closest to the table). The operator keeps the patient's sacrum perpendicular to the table by controlling the pelvis through the patient's legs. The operator then introduces flexion from below by bringing the knees craniad. If the patient's knees are against the operator's thighs, it is easier to control the flexion without tilting the pelvis forward. The flexion barrier is reached when the right sacral base begins to move posteriorly.

3.1.1.4. The operator then slides his or her right hand under the patient's legs just proximal to the ankle and lifts both legs to introduce more left side bending until the right sacral base again begins to move posteriorly (Figure 7-7F). (This is exactly opposite to the Sims position described in 3.1.2.)

3.1.1.5. The patient is instructed to pull the feet down to the table, and the operator resists equally with the right arm and hand while feeling the sacral base move posteriorly (into the left index finger) over a 3- to 5-second period. The patient is then instructed to stop pulling and relax.

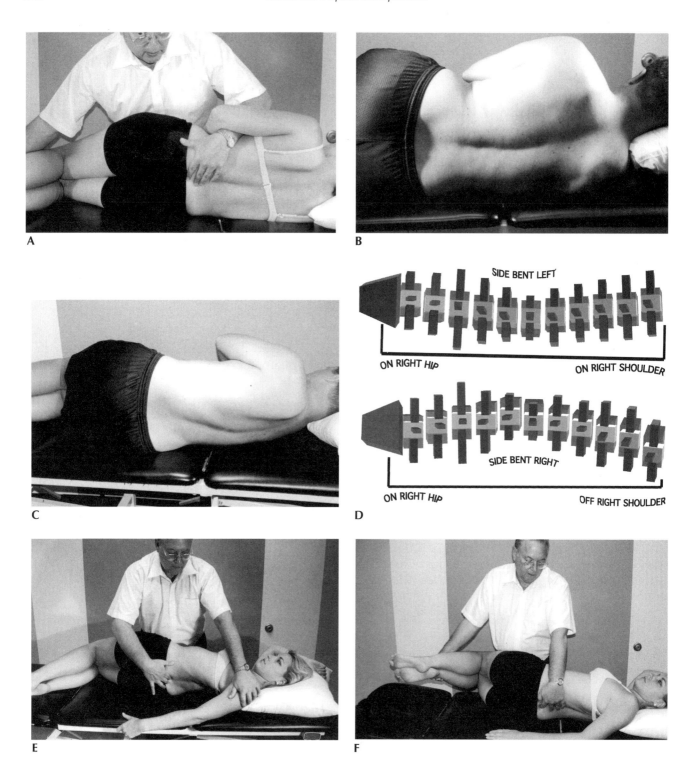

FIGURE 7-7

The preferred technique to treat a left on left sacral torsion. (A) The patient lies on the right hip and shoulder while the lumbosacral junction is positioned in its neutral range. (B) When the patient lies on the right shoulder and right hip, the lumbar spine side bends to the left. (C) If the patient's right arm is pulled out from underneath the shoulder, the lumbar spine side bends to the right. (D) Diagram showing a change in side bending with the patient lying both on and off the shoulder. (E) The patient is rotated left to L5 and stabilizes this position by grasping the table. (F) While palpating the right sacral base, the operator lifts the patient's legs to introduce flexion from below up until tension is palpated at the right sacral base. Then the operator introduces left side bending to the barrier palpated as tension builds at the right sacral base as the legs are lifted toward the ceiling.

3.1.1.6. The new barrier for posterior nutation of the right base can be found by increasing the side bending by lifting the legs or by flexion through the hips. The barrier is detected when the right sacral base begins to move posteriorly. The degree of side bending needed is determined by the degree of hip flexion and vice versa. The decision about which movement to use most is determined by the size of the operator relative to the patient and the operator's ability to maintain control. The movement may be repeated several times or until no further posterior nutation of the right sacral base is detected.

3.1.1.7. Retest.

3.1.2. A muscle energy technique with the patient lying on the left side (more difficult).

3.1.2.1. The patient lies prone, with the right shoulder close to the side of the table and the right arm hanging over the edge.

3.1.2.2. Using the left hand, the operator lifts both of the patient's ankles; then, using the right hand, the operator brings the patient's knees up, placing the patient into a left lateral Sims position with the sacrum perpendicular to the table. The precise position is important; the hip flexion must be stopped at the point just before the sacrum begins to move, and the movement is therefore monitored in its final stage by the fingers of the operator's right hand on the patient's right sacral base. Note that, insofar as the patient is on the left side, it is the side of the axis of the torsion (Figure 7-8*A*).

3.1.2.3. The patient is asked to breathe deeply and reach for the floor with his or her right hand during each exhalation. This movement must be monitored and is stopped when L5 just begins to move into left rotation. The operator monitors with the left hand at this stage so as to be able to use the right hand to increase the patient's rotation by pressing down on the patient's right shoulder during the exhalation effort. If necessary, exhalation and reaching for the floor are repeated until the tension reaches L5.

3.1.2.4. The operator switches hands so that the right hand monitors the patient's right sacral base, and the left hand grasps the patient's lower legs at the ankles. The patient's feet are allowed to drop toward the floor until the right sacral base is felt to move posteriorly (against the operator's palpating right finger) (Figure 7-8*B*).

3.1.2.5. The necessary left side bend introduced by dropping the patient's feet over the edge of the table can be uncomfortable due to the pressure of the table edge on the under thigh. To avoid this discomfort,

3.1.2.5a. Place a small cushion under the thigh to protect it from the edge of the table, or

3.1.2.5b. Stand so that the patient's knees can be supported on or over your left thigh or knee and balance the patient's legs, supporting under the upper tibiae so that the thighs remain clear of the table top (Figure 7-8*C*), or

3.1.2.5c. Sit at the foot of the table and, with legs apart, support the patient's knees with your left thigh. Sometimes known as the *lazy man's technique*, its disadvantage is that it is no longer possible for the operator to control the trunk with the right forearm. To monitor over the right sacral base, the operator must change hands, and the right hand now provides the resistance to the patient's effort in 3.1.2.5. The patient should be told to maintain the twisted position. This technique is less easy if the operator wears a skirt, as the abduction of the operator's legs must be wide enough to allow the patient's feet to drop between them (Figure 7-8*D*).

3.1.2.6. The patient is instructed to raise his or her feet toward the ceiling, and the operator resists with an equal and opposite force by using the left hand in variants 3.1.2.5a and 3.1.2.5b and the right hand in variant 3.1.2.5c. The pressure is maintained for 3 to 5 seconds, and the patient must then relax. It helps to tell the patient to drop his or her feet. If the positioning is correct, it should be possible to feel the right sacral base move posteriorly against the monitoring fingers during the patient's effort.

3.1.2.7. After full relaxation, the slack is taken up to the new point of tension, as monitored by the fingers. Allowing the patient's feet to drop is usually enough to take up the slack and bring the tension back (barrier) to the sacral base, but sometimes an adjustment by flexion of the hips can help.

3.1.2.8. Repeat steps 3.1.2.5 and 3.1.2.6 two or more times.

3.1.2.9. Retest.

3.1.3. Thrust (sitting).

3.1.3.1. The patient sits astride the table, holding the right shoulder with the left hand.

3.1.3.2. The operator stands on the right side of the patient. Using the left pisiform, the operator contacts the patient's left sacral base.

3.1.3.3. With the operator's right axilla over the patient's right shoulder, the operator grasps the patient's left humerus and bends the patient forward, down to and including the sacrum, but not so far as to lock the SI joint (Figure 7-9*A*).

3.1.3.4. Side bending and rotation are introduced to the right by the operator's right arm, again including the sacrum but not the innominates (Figure 7-9*B*). Note that this technique uses non-neutral mechanics to move the sacrum, whereas the muscle energy techniques locked the spine with neutral mechanics, side bending and rotation being to opposite sides.

3.1.3.5. A high-velocity, low-amplitude thrust is now given by the operator's left pisiform against the left sacral base at the same time that the patient's trunk is taken into further side bending and rotation. To allow the sacrum to nutate anteriorly on the left and rotate right,

FIGURE 7-8

(A) Left lateral Sims position. (B) Monitoring the patient's right sacral base with the right hand. The legs are allowed to drop until the sacral base begins to move. (C) Supporting the patient's knees against operator's thigh while standing.

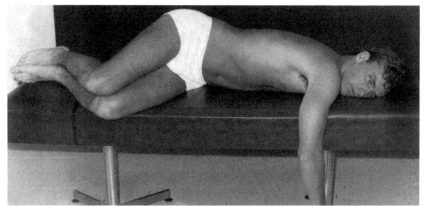

A

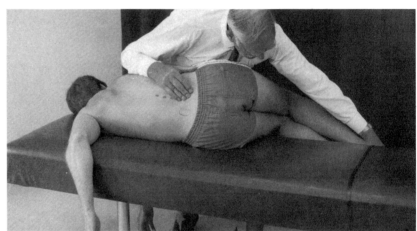

B

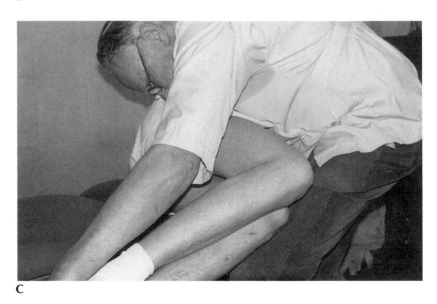

C

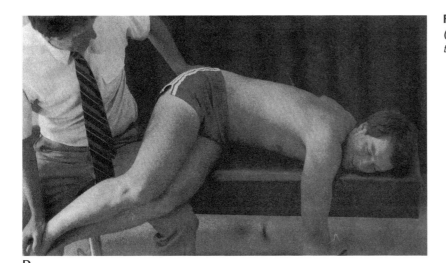

FIGURE 7-8 *continued.*
(D) Supporting the patient's knees against operator's thigh while sitting.

D

the flexion of the lumbosacral joint should be released at the same time.

3.1.3.6. Retest.

3.1.4. Thrust (side-lying).

3.1.4.1. The patient lies on the left side with shoulders perpendicular to the table and the trunk in slight flexion. The flexion must not take the spine out of the neutral range.

3.1.4.2. The operator stands in front of the patient and first extends, then flexes, both hips with the left hand while palpating the right sacral base with the right hand until the base first starts to posteriorly nutate.

3.1.4.3. The operator contacts the left ILA of the sacrum using the left pisiform, keeping the left elbow bent so that the operator's forearm is nearly in line with the intended thrust.

3.1.4.4. With the operator's right hand on the patient's right shoulder, the operator introduces right side bending by taking the shoulder caudad until all slack has been taken out, and, as the spine is in neutral, left rotation is produced (Figure 7-10). This time, the spinal lock is accomplished by using neutral mechanics.

3.1.4.5. The operator presses on the patient's left ILA with the left pisiform in the direction of the patient's right shoulder until all the slack of that move-

FIGURE 7-9
Thrust treatment for left on left sacral torsion with patient sitting. (A) Starting position. (B) Final position.

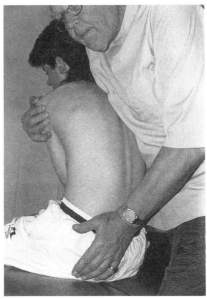

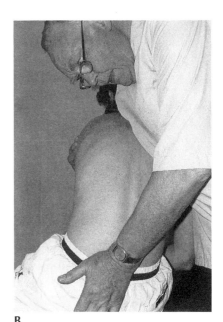

A   **B**

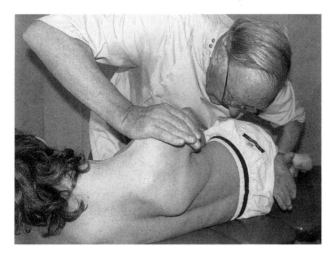

FIGURE 7-10
Thrust treatment for left on left sacral torsion with patient lying on his or her left side.

ment has been removed.

3.1.4.6. A high-velocity, low-amplitude thrust is given by the pizsiform, with a scooping motion on the left ILA directed toward the patient's right shoulder, to bring the right side of the sacral base posterior.

3.1.4.7. Retest.

3.2 Posterior Sacral Torsion

Described for Posterior Torsion to the Left (Left on Right)

Clinically, posterior torsions are almost always symptomatic. Posterior torsion is not a sacral motion that occurs during the normal walking cycle, and, when present and symptomatic, it interferes with the gait cycle, because the sacral base is unable to nutate anteriorly (see Chapter 4, Figure 4-22). In a left-on-right posterior sacral torsion, the left sacral base is restricted for anterior nutation, shortening the length of stride for the left leg. The patient may feel and walk as though the left leg is shorter. This dysfunction occurs when the lumbar spine and sacrum are operating in non-neutral mechanics. Typically, the history includes flexion of the spine followed by the addition of coupled lumbar rotation and side bending to one side. In other words, this dysfunction occurs as a result of bending, twisting, and reaching followed by an attempt to directly assume the upright posture. The actual mechanism of injury that results in a backward sacral torsion is debatable and is thought to occur by two different sets of mechanics operating at the time of injury. We therefore propose that a posterior sacral torsion can either occur as the result of a physiological motion or nonphysiological motion that becomes restricted. Nonphysiological posterior torsion

occurs as the consequence of a total ligamentous and facet opposition lock at the lumbosacral junction that forces the sacrum to follow the rotation of L5 when the lumbar spine is at the extremes of its motion for flexion and combined side bending and rotation. We further believe that physiological posterior sacral torsional movement can and does occur as a consequence of lumbar flexion with coupled side bending and rotation to one side. In this scenario, for example, if left side bending and left rotation are introduced when the lumbar spine is in flexion, but the lumbosacral junction is not fully locked, then the sacral base is free to rotate posteriorly on the right side across the left oblique axis, resulting in a right on left (ROL) backward torsion (see Chapter 4, Figure 4-21). If, however, the patient is fully flexed forward, fully side bent, and rotated to the left, as can occur with the act of bending and turning to the left and then lifting a load, then the lumbar spine can act as a long lever and force the left sacral base to move posteriorly with it. We consider this a nonphysiological movement resulting in a left on right backward sacral torsion. Whether the sacrum rotates posteriorly on the left or right oblique axis therefore depends on the degree of forward flexion mobility and the degree of side bending and rotation coupled at the lumbosacral junction at the time of strain, overload, or injury. Tropism at L5-S1 with a coronally facing facet joint on one side and a sagittal facet joint on the other side also may play an important role in deciding which direction the sacrum ultimately rotates. In either case, a backward sacral torsion that remains on the patient's return to upright standing severely disrupts normal neutral lumbopelvic mechanics, and the treatment approach is exactly the same.

The combination of a strain, non-neutral spinal mechanics, and altered muscle tone, along with other somatic changes, often results in a persistence of this backward sacral torsion in combination with restricted lumbar extension. When acute, there may be immediate pain and inability to assume the upright posture, but often the signs and symptoms evolve over 24 hours, initially having been felt as a "twinge" of discomfort. Although probably the most common cause of low back pain, these symptoms can subside after several days; however, because the dysfunction remains, recurrences of severe symptoms force the patient to self-restrict from many activities. When severe symptoms persist, patients with this dysfunction comprise the majority of those experiencing chronic disabling low back pain. Typically, these patients describe increased discomfort when rising from a flexed or seated position. They are uncomfortable lying prone and prefer to sleep on their sides with a pillow between the legs; usually, they cannot lie on the side of the posterior torsion. Sleep is often interrupted, and, as with any reduction in physical activity, there is increased back stiffness on rising. This stiffness can be reduced by applying heat and, at times, by morning exercises. Dressing is difficult because of an inability to cross the right leg over the left thigh. After early morning symptoms subside, they increase during the day and worsen with prolonged sitting or increased physical activity. Vacuuming is noted to aggravate the pain. Medications, including nonsteroidal anti-inflammatory drugs, narcotic analgesics, muscle relaxants, antidepressants, and anticonvulsants, are usually of little or no help.

The loss of normal lumbosacral motion may, at least in part, be responsible for the desiccation of the intervertebral disc at L5-S1 seen by MRI. Because the injury involved a torsional motion, annular tears are not uncommon along with subsequent lumbar disc herniation. The major source of pain often originates from the SI joint and usually radiates down the back of the leg, mimicking sciatica. This may be the reason for continued pain after surgical intervention for a herniated nucleus pulposus. However, it should be noted that the vast majority of those having chronic low back pain have never had surgery and represent the failures of current "conservative" nonsurgical care.[1]

Diagnostic Points

The stork test is positive on the left (upper pole only*). The sitting FFT is positive on the left. The sacral base and the ILA are posterior on the left in extension and when prone but become level in flexion. The lumbar spine is flat and the spring test positive. There often is a non-neutral dysfunction at L5-S1; usually, L5 appears level in the prone-propped position, which in relation to the sacral base means that is actually flexed, rotated, and side bent right (FRSrt). Because the correction of a posterior sacral torsion requires normal neutral lumbar spinal mechanics, L5 must be able to freely rotate opposite to the sacrum when in the neutral position. Thus, if L5 is dysfunctional, it must be treated first, along with any other non-neutral lumbar dysfunctions (see Chapter 8, Sections 1.1 and 1.2). When the patient is in the prone position and neutral mechanics are operative, the lumbar spine adapts to the unlevel sacral base by side bending left and rotating right, which shortens the left leg. If the leg lengths appear equal or if the left leg is longer, suspect an inability for lumbar adaptation to occur due to one or more non-neutral dysfunctions that are severe enough to interfere with neutral mechanics in the prone (neutral) position.

---

*Unpublished personal observations by the editor (E. R. I.) suggest a high correlation between specific sacral dysfunctions and the stork test. Notation is made of the response when testing the upper pole and the lower pole as described in Chapter 3, Figures 3-11 and 3-12. These observations are noted in parentheses.

3.2.1. Muscle energy technique.

3.2.1.1. The patient lies on the right side, which is the side of the axis around which the torsion has taken place. The operator stands in front of the patient.

3.2.1.2. Monitoring with the right middle or index finger at L5, the operator takes the patient's right arm and pulls it forward, out from under the patient's right shoulder, to induce left rotation and right side bending of the lumbar spine. Rotation must be continued until it reaches L5, as detected by an increase in tension under the monitoring fingers (Figure 7-11A). If necessary, added rotation can be accomplished by rotating the patient's left shoulder backward. When that position is adjusted, the patient should grip the back of the table edge with his or her left hand to maintain it.

3.2.1.3. The operator's left index or middle finger monitors the patient's left sacral base while using the right hand to move the patient's right leg backward from hip flexion toward the extension barrier. Some indication as to the extent of the restriction imposed by the left posterior sacral torsion can be estimated by the position needed to observe symmetry of the ILAs during the seated FFT. The operator can then ease the patient's right leg toward the back of the table to localize extension from below, leaving the left leg in front. Positioning of the right leg must be done by the operator, with the patient relaxed. Any attempt by the patient to help must be stopped. The movement is taken to the point at which the left sacral base just begins to move anteriorly but L5 does not (Figure 7-11B).

3.2.1.4. Monitoring again with the left hand over the patient's left sacral base, the operator uses the right hand to bring the patient's left leg forward, supporting the leg proximal to the knee. The operator also uses his or her right thigh in combination with the right hand for additional support of the patient's left leg. This position helps keep the pelvis perpendicular to the table throughout the technique. The operator's right hand is placed above the patient's left knee to provide the counter force to hip abduction (Figure 7-11C).

3.2.1.5. The instruction is "try to raise your left knee against my hand." The pressure should be maintained for 3 to 5 seconds, and then the patient must relax. If the positioning is correct, it should be possible to feel the left sacral base move anteriorly or away from the monitoring fingers during the patient's effort.

3.2.1.6. When relaxation is complete, the remaining barrier(s) for left sacral base anterior nutation is approached by further extension of the right hip, left rotation of the spine, or allowing the left leg to drop closer to the floor, separately or in any combination, remembering that the introduction of one new position lessens the amount of movement in the other two positions necessary to reach the next barrier.

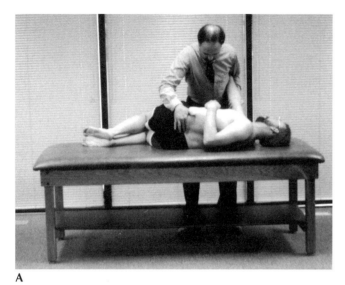

A

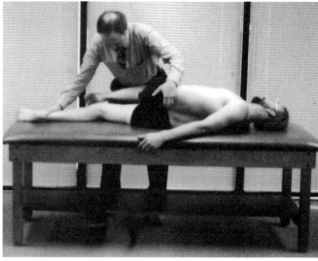

B

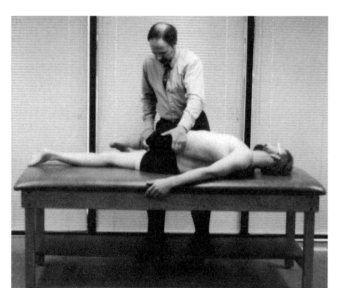

C

FIGURE 7-11

Muscle energy technique for treating a backward sacral torsion, left on right. (A) Patient's right arm is pulled out from underneath the body to induce right side bending and left rotation down to L5. The operator monitors at the L5, S1 interspace. (B) With the operator palpating the patient's left sacral base, the right leg is brought back into extension from below up until the operator perceives movement at the left sacral base. (C) The operator then slowly lowers the left leg in adduction until tension is palpated at the left sacral base. Note that the patient's pelvis stays perpendicular to the table throughout the technique.

3.2.1.7. Steps 3.2.1.5 and 3.2.1.6 are repeated three or more times, until no further anterior motion of the left sacral base occurs.

3.2.1.8. Retest.

3.2.2. Thrust (sitting). This technique also may be used to correct a right unilateral posteriorly nutated sacrum (see 3.4, below).

Described for Right on Left Sacral Torsion

3.2.2.1. The patient sits astride the table while holding the right shoulder with the left hand.

3.2.2.2. While standing on the left side, the front of the operator's left shoulder is pressed against the side of the patient's left shoulder; then the left hand is used to grasp the patient's right shoulder.

3.2.2.3. The operator uses the right pisiform bone or thumb to contact the patient's right sacral base. The operator then locks the patient's spine down to and including the sacrum by side bending the trunk to the right and rotating to the left to start the right sacral base moving forward (Figure 7-12). The mechanics involve sacral rotation to start the movement and then extension of L5 to encourage the right sacral base to nutate anteriorly.

3.2.2.4. The operator extends the patient's spine down to L5 until all the slack has been taken out and then a high-velocity, low-amplitude thrust is directed forward on the right sacral base by the operator's right pisiform while the extension of the trunk is exaggerated. The thumb could be used, but the small pisiform fits more easily in the narrow sulcus so that the sacral base itself is contacted.

3.2.2.5. Retest.

3.2.3. Thrust (supine). This technique may also be used to correct a right unilateral posteriorly nutated sacrum (see 3.4, below) or reversed to correct a left on right posterior sacral torsion.

Described for a Right on Left Posterior Sacral Torsion

3.2.3.1. The patient lies supine, with fingers laced together behind the neck and elbows forward. The patient's pelvis should be close to the operator (at the left side of the table); then, the feet and upper trunk are moved to the right side of the table, producing right side bending of the trunk (Figure 7-13*A*).

3.2.3.2. Leaning over, the operator threads his or her right forearm through the gap between the patient's right arm and chest and then rests the back of the right hand on the patient's sternum.

3.2.3.3. The operator pulls the patient's right arm forward, bringing the trunk into left rotation without losing the right side bend, until the right ilium begins to lift off the table (Figure 7-13*B*).

3.2.3.4a. The operator holds the right ilium down using the left hand, and the correction is produced by a sharp increase in left rotation of the trunk *without losing the side bend*. Note that, to achieve correction, the spine must be locked down to and including the sacrum (Figure 7-13*C*).

3.2.3.4b. Alternatively, the dysfunction can be corrected by a high-velocity, low-amplitude posteriorly directed thrust by the operator's left hand on the patient's right ASIS while maintaining the trunk in the left rotated and right side bent position.

3.2.3.5. Retest.

3.3 Unilateral Anterior Sacral Nutation

Unilateral anterior sacral nutation (formerly known as an *inferior sacral shear* or *unilateral flexed sacrum*) is a nonphysiological dysfunction.

Described for the Left Side (Most Common)

Clinically, patients with this dysfunction frequently describe a history of aching low back pain that gets worse the longer they stand and is relieved by sitting down. Symptoms usually peak within 20 to 30 minutes of standing, and, if they cannot sit down, they tend to pace. They are most uncomfortable at cocktail parties or standing in line. The mechanism of injury is thought to be due to landing hard on one leg after jumping, as can occur while playing volleyball or bas-

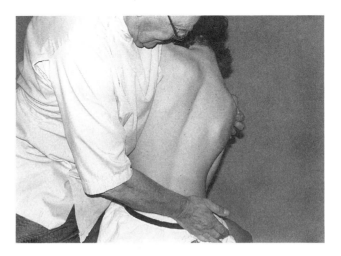

FIGURE 7-12
Thrust treatment for right on left sacral torsion with the patient sitting.

ketball, when a force from above, coupled with an extended lumbar spine, drives the sacrum deep into the pelvis on one side. Because no two SI joints are the same from side to side, this dysfunction may also occur secondarily to the failure of the sacral base on one side to return to its neutral position after being anteriorly nutated during hyperextension of the lumbar spine. For some as-yet unexplained reason, this dysfunction almost always occurs on the left side and is usually associated with a non-neutral dysfunction at L5, which will be extended, rotated left, and side bent left (ERSlt). L5 must be treated first, because its side-bending component will block the sacral base from moving craniad during the corrective treatment. The anteriorly nutated sacrum is also commonly found with a concurrent left posterior innominate dysfunction (see 4.1, below).

A unilateral anteriorly nutated sacrum is not a consequence of normal physiological motion and can be likened to a desk drawer that is off track on one side. The left ILA is in a posterior and inferior position, but the left sacral base is in an anterior position (see Chapter 4, Figure 4-18). This arrangement is unlike the torsions, in which both the ipsilateral base and ILA are equally in a posterior or anterior position. The unilateral anterior sacral nutation does not become level at the ILAs with flexion or extension of the lumbar spine and is therefore differentiated from the sacral torsions. Recall that with the anterior sacral torsions, the ILAs become worse (more asymmetrical) with flexion and symmetrical with extension of the lumbar spine; with posterior sacral torsions, the ILAs become worse with extension and symmetrical with lumbar flexion.

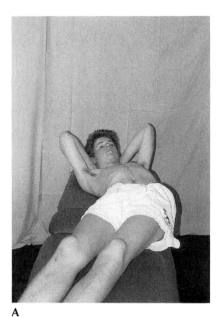

A

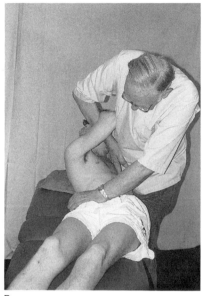

B

FIGURE 7-13
Thrust treatment for right on left sacral torsion with the patient supine. (A) Starting position. (B) Thrust position as seen from patient's feet. (C) Thrust position as seen from right side of patient.

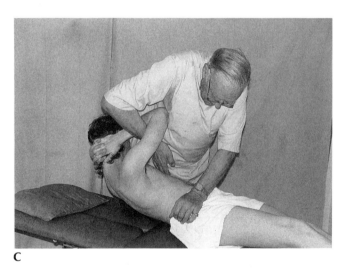

C

Diagnostic Points

The stork test is positive on the left (the lower pole only). The sitting FFT is positive on the left. The sacral base is anterior on the left in flexion, neutral, and extension. The ILA is posterior on the left in flexion, neutral, and extension. The lumbar spine is in lordosis, and the spring test is negative. The right leg is shorter than the left leg in the prone (neutral) position, and the sacrum is rotated to the right and faces the adaptive lumbar concavity, which is side bent to the right.

3.3.1. Articulatory technique with direct action and thrust variant.

3.3.1.1. The patient lies prone with both feet resting on the tabletop.

3.3.1.2. The operator stands on the left side and monitors the patient's left sacral sulcus using the left index and middle fingers.

3.3.1.3. With the right hand, the operator lifts the patient's left thigh and moves it to the point at which the left SI joint is "loose packed." This is the point of maximum ease, as detected by the monitoring fingers, and is usually found in 10 to 15 degrees of hip abduction. Rotating the thigh internally helps to open the posterior aspect of the SI joint. The patient is then told to keep the leg in internal rotation, which is easier to do if the foot remains on the table (Figure 7-14A).

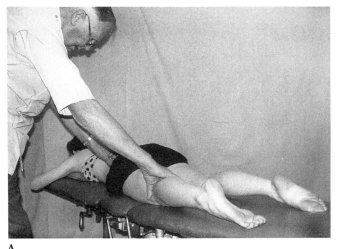

A

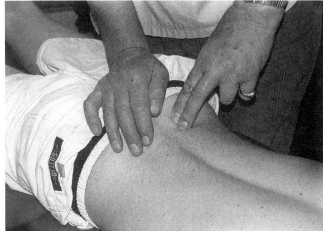

B

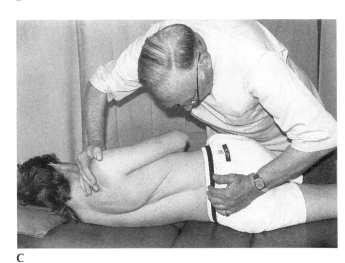

FIGURE 7-14
Unilateral anterior sacral nutation on the left. (A) Positioning the leg. (B) Articulatory treatment with respiratory assist. (C) Thrust with patient lying on his or her side.

C

3.3.1.4. The heel of the operator's right hand is placed on the left ILA of the patient's sacrum so that a springing pressure can be applied. By keeping the right elbow straight, the operator can adjust the direction of force through the right arm so that the springing pressure being applied to the left ILA produces the most movement of the left sacral base toward posterior nutation. The operator uses his or her left fingertips to monitor the motion of the left sacral base (Figure 7-14*B*).

3.3.1.5. The patient is instructed to breathe in as deeply as possible (which promotes posterior nutation of the sacrum) and holds the breath while the operator presses firmly in an anterior and especially a superior direction on the left ILA. The operator keeps the right arm extended while transferring his or her body weight down from the shoulder onto the patient's left ILA, using a springing motion.

3.3.1.6. After approximately 5 seconds, the patient should exhale slowly; the operator does not release the pressure on the left ILA.

3.3.1.7. Steps 3.3.1.5 and 3.3.1.6 are repeated, repositioning the direction of springing force to the ILA to maintain maximal posterior nutation and superior translation of the left sacral base. It may be necessary to adjust and redirect the force from the ILA as the sacral base moves posteriorly and superiorly along its unique SI articulation. These steps are repeated until the left sacral base is once again level to the right base, and finally the operator *slowly* releases the pressure. Too rapid a release may allow the sacrum to spring forward.

3.3.1.8. The common association of a left posterior innominate dysfunction may require that the innominate be treated after correction of the left unilateral anterior sacral nutation. If this is the case, then special precautions should be taken to avoid bringing the left sacral base anterior again when the left innominate is rotated anteriorly. This movement can be prevented by a modification of the technique, as described in section 4.1.2, in which pressure is maintained on the left ILA during the correction of the innominate rotation.

3.3.1.9. Retest.

3.3.2. Thrust, side lying.

3.3.2.1. The patient lies on the left side.

3.3.2.2. The operator stands in front and flexes the patient's hips and knees with the left hand to start posterior nutation of the sacrum; the operator monitors with the right hand at the left sacral base to ensure that the lumbosacral joint is not also flexed.

3.3.2.3. Using the right hand, the operator pulls the patient's left shoulder forward and caudad to lock the spine by neutral mechanics down to L5.

3.3.2.4. Flexing the patient's right (upper) knee and hip a little further, while being careful not to lock the lumbosacral joint, the operator's left pisiform can make contact with the left ILA of the patient's sacrum.

3.3.2.5. Keeping the left forearm parallel to the table, the operator presses forward and cranial on the patient's ILA to take out the slack from below.

3.3.2.6. Using the right hand, the operator takes out the slack down to L5 by adding pressure directed posteriorly through the patient's right shoulder (Figure 7-14C).

3.3.2.7. After all the slack is taken up, a high-velocity, low-amplitude thrust is directed cranially by the operator's left hand on the patient's left ILA. This technique is similar to the one used for an LOL anterior sacral torsion (3.1.4), except that the thrust is directed cranially and not with a scooping motion toward the right shoulder.

3.3.2.8. Retest.

3.3.3. Thrust, prone.

3.3.3.1. The prone thrust is almost the same as the muscle energy technique, 3.3.1, but at the time of the third inhalation the operator gives a high-velocity, low-amplitude thrust in the direction that the springing has shown to be most effective in producing motion at the left SI joint.

3.4 Unilateral Posterior Sacral Nutation

Unilateral posterior sacral nutation (formerly known as a *superior sacral shear* or *unilateral extended sacrum*) is a nonphysiological dysfunction.

Described for the Right Side (Most Common)
Clinically, these patients present much like those with an ROL posterior sacral torsion, often with a history of bending and twisting followed by asymmetrical forceful extension, as with lifting a load. The upper lumbar and lower thoracic spine may be the focus of the strain

rather than the lumbosacral region with hypertonus of the ipsilateral longissimus thoracis. This dysfunction is most commonly found on the right, is rare on the left side, and is often associated with an anterior innominate dysfunction on the same side.

> ### *Diagnostic Points*
> The stork test is positive on the right (the upper pole, only). The sitting FFT is positive on the right. The right sacral base is posterior, and the right ILA is anterior and superior (craniad) compared to the left (see Chapter 4, Figure 4-19). Although the asymmetry may worsen in extension and improve with flexion, the sacral base and ILAs never become symmetrical, thereby helping to differentiate them from ROL torsions. The lumbar spine is flat, and the spring test is positive. In the prone position, the right leg is shorter than the left, if the lumbar spine is freely adaptive. There is usually an associated FRSrt at L4 or L5 and hypertonus of the right longissimus thoracis. Non-neutral dysfunctions are also usually present at the thoraco-lumbar junction and lower thoracic spine.
>
> Correction of those dysfunctions, which contribute to the right longissimus hypertonicity, may actually correct the right posterior sacral nutation. Treatment for the sacral dysfunction with the muscle energy technique sometimes can only be accomplished by first treating the FRSrt at L5, if present. Occasionally, the FRSrt at L5 is not detected until after correction of the sacral dysfunction.

3.4.1. Articulatory technique.

3.4.1.1. The patient lies prone on the table, and the operator stands on the right side and uses the right hand to monitor the patient's right sacral sulcus (Figure 7-15A).

3.4.1.2. The operator uses the left hand to lift the patient's right thigh above the knee, avoiding the patellofemoral joint, and adjusts the ad- and abduction position until the SI joint is loose packed. The operator then externally rotates the patient's thigh to open the anterior aspect of the right SI joint and puts the leg back on the table, asking the patient to maintain that position.

3.4.1.3. Facing the patient's feet, the operator's right pisiform is placed in contact with the right side of the patient's sacral base, and the patient assumes the prone-propped position, because extension of the lumbar spine promotes anterior nutation of the sacrum (Figure 7-15B).

3.4.1.4. The operator's left hand is placed under the patient's right ASIS to provide counter pressure (Figure 7-15C).

3.4.1.5. The patient is asked to exhale as far as possible and to then hold the breath. This tends to bring

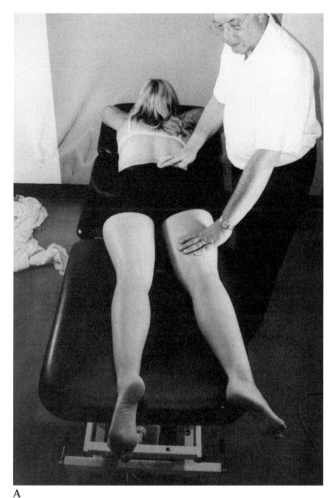

A

B

FIGURE 7-15

Treatment for a right posteriorly nutated sacrum. (A) The patient's right leg is abducted to find the loose-packed position for the sacroiliac joint and externally rotated to open the anterior aspect of the joint. (B) The patient is placed in a prone-propped sphinx position. The operator's right pisiform contacts the patient's right sacral base. (C) The operator's left hand is placed under the patient's right anterior superior iliac spine to stabilize the innominate on the right side.

C

the sacrum into anterior nutation. During exhalation, the operator applies firm anterior and inferior pressure on the patient's right sacral base with the right pisiform while exerting a similar counter force posteriorly against the patient's right ASIS with the left

hand (see Figure 7-15C). After exhalation, the patient attempts to pull the right ASIS down toward the table, activating the left spinal rotators to assist in the correction. The patient's attempt to pull the right ASIS down toward the table is resisted by the opera-

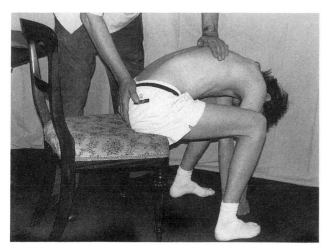

FIGURE 7-16
Muscle energy treatment for bilateral anterior sacral nutation.

tor's left hand while pressure is maintained by the operator's right hand on the right sacral base. It is wise to warn the patient that the sacral base contact will probably be uncomfortable. If possible, the operator should try to keep both elbows fully extended so that the forces are provided through the trunk and not by the arms.

3.4.1.6. After 4 or 5 seconds, the patient is asked to inhale slowly while the operator maintains firm pressure on the right sacral base.

3.4.1.7. Steps 3.4.1.4 and 3.4.1.5 are repeated two or three times. The patient is then asked to lie flat from the prone-propped position before the pressure is gradually released.

3.4.1.8. After this treatment, it may be necessary to correct a right anterior innominate dysfunction. The technique to correct an anteriorly rotated innominate can be modified so that the operator's left pisiform is placed over the right sacral base to prevent the base from nutating posteriorly while the innominate is rotated posteriorly (see Figure 7-21*B*).

3.4.1.9. Retest.

3.4.2. Thrust. See the description of the thrust techniques for posterior sacral torsions (Sections 3.2.2 and 3.2.3) that also correct these dysfunctions (see Figures 7-12 and 7-13).

3.5 Bilateral Anterior Sacral Nutation

Clinically, bilateral anterior sacral nutation (formerly known as a *bilateral inferior sacral shear* or *flexed sacrum*) is an uncommon diagnosis. These patients have persistent low back pain, cannot flex, prefer to sleep in the prone position, and are uncomfortable sitting. This dysfunction is commonly associated with hyperextension at the lumbosacral junction as might occur from jumping from a height and landing equally on both legs or lifting up with both shoulders while in a hyperlordotic stance.

> **Diagnostic Points**
> The stork test will be positive bilaterally (at the lower poles). The seated FFT will also be positive bilaterally and is identified by the observation that both PSISs begin to move superiorly at the start of forward flexion of the spine. The standing FFT also is positive, bilaterally. All landmarks are level, but motion tests reveal stiffness for posterior nutation of the sacral base bilaterally, and the lumbar spine is in lordosis with a negative spring test. Both sacral bases are deep, and the ILAs are posterior and inferior, along with innominates that appear posteriorly rotated. The lumbar lordosis does not reverse with forward flexion.

3.5.1. Muscle energy technique. Treat first one side and then the other, as described in 3.3.1.

3.5.2. Alternative muscle energy technique.

3.5.2.1. The patient sits on a stool or on the front of a firm chair, with feet separated and toes turned in (to start opening the posterior aspect of both SI joints). The patient bends forward as far as possible, with arms between the legs.

3.5.2.2. The operator stands to either side of the patient and places the heel of the hand closest to the sacrum (the right hand is used if standing on the left) over the ILAs of the patient's sacrum.

3.5.2.3. Using the other hand to contact the patient's upper trunk, the operator prepares to resist an extension effort.

3.5.2.4. While the operator maintains anterior pressure on the sacral apex, the patient is asked to take a deep inhalation and then, while holding the breath, make an extension effort to raise both shoulders toward the ceiling, a movement that is resisted by the operator's other hand (Figure 7-16).

3.5.2.5. After 3 to 5 seconds, the patient should relax and exhale. The operator holds the patient in position while maintaining force against the apex of the sacrum. The new barrier is identified by a return of resistance to increased trunk flexion, which is passively introduced by the operator's other hand.

3.5.2.6. Steps 3.5.2.5 and 3.5.2.6 are repeated two to four times.

3.5.2.7. Correct bilateral posterior innominate rotations, if present, in the same fashion as described in section 3.3.1.8 on each side.

3.5.2.8. Retest.

3.6 Bilateral Posterior Nutation

Clinically, bilateral posterior nutation (formerly known as a *bilateral superior sacral shear* or *extended sacrum*) is an uncommon diagnosis. These patients have constant low back pain and prefer to sit slumped, resting their elbows on their laps. They prefer to lie supine or, more likely, on either side in a fetal position. By history, the injury can occur when lifting a heavy load while fully flexed and in the midline position. For example, one patient reported being injured while a passenger in a truck that struck another truck broadside. Seeing what was about to happen, he braced himself by putting both feet on the dashboard before impact.

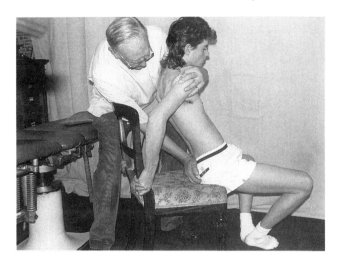

FIGURE 7-17
Muscle energy treatment for bilateral posterior sacral nutation.

> #### *Diagnostic Points*
> The stork test is positive bilaterally (for both upper poles). The seated and standing forward-bending tests are bilaterally positive, with motion occurring at the onset of flexion. Both sacral bases are posterior, and the ILAs are inferior and anterior. There may be a bilaterally flexed dysfunction at L5 (extension restriction) and bilateral hypertonicity of the longissimus muscles. The spring test is positive. Often, there is also an associated anterior innominate dysfunction (see 4.2).

3.6.1. Muscle energy technique. Treat first one side and then the other, as described in 3.4.1.

3.6.2. Alternative muscle energy technique.

3.6.2.1. The patient sits on a stool or on the end of a table, with feet together and knees apart (to begin to open the anterior aspect of the SI joints). If on a table that is too high for the patient's feet to reach the ground, a stool may be used to support the feet. Leaning backward, the patient can take hold of the edges of the stool or table behind.

3.6.2.2. The operator prepares to resist the sacral posterior nutation that occurs in response to the patient's flexion effort by standing to one side and placing the heel of a hand against the base of the patient's sacrum to press anteriorly while keeping the arm extended. Alternatively, if the patient is sitting on a stool, the operator's arm can be flexed, with the elbow braced against the thigh of one leg to deliver sufficient anterior force to promote anterior nutation of the sacral base. The operator's other arm is placed around the patient, over the sternum, to grasp the opposite shoulder and resist a future flexion effort (Figure 7-17).

3.6.2.3. As the patient exhales and makes an effort to bend forward, the operator resists with the hand on the patient's sternum. After 3 to 5 seconds of flexion effort, the patient should relax.

3.6.2.4. The operator approaches the new barrier by further extending the lumbar spine over the sacrum while maintaining anterior pressure with the palm of the hand on the sacral base.

3.6.2.5. Steps 3.6.2.4 and 3.6.2.5 are repeated two to four times.

3.6.2.6. Retest.

The bilaterally flexed L5 can best be treated with the patient supine and arms overhead, held above the wrists by the operator. The patient is asked to take a deep breath and, after full exhalation, the operator rapidly tugs both arms with modest force. The patient may feel some discomfort at the lumbosacral junction. Any remaining nonneutral lumbar and thoracic dysfunctions should be treated to ensure resumption of normal longissimus tone. If present, bilateral anterior innominate dysfunctions are treated, individually, using the modifications described in Section 4.2.2 and depicted in Figure 7-21B.

3.7 Bilateral Sacral Dysfunctions, Anterior Nutated Left and Posterior Nutated Right

Clinically, bilateral sacral dysfunctions, anterior nutated left and posterior nutated right occur more commonly than one might expect and are probably the consequence of two injuries. It is not known how the dysfunction happens, but it would seem most probable that the left anterior nutation occurs first and then, because of postural accommodations to the discomfort, the patient moves more carefully, thus increasing the risk for a unilateral posterior nutation caused by bending and twisting (as described in Section 3.4). A bilateral dysfunction should be suspected when correction of one dysfunction does not provide the expected symmetry when retesting.

3.7.1. Muscle energy technique.

> *Diagnostic Points*
> The left sacral base is anterior, and the right sacral base is posterior; the left ILA is posterior and inferior, and the right is anterior and superior. In short, the sacrum appears as it would for either dysfunction alone; however, the stork test is positive for the left lower pole and the right upper pole. The seated forward-bending test and the standing forward-bending test are bilaterally positive. The spring test is positive. While prone, leg length measurement reveals a short right leg.

3.7.1.1. Treat the right posteriorly nutated sacrum first by treating the lumbar or thoracic dysfunctions that may be responsible for the increase in tone in the right longissimus muscle. If this approach is not successful, then treat either the posteriorly nutated sacrum directly, as described in 3.4, or

3.7.1.2. Treat the anteriorly nutated sacrum as described in 3.3.

3.7.1.3. Retest and, if not successful, reverse the order of treatment.

4. ILIOSACRAL DYSFUNCTIONS

4.1 Posterior Innominate on the Left

Clinically, a posterior innominate is more common on the left side than on the right and often is associated with other lumbopelvic dysfunctions and muscle imbalances in the lower quarter. It can be a cause of local or referred pain and, as in other dysfunctions of the SI joint, the pain often is felt on the opposite side. When one innominate is in the posterior position, the opposite side usually appears to be in an anterior position, but it should be capable of posterior rotation unless it, too, is restricted. The innominate dysfunctions may be responsible for residual symptoms of low back or SI pain after the sacral dysfunctions have been treated.

> *Diagnostic Points*
> The standing FFT is positive on the left. The left ASIS is high, the PSIS a little low, and the left sulcus deep. The left medial malleolus is craniad in the supine position if the legs are structurally equal in length.
>
> Note that this dysfunction often accompanies a unilateral anterior sacral nutation on the left. *The effort required for treatment of the posterior innominate may cause recurrence of the anterior sacral nutation unless the sacral position is protected* (see steps 4.1.2.2 and 3.3.1.8).

4.1.1. Muscle energy technique, side lying.

4.1.1.1. The patient lies on the right side, and the operator stands behind, at the level of the pelvis.

4.1.1.2. The operator's right hand contacts the posterior part of the patient's left iliac crest, preferably with the thumb placed to monitor the tension at the patient's left SI joint.

4.1.1.3. The operator's left hand is place underneath and anteriorly around the patient's flexed left knee to lift and move the patient's leg into adduction, or abduction and external or internal hip rotation, until the monitoring right thumb senses the loose-packed position or minimal tension at the left SI joint.

4.1.1.4. The operator then extends the patient's left hip until the tension just reaches the SI joint and, finally, approximates the barrier to anterior innominate rotation by gently pressing forward on the iliac crest (Figure 7-18*A*).

4.1.1.5. The instruction is "pull your knee forward," a movement that the operator resists with an equal and opposite counter force.

4.1.1.6. After 3 to 5 seconds, the patient should be told to relax and, when full relaxation has occurred (and not before), anterior rotation is increased by adding further extension of the hip until tension builds at the SI joint. It may also be necessary to readjust to a new loose-packed position after each muscle contraction.

4.1.1.7. Steps 4.1.1.5 and 4.1.1.6 are repeated two or more times.

4.1.1.8. Retest.

Note: The operator may grip the ankle (Figure 7-18*B*) instead of holding the knee. The advantage is that small operators do not have to reach as far. The disadvantage is that it is not as easy to position the limb properly to loose pack the SI joint.

4.1.2. Muscle energy technique, prone. (This is technique 4.1.1 turned 90 degrees to the prone position.)

4.1.2.1. The patient is prone, and the operator stands to either side. The left side may be easier for short operators, but the right side is easier for many.

4.1.2.2. With the hand nearer the patient's head, the operator contacts the back of the patient's left iliac crest to monitor and act as a counter force (Figure 7-18*C*). If a unilateral anterior sacral nutation has been present and recently treated, the sacrum should be protected by the counter force being applied to the left ILA of the sacrum instead of the back of the crest (Figure 7-18*D*). If this is not done, the anterior sacral nutation on the left may recur when the innominate is rotated anteriorly.

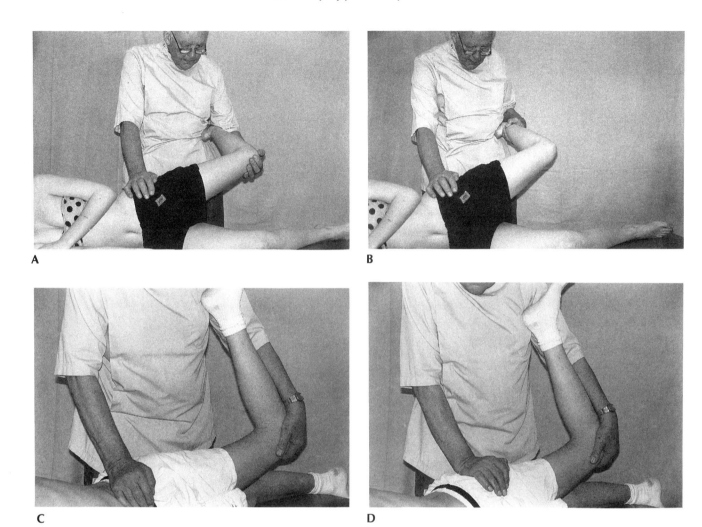

FIGURE 7-18

*Muscle energy treatment for left posterior innominate. **(A)** Patient is lying on his or her side, knee grip. **(B)** Patient is lying on his or her side, ankle grip. **(C)** Patient is lying prone with operator's right hand on the patient's iliac crest. **(D)** Patient is prone with operator's right hand placed on the patient's left ILA protecting an anterior sacral correction.*

4.1.2.3. With the caudally placed hand, the operator lifts the patient's left thigh, avoiding the patello-femoral joint. It is easier to lift the knee if it is flexed to 90 degrees.

4.1.2.4. With the SI joint loose packed and the anterior innominate barrier approximated by lifting the thigh, the operator instructs the patient to pull the knee down toward the table. This movement is resisted with equal counter force, and it is wise to caution the patient not to pull too hard.

4.1.2.5. After 3 to 5 seconds, the effort should end and the patient should relax. When relaxation is complete, the new barrier is found by increasing the newly achieved anterior innominate rotation through further lifting of the thigh. It may also be necessary to readjust

to a new loose-packed position after each muscle contraction.

4.1.2.6. Steps 4.1.2.4 and 4.1.2.5 are repeated two or more times.

4.1.2.7. Retest.

4.1.3. Muscle energy technique, supine. (Compare to the superior pubis dysfunction technique described in Section 1.1.) The major difference between this technique and the technique used for a superior pubic dysfunction is that the SI joint is loose, rather than close, packed, with the PSIS off the edge of, rather than on, the table to allow the innominate to rotate anteriorly. The instruction to the patient is to flex the hip using the rectus femoris isotonically rather than using the hip adductors to make the correction.

4.1.3.1. The patient is supine, and the pelvis is moved to the edge of the table so that the left PSIS is just *off* the tabletop. For stability, the patient's shoulders should remain in the center of the table (see Figure 7-1*A*).

4.1.3.2. The operator stands on the patient's left side and takes the left leg off the table, supporting the patient's ankle with both legs (see Figure 7-1*B*). Alternatively, while standing on the right leg, the operator can bend the left leg at the knee, using the left ankle to hook around and support the patient's left leg (see Figure 7-1*C*).

4.1.3.3. The operator's left hand is placed on the patient's right ASIS to provide the patient with a sense of stability and to monitor the motion barrier for anterior innominate rotation, which is detected when the ASIS just begins to move inferiorly.

4.1.3.4. The operator's right hand is placed on the front of the patient's lower left thigh to resist a future hip flexion effort, being careful to avoid pressure over the patello-femoral joint.

4.1.3.5. The instruction is "try to raise your left thigh against my hand." The pressure should be no more than moderate and maintained for 3 to 5 seconds.

4.1.3.6. After the hip flexion effort ends, wait for the second phase, when relaxation is complete; if necessary, ask again for full relaxation. When the patient is fully relaxed, allow the leg to slide down between your legs (or lower your ankle) until you reach the next barrier, which is sensed by the return of resistance detected by the hand palpating the right ASIS. The patient's left knee should not be allowed to hang bent and unsupported at any time during this treatment technique.

4.1.3.7. Repeat steps 4.1.3.5 and 4.1.3.6 three or four times or until there is no further gain on relaxation.

4.1.3.8. Retest.

Note: The supine technique to correct a posteriorly rotated innominate may also stabilize the sacrum enough to prevent the recurrence of an anteriorly nutated sacrum, perhaps proving to be an acceptable alternative to step 4.1.2.2 (Steele C., personal communication, June 2000).

4.1.4. Thrust. First technique.

4.1.4.1. The patient lies on the right side with the right leg moderately extended.

4.1.4.2. The operator stands in front of the patient's pelvis and uses the right hand to monitor over the sacral base and then pulls the patient's right shoulder forward ("out from under"). In this way, the operator induces right side bending and left rotation of the spine down to and including the sacrum, locking the spine in neutral mechanics.

4.1.4.3. Changing to monitor with the left hand, the operator flexes the patient's left leg to approximately 90 degrees, leaving the left SI joint loose packed.

4.1.4.4. The operator finds the ledge under the patient's left PSIS and, leaning forward, contacts it with the heel of the right hand, usually with the pisiform bone. The operator's forearm should be parallel to the tabletop and extend posteriorly and caudad at an angle of approximately 30 degrees to the axis of the patient's trunk (Figure 7-19*A*).

4.1.4.5. The operator's left hand moves to the front of the patient's left shoulder and takes up the slack, to the barrier, slightly increasing the left rotation of the trunk by moving the patient's left shoulder backward.

4.1.4.6. The thrust is given by a high-velocity, low-amplitude movement of the operator's right hand in the direction in which the forearm points, and the pressure on the patient's left shoulder simultaneously is increased slightly to provide the counter force.

4.1.4.7. Retest.

4.1.5. Thrust. Second technique.

Steps 4.1.5.1 to 4.1.5.3 are the same as steps 4.1.4.1 to 4.1.4.3.

4.1.5.4. The operator's upper right forearm contacts the anterior part of the patient's left ischial tuberosity; then, moving it in a craniad and posterior direction, it takes up the slack (Figure 7-19*B*).

4.1.5.5. The thrust is given by the operator's right forearm against the patient's ischial tuberosity, directed craniad and posteriorly while using the left hand to prevent loss of the position from above.

4.1.5.6. Retest.

4.2 Anterior Innominate on the Right

Clinically, an anterior innominate is more common on the right than the left and often is associated with other lumbopelvic dysfunctions and muscle imbalances in the lower quarter. Anterior innominate dysfunctions can be responsible for residual symptoms of low back or SI pain after the sacral dysfunctions have been treated.

Diagnostic Points

The standing FFT is positive on the right. The right ASIS is low and anterior, the PSIS is a little high, and the right sulcus is shallow. The right medial malleolus is caudad in the supine position if the legs are structurally equal in length.

This dysfunction is common in association with a right unilateral posterior sacral nutation. *If the patient has recently had such a nutation treated, the effort for treatment of the anterior innominate may cause recurrence of the nutation, and the sacrum should be protected* as in Section 4.2.2.4.

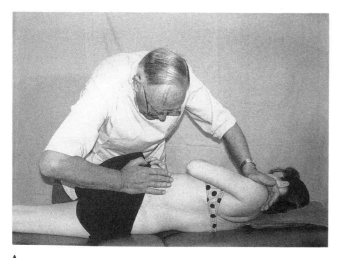
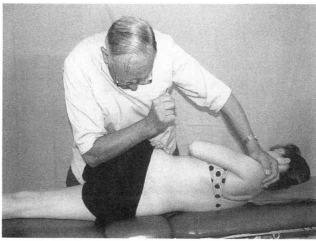

A   B

FIGURE 7-19

Thrust treatment for left posterior innominate. **(A)** *Using pisiform contact on posterior superior iliac spine.* **(B)** *Using forearm contact on ischial tuberosity.*

4.2.1. Muscle energy technique, supine. Compare this technique to the one described in Section 1.2 for an inferior pubic dysfunction and note the differences, in that the thigh is abducted to loose pack the SI joint and the ischium is lifted toward the right ASIS and not toward the pubic symphysis.

4.2.1.1. The patient lies supine and the operator may stand to either side. For a small operator, it may be easier to stand on the right side; for a larger operator, it is easier to apply the force in the required direction if standing on the left side. This description is for the operator standing on the left side; differences are noted in parentheses.

4.2.1.2. The patient's right knee and hip are flexed almost fully, and the operator rolls the patient so that the operator's left (right) hand can be placed under the patient's right buttock. The operator's index and middle fingers should reach to be on either side of the patient's right PSIS for monitoring (if they are long enough) while holding the patient's right ischial tuberosity in the palm of the hand (Figure 7-20*A*).

4.2.1.3. The operator's axilla or shoulder (or other hand and trunk) is placed against the patient's leg near the knee to block hip extension. While monitoring with the fingertips, the operator identifies the barrier by further hip flexion and by lifting the patient's right ischial tuberosity in the direction of the right ASIS. If standing to the left, the operator may increase control by pressing posteriorly with the right hand on the patient's right ASIS (Figure 7-20*B*). If the operator is standing on the right side, the patient's

right ASIS will be in contact with the operator's left hand.

4.2.1.4. When at the barrier to posterior innominate rotation, the instruction is "*gently* push your right foot toward the foot of the table." This is resisted by an equal counter force and, as the muscles concerned are powerful, the caution to be gentle is important.

4.2.1.5. After 3 to 5 seconds, the patient should relax and, after full relaxation, the operator takes up the slack created by restored motion to the new barrier by pulling with the palm of his or her left hand *in the direction of the right ASIS*. Once the new barrier is encountered, the loose-packed position should be reconfirmed.

4.2.1.6. Steps 4.2.1.4 and 4.2.1.5 are repeated two or more times.

4.2.1.7. Retest.

Note: When using the supine technique to correct an anterior innominate rotation, the sacrum is stabilized on the tabletop. This might prove to be a reasonable alternative technique (Steele C., personal communication, June 2000) for treatment of this dysfunction when it is found in association with a posteriorly nutated sacrum as opposed to having to use the prone correction technique described in the next section.

4.2.2. Muscle energy technique, prone.

4.2.2.1. The patient lies prone, with the right hip at the edge of the table.

4.2.2.2. The operator stands at the patient's right side and takes the patient's right leg and ASIS off the table,

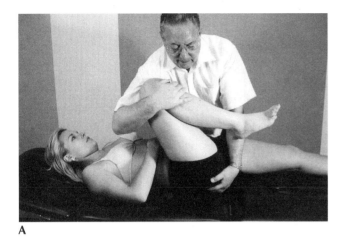

A

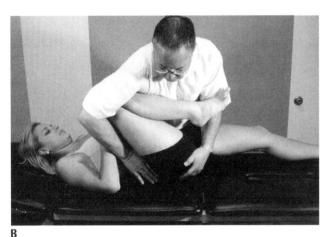

B

FIGURE 7-20

*Treatment for an anteriorly rotated innominate on the right with patient supine. **(A)** Operator palpates the sacroiliac (SI) joint to find the loose-packed position and posteriorly rotates the innominate until tension builds at the palpating fingers. Note that the operator keeps the patient's thigh abducted in line with the plane of the SI joint. **(B)** Operator applies pressure over patient's right anterior superior iliac spine.*

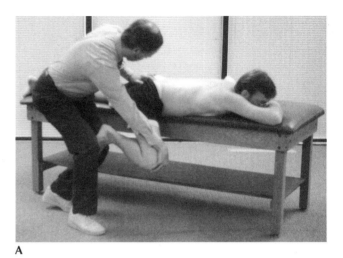

A

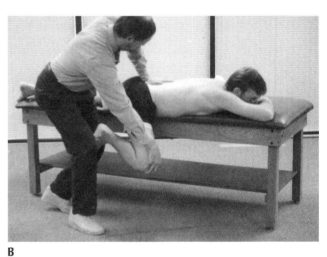

B

FIGURE 7-21

*Treatment for an anteriorly rotated innominate on the right with patient prone. **(A)** The patient's right innominate is placed off the side of the table so that the right anterior superior iliac spine is clear of the table. The operator's left hand palpates the patient's right SI joint to find the loose-packed position and the motion barrier. **(B)** In the presence of a previously treated posteriorly nutated right sacral base, the right sacroiliac (SI) joint is stabilized by the operator's left hand, which is placed firmly on the right sacral base during the treatment of an anteriorly rotated innominate on the right.*

allowing the knee to hang down in a position controlled by the operator's right hand.

4.2.2.3. The operator positions his or her legs so that the patient's right foot can be trapped against the operator's left leg.

4.2.2.4. While monitoring in the sacral sulcus with the tips of the left index and middle fingers, the operator's right hand supports the patient's right knee and, by rotation, abduction or adduction, and flexion or extension of the hip, moves that right knee to loose pack the patient's right SI joint (Figure 7-21*A*). If the patient has recently had a posterior sacral nutation on the right side, the sacrum must

be protected. Protection is conveniently achieved by the operator pressing anteriorly on the right sacral base, using the heel of the left hand (or left pisiform), the fingers of which would otherwise simply be used as monitors of the position and tension (Figure 7-21*B*).

4.2.2.5. The instruction is "gently push your right foot toward the foot of the table." The operator's left leg resists this movement, and, after 3 to 5 seconds, the patient is told to relax.

4.2.2.6. When full relaxation has occurred, the slack is taken up to the new barrier, this time by the operator's easing the patient's right leg craniad. The monitoring fingers indicate that the new barrier for posterior innominate rotation has been reached when sensing an increase in tension at the right SI joint. An adjustment to ensure a loose-packed position may be necessary before proceeding.

4.2.2.7. Steps 4.2.2.5 and 4.2.2.6 are repeated two or more times.

4.2.2.8. Retest.

4.2.3. Muscle energy technique, side lying.

4.2.3.1. The patient lies on the left side and the operator stands in front, near the pelvis.

4.2.3.2. Using the right hand, the operator picks up the patient's right knee and flexes the knee and hip until the fingers of the left hand feel tension begin to increase in the patient's right sacral sulcus between the PSIS and the sacral base (Figure 7-22).

4.2.3.3. The operator can either stand in front of the patient and use the trunk or thigh to block motion of the patient's knee or stand level with the patient's right knee; the operator resists motion by placing the right hip (or left thigh) against the patient's right foot.

4.2.3.4. When all the slack has been taken out to the barrier by further controlled hip flexion, the patient is instructed to try gently to push the right foot toward the foot of the table, against the operator's hip or thigh.

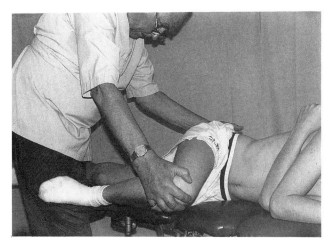

FIGURE 7-22

Muscle energy treatment for a right anterior innominate dysfunction with the patient lying on his or her side.

4.2.3.5. The pressure is maintained for 3 to 5 seconds and then relaxed.

4.2.3.6. After full relaxation, the slack is taken out for the restored free motion by further hip flexion up to the new barrier, with an adjustment made to ensure maintaining the loose-packed position of the SI joint; steps 4.2.3.4 and 4.2.3.5 are repeated two or more times.

4.2.3.7. Retest.

4.2.4. Thrust. First technique.

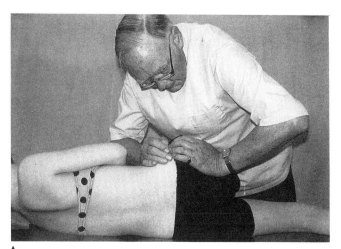

A

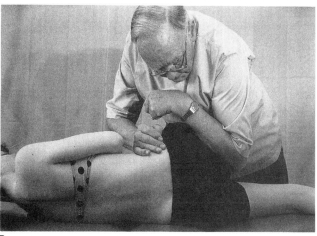

B

FIGURE 7-23

*Thrust treatment for right anterior innominate. (**A**) Using heel of hand on ischial tuberosity. (**B**) Using forearm on ischial tuberosity.*

A

B

FIGURE 7-24
Treatment of a right iliac out-flare. (A) Operator grips medial to the right posterior superior iliac spine to distract it laterally. (B) Operator applies a counter force to the patient's right knee to resist hip abduction.

4.2.4.1. The patient lies on the left side, and the operator stands in front of the patient's pelvis.

4.2.4.2. The operator pulls the patient's left shoulder out to lock the spine by using neutral mechanics of left side bending and right rotation down to and including the sacrum.

4.2.4.3. With the left hand, the operator picks up the patient's right knee and flexes the knee and hip until increasing tension is felt to begin by the monitoring fingers of the right hand, which have been placed in the patient's right sacral sulcus between the PSIS and the sacral base. The patient's foot may remain on the table.

4.2.4.4. Allowing the patient's right thigh to rest on the edge of the table, the operator uses the left hand to contact the patient's right ischial tuberosity posteriorly and the right hand to contact the front of the patient's iliac crest (Figure 7-23A).

4.2.4.5. Slack is taken out by a rotatory motion of the right innominate, by the operator's using the right hand to press posteriorly on the anterior part of the patient's right iliac crest or ASIS and the left hand to push anteriorly on the patient's ischial tuberosity.

4.2.4.6. When the slack has been taken out (determining this requires judgment, as there is no monitor in the sulcus), a high-velocity, low-amplitude thrust is given by the operator's left hand, pushing the patient's right ischial tuberosity forward. The pressure of the operator's right hand is increased slightly at the same time.

4.2.4.7. Retest.

4.2.5. Thrust. Second technique.

Steps 4.2.5.1 and 4.2.5.2 are the same as steps 4.2.4.1 and 4.2.4.2.

4.2.5.3. The patient's right thigh is allowed to hang over the edge of the table, and the operator's left upper forearm contacts the posterior part of the patient's right ischial tuberosity, taking up the slack with pressure anteriorly and craniad.

4.2.5.4. The operator's right hand controls the position of the patient's right ASIS, and the thrust is given by the operator's left forearm on the patient's ischial tuberosity, directed anteriorly and craniad (Figure 7-23B).

4.2.5.5. Retest.

Note: Because both the anterior and posterior innominate dysfunctions are greatly influenced by, and perhaps perpetuated from, muscle imbalances of the lower quarter, a specific home exercise program to balance the length and strength of the lower extremities is needed to maintain normal and reciprocal innominate rotation (see Chapter 14).

4.3 Iliac Out-flare

Described for the Right Side
Clinically, an iliac out-flare is extremely rare; therefore, an accurate diagnosis is critical. An anterior innominate dysfunction is often mistaken for an out-flare because, when present, the ASIS is positioned further laterally from the midline when compared to the opposite side.

Diagnostic Points
An out-flare dysfunction is suspected if, after all other pelvic dysfunctions, especially the innominate rotations, have been treated, the standing FFT remains positive on the right, and the ASIS is farther from the midline on the right side than on the left. The lateral placement of the ASIS should not be associated with a more inferior position as compared to the other side. The right PSIS should be medial and likewise level with its counterpart.

4.3.1. Muscle energy technique.

4.3.1.1. The patient lies supine, and the operator stands on the right side.

4.3.1.2. The patient's right hip is flexed to approximately 90 degrees, and the pelvis is rotated slightly to the left to allow placement of the operator's left hand under the right innominate.

4.3.1.3. The operator uses the left fingertips to reach under the patient to monitor and to grip the right PSIS and pull it laterally (Figure 7-24*A*).

4.3.1.4. The operator's right hand is used to control the position of the patient's right thigh and introduce hip adduction and internal rotation (Figure 7-24*B*).

4.3.1.5. The slack is taken out by further adduction of the patient's right thigh to the point of tension (before the sacrum begins to move), and the instruction is then "try to push your right knee to the right."

4.3.1.6. After 3 to 5 seconds, the patient should relax.

4.3.1.7. When relaxation is complete and the new motion barrier is reached by the addition of further hip adduction and internal rotation, steps 4.3.1.5 and 4.3.1.6 are repeated two or more times.

4.3.1.8. Retest.

4.4 Iliac In-flare

Described for the Left Side

Clinically, iliac in-flare is also extremely rare, so an accurate diagnosis is again critical. A posterior innominate dysfunction is often mistaken for an in-flare because, when present, the ASIS is positioned more medially from the midline when compared to the opposite side.

Diagnostic Points

An in-flare dysfunction is suspected if, after all other pelvic dysfunctions, especially the innominate rotations, have been treated, the standing FFT remains positive on the left, and the ASIS is closer to the midline on the left side than on the right. The medial placement of the ASIS should not be associated with a more superior position as compared to the other side. The left PSIS should be more lateral and likewise level with its counterpart.

4.4.1. Muscle energy technique.

4.4.1.1. The patient lies supine. The operator stands to the left of the patient's lower thighs.

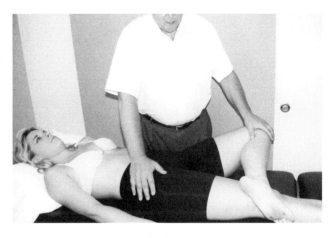

FIGURE 7-25
Muscle energy technique for treatment of a left iliac in-flare.

4.4.1.2. The patient's left hip is fully flexed and abducted, and the knee flexed enough to allow the left foot to rest over the right thigh.

4.4.1.3. The operator holds the patient's left knee, using the left hand to keep the hip abducted and externally rotated, and then places the right hand against the medial side of the patient's right ASIS for counter force (Figure 7-25).

4.4.1.4. When the slack has been taken out by abduction of the patient's left thigh as far as it easily goes (and without moving the right ilium), the instruction is "try to pull your left knee medially [into adduction] against my hand."

4.4.1.5. After 3 to 5 seconds, the patient should relax.

4.4.1.6. When relaxation is complete and the new motion barrier is reached by the addition of further hip abduction and external rotation, steps 4.4.1.5 and 4.4.1.6 are repeated two or more times.

4.4.1.7. Retest.

REFERENCE

1. Greenman PE. Principles of Manual Medicine (2nd ed). Baltimore: Lippincott Williams & Wilkins, 1996; 545.

8

Treatment of the Lumbar Spine

Both muscle energy and thrusting techniques are described in this chapter. All of the thrust techniques for the lumbar spine can be modified to become muscle energy procedures, but the reverse is not always true. The modification to either technique can be made after localization to the barrier is completed. Instead of an external force being used to break through the barrier while the patient is as relaxed as possible, using a muscle energy technique requires the patient to attempt to gently push away from the barrier, using minimal muscle effort and contracting for 3–5 seconds. The operator blocks this movement, usually with an unyielding counter force. The treatment relies on the postisometric muscle relaxation that follows, which enables the barrier to recede and allows passive repositioning to a new barrier. The motion barrier is usually removed in stages after two to three sequential isometric contractions or until full range of motion has been restored. As previously noted in Chapter 6, muscle energy and thrust techniques work well only if localization is accurate. It should be emphasized that the use of more force with either a muscle energy or thrust technique is not an appropriate substitute for the lack of localization. If a restriction is resistant to a thrusting technique, reassess the location of the barrier before adding additional force and be sure the patient is totally relaxed and reasonably comfortable.

To review from Chapter 5, the diagnosis of a dysfunctional vertebral segment is based on a comparison of the position of the transverse processes (TPs) of one vertebra to the position of the TPs of the vertebra immediately below to determine whether they lie in the same or different coronal plane(s). A non-neutral dysfunction is diagnosed when the vertebra above and its corresponding TPs are in a different position from the vertebra below when the spine is examined in flexion or extension. Major dysfunctions are diagnosed when asymmetries of the TPs are also present in the neutral position. The asymmetries of the TPs seen in extended, rotated, and side bent (ERS) dysfunctions improve with extension and worsen with flexion. The asymmetries of the TPs seen in flexed, rotated, and side bent (FRS) dysfunctions improve with flexion and worsen with extension. If there is no dysfunction between the vertebrae above a non-neutral dysfunction, each vertebra will follow the rotation from below when challenged to do so in either flexion or extension of the spine and appear to be rotated to the same degree as the dysfunctional level. Comparisons between the TPs of nondysfunctional vertebrae show no difference in position between the vertebra above and the one below. Additional non-neutral dysfunctions are identified when there *is* a difference in position, and the vertebrae appear *less rotated, level,* or *rotated in the opposite direction* in comparison to the vertebra below. Consider the following examples.

A non-neutral dysfunction between L3 and L4 is identified by the observation that the TPs of L3 are rotated to the left (abbreviated *lt* when used with ERS and FRS) in comparison to the TPs of L4. If this left rotation at L3 becomes greater with increasing lumbar extension and becomes less obvious or disappears with lumbar flexion, then L3 can be described as FRSlt in comparison to L4.

If the position of the left TP of L2 appears as equally rotated as that of L3 in extension, then there is no difference in the position of L2 in comparison with L3; with increasing lumbar extension, the position of L2 matches the increased left rotation of L3. Thus, there is no FRS non-neutral dysfunction between L2 and L3. The same can be said for T12 and L1 in relation to L2, if there is no difference in the position of the TPs when comparing the vertebra above to the vertebra below in extension.

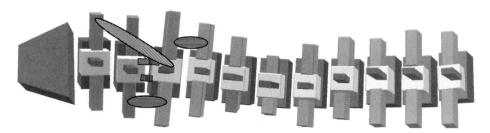

FIGURE 8-1

Diagram of Step 1 for treatment of an FRSrt at L3-4 in the right side-lying position showing an open facet on the left between L3 and L4 and hypertonic right intertransversaris and left multifidus muscles, which may participate in maintaining this dysfunction. The TPs of L3 are perpendicular to the tabletop.

In another example, if the TPs of L4 appear rotated to the left in extension, but the TPs of L3 appear to be level (i.e., the left TP of L3 is not rotated posteriorly to the left to the same degree as L4 in extension), then L3 is in a different position than L4, and a non-neutral FRS dysfunction is present at L3 in comparison to L4. *Because L4 appears rotated to the left and L3 appears level, then L3 is actually rotated to the right (abbreviated* rt *when used with ERS and FRS) in comparison to the position of L4. The positional diagnosis of L3, then, is FRSrt.*

For this reason, to arrive at the most accurate structural diagnosis, the operator repeatedly asks the question: "Are the TPs the same, or are they different?" *What appears to be rotated may be quite normal, and what appears to be level may be dysfunctional if comparisons are consistently made between the position of the TPs palpated under the thumbs relative to the position of the TPs palpated at the level below.*

1. SIDE-LYING, SIDE-BENDING ACTIVATION TECHNIQUES

The following techniques use the activation of side bending to make the correction for the non-neutral FRS and ERS dysfunctions. To allow the required rotation, the patient lies on the side of the most posterior TP for either the FRS or ERS non-neutral dysfunction. For example, with an FRSrt or an ERSrt, the patient lies on the right side. This positioning is used both for the muscle energy and thrust techniques.

When side bending is used to correct a neutral group dysfunction, rotation is not considered in the treatment because it is automatically coupled with the side bending. Therefore, for the neutral dysfunction, the posterior TPs are up so that the concavity of the curve faces the tabletop (i.e., a neutral group rotated to the left [NRlt], the patient lies on the right side).

When the patient is lying on the right side and resting on the right shoulder and right hip, the spine is slightly side bent to the left (see Figure 7-7B and D). If the patient's right shoulder is pulled forward or if the patient is allowed to roll backward off the right shoulder, the spine is then slightly side bent to the right (see Figure 7-7C and D).

Muscle Energy Technique for an FRS Dysfunction

1.1 Described for L3 That Is Flexed, Rotated, and Side Bent to the Right in Relation to L4 (FRSrt)

This is a non-neutral dysfunction with restriction for extension and for rotation and side bending to the left between L3 and L4. The left facet between L3 and L4 does not close completely.

> ### *Diagnostic Points*
> There is tissue texture change at the segment. The right TP of L3 is posterior to the TP on the left in extension (prone-propped) when compared to the TPs of the level below (L4). The TPs of both L3 and L4 appear level in flexion. There may be some prominence of the right TP of L3 in the neutral position if the dysfunction is due to a major motion barrier that encroaches on the neutral zone of a normal joint.

1.1.1. The patient lies on the right side, resting on the right shoulder and right hip while supporting the neck with the right hand and a pillow. This position causes the spine to side bend slightly to the left. The TPs of L3 should be perpendicular to the table (Figure 8-1). The operator stands facing the patient and moves the patient's pelvis near the front of the table, while monitoring at the segment to avoid moving too far. This position can be estimated beforehand by judging the degree of flexion necessary to level the TP on the right with the left. If there is a major restriction, the extension barrier may be found on the flexion side of the neutral

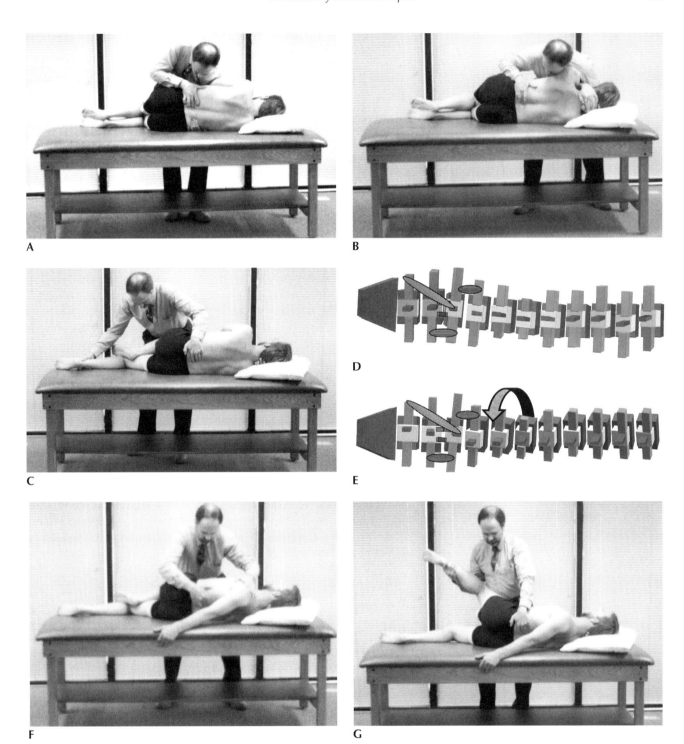

FIGURE 8-2

*Muscle energy technique for an FRSrt at L3-4. (**A**) The operator's hands are positioned at the level of the dysfunction, and extension can be introduced by pulling the bottom hand with the top hand in a posterior-to-anterior direction to introduce extension to the interspinous space of the dysfunctional segment. (**B**) To further refine extension from above down through the shoulders. (**C**) Extension is introduced from below up through the patient's bottom leg with the top knee (left) resting on the operator's right thigh. (**D**) Step 2 of treatment. Diagram of spine at extension barrier for L3-4. (**E**) Step 3 of treatment. Diagram showing left rotated spine to L3. Arrow indicates direction of rotation. (**F**) Left rotation is introduced from above down, and, if able, the patient grasps the table to secure the left rotation. (**G**) Left side bending is introduced by the operator lifting the top leg (left). Further refinement for rotation can be obtained by internally rotating the left hip.*

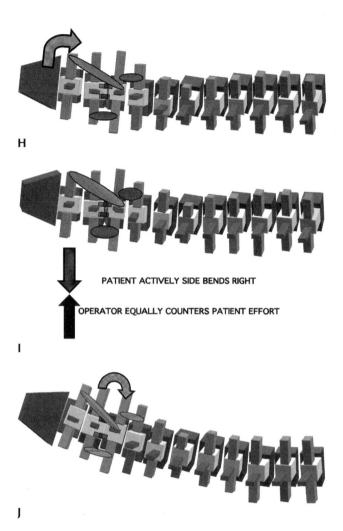

H

PATIENT ACTIVELY SIDE BENDS RIGHT

OPERATOR EQUALLY COUNTERS PATIENT EFFORT

I

J

FIGURE 8-2 *continued.*
(H) Step 4 of treatment. Diagram of spine showing left side-bending motion. Arrow indicates direction of side bending. (I) Step 5 of treatment. The patient is asked to pull the left leg toward the table, activating the hypertonic right side benders and rotators for 5–7 seconds. Arrows indicate directions of patient and operator effort. (J) Step 6 of treatment. On relaxation of the right side-bending effort, additional left side bending is introduced. Arrow indicates additional side bending.

position, and localization to the barrier must begin with the patient's lumbar spine still flexed. If a minor restriction is to be treated, the location of the extension barrier is on the extension side of the neutral position. When positioning the patient from a flexed position into extension, the degree of extension necessary is signaled when the palpating finger at the interspinous space senses the end of free motion (closure) or the approximation of the spinous processes of L3 and L4. Movement of the patient's lumbar spine up to the extension barrier can initially be

done by lifting with one hand under the patient's waist and translating the spine anteriorly while using the other hand as a monitor (Figure 8-2*A*).

1.1.2. The operator now monitors at L3-4 with the right hand while localizing from above down. The operator reaches under the pillow that supports the patient's neck and slides the patient's right shoulder forward to first fully flex the spine and be sure that passive extension will begin on the free side of any barrier to extension. The operator then slides the patient's shoulder backward to engage the extension barrier palpated as the tension just reaches the monitoring finger at L3 (Figure 8-2*B*). When the patient is lying on the right shoulder and right hip, the spine is side bent left. Care must be taken that the right shoulder is not pulled out from under the patient or that the patient has not rolled backward off the shoulder, because such a movement would reverse the side bending (see Figure 7-7*D*).

1.1.3. Monitoring at the L3-4 interspace with the left hand, the operator extends the patient's right leg from a flexed starting position just until movement occurs at L4, which is noted by a change in tissue tension between the spinous processes of L3 and L4 (Figure 8-2*C*). The lumbar spine position should now be localized to the extension barrier (Figure 8-2*D*).

1.1.4. Rotation is introduced to its barrier when the operator picks up the patient's left hand and pulls the left arm down and back until tension is felt at L3. Again, be careful not to allow the patient's right shoulder to slide forward and change the thoraco-lumbar side bend from left to right. The patient is then asked to hold on to the table edge with his or her left hand to maintain the position (Figure 8-2*E* and *F*).

Note: There is a major difference in the positioning for treatment of posterior sacral torsions when the patient's underneath shoulder is pulled forward, reversing the side bending of the lumbar spine as noted in Chapter 7, Section 3.2.1.

1.1.5. To localize the left side bending to its barrier, the operator changes hands to monitor with his or her left hand while, with the right hand, lifting the patient's left ankle directly above the patient's right knee by abduction. The operator can fine-tune the patient's position, achieving a more precise localization to the restrictive barrier, by slightly internally rotating the patient's left leg until tension is felt under the monitoring fingers of the operator's left hand between L3 and L4 (Figure 8-2*G* and *H*). If internal rotation of the leg causes discomfort at the hip joint, then localization must be achieved solely by abduction of the hip.

1.1.6. The instruction is, "pull your left foot down toward your right knee." When the patient does so, the operator should feel the muscles tighten on the right side of L3 with the monitoring fingers of the left hand (Figure 8-2*I*). A focal muscle contraction at the level of L3 indicates that the localization to the barrier is probably correct.

1.1.7. After 3–5 seconds, the patient is asked to stop pulling his or her leg down, but the position must be maintained.

1.1.8. After full relaxation that is monitored by the decrease in tone of the contracting muscles to the right of L3, the slack is taken up to the new left side-bending barrier by lifting the patient's left leg (Figure 8-2*J*). The operator could add additional rotation by asking the patient to grip further down the table with his or her left hand, which increases both extension and left rotation, or by gently moving the patient's left shoulder backward to increase the left rotation alone.

1.1.9. Steps 1.1.6, 1.1.7 and 1.1.8 are repeated two or more times, always checking the position of the patient's right shoulder.

1.1.10. Retest.

Alternative Side-Bending Technique for an FRS Dysfunction

1.1.a Described for L3 That Is Flexed, Rotated, and Side Bent to the Right (FRSrt)

1.1.1.a The patient lies on the right side (most posterior TP down), and the extension and left rotation barrier at L3-4 is localized as above in steps 1.1.1, 1.1.2, 1.1.3, and 1.1.4.

1.1.2.a The patient's left leg and hip are flexed, and the left knee is allowed to rest on the tabletop with the left foot resting over the right knee. The operator's right hand is placed against the patient's left ischial tuberosity to direct a counter force craniad and anteriorly in front of the patient's left shoulder (Figure 8-3).

1.1.3.a This time, the patient is asked to push the buttock (left ischial tuberosity) against the operator's right hand, which resists this right side-bending effort. The patient's force must not be greater than the operator's ability to resist. The operator can add his or her own body weight by "locking" the forearm against the trunk through the shoulder. Probably the best verbal cue is, "don't let me push your hip up," which will cause the patient to match the operator's counter force with an isometric contraction of the right side-bending muscles.

1.1.4.a While monitoring at L3-4 with the left hand, the new barrier to left side bending can be reached by pushing the left ischial tuberosity craniad and anteriorly, directing the force in front of the patient's left

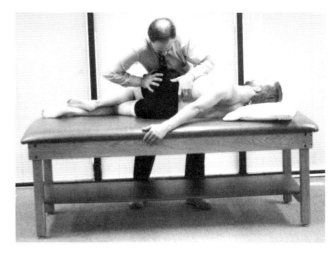

FIGURE 8-3
Alternative technique to reach left side-bending barrier and to resist left side bending through the left ischial tuberosity. A pelvic diagonal is introduced by the operator's right hand placed on the patient's left ischial tuberosity, with the force directed craniad and anteriorly to introduce left side bending and extension to their respective barriers.

shoulder during the postcontraction, relaxation period, closing the left L3-4 facet joint.

1.1.5.a The isometric contraction for right side bending can be repeated two or more times, until there is no apparent increase in motion obtained in left side bending.

1.1.6.a The last step in this technique is to ask the patient to "hike the left hip up," with an active contraction of the left quadratus lumborum and left lumbar side benders, while the operator guides the motion with continued contact on the left ischial tuberosity. This final addition provides the opportunity for the left quadratus and left lumbar side benders to be recruited by voluntary contraction, further inhibiting the abnormally hypertonic right side-bending muscles by reciprocal inhibition.

Muscle Energy Technique for an ERS Dysfunction

1.2 Described for L3 That Is Extended, Rotated, and Side Bent to the Right in Relation to L4 (ERSrt)

This is a non-neutral dysfunction with restriction for flexion and for rotation and side bending to the left between L3 and L4. The right facet between L3 and L4 does not open completely. Compare this technique with the technique for an anterior sacral torsion dysfunction, described in Chapter 7, Section 3.1.1.

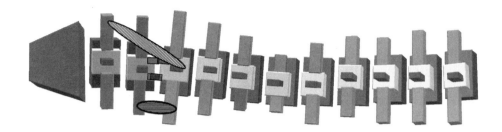

FIGURE 8-4

Diagram of Step 1 for treatment of an ERSrt at L3-4 in the right side-lying position showing a closed facet joint on the right between L3 and L4 and hypertonic right intertransversaris and left multifidus muscles, which may participate in maintaining this dysfunction. The TPs of L3 are perpendicular to the tabletop.

Diagnostic Points

There is tissue texture change at the segment. The right TP of L3 is more posterior than the left in flexion when compared to the TPs of the level below (L4). The TPs of both L3 and L4 appear level in extension. There may be some prominence on the right in the neutral position if there is a major restriction. To see L3 become level, it may be necessary to hyperextend the lumbar spine by prone propping with the patient's arms fully extended instead of resting on the elbows.

Occasionally, there is both an FRS and an ERS dysfunction on the same side, and there is little or no change in position of the TPs between full flexion and full extension. An anatomical variation should be ruled out by the presence of tissue texture changes. If such a double non-neutral dysfunction exists, treatment is directed to each dysfunction individually, alternating from one technique to the other, if necessary, until full motion is restored to both facet joints.

Preferred Muscle Energy Technique with Posterior Transverse Process Down

1.2.1. The patient lies on the right side with hips and knees flexed and the right arm bent, placing the right hand under the head. A pillow to support the head and neck is recommended. In this position, the lumbar spine is slightly side bent to the left, and the TPs of L3 should be perpendicular to the tabletop (Figure 8-4).

Note: This technique is a modification of what is described in Chapter 7, Section 3.1.1 for an anterior sacral torsion when the right shoulder is pulled forward to reverse the side bend from left to right to incorporate neutral mechanics. In treating a non-neutral lumbar dysfunction, non-neutral coupling mechanics must be maintained in the flexed lumbar spine.

1.2.2. Standing in front of the patient, the operator uses the left hand to monitor at L3-4 and the right hand to grasp the patient around both ankles. Initially, the operator fully extends the spine by moving the patient's legs posteriorly to be sure to begin on the free side of any barrier to flexion. The operator then moves the patient's legs anteriorly, flexing the spine until L4 just begins to move (Figure 8-5*A*).

1.2.3. The operator switches hands and monitors L3-4 with the right hand and brings the patient's upper trunk into flexion by either sliding the left hand under the patient's right shoulder and sliding the patient forward or by pulling the pillow forward. The tabletop should be smooth enough to slide the patient into flexion, until motion is felt at L3 (Figure 8-5*B*). The lumbar spine should now be positioned at the flexion barrier for L3-4 (Figure 8-5*C*).

1.2.4. The operator's left hand is used to rotate the patient to the left by guiding the patient's left shoulder posteriorly, using the index finger or middle finger of the right hand to monitor for the first rotational movement at L3 (Figure 8-5*D* and *E*). Care must be taken not to let the patient roll back off the right shoulder and reverse the lumbar side bending from left to right.

1.2.5. The right TP of L3 should remain perpendicular to the table. The operator switches hands again and monitors L3-4 with the left hand and, with the right hand grasping under the right leg proximal to the ankle, lifts both legs toward the ceiling, introducing more left side bending, until tension is felt between L4 and L3 (Figure 8-5*F* and *G*).

1.2.6. The operator monitors over the interspinous space between L3 and L4, instructs the patient to *gently* pull the feet back down toward the table and resists with equal force (Figure 8-5*H*). The muscle contraction should easily be felt localized to the

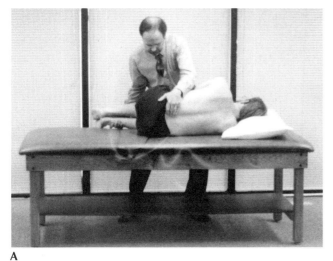
A

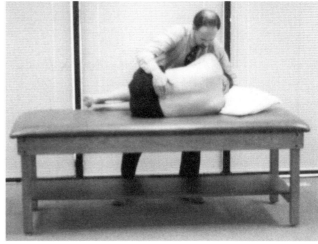
B

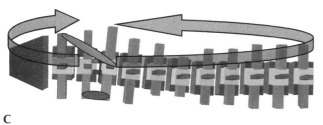
C

D

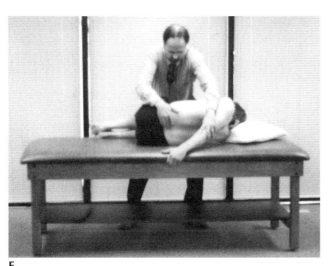
E

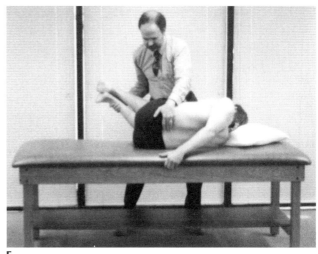
F

FIGURE 8-5

*Muscle energy technique for an ERSrt at L3-4. (**A**) The patient is positioned in right side-lying, and flexion is introduced through the legs from below up. (**B**) Flexion is introduced from above down to the dysfunctional segment. (**C**) Step 2 of treatment. Diagram showing lumbar spine flexed to the flexion barrier. Arrows indicate direction of flexion from above and below. (**D**) Step 3 of treatment. Diagram showing left rotated spine to L3. Arrow indicates direction of rotation. (**E**) Rotation to the left is introduced from above down. (**F**) Left side bending is introduced by lifting both feet toward the ceiling.*

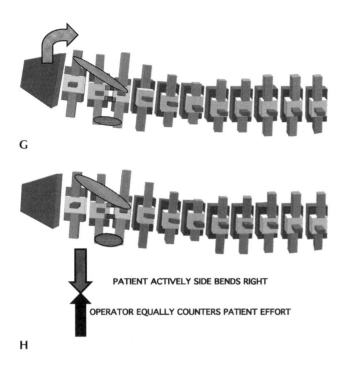

G

PATIENT ACTIVELY SIDE BENDS RIGHT

OPERATOR EQUALLY COUNTERS PATIENT EFFORT

H

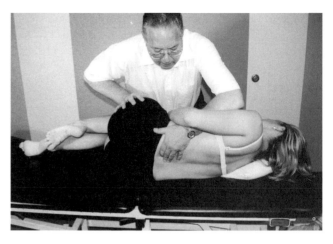

I

FIGURE 8-5 *continued.*
(G) Step 4 of treatment. Diagram showing the introduction of left side bending from below with the right facet between L3 and L4 still closed. Arrow indicates direction of side bending. (H) Step 5 of treatment. Diagram showing isometric right side bending effort when patient is asked to pull both feet toward the floor to activate the hypertonic right side benders and multifidus down against equal resistance. Arrows indicate directions of patient and operator effort. (I) Step 6 of treatment. After postisometric relaxation of hypertonic restricting muscles, the left side bending is increased to open the right L3-4 facet. Arrow indicates direction of additional side bending.

region between the spinous process and the tabletop, over the right TP of L3.

1.2.7. After 3–5 seconds, the patient is instructed to stop pulling his or her feet down to the table and relax. When the muscles overlying the right TP of L3 are felt to relax, more left side bending is introduced by lifting the legs higher (Figure 8-5*I*). A new barrier to motion between L3 and L4 can be reached by increasing the side bending, adding more flexion from below, or increasing the left rotation from above.

FIGURE 8-6
Alternative technique to reach left side-bending barrier and to resist right side bending through the left ischial tuberosity. A pelvic diagonal is introduced by the operator's right hand placed on the patient's left ischial tuberosity, with the force directed posteriorly and craniad to introduce flexion and left side bending to their respective barriers.

1.2.8. Steps 1.2.6 and 1.2.7 are repeated two or three times.

1.2.9. Retest.

Alternative Side-Bending Technique for an ERS Dysfunction

1.2a Described for L3 That Is Extended, Rotated, and Side Bent Right (ERSrt)

1.2.1.a The patient lies on the right side (most posterior TP down), and the flexion and left rotation barrier at L3-4 is localized as in steps 1.2.1 through 1.2.5.

1.2.2.a The patient's left leg and hip are flexed, and the left knee is allowed to rest on the tabletop with the left foot resting over the right knee.

1.2.3.a The operator's right hand is placed against the patient's left ischial tuberosity to direct a counter force craniad and posteriorly, behind the patient's left shoulder. The patient is asked to push the buttock (left ischial tuberosity) against the operator's right hand, which resists this right side-bending effort (Figure 8-6). The patient's force must not be greater than the operator's ability to resist. The operator can add his or her own body weight by "locking" the forearm against the trunk through the shoulder. Probably the best verbal cue is "don't let me push your hip up," which causes the patient to match the operator's counter force with an isometric contraction of the right side-bending muscles.

1.2.4.a While monitoring at L3-4 with the left hand, the new barrier to left side bending can be reached by pushing the left ischial tuberosity craniad and posteriorly, directed behind the patient's left shoulder during the postcontraction, relaxation period, opening the right L3-L4 facet joint.

1.2.5.a The isometric contraction of the right side benders can be repeated two or more times, until there is no apparent increase in motion obtained for left side bending.

1.2.6.a The last step in this technique is to ask the patient to "hike the left hip up" in an active contraction of the left quadratus lumborum and left lumbar side benders, while the operator guides the motion with continued contact on the left ischial tuberosity. This final addition provides the opportunity for the left quadratus and left lumbar side benders to be recruited by voluntary contraction, further inhibiting the abnormally hypertonic right side-bending muscles by reciprocal inhibition.

Alternative Muscle Energy Technique for an ERS Dysfunction

1.3 Described for L3 That Is Extended, Rotated, and Side Bent to the Right in Relation to L4 (ERSrt)

This is a non-neutral dysfunction with a restriction for flexion and for rotation and side bending to the left between L3 and L4. The right facet between L3 and L4 does not open completely. This muscle energy technique is a more difficult technique using the Sims position (most posterior TP up). Compare this technique with the technique for an anterior sacral torsion dysfunction, described in Chapter 7, Section 3.1.2.

1.3.1. The patient lies prone with the right shoulder placed close to the side of the table so that his or her right arm can hang over the edge.

1.3.2. Using the left hand, the operator lifts both of the patient's ankles and, with the right hand under the patient's knees, pulls the knees forward to rotate the patient onto the left side into a left lateral Sims position. The precise position is important for localization; the hip flexion must be stopped just as L4 begins to move. Therefore, the movement is monitored in its final stage by the fingers of the operator's right hand at the L3–4 interspinous space. Note that, insofar as the patent is lying on the left side, the more posterior TP is on the right side, which is up from the tabletop (Figure 8-7A).

1.3.3. The patient should then breathe deeply and, while exhaling, reach for the floor with his or her right hand. This left rotational movement must be monitored and is stopped just as L3 begins to move. The operator uses the left hand to

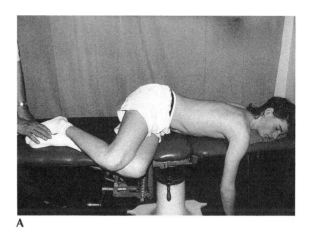

A

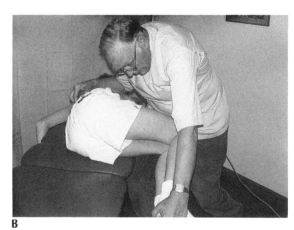

B

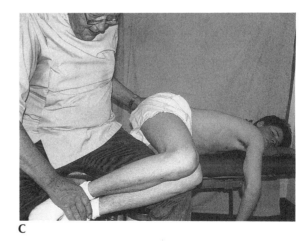

C

FIGURE 8-7

Muscle energy, side-bending activation treatment for an ERSrt dysfunction. (A) Left lateral Sims position. (B) Position for effort, supporting patient's knees on operator's thigh. (C) Alternative position for effort, operator seated.

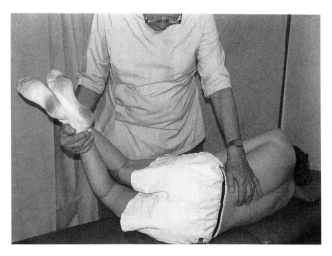

FIGURE 8-8
Muscle energy, side-bending activation treatment for NRlt.

monitor at this stage, because he or she may need to use the right hand to increase the patient's rotation by pressing down on the patient's right shoulder during the exhalation. If necessary, the exhalation and reaching for the floor are repeated until the point of tension at L3 is reached. It is important to make sure, at this point, that the level to be treated (i.e., L3) is held perpendicular to the tabletop.

1.3.4. The necessary left side bending is introduced by dropping the patient's feet over the edge of the table without losing the localization from below (Figure 8-7*B*). Pressure of the table edge under the thigh is usually uncomfortable for the patient. To avoid this pressure, one of the following three methods is commonly used:

1.3.4a. The operator places a small cushion under the thigh to protect it from the edge of the table.

1.3.4b. The operator's left thigh can be used to support the patient's knees (see Figure 8-7*B*).

1.3.4c. The operator sits at the foot of the table and, with legs apart, uses the left knee to support both of the patient's knees. This is sometimes known as the *lazy man's technique* (Figure 8-7*C*). The technique's disadvantage is that it is no longer possible for the operator to control the trunk with his or her right arm. To monitor at L3-4, the operator must change hands and use the right hand to provide the resistance to the patient's effort.

1.3.5. The patient should be told to maintain the twisted position. Whereas this technique is easier for the small operator, the lazy man's technique is difficult for operators wearing skirts because of the abduction required to allow the patient's feet to drop.

1.3.6. The instruction to the patient is to raise the feet toward the ceiling, which the operator resists with an equal

and opposite force with the left hand (in variants 1.3.4a and 1.3.4b) or the right hand (in variant 1.3.4c). The pressure is maintained for 3–5 seconds, and the patient must then relax. It helps to tell the patient to let his or her feet drop.

1.3.7. After full relaxation, the legs are allowed to drop further, until the left side-bending barrier is sensed between L3 and L4 by feeling the new point of interspinous tension as monitored by the fingers. A new flexion barrier can also be introduced by increasing flexion of the hips until there is an increase in the tension between L3 and L4. Using both flexion and side bending reduces the degree of passive motion needed to reach either barrier alone.

1.3.8. Steps 1.3.6 and 1.3.7 are repeated two or more times.

1.3.9. Retest.

Muscle Energy Technique for a Neutral Group Dysfunction

1.4 Described for a Neutral Group Dysfunction That Is Rotated to the Left and Side Bent Right (NRlt)

There is a restriction of right rotation and left side bending from L2-4. The most posterior TP is that of L3 on the left. This technique is applied with the patient side lying on the right with the most posterior TPs up from the tabletop.

> ### *Diagnostic Points*
> There is tissue texture change at the group. The left TPs of L2-4 are more posterior than the TPs on the right. This feature is most marked in the neutral position and may improve in flexion or extension, but there is no position in which the TPs all become level.

1.4.1. The patient lies on the right side, and the operator stands in front of the patient.

1.4.2. Using the right hand, the operator flexes the patient's hips and thighs, while using the left hand to monitor at L2-3. In this technique, because neutral is required in the sagittal plane, the end point is not tension but *maximum ease* at the apex of the group (L3).

1.4.3. The operator then introduces left side bending by lifting the patient's feet until tension develops between L3 and L4, remembering that the most common fault is to go too far (Figure 8-8). Because this is a neutral dysfunction treated in the neutral position, the rotation is coupled in the opposite direction to the side bending and occurs automatically by correction of the side-bending component alone.

1.4.4. The instruction is to try to pull the feet down to the table, which the operator resists. The effort is maintained for 3–5 seconds, and then the patient should relax. It is necessary for the patient to exert more effort in contracting the side-bending muscles in the concavity of the neutral curve than in correction of a non-neutral dysfunction, because the restricting muscles are much larger and cross several segments.

1.4.5. After relaxation is complete, the patient's feet are lifted to the new barrier, and steps 1.4.4 and 1.4.5 are repeated two or more times.

1.4.6. Retest.

2. SIDE-LYING, ROTATORY TECHNIQUES

These three techniques are easy to remember because, in each, the patient lies on the same side as the most posterior TP. When thrust is used, it is important to remember the "low amplitude" part of the description, because the morphology of the lumbar joints allows for, on average, only 3 degrees of intersegmental rotation before reaching the anatomical barrier.

Thrust and Muscle Energy Technique for an FRS Dysfunction

2.1 Described for L3 That Is Flexed, Rotated, and Side Bent to the Right in Relation to L4 (FRSrt)

This is a non-neutral dysfunction with a restriction for extension and for rotation and side bending to the left between L3 and L4. The left facet between L3 and L4 does not close completely.

> *Diagnostic Points*
> There is tissue texture change at the segment. The right TP of L3 is more posterior to the left TP in extension (prone-propped) compared to the TPs of the level below (L4). The TPs of both L3 and L4 appear level in flexion. If there is a major restriction, there may be some prominence of the right TP in the neutral (prone) position.

2.1.1. The patient lies on the right side, with the right TP of L3 perpendicular to the table, and the operator stands in front of the patient. The operator translates the patient's abdomen anteriorly, near to the front of the table, which starts extension of the spine; the operator simultaneously monitors at the dysfunctional segment to avoid moving too far.

2.1.2. Monitoring at L3-4 with the left hand, the operator initiates extension from below up by moving the right leg underneath and behind the left leg until tension is felt to build between L3 and L4, and L4 just begins to move. The patient's left leg lies on the table with the

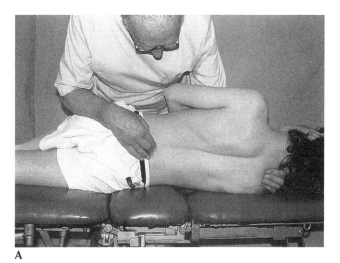

A

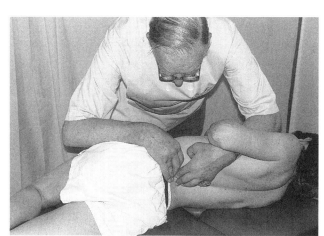

B

FIGURE 8-9
*Rotatory activation treatment for an FRSrt. Muscle energy or thrust. **(A)** Localization from above. **(B)** Final position for patient effort or operator's thrust.*

knee bent, and, if the foot is placed in front of the right leg, the tendency for the patient to flex the right leg (and spoil the localization) can be reduced.

2.1.3. The operator's right hand monitors at L3 while localizing with left rotation to L3 from above. If step 2.1.1 has been carried out, it may be found that only slight rotation is needed to bring the tension to the right place (between L3 and L4). If more than a slight rotation is needed to reach L3-4, then the position of the upper spine should be changed by lifting under the patient's neck and sliding his or her right shoulder backward, extending the spine from above down until the tension reaches the monitoring finger at L3 (Figure 8-9A). To preserve the left side-bent position, the right shoulder must not be pulled out from under the patient.

2.1.4. The operator's left forearm slides through the patient's left axilla. The operator then places the left fingers as an additional monitor at L3, while maintaining contact with his or her upper forearm against the front of the patient's left shoulder. Alternatively, the operator's left hand can press backward on the front of the patient's left shoulder, but then the additional monitor is not available.

2.1.5. The operator's right forearm is placed over the upper part of the patient's left buttock, between the iliac crest and the greater trochanter, while monitoring at L4 by reaching around with the fingers of the right hand (Figure 8-9*B*).

2.1.6. The position is fine tuned by backward rotation of the patient's left shoulder and forward rotation of the left buttock, until all slack is taken out, and the tension is localized between L3 from above and L4 from below. Fine tuning is also enhanced by taking up the available motion and focusing the tension, after one or more forced exhalations, to the remaining elastic barrier between L3 and L4. *At times, mobilization occurs with the proper positioning and the exhalation alone, without the need for a thrusting force.*

T.2.1.7. Thrust variant. The high-velocity, low-amplitude thrust is given by the right forearm on the patient's left buttock. The forearm is placed so that, while rotating the ilium forward, it helps increase lumbar extension and left side bending at L3-4. The motion may be imagined as though the operator were rolling a large ball with the forearm. Placing the forearm to the right of the top of the ball and then pulling the arm toward the operator causes the ball to roll to the left, resulting in side bending the lumbar spine to the left. Pulling the forearm forward toward the operator extends the spine while rotating L4 to the right, increasing the relative left rotation of L3. The pressure with the left forearm must be increased enough to stabilize the patient's upper trunk. To control the amplitude and force available for the thrust and make this a safer technique, the operator should try to "lock" his or her right forearm against his or her own trunk, providing the thrust with a combined trunk-forearm movement by a rapid, but slight, flexion of the operator's trunk.

The thrust may be given against the ischial tuberosity and directed craniad to produce side bending but directed slightly anteriorly, toward the front of the patient's left shoulder, to produce lumbar extension. By using the forearm contact, the fingers of the operator's right hand can no longer be used to monitor from below.

M.2.1.7a. Muscle energy variant. Instead of a thrust, the patient is asked to try to change his or her position against resistance. This resistance can be accomplished by the operator's maintaining the position at the barrier, while the patient is instructed to "try to untwist yourself" or "push your left shoulder forward"; if the operator moves the right hand to the lateral aspect of the patient's left knee, the instruction is to "try to lift your left knee against my hand." Some patients push too hard and need to be cautioned to be gentle because, for the technique to be isometric, the operator must be able to prevent motion.

M.2.1.7b. After 3–5 seconds, the patient should be told to relax, and, when relaxation is complete, the operator adjusts the patient's position by rotating the left shoulder backward and the left hip forward to reach the new rotation barrier. This barrier also can be reached by increasing extension from above and/or below, if required.

M.2.1.7c. The last two steps are repeated twice, or sometimes more, depending on the response. The important step of taking up all of the available slack each time ensures that the total gain in range of motion is achieved.

2.1.8. Retest.

Thrust or Muscle Energy Technique for an ERS Dysfunction

2.2 Described for L3 That Is Extended, Rotated, and Side Bent to the Right in Relation to L4 (ERSrt)

This is a non-neutral dysfunction with a restriction for flexion and for rotation and side bending to the left between L3 and L4. The right facet between L3 and L4 does not open completely.

> *Diagnostic Points*
> There is tissue texture change at the segment. The right TP of L3 is more posterior to the left TP in flexion when compared to the TPs of the level below (L4). The TPs of both L3 and L4 appear level in extension. If there is a major restriction, there is prominence of the right TP when the patient is in the neutral position.

2.2.1. The patient lies on the right side with the right TP of L3 perpendicular to the table. The operator stands in front of the patient. The patient should be positioned toward the farther side of the treatment table.

2.2.2. While monitoring at L3-4 with the left hand, the operator flexes the patient's right leg until L4 just begins

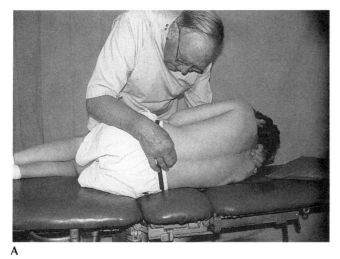
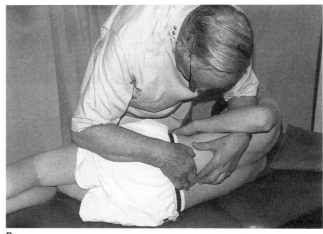

A   B

FIGURE 8-10

*Rotatory activation treatment for an ERSrt. Muscle energy or thrust. (**A**) Localization from above. (**B**) Final position for patient effort or operator's thrust.*

to move or tension begins to build between L4 and L3. The patient's left foot may be hooked onto the back of the right knee, or the legs may be moved together.

2.2.3. The operator must now monitor at L3 with the right hand, while localizing from above. Flexion of the spine from above down is introduced by lifting under the patient's neck and sliding his or her right shoulder forward, until the tension just reaches L3. To preserve the left side-bent position, the right shoulder (the shoulder resting on the table) must *not* be pulled out from under the patient (Figure 8-10*A*).

2.2.4. The operator's left forearm slides through the patient's left axilla; the operator uses the fingers of the left hand as an additional monitor at L3, while the upper forearm rests against the front of the patient's left shoulder. Alternatively, the operator's left hand can press on the front of the patient's left shoulder, but then the additional monitor is not available.

2.2.5. With the right fingers monitoring at L4, the operator places the right forearm over the patient's left buttock, roughly halfway from the ischial tuberosity to the anterior superior iliac spine, behind and just below the greater trochanter.

2.2.6. The position is fine tuned by backward rotation of the patient's left shoulder and forward rotation of his or her left buttock, until all slack has been taken out and the tension is localized at the L3-4 joint (i.e., when the tension just reaches L4 from below and L3 from above) (Figure 8-10*B*).

T.2.2.7. Thrust variant. The high-velocity, low-amplitude thrust is given mainly on the buttock to produce left

side bending, right pelvic rotation (increasing the left lumbar rotation of L3 on L4), and flexion of the pelvis and lumbar spine between L3 and L4. The thrust is given by having the forearm contact posterior and caudal to the greater trochanter. Using the analogy of resting the forearm on a large ball, in this treatment, placement is just to the right of the apex. By pulling the arm toward the operator, the ball will roll left and turn to the operator's left, resulting in left rotation, left side bending, and flexion of the lumbar spine. Pressure with the left forearm must be increased enough to stabilize the patient's upper trunk. To control the amplitude and force available for the thrust and make this a safer technique, the operator should try to "lock" his or her forearm against the trunk, and use a trunk-forearm movement, generating the thrusting force from the trunk.

The thrusting force can be applied against the ischial tuberosity and directed craniad to produce left side bending and slightly posteriorly (toward the back of the patient's left shoulder) to produce additional lumbar flexion. With this variation, the fingers of the operator's right hand may no longer be used to monitor from below.

M.2.2.7a. Muscle energy variant. Instead of a thrust, the patient is asked to try to change position against resistance. This resistance can be accomplished by the operator's maintaining the position at the barrier while the patient is instructed to "try to untwist yourself" or "push your left shoulder forward"; if the operator moves his or her right hand to the lateral aspect of the patient's left knee, the instruction is, "try to lift your left knee against

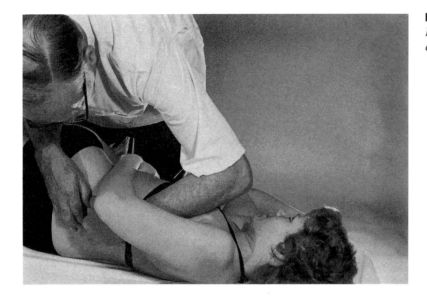

FIGURE 8-11
Rotatory activation treatment for an NRrt. Muscle energy or thrust.

my hand." Some patients push too hard and need to be cautioned to be gentle because, for the technique to be isometric, the operator must be able to prevent motion.

M.2.2.7b. After 3–5 seconds, the patient should be told to relax, and, when relaxation is complete, the operator adjusts the patient's position to reach the new barrier by pushing the ischial tuberosity craniad along the line of force toward the back of the patient's left shoulder. This adjustment results not only in side bending the spine to the left, but also flexes the lumbar spine to the next barrier.

M.2.2.7c. The last two steps are repeated twice, or sometimes more, depending on the response. The important step of taking up all of the available slack each time ensures that the total gain in range of motion is achieved.

2.2.8. Retest.

Thrust or Muscle Energy Technique for a Neutral Group Dysfunction

2.3 Described for a Neutral Group Dysfunction That Is Rotated to the Right and Side Bent Left (NRrt)

There is a restriction of left rotation and right side bending at L2, 3, and 4. The most posterior TP is that of L3 on the right.

> *Diagnostic Points*
> There is tissue texture change at the group. The right TPs of L2-4 are more posterior than the TPs on the left. This feature is most marked in neutral and less in flexion or extension; in no position do the TPs become level.

2.3.1. The patient lies on the right side, and the operator stands in front.

2.3.2. The patient's left foot should be hooked behind his or her right knee. The operator palpates the interspinous space between L3 and L4 with the left hand and introduces flexion and extension of the spine through the legs, using the right hand to find the neutral range at L3-4.

2.3.3. The rotation required is the same as in Sections 2.1 and 2.2, but the side bend has to be reversed. To achieve this, the operator monitors with the right hand while pulling the patient's right shoulder out from underneath the patient. The left rotational movement is continued caudad, until the barrier is identified by palpating the beginning of tissue tension at the L3 level from above (Figure 8-11).

2.3.4. With both arms positioned as in Sections 2.2.4 and 2.2.5, the operator fine tunes the position by rotation. The point of localization should be just below the apex of the group (on and just below the TP of L3).

T.2.3.5. Thrust variant. The high-velocity, low-amplitude thrust is given by the right forearm on the patient's buttock by rotation anteriorly without a flexion or extension component. This thrust is analogous to rolling a large ball by placing an arm directly on the middle of the top of the ball and pulling the arm over the ball. To control the amplitude and force available for the thrust and make this a safer technique, the operator should try to "lock" his or her forearm through the shoulder against his or her own trunk and use a trunk-forearm movement for the thrust. The thrust is given after the patient's exhalation effort, taking up the additional slack provided.

M.2.3.5a. Muscle energy variant. Instead of a thrust, the patient is asked to try to change position against resistance. This resistance can be accomplished by the operator maintaining the position at the barrier, while the patient is instructed to "try to untwist yourself" or "push your left shoulder forward"; if the operator moves his or her right hand to the lateral aspect of the patient's left knee, the instruction is, "try to lift your left knee against my hand." Some patients push too hard and need to be cautioned to be gentle because, for the technique to be isometric, the operator must be able to prevent motion.

M.2.3.5b. After 3–5 seconds, the patient should be told to relax, and, when relaxation is complete, the operator adjusts the patient's position to reach the new barrier.

M.2.3.5c. The last two steps are repeated twice, or sometimes more, depending on the response. The important step of taking up all of the available slack each time ensures that the total gain in range of motion is achieved.

2.3.6. Retest.

3. SITTING TECHNIQUES

Sitting techniques can be used for thoracic dysfunctions up to approximately T5. Except for the first technique, they are described with the patient sitting astride the table, because such a position improves stability. These techniques can also be done with the patient on a stool or sitting across the table, if necessary, but both feet should be flat on the floor. Alternative grips for the operator can be used, especially for the muscle energy variants, and some of these grips are described at the end of this chapter.

Overview of the Treatment Technique for an FRS Dysfunction with the Patient Seated

When treating in the seated position, FRS dysfunctions of the lower thoracic and lumbar region pose a unique problem. When in the flexed position, the inferior facet of the superior vertebra has not only moved in a superior direction, but it has moved anteriorly as well. Any treatment designed to restore extension through this area must account for the possibility that the inferior facet of the superior vertebra may be too far forward (anterior); thus, the joint may bind when any attempt is made to directly close the joint from above down. For this reason, when the patient is sitting, it may be best to begin the treatment for an FRSrt dysfunction by first restoring left rotation using neutral mechanics to gap the left facet joint, taking the

inferior facet of the superior vertebra posteriorly. After left rotation is restored, it must be maintained to keep the inferior facet of the superior vertebra posterior relative to the superior facet of the vertebra below while reversing the side bending from the right to the left side. Extension is added last by sliding the inferior facet of the superior vertebra down from above, while translating the superior facet of the inferior vertebra anteriorly underneath.

Seated Muscle Energy Technique for an FRS Dysfunction

3.1 Described for L3 That Is Flexed, Rotated, and Side Bent to the Right in Relation to L4 (FRSrt)

This is a non-neutral dysfunction with a restriction for extension and for rotation and side bending to the left between L3 and L4. The left facet joint between L3 and L4 does not close completely.

> ***Diagnostic Points***
> There is tissue texture change at the segment. The right TP of L3 is more posterior to the left TP in extension (prone-propped or seated) when compared to the TPs of the level below (L4). The TPs of both L3 and L4 appear level in flexion. There may be some prominence of the right TP in the neutral position if there is a major extension restriction. The position, which signals the location of the barrier for extension, can be appreciated by observing the degree of flexion necessary for the TPs of L3 to become symmetrical. The barrier needs to be redefined in the sitting position if it was initially found in the prone-propped position.

3.1.1. The patient sits on a stool. The operator sits behind the patient on a stool or a chair.

3.1.2. The patient should sit in "erect neutral"—a position in which the patient is erect or nearly erect and can still preserve the flexion-extension ease. The operator's right thumb monitors at the L3-4 interspinous space (Figure 8-12A and B). The patient is asked to actively flex and extend ("slump" or "sit up tall") the lumbar spine to find the midrange neutral at L3-4. The operator's left hand is then placed on the patient's left shoulder. The patient's right hand and arm should be lying anteriorly across his or her own left thigh.

3.1.3. The first part of the technique is designed to restore the lost left rotation, and for this, "neutral" mechanics are used by side bending the patient's spine to the right and then rotating the spine to the left. First, the operator side bends L3-4 to the right through a combination of right-to-left translation, using the right thumb to the right side of L3-4 as both a monitor and guide for

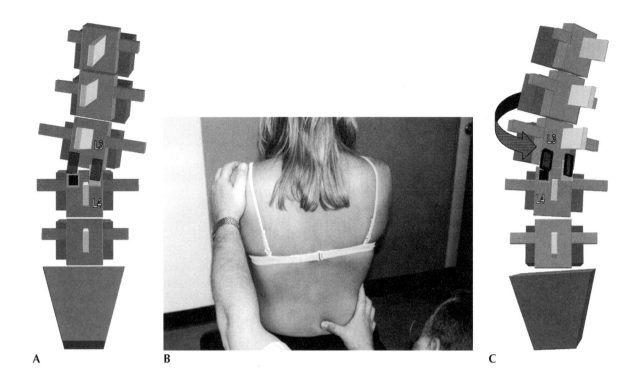

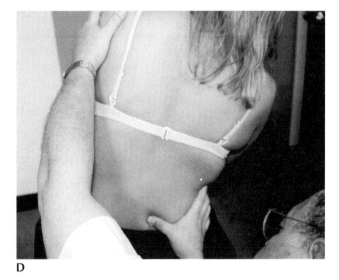

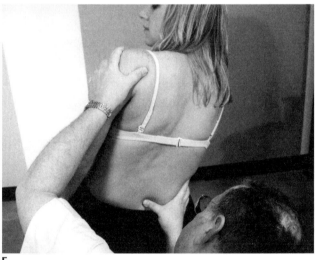

FIGURE 8-12

Seated muscle energy technique for an FRSrt L3-4. (A) Diagram showing position of lumbar spine with FRSrt L3-4. (B) The patient is seated, and the operator monitors to the right of the L3-4 interspace. (C) Diagram showing lumbar spine side bent right and rotated left. Arrow indicates direction of rotation. (D) By using neutral mechanics, the patient is first side bent to the right. (E) The patient is then rotated to the left, followed by increasing the right side bending and left rotation, which brings the left inferior facet of L3 behind the left superior facet of L4. (F) The patient's side bend is now reversed to the left. (G) Diagram showing closure of left L3-4 facet joint to achieve more left side bending after resisted isometric effort to the right side benders. Arrows indicate direction of side bending at L3-4. (H) Diagram showing the restoration toward lumbar extension without losing the left rotation. Arrows indicate direction of extension. (I) Maintaining the extension, the patient is de-rotated back to the midposition. L4 is blocked by the operator's right hand, and a forward flexion motion is blocked by the operator's left arm. After an isometric flexion effort, the patient is taken into full extension. (J) Diagram showing spine hyperextended by translating L4 anteriorly to close both facet joints at L3-4 equally. Arrows indicate direction of translation.

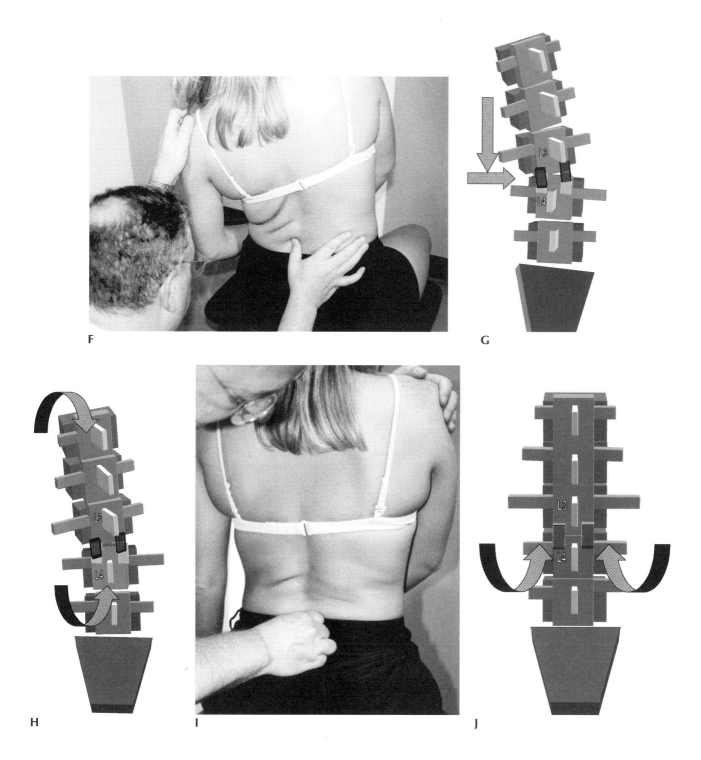

F

G

H

I

J

translation from below, while the operator's left hand side bends and translates the patient's shoulders to the right, down to L3-4 from above (Figure 8-12C). When side bending with translation is done properly, the patient sits with his or her body weight shifted over the left ischial tuberosity.

3.1.4. The operator asks the patient to rotate to the left by reaching forward and to the left with his or her right hand, which lies across the left thigh. The operator monitors the tissue tension as it reaches the L3-4 level and controls the rotational movement through the patient's left shoulder, making sure that the patient does not move into flexion or extension at L3-4 during the introduction of left rotation (Figure 8-12*D* and *E*). If the patient is allowed to bring the left shoulder backward, rather than guiding the right shoulder forward, the lumbar spine can be extended inadvertently, and the neutral position can be lost.

3.1.5. The patient is asked to gently attempt to side bend to the left or to pull the left shoulder forward; this movement is equally resisted by the operator's left hand. The effort is maintained for 3–5 seconds, and when the patient relaxes, the slack is taken up for additional right side bending, combining translation from right to left at L3-4 by the operator's right hand and increasing pressure through the left hand on the patient's left shoulder. The patient is once again instructed to reach forward and to the left with his or her right hand to reach the new left rotation barrier. Steps 3.1.4 and 3.1.5 are repeated, until there is no further gain in left rotation and right side bending (Figure 8-12*D* and *E*).

3.1.6. The treatment then is converted to a technique that uses non-neutral mechanics by reversing the side bending from right to left, while the left rotation is maintained. The operator's right thumb contact switches from the right side of L3-4 to the left side of L3-4 to monitor and guide the lumbar translation from left to right to the left side-bending barrier, as the patient's weight is shifted from the left ischial tuberosity to the right ischial tuberosity. The patient is asked to drop the left shoulder down toward the tabletop; this movement encourages left side bending until the motion barrier on the left side of L3-4 is palpated (Figure 8-12*F*).

3.1.7. With the patient sitting with the spine translated from left to right, and weightbearing more heavily on the right ischial tuberosity, the extension barrier is introduced by asking the patient to push the stomach forward toward the right knee. The movement must be monitored by the operator's right thumb at L3-4, until the interspinous space between L3 and L4 starts to close. If the patient extends too far, an adjustment can be made by asking the patient to stop the extension, relax, slump a little, and reposition again to the extension barrier.

3.1.8. The patient's effort now is either to pull the left shoulder forward or to attempt right side bending. The effort is resisted by the operator's left hand contact on the patient's left shoulder.

3.1.9. After 3–5 seconds, the patient should relax, and the operator uses the newly achieved increase in motion to either increase left side bending or extension of L3 on L4. To locate the next left side-bending barrier, the operator applies a translatory movement from left to right at L4, while monitoring at the interspinous space above with the right thumb or fingers. To locate the next extension barrier at L3-4, the patient is asked to push his or her stomach a little further forward and slightly to the right, translating

L4 in an anterior direction underneath L3. The operator monitors closure of the interspinous space at L3-4 while the additional translation is added. Increased left side bending or extension requires further closing of the left L3-4 facet joint (Figure 8-12*G* and *H*). One motion may be easier than the other to achieve, so fine tuning may require reducing the extension and then increasing the side bending, or reducing the side bending and then increasing the extension, trading one for the other, according to the third concept of spinal mechanics. No further adjusting of the rotation is required, but left rotation must be maintained throughout the treatment until the final step.

3.1.10. Steps 3.1.8 and 3.1.9 are repeated two or more times, or until there is no further gain of motion.

3.1.11. Finally, to finish the treatment, the patient is de-rotated from the left rotated position back to the midline while maintaining the extended position at L3-4. To accomplish this de-rotation, the operator's left hand is moved and placed either on the patient's sternum or across the chest to grip the patient's right shoulder. The operator places the right thumb or the middle phalanx of the index finger on the spinous process of L4, or contacts both TPs of L4, and, while maintaining a forward pressure at L4, brings the patient's right shoulder back to the midline. The patient is then asked to pull his or her chest forward toward the floor, and the effort is blocked by the operator's left arm and hand above and by the right hand below at L4 (Figure 8-12*I*).

3.1.12. After 3–5 seconds of effort, the patient is asked to relax. After relaxation, extension is increased from above with the operator's left hand, while L4 is guided anteriorly by the operator's right thumb and fingers, translating L4 under L3 to achieve bilateral facet joint extension (closure) (Figure 8-12*J*).

3.1.13. Retest.

Alternative Seated Muscle Energy Technique for an FRS Dysfunction

3.1.a Described for L3 That Is Flexed, Rotated, and Side Bent to the Right in Relation to L4 (FRSrt)

This is a non-neutral dysfunction with a restriction for extension and for rotation and side bending to the left between L3 and L4. The left facet joint between L3 and L4 does not close completely.

The benefit of the alternative seated muscle energy technique is that more precise control and localization of side bending and lateral translation can be achieved by working from below up as a consequence of raising or lowering the patient's ischial tuberosity.

3.1.1a. The operator sits behind the patient. The patient sits on a stool, with the left buttock near the right edge of the stool and the right buttock resting on the operator's right knee. The patient should be seated at a height that allows the operator to support comfortably the patient's right buttock; this height can be achieved either above or below the top of the stool by simply raising or lowering the operator's right knee. When the operator raises the right knee, the patient's right hip is raised higher than the left hip, which side bends the patient's lumbar spine to the right. Likewise, when the operator lowers his or her right knee below the height of the stool on which the patient sits, left lumbar side bending can be induced (Figure 8-13*A*).

3.1.2a. The patient should sit in an "erect neutral position"—a position in which the patient is erect or nearly erect and can still preserve the flexion-extension ease. The operator's right thumb is used to monitor the L3-4 interspinous space while the patient flexes and extends the lumbar spine, until the midrange (neutral) position is determined for L3-4. The operator then reaches with his or her left hand under the patient's left arm to grasp the patient's right arm above the elbow. The operator uses this grip to assist in translating the patient's spine from right to left to induce right side bending (Figure 8-13*B*).

3.1.3a. The first part of the technique is designed to restore the lost left rotation, and for this technique, "neutral" mechanics are used. The operator raises his or her right knee and elevates the right side of the patient's pelvis enough to produce right side bending from below up to the L3-4 level. At the same time, the operator's left hand pulls the patient's right arm across to side bend the patient to the right from above down to the top of L3. By using the right thumb on the right side of L3-4, the operator guides translation of the patient's lumbar spine to the left while still monitoring the tension and motion at the L3-4 level. This position ultimately results in translation of L3-4 to the left (see Figure 8-13*A*).

3.1.4a. The operator then rotates the patient to the left, using his or her left hand contact on the patient's right arm, pulling the right arm forward to the left rotation barrier. This rotation is monitored until tissue tension reaches the L3-4 level. Rotating the patient to the left by bringing the right shoulder forward helps to prevent the inferior facet of the superior vertebra from jamming down onto the lower facet (superior facet of the inferior vertebra), because neutral mechanics are maintained and the extension barrier is not engaged. The restoration of rotation to the left is accomplished using neutral mechanics with the patient side bending to the right and rotating to the left (see Figure 8-13*B*).

3.1.5a. The patient is asked to attempt to gently side bend to the left, and the operator resists by blocking the patient's left shoulder with his or her left shoulder, while controlling the patient's spine with the left hand contact on the patient's right arm and

with the operator's right thumb contact at L3-4. The effort is maintained for 3–5 seconds, and after the patient relaxes, there should be more freedom to increase right side bending and left rotation. Steps 3.1.4a and 3.1.5a are repeated until there is no further gain in left rotation.

3.1.6a. The second step in the treatment sequence is then converted to one that uses non-neutral mechanics, changing the side bending from the right to the left side. This step is accomplished by the operator lowering his or her right knee to introduce left side bending from below up while maintaining the patient in left rotation. The patient is asked to place his or her right hand on the left shoulder after it has been released by the operator. The operator's left hand is then placed on top of the patient's right hand, which is on top of the patient's left shoulder, and the operator depresses the left shoulder to induce left side bending from above down to L3-4. The degree of left side bending is further controlled by the height of the operator's knee underneath the patient's right buttock and is monitored by the operator's right thumb, which has now shifted from the right side of L3-4 to the left side. The patient is now rotated left and side bent left with a slight introduction of extension (Figure 8-13*C*).

3.1.7a. Extension to the barrier between L3 and L4 is now needed and can be introduced by asking the patient to push the stomach forward toward the right knee (Figure 8-13*D*). The movement must be monitored by the operator's right thumb. Using verbal instructions, care is taken not to let the patient overextend at the dysfunctional level; if the patient has over extended, an adjustment can be made by having the patient slump a little into flexion before extending back to the barrier.

3.1.8a. The corrective effort can then be made by having the patient pull his or her left shoulder forward or attempt to side bend to the right. Either effort is resisted by equal counter force from the operator's left hand.

3.1.9a. After 3–5 seconds, the patient should relax, and the operator uses the newly achieved increase in motion to side bend L3 on L4 by further lowering the right knee and translating the patient from left to right through increased pressure on the patient's left shoulder or to extend L3 on L4 from below by an anterior translatory movement of L4, which is achieved by having the patient push his or her stomach a little further forward. Any additional increase in left side bending or extension mobility requires further closing of the left L3-4 facet joint. One motion may be easier to achieve than the other, so fine tuning may require reducing the extension to increase the side bending or reducing the left side bending to increase the extension, trading one for the other, according to the third concept of spinal mechan-

FIGURE 8-13

Alternative seated technique for an FRSrt dysfunction. (A) The patient's right ischial tuberosity is seated on the operator's right knee so that the operator can raise the patient's right buttocks and introduce right side bending. (B) Left rotation is introduced by the operator pulling the patient's right arm forward and across. The patient attempts to left side bend and is resisted by the operator three or four times, introducing more right side bending and left rotation. (C) The patient is then shifted into left side bending through a combination of depression of the left shoulder by the operator's left hand and lowering of the operator's right knee. (D) The patient is then asked to stick the stomach forward toward the right knee to introduce extension. (E) The patient is brought back to the midline after sliding the right buttock onto the top of the seat and is asked to pull the chest forward against isometric resistance. On relaxation, the operator's right thumb guides the inferior segment in a posterior to anterior direction.

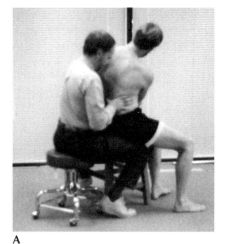

A

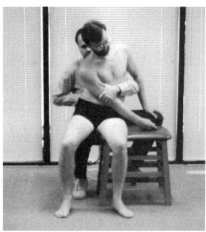

B

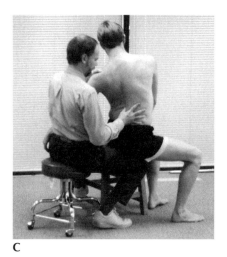

C

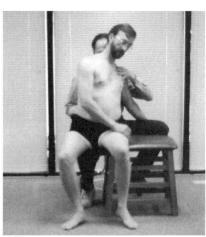

D

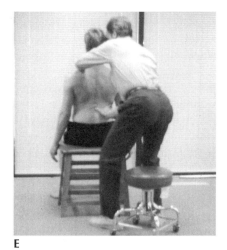

E

ics. It should be noted that, once achieved in step 3.1.4a, the left rotation must be maintained.

3.1.10a. Steps 3.1.8a and 3.1.9a are repeated two or more times or until there is no further gain in motion for left side bending or extension.

3.1.11a. A final further extension effort can be made by having the patient de-rotate the spine, bringing the right shoulder back in alignment with the left shoulder while maintaining the extended position. The patient's hips should now be level as the operator's right knee is raised to the height of the top of the stool. The operator's left hand and arm are then placed across the patient's chest and sternum, while maintaining a posterior-to-anterior pressure on the spinous process of L4 or TPs of L4 with the right hand. The patient is asked to pull the chest forward toward the floor, and this flexion effort is blocked by the operator's left arm from above and right hand from below (Figure 8-13*E*).

3.1.12a. After 3–5 seconds of effort, the patient is asked to relax, and after having done so, further extension is increased from above down to L3-4, while L4 is actively translated anteriorly under L3 by the operator's thumb or flexed index finger applied to the spinous process or both TPs of L4 to achieve bilateral symmetrical extension (closure) at L3-4.

3.1.13a. Retest.

At times, it may be possible to correct an FRS dysfunction in the seated position without first restoring the rotation. In this situation, the barrier is directly engaged by a combination of extension, rotation, and side bending, as described in step 3.1.6 and so on, with the addition of rotation. Remember that more motion in one direction can substitute for motion in the other two directions. For instance, more side bending can be used instead of more rotation or extension. The seated FRS technique is usually more successful, however, when rotation is restored first, using neutral lumbar mechanics as previously described.

Seated Thrust Technique
for an FRS Dysfunction

3.2 Described for L3 That Is Flexed, Rotated, and Side Bent to the Right in Relation to L4 (FRSrt)

This is a non-neutral dysfunction with a restriction for extension and for rotation and side bending to the left between L3 and L4. The left facet joint between L3 and L4 does not close completely.

T.3.2.1. The patient sits astride the table, with his or her back close to the end, and places the right hand on the left shoulder. The patient may sit on a stool with both feet on the floor or sit across a table, but in the latter position, the pelvis is less well controlled.

T.3.2.2. The operator stands behind and to the left of the patient. Using the left hand and arm, the operator reaches around the front of the patient to grasp the patient's right shoulder. The operator's left axilla should be resting on top of the patient's left shoulder, or, as an alternative position, the operator's left hand can be placed on top of the patient's left shoulder.

T.3.2.3. Using the right thumb (Figure 8-14*A*) or the heel of the hand (Figure 8-14*B*), the operator contacts the right TP or the left side of the spinous process of

L3. This movement serves as a monitor and a thrusting contact.

T.3.2.4. Extension is introduced by having the patient push his or her stomach out to obtain anterior translation, bringing the tension just down to L3 and just up to L4. Translation to the right by downward pressure on the patient's left shoulder is then used to side bend to the left from above and below with the same monitor. Rotation to the left fine tunes the barrier so that the tension just reaches L3 from above.

T.3.2.5. When all the slack is taken out, the operator brings his or her right hip close behind the right elbow. The high-velocity, low-amplitude thrust is given through the thumb or the heel of the hand against the right TP or on the left side of the spinous process of L3. At the same time that the thrust is given, the patient is further extended and rotated to the left from above. Control is improved by the thrust coming mainly from movement of the operator's right hip.

Seated Muscle Energy Technique
for an ERS Dysfunction

3.3 Described for L5 That Is Extended, Rotated, and Side Bent to the Left in Relation to the Sacrum (ERSlt)

This is a non-neutral dysfunction with a restriction for flexion and for rotation and side bending to the right between L5 and the sacrum. The left facet between L5 and S1 does not open completely.

> *Diagnostic Points*
> There is tissue texture change at the segment. The left TP of L5 is more posterior to the right TP in flexion when compared to the sacral base below. The TPs of L5 and the sacral base both appear level in extension. There may be some prominence of the left TP in the neutral position if there is a major restriction to flexion. The degree of extension necessary to produce a leveling of the TPs of L5 provides a good estimate of the location of the beginning of the flexion barrier. The barrier can be found with the patient in the seated position, extending by sitting up tall and arching and then slowly slumping or flexing, while the operator palpates the TPs.

Note: When treating an ERS dysfunction with the patient in the seated position, side bending to the barrier can be accomplished using translation by two different methods. The first technique uses distraction; the other involves compression. In the first technique, the operator stands on the side of the dysfunction, places his or her arm under the patient's axilla, and contacts the patient's opposite shoulder. The patient is side bent away from the

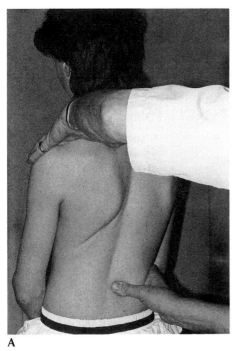

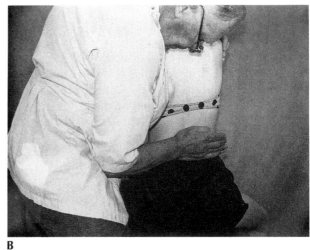

A   B

FIGURE 8-14

*Thrust treatment for FRSrt at L3-4 without preliminary correction of rotation. **(A)** Starting position with operator's left hand on patient's left shoulder and operator's thumb against the right transverse process (TP) of L3. **(B)** Alternative position with operator's left axilla over patient's left shoulder and right hypothenar eminence against the right TP of L3. The operator's right elbow is supported by his or her right hip, from which the thrusting force is delivered.*

operator to engage the side bending barrier by lifting the patient's near shoulder while translating the opposite shoulder toward the operator (Figure 8-15A). By lifting the shoulder on the side of the closed facet, the operator provides a direct ipsilateral force of distraction to open the facet joint. In the other technique, the operator stands on the opposite side of the closed facet joint and places his or her axilla over the patient's shoulder to translate that shoulder down and away from the operator. In this technique, the operator uses compression through the patient's shoulder to induce side bending and to open the dysfunctional facet joint on the opposite side (Figure 8-15B). Fred Mitchell, Sr., described a seated technique to treat an ERS dysfunction in the lower lumbar region that combines both approaches, providing distraction and compression with an easier way to control rotation; this technique is described.

3.3.1. The patient sits on a stool with both feet on the floor or astride a table, with his or her back close to the end and the right arm hanging freely to the side. The patient places the left hand between the legs. If the patient sits on a table with his or her legs hanging down, there is less pelvic stability.

3.3.2. The operator stands to the left of the patient with the patient's left shoulder placed against the operator's left chest wall. The operator reaches around the front of the patient to grasp the patient's right shoulder with his or her left hand. The operator uses the fingers of the right hand to palpate the interspinous space and the left TP of L5 (Figure 8-16A).

3.3.3. The operator introduces flexion by translation of the patient's trunk from above down and below up into a slumped posture, until tension is palpated by the operator's right fingers at L5. For major restrictions, it is necessary to begin translation into flexion from the extended position. Side bending to the right side-bending barrier is accomplished by translating the patient's shoulders from right to left using the operator's left hand, while simultaneously lifting the patient's left shoulder with the operator's chest wall until tension is palpated at L5 (Figure 8-16B). This maneuver starts to open the left facet joint at L5-S1 because of the upward distracting force on the left and the compressive force on the right. The patient may be asked to actively right side bend by reaching toward the floor with the right hand to further define the right side-bending barrier. Rotation of the patient to the right fine tunes the position so that the tension just reaches L5 from above, and all the slack is taken out (Figure 8-16C).

3.3.4. The patient is then asked to side bend to the left or to sit up tall (extension); the operator resists with equal counter force.

3.3.5. After 3–5 seconds, the patient is asked to stop the effort. When relaxation of the paraspinal muscles at L5 is palpated, more right side bending, flexion, and rotation are added to the next barrier, if one exists.

3.3.6. Steps 3.3.4 and 3.3.5 are repeated two or three times or until there is no further gain in the ability to right side bend, right rotate, and flex the patient.

3.3.7. While maintaining the patient in the flexed, right side bent, and right rotated position achieved in step 3.3.6, the operator removes his or her left hand from the patient's right shoulder and places it on the patient's left shoulder. The operator also moves his or her right hand to the patient's right shoulder. The patient's left arm is allowed to hang freely between his or her knees, and the patient is asked to reach toward the floor with the left hand to further open the left L5-S1 facet joint. The operator maintains the patient in the right rotated position as the patient reaches toward the floor with the left hand (Figure 8-16D).

3.3.8. The patient is then de-rotated back to the midline by bringing the right arm between his or her knees to match the left arm and to maximize spinal flexion. The operator places his or her left hand above L5 and the right hand below L5 and asks the patient to try to lift upward against the operator's equal resistance. This effort is followed by relaxation and guidance into further flexion (Figure 8-16E). This last step further reduces the tone of the spinal extensors and promotes bilateral and symmetrical facet joint opening at L5-S1.

3.3.9. Re-examine to see if the ERSlt at L5 has been corrected.

Alternative Seated Muscle Energy and Thrust Techniques Using Compression for an ERSrt Dysfunction

3.3.a Described for L3 That Is Extended, Rotated, and Side Bent to the Right in Relation to L4 (ERSrt)

This is a non-neutral dysfunction with a restriction for flexion and for rotation and side bending to the left between L3 and L4. The right facet between L3 and L4 does not open completely.

3.3.1a. The patient sits astride the table with his or her back close to the end and places the right hand on the left shoulder. The patient may sit on a stool with both feet on the floor or sit across a table, but in the latter position, the pelvis is less well controlled.

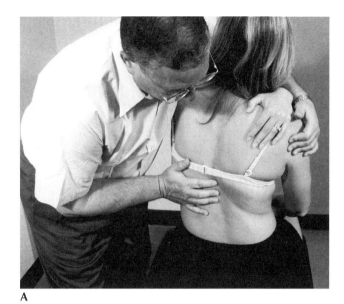

A

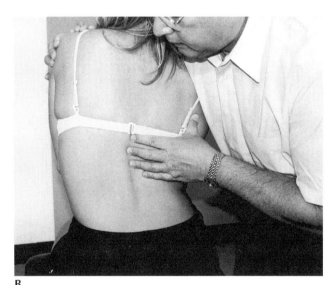

B

FIGURE 8-15
Alternative techniques to treat an ERSlt with the patient seated. (A) By distraction, lifting the left side to open the dysfunctional facet joint. (B) By compression, depressing the opposite (right) side to open the dysfunctional facet joint on the left.

3.3.2a. The operator stands behind and to the left of the patient. Using the left hand and arm, the operator reaches around the front of the patient to grasp the patient's right shoulder. The operator's left axilla should be resting on top of the patient's left shoulder.

3.3.3a. Using the right thumb or the heel of the hand, the operator contacts the right TP or the left side of the spinous process of L3. This position serves both as monitor and thrusting contact.

FIGURE 8-16

Muscle energy technique in the seated position to correct an ERSlt. (A) The patient's left shoulder is against the operator's left chest wall, and the operator's left hand is placed on the patient's right shoulder. (B) Flexion is introduced from above down and below up, while the operator's right hand palpates at the dysfunctional segment. Using the left hand, the patient's shoulders are translated from right to left, and the right side-bending barrier is defined further by having the patient reach toward the floor with the right hand. (C) Right rotation is then added to further define the barrier. (D) After isometric left side bending or extension efforts, maximum flexion, right side bending, and right rotation are maintained with the operator's left hand on the patient's left shoulder and the right hand on the patient's right shoulder to guide the patient as he or she reaches toward the floor with the left hand. (E) Maximum flexion is obtained when the patient's right hand is placed between the knees to match the left hand. The patient attempts to lift up and, after an isometric extension effort, relaxes to allow further flexion to bilaterally and symmetrically open both facet joints at the dysfunctional level.

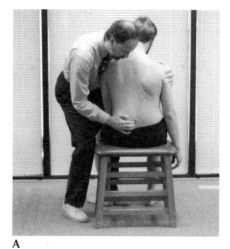

A

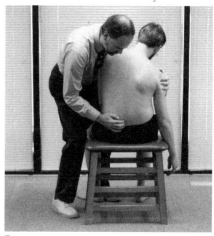

B

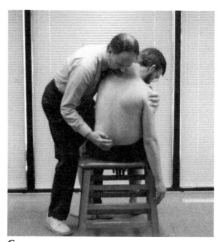

C

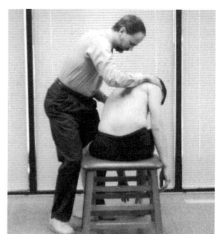

D

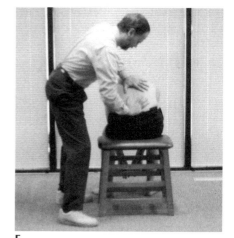

E

3.3.4a. The operator introduces flexion by translation of the patient's trunk in an anterior to a posterior direction ("allow yourself to slump") and side bending by translation from left to right. Both positions are adjusted to bring the tension from above down just to L3 and from below up just to L4. For major restrictions, it may be necessary to begin translation into flexion from the extended position. Rotation to the left fine tunes the position so that the tension just reaches L3 from above, and all the slack is taken out (Figure 8-17).

T.3.3.5. Thrust variant. A high-velocity, low-amplitude thrust is given against the right TP or the left side of the spinous process of L3 by the operator's right thumb or the heel of the hand, supported by the hip, which is brought up behind the elbow (see Figure 8-14*B*). At the same time as the thrust, the patient's trunk position is slightly exaggerated into flexion and left rotation.

M.3.3.5. Muscle energy variant. The patient is asked to try to raise the left shoulder or to side bend to the right. This effort is equally resisted by the operator. To keep the contraction isometric, it may be necessary to tell the patient to be gentle in the effort.

M.3.3.6. After 3–5 seconds, the patient is asked to relax, and, when relaxation is complete, the operator adjusts the patient's position to reach the new barrier in flexion, side bending, and rotation.

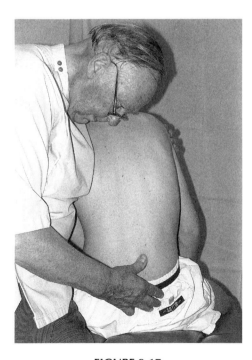

FIGURE 8-17
Muscle energy or thrust technique for the treatment of an ERSrt dysfunction.

M.3.3.7. The last two steps are repeated twice, or more if desired, and the slack is finally taken up.

M.3.3.8. If necessary, an isometric extension effort may be used as well or instead. The patient is asked to bend backward. The operator resists the effort, and, after 3–5 seconds, the contraction is stopped and then repeated after repositioning to the new flexion barrier. After de-rotating the spine back to the midline while maintaining the regained flexion, the operator resists the patient extension effort for 3–5 seconds. This effort is used to balance and reset both L3-4 facet joints with the additional flexion gained, postisometrically.

3.3.9. Retest.

Seated Muscle Energy and Thrust Techniques for a Neutral Group Dysfunction

3.4 Described for a Neutral Group Dysfunction That is Rotated to the Right and Side Bent Left (NRrt) L2-4

There is a restriction of left rotation and right side bending from L2-4. The most posterior TP is that of L3 on the right.

> *Diagnostic Points*
> There is tissue texture change at the group. The right TPs of L2-4 are more posterior than the TPs on the left. This feature is most apparent in the neutral position and still present in flexion or extension. In no position do the TPs become level.

3.4.1. The patient sits astride the table, with his or her back close to the end, and places the right hand on the left shoulder. The patient may sit on a stool with both feet on the floor or sit across a table, but in the latter position, the pelvis is less well controlled.

3.4.2. The operator stands behind and to the left of the patient. The operator then threads his or her left forearm through the patient's left axilla to grip the patient's right shoulder from in front (Figure 8-18*A* and *B*).

3.4.3. Using the right thumb or the heel of the hand, the operator contacts the right side of L3 at and a little below the right TP; *this contact is not made on the left side of the spinous process,* because that would prevent the necessary right side bending.

3.4.4. The patient's lumbar spine should remain in the neutral position, neither flexed nor extended. By lifting the left arm under the patient's left axilla, the operator introduces right side bending of the patient's trunk down to L3. Left rotation is coupled to the side bend and need not be added by the operator.

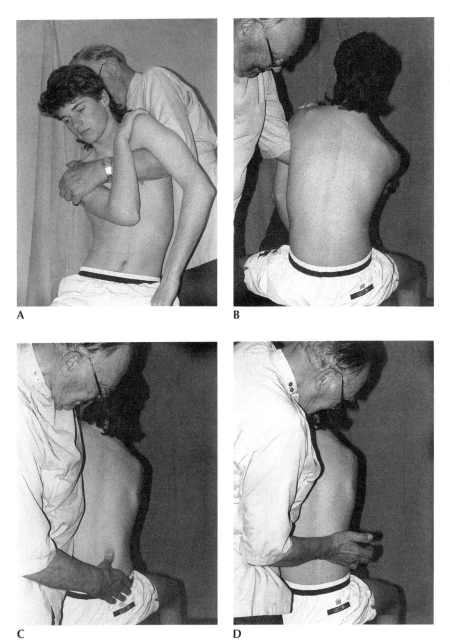

A

B

C

D

FIGURE 8-18
*Sitting treatment for NRrt. Muscle energy or thrust. (**A**) Operator's grip with left forearm through axilla. (**B**) The same grip seen from behind. (**C**) Position for patient effort. (**D**) Thrust variant.*

T.3.4.5. Thrust variant. The high-velocity, low-amplitude thrust against and a little below the right TP of L3 is given by the operator's right thumb or the heel of the hand and is supported by bringing the right hip behind the right elbow, using body movement (Figure 8-18C and D).

M.3.4.5. Muscle energy variant. The patient is asked to attempt to side bend to the left, and the operator resists the movement by blocking with the left arm placed under the patient's left arm.

M.3.4.6. After 3–5 seconds, the patient is asked to relax, and, when relaxation is complete, the operator adjusts the patient's position to reach the new barrier in right side bending. Coupled rotation left automatically occurs as side bending to the right is increased.

M.3.4.7. The last two steps are repeated twice, or more if desired, and the slack is taken up after each effort.

3.4.8. Retest.

Seated Muscle Energy and Thrust Techniques for a Bilaterally Flexed Non-Neutral Dysfunction

3.5 Described for a Bilaterally Flexed L3 in Relation to L4

There is a restriction of backward bending or extension of L3 on L4 bilterally. Both facet joints between L3 and L4 do not close completely.

> **Diagnostic Points**
> The TPs are level in neutral, forward bending, and backward bending, but there is tissue texture change at the segment. The interspinous space between L3-4 will move further apart with flexion but motion between the two spinous processes stops immediately at the barrier for extension.

3.5.1. The patient sits astride the table with his or her back close to the end and with both hands laced tightly together behind the neck.

3.5.2. The operator stands either behind or to one side of the patient and places the heel of one hand (the right hand, if standing on the patient's left) across the spinous process and both TPs of L4 (Figure 8-19*A*).

3.5.3. The operator then grasps the patient's elbows with the free hand and extends the patient's spine from above down until the tension reaches L3, which should be close to the position determined by the diagnostic motion testing (Figure 8-19*B*).

T.3.5.4. Thrust variant. The thrust is given by a high-velocity, low-amplitude, and forward translation of L4

with the operator's lower hand with the addition of further extension of the trunk with the upper hand.

M.3.5.4. Muscle energy variant. At the extension barrier, the patient is asked to attempt to bend forward or pull the elbows down against the operator's resistance.

M.3.5.5. After 3–5 seconds, the patient is asked to relax, and, when relaxation is complete, the operator adjusts the patient's position by translating L4 anteriorly with the right hand to reach the new extension barrier.

M.3.5.6. The last two steps are repeated twice, or more if desired, and the slack is taken up after each effort.

3.5.7. Retest.

Note: A bilateral dysfunction for flexion or extension can be treated in the usual fashion by treating one side and then the other.

There are several positions for the patient's arms by which the operator can control the patient's upper trunk in the manner that is needed before a treatment can be given with accuracy. These positions are not all as applicable as each other in any given situation. For instance, if the operator wishes to side bend the patient away to the opposite side from which the operator is standing, the under-axilla grip has certain advantages, as noted in Section 3.3. With the under-axilla grip, however, it is not easy to control the patient in flexion, but control of extension is easier. If, on the other hand, side bending toward the operator is required, the over-the-shoulder position gives better control, but, in this instance, flexion is easier to control and extension is more difficult to control. In both grips, the operator stands behind and to one side of the patient. For the under-axilla grip, the operator threads his or her left

FIGURE 8-19

*Treatment for a bilaterally flexed segment (bilateral extension restriction). Muscle energy or thrust. (**A**) Position from behind. (**B**) Position from in front.*

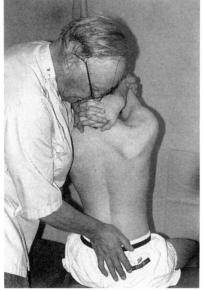
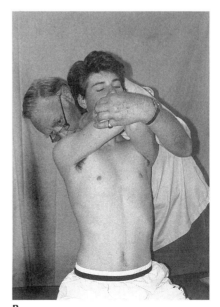

A   B

A

B

FIGURE 8-20
(A, B) Alternative placements of arms to enhance control.

arm through the patient's left axilla (or the right arm through the patient's right axilla) and grips the opposite shoulder from in front (see Figure 8-15A). For the over-the-shoulder grip, the operator grasps the patient's far shoulder from in front with the hand and brings his or her axilla down on top of the patient's near shoulder (see Figure 8-15B).

When muscle energy treatment is planned, the operator can stand on either side of the patient, and the decision as to the grip used will depend on convenience and the considerations just mentioned. However, for thrust treatment with the patient sitting, the operator should stand on the side away from which the thrust is to be applied. It follows that in those cases for which thrust may be needed, even if the primary corrective attempt uses muscle energy, it may be that the operator should use a position from which either technique can be done without the operator having to move.

There are also several variations of grips by which the patient can stabilize his or her shoulder-trunk connection so that motion introduced by the operator holding the patient's shoulders is transmitted accurately to the dysfunctional joint. The simplest varia-

tion is for the patient to hold one shoulder with the other hand. This position can be done with either side and can provide reasonable stability. If more stability is needed, the patient can use the other hand to hold the elbow of the arm holding the shoulder (Figure 8-20A). This position also can apply to either side; the objective is to enhance the patient's stability rather than the operator's contact. Some operators prefer to have the patient use one hand to hold the neck on the same side and use the other hand to hold the fully flexed elbow (Figure 8-20B). This position provides excellent stability, but some patients find it uncomfortable. For certain thrusting techniques, the patient's hands are laced tightly together behind the neck; this grip could be used for muscle energy techniques if circumstances made it necessary (see Figure 8-19B).

The position with the patient astride the table is useful for certain techniques because it increases the stability of the innominates. The model in Figure 8-18B illustrates this position. This position can only be used on tables that are not so wide that it is too uncomfortable for the patient to separate his or her knees that far.

9

Treatment of the Thoracic Spine

Manipulative treatment for the thoracic spine can be done in a variety of positions, some of which lend themselves to muscle energy variants. Only in the thoracic region are there more thrusting than muscle energy techniques available. At the lower end of the thoracic spine, both the rotary and the side-bending activation lumbar techniques done in side-lying can be used, but accurate localization becomes more difficult when treating thoracic dysfunctions found higher up. Only the rotary activation techniques are available for thrusting techniques in the lower thoracic spine. For descriptions of the lumbar side-lying techniques that can be used in the lower thoracic spine, see Chapter 8, Sections 1.1, 1.2, 2.1, 2.2, and 2.3.

The sitting techniques described for the lumbar spine (Chapter 8, Sections 3.1 through 3.5) are also applicable for the thoracic spine below T5—both in their muscle energy and thrust variants. The sitting techniques described in this chapter are similar in many respects (1.2.1, 1.2.2, and 1.2.3) and are the great standbys for treatment of the upper thoracic joints. These techniques can be used as either muscle energy or thrusting manipulative procedures. There are also the "knee-in-back" techniques, which are only used with thrust activation.

The prone position can be used for thrust treatment of restrictions of extension and, in the upper joints, for neutral dysfunctions. Care is required when treating a patient in the prone position, because anterior rib subluxations can be produced by incorrect technique.

Supine techniques are available for high-velocity thrust treatment of dysfunctions that are flexed, rotated, and side bent (FRS), extended, rotated, and side bent (ERS), and neutral.

For all of these techniques, when positioning the patient by using translation, the apex of the antero-posterior (sag-

ittal plane) curve should coincide with the apex of the lateral (coronal plane) curve.

Occasionally, it may be found that there is an ERS dysfunction of a joint, usually between T4 and T10, with which there is also an external rib torsion. This combination sometimes proves difficult to resolve, unless both dysfunctions are treated at the same time. A combined muscle energy technique and a high-velocity thrust technique are described in Chapter 10, Sections 5.8 through 5.10.

Bilateral restrictions of flexion or extension are not uncommon in the lower thoracic spine. Often, these restrictions are harder to find and diagnose than they are to treat, especially if the facet joints are symmetrically restricted so that there is no positional asymmetry of the transverse processes (TPs) palpable in flexion or extension.

Clinically, patients with dysfunctions affecting the upper thoracic spine commonly present with more neck pain and, sometimes, more arm pain than upper back pain. Functionally, normal neck motion is the result of a combination of normal cervical and upper thoracic motion. Flexion-extension neck injuries, so often seen as a consequence of a motor vehicle accident, often result in chronic neck pain with restricted mobility originating primarily from upper thoracic non-neutral dysfunctions. All too often, only the cervical component is treated, and it is usually treated unsuccessfully. This may be because the pain is felt and described by the patient as occurring primarily in the neck, whereas only tightness, if anything, is felt in the upper thoracic region. Upper thoracic and rib cage dysfunctions are also common causes of restricted motion and pain in the shoulder. FRS dysfunctions, in particular, limit the patient's ability to reach above shoulder height. ERS dysfunctions in the upper thoracic spine restrict neck flexion and inhibit the deep neck flexors, which are important in helping to stabilize the cervical spine. ERS dysfunctions in both the upper and lower thoracic spine contribute to rib dysfunctions, which twist the rib shaft, often causing chest wall pain. Both ERS and FRS dysfunctions interfere with the respiratory mechanics of inhalation or exhalation. It is also important to realize that any dysfunction affecting the upper thoracic spine can also be the primary cause of headaches, which are usually occipital and frontal in location and are usually associated with altered cervical mobility. Finally, dysfunctions of the upper thoracic spine can influence spinal function below, even into the lumbar segments. This influence can be seen clinically when an apparent multisegmental rotation in the thoracolumbar area is palpable all the way up to an upper thoracic level, where the rotation appears to stop abruptly. This level-appearing vertebra does not follow the one below it and is therefore a non-neutral dysfunction, and it may have a significant influence on the more caudal vertebral segments, which become locally symptomatic.

Dysfunctions involving the lower thoracic spine can cause altered upper trunk and especially head and neck posture and can contribute to both shoulder and neck pain. More commonly, lower thoracic dysfunctions contribute to lower rib dysfunctions, chest wall pain, upper abdominal pain, and lumbar and sacroiliac pain. At times, lower thoracic dysfunctions are painful but, more often, are unnoticed by the patient.

1. SITTING TECHNIQUES

The accurate diagnosis and effective positioning for treatment of any spinal dysfunction require an initial determination of the range of the remaining neutral zone for that dysfunctional joint. It must be remembered that, for major restrictions in which the barrier extends into the midrange, the neutral zone has significantly shifted and now is found in the region of residual free motion, midway between the pathological barrier in one direction and the physiological barrier in the other direction. For unilateral dysfunctions, the observation of the position in which the TPs become level and when rotational asymmetry begins during flexion or extension defines this free range. The free range of motion available in bilateral dysfunctions can be determined by using passive mobility testing, palpating the interspinous space, and observing the range of motion available between separation (opening) of the spinous processes during flexion and approximation (closure) of the spinous processes with extension. A key point to remember is that more accurate localization during treatment can be achieved by always approaching the motion barrier from the pathological neutral zone.

Thrust or Muscle Energy Techniques for the Lower Thoracic Spine, T6 Down

1.1 Described for Non-Neutral ERS and FRS Dysfunctions from T6 Down to L5

The seated techniques described for the lumbar spine in Chapter 8, Sections 3.1 through 3.5, may be used for thrusting or muscle energy treatment, or the knee-in-back method may be used if thrusting is the treatment of choice (see 1.3, below).

Thrust or Muscle Energy Techniques for FRS Dysfunctions in the Upper Thoracic Spine, C7-T5

When treating FRS dysfunctions in the upper half of the thoracic spine, positioning the neck is important for both thrust and muscle energy treatments. To bring the dysfunctional segment to the extension barrier, the spine must be extended, but in many patients with these dysfunctions, the pain is felt and described as occuring primarily in the neck, and this discomfort increases if extension of the upper thoracic spine is not introduced correctly. The intent is not for the head to be extended on the neck (Figure 9-1A) but for the neck itself to be extended. Having the operator protect the neck by supporting it with his or her forearm is not always enough. To protect the neck, the operator must ensure that only the lower cervical segments are extended, using anterior-to-posterior translation down to the dysfunctional level in the thoracic spine. This protection can be achieved by having the patient tuck the chin down or pull the chin back while leaving the head upright (Figure 9-1B). Some patients have difficulty understanding what is being asked of them, but the request "let me bring your chin back" is usually successful. There may be some difficulty in persuading the patient to relax in that position. The use of the operator's forearm to guide and support the neck is an additional help (Figure 9-1C).

There is another variant applicable to muscle energy treatment for FRS dysfunctions. To treat an FRSrt at T3, the operator can have the patient hold his or her right shoulder with the left hand. The operator then lifts the patient's elbow in front of the patient's face while monitoring with the other hand and, at the same time, introduces left side bending and left rotation, until the barrier is reached (Figure 9-1D). The patient may use the right arm to hold the shoulder, if preferred. Localization occurs by translation, rather than by simple extension or side bending, and it may help to ask the patient to push his or her stomach forward to produce anterior translation from below up. Then, the patient's effort is to try to pull his or her elbow down as the elbow is raised. The operator equally resists this effort by holding the patient's elbow in

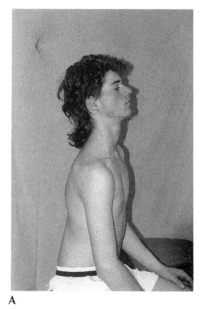
A

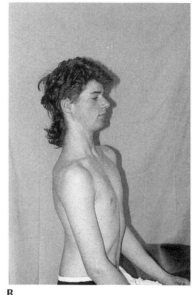
B

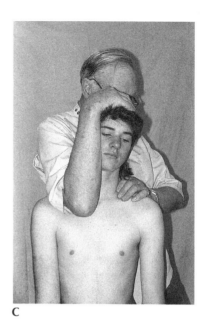
C

FIGURE 9-1
*Methods of protecting the cervical spine when treating FRS dysfunctions in the upper thoracic region. (**A**) Head extension is to be avoided. (**B**) The chin is tucked in, and the head is translated posteriorly to extend the neck. (**C**) Protecting the neck with the operator's forearm. (**D**) Variant using the patient's elbow.*

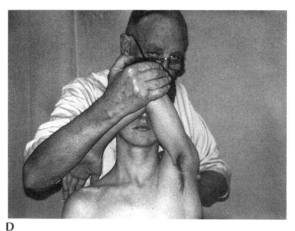
D

place. This variant may be used down to the midthoracic region and is particularly useful in the upper thoracic spine in patients who have additional dysfunctions in the cervical region that make it undesirable to use the neck as a lever.

When there is difficulty in lateral translation of the upper thoracic region, another technique may be useful. The operator places his or her foot on the tabletop, with the thigh beside the patient's chest and on the side toward which the patient is to be translated. If the patient's arm is placed over the operator's thigh, the operator has an extra means of controlling the patient's lateral translational movement by moving the thigh to one side or the other, as required (Figure 9-2).

1.2 Described for T3 That Is Flexed, Rotated, and Side Bent to the Right in Relation to T4 (FRSrt)
This is a non-neutral dysfunction with restriction for extension and for rotation and side bending to the left

between T3 and T4. The left facet between T3 and T4 does not close completely.

> **Diagnostic Points**
> There is tissue texture change at the segment. The right TP of T3 is more posterior to the left TP in extension when compared to the TPs of the level below (T4). The TPs of both T3 and T4 appear level in flexion. There may be some prominence of the right TP of T3 in the neutral position if there is a major restriction that encroaches on the neutral zone. If motion testing with lateral translation in the seated position, the spinous process of T4 feels restricted for translation from left to right but not from right to left when the spine is extended (see Figure 5-11).

1.2.1. The patient sits on a table or stool, and the operator stands behind the patient.

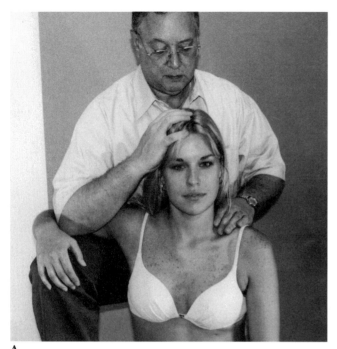 

A   B

FIGURE 9-2

(A) Position that can be used to treat dysfunctions in the upper thoracic spine. The operator's right leg supports patient's right arm. The operator's right hand supports and resists the patient's head, while the left hand is used to palpate. (B) Patient translated from left to right by the operator moving his or her right leg to the right and holding the patient's head in place. This position is also used to treat a neutral dysfunction in the upper thoracic spine that is rotated left and side bent right.

1.2.2. The operator's left hand is placed over the shawl area of the patient's left shoulder, placing the left thumb to the left side of the base of the spinous process of T3 (Figure 9-3A). The left thumb is positioned not only to monitor the motion of T3, but also to monitor the motion of the interspinous space between T3 and T4. Using the right hand and forearm, the operator controls the patient's head (Figure 9-3B). The operator's right elbow can also be placed in front of the patient's right shoulder to help with stabilizing and localization. At the same time, the operator's right hip can be placed against the patient's back to help reinforce extension from below.

1.2.3. By asking the patient to push his or her abdomen forward and bring the chin back, T3 is translated posteriorly to reach the barrier in extension from above and below. This movement should be monitored by the operator's left thumb. The cervical joints are protected by the operator's right forearm (see Figure 9-1C). For an alternative position that does not put as much stress through the neck, the technique that uses the patient's elevated elbow can be used, as described in Section 1.1 and Figure 9-1D.

1.2.4. By pressure through the left hand caudad and to the right, and by side bending the patient's head to the left with the right hand, the operator introduces left side bend-

ing of T3 to its barrier from above and below. Both of these movements must be monitored by the operator's left thumb and stopped as soon as tension begins to reach the area.

1.2.5. Left rotation is introduced by the operator turning the patient's head to the left. This rotation can be used to fine tune the position and to take up all remaining free motion to the barrier. Because extension and left side bending were introduced first to their barriers, there should be very little remaining available motion for rotation.

T.1.2.6. Thrust variant. The thrust is given by a high-velocity, low-amplitude movement of the operator's left hand, caudad and to the right, and mainly over the shawl area with the web of the hand. The thrust can also be given by the operator's thumb moving from left to right at the base of the spinous process of T3, or as close to the base as possible (see Figure 9-3B). By having the thumb contact at the base of the spinous process of T3, and by directing the movement of the spinous process of T3 caudad and to the right, left rotation and extension are introduced against the restrictive barrier. To have enough power for the movement to be controlled easily, the operator's left forearm should be in line with the direction of the thrust. As with all thrust techniques, the force is applied at the end of the patient's full exhalation, while the operator maintains the localization to the beginning of the barrier. This technique may require slight additional extension, side bending, and rotation by following the tissue tension as the patient relaxes with exhalation.

M.1.2.6a. Muscle energy variant. The patient is asked to attempt to push his or her head to the right gently, and the operator resists with an equal and opposite force. A flexion effort could be used instead and may be valuable if the response to side bending is inadequate. A rotational effort on the part of the patient is best avoided, because it will be more difficult to control.

M.1.2.6b. After maintaining the effort for 3–5 seconds, the patient is asked to relax. When relaxation is complete, the operator takes the patient's head and upper thoracic spine position to the new barrier in all three planes, and steps M.1.2.6a and M.1.2.6b are repeated two or more times.

1.2.7. Retest.

Thrust or Muscle Energy Techniques for ERS Dysfunctions in the Upper Thoracic Spine, C7-T5

1.3 Described for T3 That Is Extended, Rotated, and Side Bent to the Right in Relation to T4 (ERSrt)

This is a non-neutral dysfunction with restriction for flexion and for rotation and side bending to the left between T3 and T4. The right facet between T3 and T4 does not open completely.

Diagnostic Points
There is tissue texture change at the segment. The right TP of T3 is more posterior to the left TP in flexion when compared to the TPs of the level below (T4). The TPs of both T3 and T4 appear level in extension. There may be some prominence of the right TP of T3 in the neutral position if there is a major restriction that encroaches on the neutral zone. If motion testing with lateral translation in the seated position, the spinous process of T3 feels restricted for translation from left to right but not from right to left when the spine is flexed (see Figure 5-11).

1.3.1. The patient sits on a table or stool, and the operator stands behind the patient.

1.3.2. The operator's left hand is placed over the shawl area of the patient's left shoulder. The operator uses the left thumb (as monitor) to the left side of the spinous process of T3 and the interspinous space of T3-4. The operator's right hand is used to control the patient's head (Figure 9-4).

1.3.3. The flexion barrier is obtained by helping the patient translate T3 backward through flexion and

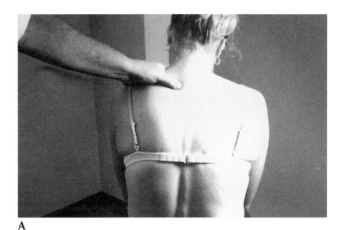

A

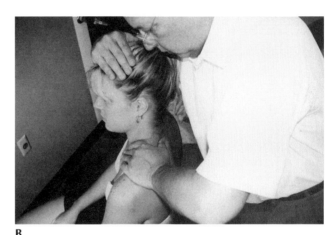

B

FIGURE 9-3
Treatment for an FRSrt dysfunction in the upper thoracic spine, using muscle energy or thrust techniques. (A) Placement of thumb. (B) Monitor and side bend by translation. Note position for thrust with the operator's forearm in line with the thumb.

slight compression of the head, while the operator maintains extension of the thoracic spine from below with the left hand. It is necessary for the patient to maintain a lumbar lordosis to establish an apex for flexion at T3-4. If this apex is not achieved, the tendency is for the patient to slump and create an apex for flexion in the midthoracic spine, resulting in a loss of localization. Further localization can be achieved by forward bending the patient's neck, until the tension just reaches the upper border of T3 from above, as monitored by the operator's left thumb. The flexion barrier should be close to the position at which the TPs of T3 first became asymmetrical with flexion of the neck from the extended position.

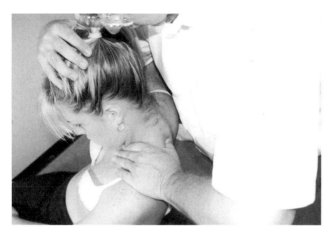

FIGURE 9-4
Treatment for an ERSrt dysfunction in the upper thoracic spine, using muscle energy or thrust techniques. Monitor and side bend by translation. Note position for thrust with the operator's forearm in line with the thumb.

1.3.4. By pressure with the left hand caudad and to the right, and by side bending the patient's head to the left with the right hand, the operator introduces translation of T3 to the right, inducing left side bending to its barrier from above and below. Both of these movements must be monitored by the operator's left thumb and stopped as soon as tension begins to reach the area.

1.3.5. Left rotation is introduced by the operator turning the patient's head to the left. This rotation can be used to fine tune the position and to remove all remaining available free motion to the barrier.

T.1.3.6. Thrust variant. The thrust is given by a high-velocity, low-amplitude movement of the operator's left hand on the shawl area, increasing both the left side bending and the flexion of T3 with the right hand and translating the spinous process of T3 to the right with the left thumb (see Figure 9-4). To have enough power for the movement to be easy to control, the operator's left forearm should be in line with the direction of the thrust. As with all thrust techniques, the force is applied at the end of the patient's full exhalation, while the operator maintains the localization to the beginning of the barrier. This technique may require slight additional flexion, side bending, and rotation by following the tissue tension as the patient relaxes with exhalation.

M.1.3.6a. Muscle energy variant. The patient is asked to attempt to push his or her head to the right gently, and the operator resists with an equal and opposite force. An extension effort could be used instead and may be valuable if the response to side bending is inadequate. A rotational effort from the patient is best avoided, because it is more difficult to control.

M.1.3.6b. After maintaining the effort for 3–5 seconds, the patient is asked to relax. When relaxation is complete, the operator takes the patient's head and upper thoracic spine position to the new barrier in all three planes, and then steps M.1.3.6a and M.1.3.6b are repeated two or more times.

1.3.7. Retest.

Note: Alternative positions are useful for the muscle energy technique, but they cannot be converted to a thrust technique. It is best if the operator stands on the patient's left side, where left-to-right translation can be introduced by applying pressure on the patient's left shoulder with the operator's chest. This position also provides additional support of the patient's trunk. By placing the left hand over the top of the patient's head (just above his or her right ear), or by wrapping the left forearm and hand around the patient's forehead like a turban, the barrier to flexion, left side bending, and left rotation can be controlled by the operator's left hand and monitored with the right hand over the dysfunctional segment (Figure 9-5). Typically, in this example, the operator's right middle finger either palpates the right TP of T3 or the interspinous space at T3-4. The patient's effort for right side bending can be opposed by the operator's left hand, and the new barriers can be introduced after relaxation.

Thrust or Muscle Energy Technique for a Neutral Group Dysfunction

1.4 Described for a Neutral Group Dysfunction That Is Rotated to the Left and Side Bent Right (NRlt)

There is a restriction of right rotation and left side bending from T2-4.

> **Diagnostic Points**
>
> There is tissue texture change at the group. In the neutral position, the TPs of T2-4 are all rotated to the left. The most posterior TP is that of T3 on the left. In both flexion and extension, the rotation remains but may vary in degree. T2-4 appear most rotated in the neutral position.

1.4.1. The patient sits on a table or stool, and the operator stands behind the patient.

1.4.2. The operator's left hand is placed over the shawl area of the patient's left shoulder. The left thumb is used (as monitor) between the TPs of T3 and T4, with pressure anteriorly but *not* against the spinous process. The operator's right arm is used to control the patient's head and neck, and the operator's right knee is placed under the patient's right arm (see Figure 9-2A).

1.4.3. Because this is a neutral dysfunction, localization occurs by monitoring the interspinous space at the apex of the group with the left thumb and by introducing flexion and extension with the operator's right hand to find the neutral zone for the apex of the group. The operator's right leg and knee help the patient maintain this posture.

1.4.4. While monitoring at T3 with the left thumb and holding the patient's head with the right arm and hand, left-to-right translation can be accomplished when the operator moves the right knee to the right, until left side-bending tension is felt at T3 (see Figure 9-2*B*). This technique can also be used for treatment of the non-neutral dysfunctions, but it is particularly helpful here, because supporting the patient's right arm reduces the tension in the restricting, long, side-bending muscles to the right of T2-4. There is no need to add right rotation, because rotation is automatically coupled to left side bending when the spine is in neutral.

T.1.4.5. Thrust variant. A high-velocity, low-amplitude movement anteriorly and to the right by the operator's left thumb restores the left side bend. The operator's left forearm should be in line with the thrust.

M.1.4.5.a. Muscle energy variant. The patient is asked to attempt to push his or her head to the right gently, and the operator resists with an equal and opposite force. Extension or flexion efforts are not appropriate for this dysfunction.

M.1.4.5.b. After maintaining the effort for 3–5 seconds, the patient is asked to relax. When relaxation is complete, the operator positions the patient's head and thoracic spine to the new left side-bending barrier with left-to-right translation by moving the right leg further to the right. The rotation to the right follows automatically if the spine is maintained within the neutral zone.

1.4.6. Steps M.1.4.5.a and M.1.4.5.b are repeated two or more times.

1.4.7. Retest.

Note: When treating neutral dysfunctions, the point at which to monitor and to apply any external force is a little below the apex of the group. This is because the upper vertebra is less rotated than the middle one and does not usually require individual attention. When there are an even number of vertebrae in the group, the monitoring point is between the TPs of the middle two vertebrae of the group.

Alternative Seated Muscle Energy Technique for T5-7

1.5 Described for the Non-Neutral Dysfunctions ERSrt or FRSrt and the Neutral Dysfunctions NRlt (Rotated Left and Side Bent Right)

Occasionally, it is difficult to obtain the proper localization and muscle energy effort for dysfunctions that affect the T5-7 area within the thoracic spine. Localiza-

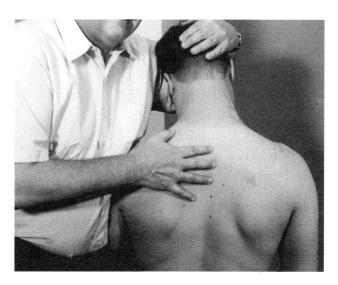

FIGURE 9-5
Alternative "turban" head-hold for an ERSrt dysfunction in the upper thoracic spine.

tion from above through the head and cervical spine does not quite reach these vertebrae; the techniques described in Section 1.1 are also limited, because the dysfunctional vertebrae are too high up. In such situations, a modification of the muscle energy technique may prove quite useful.

In each of these examples, the restricting muscles are on the right side, as described in the structural diagnoses. These are the muscles that must be lengthened during the postisometric contraction or relaxation period. The ERS dysfunctions are modified in that the positioning is from extension into flexion, whereas the FRS treatment requires positioning from flexion into extension. Both treatments use translation from above and below. The neutral dysfunction is treated in the neutral position.

1.5.1. The patient sits on a table or stool, and the operator stands behind the patient.

1.5.2. The operator's right foot is placed on the stool or tabletop, and the patient's right arm is draped over the operator's right thigh. If the patient's hand and upper extremity quickly feel numb and tingly, this numbness can interfere with the treatment. The arm position can be modified by resting the patient's entire arm and hand on the operator's leg (Figure 9-6*A*).

1.5.3. The operator translates the patient to either the flexion barrier while asking the patient to slump (Figure 9-6*B*) or the extension barrier while asking the patient to sit up tall (Figure 9-6*C*). For the neutral group dysfunction, the neutral range is found by having the patient both slump and sit up tall and is assisted by the operator's knee controlling the translation by moving it back-

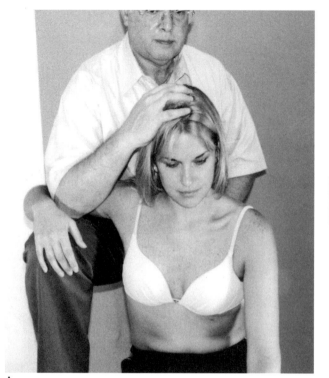

A

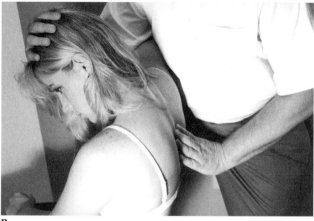

B

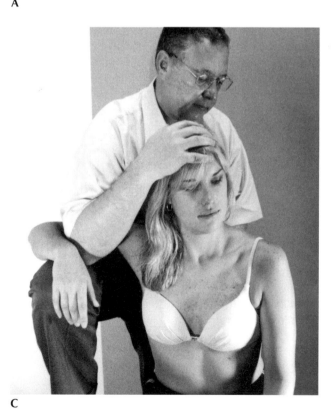

C

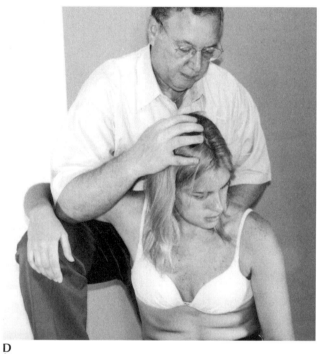

D

FIGURE 9-6
(A) Alternative technique for treating non-neutral dysfunctions in the transitional zone between upper and lower thoracic regions. The treatment is shown for right-sided dysfunctions. *(B)* Creating an apex for flexion at the dysfunctional segment. *(C)* Creating an apex for extension at the dysfunctional segment. *(D)* Treatment for an ERSrt dysfunction. *(E)* Treatment for an FRSrt dysfunction. After an isometric muscle contraction by the patient pushing his or her right arm down over operator's right leg, the operator repositions the patient to the next barrier.

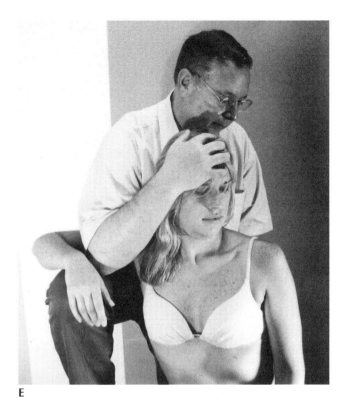

E

A

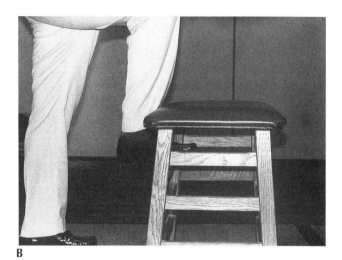

B

FIGURE 9-7
(A) "Ladder" stool. (B) Possible foot placement on stool.

ward or forward appropriately. Monitoring for the flexion or extension barrier at the appropriate level is done with the operator's left hand (see Figure 9-6B).

1.5.4. The operator introduces left side bending via translation to the right by moving his or her right knee laterally away from the patient, while monitoring for the side-bending barrier with the left hand. Rotation to the left is accomplished by rotating the patient's head left, using the operator's right hand and forearm, which are placed alongside the patient's head (Figure 9-6D and E). In the neutral dysfunction, rotation to the right occurs automatically with the introduction of left side bending and does not need to be introduced by the operator (see Figure 9-2B).

1.5.5. At the barrier, the patient is asked to push down on the operator's right thigh for 3–5 seconds using his or her right arm to contract the right side-bending muscles.

1.5.6. After complete relaxation, the new barrier is engaged, and steps 1.5.4 and 1.5.5 are repeated two or more times.

1.5.7. Retest.

"Knee-in-Back" Alternative Seated Thrust Techniques for the Lower Thoracic Spine

Knee-in-back techniques are applicable to the lower two-thirds of the thoracic spine. Except for the neutral

dysfunctions, these techniques are described with the knee supporting and stabilizing the lower member of the motion segment being treated. There are variants in which the upper vertebra is contacted by the knee, which then becomes the thrusting agent, but when this variant is performed, the lower vertebra is not as well stabilized.

The position of the knee requires careful adjustment. The "ladder" stool (Figure 9-7A) is useful for this purpose because of the bars at various heights (Figure 9-7B). Without such a stool, the required position often can be obtained by using whatever support is available and, if necessary, having the leg tilted to one side to adjust the height of the knee.

1.6 Described for T6 That Is Flexed, Rotated, and Side Bent to the Left in Relation to T7 (FRSlt)

This is a non-neutral dysfunction with a restriction for extension and for rotation and side bending to the right between T6 and T7. The right facet joint between T6 and T7 does not close completely.

Diagnostic Points

There is tissue texture change at the segment. The left TP of T6 is more posterior to the right TP in extension when compared to the TPs of the level below (T7). The TPs of both T6 and T7 appear level in flexion. There may be some prominence of the left TP of T6 in the neutral position if there is a major restriction that encroaches on the neutral zone. If motion testing with lateral translation in the seated position, the spinous process of T7 feels restricted for translation from right to left but not from left to right when the spine is extended (see Figure 5-11).

1.6.1. The patient sits on a table or stool with hands clasped behind the neck.

1.6.2. The operator stands behind the patient and places his or her right foot on the tabletop or on a support of suitable height, placing the knee against the patient's right TP of T7 (the lower vertebra).

1.6.3. The operator threads his or her right hand through the patient's right axilla and grasps the patient's right wrist (Figure 9-8).

1.6.4. Monitoring at T6 with the left hand, the operator introduces posterior to anterior translation with the right knee, increasing pressure anteriorly from the knee and extending the patient's spine from below up while using the right arm under the patient's right axilla to lift the patient and provide extension of

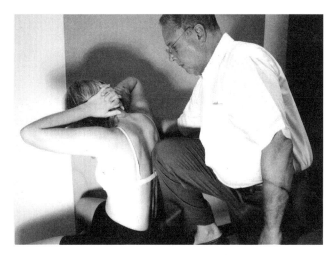

FIGURE 9-8
Knee-in-back treatment for an FRSlt dysfunction, using thrust only. Knee in position with operator's right hand gripping patient's right wrist.

the trunk from above down. By moving the knee from right to left, lateral translation is guided by the operator from right to left, introducing right side bending to the barrier. The right rotation is added by bringing the patient's right shoulder backward until the right rotation reaches T6 from above down. In this fashion, all of the forces are localized to T6 from above down and to T7 from below up.

1.6.5. The operator then grips the patient's other (left) wrist by threading the free (left) hand through the patient's other (left) axilla (Figure 9-9). Any remaining slack is taken out by adjustment of rotation. After complete exhalation, the thrust is given through the operator's arms by a high-velocity, low-amplitude movement that translates the patient's upper trunk backward and slightly craniad, while the operator maintains the side bend and the rotation.

1.6.6. Retest.

1.7 Described for T6 That Is Extended, Rotated, and Side Bent to the Left in Relation to T7 (ERSlt)

This is a non-neutral dysfunction with a restriction for flexion and for rotation and side bending to the right between T6 and T7. The left facet joint between T6 and T7 does not open completely.

Diagnostic Points

There is tissue texture change at the segment. The left TP of T6 is more posterior to the right TP in flexion when compared to the TPs of the level below (T7). The TPs of both T6 and T7 appear level in extension. There may be some prominence of the left TP of T6 in the neutral position if there is a major restriction that encroaches on the neutral zone. If motion testing with lateral translation in the seated position, the spinous process of T6 feels restricted for translation from right to left but not from left to right when the spine is flexed (see Figure 5-11).

1.7.1. The patient sits on a table or stool with hands clasped behind the neck.

1.7.2. The operator stands behind the patient and places the right foot on the tabletop or support of suitable height, placing the right knee against the patient's right TP of T7 (the lower vertebra).

1.7.3. The operator threads his or her right hand through the patient's right axilla and grasps the patient's right wrist (see Figure 9-8).

1.7.4. Monitoring at T6 with the left hand, the operator introduces anterior to posterior translation with the right knee, decreasing pressure anteriorly from the knee and flexing the patient's spine from below up while using the right arm under the patient's right axilla to lower the patient and provide flexion of the trunk from above down. By moving the knee from right to left, lateral translation is guided by the operator from right to left, introducing right side bending to the barrier. The right rotation is added by bringing the patient's right shoulder backward until the right rotation reaches T6 from above down. In this fashion, all of the forces are localized to T6 from above down and to T7 from below up.

1.7.5. The operator then grips the patient's other (left) wrist by threading the free (left) hand through the patient's other (left) axilla (see Figure 9-9). Any remaining slack is taken out by adjustment of rotation. After complete exhalation, the thrust is given by a high-velocity, low-amplitude movement that translates the patient's upper trunk craniad and posteriorly to produce flexion at T6-7, while the operator maintains the side bend and the rotation.

1.7.6. Retest.

1.8 Described for a Neutral Group Dysfunction That Is Rotated to the Right and Side Bent Left (NRrt)

There is a restriction of left rotation and right side bending from T6-8.

> ### Diagnostic Points
> There is tissue texture change at the group. In the neutral position, the TPs of T6-8 are all rotated to the right. The most posterior TP is that of T7 on the right. In both flexion and extension, the rotation remains. T6-8 appear most rotated in the neutral position.

1.8.1. The patient sits on a table or stool with hands clasped behind the neck.

1.8.2. The operator stands behind the patient and places the right foot on the tabletop or support of suitable height, placing the right knee just below the right TP of T7 (or just below the apex of the curve). See note after the technique described in Section 1.2.3.

1.8.3. The operator then threads the right hand through the patient's right axilla and grasps the patient's right wrist. At this point, the operator must see that the patient's spine is in neutral (in the sagittal plane).

1.8.4. Monitoring at T7 with the left hand, the operator introduces right side bending to the barrier by translation, moving the knee from right to left. Left rotation is then added to fine tune and localize the tension to T7.

1.8.5. The operator then grips the patient's other (left) wrist by threading the free (left) hand through the patient's other (left) axilla. Any remaining slack is taken

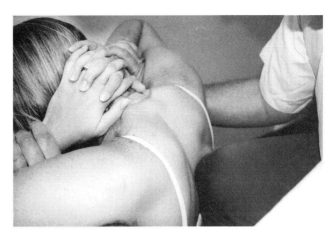

FIGURE 9-9
Knee-in-back treatment for an ERSlt dysfunction at T6.

out by adjustment of rotation. After complete exhalation, the thrust is given by a high-velocity, low-amplitude movement that translates the patient's upper trunk backward and slightly craniad, rotating the group to the left while maintaining the trunk at the right side-bending barrier (Figure 9-10).

1.8.6. Retest.

1.9 Described for a Bilaterally Extended T9 in Relation to T10 with a Restriction of Forward Bending or Flexion of T9

There is a bilateral and equally restricted loss of flexion at both facet joints. Both facet joints between T9 and T10 do not open completely.

> ### Diagnostic Points
> There is tissue texture change at T9. The TPs of T9 and T10 remain level in the neutral position and during flexion and extension. Passive mobility testing demonstrates little or no movement between T9-10 during flexion, and the interspinous space is often unusually narrow but should still be able to further narrow as the spinous processes approximate during hyperextension. If motion testing with lateral translation in the seated position, the spinous process of T9 feels restricted for translation from left to right and from right to left when the spine is flexed. Lateral translation to the right or left at T9 should not feel restricted when the spine is extended (see Figure 5-11).

1.9.1. The patient sits on a table or stool with hands clasped behind the neck.

1.9.2. The operator stands behind the patient and places his or her foot on the tabletop or a support of

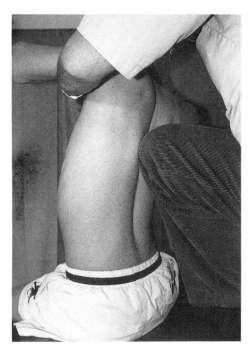

FIGURE 9-10
Knee-in-back treatment for an NRrt dysfunction.

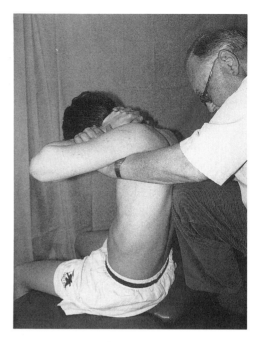

FIGURE 9-11
Knee-in-back treatment for bilateral restriction of flexion.

suitable height, placing the knee against the spinous process of T10 (the lower vertebra). If the spinous process is tender, a folded towel may be placed between the operator's knee and the spinous process.

1.9.3. The operator threads his or her hand through the patient's axilla on the same side and grasps the patient's wrist.

1.9.4. Monitoring at T9 with the other hand, the operator introduces flexion, beginning from the extended position. Flexion is introduced by posterior translation from above down and is controlled by the operator's knee pressing anteriorly on T10, while the patient is slumped to the flexion barrier at T9-10.

1.9.5. The operator grips the patient's other wrist by threading the free hand through the patient's other axilla. When all slack is taken out by additional flexion after full exhalation, the thrust is given by a high-velocity, low-amplitude movement of the operator's arms and is directed posteriorly and slightly craniad (Figure 9-11).

1.9.6. Retest.

1.10 Described for a Bilaterally Flexed T9 in Relation to T10 with a Restriction of Backward Bending or Extension of T9

There is a bilateral and equally restricted loss of extension at both facet joints. Both facet joints between T9 and T10 do not close completely.

> ### Diagnostic Points
> There is tissue texture change at T9. The TPs of T9 and T10 remain level in the neutral position and during flexion and extension. Passive mobility testing demonstrates little or no movement between T9-10 during extension and the interspinous space is often unusually wide, but it should still be able to further widen as the spinous processes move further apart during hyperflexion. If motion testing with lateral translation in the seated position, the spinous process of T10 feels restricted for translation from right to left and from left to right when the spine is extended. Lateral translation to the left or right at T10 should not feel restricted when the spine is flexed (see Figure 5-11).

1.10.1. The patient sits on a table or stool with hands clasped behind the neck.

1.10.2. The operator stands behind the patient and places his or her foot on the tabletop or a support of suitable height, placing the knee against the spinous process of T10 (the lower vertebra).

1.10.3. The operator threads his or her hand through the patient's axilla on the same side and grasps the patient's wrist.

1.10.4. Monitoring at T9 with the other hand and starting from full flexion, the operator introduces extension by forward translation of T10, which is controlled by increasing the anterior pressure from his or her knee (see Figure 9-8).

1.10.5. The operator grips the patient's other wrist by threading the free hand through the patient's other axilla. After full exhalation, and when all the slack is taken out by additional extension, the thrust is given by a high-velocity, low-amplitude movement that lifts and translates the patient's upper trunk posteriorly over the fulcrum of the operator's knee.

1.10.6. Retest.

2. THORACIC SUPINE TECHNIQUES

Thoracic supine techniques are all thrust techniques and are most easily used between T3 and T8. Above T3, localization becomes very difficult, and below T9-12 (and, in some patients, down to L2 or L3), the upper trunk needs to be flexed and lifted off the table. As with any of the techniques described, modifications may be required, depending on the relative sizes of the operator and the patient. When the patient is very large, these supine techniques are impossible, unless the operator is also very large. The supine technique can be slightly modified to correct certain rib dysfunctions associated with thoracic ERS dysfunctions.

Thrust Technique for FRS Dysfunctions in the Thoracic Spine

2.1 Described for T7 That Is Flexed, Rotated, and Side Bent to the Right in Relation to T8 (FRSrt)
This is a non-neutral dysfunction with a restriction for extension and for rotation and side bending to the left between T7 and T8. The left facet between T7 and T8 does not close completely. This technique is used from T6-8 or T9.

Diagnostic Points
There is tissue texture change at the segment. The right TP of T7 is more posterior to the left TP in extension when compared to the TPs of the level below (T8). The TPs of both T7 and T8 appear level in flexion. There may be some prominence of the right TP of T7 in the neutral position if there is a major restriction that encroaches on the neutral zone. If motion testing with lateral translation in the seated position, the spinous process of T8 feels restricted for translation from left to right but not from right to left when the spine is extended (see Figure 5-11).

Note: Ribs can be viewed as an extension of the TPs and, if the rib is otherwise normal (see Chapter 10), rib asym-

metry can be used to make a structural diagnosis of a non-neutral vertebral dysfunction in the thoracic spine. When the patient is seated, the anterior portions of both left and right ribs at the same level can be examined simultaneously from the front by palpating each rib at symmetrical sites near their costochondral junctions. If there is a non-neutral dysfunction in the thoracic spine that corresponds to the same level as the palpated ribs, there will be an observed rotation of both left and right ribs around a vertical axis in the appropriate direction when the thoracic spine is flexed and there is an ERS dysfunction or when the thoracic spine is extended and there is an FRS dysfunction.

The relative rotation of both left and right ribs at the same level is determined by comparing their positions to the ribs immediately below them. If, for example, there is an FRSrt at T7, both left and right seventh ribs will be symmetrical (not rotated) when the thoracic spine is fully flexed, but they will rotate to the right as the thoracic spine extends past the barrier to extension between T7 and T8. This rotation causes the seventh rib on the right to move posteriorly (away from the examiner) and the seventh rib on the left to move anteriorly (toward the examiner) in the same fashion as the position of the TPs are determined when the patient is examined from behind. There should be no rotation of the eighth ribs. If there is a major barrier for extension at T7, there will be a rotation of the seventh ribs to the right (e.g., right rib posterior and left rib anterior, right TP posterior and left TP anterior) when the patient is sitting in the neutral position. Similarly, rib rotation will occur at the same level as a thoracic ERS dysfunction when the thoracic spine is flexed. When non-neutral dysfunctions are present in the thoracic spine, the associated ribs will not move normally with inhalation or exhalation, or both (see Chapter 10).

2.1.1. The patient is supine, and the operator stands to the right (the side of the most posterior TP). The patient should cross arms (left over right) on the chest so that the left elbow is directly in front of the right and the hand is in the opposite axillae.

2.1.2. The operator uses the left hand to reach across and lift the patient's left shoulder so that the right hand can be inserted under the patient with the base of the thenar eminence in contact with the left TP of T8; the thumb points craniad, and the patient's spinous processes are in the hollow of the operator's hand. The operator's fingers support the right side of the patient's spine (Figure 9-12*A*). For those operators whose knuckle joints flex fully without pain, the fingers can be flexed (Figure 9-12*B*) to provide more support to the right side of the spine. If it is necessary, but painful, to use the fingers fully flexed, a small fold of material held in the bent knuckles can stabilize the position and prevent full flexion of the digits. The

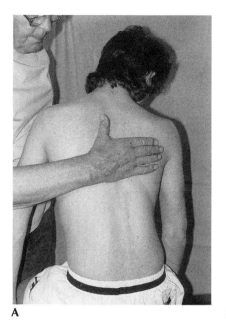
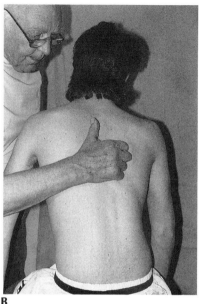

A   **B**

FIGURE 9-12
*Supine thrust treatment for an FRSrt dysfunction at T7. **(A)** Position adopted by right hand with fingers extended. **(B)** Position adopted by right hand with fingers flexed. **(C)** Placing the hand under the supine patient. **(D)** Thrust position using lower chest on elbows.*

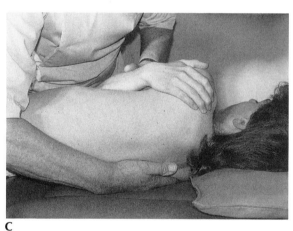
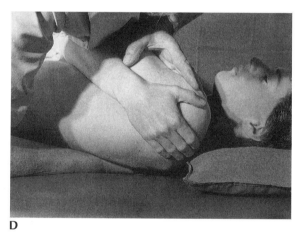

C   **D**

index finger of the operator's right hand should contact the right TP of T8.

2.1.3. The operator returns the patient to the supine position with the right hand in place underneath the patient (Figure 9-12*C*).

2.1.4. With the left hand over the patient's elbows, the operator introduces flexion until movement is just felt at T7. The operator then allows the patient to extend slowly, until the T7-8 joint is at the extension barrier.

2.1.5. The operator moves the patient to the left rotation and the left side-bending barrier through the patient's elbows and by using the right hand to translate the patient toward the operator. The operator also uses the right hand as a monitor so that the tension just reaches T7.

2.1.6. Bringing the chest or upper abdomen over the left hand, the operator instructs the patient to exhale fully,

applies increasing body weight across the patient's crossed elbows, and takes up the slack provided by the exhalation. The operator then delivers a high-velocity, low-amplitude thrust by dropping his or her weight on the patient's arms in the direction of T7 to extend T7 on T8, closing the left facet (Figure 9-12*D*). As with all thrust techniques, the patient's position at the barrier, along with the relaxation provided by full exhalation, may be enough to correct the dysfunction without the need for additional thrusting.

2.1.7. Retest.

Note: It may be awkward to side bend and rotate the patient away from the operator. An alternate position might be easier if the operator stands on the side opposite the posterior TP or on the side of the facet joint that does not close. For example, the operator stands

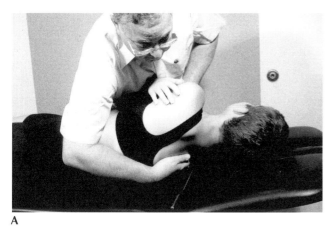

A

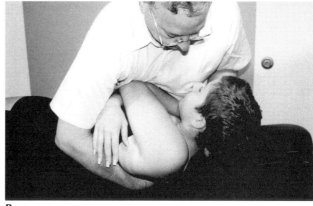

B

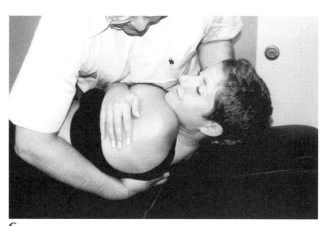

C

FIGURE 9-13
Thrusting technique for an upper thoracic spine FRSrt dysfunction with patient supine. (A) The operator's right hand is positioned under the transverse processes of the lower vertebra of the dysfunctional segment. (B) The operator holds the patient's head with the left hand and extends the neck from the flexed position, until tension reaches the upper vertebra of the dysfunctional segment. (C) The operator side bends and rotates the patient's head to the left until tension is localized to the dysfunctional segment. After the patient exhales, the operator takes up all slack to the barrier and gives the thrust.

on the patient's left side and reaches around with the left hand. In this circumstance, it is necessary for the operator to be able to fully flex the left index finger so that the second phalangeal bone can come into direct contact under the left TP of T8, while the thenar eminence lies under the right TP and the operator's thumb supports the right side of the patient's spine. Side bending and rotation to the left to the barrier may be easier, because the patient is brought toward, rather than away from, the operator. The extension barrier is reached in the same fashion as previously described, except that the operator uses the right hand. After full exhalation and taking up the slack from the relaxation, the thrust is still toward T7.

2.1a Described for T4 That Is Flexed, Rotated, and Side Bent to the Right in Relation to T5 (FRSrt)
This is a non-neutral dysfunction with a restriction for extension and for rotation and side bending to the left between T4 and T5. The left facet between T4 and T5 does not close completely. This technique is used from T3-5 or T6.

> **Diagnostic Points**
> There is tissue texture change at the segment. The right TP of T4 is more posterior to the left TP in extension when compared to the TPs of the level below (T5). The TPs of both T4 and T5 appear level in flexion. There may be some prominence of the right TP of T4 in the neutral position if there is a major restriction that encroaches on the neutral zone. If motion testing with lateral translation in the seated position, the spinous process of T5 feels restricted for translation from left to right but not from right to left when the spine is extended (see Figure 5-11).

The technique is the same as in Section 2.1, except that the operator localizes to the extension barrier by controlling the patient's head and neck. The operator places his or her right thenar eminence against the left TP of T5 and places the second phalanx of the index finger on the right TP of T5 (Figure 9-13A). Lifting the patient's head with the left hand accomplishes localization through the cervical spine by first flexing the neck and then extending the neck, until the tension increases at T4 (Figure 9-13B). Side

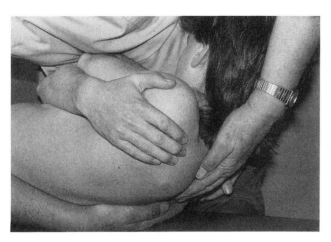

FIGURE 9-14
Supine thrust for an ERSlt dysfunction. Note position of the hand giving flexion.

bending and rotation to the left to the barrier are achieved by tilting the patient's head left, then rotating it left until tension is again felt at T4 (Figure 9-13*C*). The patient's arms are crossed as described in Section 2.1.1. The force is delivered in the direction of T4 extending T4 on T5 and closing the left facet.

Thrust Technique for ERS Dysfunction in the Thoracic Spine

2.2 Described for T7 That Is Extended, Rotated, and Side Bent to the Left in Relation to T8 (ERSlt)

This is a non-neutral dysfunction with a restriction for flexion and for rotation and side bending to the right between T7 and T8. The left facet between T7 and T8 does not open completely. This technique is used from T6-T8 or T9.

> *Diagnostic Points*
> There is tissue texture change at the segment. The left TP of T7 is more posterior to the right TP in flexion when compared to the TPs of the level below (T8). The TPs of both T7 and T8 appear level in extension. There may be some prominence of the left TP of T7 in the neutral position if there is a major restriction that encroaches on the neutral zone. If motion testing with lateral translation in the seated position, the spinous process of T7 feels restricted for translation from right to left but not from left to right when the spine is flexed (see Figure 5-11).

2.2.1. The patient is supine, and the operator stands to the right (opposite the most posterior TP). The patient should cross both arms over his or her chest so that the left elbow is directly in front of the right elbow, and the hands are in the opposite axillae.

2.2.2. The operator reaches across and lifts the patient's left shoulder with the left hand so that the right hand is inserted under the patient with the base of the thenar eminence in contact with the left TP of T8, the thumb is pointing craniad, and the patient's spinous processes are in the hollow of the operator's hand. The operator's fingers are used to support the right side of the patient's spine. For the alternative finger position, see Section 2.1.2.

2.2.3. After returning the patient to the supine position, the operator reaches down with the left hand under the upper thoracic vertebrae to support the patient's head and neck. The operator then flexes, rotates, and side bends the patient to the right (toward the operator), until movement just begins at T7 (Figure 9-14).

2.2.4. Bringing his or her chest or upper abdomen over the patient's elbows, the operator asks the patient for a full exhalation and, after taking up the slack provided by the associated relaxation, gives a high-velocity, low-amplitude thrust by dropping his or her weight onto the patient's elbows in the direction of T7 (i.e., in the direction of the operator's right hand), producing flexion of T7 on T8 and opening the left facet joint.

2.2.5. Retest.

2.2a Described for T4 That Is Extended, Rotated, and Side Bent to the Left in Relation to T5 (ERSlt)

This is a non-neutral dysfunction with a restriction for flexion and for rotation and side bending to the right between T4 and T5. The left facet between T4 and T5 does not open completely. This technique is used from T3-T5 or T6.

> *Diagnostic Points*
> There is tissue texture change at the segment. The left TP of T4 is more posterior to the right TP in flexion when compared to the TPs of the level below (T5). The TPs of both T4 and T5 appear level in extension. There may be some prominence of the left TP of T4 in the neutral position if there is a major restriction that encroaches on the neutral zone. If motion testing with lateral translation in the seated position, the spinous process of T4 feels restricted for translation from right to left but not from left to right when the spine is flexed (see Figure 5-11).

This technique is the same as described in Section 2.2, except that the operator localizes to the flexion barrier by controlling the patient's head and neck. The operator places his or her right thenar eminence against the left TP of T5 and the right index finger

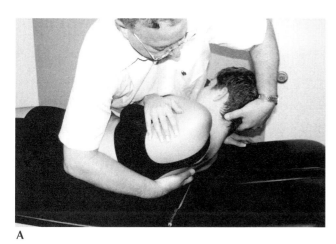

A

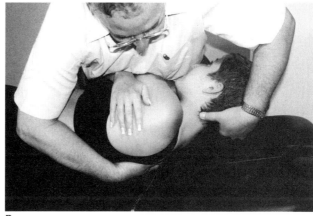

B

FIGURE 9-15
Thrusting technique for an upper thoracic spine ERSlt dysfunction with patient supine. (A) The operator's hand is placed to the left on the lower vertebra of the dysfunctional segment. (B) The operator supports the patient's head and flexes the neck, until tension reaches the upper vertebra of the dysfunctional segment. (C) The operator side bends and rotates the patient's head to the right, until tension is localized to the dysfunctional segment. After the patient exhales, the operator takes up all slack to the barrier and gives the thrust.

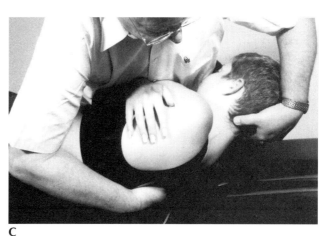

C

on the patient's right TP of T5 (Figure 9-15*A*). Localization to the barrier is accomplished through the cervical spine by lifting the patient's head with the operator's left hand, flexing the cervical spine until tension reaches T4 (Figure 9-15*B*). Side bending and rotation to the right to the barrier are done by tilting the patient's head right and rotating it right, until tension is felt at T4 (Figure 9-15*C*). The patient's arms are crossed as described in Section 2.2.1, and the force is delivered as described in Section 2.2.4. In this technique, the force is applied in the direction of T4, flexing T4 on T5 and opening the left facet.

Thrust Technique for Neutral Group Dysfunction in the Thoracic Spine

2.3 Described for a Neutral Group Dysfunction That Is Rotated to the Left and Side Bent Right (NRlt)
There is a restriction of right rotation and left side bending from T6-8.

> *Diagnostic Points*
> There is tissue texture change at the group. In the neutral position, the TPs of T6-8 are all rotated to the left. The most posterior TP is that of T7 on the left. In both flexion and extension, the rotation remains. T6-8 appear most rotated in the neutral position.

2.3.1. The patient is supine, and the operator stands to the opposite side from which the group is rotated. For example, the operator stands on the patient's right side. The patient crosses both arms over his or her chest with the left elbow anterior to the right and hands in the opposite axillae.

2.3.2. The operator lifts the patient's left shoulder with the left hand so that the right hand is inserted under the patient with the base of the thenar eminence just below the left TP of T7, the thumb points craniad, and the patient's spinous processes are in the hollow of the operator's hand. The operator's fingers are used to support the right side of the patient's spine. For an alternative finger position, see Section 2.1.2. See note after the technique described in Section 1.2.3.

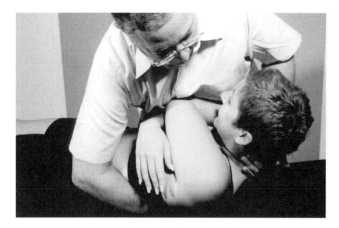

FIGURE 9-16
Thrusting technique for a lower NRlt dysfunction with patient supine. The operator's right hand is positioned on the left side of the spine, just below the most posterior transverse process at the apex of the neutral curve. While supporting the upper back and neck, the patient is side bent to the left to the lower thoracic side-bending barrier. The thrust is directed toward the operator's right hand.

2.3.3. After the patient is returned to the supine position, the operator leans over the patient with the chest or upper abdomen to bring the tension to the right thumb. With the left hand, the operator supports and lifts the patient's neck and upper thoracic spine, but not beyond the neutral range, and then side bends the upper trunk to the left down to T7 (Figure 9-16).

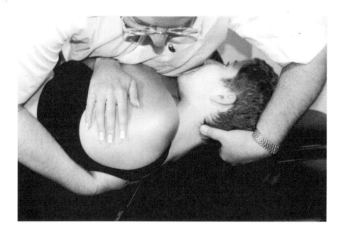

FIGURE 9-17
Thrusting technique for an upper NRlt dysfunction with patient supine. The operator's right hand is positioned on the left side of the spine, just below the most posterior transverse process at the apex of the neutral curve. The patient's head and neck are side bent to the left, until the thoracic side-bending barrier is palpated. The thrust is directed toward the operator's right hand.

2.3.4. After the patient is instructed to exhale completely, and after any additional slack for left side bending is taken up, the thrust is given by the operator by dropping his or her body weight onto the patient's elbows in the direction of the operator's right thenar eminence.
2.3.5. Retest.

2.3a Described for a Neutral Group Dysfunction That Is Rotated to the Left and Side Bent Right (NRlt)
There is a restriction of right rotation and left side bending from T3-5.

Diagnostic Points
There is tissue texture change at the group. In the neutral position, the TPs of T3-5 are all rotated to the left. The most posterior TP is that of T4 on the left. In both flexion and extension, the rotation remains. T3-5 appear most rotated in the neutral position.

This technique is the same as described in Section 2.3, except that the operator lifts the patient's head and accomplishes localization through the cervical spine with the left hand, placing the thenar eminence of the right hand just below the left TP of T4. Side bending to the left barrier is accomplished by tilting the patient's head to the left until tension is felt at T4 (Figure 9-17). The patient's arms are crossed as described in Section 2.3.1, and the force is delivered as described in Section 2.3.4.

Thrust Technique for a Bilateral Non-Neutral Dysfunction

2.4 Described for a Bilaterally Extended T9 in Relation to T10 with a Restriction of Forward Bending or Flexion of T9
There is a bilateral and equally restricted loss of flexion at both facet joints. Both facet joints between T9 and T10 do not open completely.

Diagnostic Points
There is tissue texture change at T9. The TPs of T9 and T10 remain level in the neutral position and during flexion and extension. Passive mobility testing demonstrates little or no movement between T9-10 during flexion, and the interspinous space is often unusually narrow but should still be able to further narrow as the spinous processes approximate during hyperextension. If motion testing with lateral translation in the seated position, the spinous process of T9 feels restricted for translation from the left to right and from the right to left when the spine is flexed. Lateral translation to the right or left at T9 should not feel restricted when the spine is extended (see Figure 5-11).

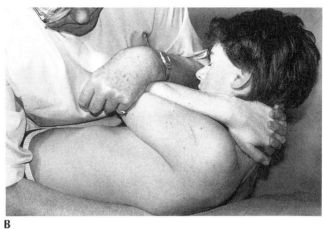

A   **B**

FIGURE 9-18

Supine thrust for bilateral restriction of flexion. (A) Position of hands at base of neck. (B) Thrust position with the operator's right hand under the patient, with the base of the thenar eminence in contact with the left TP of T10 and the fingers supporting the right TP of T10. The operator's left arm overlies the patient's flexed elbows.

2.4.1. The patient is supine, with fingers laced together at the base of the neck and elbows together in front (Figure 9-18*A*).

2.4.2. The operator stands at either side of the patient. If standing on the right side, the operator uses the left hand to lift the patient's left shoulder so that the right hand can be inserted under the patient and the base of the thenar eminence can be in contact with the left TP of T10. The operator's fingers support the right TP of T10, and the thumb points craniad. For an alternative finger position, see Section 2.1.2.

2.4.3. The patient is returned to the supine position with the operator's hand underneath.

2.4.4. The operator uses the left hand to flex the patient's trunk by pressing posteriorly and caudad on the patient's elbows, until the tension is brought down to T9.

2.4.5. When all slack is taken out after full exhalation, the high-velocity, low-amplitude thrust is given by the operator by leaning his or her chest (or upper abdomen) over the left hand on the patient's elbows and dropping his or her weight on the patient in the direction of T9 (Figure 9-18*B*).

2.4.6. For treatment of the upper thoracic joints, the arm position described in Sections 2.1.1, 2.2.1, and 2.3.1 may be easier. In such treatment, the operator's left hand lifts the patient's head and upper trunk to reach the barrier. After full exhalation, the thrust is given as the operator's chest is placed directly against the patient's elbows; a folded towel

or a small cushion may be placed over the elbows for the operator's comfort. For bilateral restrictions between T3 and T5 (and sometimes T6), localization is accomplished by lifting the patient's head and flexing the cervical spine.

2.4.7. Retest.

2.5 Described for a Bilaterally Flexed T9 in Relation to T10 with a Restriction of Backward Bending or Extension of T9

There is a bilateral and equally restricted loss of extension at both facet joints. Both facet joints between T9 and T10 do not close completely.

Diagnostic Points

There is tissue texture change at T9. The TPs of T9 and T10 remain level in the neutral position and during flexion and extension. Passive mobility testing demonstrates little or no movement between T9-10 during extension, and the interspinous space is often unusually wide but should still be able to further widen as the spinous processes move further apart during hyperflexion. If motion testing with lateral translation in the seated position, the spinous process of T10 feels restricted for translation from left to right and right to left when the spine is extended. Lateral translation to the right or left at T10 should not feel restricted when the spine is flexed (see Figure 5-11).

FIGURE 9-19
Supine thrust for bilateral restriction of extension.

2.5.1. The patient is supine, with fingers laced together at the base of the neck and elbows together in front.

2.5.2. The operator stands at either side of the patient. If the operator stands on the right side, the left hand is used to lift the patient's left shoulder so that the operator can insert the right hand under the patient with the base of the thenar eminence in contact with the left TP of T10. The operator's fingers support the right TP of T10, while the thumb points craniad. For an alternative finger position, see Section 2.1.2.

2.5.3. The patient is returned to the supine position with the operator's hand underneath.

2.5.4. The operator uses the left hand to flex the patient down to T9 by pressing posteriorly on the patient's elbows, until tension is brought down toT9. Then, the patient is allowed to extend so that T9 is extended on T10 (Figure 9-19).

2.5.5. When all slack is taken out after a full exhalation, the high-velocity, low-amplitude thrust is given by the operator by leaning his or her chest (or upper abdomen) over the left hand on the patient's elbows and dropping his or her weight on the patient in the direction of T9.

2.5.6. For treatment of the upper thoracic joints, the arm position described in Sections 2.1.1, 2.2.1, and 2.3.1 may be easier. In such treatment, flexion is introduced by pressure of the operator's chest on the patient's elbows, until the tension reaches the vertebra to be moved. Then, the patient is allowed to extend by a slight reverse movement, until that vertebra is extended on the one below. After full exhalation, the thrust is given by the operator's chest against the patient's elbows in the direction of the upper vertebra, or even the next (higher) vertebra. For bilateral restrictions between T3 and T5 (and sometimes T6), localization is achieved by lifting the patient's head, flexing the cervical

spine, and extending the thoracic spine over the fulcrum created by the operator's hand on the inferior segment.

2.5.7. Retest.

3. THORACIC PRONE TECHNIQUES

Thoracic prone techniques are used for FRS dysfunctions, and in the upper joints, there is a technique for neutral dysfunctions. All of these prone techniques described use thrusting force only, but they can be modified and used as articulatory techniques.

Crossed Pisiform Techniques for FRS Dysfunctions

The crossed pisiform technique is powerful, but it is only useful for restrictions of extension (FRS), primarily between T4 and T10. This technique must be done correctly and accurately, because a repeated force applied to the posterior aspect of the ribs can result in an anterior subluxation of the rib.

3.1 Described for T7 That Is Flexed, Rotated, and Side Bent to the Right in Relation to T8 (FRSrt)
This is a non-neutral dysfunction with a restriction for extension and for rotation and side bending to the left between T7 and T8. The left facet joint between T7 and T8 does not close completely.

> *Diagnostic Points*
> There is tissue texture change at the segment. The right TP of T7 is more posterior to the left TP in extension when compared to the TPs of the level below (T8). The TPs of both T7 and T8 appear level in flexion. There may be some prominence of the right TP of T7 in the neutral position if there is a major restriction that encroaches on the neutral zone. If motion testing with lateral translation in the seated position, the spinous process of T8 feels restricted for translation from left to right but not from right to left when the spine is extended (see Figure 5-11).

3.1.1. The patient is prone, with his or her head turned to the left.

3.1.2. The operator stands on the left side of the patient and puts the left pisiform in contact with the superior aspect of the patient's left TP of T7 (Figure 9-20A). It is important that the contact is on the TP and not on the rib.

3.1.3. Using the right pisiform, the operator contacts the posterior aspect of the patient's right TP of T7 (Figure 9-20B). Again, the rib must be avoided.

3.1.4. The slack is taken out by a combination of full exhalation, caudad pressure with the left pisiform on the patient's left TP, and anterior pressure by the right pisiform on the patient's right TP. At the end of exhalation, the high-velocity, low-amplitude thrust is given, introducing left rotation and left side bending. Because this is a short lever technique with contact on the TPs on either side, the distance to be traveled by the force is very small, so the "low amplitude" part of the instruction is important.

3.1.5. Retest.

Prone Thrust Techniques
for the Upper Thoracic Spine, T1-T5

3.2 Described for T3 That Is Flexed, Rotated, and Side Bent to the Left in Relation to T4 (FRSlt)

This is a non-neutral dysfunction with a restriction for extension and for rotation and side bending to the right between T3 and T4. The right facet joint between T3 and T4 does not close completely.

Diagnostic Points

There is tissue texture change at the segment. The left TP of T3 is more posterior to the left TP in extension when compared to the TPs of the level below. The TPs of both T3 and T4 appear level in flexion. There may be some prominence of the right TP of T3 in the neutral position if there is a major restriction that encroaches on the neutral zone. If motion testing with lateral translation in the seated position, the spinous process of T4 feels restricted for translation from right to left but not from left to right when the spine is extended (see Figure 5-11).

3.2.1. The patient is prone, and the operator stands a little to the patient's right at the head of the table.

3.2.2. The operator lifts the patient's head and moves the patient's chin to the right. At the same time, the operator rotates the patient's head to face right, allowing it to rest on the left side of the chin (Figure 9-21*A*).

3.2.3. With the pisiform of the left hand, the operator contacts the posterior surface of the right TP of T4 and takes up the slack by pressing anteriorly.

3.2.4. The operator's right hand fine tunes and maintains the right side bending and right rotation of the patient's head.

3.2.5. After full exhalation, the high-velocity, low-amplitude thrust is given by the left hand in an anterior direction. This thrust produces extension and left rotation of T4 under T3, thereby producing relative right rotation of T3 and facet closure on the right at T3-4 (Figure 9-21*B*). It would be possible to use the left-hand contact on the left TP to rotate T3 directly, but then there would be no way to block rotation of T4. The operator should never thrust through the head and neck with this technique.

3.2.6. Retest.

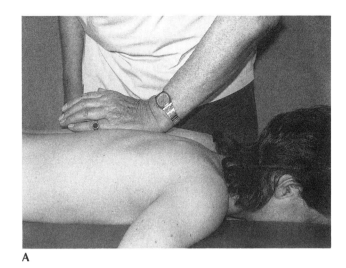

A

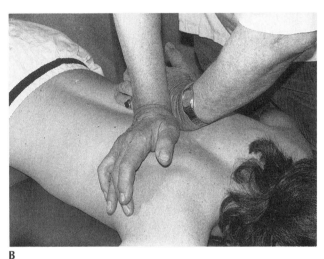

B

FIGURE 9-20
*Crossed pisiform thrust with the patient prone. (**A**) Left pisiform contacts the superior surface of left transverse process (TP) of T7. (**B**) Right pisiform on the posterior aspect of the right TP of T7.*

3.3 Described for Neutral Group Restrictions, T1-5

The following treatment is described for T3-5 with restriction of left rotation and right side bending, or NRrt (rotated right and side bent left).

Diagnostic Points

There is tissue texture change at the group. In the neutral position, the TPs of T3-5 are all rotated to the right. In flexion and extension, the rotation may change in degree, remaining maximal in the neutral position.

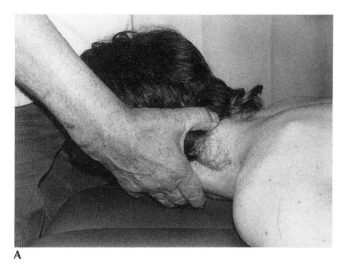

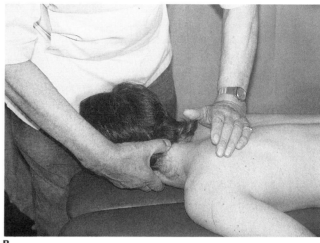

A   B

FIGURE 9-21
*Prone upper thoracic thrust for an FRSlt dysfunction at T3. (**A**) Chin and head position. (**B**) Thrust position.*

3.3.1. The patient is prone, with his or her head resting on the chin in the midline. The operator stands at the head of the table and controls the patient's head with the right hand (Figure 9-22*A*).

3.3.2. The operator places his or her left thumb on the right side of the patient's spine just below the apex (T4), pressing in the direction of the facet joint between T4 and T5.

3.3.3. Using the right hand to roll the patient's head on the chin and to the right, the operator introduces right side bending and left rotation, until the tension approaches the left thumb. If rolling the head does not bring the tension to the required level, the head should be lifted and side bent slightly to the right before putting the chin down and trying the rotation again (Figure 9-22*B*). Rotation is used in this technique to reduce the amount of side bending that might be needed to reach the barrier, according to the third rule of spinal mechanics.

3.3.4. When all slack has been taken out after full exhalation, the high-velocity, low-amplitude thrust is given by the operator's left thumb on the right TPs ventrally and to the left, while the position of the head is slightly exaggerated to help increase the rotation and side bending.

3.3.5. Retest.

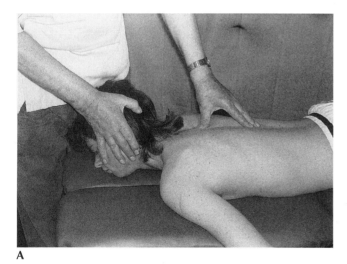

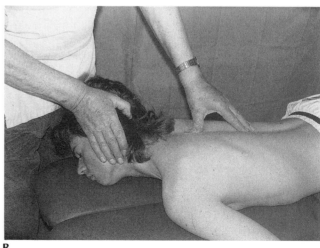

A   B

FIGURE 9-22
*Prone upper thoracic thrust for an NRrt dysfunction. (**A**) Chin and head position. (**B**) Position if more side bend is required for localization.*

10

Diagnosis and Treatment
of Dysfunctions of the Rib Cage

DESCRIPTION AND DIAGNOSIS

There are several dysfunctions to which ribs are subject. Many rib dysfunctions are associated with spinal zygapophyseal joint dysfunctions. For example, the typical ribs (i.e., ribs 2–9) articulate posteriorly at the costotransverse joint and at the costovertebral joint. These ribs have two demifacets at the costovertebral joint: One demifacet articulates with the vertebra at the same segmental spinal level, and the other articulates with a demifacet to the vertebra above. Subsequently, these ribs are influenced not only by rotation of the vertebra to which they are attached at the costotransverse joint, but also by rotation and dysfunction of the vertebra above through the costovertebral joint. For instance, the fifth rib is often influenced by dysfunction of T4, which occurs above at the T4-5 zygapophyseal joint and results in rotation or torsion of the rib. Therefore, these dysfunctions are referred to as *rib torsions.*

In addition to rib torsions, there are other rib dysfunctions that can occur independently of any disturbance of the thoracic spine. All of these dysfunctions also are accompanied by hypertonus in the intercostal muscles, are known as *structural ribs* or *structural rib dysfunctions,* and comprise a diverse group. These dysfunctions are important because they are often the cause of chest wall pain, which may be severe and may erroneously be mistaken for pain of cardiac origin. It is always comforting to know that chest wall pain of a nonmusculoskeletal origin has been fully evaluated before a musculoskeletal

evaluation. Often, because the pain from a structural rib dysfunction may be maximal at the costochondral junction, a previous diagnosis of costochondritis has been made. Certain types of structural rib dysfunctions are also a cause of shoulder pain and the so-called thoracic outlet syndrome.

For the rib torsions and some of the other structural rib dysfunctions, successful treatment of the associated spinal zygapophyseal joint dysfunction may allow the rib function to return to normal, and, if it does, treatment of the rib itself is unnecessary. For this reason, it is usually recommended to treat non-neutral thoracic joint dysfunctions before dysfunctions of the ribs.

The third and simpler type of rib dysfunctions consists of restrictions in excursion of the rib when tested with inhalation and exhalation. These dysfunctions are commonly known as *respiratory rib dysfunctions* or, simply, *respiratory ribs.* Respiratory rib dysfunctions are associated with hypertonus in the intercostal muscles above or below the rib, and, although the dysfunctions may not cause much pain if left untreated, the restriction of motion may contribute to recurrence of the spinal non-neutral dysfunction. For this reason, it is important to add to an operator's armamentarium techniques for treatment of these respiratory rib dysfunctions.

RESPIRATORY RIBS

Rib motion may be restricted during either inhalation or exhalation, and because the treatment for an inhalation or an exhalation restriction is different, it is important to distinguish between them. Inhalation restriction is common in the upper ribs on the right, whereas exhalation restriction is common in the lower ribs on the left.

Excerpts from this chapter have previously been published[1,2] in *The Journal of Orthopaedic Medicine,* and are included with minor modifications.

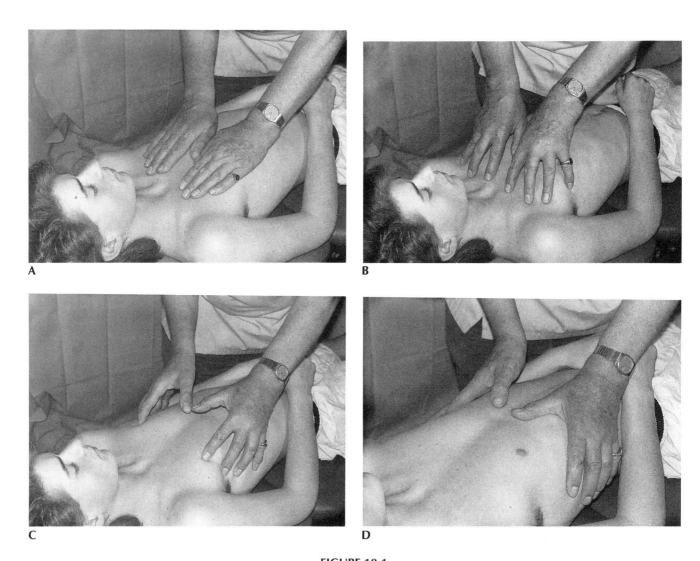

A   B

C   D

FIGURE 10-1
*Examination for restriction of respiratory motion. (**A**) Upper ribs, using flat hand. (**B**) Upper ribs, using fingertips. (**C**) Middle ribs. (**D**) Lower typical ribs.*

The diagnosis of a respiratory motion restriction of a rib is made by observing the range of the excursion of the ribs during forceful inhalation and exhalation. For this observation to be accurate, precautions must be taken, because the difference in excursion of the ribs between one side and the other may be quite small.

1. The operator must stand with his or her dominant eye over the midline of the patient. Inaccurate observations often are made if the operator is positioned to the side or attempts to visualize with the nondominant eye. Determination of the dominant eye is described in Chapter 3 (see Figure 3-3). For operators who have so little eye dominance that they

are unable to be certain with which eye they are looking, it is wise to close one eye and look with the open eye over the patient's midline. Determination of asymmetry of either inhalation or of exhalation is difficult by palpation alone.

2. The observations are made with both the eye and the hands. The eye should focus on the midline of the patient so that, with peripheral vision, the operator observes the rib movement on both sides at the same time. The hands should be placed symmetrically on the patient's chest, and, if possible, the operator should use either the flat hand or the tips of the fingers (Figure 10-1). The fingertips are sometimes more suitable for a male operator examining a female patient.

It is important that the hands make very light contact with the ribs. This light contact is necessary because firm contact tends to modify the rib movement and partly because the operator's proprioceptors are more sensitive if they are not overloaded by too much pressure. The point of palpation can be either the rib itself or the intercostal space. It is important that the same point is used on both sides of the rib cage and that the fingers are on symmetrical parts of the rib or intercostal space on the two sides. The contact must be such that the motion of the ribs can be followed without interference, and the examiner should find that he or she must move both arms in synchrony with the movement of the chest wall.

3. To identify a rib dysfunction, the question to be answered in evaluating rib motion is the following: On which side does the movement *stop* first? This is a much easier observation than that sometimes taught in medical schools, such as the observation of estimating which side moves furthest. It is also important to remember the possibility of hyperventilation from overbreathing and the discomfort caused by it. Hyperventilation can be avoided if, after finding out at which end of the respiratory range there appears to be a restriction, repeated examinations are limited to that end of the range. For example, if an inhalation restriction is suspected, the instruction should be "breathe out a little, and then breathe in as far as you can," rather than "breathe in and out deeply."

4. For descriptive purposes, normal rib motion can be divided into two types. These types are commonly referred to as *pump-handle* and *bucket-handle*. The terms refer to the rise and fall of the anterior end of the rib (pump-handle) and the rise and fall of the lateral part of the rib (bucket-handle). All ribs have some component of each type in their motion; the relative proportion varies from above down and is determined by the angle formed between the line joining the costovertebral and costotransverse joints with the coronal plane (see Figure 2-9*B*). The upper ribs have mainly a pump-handle motion and a very small bucket-handle component, whereas the lower ribs have mainly a bucket-handle motion and a very small pump-handle component. However, bucket-handle restrictions can be found at the first rib, and pump-handle restrictions sometimes are found in the lower ribs. It is less important to distinguish between pump- and bucket-handle motion restriction than to distinguish an inhalation from an exhalation restriction.

5. Although the proportion of sagittal plane to coronal plane motion for each rib is determined by the angle of an axis that transverses the costovertebral and costotransverse joints, the direction of the restriction in rib motion depends more on whether the intercostal muscle tightness is above or below the dysfunctional rib. Inter-costal muscle tightness above the rib holds the rib in an elevated position (inhalation) that restricts exhalation. Intercostal muscle tightness below the rib holds the rib in a depressed position (exhalation) that restricts inhalation. Both inhalation and exhalation restrictions have either a bucket-handle or pump-handle component that predominates, depending on whether the intercostal muscle tightness is found more medially (pump-handle) or more laterally (bucket-handle).

6. Some patients play wind instruments, sing, or are avid joggers and have taught themselves to emphasize diaphragmatic breathing. These patients are obviously difficult to examine because the chest wall excursions are minimal to absent. Still, if instructed to so, these patients may be able to voluntarily expand and contract the chest wall enough to determine whether there are rib restrictions present.

Diagnosis of Respiratory Dysfunctions of Ribs 1–10

To assess restriction of pump-handle motion, the hands need to be near the anterior end of the ribs; to assess bucket-handle motion, the hands should be placed further laterally on the rib shaft. The first rib presents some difficulty, because much of it is covered by the clavicle or by the brachial plexus and its associated vessels. The costal cartilage of the first rib can be felt immediately inferior to the medial end of the clavicle (see Figure 10-1*B*), but to assess bucket-handle motion, palpation must be in the anterior triangle of the neck, posterolateral to the neurovascular bundle.

First, the rib cage is examined to find out whether there is a group of restricted ribs. This examination is started in the front for the upper ribs, and the upper three or four ribs can be assessed together (see Figure 10-1*A*). Moving more laterally because of the increasing bucket-handle component of the motion, the next group down is tested (see Figure 10-1*C*). Then, with the hands near the midaxillary line, the lower rib motion is estimated (see Figure 10-1*D*). The rib cage down to R10 can normally be tested by using just three contact positions of the hands.

Respiratory rib restrictions tend to occur in groups, and when a restriction of inhalation or exhalation is found, it is important to discover the "key" rib. The key rib is the uppermost restricted rib in an inhalation restriction and the lowest restricted rib in an exhalation restriction. The importance of the key rib is that, partly for mechanical reasons and partly by neurophysiological reflex mechanisms, the key rib prevents its neighboring ribs either above or below from moving fully.

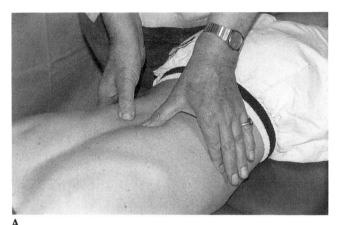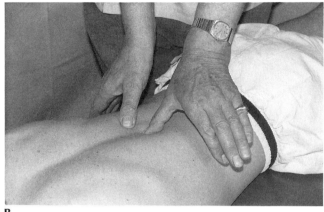

A   B

FIGURE 10-2
Examination for restriction of respiratory motion of ribs 11 and 12. **(A)** *Position in exhalation.* **(B)** *Position in inhalation.*

Sometimes, there is more than one key rib in a group, and partly for this reason, it is always wise to re-examine the area after treatment.

The key rib is found by testing the movement of individual paired ribs, starting at the top of the group for an inhalation restriction and at the lower end of the group for an exhalation restriction. The testing is done by palpation and observation, using the index or middle finger on each side to compare motion of a corresponding pair of ribs. Once a key rib is identified, the anterior ends and lateral aspects of that rib need to be examined to discern between a pump- or bucket-handle restriction. Structural rib dysfunctions also cause respiratory restrictions and can present as the key rib either for an inhalation or exhalation restriction, or both.

Diagnosis of Respiratory Dysfunctions of Ribs 11 and 12

Examination of the motion of the eleventh and twelfth ribs is performed with the patient prone. The movement characteristics of these ribs are different because they have no anterior attachment; their motion is usually described as a "caliper" type of movement. The examination is made by placing the thumbs symmetrically over the medial ends of the rib on each side and placing the index finger of the same hand on the shaft of the rib as far laterally as the rib can be felt. If the rib on one side is short, the finger on the other side should not be further from the midline than the finger on the short rib side (Figure 10-2).

The purpose of the examination is to assess the relative opening and closing of the caliper formed by the rib on each side at the same level. Failure of one side to close

properly indicates an exhalation restriction, whereas failure to open indicates an inhalation problem.

STRUCTURAL RIBS

There are several types of structural rib dysfunctions. They are as follows:

1. Subluxation, anterior, posterior, or superior
2. Torsion, external, or internal
3. Lateral flexion
4. Antero-posterior compression
5. Lateral compression

Structural rib dysfunctions are most frequently found after injury or in patients who have been subjected to major chest wall trauma, including surgery. In postsurgical patients, dysfunctions are often multiple and may be difficult to treat. Structural rib dysfunctions are the cause of the pain in most cases of "costochondritis," and manual treatment often removes the symptoms immediately. Structural rib dysfunctions in the upper four ribs are frequent causes of shoulder pain and adverse neural tension signs in the ipsilateral upper extremity.

In patients with chest wall pain, if there is no structural rib dysfunction, there is likely to be some other truly pathological cause. Of the possibilities, one of the most common is herpes zoster.

Diagnosis of structural rib dysfunctions depends on finding asymmetry of rib position and tissue texture changes at the rib angle and costochondral junction. There is often acute tenderness to palpation as well.

Remember, a rib with a structural rib dysfunction is often the key rib for a group of ribs with a respiratory restriction for inhalation or exhalation.

An important landmark used for diagnosing most of the structural rib dysfunctions is the rib angle. The rib angle is the most posterior part of the rib, and, being the point of insertion of the iliocostalis muscle, it is the place at which tissue texture changes may easily be palpable. In the upper ribs (ribs 2–5, particularly), the rib angle is usually concealed by the scapula; to palpate it, the shoulder must be protracted. It is usually enough to instruct the patient to cross his or her hands on the lap to expose the rib angles.

The line of the rib angles normally forms a smooth posterior convexity. The rib angles also become progressively more lateral when sighting and palpating from above down. This line might be best observed by standing in front of a seated patient who has slumped into a flexed posture with the shoulders protracted, sighting the posterior chest wall from above down. Any deviation from either curve is a cause for further examination. Observation and palpation of the ribs anteriorly help to confirm whether a rib's position has been altered. An alteration in a rib's position in the same direction found ipsilaterally both in front and in back suggests an anterior or posterior rib subluxation. However, if the anterior end of a rib is prominent, and the rib angle of the same rib is also prominent posteriorly, a lateral compression is likely. Similarly, if both the front and back of the same rib are depressed, suspect an antero-posterior compression.

Note: Normally, the ribs can be thought of as an extension of the transverse processes (TPs) to which they are attached. Therefore, a pair of ribs can also be palpated from the front or the back and be used to make a positional diagnosis of vertebral non-neutral dysfunctions. For example, with an ERSlt dysfunction at T4-5, the left fourth rib will be posterior in comparison to the right fourth rib when the patient is flexed, but the rib pair appears symmetrical when the spine is extended. With structural rib dysfunctions, flexion or extension of the spine does not influence the rib position, and the asymmetry persists. Thus, noting the response of the ribs to flexion and extension of the spine helps to differentiate true structural rib dysfunctions from ribs that appear asymmetrical secondary to non-neutral thoracic spinal dysfunctions.

Subluxations

Subluxations are true subluxations of the costovertebral and costotransverse joints, with the whole rib moving slightly anteriorly or posteriorly; in the case of the first rib, the posterior end moves superiorly.

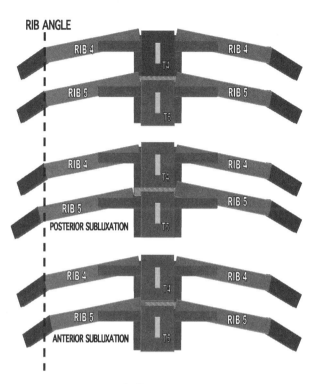

FIGURE 10-3

Diagram showing normal rib position, posterior view, and rib position for posterior subluxation with rib angle laterally displaced and for anterior subluxation with rib angle medially displaced.

Anterior Rib Subluxations

Anterior subluxations may be seen in patients who have had repeated treatment for thoracic joint problems by the crossed pisiform technique. Although, when performed correctly (i.e., with contact on the TPs only), the crossed pisiform technique is an excellent treatment for vertebral joints with restriction of extension (FRS). The crossed pisiform technique often is applied incorrectly with contact on the ribs, and if the ribs are repeatedly thrust forward, an anterior subluxation may result. Anterior rib subluxations can also be the consequence of any blow to the back or a backward fall in which the patient lands on a hard obstacle.

It is important to remember that these joints are hypermobile and should not be treated with a high-velocity thrust.

Diagnosis   The head of the rib slides forward on the vertebrae with which it articulates. Because of the direction of the line joining the costovertebral and costotransverse joints, the rib angle not only becomes less prominent posteriorly (out of line in the antero-posterior curve), but it also becomes more medial (out of line in the lateral curve) (Figure 10-3). The rib angle is usually tender and is the site of tissue texture changes in the ilio-costalis muscle.

When examined in front, the anterior end of the same rib is prominent and usually tender. The examination is best performed with the patient sitting. If the patient is supine, the other ribs may be pushed forward by contact with the table, making the asymmetry less easy to see. Similarly, if the patient is prone, the anterior rib may be pushed back enough to make it difficult to find.

Posterior Rib Subluxations

The posterior subluxation is a true subluxation. The joint is hypermobile, and thrusting manipulation is contraindicated. Posterior subluxations may be caused by a blow to the front of the chest, as in motor vehicle accidents, especially if the injury is associated with a shoulder harness or if the patient's chest strikes the steering wheel or dashboard. This subluxation often is found in patients who have had sternal splitting surgery.

Diagnosis In the posterior subluxation, the rib has moved laterally and posteriorly in relation to the vertebrae with which it articulates. The rib angle is more prominent posteriorly and more lateral than the angles of neighboring ribs (see Figure 10-3). There are tissue texture changes at the insertion of the iliocostalis and associated tenderness at the rib angle. Anteriorly, the costochondral junction is posterior to that of the neighboring ribs, but if the patient is supine, the rib may be pushed forward enough to make the position appear normal. Therefore, as with the anterior subluxed rib, the examination is best performed with the patient sitting. Tenderness at the anterior end of the rib (i.e., costochondral junction) is common.

First Rib Superior Subluxation

In the first rib only, the costotransverse joint may be subluxed superiorly by the pull of the scalene muscles. This dysfunction is often the result of a motor vehicle accident in which the patient's vehicle is struck from the side. This dysfunction also can occur as a consequence of any acute side-bending strain of the cervical spine. Symptomatically, patients with this dysfunction have severe shoulder pain on the side of the subluxation and numbness or paresthesias along the C8 nerve root, which lies directly on top of the rib. Patients obtain some relief by pulling the shoulder down with the opposite hand, and the diagnosis can be suspected when the patient is seen in this posture while seated in the waiting or examination room. These patients may have severe pain when trying to rotate the head in the direction of the superiorly subluxed rib. These patients are often diagnosed as having a thoracic outlet syndrome; some of these patients have already had their first ribs resected. Usually, there are associated spinal dysfunctions at either C7-T1 or T1-2. These spinal zyga-pophyseal joints should always be checked for non-neutral dysfunctions and treated first, if dysfunctional. Additional associated dysfunctions are common and involve the remaining cervical vertebrae, the sternoclavicular joint, and the second rib, which can be laterally flexed superiorly by the same injury. These dysfunctions, too, must be treated before attempting to treat the first rib. When the first rib is pulled up, its articular head may become "hitched" and lie on top of the superior aspect of the TP of T1. The rib, therefore, needs to be pushed forward (anteriorly) before the subluxation can be reduced.

Diagnosis The first rib position can be felt by the operator standing behind the seated patient. With one index finger on each side, the operator pulls the trapezius posteriorly to find the superior aspect of the rib in front of the main part of the muscle (Figure 10-4). In a first rib subluxation, the difference in height of the rib on the two sides is greater than 6 mm (1/4 in.). Examination for this dysfunction must be gentle because even in patients without this dysfunction, the posterior end of the rib is usually tender, and when subluxation is present, the tenderness may be severe. There are marked restrictions of respiratory excursions, especially exhalation, and if the patient is asked to forward flex the neck, the rib can often be felt to move forward immediately on the subluxed side. Lindgren, Manninen, and Rytkonen[3] have presented three-dimensional computed tomography (CT) scan findings that show a superior subluxation of the first rib at the costotransverse joint. They have also described a cervical rotation lateral flexion (CRLF) test to evaluate for a superiorly subluxated first rib. The test is performed by passively and maximally rotating the cervical spine away from the side being examined. Then, taking the cervical spine gently into flexion as far as possible, the operator moves the ear toward the chest. A restriction of this movement indicates a positive CRLF test. In Lindgren, Manninen, and Rytkonen's[3] study of patients with thoracic outlet syndrome, 12 of 13 patients who presented with a positive CRLF test also were shown to have subluxation of the first rib at the costotransverse joint by three-dimensional CT scanning. These findings support the hypothesis that the first rib is often subluxated superiorly at the costotransverse joint in patients with thoracic outlet syndrome.

Rib Torsions

When one thoracic vertebra is rotated on the vertebra below, the two demifacets that make up the ver-

FIGURE 10-4
Method to find the superior aspect of the head of rib 1.

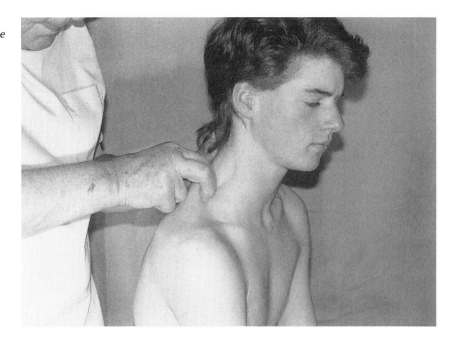

tebral component of the costovertebral joint are no longer correctly aligned and impart a twist to the head of the rib below. This twist of the rib head—also referred to as *rib torsion*—is more pronounced with the vertebra extended (ERS) on the lower vertebra, because extension closes down on the rib head and leaves less room for the rib head to accommodate the rotation of the vertebra above. Normally, the inferior border of the rib is more easily palpable posteriorly than the superior border. If, however, the upper vertebra is rotated to the left on the lower vertebra (ERSlt), the rib head on the left side is twisted so that the superior border of that rib becomes more prominent posteriorly than the inferior border. This twist is known as an *external torsion* of the rib. At the same time, the rib head on the right side is twisted so that the inferior border of the right rib becomes relatively more prominent. This twist is called an *internal torsion* of the rib. Rib torsion occurs normally as a coupled response to rotational movement of the thoracic spine, and it is only likely to persist if there is an intervertebral non-neutral dysfunction. For example, with an ERSlt at T4, the left fifth rib is found in external torsion, and the right fifth rib is found in internal torsion (Figure 10-5). The rib torsion usually is corrected as a consequence of successful treatment of the non-neutral intervertebral joint dysfunction.

Rib torsions only need treatment when the rib position has been present long enough to become self-per-

petuating and when the torsion fails to correct after treatment of the non-neutral dysfunction. The restriction in rib torsions is within the normal range of motion at the costovertebral joints, and in the absence of hypermobility, thrusting techniques are permitted

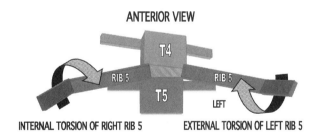

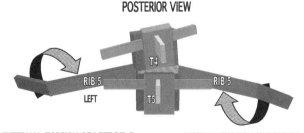

FIGURE 10-5
Diagram with an anterior and posterior view showing external torsion of left fifth rib and internal torsion of right fifth rib due to ERSlt at T4. Arrows indicate direction of torsion.

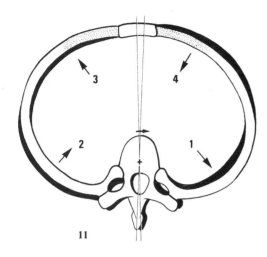

FIGURE 10-6
Illustration of rib torsion caused by rotation of the vertebra above. Horizontal arrow indicates direction of rotation. Note the reverse torsion of the rib anteriorly. Angled arrows indicate external torsional movement of rib at #1 and #3 and internal torsional movement of rib at #2 and #4. (Reproduced with permission from IA Kapandji. The Physiology of the Joints [Vol 3]. London: Churchill Livingstone, 1974.)

and sometimes essential. Occasionally, it proves almost impossible to correct the thoracic non-neutral dysfunction when there is an associated rib torsion, except by a combined thrust technique, as described later in Section 5.9.

Owing to the curvature of the rib and its attachments in front and behind, the direction of the twist changes as the rib passes forward through the axilla and is reversed at the anterior end. What is seen on examination is that, with external torsion of a rib, the inferior margin of the anterior end of the same rib is the more prominent (Figure 10-6). If the bone is thought of as the kind of rigid structure handled in anatomy classes, such torsional changes seem impossible. However, evidence suggests that living bone is deformable and in some ways, plastic, in nature. Trained fingers can appreciate the differences in shape before and after treatment, but it is fair to say that accurate rib diagnosis demands a degree of palpatory skill and is difficult for a beginner.

The Diagnosis of Structural Rib Dysfunctions

External Rib Torsion
Ribs restricted in external torsion are much more common than ribs restricted in internal torsion.

Diagnosis
1. The dysfunctional rib is often the key rib of a respiratory restriction for inhalation or exhalation.
2. The superior border of the rib is prominent posteriorly, and the inferior border is less prominent than normal.
3. The intercostal space above the rib is wide, and the intercostal space below the rib is narrow.
4. There is tissue texture change and tenderness at the insertion of iliocostalis at the rib angle and, often, in the intercostal muscles in the space below.
5. The vertebral body immediately above the rib is (was) rotated toward the side of the rib and is (was) probably extended. For example, if there is an external torsion of the left fifth rib, there is (was) an associated ERSlt at T4.
6. Palpation over the rib with the patient supine presents an increased rigidity when compared to palpation of the other ribs. The dysfunctional rib stands out if the chest wall is compressed by springing it.

Internal Rib Torsion
Diagnosis
1. The dysfunctional rib is often the key rib of a respiratory restriction for inhalation or exhalation.
2. The inferior border of the rib is more prominent posteriorly than normal.
3. The intercostal space below the rib is wide, and the intercostal space above the rib is narrow.
4. There is tissue texture change and tenderness at the insertion of iliocostalis at the rib angle and, often, in the intercostal muscles in the space above.
5. The upper vertebra is (was) rotated away from the side of the rib and is (was) probably extended (ERS). For example, if there is an internal torsion of the fifth rib on the right, it could be the result of an ERSlt dysfunction at T4.

Laterally Flexed Rib

A laterally flexed rib is often a very painful condition in which the rib is elevated acutely. This condition usually is caused by a sudden side-bending strain of the neck and upper thoracic spine. The rib acts as if it had a fixed pivot in front, as well as at the back; the pivot really more closely resembles a bucket handle. Although this is a more accurate description than "laterally flexed," it would be confused with the terminology for respiratory rib motion. A laterally flexed rib is painful at any level, but when it affects the second rib, there may be severe arm pain from the effect on the brachial plexus, and the shoulder often is carried high to avoid pressure on the neurovascular bundle. Treatment is painful, especially at the second rib. This condition is often associated with a concomitant ipsilateral superior subluxation of the first rib.

Diagnosis

The history of injury is very suggestive. A rib is found with severely restricted respiratory motion, most marked for exhalation. In the axilla, the rib is found elevated with a narrow space above and a wide space below. The rib is exquisitely tender, which is most easily noted just medial and above the coracoid process. This is always a tender area, but it is much more tender in comparison to the other side. There may be signs of sympathetic dysfunction in the arm, and any attempt to lower the shoulder causes an increase in the pain. Imaging and electromyographic (EMG) studies are usually normal, and the severity of the patient's symptoms is not at all obvious to those who are unaware of this dysfunction. It is equally possible to view the problem as a "frozen shoulder" with signs of a complex regional pain syndrome, especially when there are associated signs of increased sympathetic activity.

Antero-Posterior Compression

The possibility of the occurrence of an antero-posterior compression deformity also depends, as does the lateral compression, on the plastic nature of living bone. Antero-posterior compression occurs when there is a simultaneous impact to the front and back of the chest. This impact can be the consequence of a sports injury when two players collide against a third, or when the chest is struck while lying prone or supine. Usually, several adjacent ribs are affected at the same time.

Diagnosis

Both anterior and posterior ends of the affected rib or ribs are less prominent than the neighboring ribs, and the rib (or ribs) is prominent laterally in the midaxillary line. The affected rib(s) are also tender, particularly in the midaxillary line.

Lateral Compression

The lateral compression deformity is produced by a blow to the side of the chest, as when struck from the side in a motor vehicle collision. This condition is usually accompanied by severe pain.

Diagnosis

The findings are the reverse of the antero-posterior compression, with a prominent anterior end of the rib, a prominent rib angle, and flattening of the lateral aspect of the rib in the axilla or midaxillary line. As with antero-posterior compressions, lateral compressions are painful (like rib fractures), but imaging is negative. Both types of compression dysfunctions may be associated with nondisplaced rib fractures.

TREATMENT OF RESPIRATORY RIB DYSFUNCTIONS

The most important point in the diagnosis of respiratory rib dysfunctions is the difference between inhalation and exhalation restriction. The second most important point is to identify the key rib. Because there can be more than one key rib, re-examination after treatment is always necessary. If present, the additional key ribs should also be treated. Muscle energy is the most frequently used technique for treatment of respiratory rib dysfunctions. Because respiratory ribs are not subluxations, thrusting techniques also can be used, if necessary.

Muscle Energy Treatment

1 Restrictions of Inhalation

Described for Right-Sided Inhalation Restrictions for Ribs 1–10 There are three components to the treatment of restrictions of inhalation:

1. Inhalation effort by the patient
2. Muscle effort by the patient resisted by the operator
3. Rib elevation assistance by the operator

Operator resistance is used in these techniques to stabilize one end of the muscle attachment and to allow the other end of the muscle to move the restricted rib. In this manner, the muscle energy technique is isotonic. As in all muscle energy procedures, some of the gain takes place after relaxation when the slack is taken up.

The operator helps to elevate the rib anteriorly by pulling laterally and caudad on the angle of the rib posteriorly. Because the rib angle is behind the axis of motion, pulling caudally on the angle elevates the rib anteriorly.

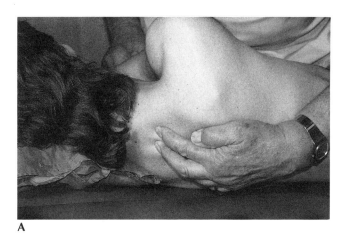
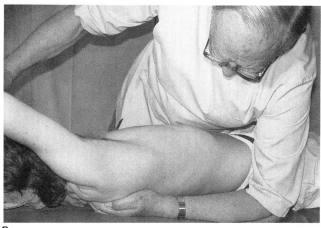

A   B

FIGURE 10-7
*Treatment for inhalation restriction of ribs 1 and 2. **(A)** Fingertips hooked over posterior shafts of ribs 1 and 2. **(B)** Position for patient effort with the operator's forearm on the table.*

The patient's starting position with the arm elevated helps by stretching any tight fascial tissue that may be restricting inhalation. Alternative techniques are required for patients with stiff shoulders.

1.1 Ribs 1 and 2

> **Diagnostic Points**
> The first or second rib is the uppermost or the key rib that limits the inhalation motion of all the ribs below it, and it is the first rib to stop moving during an inhalation effort when compared to the same rib on the other side.

Both ribs 1 and 2 on the same side are usually treated at the same time. An isotonic contraction of the scalene muscles is used.

1.1.1. The patient is supine with the operator standing on the patient's left side. The operator uses the right hand to lift the patient's right shoulder and then hooks the terminal phalanges of the left index and middle fingers over the superior edges of the shafts of ribs 1 and 2 (Figure 10-7A).

1.1.2. The patient's shoulder is then returned to the table. The operator's left arm lies underneath the patient, and the left forearm rests on the tabletop.

1.1.3. The patient's head is rolled 15 to 20 degrees to the left; this movement also side bends the neck, putting the scalenes on stretch. The patient's right forearm is placed on his or her forehead and held there by the operator (Figure 10-7B).

1.1.4. The patient then inhales fully and attempts to lift his or her head against the operator's resistance. If the patient's shoulder is not mobile, the operator's right hand

can be used to provide the counter force directly on the patient's forehead without elevating the patient's arm.

1.1.5. After 3–5 seconds, the patient is told to relax, and while doing so, the operator takes up the slack by pulling the ribs laterally and caudad along the direction of the operator's resting left forearm.

1.1.6. Steps 1.1.4 and 1.1.5 are repeated two to four times, while the operator maintains the pull with the left hand.

1.1.7. After a slow release of the caudal pull, the operator should re-examine the patient for any residual inhalation restrictions for these ribs.

1.2 Ribs 3, 4, and 5

> **Diagnostic Points**
> The third, fourth, or fifth rib is the uppermost or the key rib of the group that limits the inhalation motion of all the ribs below it, and it is the first rib to stop moving during inhalation effort when compared to the same rib on the other side.

An isotonic contraction of the pectoralis minor muscle is used.

1.2.1. The patient lies supine with the operator standing on the patient's left side. The operator hooks the tips of the left index, middle, and ring fingers posteriorly over the shafts of the patient's third, fourth, and fifth ribs, medial to the rib angles so that, with the left forearm on the table, the operator can pull laterally and caudad. See Sections 1.1.1 and 1.1.2.

1.2.2. The patient's right arm is raised overhead so that it lies beside his or her head. The operator's right

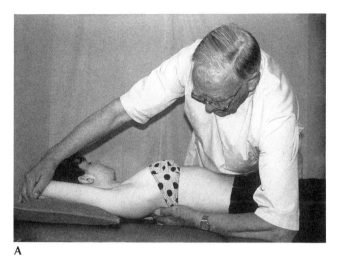

A

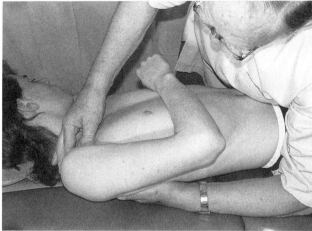

B

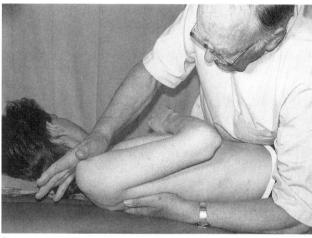

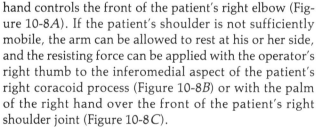

C

FIGURE 10-8

Treatment for inhalation restriction of ribs 3 to 5. (A) With the patient's arm beside the head and the operator's hand on the elbow. (B) With the thumb on the coracoid process. (C) With the hand on the front of the shoulder.

hand controls the front of the patient's right elbow (Figure 10-8*A*). If the patient's shoulder is not sufficiently mobile, the arm can be allowed to rest at his or her side, and the resisting force can be applied with the operator's right thumb to the inferomedial aspect of the patient's right coracoid process (Figure 10-8*B*) or with the palm of the right hand over the front of the patient's right shoulder joint (Figure 10-8*C*).

1.2.3. The patient inhales deeply and tries to elevate his or her right arm—anteriorly for a pump-handle restriction, or more laterally for a bucket-handle restriction. If the operator's resistance is on the front of the shoulder, the patient's effort is to move the shoulder anteriorly and slightly medially for the pump-handle restriction or laterally for the bucket-handle restriction.

1.2.4. After 3–5 seconds, the patient relaxes, and, as before, the slack is taken up by pulling laterally and caudad on the medial rib shafts with the operator's left hand.

1.2.5. The process is repeated two to four times, with the operator taking up the slack with a lateral and caudal pull posteriorly on the rib after each effort.

1.2.6. Re-examine.

1.3 Ribs 6 to 10   An isotonic contraction of the serratus anterior is used to treat these ribs.

Diagnostic Points
One of the sixth through tenth ribs is the uppermost or the key rib that limits the inhalation motion of all the ribs below it, and it is the first rib to stop moving during an inhalation effort when compared to the same the rib on the other side.

1.3.1. The patient is supine with the operator on the left side. The operator hooks the tips of the left index, middle, ring, and little fingers individually posteriorly

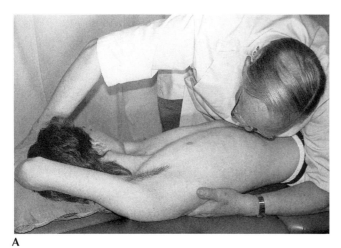

A

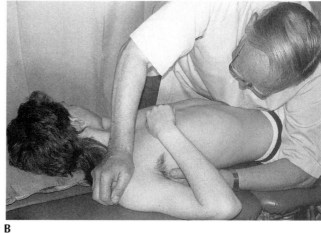

B

FIGURE 10-9

*Treatment for inhalation restriction of ribs 6 to 10. (**A**) With the arm over the top of the head. (**B**) With the hand on the front of the shoulder.*

over each of the shafts of the patient's ribs (ribs 6–9), medial to the rib angles with the left forearm still resting on the tabletop. Rib 10 can also be treated this way, but it is not often the key rib.

1.3.2. The patient's arm is elevated as before, but this time, the forearm is brought above the head, and the patient's wrist is grasped by the operator's right hand to provide resistance (Figure 10-9A). If the patient's shoulder is too stiff to permit this much movement, the serratus anterior can be resisted by the operator's right hand's pushing backward and medially on the patient's right humeral head and acromion (Figure 10-9B). If the shoulder is sufficiently mobile, it may be flexed to a right angle, and the resistance may be applied to the patient's elbow, while the patient attempts to protract the shoulder.

1.3.3. For the more common bucket-handle restriction, the patient's effort at the top of forced inhalation should be to pull his or her right arm down to the side (adduction). If there is more of a pump-handle component, the patient is instructed to pull his or her arm toward the feet (extension). In each case, the effort is resisted by the operator. If resistance is applied to the front of the shoulder, the patient's effort is to move the shoulder anteriorly and caudad.

1.3.4. After 3–5 seconds, the patient should relax, and the operator takes up the slack as before. The process is repeated two to four times, with the lateral and caudad pull maintained by the operator's left hand.

1.3.5. Re-examine.

2 Restriction of Exhalation

Described for Right-Sided Restrictions for Ribs 1–10

There are three components to the treatment for restriction of exhalation:

1. Patient positioning by the operator
2. Exhalation effort by the patient
3. Control of inhalation of the rib by the operator

The exhalation effort and the patient positioning are designed to allow the maximum caudal motion of the restricted rib. The operator's thumb and thenar eminence rest on the superior margin of the rib and blocks the craniad motion of the rib while the patient inhales. The operator then follows the rib caudally on the next exhalation. It should be emphasized that the rib is not forced down but is held in position against the inspiratory effort. The costochondral junction must be spanned by the operator's thumb when holding the rib down; otherwise, strain to the joint can occur, even with simple patient effort.

2.1 Rib 1 The first rib is unique because of its anatomy.

Diagnostic Points
On exhalation, the first right rib stops moving caudally before the left first rib, but the second ribs move symmetrically.

2.1.1. The patient is supine, and the operator sits at the head of the table.

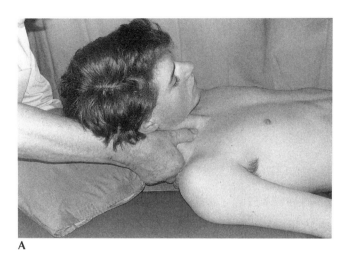 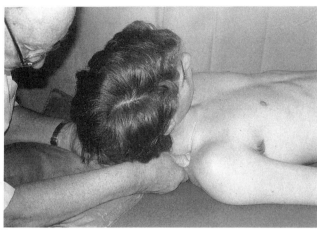

A   B

FIGURE 10-10
Treatment for exhalation restriction of rib 1. **(A)** *For pump-handle restriction.* **(B)** *For bucket-handle restriction.*

2.1.2. To relax the tissues, the operator uses the hand to lift the patient's head, producing flexion and a slight right side bend.

2.1.3. The operator's right thumb finds the rib. For the common pump-handle restriction, the anterior end of the rib is found, from above, deep to the medial end of the clavicle and immediately lateral to the sternocleidomastoid insertion. For patients who have a wide sternocleidomastoid muscle, it is often easier to approach the rib between the sternal and clavicular heads (Figure 10-10A). For bucket-handle restrictions, contact is made with the shaft of the rib posterolateral to the neurovascular bundle (Figure 10-10B).

2.1.4. The patient exhales, and the operator follows the downward motion of the rib with the right thumb. At the same time, the operator increases the forward flexion of the patient's neck, adding more right side bending for the bucket-handle restriction.

2.1.5. During the inhalation phase, the operator keeps the rib down by holding its position with his or her right thumb.

2.1.6. The cycle is repeated two or more times, and after the last exhalation, the patient is asked to push his or her head back to the table against slight resistance. This movement reduces any discomfort caused by keeping pressure contact on the rib by using reciprocal inhibition to relax the muscles that elevate the rib. The rib is held down until after another inhalation phase.

2.1.7. Re-examine.

2.2 Ribs 2 to 10 The technique is the same for ribs 2–10, except that, for the upper ribs with more pump-handle

restriction, the head and neck should be raised forward; for the lower ribs, typically, more side bending of the trunk is required to correct the bucket-handle restrictions.

Diagnostic Points
The rib to be treated is the lowest or the key rib that limits exhalation motion of all the ribs above it, and it is the first rib to stop moving during an exhalation effort when compared to the same rib on the other side. Tissue texture changes are noted anteriorly in the intercostal muscles above the restricted rib.

2.2.1. The patient is supine, and the operator stands or sits at the head of the table. With the right thumb and thenar eminence (first metacarpal) aligned in abduction, the operator contacts the upper border of the dysfunctional rib *so that hand contact spans the costochondral junction*, which should be near the operator's first metacarpal-phalangeal joint. For bucket-handle restrictions, the contact should be more lateral; for pump-handle restrictions, the contact should be more medial, but the junction must always be protected (Figure 10-11A).

2.2.2. Using the left hand, the operator reaches down so that the fingertips are under the patient's upper thoracic vertebrae. The operator lifts the patient's head and neck down to the point at which the tissue tension just reaches the operator's right thumb (Figure 10-11B). Because the lower ribs often have a bucket-handle restriction, side bending of the thoracic spine down to the restricted rib is often needed in addition to flexion (Figure 10-11C).

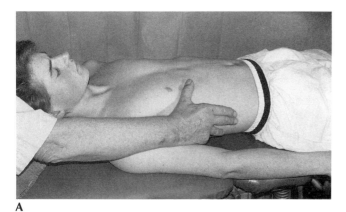

A

B

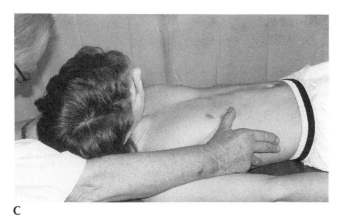

C

FIGURE 10-11
Treatment for exhalation restriction of typical ribs. (A) Protecting the costochondral junction. (B) Lifting the head, neck, and upper thoracic spine forward for pump-handle restriction. (C) Lifting the head, neck, and upper thoracic spine sideways for bucket-handle restriction.

2.2.3. The patient exhales fully, and the operator follows the movement with the right hand. By further lifting the patient's head, neck, and shoulders with the left hand, the operator introduces additional flexion down to the new point of tension.

2.2.4. On inhalation, the operator maintains the position. The cycle is repeated two or more times, and the patient then pushes his or her head and trunk back to the tabletop against light resistance by the operator's left hand. The operator's right thumb continues to hold the patient's rib down, releasing the pressure after another inhalation phase and after the head is again resting on the table.

2.2.5. Re-examine.

3 Ribs 11 and 12, Inhalation and Exhalation Restrictions

The treatments for inhalation and exhalation restrictions for ribs 11 and 12 are similar. The main muscles used are the quadratus lumborum and those of the abdominal wall, and the differences in treatment are in the patient positioning and the direction of the operator's effort. The effectiveness of treatment appears to be

the result of positioning, because the desired corrective movement is the only one permitted when the muscle effort is made.

> ### Diagnostic Points
> On inhalation, the eleventh or twelfth rib does not open the caliper as widely as the opposite rib when there is an inhalation restriction. If there is an exhalation restriction, the rib does not close as narrowly as the rib on the other side. There is likely to be tissue texture change on the restricted side.

3.1 Restriction of Inhalation   The following treatment is described for the left side.

3.1.1. The patient is prone. To assist the inhalation movement on the left, the patient is side bent to the right with the left arm abducted over his or her head. The operator stands on the patient's right side (Figure 10-12A).

3.1.2. The operator contacts the medial ends of the eleventh and twelfth ribs with the heel of the right hand so that the ribs can be "scooped" away laterally. The operator's arm position directs a lateral force and, with

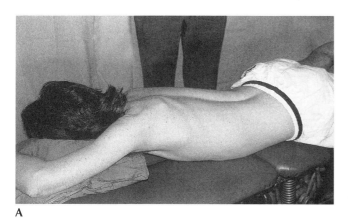
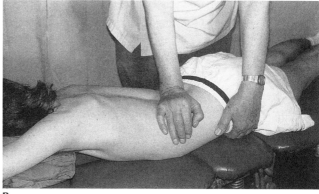

A   B

FIGURE 10-12
Treatment for inhalation restriction of ribs 11 and 12. (A) Side-bent position on the table. (B) Position for patient effort (or for thrust).

a slight lateral rotation of the arm, directs this force *craniad* as well.

3.1.3. With the left hand under the patient's anterior superior iliac spine (ASIS), the operator lifts the left side of the patient's pelvis until tension is felt to build at these lower ribs (Figure 10-12*B*).

3.1.4. The patient takes a deep breath *in* and, while holding the breath, attempts to pull his or her pelvis back to the table. The operator resists with the left hand, while pushing the ribs craniad with the right hand, using the muscle energy effort from the abdominal muscles, along with the inhalation effort, to make the correction.

3.1.5. After 3–5 seconds, the patient relaxes and breathes out. The operator blocks exhalation of the rib using the right hand. When the patient is fully relaxed, the left hip is lifted a bit more by the opera-

tor's left hand until the tissue tension reaches these ribs.

3.1.6. Two to four repetitions are made, and the position is re-examined.

3.2 Restriction of Exhalation 3.2.1. The patient is prone. To assist the exhalation movement on the left, the patient is side bent to the left with the left arm down by his or her side (Figure 10-13*A*). The operator stands on the patient's right side.

3.2.2. With the heel of the right hand, the operator contacts the medial ends of the eleventh and twelfth ribs so that the ribs can be scooped away laterally. The operator's arm is positioned to direct a lateral force and is rotated slightly internally to direct this force *caudad* as well.

3.2.3. The operator's left hand is placed under the patient's ASIS, and the left side of the patient's pelvis is

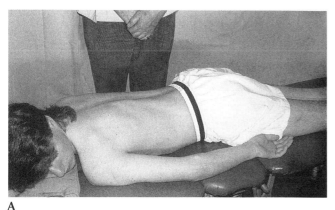
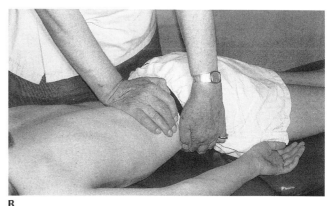

A   B

FIGURE 10-13
Treatment for exhalation restriction of ribs 11 and 12. (A) Side-bent position for exhalation restriction. (B) Position for patient effort (or for thrust).

lifted off the tabletop, until tissue tension begins to build at the level of these lower ribs (Figure 10-13B).

3.2.4. The patient exhales fully and, while holding the breath in exhalation, attempts to pull his or her pelvis back to the table. The operator resists this movement with the left hand, while applying lateral and caudal pressure to the patient's ribs with the right hand.

3.2.5. After 3–5 seconds, the patient relaxes and breathes in, but inhalation motion of the ribs is resisted by the operator's right hand. When the patient has fully relaxed, the slack is taken up to the next barrier as the operator's left hand lifts the pelvis further off the table.

3.2.6. Two to four repetitions are made, and the position is re-examined.

4 Thrust
4.1 Typical Ribs, Supine Techniques
All supine techniques can be used for treatment of inhalation or exhalation restrictions. These techniques are useful for ribs 3 to 9 but are easier for ribs 4 to 7. These methods are variants of the supine thoracic techniques; the chief difference is in the position of the fulcrum at the back. The arm positions described in Chapter 9 can be used, but a thrust through the patient's elbow on the ipsilateral side is usually better.

The following treatment is described for the sixth left rib with an inhalation or exhalation restriction.

> **Diagnostic Points**
> The left sixth rib is the key rib of a group that stops moving earlier than the rib on the other side during either inhalation or exhalation.

4.1.1. The position for this treatment is similar to the position for the supine thoracic techniques. The patient is supine, and the operator stands on the right side. The patient crosses the left arm (*one arm only*) over the chest and holds the right shoulder with the left hand (Figure 10-14A).

4.1.2. The operator uses the left hand to lift the patient's left shoulder so that the operator's right hand can be inserted under the patient and the base of the thenar eminence can be in contact with the posterior shaft of R6. For an inhalation restriction, the thenar eminence should be above the rib shaft near the angle; for an exhalation restriction, it should be below the rib shaft. The operator's fingers are used to support the left side of the patient's spine (Figure 10-14B). Because of the thoracic kyphosis, some flexion of the spine may be needed to allow the rib angles of the lower ribs to come closer to the tabletop.

4.1.3. The operator leans over to use his or her chest or upper abdomen to direct a downward force over the patient's chest. The force is directed toward the right thenar eminence underneath the rib.

4.1.4. The thrust is given through the patient's left arm at the end of a deep respiratory effort in the appropriate phase of respiration (inhalation for an inhalation restriction; exhalation for an exhalation restriction), and, at the same time, the operator makes a rotatory movement with the right thenar eminence. For inhalation restrictions on the left side, the rotation is clockwise (as seen from the front) so that the posterior rib shaft is taken caudad (Figure 10-14C); for the exhalation restriction, the rotation is counterclockwise so that the posterior rib shaft is taken craniad (Figure 10-14D).

4.1.5. Retest.

4.2 Middle Ribs, Side-Lying
The following treatment is described for the fifth right rib.

4.2.1. The patient lies on the left side with the spine in neutral, and the operator stands in front of the patient (Figure 10-15A).

4.2.2. With the pisiform of the left hand, the operator contacts the patient's fifth rib at the rib angle. For an inhalation restriction, the contact needs to be above (craniad) the angle; for an exhalation restriction, the contact is below (caudad) the angle.

4.2.3. With the right hand, the operator rotates the patient's upper trunk to the right by backward pressure on the patient's shoulder, until the operator's left hand can feel the tension reach the level of the fifth rib.

4.2.4. After the slack has been taken out, the thrust is given at the end of the appropriate phase of respiration in a direction that is anterior and craniad for an exhalation restriction to tilt the anterior portion of the rib downward. The thrust is directed anterior and caudad for an inhalation restriction to tilt the anterior portion of the rib upward (Figure 10-15B).

4.2.5. Retest.

4.3 Rib 1, Supine Technique
The following treatment is described for the left side.

> **Diagnostic Points**
> In inhalation or exhalation, the left first rib stops moving before the first rib on the right. In an inhalation restriction, this rib may be the uppermost of a group. For an exhalation restriction, if rib 1 is to be treated, it is the only restricted rib.

4.3.1. The patient is supine, and the operator stands at the patient's right side. The operator slides the right hand diagonally under the patient's upper trunk so the left first rib can be gripped with the fingers of the right hand (Figure 10-16).

4.3.2. By pulling back the edge of the left trapezius muscle with the fingertips of the right hand, the operator can contact the back of the patient's first rib. For an exhalation restriction, the operator's fingers are used to roll

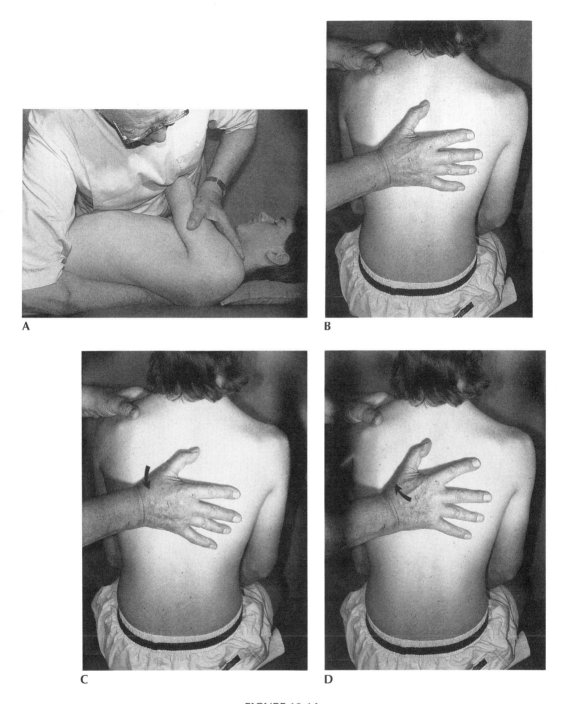

FIGURE 10-14
Thrust treatment for typical ribs. (A) Position for elbow thrust on one arm. (B) The hand position when the patient is seated. (C) Showing hand rotation for inhalation restriction. (D) Showing hand rotation for exhalation restriction. Arrows indicate direction of rotation.

the rib forward and down, whereas for an inhalation restriction, the fingers roll the rib backward and up.

4.3.3. Using the left hand, the operator side bends the patient's head and neck to the left, rotating it to the right until the tension comes to the rib.

4.3.4. The thrust is with the operator's left hand on the back of the patient's head, rotating it to the right at the end of the appropriate phase of respiration (inhalation or exhalation). The head is turned further to the right, which rotates T1 to the right and pushes forward

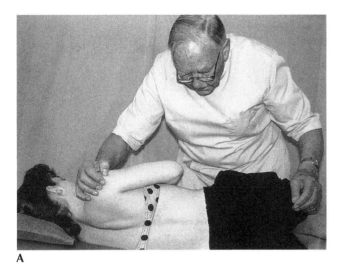

A

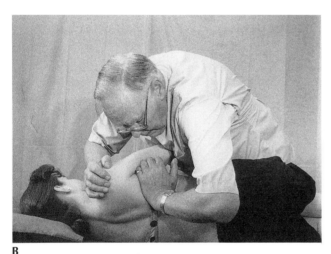

B

FIGURE 10-15
Side-lying thrust treatment for middle ribs. (A) Patient position. (B) Operator position for thrust.

on the back of the rib, while the fingers of the operator's right hand guide the rib into the corrective position.

4.2.5. Retest.

4.4 Rib 1, Sitting Technique The following treatment is described for the left side.

Diagnostic Points
In inhalation or exhalation, the left first rib stops moving before the first rib on the right. In an inhalation restriction, this rib may be the uppermost of a group. For an exhalation restriction, if rib 1 is to be treated, it is the only restricted rib.

4.4.1. The patient sits up tall, with legs over the side of the table, and the operator stands behind the

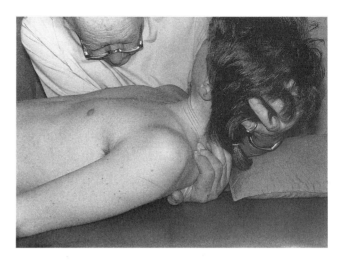

FIGURE 10-16
Position for supine thrust for rib 1, inhalation or exhalation.

patient with the right foot on the tabletop, close to the patient's right side. The patient drapes the right arm over the operator's right knee, giving the operator the ability to change the degree of the patient's left side-bending position through medial or lateral translation by the positioning of the operator's right leg.

4.4.2. The operator places the web of the left hand over the inner part of the patient's left first rib. The operator uses his or her right forearm and hand to control the patient's head and protect the neck. Because the operator thrusts with the left hand, the left elbow needs to be raised to bring the forearm in line with the thrust direction (Figure 10-17). For an inhalation restriction, the left hand contacts the posterior part of the rib. For an exhalation restriction, the side of the index finger is used to contact the shaft of the rib laterally (but behind the neurovascular bundle).

4.4.3. The operator uses the left hand to monitor the patient while introducing left side bending by translation, using the right thigh from below and the right forearm from above.

4.3.4. The high-velocity, low-amplitude thrust is given in a diagonal to the right by the operator's left hand, with slight exaggeration of the left side bend from above through the operator's right forearm.

4.3.5. Retest.

4.5 Rib 2 The following treatment is described for the second right rib with an inhalation or exhalation restriction.

4.5.1. The patient sits on a table or stool with his or her upper spine in neutral. The operator stands behind the patient.

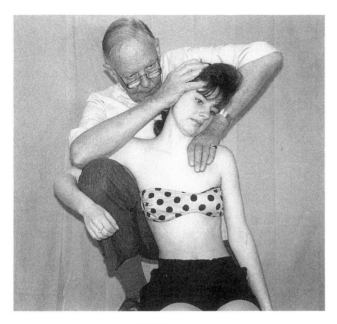

FIGURE 10-17
Sitting thrust for rib 1, inhalation. For exhalation, the index finger of the left hand is more lateral. Note use of the leg by the operator to control sideways translation of the trunk.

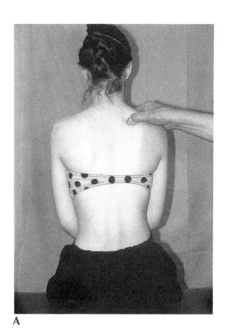

A

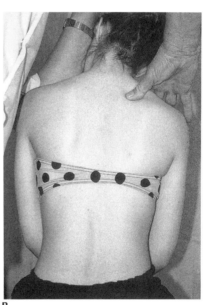

B

FIGURE 10-18
Sitting thrust for rib 2, inhalation or exhalation. (A) Thumb contact on the posterior rib shaft. (B) Thrust position (operator to the side for clarity).

4.5.2. The operator's right thumb is placed against the back of the shaft of the second right rib so that the rib can be pushed either up (craniad) or down (caudad), as required (Figure 10-18*A*).

4.5.3. With the left hand, the operator takes the patient's head into right side bending and left rotation, until the tension reaches the upper edge of the rib.

4.5.4. At the end of the appropriate respiratory phase, and when all the slack has been taken out, the thrust is given on the rib by the operator's right thumb. The direction should be anterior and craniad for an exhalation restriction; the direction should be anterior and caudad for an inhalation restriction (Figure 10-18*B*).

4.5.5. Retest.

Ribs 11 and 12 The thrust techniques for ribs 11 and 12 are very similar to the techniques that use muscle energy activation.

The following treatment is described for the left side.

> ***Diagnostic Points***
> The eleventh or twelfth rib does not open the caliper as widely on inhalation or close the caliper as tightly on exhalation as does the rib on the other side. There is likely to be tissue texture change on the restricted side.

4.6 Described for Restriction of Inhalation 4.6.1. The patient is prone. To assist the inhalation movement on the left, the patient is side bent to the right with the left arm abducted above the patient's head. The operator stands on the patient's right side.

4.6.2. With the heel of the right hand, the operator contacts the medial ends of the eleventh and twelfth ribs so that he or she can scoop them away laterally. The operator's arm should point laterally and *craniad*.

4.6.3. The operator's left hand is placed under the patient's left ASIS and lifts the left side of the patient's pelvis (see Figure 10-12*B*).

4.6.4. When all slack has been taken out by lifting the pelvis, the patient takes a deep breath in, and the operator gives a high-velocity, low-amplitude thrust laterally and craniad.

4.6.5. Retest.

4.7 Described for Restriction of Exhalation The following treatment is described for the left side.

4.7.1. The patient is prone. To assist the exhalation movement on the left, the patient is side bent to the left with the left arm down by his or her side. The operator stands on the patient's right side.

4.7.2. With the heel of the right hand, the operator contacts the medial ends of the patient's eleventh and twelfth ribs so that he or she can scoop them away laterally. The operator's arm should point laterally and *caudad*.

4.7.3. The operator's left hand is placed under the patient's left ASIS and lifts the left side of the patient's pelvis (see Figure 10-13*B*).

4.7.4. When all slack has been taken out by lifting the pelvis, the patient breathes out deeply, and the operator gives a high-velocity, low-amplitude thrust laterally and caudad.

4.7.5. Retest.

TREATMENT OF STRUCTURAL RIB DYSFUNCTIONS

Structural rib dysfunctions are likely to be associated with intervertebral joint dysfunctions, and the general rule is that the intervertebral zygapophyseal joint is treated first. Indeed, many rib dysfunctions return to normal if the intervertebral problem is corrected.

Accurate diagnosis is important because the treatment varies widely, depending on precisely what is wrong. The diagnosis depends on finding a rib positioned out of the normal contour of the rib cage, usually with the rib asymmetry being present both anteriorly and posteriorly. There will also be tissue texture abnormality found at the insertion of the iliocostalis muscle on the rib angle of that rib. The rib angle and the costochondral junction are usually tender, so all of these treatments are likely to be painful. Often, it is found that the anterior tenderness at the costochondral junction is immediately less after treatment of a structural rib dysfunction.

5. Muscle Energy

5.1 Anterior Subluxation

Diagnostic Points
The rib angle is anterior to its expected position in the antero-posterior curve and medial to its expected position in the lateral curve. The rib also appears prominent anteriorly and tender to palpation at the costochondral junction. The respiratory excursion of the rib is diminished, and this rib is often the key rib for a group of ribs with an inhalation or exhalation restriction. The insertion of the iliocostalis is tense and often edematous and tender. It may be necessary to assess the rib cage with the patient in a seated position because of the effect of pressure on the ribs by the tabletop when the patient is supine or prone.

Described for the Left Fourth Rib 5.1.1. The patient sits with the spine in neutral. The operator stands behind the patient. The patient holds his or her right shoulder with the left hand, and the operator uses the right hand to grasp the patient's left elbow (Figure 10-19*A*).

5.1.2. The operator's left thumb contacts the patient's fourth left rib medial to the rib angle and prepares to pull it laterally. The operator adjusts the patient's elbow position by moving it upward or downward, until motion is felt at the rib to be treated, and the tension in the tissues at the back reaches the operator's left thumb (Figure 10-19*B*).

5.1.3. If there is restriction of inhalation, the next step is performed during inhalation. If there is restriction of exhalation, the treatment is performed in that phase. In the correct phase of respiration, the operator *pulls* the rib angle to the left, while the patient *pulls* his or her elbow to the left against the operator's resistance. Alternatively, for the lower ribs, the patient may pull his or her elbow down against the operator's resistance—in that case, the patient's right fist can also be inserted between his or her left elbow and the front of the rib to help to push the rib back (Figure 10-19*C*). Another alternative is to ask the patient to push his or her elbow forward against the operator's unyielding resistance, while the operator continues to pull the rib laterally. This second alternative technique uses an isotonic contraction of the patient's left serratus anterior to actively pull the rib back.

5.1.4. After 3–5 seconds, the patient should relax, but the operator retains the lateral pull on the rib angle.

5.1.5. Steps 5.1.3 and 5.1.4 are repeated two to four times, and the patient's rib position is re-examined.

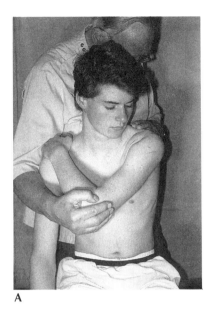
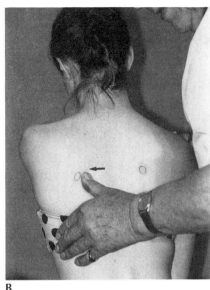
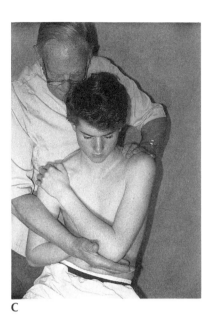

A   B   C

FIGURE 10-19

Treatment for anterior subluxation of a typical rib. (A) Position from in front. (B) Position from behind. Arrow indicates direction of force from operator's thumb, and the circles outline rib angles. (C) Alternative technique for lower ribs with the patient's right fist placed between his or her arm and the dysfunctional rib.

5.2 Posterior Subluxation

> ### Diagnostic Points
>
> The rib angle is posterior to its expected position in the antero-posterior curve and lateral to its expected position in the lateral curve. It is important to remember that the rib angles are found progressively more laterally when palpating the angles from above down. The rib also appears to be missing or posteriorly displaced in front and tender to palpation at the costochondral junction. The respiratory excursion of the rib is diminished, and this rib is often the key rib for a group of ribs with an inhalation or exhalation restriction. The insertion of the iliocostalis is tense and often edematous and tender. It may be necessary to assess the position of the ribs with the patient in a seated position because of the effect of pressure on the rib by the tabletop when the patient is supine or prone.

Described for the Left Fourth Rib 5.2.1. The patient sits, and the operator stands behind the patient. The patient holds his or her right shoulder with the left hand, and the operator's right hand grasps the patient's left elbow.

5.2.2. The operator's left thumb contacts the patient's left fourth rib lateral to the rib angle and prepares to push it anteriorly and medially (Figure 10-20*A*). The operator adjusts the patient's elbow position by moving it up or down, until the tension in the tissues at the back reaches the operator's left thumb (see Figure 10-19*A*).

5.2.3. If there is a major restriction in one phase of respiration, the treatment is performed in that phase.

5.2.4. The patient is then instructed to *push* his or her elbow forward and to the right against the operator's resistance. At the same time, the operator blocks the rib from moving posteriorly by placement of the left thumb. Alternatively, the patient may attempt to raise his or her elbow against unyielding resistance (Figure 10-20*B*).

5.2.5. After 3–5 seconds, the patient stops pushing, and the operator's left thumb pushes the patient's rib anteriorly and medially, taking up the slack gained during the relaxation phase. This technique uses a postisometric contraction and then relaxation of the serratus anterior to correct the dysfunction.

5.2.6. Steps 5.2.4 and 5.2.5 are repeated two to four times; then the rib position is re-examined.

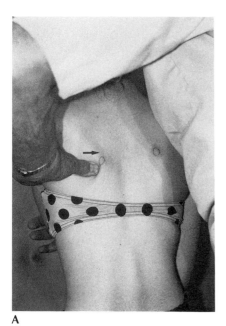

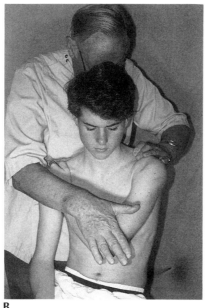

A   B

FIGURE 10-20

*Treatment for posterior subluxation of a typical rib. **(A)** Position from behind. Arrow indicates direction of force from operator's thumb, and the circles outline the rib angles. **(B)** Alternative resistance to raising elbow.*

5.3 Superior Subluxation of the First Rib

> ### Diagnostic Points
> The medial end of the first rib is at least a "thumb's width" higher on the dysfunctional side, and it will be tender. While palpating both first ribs, the introduction of cervical flexion causes the dysfunctional rib to immediately move superiorly compared to the normal side. The patient will have a positive cervical rotation lateral flexion (CRLF) test. This test is performed with the patient lying supine. The cervical spine is passively fully rotated to the opposite (normal) side and, while maintaining this rotation, the cervical spine is then laterally flexed anteriorly by tilting the head toward the chest. The test is positive when the range of lateral flexion is severely restricted when compared to the opposite side.

The C7-T1 and T1-2 joints should always be checked and, if indicated, treated before attempting to treat the first rib. Often, there is an associated elevation of the clavicle at the sternoclavicular joint. Placing an index finger on top of each clavicular head and asking the patient to shrug the shoulders can detect this dysfunction. If the left index finger moves higher than the right, dysfunction may be present. This is treated when the patient is supine with the left shoulder off the table. The operator stands on the patient's left side and palpates the sternoclavicular joint with the left hand while holding the patient's forearm with the right hand. The patient's arm is internally rotated and allowed to drop, until motion is detected at the sternoclav-

icular joint. The patient is then asked to raise the left arm against the operator's resistance for 3–5 seconds, after which the arm is again allowed to drop toward the floor until motion is detected at the sternoclavicular joint by the palpating fingers of the operator's left hand. This movement may be repeated several times and then retested.

Due to the mechanism of injury, which most often involves an acute side-bending strain of the cervical spine, there often is an associated second rib dysfunction with the rib laterally flexed upward. A laterally flexed second rib will prevent successful treatment of a superiorly subluxed first rib above it and therefore the laterally flexed second rib must be treated first when present, as described in Section 5.4. In fact, to successfully correct a first rib superior subluxation, it is necessary to treat all of the associated dysfunctions first, including non-neutral cervicothoracic dysfunctions and clavicular dysfunctions.

The following treatment is described for the left side.

5.3.1. The operator stands behind the seated patient.

5.3.2. The operator's right foot is placed on the tabletop beside the patient. The patient's right arm is draped over the operator's right thigh to provide lateral control of the patient's trunk.

5.3.3. With the index and middle fingers of the left hand, the operator palpates the superior aspect of the patient's left first rib in front of the trapezius muscle, pulling the muscle back so that the superior surface of the rib can be reached (see Figure 10-4). Feeling through the trapezius, the operator's left thumb finds the posterior aspect of the rib.

5.3.4. Using the right hand, the operator side bends the patient's neck to the left to relax the tissues around the rib and, by using translation through the right leg, helps keep the patient balanced (Figure 10-21).

5.3.5. The patient pushes his or her head to the right against the operator's resistance to contract the right scalenes and, by reciprocal inhibition, relax the left scalenes. The patient's effort must be controlled because, although easy pressure causes the antagonists to relax, if the patient presses too hard, the left scalenes may tighten again to stabilize the cervical spine. A few pounds of pressure are all that is required.

5.3.6. When the tissues on the left are relaxed, the operator pushes the rib down into position. Often, however, the rib has "hitched" on the top of the TP of T1, and the rib's caudal descent is blocked. In this event, forward pressure by the operator's left thumb is necessary to disengage the rib before it can descend. If this pressure is given during an exhalation effort, there is further relaxation of the scalenes, and, often, the rib can be felt to drop. Before releasing the anterior pressure on the rib, the operator should rotate the patient's head to the left in a circular motion, bringing the head and neck from a flexed, left side-bent and right-rotated position into left rotation. Rotating the head and neck to the left while maintaining an anteriorly directed force on the shaft of the first rib takes the TP of T1 to the left and out from under the first rib, thereby allowing the first rib to drop down, often with a "clunk" sound or feeling.

5.3.7. Re-examine.

5.4 Lateral Flexion

Lateral flexion is a painful and incapacitating condition, especially if it involves the third or, worse, the second rib.

Diagnostic Points

The rib is prominent and very tender in the axilla, and its respiratory excursion is significantly limited, particularly for exhalation. The intercostal space above the rib is narrow, and the intercostal muscle is very tight and tender. The origin of the pectoralis minor muscle from the rib also shows tissue texture change and is tender. The examination may raise suspicion, but it is the history of an acute lateral flexion strain, as occurs when struck from the side in a motor vehicle accident, which helps to confirm the diagnosis. This dysfunction commonly occurs at the second rib and often is found in association with a superior subluxation of the first rib above it, because both are caused by the same mechanism of injury. If a superiorly subluxed first rib cannot be restored to its proper position, then the operator should consider that the second rib is elevated and held in the laterally flexed position.

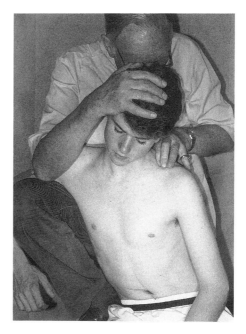

FIGURE 10-21
Treatment for superior subluxation of rib 1.

The following treatment is described for the third left rib.

5.4.1. The patient is supine, and the operator stands on the left side.

5.4.2. Placing the right hand on the patient's ribs in the left axilla, the operator must reach high enough to hook the terminal phalanges of the index and middle fingers over the superior border of the third rib. This position is not easy at the third rib and is much more difficult for the second rib, because these ribs have been pulled up higher into the axilla than their normal positions.

Reaching the superior margin of the lateral flexed ribs must be done in stages. As the operator's fingertips are slowly pushed upward into the axilla, the patient is asked to exhale while reaching down with his or her left hand toward the left knee. With the left hand, the operator can increase left side bending by bringing the patient's head toward the left shoulder with each attempt by the patient to reach further down. After each attempt to reach down and after exhalation, there is some relaxation in the axillary tissues, which allows the operator to reach up further into the axilla with the fingertips of the right hand (Figure 10-22A).

5.4.3. The final step of this treatment can be very painful, especially at the second rib level, and must be performed rapidly and firmly. Once the fingertips are over the superior margin of the rib, the rib is held in place as the patient's head and neck are straightened and

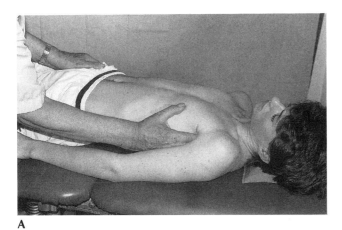

A

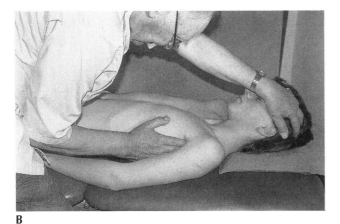

B

FIGURE 10-22

Treatment for laterally flexed rib. (A) Starting to reach fingers over top of rib. (B) Final position; correction achieved by holding the rib down while the head and trunk are straightened.

side bent to the right by the operator's left hand (Figure 10-22B).

When they are treated for the first time, it is common for patients to pull away by trying to scoot toward the top of the table, and the finger hold can be lost. Even if treatment is successful, recurrences are fairly common. However, when the patient has experienced relief from prior treatment, he or she is much more cooperative, although no less uncomfortable with the technique if the treatment needs to be repeated at a later date.

5.4.4. Re-examine.

5.5 Lateral Flexion, Alternative Technique

Because the treatment described in Section 5.4 is painful, one of the authors (M. B.) found an easier way to treat this dysfunction. This technique is based, in part, on the work described by Butler[4] and uses neural tension mobilization through the brachial plexus to help relax the anterior and posterior scalenes and intercostal muscles that hold the rib laterally flexed (upward).

Described for the Left Second Rib 5.5.1. The patient is supine with shoulders near one end of the table so that his or her head and cervical spine can be taken easily into flexion. The operator sits at the head of the table and uses the right hand to support the patient's occiput.

5.5.2. With the left hand, the operator depresses the patient's shoulder while palpating anteriorly with the fingers over the superior border of the second rib (Figure 10-23A). With the left thumb placed posteriorly on the rib shaft of the second rib, the operator depresses and holds the rib inferiorly (Figure 10-23B).

5.5.3. With the right hand, the operator lifts the patient's head, bringing the cervical spine into flexion, and then rotates and side bends the patient's head and cervical spine to the right, until tension reaches the second rib. The patient's head can be further supported by the operator's right upper chest wall and anterior shoulder placed against the patient's forehead (Figure 10-23C).

5.5.4. The patient is asked to abduct his or her left arm to approximately 90 degrees, to externally rotate the shoulder, to supinate the forearm with the elbow flexed, and then to extend his or her wrist and fingers (see Figure 10-23C).

5.5.5. The patient is asked to extend his or her elbow while maintaining the extended hand and wrist position. An assistant operator, if available, can help by depressing the left shoulder, holding the patient's wrist and fingers extended, and extending the elbow to the extension barrier. At the extension barrier, there is a sudden increase in tone in the biceps or upper trapezius muscle, and tension is palpated over the second rib (Figure 10-23D). Once the barrier to elbow extension is found, the assistant flexes and extends the left elbow in a fairly rapid and cyclical fashion toward and away from the barrier. The operator maintains the cervical flexion, right side bending, right rotation, and caudal pressure over the left second rib throughout the technique. This treatment is continued until full elbow extension is possible. Often, the operator feels a sudden release of tension at the second rib at the same time full elbow extension is achieved.

5.5.6. Once full elbow extension is possible, the operator slowly returns the head and neck to the table and releases the second rib.

5.5.7. Re-examine.

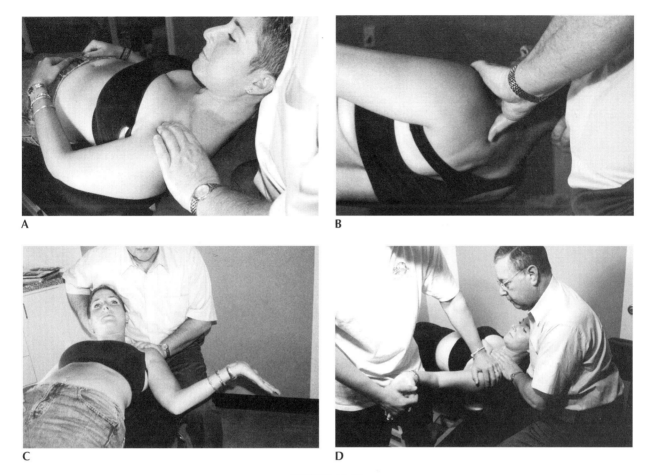

FIGURE 10-23

*Alternative treatment technique to correct a left laterally flexed second rib using adverse neural tension. **(A)** The operator uses the left hand to depress the patient's left shoulder and, at the same time, uses the fingers to palpate over the superior surface of the second rib. **(B)** The operator's left thumb contacts the second rib posteriorly. **(C)** The patient's head is flexed, side bent right, rotated right, and supported by the operator's right hand and chest. The patient extends the wrist and fingers and then flexes and extends at the elbow. Tension at the second rib should be felt when the patient's head and neck are properly positioned and when the patient extends the elbow. **(D)** With an assistant to hold the patient's shoulder down and assist in extending the elbow (until adverse neural tension develops) and in flexing the elbow to release the tension. The cycle is repeated, until tension with extension diminishes, and the second rib releases.*

5.6 External Torsion

> ### Diagnostic Points
> External torsion is nearly always associated with a non-neutral thoracic spine dysfunction and it is often the key rib in a respiratory restriction for inhalation or exhalation. The vertebra forming the upper half of the costovertebral joint is (or has been) rotated to the side of the dysfunctional rib and has limited flexion (ERS). The dysfunctional rib shaft has a prominent superior border, and the inferior border is difficult to feel. The intercostal space above is wide, and the intercostal space below is narrow. The intercostal muscles in the narrow space are likely to be tense and tender.

Described for a Left Rib 5.6.1. The patient is seated and holds his or her right shoulder with the left hand.

5.6.2. The operator stands behind the patient and puts his or her right hand on the patient's left elbow so that a lifting effort can be resisted (see Figure 10-19*A*).

5.6.3. The operator's left thumb is placed vertically over the dysfunctional rib at the rib angle, and the patient's left elbow is raised and lowered until tension is palpated at the rib angle (Figure 10-24).

5.6.4. The operator pushes forward on the superior border of the angle of the rib with the left thumb, while the patient attempts first to elevate and then to depress his or her left elbow through a number of cycles against the operator's resistance.

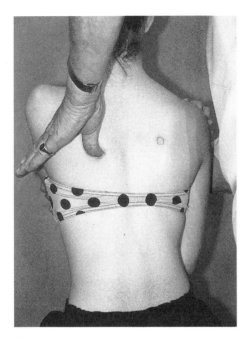

FIGURE 10-24
Treatment for an external rib torsion, showing position and mark (circle) at rib angle.

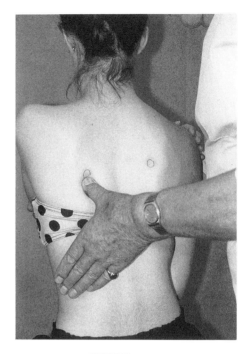

FIGURE 10-25
Treatment for an internal rib torsion, showing position and mark (circle) at rib angle.

5.6.5. Re-examine.

Note: In rib torsion techniques, the operator's thumb lies directly over the rib angle, as opposed to the position of the thumb when treating anterior and posterior subluxations. Because the iliocostalis is tender, tense, and attached to the rib angle, techniques to correct rib torsions are usually very uncomfortable for the patient.

5.7 Internal Torsion
The dysfunction of internal torsion is less common than that of external torsion.

> *Diagnostic Points*
> Internal torsion is nearly always associated with a non-neutral thoracic spine dysfunction and it is often the key rib in a respiratory restriction for inhalation or exhalation. The vertebra forming the upper half of the costovertebral joint is rotated away from the side of the dysfunctional rib and probably has limited extension (ERS). The rib shaft has a prominent inferior border; the superior border is difficult to feel. The intercostal space above is narrow and is probably tense and tender. The intercostal space below is wider than usual.

Described for a Left Rib   5.7.1. The patient is seated and holds his or her right shoulder with the left hand.

5.7.2. The operator stands behind the patient and puts his or her right hand on the patient's left elbow so that a downward pressure can be resisted.

5.7.3. The operator's left thumb is placed vertically over the dysfunctional rib at the rib angle, and the patient's left elbow is raised and lowered by the operator's right hand, until tension just reaches the thumb.

5.7.4. The operator pushes forward on the inferior border of the dysfunctional rib at the angle, while the patient attempts first to elevate and then to depress his or her left elbow through a number of cycles against the operator's resistance (Figure 10-25).

5.7.5. Re-examine.

There are times, especially in patients who have a chronic torsional rib dysfunction, when attempting to reduce the torsion from the rib angle does not result in a successful resolution. An alternative technique was uncovered by Dr. Philip Greenman while he sorted through some of the written notes of Dr. Fred Mitchell, Sr. This alternative technique had never before been mentioned or demonstrated. Greenman first demonstrated this technique at a continuing medical education course in manual medicine in October 1992 at the Kellogg Center in East Lansing, MI, when he was called on to assist the faculty because of the sudden loss of Dr. John Bourdillon the day before.

This alternative technique combines treating an external rib torsion with the positioning used to treat an ERS dysfunction and takes advantage of the normal torsional movement of the ribs that occurs with rotation of the thoracic spine. When there is torsion of a rib, the direction of the torsion reverses at the rib angle (see Figure 10-6). For example, if there is an external torsional dysfunction of a rib, the upper edge of that rib is most prominent between the TP and the rib angle. Once beyond the rib angle, the torsion reverses, and the lower edge of that rib becomes more prominent anteriorly. The length of the rib between the rib angle and the costochondral junction is considerably longer than the length between the thoracic spine and rib angle. Therefore, this technique takes advantage of the fact that a longer lever for treatment is available when contact on the rib is made lateral and anterior to the rib angle.

6.1 Combined Muscle Energy Technique for Treatment of an External Rib Torsion and an Associated Non-Neutral Thoracic Dysfunction

Described for a Left Rib External Torsional Dysfunction with an Associated ERS Left   6.1.1. The patient is seated and holds his or her left shoulder with the right hand. The operator stands on the right side of the patient.

6.1.2. The operator places his or her right axilla over the patient's right shoulder and grasps the patient's left shoulder with the right hand. The operator then reaches his or her left arm behind the patient and places the left thumb and thenar eminence along the inferior margin of the dysfunctional rib shaft anteriorly, spanning the costochondral junction. It is natural and comfortable to allow the thumb to angle downward along the rib, lateral to the rib angle, palpating toward the costochondral junction (Figure 10-26A).

6.1.3. Using the right arm and chest, the operator can translate the patient's thoracic spine posteriorly into flexion, until tension is felt to build under the operator's left thumb along the patient's rib. The operator can then rotate the patient to the right by bringing the patient's left shoulder forward, until the beginning of rib motion is palpated. To fine tune to the barrier, side bending the patient to the right is initiated by depressing his or her right shoulder, until the last motion barrier is detected at the dysfunctional rib.

6.1.4. The patient is asked to side bend or rotate to the left, while this motion is blocked by the operator's right arm, hand, and shoulder. The operator applies an internal rotatory force anteriorly with the left thumb to the prominent inferior border of the rib (Figure 10-26B).

A

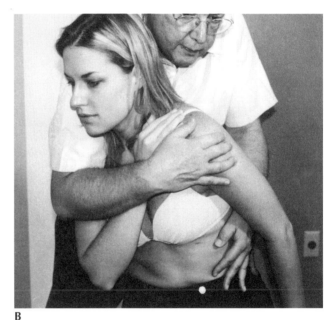

B

FIGURE 10-26

Combined muscle energy technique to correct an ERSlt dysfunction in the thoracic spine with a left external rib torsion below it. (A) The operator is positioned to the patient's right side and monitors the rib anteriorly with the left thumb and thenar eminence over the inferior margin of the rib. The rib margin, instead of the dysfunctional thoracic segment, is palpated for the right side bend, right rotation, and flexion barrier. (B) During an isometric, left side-bending effort by the patient, the operator maintains pressure on the lower rib margin. The operator continues to maintain this pressure when repositioning the patient to the next barrier.

6.1.5. After 3–5 seconds, the patient is asked to relax this effort. The operator increases the pressure on the rib to further reduce the torsion and then repositions the patient with more flexion, right side bending, and right rotation, until the next barrier is felt as a slight motion or increased tension along the rib.

6.1.6. Steps 6.1.4 and 6.1.5 are repeated two or more times.

6.1.7. Re-examine.

Note: Because it was the ERS dysfunction that caused the rib torsion, by using the combined muscle energy technique in the sitting position or the thrust technique in the supine position (described in Section 5.9), it is possible to treat both the ERS and rib torsion at the same time.

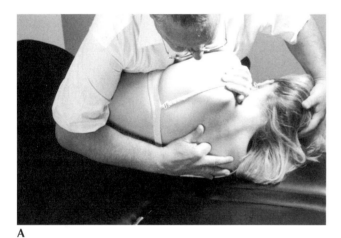

A

B

FIGURE 10-27
*Combined thrust technique for an external torsion of the left fifth rib and an ERSlt at T4-5. **(A)** Hand position to place counterclockwise (craniad) pressure on the rib. **(B)** Final head and trunk position.*

6.2 Combined Thrust Technique for Treatment of an External Rib Torsion and an Associated Non-Neutral Thoracic Dysfunction

Described for a Left Rib External Torsion Dysfunction with an Associated ERS Left   The combined technique for an external rib torsion and ERS dysfunction is performed by an addition to the supine technique used for ERS dysfunctions in the thoracic spine. This technique is valuable for ERS dysfunctions associated with external torsion of the rib, because sometimes successful treatment can be achieved only by treating both at the same time.

The following technique is described for the left fifth rib with T4 ERSlt in relation to T5. The aim of this technique is to open the left T4-5 facet joint and internally rotate the left fifth rib at the costovertebral joint.

> *Diagnostic Points*
> The left fifth rib has a prominent upper border with a wide interspace above, and the lower border of the rib is difficult to feel. The TPs of T4 are rotated to the left when the spine is taken into full flexion. There is marked tissue texture change around the left spinal and costovertebral joints.

6.2.1. The patient is supine, and the operator stands to his or her right (opposite the most posterior TP). The patient crosses the arms over the chest so that the left elbow is directly in front of the right and the hands rest over the opposite shoulders.

6.2.2. The operator reaches across with the left hand and lifts the patient's left shoulder so that the right hand can be inserted under the patient. In this technique, the lower vertebra (T5) is supported by the operator's right thumb and fingers. The operator uses the thenar eminence to contact the inferior part of the angle of the dysfunctional rib so that, by rotation of the hand, correction of the rib torsion occurs at the same time as the main thrust corrects the vertebral dysfunction (Figure 10-27*A*).

6.2.3. The operator reaches down with the left hand behind the patient's neck to support the head and then flexes and side bends the patient to the right, until movement just begins at T4. Rotation is introduced by turning the patient's head to the right, again until motion just begins at T4 (Figure 10-27*B*).

6.2.4. Bringing the chest or upper abdomen over the patient's elbows, the operator waits until the patient has fully exhaled and then gives a high-velocity, low-amplitude thrust. When giving the thrust, the operator drops his or her weight on the patient's elbows in the direction of the operator's right thumb, while he or she twists the thenar eminence counterclockwise (as seen from the front) to raise the left rib angle superiorly.

6.2.5. Retest.

FIGURE 10-28
*Treatment for antero-posterior compression of a left rib. **(A)** With the arm over the operator's shoulder. **(B)** With the arm at the patient's side.*

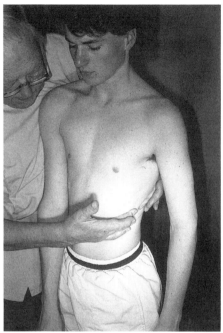

A   B

7. Muscle Energy

7.1 Anterior-Posterior Compression

> *Diagnostic Points*
> The rib(s) are identified as the key rib(s) of a respiratory restriction for inhalation and/or exhalation. The anterior and posterior ends of the rib are less prominent than the expected position in the curves. The rib shaft is prominent in the axilla, but the intercostal spaces above and below remain symmetrical.

7.1.1. The patient is sitting or standing, and the operator stands on the patient's normal side. For the higher ribs, the patient should have his or her arm over the operator's shoulder (Figure 10-28A), but for the lower ribs or for a patient with restricted shoulder mobility, the patient's arm can be kept at his or her side (Figure 10-28B).

7.1.2. With the middle fingers, the operator circles the dysfunctional rib, pulling the patient's trunk toward the operator and putting medial pressure with the fingertips over the rib in the mid axilla.

7.1.3. The patient should take a deep breath in to expand the rib cage anteriorly and posteriorly, while the operator maintains medial compression on the dysfunctional rib.

7.1.4. While holding deep inhalation, the patient attempts to side bend his or her trunk against the operator; for the upper ribs, the patient pulls his or her arm downward on top of the operator's shoulder, while the medial compression on the rib is maintained.

7.1.5. After two to four repetitions, and taking up the slack after each repetition, the rib(s) are re-examined.

7.2 Lateral Compression

> *Diagnostic Points*
> The rib(s) are identified as the key rib(s) of a respiratory restriction for inhalation and/or exhalation. The anterior and posterior ends of the rib are prominent, but the rib is "missing" in the axilla. The intercostal spaces are even.

7.2.1. The patient sits, and the operator stands at the patient's affected side. The patient is asked to abduct the arm on the affected side and place it over the operator's shoulder.

7.2.2. The operator places one hand anteriorly over the costochondral junction and the other hand posteriorly over the rib angle of the dysfunctional rib. Recall that the rib angle is more craniad than the costochondral junction, so the hand in back is higher than the hand in front. It is best to palpate the entire length of the rib shaft to ensure bilateral hand contact on the same rib (Figure 10-29).

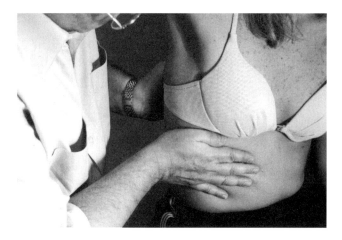

FIGURE 10-29

Treatment for a lateral compression of a right rib with hand contacts in front and back on the same (dysfunctional) rib.

7.2.3. While the operator compresses the rib from front to back, the patient inhales deeply and pulls his or her arm down onto the operator's shoulder.

7.2.4. This technique is repeated two to four times, taking up the slack after each repetition. The rib(s) are then re-examined.

REFERENCES

1. Bourdillon J. Treatment of respiratory rib dysfunctions. J Orthop Med 1990;12:63–68.
2. Bourdillon J. Treatment of structural rib dysfunctions. J Orthop Med 1991;13:20–22.
3. Lindgren KA, Manninen H, Rytkonen H. Thoracic outlet syndrome: a functional disturbance of the upper thoracic aperture? Muscle Nerve 1995;5:526–530.
4. Butler DS. Mobilisation of the Nervous System. Melbourne: Churchill Livingstone, 1991.

11

Treatment of the Cervical Spine

The most serious accidents caused by manipulation without anesthesia have been from treatment of the upper cervical spine in extension and nearly full rotation. This position is not necessary to effectively treat the upper cervical spine, and it is important to avoid the risk that such positioning involves. The problem is caused by injury to the vertebrobasilar arterial system, and it has been shown that the mechanism is usually an intimal dissection[1] rather than a direct obstruction. Thrusting manipulation is not the only cause; this injury has even been recorded as happening when the person has held his or her own neck voluntarily extended and rotated for a period of time without an external force of any kind.

Millions of high cervical manipulations using high-velocity techniques are performed every year, and the number of reported accidents is very small. When an accident does happen, the results are serious and may be fatal. Permanent paresis is common after such an accident. An excellent review of this data is given by Kleynhans.[2]

Lewit[3] quotes a test ascribed to De Kleyn as being useful for determination of vertebral artery insufficiency. The test is performed with the patient supine with the head extended over the end of the table. The operator rotates the head first to one side and then to the other, watching for the development of nystagmus or listening for a complaint of dizziness or nausea. The risk of an ischemic catastrophe has been described in head and neck positions[4] that are similar to those normally used for the De Kleyn test. Furthermore, the results of such provocative testing do not correlate with the occurrence of cerebrovascular complications due to cervical manipulation.[5] In the opinion of the authors, the De Kleyn test or similar variations of this test should not be used. This recommendation is in spite of the fact that the test is mandatory in Germany before cervical manipulation is performed. As noted in Chapter 6, it is *anxiety*, rather than *nystagmus*, that is the earliest sign of cerebral anoxia. *Therefore, it is recommended that, if the patient becomes anxious during any procedure to the upper cervical spine, the procedure should be abandoned immediately.*

A somewhat safer test can be performed before the examination and treatment of the cervical spine. The seated patient is asked to extend the head on the neck and, in that position, to rotate first to one side and then to the other, without being touched by the operator. The rotated position is maintained for 5 seconds, and the patient is watched carefully for anxiety, dizziness, or nystagmus. The testing should be stopped immediately if any of these signs appears. If the test is positive, it is probably best to proceed with appropriate consultations or diagnostic studies to examine the integrity of the cervical and intracranial circulatory system. It is unlikely that dramatic responses to this head position have gone unnoticed by the patient before the examination, but, once again, the absence of any abnormal response does not preclude the risk of a complication. Adding to the difficulty in interpreting such tests is the fact that many patients with cervical somatic dysfunction experience vertigo with changes in head and neck position.

Serious complications from thrusting manipulation of the cervical spine performed in Switzerland over a 33-year period occurred at a frequency of 1 in 400,000 cervical manipulations and included incidents of diminished consciousness, loss of consciousness, neurological symptoms, and radiculopathies. Vertigo was noted to occur in 1 in 40,000 cases.[6] There has not been any report of a serious complication occurring in cases in which the cervical spine was treated with the muscle energy and thrust techniques described in this book, and such complications are especially unlikely when care is taken to avoid the positions that would put the vertebral artery at risk.

The cervical spine is unique in that there are no neutral dysfunctions, although, in the upper cervical spine, there is a small amount of rotation that occurs at the occipitoatlantal (OA) joint to the opposite side of side bending. This coupled movement at the OA joint is guided by the alar ligaments and the osteology of the OA joint and is not truly the consequence of neutral mechanics. Therefore, because there are no neutral mechanics in the typical cervical spine, all dysfunctions in the typical cervical spine (C2-7) are of the non-neutral type. When treating the cervical spine, the beginning operator often appears to have difficulty in locating the restrictive barrier, especially after the first patient effort. It is important, especially in the cervical spine, not to go beyond the barrier when positioning a joint for muscle energy or thrusting treatment.

Motion characteristics of the cervical spine are directly influenced by the upper thoracic spine (T1-5); therefore, the neck can be viewed functionally as a combination of both areas, which have been artificially separated by anatomical classification. Neck pain is often relieved by restoration of upper thoracic spinal function, rather than by direct treatment of the cervical spine alone. Likewise, restricted active cervical range of motion for rotation, side bending, and flexion or extension often originates in the upper thoracic spine. This fact often is not appreciated, and it is quite common to find that the cause for persistent neck pain is because the thoracic dysfunctions were never addressed. This is particularly true in patients who have experienced a flexion-extension neck injury, or so-called "whiplash" injuries. For this reason, in this edition, the thoracic spine is presented before this chapter. It should also be emphasized that headaches are often the consequence of cervical and thoracic dysfunctions, especially if they influence the upper cervical spine. Dysfunctions between the occiput and C1 can often cause unilateral headaches, which radiate behind the eye and, because of their nature and intensity, can be confused with true migraine headaches. Lower cervical spine dysfunctions can also refer pain that radiates into the upper thoracic spine and under the scapula. When treating the cervical spine, it is important to be aware of the influence of the long restrictor muscles that can act on and affect the mobility of multiple levels of the cervical spine the same way. Particularly, the scalenes and longus colli can act as long restrictors responsible for multiple ipsilateral flexed, rotated, and side bent (FRS) dysfunctions in the typical cervical spine, whereas the levator scapulae can be the long restrictor responsible for the appearance of multiple ipsi-

lateral extended, rotated, and side bent (ERS) dysfunctions in the upper cervical spine. It is probably best to lengthen these long restrictors (see Chapter 14) before treating individual segments in the cervical spine.

Flexion and extension occur maximally between C4, C5, and C6, and it is no wonder that most cervical dysfunctions include these segments. Because this is a region of maximal physical stress, it is also the region in which reactive bone growth can provide additional stabilization by osteophyte formation. If viewed as a similar process as the formation of calluses on the palm of the hand, thickened bone, like thickened skin, has a protective role and should not be considered simply a "degenerative change." Nevertheless, osteophyte formation certainly changes the osteology of the spine and thereby reduces the anatomical range of motion between vertebrae.

Radiculopathies also commonly occur at these mid-level segments of the cervical spine, usually at C5-6 with pain radiating to the shoulder and down the arm laterally to the thumb. Sensory loss over the thumb and index finger can be confused with carpal tunnel syndrome. In more severe cases, there is a loss of the biceps and brachioradialis reflexes with weakness of the biceps, infraspinatus, and supraspinatus muscles. Radiculopathies occurring above C4-5 and below C5-6 are less common, unless there has been a surgical fusion between C4 and C6. The consequence of adaptive increased mobility and subsequent increased physical stress is additional osteophyte formation at those segments above and below the fusion. Brachial plexopathies must always be considered in the differential diagnosis. Radicular symptoms that become worse or accentuated with cervical extension are usually the consequence of foraminal stenosis by osteophyte formation; symptoms that worsen with flexion are usually from cervical disc herniation. The development of large posterior osteophytes can reduce the diameter of the spinal canal and compromise the spinal cord over time, causing a progressive myelopathy. Likewise, an acute myelopathy can be the consequence of any trauma that flexes the cervical spine in the presence of a large posterior osteophyte.

1. TYPICAL CERVICAL VERTEBRAE, C2-7

Review of Examination

Most of the examination techniques for the thoracic and lumbar spines use motion testing or positional testing with flexion and extension, seeking asymmetries in the movement or position of the transverse processes. In the examination of the cervical spine, the operator avoids contact with the transverse processes because the tips of these TPs are very tender. Instead, the operator palpates over the large articular pillars of the cervical zygapophyseal joints. The examination of the cervical spine is usually performed with the patient supine. The operator is seated at the head of the table, supporting the patient's occiput with the palms and palpating over the articular pillars with the finger pads, the width of which are approximately equal to the surface of the articular pillar. The most comfortable initial placement of the fingers of both hands is usually with the fifth digit on C3 and the index finger on C6. Movement of the hand caudally allows the index finger to contact C7, whereas movement cranially allows the little finger to contact C2. Palpation at this stage provides scanning for tissue texture changes over the pillars to give the examiner a clue as to which segmental levels need to be examined further.

The identification of a motion restriction in the cervical spine is best determined by lateral translation with the index fingers supporting the segment to be tested or with the finger pads placed against the articular pillars. Two different techniques have been described to passively translate a specific, typical, cervical vertebra. In the first technique, described by Greenman,[7] a sling is formed with the index fingers of both hands that supports the vertebra to be translated; the palms support the patient's head, and the remaining fingers support and translate all of the vertebrae that are craniad to the one being examined. This technique uses lateral translation with alternating pressure from right to left and left to right as a measurement of the freedom or restriction of mobility of the zygapophyseal joints to open or close at the immediate level below the vertebral body held by the examiner's index fingers. Therefore, the dysfunctional vertebra will always be identified as the superior vertebra that is restricted for lateral translation in relation to the one below. For example, if, in extension, C5 is found to be restricted for translation from right to left, the positional diagnosis is an FRSlt at C5-6 with a restriction in closure of the right facet between C5 and C6. If, in flexion, C5 is found to be restricted for translation from right to left, the positional diagnosis is an ERSlt at C5-6 with a restriction in opening of the left facet between C5 and C6. This diagnosis is true as long as, during the examination, C5 is translated from right to left with the rest of the cervical spine and head above en bloc. When using this technique, it is important to maintain a pure lateral translatory force and avoid any tilting or side bending of the head around the index fingers, which can inadvertently result in a false sense of freedom of motion at that spinal level.

A second technique has also been used in evaluating the typical cervical spine using translation. In this technique, the operator's index or middle finger pads are placed against the articular pillars, and translation is introduced at that segment only, without supporting and moving the head and cervical spine above. Restriction in lateral translation using this technique may involve the facet joints below or above the level tested, because with this technique, it is possible to slide the superior facet of the translated vertebra underneath the level above, especially if testing by translation of the cervical spine in extension. Another tendency when evaluating the cervical spine with this technique is for the examiner to allow the patient's head and neck to side bend and rotate rather than translate during testing, which results in a false sense of movement with the restrictive barrier undetected. For these reasons, the authors prefer the first technique, as originally described by Greenman.

The barrier for an ERS dysfunction can be found by starting in extension and motion testing with translation laterally. The operator must introduce enough extension into the cervical spine to find the range in which translation is unrestricted and symmetrical from right to left and left to right (see Figure 5-19). The operator then gradually introduces flexion until tension builds at one of the fingers supporting the articular pillars during translation to the right or the left. The barrier for an FRS dysfunction is found by introducing flexion from the extended position, until translation is unrestricted and symmetrical from right to left and from left to right (see Figure 5-18). The operator then reintroduces extension until tension builds at one of the fingers supporting the articular pillars during translation to the right or the left.

An alternative method to identify flexion and extension restrictions of the lower cervical spine can be done with the patient seated and the operator standing behind in a fashion similar to that for evaluating the upper thoracic spine (see Figure 5-9). The operator palpates over the articular pillars with the thumbs and assesses for any rotational changes that might accompany spinal flexion or extension, thereby arriving at a diagnosis of an ERS or FRS dysfunction. This may actually be the preferred technique when attempting to examine a patient with a muscular or broad neck, in which lateral translation of the lower cervical spine may be difficult to accomplish with the patient supine.

Muscle Energy Treatment for an FRS Dysfunction

1.1 Described for C3 That Is Flexed, Rotated, and Side Bent to the Right in Relation to C4 (FRSrt)

This is a non-neutral dysfunction with a restriction for extension and for rotation and side bending to the left between C3 and C4. The left facet joint between C3 and C4 does not close completely.

Diagnostic Points

There is tissue texture change at the segment. With the neck fully flexed, C3 translates easily from right to left and from left to right. With the neck extended and supported to C3-4, there is restriction of translation of C3 from left to right, but translation from right to left remains free. C3 *cannot* side bend left in relation to C4, but it *can* side bend right and therefore *is* side bent right. To side bend left in extension, the left facet joint between C3 and C4 must be able to close, and it cannot.

1.1.1. The patient is supine, and the operator sits at the patient's head.

1.1.2. The operator's left index finger contacts the posterior aspect of the left lateral mass (articular pillar) of C4, the lower vertebra of the motion segment in the range of free, lateral, left-to-right translation (Figure 11-1A). C4 is lifted anteriorly by the operator's left finger, which extends the C3-4 joint until the tension is felt with the index finger. For major restrictions, there is tension at the onset. Another option to find the extension barrier is to start with the neck initially flexed by lifting the occiput with the operator's right hand and then introduce extension from below up by the operator's left index finger supporting and lifting C4 anteri-

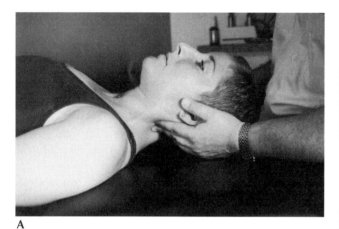

A

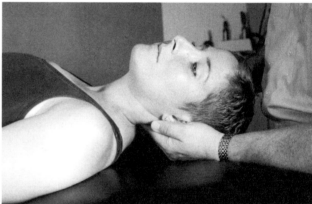

B

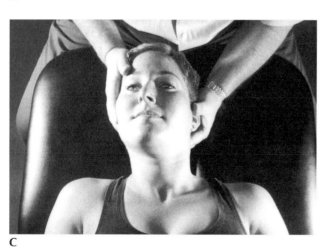

C

D

FIGURE 11-1

Muscle energy technique for an FRS right at C3-4. (A) Operator's left index finger contacts the articular pillar of C4, and the right hand supports the patient's head. (B) The extension barrier is found by lifting C4 anteriorly with the left index finger until tension is felt. (C) The operator's right hand is placed on the right side of the patient's head to stabilize and to be used later to resist right side bending. Using the left finger contact on C4, C4 is translated to the right until the left side-bending barrier is palpated. (D) Using the right hand, the operator rotates the patient's head to the left until tension builds at the C3-4 segment, signaling the presence of the left rotation barrier.

orly until tension is palpated (Figure 11-1*B*).

1.1.3. Once the extension barrier is found, the operator's right hand contacts the right side of the patient's head to stabilize, and later is used to resist right side bending. The operator's left index finger introduces translation of C4 to the right, until the left side-bending barrier is palpated (Figure 11-1*C*). The operator uses the right hand to introduce left rotation until the tension reaches the operator's left index finger (Figure 11-1*D*).

1.1.4. The patient is asked to attempt to push his or her head gently to the right or to lift it off the table. The effort is maintained for 3–5 seconds, while the operator resists so that the patient does not move. The patient then is asked to relax.

1.1.5. When the patient has relaxed fully, the operator uses his or her left index finger to either engage a new extension barrier by slightly increasing the anterior translation of C4 by lifting it or a new left side-bending barrier by translating C4 to the right. Further fine tuning can be made by using the right hand to side bend and rotate the patient's head to the left.

1.1.6. Steps 1.1.4 and 1.1.5 are repeated two or more times, depending on response. If the response is poor, it may be wise to try the other available direction for the patient's effort (flexion instead of side bending, or vice versa) or to reassess to be sure that the initial positioning for treatment was on the free side of the barrier.

1.1.7. Retest.

Note: For multilevel extension restrictions (FRS dysfunctions) on the same side, long restrictors must be considered. Most often, these restrictors are the middle and anterior scalenes and longus colli muscles. If these muscles are hypertonic, they prevent active side bending to the opposite direction at multiple cervical levels. For example, if there is hypertonus of the right anterior and middle scalenes, the longus colli muscles, or both, then there is a multisegmental restriction for active left side bending that increases with extension and decreases with flexion of the cervical spine. However, in this example, passive mobility testing of the cervical spine with lateral translation will feel restricted from right to left and may erroneously be interpreted as multiple, stacked FRSlt cervical dysfunctions.

Treatment for the hypertonic right scalenes using muscle energy techniques would begin with the patient's head cradled between the operator's left hand and left shoulder, flexing the upper cervical spine, while the operator's right hand palpates over the patient's right first rib. To introduce extension into the lower cervical spine, the patient's head and neck are supported by the operator

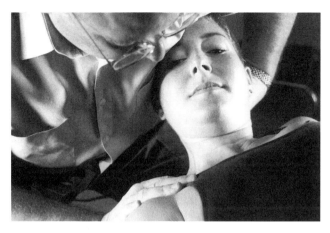

FIGURE 11-2

The positions of the patient and operator for the treatment of hypertonus in the right anterior and middle scalenes, which should be suspected when there appear to be multiple FRSlt dysfunctions.

and brought off the end of the table, down as far as T2. While maintaining pressure and depressing the patient's right shoulder caudad, the operator uses his or her left shoulder and hand to translate the patient's head and neck in an anterior-to-posterior direction to induce extension of the lower cervical spine. The patient's head is tilted to the left and rotated right until tension is felt at the first rib (Figure 11-2). The patient is asked to take a deep breath and flex the neck by pushing his or her forehead into the operator's left shoulder for 3–5 seconds. After exhalation and relaxation, the operator repositions the patient by further posterior translation, adding further left side bending and right rotation as needed. The treatment is repeated two to three times or until cervical anterior-to-posterior translation feels free. By keeping the patient's chin down, the upper cervical spine is maintained in flexion throughout the stretch. After the hypertonicity in these long restrictors has been reduced, any residual FRS dysfunctions can be treated individually with the muscle energy technique previously described.

Muscle Energy Treatment for an ERS Dysfunction

1.2 Described for C4 That Is Extended, Rotated, and Side Bent to the Right in Relation to C5 (ERSrt)

This is a non-neutral dysfunction with a restriction for flexion and for rotation and side bending to the left between C4 and C5. The right facet joint between C4 and C5 does not open completely.

Diagnostic Points

There is tissue texture change at the segment. With the neck extended, C4 translates easily from right to left and from left to right. With the neck flexed, there is restriction of translation of C4 from left to right, but translation from right to left remains free. C4 *cannot* side bend left in relation to C5, but it *can* side bend right and, therefore, *is* side bent right. To side bend left in flexion, the right facet joint must be able to open, and it cannot. When using lateral translation to assess freedom of motion during flexion, the inferior facet of the superior vertebra must be able to glide in a craniad direction over the superior facet of the inferior vertebra. If the right facet joint between C4 and C5 cannot fully open, C4 cannot translate from left to right when the spine is flexed past the point of available motion between C4 and C5.

1.2.1. The patient is supine, and the operator sits at the patient's head.

1.2.2. The operator uses the right hand to control the patient's head and upper cervical spine. The palm of the operator's left hand supports the patient's occiput, while the left thumb is placed on the left facet joint of C4-5 (Figure 11-3*A* and *B*), and the left index finger is placed under the right articular pillar of C4 (Figure 11-3*C*). Both the thumb and index finger support C4, but the thumb also serves as a pivotal block, around which left side bending is restored.

1.2.3. Using the right hand and left palm, the operator flexes the patient's neck by lifting the patient's head until tension is felt at the left index finger and thumb (see Figure 11-3*B*). Left side bending is introduced by translating C4 from left to right with the left thumb, until the barrier to left side bending is felt by increased tension between C4 and C5 (Figure 11-3*D*). If side bending is already fully restricted, the degree of cervical flexion can be reduced until some motion is possible for lateral translation from left to right at C4-5. The left rotation barrier is introduced last and is palpated when tension reaches the operator's left thumb at the left facet joint of C4-5. Turning the patient's head to the left with the right hand localizes the left rotation barrier from above down.

1.2.4. The patient is asked to make a gentle effort to side bend his or her head to the right or to press it back toward the table. The effort is maintained for 3–5 seconds and is resisted equally by the operator. The patient is then asked to relax.

1.2.5. When relaxation is complete, the operator repositions the patient's cervical spine to the new barrier

in all three planes by a slight increase in flexion, left side bending, and left rotation.

1.2.6. Steps 1.2.4 and 1.2.5 are repeated two or more times, but if there has been little or no change in the location of the restrictive barrier, successful treatment might require asking the patient to make the effort into extension (if side bending was used) or into right side bending (if extension was used).

1.2.7. Retest.

Note: For multiple flexion restrictions (ERSrt) affecting C2-4, the long restrictor may be the right levator scapula. Hypertonus in this muscle can be reduced by a muscle energy technique with the patient side lying on his or her left shoulder. The patient's left arm is positioned so that the head can lie over the upper arm and side bend to the left, with the cervical spine positioned into flexion and left rotation toward the table. The patient's right arm is placed with the hand resting on the right hip. The operator stabilizes the patient's cervical spine by placing the right hand over the right articular pillars of C1-4. The left hand is used to depress and posteriorly tilt the patient's right scapula, aligning the left forearm and wrist with the fiber direction of the levator scapulae (Figure 11-4). The patient is asked to lift the right shoulder against the operator's resistance for 3–5 seconds. After relaxation, the shoulder is further depressed inferiorly with an additional posterior tilt, while the head is further rotated to the left. This treatment is repeated two or three times, after which the cervical spine is re-examined, and any residual ERS dysfunctions can be individually treated with the muscle energy technique previously described.

Thrust Technique for an FRS Dysfunction

1.3 Described for C5 That Is Flexed, Rotated, and Side Bent to the Right in Relation to C6 (FRSrt)

This is a non-neutral dysfunction with a restriction for extension and for rotation and side bending to the left between C5 and C6. The left facet joint between C5 and C6 does not close completely.

1.3.1. The patient is supine, and the operator sits or stands at the head of the table.

1.3.2. The operator's right hand controls the patient's head, and the second metacarpophalangeal joint of the left hand is placed against the left lateral mass (articular pillar) of C5, the superior vertebra (Figure 11-5*A*).

1.3.3. Using the metacarpophalangeal joint of the left index finger and the tips of the right fingers as monitors,

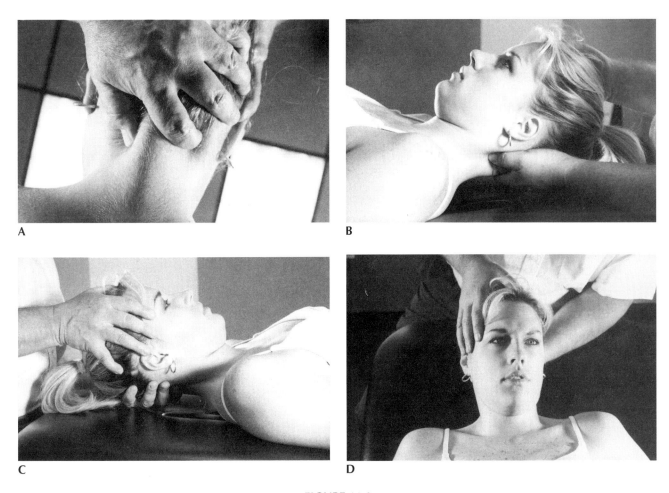

FIGURE 11-3

Muscle energy technique for an ERSrt at C4-5. (A) The operator's left thumb is placed on the left facet joint of C4-5. (B) The patient's occiput is resting in the palm of operator's left hand, and the cervical spine is flexed to the flexion barrier. (C) The operator's right hand is placed on the right side of the patient's head over the frontal, temporal, and parietal bones. The left index finger supports C4 at the flexion barrier. (D) The operator moves the left hand to the right, translating C4-5 until the tension builds and the left side-bending barrier is encountered, then rotates the patient's head to the left until tension at the operator's left thumb signals the left rotation barrier at C4-5.

the operator introduces extension and left side bending until the movement is localized to the barrier (i.e., the upper border of C5 from above and lower border of C6 from below). It is sometimes helpful to rotate the patient's head slightly to the right to "get it out of the way" (Figure 11-5*B*).

1.3.4. After full exhalation, and when all the slack has been removed by extension, left side bending, and left rotation, a high-velocity, low-amplitude thrust is given by the operator's left hand on the lateral mass of C5 in the direction of the spinous process of T1. The force should always be directed toward the spinous pro-

cess of T1 when treating any of the typical cervical levels with this technique.

1.3.5. Retest.

Thrust Technique Using Side Bending for an ERS Dysfunction

1.4 Described for ERSlt at C4-5

This is a non-neutral dysfunction with a restriction for flexion and for rotation and side bending to the right between C4 and C5. The left facet joint between C4 and C5 does not open completely.

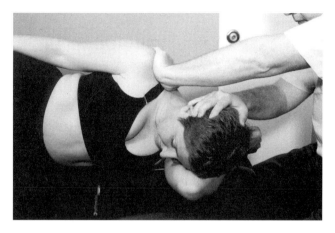

FIGURE 11-4
Muscle energy technique for a hypertonic right levator scapula muscle.

1.4.1. The patient is supine, and the operator sits or stands at the patient's head.

1.4.2. With the left hand and forearm, the operator controls the patient's head and places the second metacarpophalangeal joint of the right hand against the right zygapophyseal joint of C4-5. Typically, the operator's fingers of the left hand support the patient's chin to help introduce and control cervical flexion, and the left forearm is placed alongside the patient's head to introduce side bending to the right.

1.4.3. Using the right hand as a monitor, the operator introduces flexion and right side bending, until the movement is localized to the side-bending barrier

between C4 from above and C5 from below (Figure 11-6).

1.4.4. After full exhalation, and when all the slack has been removed by right side bending and right rotation, a high-velocity, low-amplitude thrust is given directly to the left by the operator's right hand against the C4-5 facet joint. This thrust opens the left facet joint.

1.4.5. Retest.

Thrust Technique Using Rotation for an ERS Dysfunction

1.5 Described for an ERSlt at C4-5

This is a non-neutral dysfunction with a restriction for flexion and for rotation and side bending to the right between C4 and C5. The left facet joint between C4 and C5 does not open completely.

1.5.1. The patient is supine, and the operator sits or stands at the patient's head.

1.5.2. Using the palms of both hands, the operator controls the patient's head and blocks movement at the right facet joint of C4-5 with the right index and middle fingers (Figure 11-7A).

1.5.3. The operator places the left second metacarpophalangeal joint against the posterior aspect of the left lateral mass of C4 (Figure 11-7B).

1.5.4. Using both hands to monitor, the operator introduces flexion, right side bending, and right rotation, until the movement is localized to the barrier (i.e., the upper border of C4 from above and lower border of C5 from below).

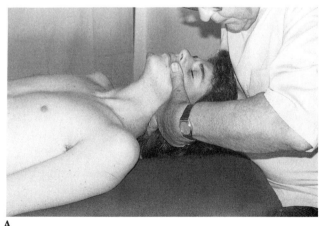

A

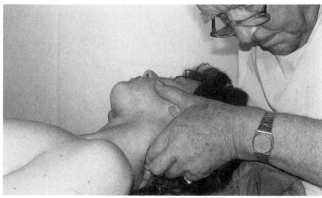

B

FIGURE 11-5
*Thrust treatment for an FRSrt at C5-6. (**A**) Lateral aspect of the operator's left index metacarpophalangeal joint is placed against the lateral mass of C5 (upper vertebra). (**B**) Position for thrust toward the spinous process of T1.*

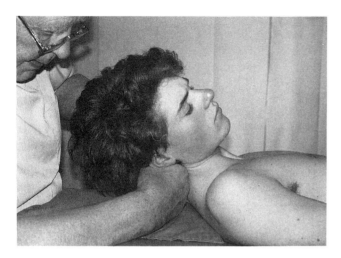

FIGURE 11-6
Side bending thrust for an ERSlt at C4.

1.5.5. After a full exhalation, and when all the slack has been removed by flexion, right side bending, and right rotation to the final barrier, a high-velocity, low-amplitude thrust is given by the operator's left hand against the posterior aspect of the left lateral mass of C4 to produce rotation to the right.

1.5.6. Retest.

2. ATLANTOAXIAL (C1-2) JOINT

The most significant motion at the atlantoaxial (C1-2) joint is rotation, even though there is a small amount of side bending and craniad to caudad translation.

Muscle Energy and Thrust Technique for a C1-2 Dysfunction

Described for a Restriction of Rotation to the Right at C1-2

Diagnostic Points

There is tissue texture change at the segment. With the neck passively held flexed by the operator as far as it easily goes, the range of rotation of the head to the right is less than the range of rotation to the left. The barrier to rotation is detected by the onset of motion of C2, which is monitored by the operator's palpating fingers on the posterior articular pillar of C2.

Note: To prevent a loss of localization while assessing mobility at C1-2, the operator must maintain cervical flexion and not allow cervical extension to occur.

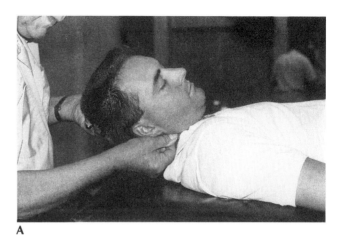

A

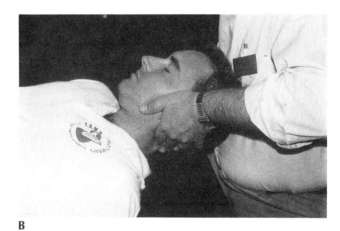

B

FIGURE 11-7
Rotatory thrust for an ERSlt at C4. (A) Blocking the right facet joint with index and thumb. (B) Left index metacarpophalangeal joint positioned behind the lateral mass of C4.

2.1 Muscle Energy Technique for Restricted Rotation to the Right at C1-2

2.1.1. The patient is supine, and the operator sits or stands at the patient's head.

2.1.2. With the palms of both hands, the operator supports the patient's head and flexes the neck as far as it easily goes, usually approximately 45 degrees.

2.1.3. Monitoring on the posterior lateral aspect of C2, the operator turns the patient's head to the right, until C2 on the left just begins to move, and then backs off the barrier by de-rotating slightly (Figure 11-8).

2.1.4. The patient is asked to turn his or her head gently to the left or simply to move his or her eyes to the left. The effort is maintained for 3–5 seconds, while the operator resists any movement.

2.1.5. On relaxation, the operator rotates the patient's head further to the right, and the patient is asked to look

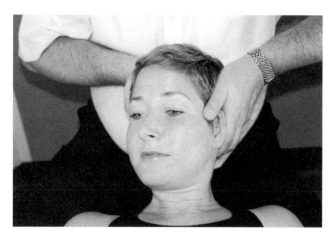

FIGURE 11-8
Treatment of a C1-2 right rotational restriction using muscle energy technique. The patient's head is rotated to the right until tension builds at C2 on the left.

to the right to help facilitate further right rotation. Steps 2.1.4 and 2.1.5 are repeated two or more times.

2.1.6. Retest to see if right rotation has been fully restored at this segment.

2.2 Thrust, First Technique for Restricted Rotation to the Right at C1-2

2.2.1. The patient is supine, and the operator sits or stands at the patient's head.

2.2.2. With the palms of both hands, the operator supports the patient's head and flexes the neck as far as it easily goes, usually approximately 45 degrees.

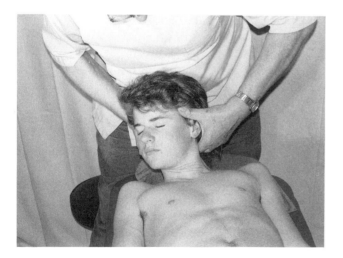

FIGURE 11-9
Position for treatment of restricted C1-2 rotation to the right. Thrust with the left index finger.

2.2.3. The operator's left second metacarpophalangeal joint is placed against the left posterior arch of the patient's atlas to monitor and localize the force. The operator rotates the patient's head to the right to reach the barrier (i.e., just before C2 begins to move).

2.2.4. When all rotatory slack has been taken out by rotation and full exhalation, the thrust is given by both hands turning the patient's head to the right. The force is localized to C1-2 through the operator's left index finger (Figure 11-9).

2.2.5. Retest.

2.3 Thrust, Second Technique for Restricted Rotation to the Right at C1-2

Steps 2.3.1 and 2.3.2 are the same as steps 2.2.1 and 2.2.2.

2.3.3. With the hands on both sides of the patient's head and with the fingers pointing caudad, the operator takes up any slack by rotating the patient's head to reach the right rotation barrier at C1-2.

2.3.4. The thrust is given by a rotatory movement of both hands while maintaining the flexion (Figure 11-10).

2.3.5. Retest.

3. OCCIPITOATLANTAL (CO-C1) JOINT

At the OA joint, the major motion is flexion and extension, but there is also a small amount of side bending. Assessment of side bending using lateral translation can be used diagnostically, because it is often easier to assess for motion loss than flexion or extension. The side-bending movement is coupled to a very small range of rotation that always occurs to the opposite side. Any loss of side-bending motion is critical and restricts the flexion-extension motion, much like a drawer that no longer glides in and out if there is a loss of side-to-side freedom. Dysfunction at the OA joint is a common cause of occipital pain and headaches that radiate frontally around the sinuses or behind one eye and are often misinterpreted as a sinus or migraine headache.

Muscle Energy Technique for Occipitoatlantal Dysfunctions

3.1 Described for an Occiput That Is Flexed and Side Bent to the Right in Relation to C1 (FSrt)

When this dysfunction is present, there is a restriction for extension between the left occipital condyle and the left superior facet of C1. As the left condyle is restricted from gliding anteriorly on the left superior facet of C1, and the right occipital condyle can glide further anteriorly on the right superior facet of C1, the occiput will rotate to the left during extension. Because the occiput has rotated to the left, and the side bending motion is coupled in the opposite direction, it will also be side bent to the right. The side-bending component for the OA joint is critical for the normal gliding motion of the joint and is considered more important to identify and restore than the coupled rotational component. The rotational component need not be considered for treatment purposes when the muscle energy technique is used.

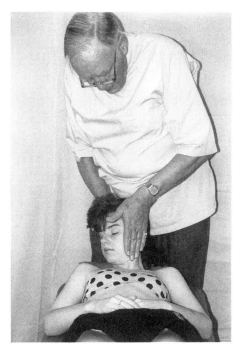

FIGURE 11-10
Position for treatment of restricted C1-2 rotation to the right. Thrust given with both hands.

> ### Diagnostic Points
> There is tissue texture change at the segment. The head does not translate as far to the right as to the left when tested with the OA joint extended (see Figure 5-23). Translation to the left and to the right may be equal when the head is flexed, as long as the joints of the lower cervical segments are free to side bend (see Figure 5-22). Anterior-posterior translation with the head rotated 30 degrees to the left demonstrates a restriction of forward translation (extension) on the left. Remember that the occipital condyles are angled approximately 30 degrees from the sagittal plane (see Figure 2-13), so that turning the head 30 degrees to the left places the left occipital condyle and the articulation at C1 vertical, whereas the joint on the right is horizontal. Comparisons between the right and left sides can be made by rotating the head 30 degrees to the right and repeating the anterior-posterior translation (see Figure 5-24). The arch of C1 is palpated laterally by the operator's index fingers (Figure 11-11*A*). A restriction for anterior translation on the left is palpated when the anterior gliding motion of the left atlanto-occipital joint binds at its extension barrier (Figure 11-11*B*) and forces C1 to rotate to the right away from the left index finger and into the operator's right index finger (Figure 11-11*C*).

3.1.1. The patient is supine, and the operator sits at the patient's head.

3.1.2. The operator holds the patient's occiput by placing the web of the left hand under the posterior cervical muscles, just below the nuchal line but not in contact with the posterior OA membrane. With the right hand, the operator controls the patient's chin position, keeping the right forearm against the right side of the patient's head. The operator places one or two fingers of the hand under the patient's chin so that a flexion effort by the patient can be resisted (Figure 11-12). The patient's head should be back at the midline, neither rotated to the right nor to the left.

3.1.3. Extension of the joint to the barrier is introduced by using both hands to rotate the patient's head backward around a horizontal axis, until the barrier is reached. This movement is extension of the skull on C1 and *not* extension of the cervical spine.

3.1.4. Fine tuning to the remaining motion barrier is accomplished by the operator using the right forearm to side bend the patient's head to the left. If the chin is allowed to remain in the midline, the right rotation occurs automatically and does not need to be introduced by the operator.

3.1.5. From this position, the patient is asked to look down toward his or her feet or, if more force is thought necessary, to push the chin down gently. Either of these commands activates the neck flexors, but the eye movement alone is almost always sufficient.

3.1.6. After 3–5 seconds, the patient is asked to relax, and, even when eye movement is used alone, the anterior muscles should "let go" and relax. When eye movement is being used, a helpful instruction is "look up above your head" to assist active extension, which reciprocally inhibits the neck flexors. When the patient has relaxed fully, the operator takes up the slack to the new barrier by extension of the head, and steps 3.1.5 and 3.1.6 are repeated two or more times.

3.1.7. Retest.

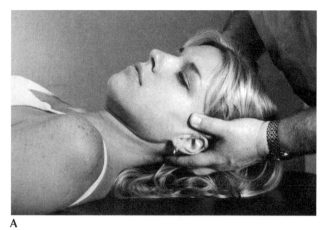

A

B

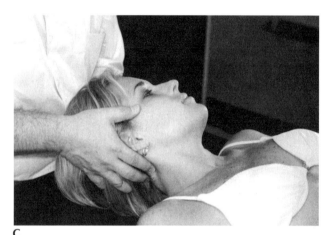

C

FIGURE 11-11

(A) Palpation of the arch of C1 laterally by operator's index fingers. (B) Motion testing at the left occipitoatlantal junction by rotating the head 30 degrees to the left and gliding the occiput vertically upward for anterior translation (extension of occiput on C1). (C) Palpating C1 rotation to the right into the operator's right index finger when anterior translation at the left occipitoatlantal joint is blocked.

FIGURE 11-12

Muscle energy technique for an occipitoatlantal FSrt with a restriction for extension and left side bending.

3.1.8. If the restriction persists, or if there is no change noted when working with the neck flexors, the patient can be asked to side bend the head to the right against the operator's right forearm or simply to move his or her eyes to the right. Movement of the head is blocked by the operator's right forearm. After relaxation and asking the patient to move the eyes to the left, left side bending can be increased.

3.2 Described for an Occiput That Is Extended and Side Bent to the Right in Relation to C1 (ESrt)

When this dysfunction is present, there is a restriction for flexion between the right occipital condyle and the right superior facet of C1. As the right condyle is restricted from gliding posteriorly on the right superior facet of C1, and the left occipital condyle can glide further posteriorly on the left superior facet of C1, the occiput will rotate to the left during flexion. Because the occiput has rotated to the left, and the side bending motion is coupled in the opposite direction, it will also be side bent to the right. The side-bending component for the OA joint is critical for the normal gliding motion of the joint and is considered more important to identify and restore the coupled rotational component. The rotational component need not be considered for treatment purposes when the muscle energy technique is used.

Diagnostic Points

There is tissue texture change at the segment. The patient's head does not translate as far to the right as to the left when tested with the OA joint flexed (see Figure 5-22). Translation to the left and to the right may be equal when tested with the OA joint extended (see Figure 5-23). Anterior-posterior translation with the head rotated 30 degrees to the right demonstrates a restriction of posterior translation on the right (Figure 11-13*A*). Because posterior glide is restricted on the right, the arch of C1 rotates posteriorly on the right into the operator's palpating right index finger when the barrier is reached.

3.2.1. The patient is supine, and the operator sits at the patient's head.

3.2.2. The operator holds the patient's occiput by placing the web of the left hand under the patient's posterior cervical muscles, just below the nuchal line but not in contact with the posterior OA membrane. The operator's left thumb and tip of the ring finger are in contact with the lateral and posterior aspect of the atlas. The patient's head should be in the midline, neither rotated to the right nor left. With the right hand, the operator controls the patient's chin and places the right forearm against the right side of the patient's head. Because the patient will be asked to elevate the chin or extend at the OA joint, the operator needs to place at least one finger on the anterior aspect of the chin (Figure 11-13*B*).

3.2.3. The flexion barrier is introduced by using both hands to rotate the patient's head forward around a horizontal axis, until the barrier is reached, as palpated by the increasing tension at the operator's left thumb and ring finger. This movement is flexion of the skull on C1 and *not* flexion of the cervical spine.

3.2.4. To engage the remaining motion barrier, the patient's head is side bent to the left with the operator's right forearm. If the chin is allowed to remain in the midline, right rotation follows automatically and does not need to be added by the operator.

3.2.5. From this position, the patient is asked to look up above his or her head or, if more force is thought necessary, to lift his or her chin gently toward the ceiling against equal resistance provided by the operator's right fingers. Either of these commands should activate

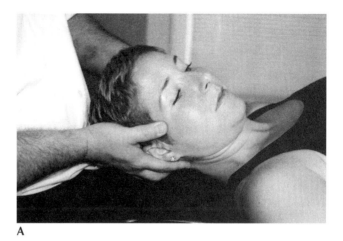

A

B

FIGURE 11-13
(A) Motion testing at the right occipitoatlantal joint by rotating the head 30 degrees to the right and gliding the occiput posteriorly (flexion of occiput on C1). *(B)* Muscle energy technique for an occipitoatlantal ESrt with a restriction for flexion and left side bending.

the neck extensors, but the eye movement alone is almost always sufficient.

3.2.6. After 3–5 seconds, the patient is asked to relax and look down toward his or her feet. This movement activates the neck flexors to reciprocally inhibit the neck extensors. When the patient has relaxed fully, the operator takes up the slack to the new barrier by flexion of the head, and steps 3.2.5 and 3.2.6 are repeated two or more times.

3.2.7. Retest.

3.2.8. If the restriction persists, or if no change is noted after activation of the neck extensors, the patient can be asked to side bend the head to the right against the operator's right forearm or simply to move his or her eyes to

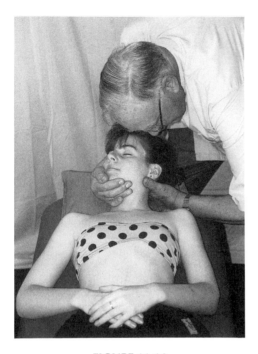

FIGURE 11-14
Position for thrust treatment for an occipitoatlantal ESrt with a restriction for flexion and left side bending.

the right. Movement of the head is blocked by the operator's right forearm. After relaxation and asking the patient to move the eyes to the left, left side bending can be increased.

Thrust Technique for Occipitoatlantal Dysfunctions

3.3 Described for an Occiput That Is Flexed and Side Bent to the Right in Relation to C1 (FSrt)

3.3.1. The patient is supine, and the operator stands at the patient's head.

3.3.2. The operator holds the patient's occiput by placing the web of the left hand under the patient's posterior cervical muscles, just below the nuchal line but not in contact with the posterior OA membrane. With the right hand, the operator controls the patient's chin and places the forearm against the right side of the patient's skull.

3.3.3. The extension movement is introduced by both hands rotating the patient's head until the barrier is reached. This movement is extension of the skull on C1 and *not* extension of the cervical spine.

3.3.4. Fine tuning the left side bending is accomplished by tilting the patient's head with the operator's right forearm. If the chin is allowed to remain in the midline, the right rotation follows automatically and needs not be added by the operator. To have the required force avail-

able for the thrust, the operator should move to the left side of the patient's head so that the thrust is given mainly with the left hand on the occiput.

3.3.5. After a full exhalation, and when all slack has been removed, the thrust is given by a high-velocity, low-amplitude movement with both hands in a craniad direction.

3.3.6. Retest.

Note: This technique is most often associated with injury to the vertebral artery if it is done incorrectly, and it is not recommended for any but the most experienced practitioners.

3.4 Described for an Occiput That Is Extended and Side Bent to the Right in Relation to C1 (ESrt)

3.4.1. The patient is supine, and the operator stands or sits at the patient's head.

3.4.2. The operator holds the patient's occiput by placing the web of the left hand under the patient's posterior cervical muscles, just below the nuchal line but not in contact with the posterior OA membrane. With the right hand, the operator controls the patient's chin, while the right forearm is placed against the right side of the patient's skull.

3.4.3. The flexion movement is introduced by both hands rotating the patient's head until the barrier is reached. This movement is flexion of the skull on C1 and *not* flexion of the cervical spine.

3.4.4. Fine tuning is accomplished by side bending the patient's head to the left with the operator's right forearm. If the chin is allowed to remain in the midline, the right rotation follows automatically and needs not be added by the operator.

3.4.5. After a full exhalation, and when all slack has been removed, the thrust is given with both hands by a high-velocity, low-amplitude movement in a craniad direction (Figure 11-14).

3.4.6. Retest.

REFERENCES

1. Dvorak J, von Orelli F. How dangerous is manipulation of the cervical spine? Case report and results of survey. Man Med 1985;2:1–4.
2. Kleynhans AM. Complications of and Contraindications to Spinal Manipulative Therapy. In S Haldeman (ed), Modern Developments in the Principles and Practice of Chiropractic. East Norwalk, CT: Appleton-Century-Crofts, 1980;359–389.
3. Lewit K. Manipulative Therapy in Rehabilitation of the Motor System. London: Butterworth, 1986.
4. Haldeman S, Kohlbeck FJ, McGregor M. Risk factors

and precipitating neck movements causing vertebrobasilar artery dissection after cervical trauma and spinal manipulation. Spine 1999;24:785–794.

5. Di Fabio RP. Manipulation of the cervical spine: risks and benefits. Phys Ther 1999;79:50–65.

6. Dvorak J, von Orelli F. [The frequency of complications after manipulation of the cervical spine.] Schweiz Rundsch Med Prax 1982;71:64–69.

7. Greenman PE. Principles of Manual Medicine (2nd ed). Baltimore: Williams & Wilkins, 1996.

12

The Lumbosacral Junction and an Overview of Treatment Strategies for the Spine

Each practitioner of manual medicine develops his or her own method of examination, because it would take too long to examine every spinal joint and the rest of the musculoskeletal system. An overall screening examination helps identify areas that require more detailed testing by a scanning examination. Following a scanning examination, the most detailed and important part of the examination can be performed: the segmental definition of a dysfunction (see Chapters 3, 4, and 5). When this is completed, the operator knows the precise directions in which motion is restricted for each joint examined so that a specific treatment plan can be determined. In addition, before treatment begins, the operator should be able to identify what appears to be the most significant dysfunction in the musculoskeletal system. We attempt to identify the most significant dysfunction by first looking for major (rather than minor) dysfunctions, as determined by positional and passive mobility testing. Once the major dysfunctions are located, we try to determine which dysfunction most likely has the greatest influence on our ability to balance the pelvis, because balancing the pelvis is thought to be a key in treating the musculoskeletal system. Once the primary restriction is identified and treated effectively, one or more secondary dysfunctions often appear to "melt away" and no longer require treatment.

THE DIAGNOSIS AND TREATMENT OF DYSFUNCTIONS AT THE LUMBOSACRAL JUNCTION

One of the most difficult and controversial areas of the spine to evaluate and treat when attempting to balance the pelvis is the lumbosacral junction. This key junc-

tional area is often the site of the primary restriction, especially for patients with chronic low back pain. Examination of the pelvis and sacrum is described in Chapter 4, and Chapter 5 addresses examination of the spine. The coupled motion that occurs between the lumbar spine and the sacrum is alluded to in both chapters and is reviewed and expanded on in this chapter.

Lumbosacral Junction

An understanding of the unique interaction between the motion of the lumbar spine and the movements of the sacrum is of great importance in the diagnosis and treatment of mechanical low back pain. The coupled movements between the lumbar spine and the sacrum and the techniques for evaluating and correcting dysfunctions in this region were originally described and demonstrated by Fred Mitchell, Sr., DO.[1] Incorporating this information into the clinical setting provides a means to identify and treat dysfunctions associated with a specific structural diagnosis; these dysfunctions are often the cause of low back pain of musculoskeletal origin. To compare outcomes and responses to treatment, it is necessary to specifically define dysfunctions of the lumbosacral junction, because the treatment approach varies accordingly. In our view, comparing outcomes of any treatment program based only on a "diagnosis" of the symptom of "low back pain" is meaningless.

The following discussion expands on Mitchell's original descriptions, serves as a useful model for the diagnosis and treatment of the lumbosacral junction, and provides some insight into the possible mechanisms of injury.

At the outset, it must be appreciated that variations in the anatomy and the osteology of the lumbosacral

L5 IS NEAR TOP OF ILIA
LUMBOSACRAL JUNCTION FUNCTIONS
BETWEEN L5 AND SACRUM

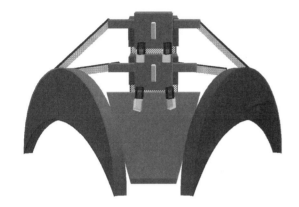

L5 IS LOW BETWEEN ILIA
LUMBOSACRAL JUNCTION FUNCTIONS
BETWEEN L4 AND L5

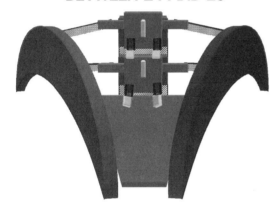

FIGURE 12-1

Diagram showing a variation of position of L5 between the ilia, which influences lumbosacral mechanics.

junction are the norm. To further complicate matters, the normal and abnormal motion characteristics of the lumbosacral junction are also influenced by the movements of the sacrum between the ilia and by the connection of the ilia to L4 and L5 through the iliolumbar ligaments. Variations in the anatomy that must be considered include the following:

1. Asymmetry of the sacroiliac (SI) joints, because no two SI joints have the same articulatory configuration

2. Facet tropism at L5-S1, which is common
3. Sacralization of L5 or the failure of the sacrum to fully fuse (i.e., lumbarization of L6)
4. The position of L5 relative to the intercrestal line (i.e., a line drawn across the top of the iliac crests), which defines the location of the actual lumbosacral junction (Figure 12-1)

Normal Physiological Neutral Mechanics at L5-S1

The model that we use in the following examples considers that the lumbosacral junction is between L5 and the sacral base. When the spine is in the neutral position, and neutral mechanics are influencing the coupled motion between L5 and the sacrum, L5 moves in a direction opposite to the sacrum. For example, when the sacrum rotates to the left and side bends to the right, L5 rotates to the right and side bends left. If the sacrum rotates to the right and side bends to the left, L5 rotates to the left and side bends right (Figure 12-2).

Starting from the neutral position with lumbar flexion (forward bending), the sacrum nutates posteriorly (sacral base tilts backward) as L5 flexes. With lumbar extension (backward bending), the sacrum nutates anteriorly (sacral base tilts forward) as L5 extends (see Figure 12-2).

Normal Physiological Non-Neutral Mechanics at L5-S1

When the lumbosacral spine moves into flexion or extension and side bending of the lumbar spine is introduced, a non-neutral lumbar spine coupling behavior occurs. The sacrum responds to non-neutral lumbar spine coupling behavior by moving around an oblique axis, resulting in a sacral torsion (non-neutral sacral mechanics). The coupled sacral torsion occurs in a posterior direction when the lumbosacral junction is flexed and side bending is introduced. The coupled sacral torsion occurs in an anterior direction when the lumbosacral junction is extended (Figure 12-3).

The following discussions are consistent with the normal physiological coupled motion, assuming fairly symmetrical facets and SI joints, and with L5 located at or above the intercrestal line. The sequence of the combined movements also may affect the coupling, because it may make a difference if side bending precedes or occurs after flexion or extension of the spine.

1. If the lumbar spine is extended, the sacrum nutates anteriorly at both sacral bases. When the extended lumbar spine side bends to the left with coupled rotation to the right, the sacrum rotates to the right on its right oblique axis, acting like a sixth lumbar vertebra. The sacral rota-

FIGURE 12-2
Diagram showing normal neutral coupled motion between L5 and the sacrum, with L5 moving in the opposite direction of the sacral base.

**FROM THE NEUTRAL POSITION
L5 MOVES IN A DIRECTION
OPPOSITE TO THE SACRAL BASE**

 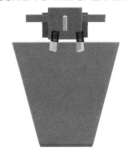 

**SACRUM ROTATES LEFT
AND SIDE BENDS RIGHT
L5 ROTATES RIGHT
AND SIDE BENDS LEFT**

NEUTRAL POSITION

**SACRUM ROTATES RIGHT
AND SIDE BENDS LEFT
L5 ROTATES LEFT
AND SIDE BENDS RIGHT**

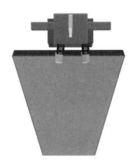  

FORWARD BENDING
**SACRUM POSTERIORLY NUTATES
AS L5 MOVES INTO FLEXION**

NEUTRAL POSITION

BACKWARD BENDING
**SACRUM ANTERIORLY NUTATES
AS L5 MOVES INTO EXTENSION**

tion probably occurs by the right sacral base moving posteriorly toward the neutral position between the ilia, while the left base is held and, perhaps taken further anteriorly, rotating to the right on the right oblique axis (right on right, or ROR). Similarly, with lumbar extension followed by right side bending with coupled rotation to the left, the sacrum rotates left on its left oblique axis (left on left, or LOL) (see Figure 12-3).

2. If the lumbar spine is flexed, the sacrum nutates posteriorly at both sacral bases. When the flexed lumbar spine side bends and rotates to the left, the sacrum rotates to the right on its left oblique axis. The sacral rotation probably occurs by the left sacral base moving anteriorly toward its neutral position between the ilia, while the right base is held and, perhaps taken further posteriorly, rotating right on the left oblique axis (right on left, or ROL). Similarly, with lumbar flexion fol-

lowed by right side bending and right rotation, the sacrum rotates left on its right oblique axis (left on right, or LOR) (see Figure 12-3).

Note: In Chapter 4, two different mechanisms of injury are discussed that can result in a posterior sacral torsion. The previous description explains the normal physiological mechanics for a posterior sacral torsion, in which the sacrum rotates in the opposite direction from L5 when the spine is flexed, then side bent and rotated. The sacrum may become dysfunctional if it becomes held or restricted in that position. A nonphysiological posterior sacral torsion has been postulated to occur when the lumbar spine is fully flexed and fully side bent, and rotated so that the lumbosacral junction is locked by facet apposition and ligamentous tension. In this case, the sacrum acts like a sixth lumbar vertebra, is forced to rotate in the

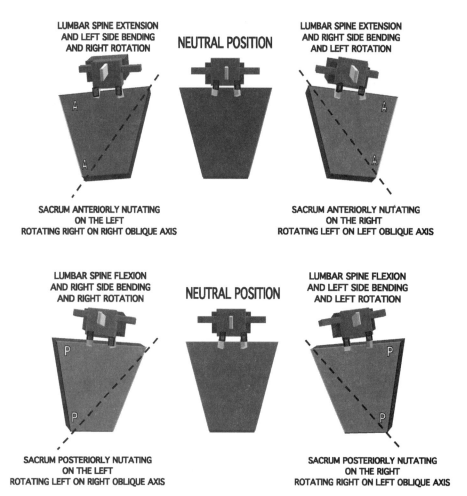

FIGURE 12-3

Diagram showing the physiological coupled lumbar and sacral motion associated with anterior and posterior sacral torsions. Dashes indicate axes. (A = anterior; P = posterior.)

same direction as L5, and becomes dysfunctional when held in that position. In either example, the treatment for a posterior sacral torsion is the same.

Diagnosing Non-Neutral Dysfunctions at L5

The strain patterns most commonly associated with persistent low back pain are a consequence of bending and twisting or side bending and then attempting to resume the upright posture diagonally, while the sacrum is rotated and posteriorly nutated, and L5 is flexed, rotated, and side bent. The strain is often, but not necessarily, associated with lifting a load. The resultant strain patterns that are most disruptive and usually highly symptomatic can either be a LOR posterior sacral torsion with an associated FRSrt at L5 (Figure 12-4A), or a right on left (ROL) posterior sacral torsion with an associated FRSlt at L5 (Figure 12-4B). The actual mechanism of injury and resulting strain pattern vary from patient to patient, depending on the degree of flexion, rotation, and side bending introduced at the time, the individual anatomy of the SI joints, the facet tropism at L5-S1, and

the position of L5 between the ilia. Regardless of an individual's anatomy and lumbosacral mechanics, the physical examination still gives the operator the ability to decide whether L5 is dysfunctional (i.e., non-adaptive) by comparing the position of the transverse processes (TPs) or lamina of L5 to the position of the sacral base when the spine is flexed, in neutral (prone), and extended. It is important to remember that when we ask the patient to forward bend, we are assessing the ability of the facet joints at each lumbar segmental level, including L5-S1, to bilaterally and symmetrically open; when the patient backward bends, we are assessing the ability of the facet joints to bilaterally and symmetrically close. Therefore, if the sacrum is dysfunctional and appears to be rotated to the right in flexion or extension of the spine, L5 should appear equally rotated to the right following the sacrum, provided that the facet joints at L5-S1 are able to bilaterally and symmetrically open or close. A non-neutral dysfunction of L5 becomes apparent when L5 does not follow the sacral base position when the lumbar spine is flexed or extended (see Figures

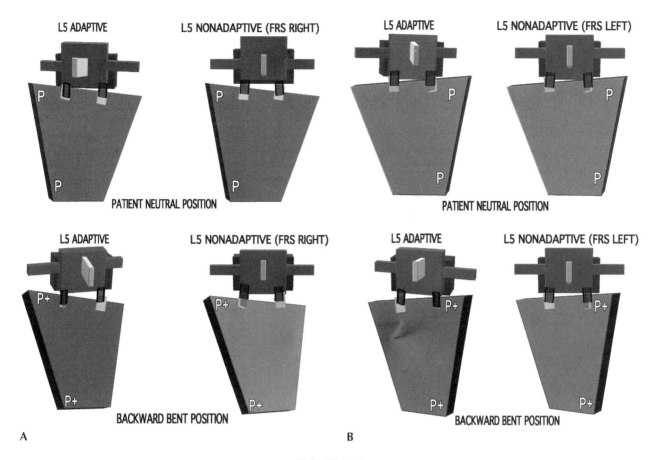

FIGURE 12-4

*The difference between adaptive and nonadaptive L5 mechanics in relation to a left on right posterior sacral torsion **(A)** and in relation to a right on left sacral torsion **(B)**. Shown in the neutral position and backward bending. (FRS = flexed, rotated, and side bent; P = posterior; P+ = more posterior than P.)*

12-4 through 12-6). At no time during positional testing with the patient in flexion or extension do we ask the patient to side bend or rotate. Therefore, a lumbar rotation seen when the spine is flexed or extended can be a consequence of a normal (i.e., not dysfunctional) L5 and the normal segments above it following the rotated (i.e., dysfunctional) sacral base.

However, when the patient is lying in the prone (neutral) position, and the sacrum is rotated and side bent (i.e., dysfunctional), L5 and the rest of the lumbar vertebrae should rotate and side bend in the opposite directions to the sacrum if the lumbar spine is normal and capable of neutral coupling behavior. Therefore, a non-neutral dysfunction of L5 is suspected when L5 fails to rotate fully in the opposite direction of a rotated sacrum in the prone neutral position (see Figures 12-4 through 12-6).

Anterior sacral torsions with an associated non-neutral dysfunction at L5 may be symptomatic, but they are less often symptomatic than the posterior sacral tor-

sions. An LOL anterior sacral torsion is often seen in combination with an ERSrt at L5. For some reason, an ROR anterior sacral torsion with an associated ERSlt at L5 is rarely seen. The diagnosis of a non-neutral ERS dysfunction at L5 is made when L5 does not follow the rotated sacral base position when the lumbar spine is flexed. A non-neutral dysfunction at L5 is also suspected when L5 fails to rotate fully in the opposite direction to the sacrum when the patient is in the prone (neutral) position (see Figure 12-5).

Unilateral sacral nutations are nonphysiological dysfunctions of the SI joint. Most commonly, the sacral dysfunction is due to either an anteriorly and inferiorly translated sacral base on the left side (i.e., a left unilateral anteriorly nutated sacrum) or a posteriorly and superiorly translated sacral base on the right side (i.e., a right unilateral posteriorly nutated sacrum). The left anteriorly nutated sacrum is thought to occur when an individual jumps and lands on the left leg while the lumbar spine is

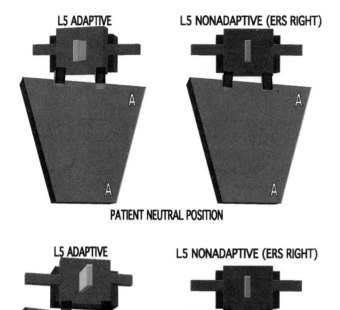

FIGURE 12-5

The difference between adaptive and nonadaptive L5 mechanics in relation to a left on left anterior sacral torsion. Shown in the neutral position and forward bending. (A = anterior; A+ = more anterior than A; ERS = extended, rotated, and side bent.)

in the hyperextended position. The right posteriorly nutated sacrum can occur with a bend-and-twist type of injury, or it can be the result of a strain and a non-neutral vertebral dysfunction higher up in the spine that results in hypertonus of the right longissimus muscle.

Non-neutral dysfunctions at L5 frequently accompany the unilateral sacral nutations. An associated ERSlt at L5 is often found with a left unilateral anterior sacral nutation. The ERSlt at L5 can be identified when the patient is in the fully flexed position and L5 appears level in the coronal plane compared to the right rotated sacral base. This dysfunction occurs because the left facet joint between L5-S1 cannot fully open and the right facet joint can. When the sacrum and lumbar spine are examined in extension (prone-propped position), L5 appears rotated to the right, following the right-rotated

sacral base, provided that both L5-S1 facet joints are able to close (i.e., no FRS dysfunctions). L5 appears level in the neutral position because it is still influenced by the ERSlt dysfunction (see Figure 12-6A).

Often, with a right unilateral posterior sacral nutation we find an associated FRSrt at L5. The FRSrt at L5 can be identified because L5 is rotated more to the right than the right-rotated sacral base when the patient is in the prone propped position. This dysfunction occurs because the left facet joint between L5-S1 cannot close completely but the right facet joint can. When the sacrum and lumbar spine are examined in flexion, L5 appears rotated to the right to the same degree as the sacral base, because the right facet joint can open and the left facet joint is already open. Normally, L5 would appear rotated to the left in the neutral position if there is no dysfunction and L5 can respond with neutral coupling mechanics. However, in this example, L5 still appears rotated to the right even in the patient-neutral position (see Figure 12-6B).

Bilateral anteriorly or posteriorly nutated sacra can occur, but they are rarely seen. When present, a bilateral anteriorly nutated sacrum can be associated with a bilaterally extended L5, and a bilateral posteriorly nutated sacrum can be associated with a bilaterally flexed L5.

Illustrative Tests for the Diagnosis of Lumbar Spine and Sacroiliac Dysfunctions

The most difficult task for the beginning operator is gaining the ability to make an accurate diagnosis of non-neutral and neutral dysfunctions. The following diagrammatic illustrations can be used to visualize and identify these dysfunctions as a learning exercise that often is applicable to the clinical setting.

The following self-tests are diagrammed using these abbreviations:

1. *L5* for lumbar 5, *L4* for lumbar 4, and so on; *T12* for thoracic 12
2. *Forward bending* for when the spine is in a position of full flexion
3. *Neutral position* for when the spine is neither flexed nor extended
4. *Backward bending* for when the spine is in a position of full extension
5. The position of individual vertebrae is diagrammed using a three-dimensional likeness
6. The up arrow (↑) signifies a craniad or superior position of the inferior lateral angle (ILA)
7. The down arrow (↓) signifies a caudad or inferior position of the ILA.

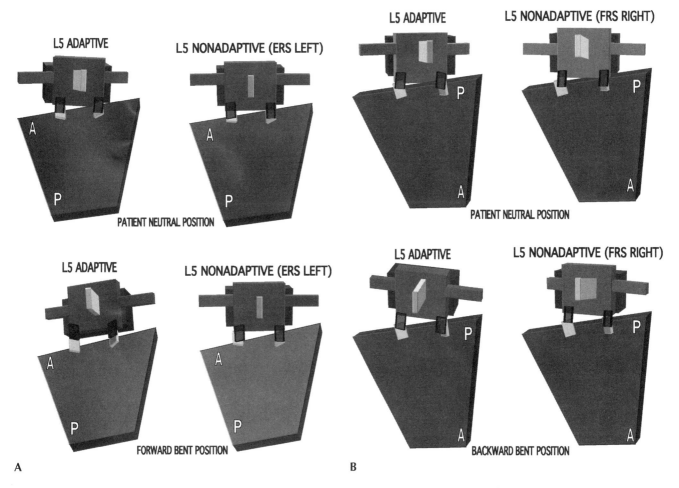

FIGURE 12-6

The difference between adaptive and non-adaptive L5 mechanics in relation to an anteriorly nutated sacrum on the left (A) and in relation to a posteriorly nutated sacrum on the right (B). Shown in the neutral position and backward bending. (A = anterior; ERS = extended, rotated, and side bent; P = posterior.)

In the clinical setting, the prominence of a TP may change as it is being examined with different positions of the spine. If a TP is prominent when the patient is in the neutral position, it may be because it represents a major restriction barrier. If the TP is only prominent when the patient is either in the forward- or backward-bending position, there is probably only a minor restriction barrier.

Test Number 1

Test number 1 is shown as Figure 12-7.

The stork test is positive left upper pole only (see editors' note in Chapter 7, section 3.2) and the seated forward flexion test is positive on the left side.

Answers for Test Number 1

1. *There is an LOR posterior sacral torsion* because the base and ILA are both posterior on the left side in the neutral position and backward bending and become level in

forward bending, which distinguishes it from a unilateral sacral nutation.

2. *There is a posterior torsion* because the ILA asymmetry disappears with forward bending (flexion) and worsens with backward bending (extension). The right sacral base can move posteriorly with flexion, but the left sacral base cannot move anteriorly during lumbar backward bending (extension).

3. *There is a major sacral dysfunction* because it is present in the neutral position.

4. *L5 is FRSrt* because L5 is not rotating left with the sacral base when the spine is in the extended position, and although it appears level in space, L5 is actually rotated to the right and side bent to the right relative to the sacral base. This is an FRSrt dysfunction because the left facet joint between L5 and the sacrum cannot close (see Figure 12-4A). The relationship between L5

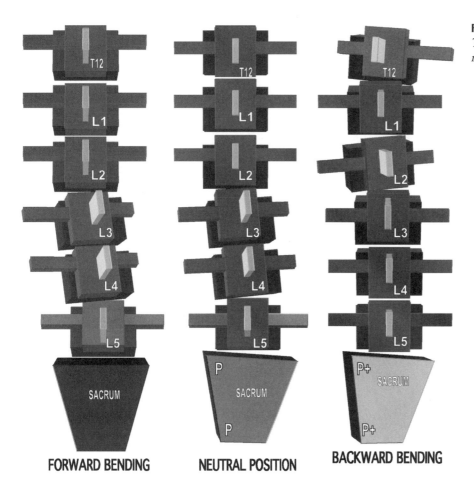

FIGURE 12-7
Test Number 1. (P = posterior; P+ = more posterior than P.)

FORWARD BENDING   **NEUTRAL POSITION**   **BACKWARD BENDING**

SEATED FORWARD FLEXION TEST POSITIVE LEFT

and the sacrum persists into the neutral position, and it must be considered a major restriction, because L5 appears level rather than rotated right. L5 is in the same position as the sacral base when the spine is in the flexed position, and therefore, both facet joints can open and there is no restriction for flexion between L5 and the sacrum.

5. *L4 is ERSlt* because L4 is rotated and side bent to the left in relation to L5 when the spine is in the flexed position. The left facet joint between L4 and L5 cannot fully open. There is a major restriction barrier for flexion, as evidenced by L4 remaining rotated and side bent left in relation to L5 when the spine is in the neutral position. L4 becomes level with L5 in the extended position, and there is no restriction for extension.

6. *L3 is normal.* It follows the position of L4 when the spine is flexed, in the neutral position, and extended.

7. *L2 is ERSrt* because even though L2 appears level in space, it is rotated and side bent to the right in relation to L3 when the spine is flexed. This relationship between

L2 and L3 remains in the neutral position and, therefore, is probably a major flexion restriction.

8. *L2 is FRSlt* because L2 is rotated and side bent to the left in relation to L3 when the spine is in the extended position. There is probably a minor restriction barrier for extension, because L2 appears right rotated in the neutral position. In this example, the right facet joint between L2 and L3 cannot completely open or close.

9. *L1 is FRSrt* because L1 is not following L2 when the spine is in the extended position, and even though L1 appears level in space, it is rotated and side bent to the right in relation to L2. Because L1 is in the same position as L2 when the spine is in a neutral position, there is only a minor restriction for extension on the left between L1 and L2.

10. *T12 is FRSrt* because T12 is rotated to the right in relation to L1 when the spine is in the extended position. This dysfunction is not seen when the lumbar spine is in the neutral position, so that only a minor restriction is

FIGURE 12-8

Test Number 2. Arrows indicate craniad position of the right inferior lateral angle and right sacral base. (A = anterior; P = posterior.)

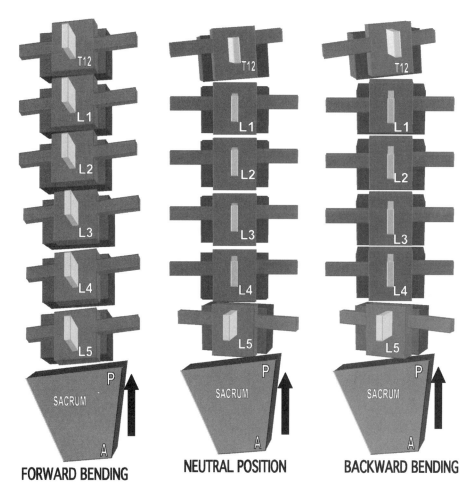

FORWARD BENDING   NEUTRAL POSITION   BACKWARD BENDING

SEATED FORWARD FLEXION TEST POSITIVE RIGHT

present; thus, the barrier to extension begins on the extension side of neutral.

11. There are no ERS dysfunctions at L1 or T12.

Treatment sequence: Treat the lumbar spine first, beginning with L5, because L5 must be free to rotate opposite to the sacrum when in the neutral position, or the sacral torsion cannot be corrected.

Test Number 2

Test number 2 is shown as Figure 12-8.

The stork test is positive right upper pole only (see editors' note in Chapter 7, section 3.2) and the seated forward flexion test is positive on the right.

Answers for Test Number 2

1. *There is a unilateral posteriorly nutated sacrum on the right* because asymmetry of the ILAs and sacral base is seen in all three test positions. The ILAs never become symmetrical, even with full flexion or full extension of the lumbar spine.

2. *This is a unilateral sacral nutation* because the sacral base and ILA are opposite on the same side (i.e., the right sacral base is posterior and the right ILA is anterior).

3. *L5 is FRSrt* because L5 is more right-rotated than the sacrum when the spine is extended and when the spine is in the neutral position (see Figure 12-6B). L5 follows the sacral base in flexion, because there is no flexion restriction between L5 and the sacrum.

4. *L4 is FRSlt* because in relation to L5, L4 is rotated to the left when the spine is extended. This is a major restriction because the dysfunction is seen in the neutral position as well.

5. *L4, L3, L2, L1, and T12* follow the sacral base and L5 in forward bending; therefore, there are no flexion restrictions (i.e., ERS dysfunctions).

6. There are no FRS dysfunctions at L3, L2, or L1.

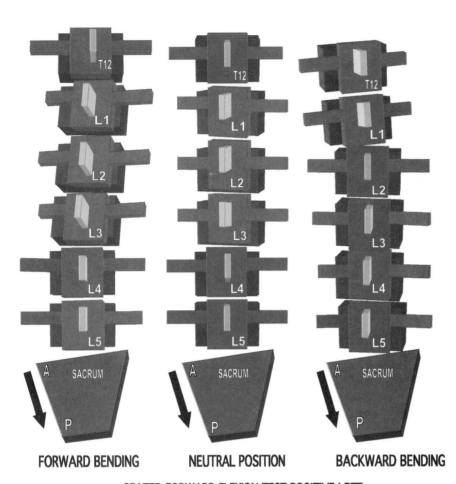

FORWARD BENDING   NEUTRAL POSITION   BACKWARD BENDING

SEATED FORWARD FLEXION TEST POSITIVE LEFT

FIGURE 12-9
Test Number 3. Arrows indicate caudad position of the left inferior lateral angle and left sacral base. (A = anterior; P = posterior.)

7. *T12 is FRSlt* and demonstrates a major restriction, because the asymmetry of the TPs is seen in the neutral position and may result in increased tone in the right longissimus muscle. Increased tone in the right erector spinae muscles may contribute to holding the sacrum in the posteriorly nutated position on the right.

Treatment sequence: Treatment should begin with T12, then L4 and L5. This sequence may resolve the sacral dysfunction by reducing the hypertonicity of the longissimus muscle. If it does not resolve the sacral dysfunction, the sacrum needs to be directly treated as well.

Test Number 3
Test number 3 is shown as Figure 12-9.

The stork test is most likely positive left lower pole only (see editors' note in Chapter 7, section 3.2) and the seated forward flexion test is positive on the left side.

Answers for Test Number 3
1. *There is a unilateral anteriorly nutated sacrum on the left* because the left sacral base is anterior, the left ILA is inferior (caudad) and slightly posterior, and the position of the ILAs does not change in the forward-bent, neutral, or backward-bent positions.

2. *L5 is ERSlt* because L5 is rotated to the left in relation to the sacral base with forward bending and in the neutral position (see Figure 12-6A). L5 appears to follow the sacral base with backward bending.

3. *L4 is normal.* It follows L5 in forward bending, in the neutral position, and in backward bending. There are no restrictions between L4 and L5.

4. *L3 is ERSrt* because L3 is rotated and side bent to the right in relation to L4 in forward bending. This is a major flexion restriction (i.e., ERS), because the relationship between L3 and L4 is still different when the lumbar spine is in the neutral position. L3 follows L4 when the lumbar spine is extended, and there is no FRS dysfunction.

FIGURE 12-10
Test Number 4. (P = posterior;
P+ = more posterior than P.)

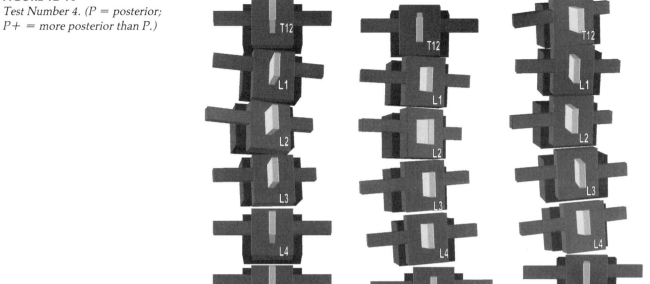

FORWARD BENDING   **NEUTRAL POSITION**   **BACKWARD BENDING**

SEATED FORWARD FLEXION TEST POSITIVE RIGHT

5. *L2 is normal.* It follows L3 in forward bending, neutral, and backward bending. There are no restrictions between L2 and L3.

6. *L1 is FRSlt* and demonstrates a minor restriction, because the asymmetry of the TPs is only in the extended position.

7. *T12 is ERSlt* because T12 is not following L1 in forward bending, and although it appears level in space, it is actually rotated and side bent to the left in relation to L1. T12 has a major ERS restriction because it is present in the prone-neutral position as well.

Treatment sequence: The ERSlt at L5 must be treated first, because its presence blocks the ability to move the sacrum superiorly and posteriorly on the left. To reduce the tension at the lumbosacral junction and the influence of the right quadratus lumborum muscle, the ERSrt at L3 should be treated next; this might make it easier to treat the sacral dysfunction. The sacrum could be treated after L5, because the treatment technique for a left unilateral anteriorly nutated sacrum does not require neutral coupling of the lumbar spine as part of the treatment technique, in contrast to treating a sacral torsion. Remember that when treating the sacral torsions, neutral coupling behavior throughout the lumbar spine is required as part of the treatment technique; thus, non-neutral lumbar spine dysfunctions need to be addressed first before attempting to treat sacral torsions.

Test Number 4
Test number 4 is shown as Figure 12-10.

The stork test is positive right upper pole only (see editors' note in Chapter 7, section 3.2) and the seated forward flexion test is positive on the right.

Answers for Test Number 4

1. *This is a right on left (ROL) posterior sacral torsion* because the sacral base and ILA are both posterior on the right.

2. *There is a posterior sacral torsion* because the ILA asymmetry is worse in the backward-bent position and disappears in the forward-bent position.

3. The ROL sacral torsion demonstrates a major restriction because it is present in the neutral position.

4. *L5 is FRSlt* because L5 is not following the sacrum in backward bending, and in relation to the sacrum, L5 is rotated to the left and side bent to the left. The relationship does not change when the patient is in the neutral position; therefore, there is a major restriction (see Figure 12-4B). L5 appears to be following the sacrum in the forward flexed position, and there is no restriction for flexion.

5. *L4 is FRSlt* and demonstrates a major restriction, because the asymmetry of the TPs is also present when the lumbar spine is in the neutral position.

6. *L1, L2, and L3 represent a neutral group dysfunction* that probably began in response to the position of L4 in the lumbar neutral position. This is a neutral group dysfunction because L1, L2, and L3 are side bent right and rotated left (Nlt) when the lumbar spine is examined in all three positions (forward-bent, neutral, and backward-bent). The dysfunction is greatest (i.e., more side bent right and rotated left) when the lumbar spine is in the neutral position.

7. *T12 is FRSlt* and demonstrates a minor restriction, because the asymmetry of the TPs is not present in the neutral position, where it assumes a normal position on top of a neutral group dysfunction.

Treatment sequence: Treat the lumbar spine first, beginning with correcting the non-neutral FRSlt L5 dysfunction. L5 must be free to rotate to the left and side bend to the right with neutral mechanics to treat the ROL sacral torsion. The FRSlt at L4 and at T12 should be treated before attempting to treat the neutral dysfunction, because the neutral group dysfunction may resolve after the non-neutral dysfunctions above and below are treated. If the neutral group dysfunction persists, then it must be treated as well. In general, it is best to treat the sacral torsion after the lumbar dysfunctions have been treated, because the torsion is corrected as a coupled response to neutral lumbar mechanics, with the lumbar spine used as a lever arm directing forces toward the lumbosacral and sacroiliac junctions.

Remember that, at times, the diagnosis of a non-neutral dysfunction in the lumbar or thoracic spine may be difficult when relying solely on the ability to palpate a predominant TP when the patient is flexed, in neutral, and extended. In this situation, it is important to have alternative motion-testing procedures (e.g., observing active side bending or using passive lateral translation of the spine, as described in Chapter 5).

It is also possible to diagnose the presence of a non-neutral dysfunction in the lumbar spine using the "Pelvic Clock," as described in Chapter 14. In general, ERS dysfunctions are suspected when the patient has difficulty moving from 9 o'clock to 12 o'clock or from 12 o'clock to 3 o'clock. FRS dysfunctions are suspected when the patient has difficulty moving from 3 o'clock to 6 o'clock or from 6 o'clock to 9 o'clock. Sacral dysfunctions are usually present when the patient has difficulty moving from 3 o'clock to 9 o'clock and back.

RECOMMENDED ORDER OF TREATMENT FOR THE PELVIS AND LUMBAR SPINE

Clinical experience has taught us that the most efficient and successful treatment sequence for the pelvis usually begins with the pubic symphysis, because dysfunctions of this mechanism significantly influence pelvic function. Dysfunction initially identified elsewhere in the pelvis may change significantly after the pubic symphysis is treated.

Next, it is best to treat those dysfunctions that occur as a consequence of a disruption of normal anatomical relationships (i.e., nonphysiological dysfunctions). These dysfunctions then become a priority when they occur.

The following is the recommended treatment sequence for the lumbar spine and pelvis:

1. *Innominate shears*: When superior shears are present, it is sometimes necessary to reduce hypertonus of the ipsilateral quadratus muscle or the iliopsoas muscle, or both by first treating any associated non-neutral dysfunctions of L3 or the thoracolumbar junction. If necessary, the hypertonic muscles may also be stretched. When inferior shears are present, they may be treated directly.

2. *Unilateral anteriorly nutated sacrum*: Because of the often associated ERSlt at L5, L5 must be treated first when dysfunctional to allow room for the sacrum to return to its proper position.

3. *Unilateral posteriorly nutated sacrum*: Because of the associated hypertonus of the ipsilateral longissimus muscle, those non-neutral dysfunctions that may be associated with this hypertonus should be treated first. These include dysfunctions of the upper thoracic spine and, especially, the thoracolumbar junction. Often, treating the thoracic spinal dysfunctions is all that is necessary, with no direct sacral treatment required.

4. *The lumbar spine* is then examined and the non-neutral dysfunctions treated next, especially if a sacral torsion has been identified.

5. *The posterior sacral torsions* are usually symptomatic, whereas the anterior sacral torsions often are not symptomatic. Asymptomatic posterior sacral torsions are often associated with a past history of significant back pain resulting in modified lifestyles that limit or delay recurrences. The patient may have received previous instruction in William's flexion exercises, touching

the toes, or drawing the knees to the chest, which are actually movements that are within the allowable range of motion because the motion loss is that of extension. Patients with lumbar FRS dysfunctions and a posteriorly torsioned sacrum have flattened lumbar spines with a loss of the normal lordosis.

The posterior sacral torsions can also have a major influence on the rest of the spinal axis and the extremities. The upper extremities can be affected by altered, adaptive upper spinal mechanics. The lower extremities are directly affected by adaptive pelvic mechanics and muscle imbalances that can develop to accommodate a sacral torsion. As noted previously, to treat a sacral torsion, L5 must be capable of neutral coupling behavior and free to move opposite to the sacral base. Correction of other non-neutral lumbar spine dysfunctions is also necessary before treating sacral torsions, because the entire lumbar spine becomes a lever arm used to de-rotate the sacrum.

6. *Innominate rotations* are treated last. To completely restore normal pelvic mechanics, it is necessary to balance the tensions between the agonistic and antagonistic muscles of the lower extremities and the trunk, especially the rectus femoris, hamstrings, glutei, hip rotators, iliopsoas, and quadratus lumborum. Some balancing of muscle function is accomplished by correcting any residual innominate anterior and posterior rotation dysfunctions, which are addressed sequentially after treating the sacrum. Modifications for the treatment of these innominate dysfunctions are necessary when they accompany either an anteriorly or posteriorly nutated sacral base. Correcting any associated hypertonicity in the iliopsoas and quadratus lumborum muscles must often follow treatment of an FRS dysfunction located at the thoracolumbar junction.

RECOMMENDED ORDER OF TREATMENT FOR THE THORACIC AND CERVICAL SPINE

The treatment sequence of the thoracic spine may vary, depending on the patient's position at the time of treatment. When the patient is side lying, it is sometimes easier to begin caudally and move craniad. When the patient is seated, it may be best to treat the upper segments and move caudally. The best place to begin is at the most dysfunctional segment, identified either by its positional presence in neutral (i.e., major dysfunction) or by the amount of resistance felt with passive motion testing. The non-neutral vertebral dysfunctions of the thoracic spine should be treated before trying to correct rib torsions or respiratory restrictions of the ribs. Sometimes, structural rib dysfunctions, especially the anterior or posterior sub-

luxations, and the anterior-posterior or lateral rib compressions may need to be treated before the thoracic spine can be treated.

The cervical spine is always treated after the upper thoracic spine has been evaluated and, if indicated, treated. If multiple FRS dysfunctions are encountered in the cervical spine on one side, suspect and treat the anterior and middle scalenes, which, when hypertonic, can interfere with normal cervical spine coupling behavior at multiple segmental levels. If there are multiple ipsilateral ERS dysfunctions in the upper cervical vertebrae, suspect and treat first the hypertonicity of the levator scapula or long extensor muscles of the cervical spine. When dysfunctional, the typical cervical vertebrae (C2-7) are treated before the upper cervical complex (atlantoaxial and occipitoatlantal joints).

After treating any cervical and upper thoracic dysfunctions, the upper extremities—including the hand, wrist, elbow, shoulder, and clavicle—should be examined and treated if necessary.

PATIENTS WITH SPECIAL PROBLEMS

Developmental Scoliosis

It is easier to detect positional asymmetry of the TPs in a patient whose spine is normally symmetrical and without curves or rotations. Patients with scoliosis can develop non-neutral and neutral dysfunctions within their scoliotic curves. These dysfunctions are more difficult to find and can be the cause of major symptoms, because a scoliotic spine does not have as much capacity to accommodate to such dysfunctions. The treatment must be directed toward restoring that patient's "normal" scoliosis. Assessing the relative rotation between each successive vertebrae and identifying tissue texture abnormalities is the key in the examination of these patients. Look for non-neutral dysfunctions at the apex of curves and at the crossover segments where the curves and rotations reverse.

Patients Who Have Had Surgery

Patients who have had lumbar surgery without fusion can develop non-neutral dysfunctions at the sight of previous surgery. Scar tissue in the skin, muscles, and ligaments can present a barrier to normal motion, and the loss of muscle tissue close to the spine leaves the area permanently weakened. Nevertheless, mobility can be restored by muscle energy, thrusting, and soft tissue techniques. The restoration and maintenance of function requires the addition of appropriate exercise programs, which support the thoracolumbar fascia (i.e., gluteals, latissimus dorsi, transverse and oblique abdominal muscles).

Patients who have had a fusion procedure that involves the lumbosacral junction must be viewed as having a new lumbosacral junction at the top of the fusion. Any fusion puts more stress on the segments above and below it. Normal mobility above and below the fusion, including mobility in the pelvis, hips, and lower extremities, is necessary to help diminish the additional stress placed on the transitional segments next to the fusion.

Patients with Spondylosis

Osteophyte formation around the vertebral margins becomes larger and more common as patients age, especially if the spine has been subjected to increased physical stress. Osteophytes are not painful, but they do change the structural anatomy of the spine and limit the anatomical range of motion. The osteophytes can also encroach on the nerve root and spinal cord. When somatic dysfunctions occur under these conditions, motion loss can be significant, and the increased stress on the less adaptable spine above and below these dysfunctions can cause additional dysfunction and pain. Restoration of motion that was available before the development of the dysfunction can result in a significant improvement in the patient. If osteophyte formation has compromised the nerve root, and especially if there is an ERS dysfunction, the nerve root may become edematous and radicular symptoms can progress. Restoration of the available foraminal opening by addressing the ERS dysfunction may help to decompress the nerve. If the spinal cord is compromised by a posterior osteophyte that narrows the spinal canal (central spinal stenosis), surgical intervention may be the best remedy.

Patients with an Intervertebral Disc Herniation

When there is a large, laterally displaced disc herniation, nerve root compression can result in a permanent radiculopathy. If there is narrowing of the spinal canal, either congenital or as a consequence of spondylosis, and a large central disc herniation occurs, there is the uncommon but real danger of severe compression of the cauda equina and paralysis of the lower extremities, preceded by loss of bowel and bladder control. In the past, there was a risk of aggravating an intervertebral disc herniation when spinal manipulation was performed under general anesthesia. It would seem reasonable to be concerned about using a rotational force when there is a known disc herniation but for the most part, properly

applied manipulative techniques can help reduce the associated abnormal spinal mechanics, decrease the tension on the intervertebral disc, and allow a better environment for nonsurgical resolution. One of the goals of manipulative intervention in a patient with a herniated lumbar disc is to restore the ability of the lumbar spine to extend. For this reason, it is particularly important to treat any lumbar FRS and sacral dysfunctions (i.e., possibly nutated sacral bases) that are commonly associated with disc herniation and restrict lumbar extension. Once this is accomplished, it is then possible to instruct the patient in self-mobilizing exercises to maintain lumbosacral extension (see Chapter 15). There are times, of course, when manipulative techniques fail to help at all and surgical intervention becomes necessary.

Patients with a Hypermobile or Unstable Joint

A restricted joint is easier to detect than one that is excessively mobile. Excessive joint mobility can be described as hypermobile or unstable, but these terms are not synonymous. The hypermobile joint maintains anatomical integrity but has excessive slack within the supporting soft tissue structures, allowing for an increased range of motion. If there is a loss of anatomical integrity of the joint, then the joint is considered unstable and generally is more symptomatic and difficult to treat.

Hypermobile joints may be the source of painful symptoms and may require treatment before the patient obtains relief. It is often found that the underlying cause of the hypermobile joint is its adaptation to a hypomobile joint nearby, of which the patient is not aware. This scenario is not uncommon, and relief of pain is often obtained by manual methods that are directed to the hypomobile joint. The relief of symptoms is believed to occur because the compensatory hypermobility imposed on other joint(s) disappears when the restricted joint regains its motion.

Joints that have been pushed beyond their anatomical barrier into subluxation may become restricted and require manual treatment (e.g., anterior or posterior [structural] ribs and innominate shears). Reduction is needed before these joints can begin to operate in their normal manner, but because the joint ligaments have already been stretched, any thrusting force is usually avoided. Reduction of a subluxation can almost always be achieved by muscle energy treatment without putting any extra strain on the ligaments. Some form of external stabilization may be needed after reduction; for example, an SI cinch belt may be used after treatment of a superior innominate shear.

Spinal joints above or below a fusion or above or below a section of the spine that has restricted motion because of degenerative changes are often hypermobile. The cause of restricted motion cannot be removed in these cases, as it can with a simple dysfunction. However, it may be possible to obtain pain relief by treating the hypermobile joint to restore as much symmetry of motion as possible. Furthermore, the hypermobile joint may also be adapting to other restrictions (dysfunctions) in the joints of the extremities or spine that may be amenable to manual treatment.

Localized hypermobility may be the result of repeated injury or the consequence of repeated overstretching as seen in dancers, acrobats, and gymnasts. Treatment is usually directed to any associated hypomobile joints but, occasionally, the hypermobile joint becomes dysfunctional and its limited mobility can significantly impede athletic performance. In this situation, localization of the barrier may be difficult, because it can be beyond what would be considered a normal range of motion.

More generalized states of hypermobility and instability with a predilection for certain joints, particularly at the upper cervical complex, are associated with Down's syndrome, rheumatoid arthritis, Marfan's syndrome, and Ehlers-Danlos syndrome. Manual therapy may not be appropriate in these conditions and should be avoided entirely in the upper cervical complex.

To make the diagnosis of hypermobility, it is necessary to appreciate the characteristic "end feel" associated with this diagnosis (i.e., the change in tissue tension that the operator senses when the joint approaches the barrier to passive motion). When a hypermobile joint is taken through its range of motion, the operator does not sense the normal increased tissue tension as the anatomical barrier is approached. The normal tightening toward the end of the range is absent, so the joint comes up to its anatomical barrier more abruptly.

Antero-posterior translation of the spine can be useful in making the diagnosis of hypermobility in the lumbar spine. The patient is side lying with the hips and knees bent, and the knees are supported against the operator's thigh. With the index or middle finger, the operator palpates the movement between the spinous processes when the patient's knees are pressed backward to posteriorly translate the lumbar spine (Figure 12-11). Different levels of the lumbar spine can be examined by introducing more or less flexion or extension of the patient's hips. In this fashion, the motion of the joint in question can be assessed and compared with the motion available in neighboring joints. A similar test of side bending can be performed, starting from the same position. Raising the feet tests side bending in one direc-

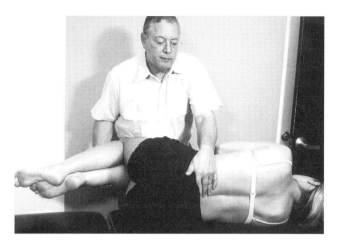

FIGURE 12-11

Examining a patient for a hypermobile lumbar joint by palpating the interspinous spaces, including the level above and below, and translating the spine posteriorly through the patient's legs.

tion; side bending is tested in the other direction by lowering the feet (Figure 12-12).

The definitive diagnostic test for instability is having stress x-ray films of the spine taken in full flexion and extension and in right and left side bending. Because of the exposure to radiation, it is wise only to take x-rays when clinical evidence suggests instability of a particular level.

It must be remembered that patients with hypermobility from any cause may present with back pain that does not arise from the hypermobile or unstable level, and in that event, treatment of the neighboring hypomobile joint by manipulation may be needed. In such patients, care must be taken during treatment to prevent further strain to the hypermobile segment.

Patients with an Anatomical Leg Length Discrepancy

As a consequence of the tendency of the pelvis to twist with one innominate rotating forward and the other innominate rotating backwards, serious errors are introduced in any attempt to measure differences in leg length from the anterior superior iliac spine to the medial malleolus. Therefore, it is recommended that this method for measuring leg length should be abandoned. Clinical and radiological methods that are more accurate are described in Chapter 3.

Structural differences in the length of the legs are sometimes the result of malunion of a fracture, limb overgrowth, or may be congenital or genetic. Differen-

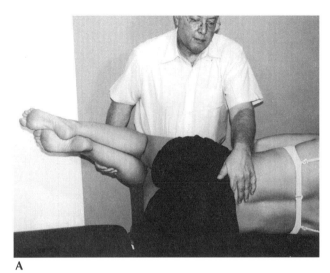 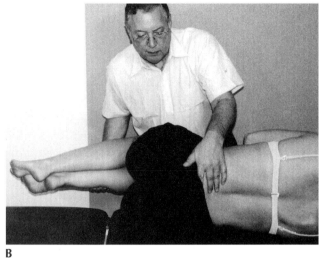

A   B

FIGURE 12-12

*Examining a patient for a hypermobile lumbar joint by palpating the interspinous spaces, including the level above and below, and side bending the spine through the patient's legs to the left **(A)** and to the right **(B)**.*

tial limb growth may result from increased circulation associated with a vascular anomaly, overuse of one side, chronic infection, or after asymmetrical neuropathies or motoneuron loss affecting one side more than the other. A natural tendency of the human body is to preserve the forward-pointing attitude of the head and level of the eyes and ears. One of the ways in which the body may attempt to do this is by a torsional movement of the pelvis so that the innominate posteriorly rotates on the side of the long leg and anteriorly rotates on the side of the short leg.

Unlevelling of the sacral base as a consequence of a difference in anatomical leg length is what is important to measure when considering a heel lift for a patient with chronic low back pain. The amount of tilt or sacral base unlevelling may differ from the measurements made from the top of the femoral heads. Unfortunately, for this reason, the only accurate method to determine sacral base unlevelling requires an AP and lateral standing x-ray of the lumbosacral junction and pelvis. Greenman[2] gives an excellent review of this subject, along with suggestions for proper lift therapy.

FREQUENCY AND DURATION OF TREATMENT

Patients who present with an acute problem (i.e., hours or days after an injury) are appropriate candidates for manual therapy, which can enhance the recovery process and certainly shorten its duration. Bed rest is a

proven failure as a treatment and really represents no treatment. Conservative treatment can still be aggressive. The soft tissue techniques and muscle energy techniques are well suited to the acutely injured and should be brief but frequent (e.g., daily or every other day). For patients with acute cervicothoracic strains, treatment should begin with the upper thoracic spine. Before treating the cervical non-neutral dysfunctions, those muscles that can act as long restrictors (i.e., scalenes, longus colli, levator scapula, and sternocleidomastoid) should be gently stretched if they are hypertonic. Restoring some, but not all, movement is better than overtreating. Sometimes, there is significant restoration of mobility with the initial treatment. The patient must be encouraged to gently move the injured area within the limits of pain or voluntary ranges that have been restored. Patients with an acute low back injury can be treated with muscle energy techniques in the same fashion as those patients with more chronic low back pain. The sequence of evaluation and treatment for the low back is: pubic symphysis, non-neutral lumbar dysfunctions (usually FRS), sacral dysfunctions (usually posterior torsions), and innominate rotations. Finally, those muscles that can act as long restrictors to lumbosacral mobility (i.e., psoas, quadratus, erector spinae) and short restrictors (i.e., pyriformis and gemelli) may also require gentle stretching by using muscle energy techniques. When no further progress is made during a treatment session, or if the patient is experiencing too much pain from the treatment technique, it is often best to stop and consider other soft tissue techniques or treatment options (e.g., analgesics, short-acting anti-inflammatories, and centrally acting muscle relaxants).

Patients with chronic pain and dysfunction have more complex problems. There have been adaptations to adaptations, and additional injuries seem to occur more easily in a spine that has a reduced capacity to accommodate to trauma. There are new patterns of movement and postures that initially occur as a response to pain and are perpetuated as a consequence of muscle imbalances and myofascial changes that have been molded into the connective tissues. These patients are usually sedentary and have limited strength and endurance throughout the musculoskeletal system. The first treatment is usually the most extensive, correcting any nonneutral spinal or pelvic dysfunctions that are thought to be the most significant or primary. Often, treatment concludes with an attempt to rebalance the muscles of the extremities and trunk, with instruction in specific self-mobilizing exercises to complement the manual treatment rendered (see Chapters 14 and 15). In chronic musculoskeletal dysfunction, a persistent imbalance between agonist and antagonist muscles is mediated, in part, by reciprocal inhibition, with the facilitated hypertonic muscle inhibiting its antagonist.[3] When the hypertonicity of the agonist is treated by postisometric relaxation, the antagonistic muscles are disinhibited and rapidly regain tone. Although the antagonist has regained tone and strength by the removal of reflex inhibition, it may not have yet regained endurance and can fatigue easily. Patients must be cautioned to maintain a reduced level of activity for several days after treatment, even if they are relieved of their symptoms, before beginning a strengthening program. It is probably best to re-examine and treat several days to a week later and compare the examination findings to the initial findings.

It is difficult to determine a numerical value that dictates the maximum duration and frequency of treatment. On the one hand, there are patients who require a prolonged period of treatment, during which they gradually improve. On the other hand, some patients require repeated treatment to maintain function, whereas other patients, often those with minor dysfunctions and major symptoms, appear to become addicted to manual therapy. The immediate goal of manual therapy is to restore function, but ultimately, it should be part of a process to empower the patient toward self-reliance. When manual therapy fails to provide a reasonable restoration of function, it should be discontinued. A patient dependent on manual therapy can be weaned with less and less hands-on treatment, with responsibility placed upon the patient to perform and follow through with an individualized home exercise program.

REFERENCES

1. Mitchell FL. Structural pelvic function. Year Book Acad Appl Osteopath 1965;2:178–199.
2. Greenman PE. Lift therapy: use and abuse. J Am Osteopath Assoc 1979;79:238–250.
3. Janda V. Muscles, Central Nervous Motor Regulation, and Back Problems. In I Korr (ed), The Neurobiologic Mechanisms in Manipulative Therapy. New York: Plenum Press, 1977;27–41.

13

Pain Patterns and Musculoskeletal Dysfunction

PRINCIPLES FOR THE DIFFERENTIAL DIAGNOSIS OF "BACK PAIN"

Even in a practice entirely made up of patients referred by physicians because of a complaint of back or neck pain, it is important to recognize that the source of this pain can still be somewhere other than the musculoskeletal system. This consideration should not be discarded, even when a treatable dysfunction seems to be responsible for the pain.

The management of any patient with back pain requires a focused differential diagnosis of the possible causes for this pain. An assessment of the patient's complaint begins at the first visit with a complete history and physical examination, including either a detailed or well-focused neurological examination. The possible causes for the patient's complaint must be reconsidered at each subsequent visit, especially if the patient does not respond as expected.

Regardless of the source, all peripheral pain begins when nociceptors are depolarized either as the result of direct mechanical or physical distortion or chemically by the production of tissue breakdown products that become inflammatory mediators (e.g., lactic acid, potassium, peptides, cystokines, serotonin, and histamine).[1] The inflammatory process also lowers the threshold for depolarization of nociceptors, thereby increasing their sensitivity to mechanical stimulation.[2] Repetitive or continuous physical distortions also seem able to increase this sensitivity and are probably mediated by neurogenic mechanisms as summarized by Willard.[3]

The location and character of the pain are determined by the nature of the noxious stimulus, the location of the nociceptor, the bias of central nervous system (CNS) activity at the moment of sensory input, and the coincidental segmental and peripheral innervation patterns shared by the stimulated nociceptor. Complicating the perception of this pain are the modifications imposed by suprasegmental pathways and the complex interactions of the limbic system that can diminish or magnify those behavioral factors that express the highly individualized reactions to the same stimulus. Any attempt to use pain reduction as the goal of a treatment protocol is challenged by all of these factors.

Primary Nociceptors of the Spine

In the lumbosacral spine,[3-5] noxious stimulation can be perceived by nociceptive nerve fibers that are branches of the sinovertebral nerve. The sinovertebral nerve arises from the dorsal root ganglion and divides into ascending and descending branches. The lesser, descending branch innervates the posterior longitudinal ligament and the outer one-third to one-half of the posterior annulus at the same level. The major, ascending branch primarily innervates the posterior longitudinal ligament, the dura, dural ligaments, and the root sleeve. Branches from the sinovertebral nerve can extend up two levels and down one and can even cross the midline, illustrating why a patient's perceived location of pain may not match the radiological findings. An example of this is finding a lumbar disc herniation that is located to the side *opposite* the pain.

The annulus is also innervated by fibers that travel in the anterior sympathetic chain and enter the CNS via the gray rami communicantes, which travel in the ventral ramus of the root. These fibers have been thought to innervate only the outer annulus, but there is evidence that nerve fibers can penetrate from one-third to one-half of the way into the disc tissue.[6] The ends of some of these fibers stain positively for substance P, identifying them as nociceptors.[7] Branches from the dorsal ramus innervate the zygapophyseal joints, whereas the sacral branches innervate the posterior sacroiliac (SI) joints.

Pain from Altered Spinal and Pelvic Mechanics

Patients who experience back pain as a consequence of mechanical dysfunctions have similar descriptions and histories. Pain may begin spontaneously, without an obvious cause or immediately after some described injury, or with a delayed onset, which can range from hours to a few days. Typically, when the pain onset is abrupt, there may be some easing of the pain intensity over the next hour, but then the pain tends to build, reaching peak levels that can last for hours or days. In time, most patients improve and, depending on the severity of the injury, experience some residual pain, stiffness, or both, described as some limitation of normal motion that is often expressed by a sense of "being out of shape." The notion that most patients spontaneously recover from low back pain without treatment comes from data that do not adequately consider long-term follow-up of the patient. The often-cited statistic that 80–85% of patients with back pain have no further difficulty 6 weeks after the initial onset of pain was dispelled in 1996.[8] After surveying patients 1 year after an episode of low back pain that was severe enough to warrant a visit to their primary care provider, 29% were still experiencing back pain and were dissatisfied with their outcome. Any physical activity that stresses residual musculoskeletal dysfunctions is probably responsible for an exacerbation of the pain and stiffness. Patients who become asymptomatic often remain so, because they consciously or unconsciously restrict activities or movements that challenge restrictive barriers and avoid any activity that was associated with the original injury or the exacerbations. These lifestyle modifications can often result in a more sedentary existence. When the pain does not remit, or if it actually worsens, there is often an accompanying history of an inability to get or remain comfortable in any position. These patients cannot sleep through the night, awaken when they turn or move, and experience increased pain and stiffness after arising in the morning or after sitting for a period of time. These patients can temporarily improve with exercise or heat, but the pain worsens at rest. Symptoms tend to fluctuate and may subside after several days or weeks of more intense pain. When less symptomatic, patients try to increase their level of activity and complete chores that had to wait when the pain

was worse. This increase in activity often causes another exacerbation that usually begins the next day and is accompanied by an increasing depression and sense of frustration.

Pain Referral Patterns

Every patient feels it is important to describe and localize the pain. However, this information can be misleading, and it should be no surprise that treatment directed only to the site of the pain often fails to resolve the problem. Most practitioners have experienced the frustration of reducing a patient's pain with symptomatic treatment in one area, only to have it emerge in another. Some approaches to pain management are directed toward silencing the local nociceptors that seem to be activated, but this is like killing the messenger. Especially in more chronic situations, the location of pain is not to be trusted, because *pain is a liar.*

The problem of referred pain is one that has received much attention from neurologists, anatomists, and physiologists. Kellgren[9] continued the work started by Lewis, in which an irritant solution of 6% saline was injected into volunteers at various sites in the low back. Kellgren showed that, by injecting the irritant beside the spinous process of the first sacral vertebra, he could produce the typical pain of sciatica with radiation down the leg. Similar experiments have been done by Sinclair et al.,[10] Feinstein et al.,[11] and Hockaday and Whitty.[12] Many workers in this field have observed that referred pain is associated with hyperalgesia in the reference zone, and, often, there is cutaneous hypoesthesia in the same area. There is a central and a peripheral mechanism in the production of referred pain and the central mechanism involves the spinal cord and higher centers.

The evidence suggests that it is not necessary to have actual damage to the segmental nerve root to have referred pain, and, indeed, experiments have shown that the referred pain from injections of an irritant is not necessarily confined to the dermatome, myotome, or sclerotome of that level.

Sacroiliac Pain

Clinically, patients with pain from certain, common SI dysfunctions have difficulty crossing the legs while putting on stockings or shoes, limp or trip, and often walk as though one leg is too long. Many patients experience increasing pain with certain activities, especially vacuuming, prolonged standing, or sitting. These patients may feel temporary relief after limited walking, but they often feel worsening pain if walking is prolonged or vigorous. Fatigue at the end of the day heralds increasing discom-

FIGURE 13-1

Pain referral patterns from sacroiliac joint and annulus from cervical and lumbar intervertebral discs.

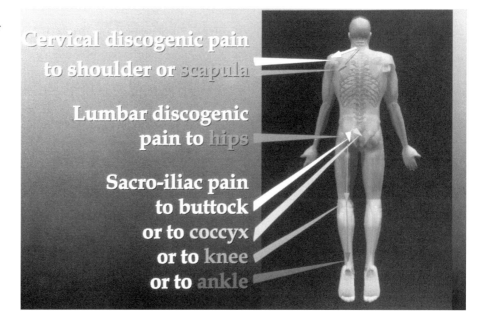

Cervical discogenic pain to shoulder or scapula

Lumbar discogenic pain to hips

Sacro-iliac pain to buttock or to coccyx or to knee or to ankle

fort in the low back and is a penalty for any increased activity. Pain typically radiates down the leg, posteriorly referred along the S1 root in a fashion reminiscent of sciatica, and although this pain often stops behind the knee, it may extend as far as the ankle (Figure 13-1).

Pain from Pelvic Articulations

Pain from a pubic symphysis dysfunction can radiate over the inguinal ligament to cause inguinal pain or dysfunction and pain posteriorly in the SI region. Restricted innominate rotation is often associated with an SI dysfunction and can contribute to pain in the hip, leg, and SI joint, especially while walking. Local tenderness can be elicited by palpation of the ligaments of the pelvic region (e.g., the inguinal ligament, pubic tubercle, and the long dorsal SI ligament) (Figure 13-2).

Hip joint dysfunction or disease can alter pelvic and lower back function significantly enough to confuse primary hip pain from pain referred to the hip. Studies have found that a loss of internal rotation of the hip correlates strongly with low back pain.[13] Patients often complain of increasing pain while walking or jogging and, at times, appear to have pelvic girdle muscle weakness, especially when trying to arise from a squatting position. A Trendelenberg gait often is observed by the examiner and positively correlates to gluteus medius weakness and hip joint pathology.

Vertebrogenic Pain

Segmental vertebral motion restrictions require adaptation by increased mobility from the zygapophyseal joints of the remaining unrestricted segments. This adaptation or compensation can result in mechanical stimulation of nociceptors distant from the dysfunctional segment. Restrictions for flexion (extended, rotated, and side-bent [ERS] or bilaterally extended) become more symptomatic when the patient is seated, bending, or supine. Restrictions for extension (flexed, rotated, and side-bent [FRS] or bilaterally flexed) become more symptomatic when the patient bends backwards, attempts to stand up straight after sitting, or is lying prone, especially when these restrictions are associated with a posterior sacral base (e.g., posterior torsion or posteriorly nutated). Patients with extension restrictions also have difficulty reaching over the head, standing on the toes, or wearing a shoe with an elevated heel; these patients prefer to sleep side lying, with a pillow between the legs. Often, these patients can bend forward but have difficulty attempting to resume an upright posture; accordingly, they may shift the hips and spine laterally around the restricted segment while returning upright. In the lumbar spine, pain from the disc or zygapophyseal joints often refers to the hips, buttocks, or legs and radiates diffusely across the low back. Although the region directly overlying the dysfunctional segments is usually tender to palpation, the patient often feels pain in those areas that have adapted to the restricted motion by becoming relatively hypermobile.

Pain from the lower thoracic region can be radicular in nature and radiate around a rib or radiate to the left or right upper quadrants and mimic intra-abdominal disease. Dysfunction in the lower thoracic spine may influence lower back and SI function and cause pain to be felt

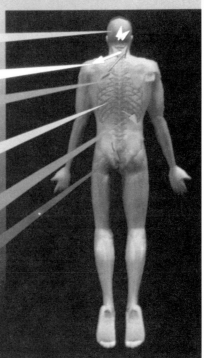

Eye pain from upper cervical complex

Shoulder pain from cervical spine

Scalenes and Rib pain

Upper abdominal pain from lower thoracic dysfunction

Inguinal pain from pubic symphysis dysfunction and SI pain

A

Upper cervical complex to eye

Mid-cervical to shoulder or scapula

Mid-thoracic to Rib "costochondritis"

Lower thoracic mimics GI symptoms

Sacro-iliac pain from pubic symphysis dysfunction

B

FIGURE 13-2
(A) Pain referral patterns from upper cervical spine, ribs, lower thoracic spine, pubic symphysis, and sacroiliac (SI) joint. (B) Additional pain referral patterns from pubic symphysis, upper cervical spine, mid thoracic spine, and lower thoracic spine as truly referred pain or by directly associated dysfunctions. (GI = gastrointestinal.)

in the SI joint region[14] (Figure 13-3*A*). This influence may arise as a consequence of the reactive hypertonicity of the longissimus muscle that occurs secondarily to the thoracic dysfunction, which then can exert a pull upward and posteriorly on the sacral base. Thoraco-lumbar dys-

functions can also influence the tone in the psoas muscles, which cross the SI joint anteriorly and, if hypertonic, can interfere with normal SI joint mobility.

Upper thoracic spinal mobility is directly associated with the movement of the cervical spine, and dysfunc-

FIGURE 13-3
*Thoracic spine dysfunctions and pain referral patterns. (**A**) From low thoracic to low back. (**B**) From upper thoracic to low back, influencing spinal mechanics at a distance through long restrictors (e.g., the longissimus and psoas muscles).*

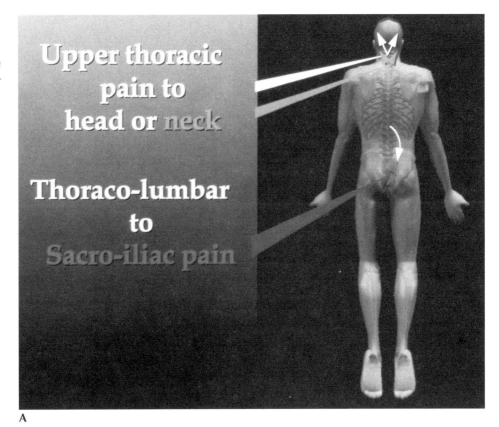

A

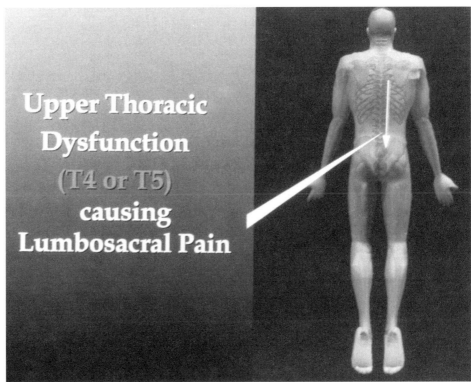

B

tions as low as T5 affect cervical spine mechanics, which can result in neck pain, headache, or both. Thoracic spine dysfunctions, especially ERS dysfunctions, are frequently associated with rib dysfunctions (i.e., torsions), which can be the source of various chest wall pains that may mimic cardiac disease, pleurisy, and herpes zoster. Rib dysfunctions are often the real cause for "costochondritis" and may compromise efficient inhalation and exhalation, adding to one of the causes for dyspnea (see Figure 13-2). Upper thoracic and associated rib dysfunctions may be causes for shoulder pain and restrict arm motion, preventing elevation of the extremity and contributing to impingement syndromes.

Pain originating from cervical spine dysfunctions can radiate down the upper extremity in a radicular fashion, down to the upper back or up to the head, causing focal or generalized pain. Zygapophyseal joint referral patterns[15] from the upper cervical vertebral dysfunctions often cause retro-orbital pain or pain frontally in regions that are commonly associated with diseased sinuses[16] (see Figures 13-1 and 13-2).

Pain Caused by Larger Muscles or Long Restrictors

Pain originating from upper thoracic dysfunctions can also contribute to low back pain due to the influence of these dysfunctions on the tone in the erector spinae muscles (i.e., longissimus and iliocostalis thoracis) (Figure 13-3B). Back and neck pain can also be caused by increased tone in the larger paraspinal muscles, which are associated with movement of the extremities. Suspicion that this increased tone is contributing to spinal pain arises from the observation of what appear to be multiple restrictions located at adjacent spinal segments. For example, increased muscle tone in the levator scapulae or the scalenes alters the function in multiple cervical segments. Likewise, increased muscle tone in the psoas, quadratus lumborum, and piriformis directly influences lumbosacral function.

Pain from Altered Mechanics of the Dura and Peripheral Nerve

Severe pain can occur as a consequence of stimulating nociceptors by stretching the shortened or scarred supporting tissues of the nervous system, particularly the dura and the peri and endoneurium of the peripheral nerve.[17] Painful sensations are described as either lancinating or burning in quality and increasing when the dura or peripheral nerve is stretched or placed under additional strain by certain body positions. This usually results in a temporary increase in muscle tension in response to the pain provoked (Figure 13-4).

Pain from Inflammation

When inflammation occurs in response to tissue injury, chemical mediators depolarize nociceptors. Inflammation is associated with redness, swelling, heat, and an influx of white blood cells. Pain is present at rest and aggravated by motion, because the inflammatory changes also lower the threshold for mechanical depolarization of the nociceptors. The pain is usually quite localized but can refer to more distant sites, depending on how deep the injured tissue is within the body. Inflammatory changes tend to evolve over a 72-hour period after injury and then slowly subside over several days to weeks. Residual pain reflects the degree of tissue injury and any alteration of tissue structure and function as a consequence of that injury.

Recall that, if a nociceptor is constantly or repeatedly stimulated, as can occur in the presence of mechanical dysfunction, the threshold for depolarization is lowered. This is probably a consequence of neurogenic inflammation by the release of substance P, calcitonin, and other polypeptides capable of inducing and maintaining a focal inflammatory reaction.[3]

Discogenic Pain

Healthy intervertebral discs are complex ligaments that imbibe water with the help of the pumping action of vertebral motion and the integrity of complex glycoproteins that act like sponges. The disc may be viewed as similar to a radial tire, filled with water instead of air. The outer one-third to one-half of the annulus is innervated by nociceptor fibers. Therefore, tears or inflammatory chemical by-products in the outer annulus can be a source of pain. When annular tears coalesce secondary to repeated torsional injuries to the spine, a lumbar disc herniation may occur. Sometimes, acute low back pain can be correlated with the appearance of a lumbar disc herniation identified by magnetic resonant imaging (MRI). In one study of patients with a disc herniation who were managed by nonsurgical intervention and whose low back pain improved had follow-up MRI scans that showed a reduction in the size of the herniated disc.[18] However, because similar disc abnormalities have been identified by MRI scans performed on people without back pain,[19] we must be careful not to assume that the presence of a lumbar disc herniation is automatically the source of the patient's symptoms. The nature of the disc herniation has also been questioned, because the nucleus pulposus "dries up" in the late teens or early twenties.[20] It has been suggested that the herniation is really just a hypertrophied annulus,[21] but most often, this herniated material contains nucleus pulposus.[22] Bogduk[6] noted that with compression injuries to the spine, especially with the subsequent development of Schmorl's

FIGURE 13-4

Supportive tissues around peripheral nerves and the dural structures are innervated by nociceptors and are thereby capable of becoming pain generators. (A) The radicular pain felt by nerve root irritation probably arises from the dural sleeve and supporting connective tissues within the nerve root or plexus. (B) Likewise, true sciatica reflects the irritation of the connective tissues supporting the lower nerve roots and their dural sleeves along the spinal canal to the cranium as a cause for generalized headaches.

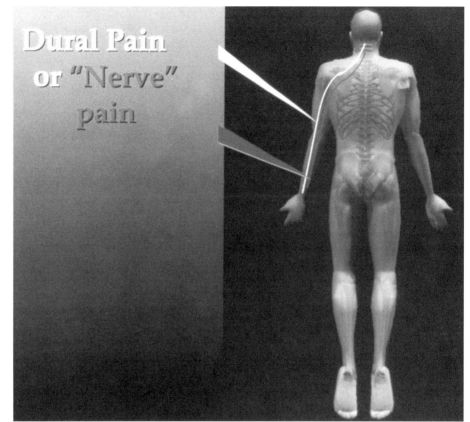

A

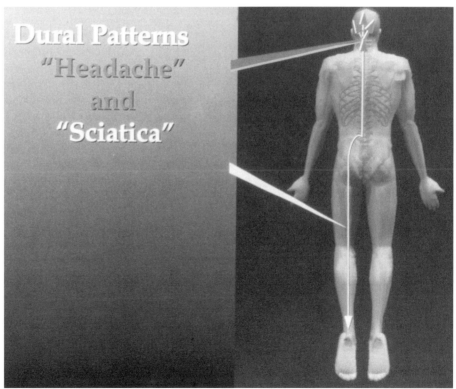

B

nodes, there is potential contact between the nuclear matrix and the circulatory system, which may cause an autoimmune reaction that destroys this matrix and results in an internal disc disruption. Subsequently, the disc's ability to hold water is diminished. If the inflammatory process from the subsequent degeneration of the disc reaches the outer one-half of the disc, annular nociceptors are stimulated, resulting in pain.[23,24] Furthermore, the mechanical deformation associated with the increased motion due to a loss of stability and integrity creates additional pain when the patient moves. In effect, a disc with internal disruption acts like a deflated radial tire. Bogduk also proposed that a compression injury resulting in internal disc disruption is a necessary precursor to disc herniation. We hypothesize that, in addition to internal disc disruption, restricted segmental vertebral motion could account for the appearance of disc desiccation because of the loss of the ability for the pumping of fluid in and out of the disc.

Discography is still a controversial technique, relying on both anatomical changes and the reproduction of the patient's pain to identify the abnormal disc. That discography can reproduce the patient's pain suggests that the disc must play some part in the production of symptoms.[25,26]

Patients with disc herniation have low back pain that typically improves by lying down and worsens while seated. Although the discogenic pain is localized to the back, it may also refer down the leg. When herniation occurs laterally, the dural covering and the intrinsic innervation of the nerve root are irritated by the concurrent inflammation, causing dural tension signs with sciatica and neurological deficits. With a lateral disc herniation, the pain tends to be in the ipsilateral hip or buttock or further down the leg and may persist even when the patient lies down. It is probably the inflammatory response that determines whether the disc herniation, as seen on MRI, is symptomatic.

Pain from Structural Abnormalities

Certain conditions pre-exist the onset of back pain and are often blamed as the primary cause of the patient's pain, despite the fact that before some injury or trauma to the spine, the patient was asymptomatic. The following conditions represent those structural changes that, by their nature, limit the available ranges of motion, possibly increasing the risk of dysfunctions and compromising the success of treatment:

1. Primary scoliosis
2. Facet tropism
3. Spondylosis
4. Spondylolisthesis
5. Congenitally or surgically fused segments
6. Healed compression fractures

Differentiating Characteristics of Pain Arising from Skeletal, Peripheral Nerve, and Visceral Structures

Skeletal

Pain from bone is mediated through the innervated periosteum and is often described as deep, sharp, aching, unremitting pain that is aggravated by motion. The operator examining a patient with a destructive process involving the axial skeleton palpates an extremely hard, resistant barrier to motion, which is also very painful and may be associated with significant muscle spasm. If a patient presents with this kind of pain on examination, it is necessary to ensure appropriate imaging studies have been done before proceeding further. On occasion, these patients demonstrate a clinical picture resembling bone pain from a destructive process before it becomes evident by diagnostic studies.

Primary Benign Tumors   Primary benign tumors, such as osteoid osteomas and intraspinal tumors (e.g., neurofibromas and meningiomas), usually cause localized pain, but only after reclining or after going to sleep. Swelling within the tumor mass associated with fluid shifts caused by a change in posture from an upright or seated position is thought to put additional pressure on the periosteum. In the case of osteoid osteomas, prophylactic aspirin ingestion can prevent nocturnal pain.

Primary Malignant Tumors   Primary malignant tumors (e.g., multiple myeloma) cause severe and continuous bone pain without inflammation and should be suspected when the spine becomes inflexible because of pain and guarding over multiple segments.

Metastatic Bone Tumors   Metastatic tumors to bone, especially from carcinomas of the breast, prostate, lung, thyroid, and kidney, may cause pain and restrictions similar to primary malignant tumors, but depending on the degree of destruction and concurrent inflammation, restoration of spinal mechanics can reduce pain, if only temporarily.

Infection   Infection also causes a combination of inflammation and bone destruction that is usually quite localized and persistent. Until the beginning of the twentieth century, tuberculosis of the spine was a common problem, and it must now be reconsidered again with the re-emergence of a virulent form of tuberculosis associated with the acquired immunodeficiency syndrome epidemic. Osteomyelitis is often a consequence of penetrating wounds or septicemia. Discitis can occur as a complication of surgery or discography when *Staph-*

ylococcus epidermis is inadvertently introduced into this avascular structure. Pain from discitis is a consequence of instability and inflammation. Discitis presents in a similar fashion as disc disruption but with fever, destructive changes, and intervertebral gas density patterns, as seen by plain x-ray studies. Disc infections are usually the consequence of an invasive procedure.

Primary Inflammatory Diseases Primary inflammatory diseases that affect the spine include rheumatoid arthritis and ankylosing spondylitis. Rheumatoid arthritis is of major concern when examining the cervical spine because of the potential to cause instability at the odontoid. Ankylosing spondylitis causes progressive restrictions at the SI and zygapophyseal joints, predisposing the patient for particular susceptibility to mechanical pain in the unaffected adaptive hypermobile regions, especially in the upper thoracic and cervical spine.

Abdominal Aneurysm The presence of an abdominal aneurysm can itself be painful and refer pain to the back or cause erosion of the anterior portion of the vertebral body, resulting in tissue breakdown and altered spinal mechanics that can help to localize the level. Similarly, localized pain and persistent focal somatic dysfunctions involving the spinal axis can identify other processes, such as paraspinal tumors, that can cause bone erosion.

Peripheral Nerve

True neuralgias originate within the sensory nerves as a consequence of inflammation, injury, and demyelination. Neuralgias occur most commonly as a consequence of herpes zoster infection or shingles. Herpes zoster, prolonged nerve compression, trauma, and vascular interruption can result in neuropathic pain that follows the sensory distribution of the peripheral nerve or nerve root. A more diffuse and distally symmetrical pain that usually involves the lower extremities more than the upper extremities is often the consequence of a nutritional, toxic, or metabolically induced polyneuropathy, most commonly seen as a consequence of diabetes mellitus.

The pain is characteristically brief, recurrent, sharp, and electric-like and often burns with associated tingling and irritating paresthesias. The pain occurs spontaneously or in response to mild stimuli (e.g., a light touch or even air currents) and typically worsens when the patient lies down to sleep. Brachial neuritis may be inherently painful or, in the case of weakened shoulder girdle muscles, cause pain because of distraction of the unsupported glenohumeral joint.

Viscera

The low back can be the site for painful sensations arising from nonspinal structures, as in the example of the aortic aneurysm. Other pelvic or abdominal conditions (e.g., diseases of bowel, kidneys, ureters, ovaries, uterus, and bladder) can result in low back pain but usually without much alteration of spinal mechanics. Likewise, diseases that affect the liver, gall bladder, stomach, heart, and lungs can cause pain in the upper back, shoulder, upper extremity, chest wall, or neck.

Diseases of the Central Nervous System

On rare occasions, patients may present with painful conditions that arise as initial manifestations of diseases of the CNS. By far, the most common of these is Parkinson's disease, which presents as pain and stiffness, usually of the upper back. The other manifestations of rigidity, tremor, and simian posture are usually evident but unnoticed by the patient. Patients with Parkinson's disease also appear to have a lowered threshold for and reduced tolerance to pain. Multiple sclerosis can begin with radicular symptoms when there is a plaque involving the white matter near the dorsal or ventral horn of the spinal cord. The spontaneous onset of focal, cramping pain and "muscle spasm" can herald the onset of amyotrophic lateral sclerosis. Spasticity associated with any myelopathy can affect the lower extremities and be associated with stiffness and pain in the low back.

Psychological Pain

A diagnosis of psychogenic pain or an emphasis on psychological factors is a common sequel to a nonrevealing diagnostic workup and lack of favorable response to treatment. Such considerations tend to intensify in the minds of the treating physicians, physical therapists, family members, and, unfortunately, even patients when the subjective complaints seem to outweigh the objective findings. Often, patients will themselves emphasize the possibilities of stress factors during their initial evaluation, perhaps in an effort to reduce concerns about more serious disease. Certainly, psychological factors can affect body posture and aggravate pain by increasing the mechanical stress while reducing the patient's ability to cope with pain. However, it is a very rare situation in which pain is the primary manifestation of a psychiatric illness. In other words, it is more likely that pain *causes* emotional distress rather than pain is *caused by* emotional distress.

The memory of a painful experience tends to linger subconsciously until it is rekindled and magnified by another experience, especially if the subsequnt pain is of the same quality as the original pain. For example, if touching something that is very hot burns a person, the memory of burning pain can be recalled when that person touches something that is very warm. This is often the case when pain has become chronic and fluctuates in intensity or when a new injury occurs that generates pain sensations similar to previous pains or discomfort. Pain has also been used as a means of punishment and connotes misbehavior or, at the least, can evoke feelings of guilt.

When pain accompanies any musculoskeletal dysfunction, it may have to be dealt with as a separate issue from the dysfunction. *The primary goal of manipulative therapy is to restore function and not necessarily to reduce pain.* The psychological aspects of persistent pain and suffering can best be identified and managed after function has been restored.

Malingering

Pure malingering is uncommon, despite what may appear to be primary or secondary reasons for pain. Unfortunately, the few patients who lie or cheat primarily for selfish, conscious reasons are remembered for their ill deeds, and their actions prejudice those responsible for the health care of or compensation payments to those patients with legitimate disability from injury. Malingering can be suspected when there is an absence of objective musculoskeletal dysfunctions or when the patient's complaints are well out of proportion to the abnormalities, if any, that can be detected by the musculoskeletal examination. Malingerers usually do not respond favorably to any treatment and are difficult to examine because of their "pain," often jumping or jerking at the slightest touch. Careful observation of these patients' posture and motion in the examination room should be compared to their behavior elsewhere, preferably when they leave the building and believe they are unobserved.

Somatic Dysfunction and the Associated Pain

It is often observed that the identification of a somatic dysfunction, although often locally tender, may not reside at the location of a perceived pain. However, successful treatment of that somatic dysfunction can result in the reduction or elimination of the pain distant from the site of the dysfunction. Physical distortion of the innervated tissues is most certainly painful if the distortion is great enough. When there is a somatic dysfunction, motion is lost. Because of the loss of motion locally, uninvolved joints are required to move more than they normally would[27] to accommodate an overall motion demand. Restoration of normal joint motion

can then reduce pain by lowering the tissue tensions locally and reducing the adaptive or resultant hypermobility of nearby or distant joints. Initially, with the restoration of motion, there seems to be proprioceptor silence in the area for a short time,[28,29] and nociceptors are no longer easily depolarized by physical distortion.

Resting muscle tone, especially around the spine, is ultimately the consequence of efferent activity from the alpha-motoneuron. The variations in this output are a consequence of the complex CNS interactions mediated by monosynaptic and multisynaptic pathways and the influences mediated by the long tract pathways that concern voluntary motion and body position in relation to gravity.[30] The pattern of hypertonic/hypotonic muscle around a particular joint can change after local injury, from an injury elsewhere, or as a patterned behavior based on activity or inactivity. Reduced mobility allows shortening in the muscle and in the connective tissues around a hypomobile joint. Reduced afferent input from joint proprioceptors further contributes to the persistence of imbalances between agonist and antagonistic muscles.

Irritation of deep muscles and other mesodermal tissues around the spinal joints causes referred pain that is similar to other painful clinical syndromes.[1,6,26,31-33] Travell and Simons[33] define *trigger points* as localized areas of increased muscle tone that can cause persistent pain within the muscle. These are to be distinguished from locally tender points in the muscle. Pressure over the trigger point causes a pain that is referred and does not follow myotomal, dermatomal, or sclerotomal patterns. The myofascial trigger point is postulated to begin with a muscular strain and perpetuates as a site of sensitized nerves, increased metabolism, and reduced circulation that eventually demonstrates histological alterations within the trigger point area. If the abnormally tight portion of the muscle is made to relax, the pain dissipates.

There is a marked similarity between the trigger point and what we find in muscle over dysfunctional spinal joints. This is not necessarily to identify the two as the same process, but some of what has been proven about trigger points is likely to be applicable to a spinal joint dysfunction. Often, the patient is unaware of the location of the spinal joint dysfunction until the operator presses on it because, like the trigger point, the patient has only noticed the pain in the reference zone, which may also be tender. The small fourth layer muscles around the spine that are found as part of the tissue texture changes associated with spinal joint dysfunction may also be a source of referred pain. It is noteworthy that stretching the hypertonic muscle either in a trigger point or in the fourth layer paraspinal muscle after an isometric muscle energy technique can relieve these referred pain patterns.

DEALING WITH THE PATIENT'S PAIN

It has been emphasized that the purpose of the musculo-skeletal examination is to detect dysfunctions that interfere with normal motion, and the purpose of manipulation is to restore that motion. In the absence of underlying structural or anatomical pathology, this restoration usually, but not always, results in pain-free motion. Pain is usually the reason for which a patient seeks help, and it cannot be ignored. Patients want to know what has caused the pain, why it is persisting, and what can be done about it. Many patients fear that their symptoms are caused by a hidden disease or malignancy.[34] When the pain is chronic, patients often seek advice from friends, relatives, other patients, and the Internet, and offer these suggestions to their physicians. Often, patients sense a disbelief in the veracity of their complaints, especially when prescribed an antidepressant medication for pain control. The use of opioids for chronic or persistent pain remains controversial, yet it is often helpful.[35,36]

In practice, there is a group of patients with back pain who respond nicely to the techniques that are described in this text, and there are others who do not. The "nonresponders" return for follow-up visits much more regularly than patients whose symptoms resolve and only return if and when there are flare-ups or new injuries. It is easy to become frustrated as the patient population of "nonresponders" grows. Why these patients do not respond to treatment can be categorized in several possibilities:

1. An underlying dysfunction has not been identified, owing to the skills of the examiner or the patient's pain behavior, and guarding makes it impossible to be sure that there is no underlying dysfunction.

2. The origin of the pain does not arise from the musculoskeletal system.

3. Pain persists, despite a restoration of normal articular motion, as though a pain-sensing mechanism has been turned on and cannot be turned off.[37]

4. There is residual pain that arises from dural structures or the connective tissues supporting a peripheral nerve remains shortened, despite the restoration of normal articular motion.[17]

5. None of the above: There is no reasonable explanation or remedy that can apply to a group of patients

whose pain appears genuine and is localized and persistent.

Other factors influence the outcome of the patient's management, including a multitude of issues associated with workers' compensation[38] or the psychosocial distresses that have been exacerbated by pain or disability.

APPLICATION OF MANIPULATIVE TECHNIQUES AND PAIN REDUCTION

The precise nature of the changes that take place in any joint and cause it to give rise to symptoms is the subject of many theories. That properly applied manipulative techniques can reduce or eliminate these symptoms has been observed over the centuries, as detailed in Chapter 1. The restoration of normal joint motion can alleviate pain that is associated with restricted joint mobility. The documentation of such success has never been enough to satisfy those who demand double-blind, controlled studies, which have become the standard for determining efficacy of any proposed treatment. Manipulative therapy and surgical procedures do not lend themselves to these methods of analysis. Instead, outcome studies are often used to evaluate the effectiveness of any treatment by comparisons to other techniques. A healthy skepticism remains for any new surgical technique until enough time has past to prove its value. Unfortunately, despite its use over the centuries, doubt remains about the value of manipulative interventions. There are good reasons for this. Although new surgical procedures are presented in a fashion that is fairly standardized and directed toward solving a particular problem, spinal manipulation is most often described as using nonspecific thrusting techniques for the nonspecific complaint of back pain. This text describes very specific techniques for very specific problems that affect the musculoskeletal system but still defy any known protocol for a double-blind study. The obstacles to such an evaluation include the inconsistencies of inter-rater reliability and the varied talent and abilities of those who use manipulative techniques. Finally, the defined outcome must be considered. If the outcome sought is the reduction of pain, it must be measured by some universally accepted means that depends on the patient's complaints and behavior. If the outcome sought is the restoration of function, pre- and post-treatment observations must be properly analyzed. For the present, the usefulness of manual therapy can only best be considered by personal experience and the success or failure of those who properly apply manipulative techniques to restore mobility and function.

REFERENCES

1. Wyke B. The Neurology of Low Back Pain. In M Jayson (ed), The Lumbar Spine and Back Pain (2nd ed). London: Pitman Medical, 1980.

2. Siddall PJ, Cousins MJ. Spine update: spinal pain mechanisms. Spine 1997;22:98–104.

3. Willard FH. The Muscular, Ligamentous and Neural Structure of the Low Back and Its Relation to Back Pain. In A Vleeming, Y Mooney, CJ Snijders, TA Dorman, R Stoeckart (eds), Movement, Stability, and Low Back Pain: The Essential Role of the Pelvis. New York: Churchill Livingstone, 1997;3–35.

4. Bogduk N, Twomey LT. Clinical Anatomy of the Lumbar Spine. Melbourne: Churchill Livingstone, 1991.

5. Bogduk N. The innervation of the lumbar spine. Spine 1983;8:286–293.

6. Bogduk N. Pathology of lumbar disk pain. J Man Med 1990;5:72–79.

7. Cavanaugh JM, Kallakuri S, Ozaktay AC. Innervation of the rabbit lumbar intervertebral disk and posterior longitudinal ligament. Spine 1995;20:2080–2085.

8. Cherkin DC, Deyo RA, Street JH, Barlow W. Predicting poor outcomes for back pain seen in primary care using patients' own criteria. Spine 1996;21:2900–2907.

9. Kellgren JH. Deep pain sensibility. Lancet 1949;1:943–949.

10. Sinclair DC, Feindel WH, Weddell G, Falconer MA. The intervertebral ligaments as a source of referred pain. J Bone Joint Surg 1948;30B:514–521.

11. Feinstein C, Langlin JNK, Jameson RM, Schiller F. Experiments in pain referred from deep somatic structures. J Bone Joint Surg 1954;36A:981–997.

12. Hockaday JM, Whitty CWM. Patterns of referred pain in normal subjects. Brain 1967;90:481–496.

13. Mellin G. Correlations of hip mobility with degree of back pain and lumbar spinal mobility in chronic low-back pain patients. Spine 1988;13:668–670.

14. Maigne R. Low back pain of thoracolumbar origin. Arch Phys Med Rehabil 1980;61:389–395.

15. April C, Dwyer A, Bogduk N. Cervical zygapophyseal joint pain patterns II: a clinical evaluation. Spine 1990;15:458–461.

16. Campbell DG, Parsons CM. Referred head pain and its concomitants. J Nerv Ment Dis 1944;99:544–551.

17. Butler DS. Mobilisation of the Nervous System. Melbourne: Churchill Livingstone, 1991.

18. Bozzoa A, Massimo G, Aprile I, Antonio B, Passariello R. Lumbar disk herniation: MR imaging assessment of natural history in patients treated without surgery. Radiology 1992;185:135–141.

19. Jensen MC, Brant-Zawadzki MN, Obuchowski N, Modic MT, Malkasian D, Ross JS. Magnetic resonance imaging of the lumbar spine in people without back pain. N Engl J Med 1994;331:69–73.

20. Vanharanta H. Etiology, Epidemiology and Natural History of Lumbar Disk Disease. In RD Guyer (ed), Spine: State of the Art Reviews (vol. 3). Philadelphia: Hanley & Belfus, 1989;1–12.

21. Yasuma T, Makinol I, Saito S, Inui M. Histological development of intervertebral disk herniation. J Bone Joint Surg 1986;68:1066–1072.

22. Moore RJ, Vernon-Roberts B, Fraser RD, Osti OL, Schembri M. The origin and fate of herniated lumbar intervertebral disk tissue. Spine 1996;21:2149–2155.

23. Franson RC, Saal JS, Saal JA. Human disk phospholipase A2 is inflammatory. Spine 1992;17:S129–S131.

24. Saal JS. The role of inflammation in lumbar pain. Spine 1995;20:1821–1827.

25. Lindblom K. Technique and results of diagnostic disk puncture and injection. Acta Orthop Scand 1951;20:315–326.

26. Perey O. Contrast medium examination of the intervertebral disks. Acta Orthop Scand 1951;20:327–334.

27. Froning EC, Frohman B. Motion of the lumbar spine after laminectomy and spinal fusion. J Bone Joint Surg 1968;50:879–918.

28. England R, Deibert P. Electromyographic studies. I. Consideration in the evaluation of osteopathic therapy. J Am Osteopath Assoc 1972;72:221–223.

29. Grice AA. Muscle tonus changes following manipulation. J Can Chiropractic Assoc 1974;19:29–31.

30. Davidoff RA. Skeletal muscle tone and the misunderstood stretch reflex. Neurology 1992;42:951–963.

31. Travell J, Simons DG. Myofascial Pain and Dysfunction. Baltimore: Williams & Wilkins, 1983;5.

32. Kellgren JH. On the distribution of pain arising from deep somatic structures. Clin Sci 1939;4:35–46.

33. Lewis T, Kellgren JH. Observations relating to referred pain. Clin Sci 1939;4:47–71.

34. Roland M, van Tulder M. Should radiologists change the way they report plain radiography of the spine? Lancet 1998;352:229–230.

35. Ytterberg SR, Mahowald ML, Woods SR. Codeine and oxycodone use in patients with chronic rheumatic disease pain. Arthritis Rheum 1998;41(9):1603–1611.

36. Shofferman J. Long Term Opioid Analgesic Therapy for Severe Refractory Lumbar Spine Pain. Presented at the Annual Meeting of the International Society for the Study of the Lumbar Spine, Brussels, 1998. In The Joint Letter. Philadelphia: Lippincott Williams & Wilkins, 1998;4(10):112.

37. Li L, Zhuo M. Silent glutameric synapses and nociception in mammalian spinal cord. Nature 1998;393:695–698.

38. Mont MA, Mayerson JA, Krackow KA, Hungerford DS. Total knee arthroplasty in patients receiving workers' compensation. J Bone Joint Surg 1998;80A:1285–1290.

14

Examination and Treatment of Muscle Imbalances

Manual treatment of spinal dysfunction traditionally has focused on mobilization of joints and paid little attention to the surrounding soft tissue structures. Normal spinal function is dependent not only on passive joint mobility, but also on normal muscle activity and central nervous system regulation of movement patterns.[1] In earlier editions of this book, focus was directed toward the restoration of joint mobility. This chapter emphasizes the examination and treatment of muscle imbalances that involve the upper and lower quarters and have a particular influence on the mobility of the spine and pelvis. Attention is paid not only to muscle length and strength, but, more important, to the observation and correction of faulty movement patterns that can perpetuate recurrent and chronic musculoskeletal dysfunction.

The evaluation and treatment of muscle imbalances traditionally has been primarily concerned with strength testing and restoration of muscle strength by resistance training, with only cursory attention paid to muscle tightness and stretching. A more effective approach toward the treatment of muscle imbalances using the principles of neuromotor retraining comes from the work of Janda[1,2] and Lewit.[3] Janda observed that certain muscle groups respond to dysfunction (i.e., pain or impaired afferent impulses from a joint or other soft tissue structures) by tightening and shortening, whereas other muscle groups react by inhibition, atrophy, and weakness. These responses are not random occurrences, but they are fairly predictable from joint to joint and from patient to patient. Janda[1] also believes that normalization of the length of a tight (hypertonic) muscle plays a very significant role in a therapeutic exercise program and that the importance of muscle tightness has been underestimated. Moreover, according to Janda, it

is futile to attempt to strengthen an apparently weakened muscle if it is inhibited by its shortened antagonist or from abnormal afferent information emanating from other soft tissues. Most commonly, in our experience, this abnormal afferent information is coming from a dysfunctional joint. Janda[4] has also reported that an inhibited muscle does not respond to resistance training, as expected, but often becomes further inhibited.

The muscle groups that respond to dysfunction and abnormal afferent information by tightening and shortening have been labeled by Janda[1,2] as *postural muscles*. These are muscles that are usually active in maintaining postural balance and are readily activated in most movement patterns. Muscles that respond by inhibition, atrophy, and weakness are referred to as *dynamic* or *phasic muscles*. The physiological basis for this clinically observed patterning between postural and dynamic muscles remains unclear. As yet, there is no correlation between postural and dynamic muscles by muscle fiber typing in human histological studies.

Janda[1,2,5] believes that there are two major body regions in which muscle imbalances are more evident or in which they begin to develop. These regions are

1. The shoulder girdle (upper quarter)
2. The pelvic girdle (lower quarter)

UPPER QUARTER

In addition to length and strength considerations for the muscles in the upper quarter, patterns of participation of various muscle groups during functional activities must also be evaluated, because faulty movement patterns may lead to joint strain and eventual osteoarthritic

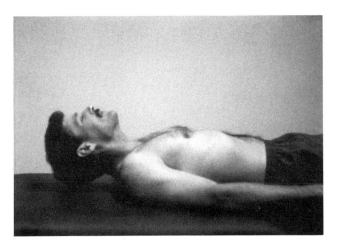

FIGURE 14-1

Incorrect movement pattern for cervical spine flexion. Note activation of the sternocleidomastoid muscle and protrusion of the chin.

changes. Janda[1,5] has noted a particular syndrome of the upper quarter that he has called the *proximal* or *shoulder crossed syndrome*. This syndrome describes an imbalance of the following muscle groups: tight and shortened pectoralis major and minor, upper trapezius, levator scapulae, and sternocleidomastoid accompanied by weakness of the lower stabilizers of the scapula and deep neck flexors. This muscular imbalance allows a forward head posture with extension of the cervicocranial junction, straightening of the cervical lordosis, increased kyphosis at the cervico-thoracic junction, and protraction with internal rotation of the shoulder girdles. Joint restrictions may result from these imbal-

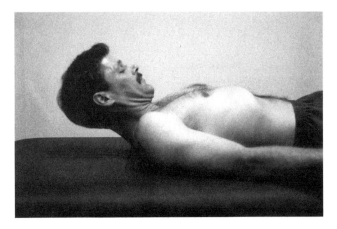

FIGURE 14-2

Correct movement for cervical spine flexion. Note that the chin stays tucked down.

FIGURE 14-3

Bilateral shoulder abduction. Note faulty elevation of the left shoulder.

ances, leading to a loss of mobility for upper cervical spine flexion (ERS dysfunctions) and lower cervical and cervico-thoracic spinal extension (FRS dysfunctions). In addition, because of the change in position of the shoulder girdle, there is an alteration in shoulder mechanics that can create a strain of the shoulder joints.[1,5]

Upper Quarter Evaluation

To evaluate for muscle imbalances and faulty movement patterns in the upper quarter, the following tests can be used:

1. *Supine cervical flexion.* The patient lies supine, with knees bent and feet flat on the table, and is asked to raise the head off the table and look toward the feet. The operator should watch for activation of the sternocleidomastoid muscles, which substitute for inhibited deep neck flexors and cause the head to extend on the neck, rather than allowing smooth cervical spine flexion (Figures 14-1 and 14-2). This dysfunctional movement pattern may perpetuate or be the result or cause of ESR dysfunctions commonly seen at the occipitoatlantal joint. The movement pattern implicates the sternocleidomastoid as a long restrictor muscle for flexion restrictions at this joint.

2. *Bilateral shoulder abduction.* The patient sits with his or her back to the operator and is asked to abduct the arms over the head. The operator observes the scapulohumeral rhythm, looking particularly for premature and excessive abduction of one scapula, elevation of the shoulder, or both (Figure 14-3). Faulty elevation of one shoulder girdle may be due to imbalance (on that side) between the levator scapulae and upper trapezius mus-

FIGURE 14-4
Scapular stabilization test in the hands-and-knees position.

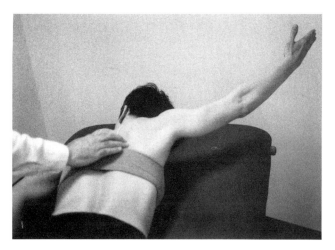

FIGURE 14-5
Lower trapezius recruitment test.

cles, which are tight, and the lower trapezius, serratus anterior, and supraspinatus, which are weak. This muscular imbalance typically leads to an impingement syndrome of the shoulder with involvement of the rotator cuff of the shoulder and frequently creates a strain in the cervical spine secondary to the hyperactivity of the levator scapulae as it attaches to the upper four cervical segments. When evaluating the flexed cervical spine, if multiple level ERS dysfunctions are found from C2 to C4—all with restricted translation to the same side when the cervical spine is in flexion—the operator should suspect involvement of the levator scapulae, perpetuated by dysfunctional scapular control.

3. *Scapular stabilization.* The patient is on hands and knees, with elbows bent enough to hold the shoulders at the same height as the hips. The operator looks for winging of the medial border of the scapula, which indicates weakness of and lack of stabilization by the lower trapezius, serratus anterior, and rhomboid muscles (Figure 14-4). To further challenge these muscle groups, the patient is instructed to lift one hand slightly off the table to see if this causes scapular winging on the side of the support arm. Clinically, we have found that ERS dysfunctions in the thoracic spine (i.e., from T3 to T6) have a strong tendency to inhibit the serratus anterior. The thoracic spine often appears straight or, in worse cases with multiple stacked ERS dysfunctions, appears lordotic in this area. Therefore, restoring joint mobility for flexion from T3 to T6 by addressing any ERS dysfunctions sometimes dramatically improves the patient's ability to recruit (activate) the serratus anterior.

4. *Lower trapezius recruitment.* The patient is prone, with the arm abducted to 125 degrees and externally rotated. The operator resists scapular retraction and depression at the inferior angle of the scapula (Figure 14-5). Clinically, we have found that FRS dysfunctions in the thoracic spine from T6 to T10 have a strong tendency to inhibit lower trapezius function on the ipsilateral side (e.g., FRSrt T8-9 with an inhibited right lower trapezius). Warmerdam[6] has reported a similar clinical observation.

5. *Length of the latissimus dorsi.* The patient is supine, with the knees bent and feet flat on the table, and puts both shoulders through a full range of flexion. The operator watches for recruitment of extension of the lumbar spine, failure to obtain adequate shoulder flexion, or both (Figure 14-6). The latissimus dorsi attaches to the lower six thoracic spinous processes and all of the lumbar spinous processes through the thoracolumbar fascia. Tightness of the latissimus dorsi pro-

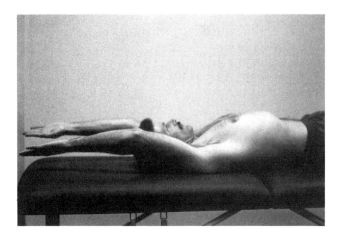

FIGURE 14-6
Latissimus dorsi length test. Note that the limitation of shoulder flexion is evident bilaterally.

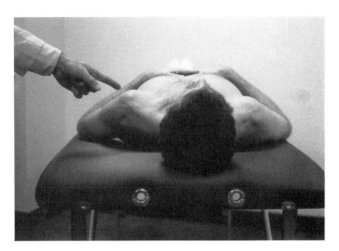

FIGURE 14-7
Forward shoulder position test (supine). Note the anterior position of the left shoulder.

motes or results in an increase in the lower thoracic kyphosis and perpetuates FRS dysfunctions in the thoracic spinal segments from T6 to T12.

6. *Shoulder position test supine.* With the patient supine, the operator observes the relative antero-posterior position of the shoulders. Tightness of the left shoulder is illustrated in Figure 14-7. In the past, finding an anteriorly displaced shoulder was interpreted as a consequence of pectoral tightness. We now believe, however, that an anteriorly displaced shoulder is more commonly due to a tight posterior shoulder capsule or restricted anterior to posterior glide of the upper ipsilateral ribs, or both. To differentiate the cause of the shoulder tightness, the operator applies an anterior-to-posterior glide to the humeral head and then to ribs 2–5 on each side. If the operator notes a restriction with anterior-to-posterior glide of the humeral head, the patient has a tight posterior shoulder capsule. If the operator notes a restriction with anterior-to-posterior glides applied to ribs 2–5, the rib cage needs to be mobilized, followed by stretching the pectorals, if needed. This is an important differentiation to make, because giving a patient with a tight posterior shoulder capsule a pectoral stretch may further compromise and jeopardize the integrity of the anterior capsule of the shoulder.

Upper Quarter Treatment, Mobilization and Stretching

Mobilization for Treatment of Muscle Imbalances and Faulty Movement Patterns

The movement and length tests presented not only give the examiner information regarding motor control and muscle function of the upper quarter, but also help in identifying corresponding areas of joint dysfunction. Consequently, we find mobilization of specific dysfunctional spinal joints helpful in restoring more normal movement patterns. For example, in patients with dysfunctional movement control seen with the supine cervical flexion test, muscle energy or high-velocity techniques directed toward ERS dysfunctions in the upper thoracic spine or upper cervical spine may help to restore the range of cervico-thoracic flexion. Restoration of mobility for cervico-thoracic flexion often results in an increase in the ability to activate the deep neck flexors. For patients with dysfunctional shoulder abduction with a loss of scapular stabilization, the operator should look for and treat ERS dysfunctions from T3 to T6 and FRS dysfunctions from T6 to T10 (see Chapter 9). Clinically, we have found that it is very difficult to improve movement patterns and address muscle imbalances in the upper quarter and cervical musculature in the presence of the non-neutral thoracic spinal dysfunctions mentioned above. Therefore, our approach to treatment of muscle imbalances includes the mobilization of joints to help normalize articular reflexes along with stretching the muscles found to be hypertonic and shortened, followed by retraining motor control with functional movement patterns.

Stretching for the Upper Quarter

To stretch commonly tight muscles, the patient is instructed to use a static stretch that is held for 20–30 seconds and repeated several times or use postisometric relaxation (i.e., muscle energy technique). Postisometric relaxation requires the patient to make an isometric muscle contraction that is held for 5–7 seconds, followed by relaxation, and then the operator passively lengthens the muscle up to the next motion barrier.

The muscles commonly found to be tight in the upper quarter can be treated by the following exercises:

1. *Upper trapezius and levator scapulae.* To stretch the right levator scapulae muscle, the patient sits and looks downward and to the left, with the head tilted to the left. The left hand may be placed on the top of the head to support the head and neck, but the patient is cautioned not to pull with the hand, because this movement could cause a strain of the joints of the cervical spine. The patient is sitting and grasps the edge of the seat, with the right hand placed behind the right hip, and then leans to the left and slightly forward, giving a passive stretch to the right levator scapulae (Figure 14-8). To isolate the right upper trapezius muscle, the patient's head and neck are slightly flexed, side bent to the left, and then rotated to the right. Leaning to the left while grasping the edge of the seat with the right

FIGURE 14-8
Self-stretch of the right levator scapulae.

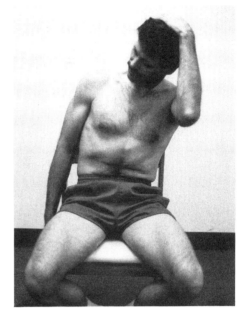

FIGURE 14-9
Self-stretch of the right upper trapezius.

hand stretches the right upper trapezius (Figure 14-9). An additional stretch may be achieved by instructing the patient to actively depress the right shoulder by contracting the right lower trapezius. To stretch the left levator scapulae and upper trapezius muscles, the reverse positioning is used, and the patient grasps the edge of the seat with the left hand.

2. *Scalenes and sternocleidomastoid.* The patient sits and, if stretching the right side, grips the chair with the right hand. The patient places the left hand over the right first rib and clavicle to stabilize both. The patient is instructed to extend the head and neck back slightly while keeping the chin down, side bend the head to the left, and rotate it to the right until tension is felt in the front of the right side of the neck (Figure 14-10).

3. *Posterior shoulder capsule and external rotators.* The patient side lies on the same side as the shoulder to be stretched and rotates backward enough to stabilize the scapula against the table. The shoulder and elbow are each flexed to 90 degrees, and the shoulder is internally rotated to its barrier (Figure 14-11). The patient is instructed to hold the shoulder internally rotated by using the opposite hand to grasp above the wrist of the shoulder to be stretched. The patient rolls forward and backward over the arm six to eight times to stretch the posterior capsule while maintaining the internal rotation. Alternatively, the patient can perform an isometric contraction of the exter-

nal rotators by resisting with the opposite hand for 5–7 seconds. On relaxation, the shoulder is taken into further internal rotation to the new barrier.

4. *Pectoralis minor and sternal fibers of pectoralis major.* To stretch the left side, the patient stands facing the wall, with the left shoulder abducted to 90 degrees, the palm of the left hand placed against the wall, and the elbow slightly bent. The patient turns the feet to the right to be parallel to the wall and, while keeping the left shoulder down and back, presses against the wall with the right hand to turn the upper trunk to the right. Most of the stretch should be felt in the pectorals, anterior shoulder, and, perhaps, the biceps. The stretch may be static or performed with a series of contract-relax cycles by having the patient press the left hand into the wall for 5–7 seconds (Figure 14-12). Caution: This stretch should not be given in the presence of a tight posterior shoulder capsule, because it may contribute further to anterior capsular laxity.

5. *Latissimus dorsi.* Acting with the teres major, the latissimus extends, adducts, and internally rotates the humerus. Particularly when tight bilaterally, the latissimus dorsi can restrict extension throughout the lower thoracic spine and, therefore, have a profound effect on head and neck posture, as well as limiting shoulder flexion. The stretch for the latissimus dorsi is performed with the patient kneeling, with hands and elbows held together and supported on a chair or stool. By sitting back toward the heels, elongation is obtained through

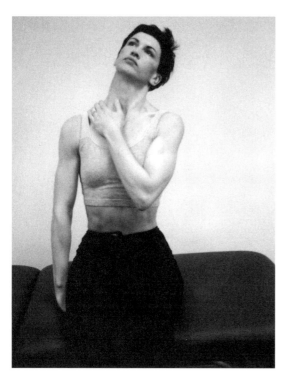

FIGURE 14-10
Self-stretch of the right scalenes.

FIGURE 14-12
Patient attempting to stretch the left anterior shoulder and pectorals. Note patient's inability to correctly depress the left scapula during the stretch.

the thoracic and lumbar areas, straightening the spine as much as possible. To promote external rotation of the shoulders, the hands and elbows should be held together as much as possible throughout the stretch. Moving the pelvis into a posterior tilt while maintaining thoracic extension places an even greater stretch on the latissimus dorsi (Figure 14-13). The stretch is typically held for 20–30 seconds and repeated two to three times.

Upper Quarter Treatment, Retraining

Exercises for strengthening (facilitating) weakened muscles are performed after addressing the tightness found

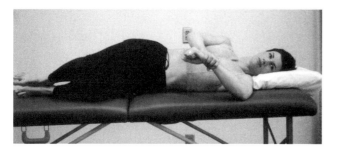

FIGURE 14-11
Self-stretch of the posterior shoulder capsule.

in the related joints and antagonistic musculature. In our clinical experience, we have had greater success by mobilizing hypomobile joints and stretching the tight and shortened muscles before attempting to strengthen a weakened (inhibited) muscle group. A shortened and tight muscle will appear to be overactivated in various movement patterns, and this activation (facilitation) may be so intense that it makes strengthening of a weakened antagonistic muscle impossible, due to the reflex inhibition.[1] The exercises used for retraining are often simply a modification of the testing procedures previously described and include the following:

1. *Deep neck flexors.* Activation of these muscles is first attempted in the seated position. Ask the patient to nod the chin toward the chest without participation of the superficial neck flexors (Figure 14-14). The patient should feel a slight stretch in the posterior occipitoatlantal region. The position is held for 5–10 seconds and is repeated five to six times. Once this movement is well controlled, the patient can attempt more aggressive strengthening in the supine position. The patient is instructed to place a hand under the cervical lordosis and gently nod the head enough to place pressure against the hand. The isometric contraction of the deep neck flexors is held for 10 seconds and repeated up to 10 times. This

FIGURE 14-13
Latissimus dorsi stretch in the kneeling position.

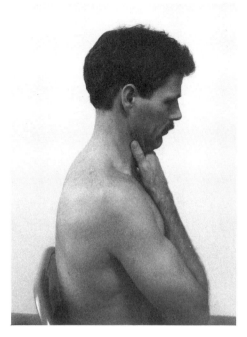

FIGURE 14-14
Re-education of the deep neck flexors. Palpation of the superficial neck flexors to ensure that they remain relaxed.

method of retraining of the deep neck flexors is reportedly being investigated for its usefulness in treating cervicogenic headaches.[7] Once the patient can hold the activated position for 10 seconds and repeat the contraction 10 times, the patient is instructed to progress to active cervical spinal flexion antigravity in the supine lying position, assisted by the use of the hands, as needed (Figure 14-15). The patient is instructed to clasp the hands behind the head and passively flexes the head so that the chin is brought toward the chest. The head is slowly lowered to the table segmentally from below up, using the deep neck flexors eccentrically to lower the head to the table. The patient uses the hands to support the head, as needed, and an emphasis is placed on keeping the chin down as the head is returned to the table. Initially, this exercise is performed for two or three repetitions, progressing up to 10 repetitions, as tolerated. This last exercise is not added until the patient has regained full passive range of motion for cervico-thoracic flexion in the supine lying position. Therefore, any residual ERS dysfunctions in the upper cervical or upper thoracic spine may need to be addressed, because they can restrict the full range of neck flexion and contribute to the inhibition of the deep neck flexors.

2. *Lower trapezius.* Retraining to facilitate the lower trapezius can be done in the prone lying position with various angles of shoulder abduction. Emphasis is placed on the patient learning to move the scapula medially and inferiorly to activate the lower trapezius (Figure 14-16). As mentioned earlier, we have found clinically that restoring thoracic extension mobility by addressing FRS dysfunctions from T6 to T10 significantly helps to improve lower trapezius recruitment.

3. *Serratus anterior.* The patient is on the hands and knees, with elbows bent enough so that the shoulders and hips are at the same height. The thoracic spine is straight, and the scapulae are stabilized against the rib cage. Once this position is attained successfully, the patient is asked to lift one hand off the floor while keeping the shoulders level, avoiding winging of the scapula on the supporting side (Figure 14-17). The position is held for approximately 10 seconds and repeated five to six times. If the patient is having difficulty recruiting the serratus anterior, be sure to check for and treat any residual ERS dysfunction(s) from T3 to T6.

4. *Shoulder abduction.* Before the shoulder abduction exercise is attempted, the patient should be able to acti-

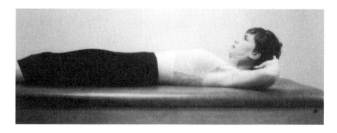

FIGURE 14-15
Strengthening of the deep neck flexors in the supine lying position, working eccentrically.

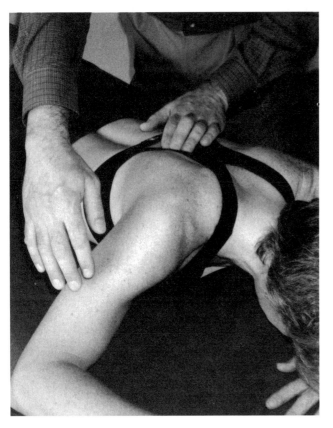

FIGURE 14-16
Retraining of the right lower trapezius.

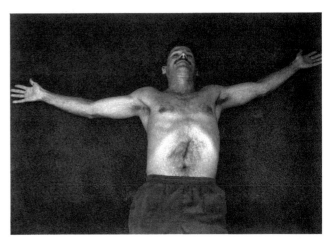

FIGURE 14-18
Retraining for shoulder abduction when the patient is supine. Note the elevation of the left shoulder girdle complex, indicating an abnormal movement pattern that must be avoided during the retraining process.

vate the lower trapezius when prone. The patient lies supine with knees bent, feet flat, and arms externally rotated at the side. Bilateral shoulder abduction is initiated while stabilizing the medial border of the scapula in retraction and depression. The patient maintains a neu-

tral lumbar spine with transversus abdominis activation and should only abduct the arms as far as possible, without elevating the shoulder girdle or losing the contact of the dorsum of the hands with the floor. When the patient reaches a point in the range at which the shoulder or hand starts to elevate or the neutral lumbar spine position is lost, he or she is instructed to back away from the barrier, elongate by reaching through the arm, shoulder, and trunk, and return the arm down to the side (Figure 14-18). This sequence is repeated five to six times. Once the full range of abduction is achieved in the supine lying position, shoulder abduction can be repeated with elongation in the seated position (see Figure 15-11).

LOWER QUARTER

In the presence of neuromotor dysfunction, Janda[1] has also identified a common pattern of muscle imbalances that occur in the lower quadrant with the hypertonic and tightened postural muscles, including the iliopsoas, rectus femoris, tensor fasciae latae, quadratus lumborum, the thigh adductors, piriformis, the hamstrings, and the thoraco-lumbar erector spinae musculature. The muscle groups showing a tendency toward inhibition and reflex weakness include the gluteus maximus, medius, and minimus and the rectus abdominus, as well as the external and internal obliques. Moreover, inhibition and delayed activation of the transversus abdominis have been confirmed in patients with low back pain.[8,9]

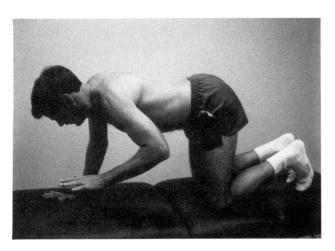

FIGURE 14-17
Retraining of the right serratus anterior.

Janda[1] refers to a pelvic crossed syndrome characterized by imbalances between the shortened and tight hip flexors, and thoraco-lumbar erector spinae musculature, and the weakened and inhibited gluteus maximus and abdominal muscles. Because the range of hip extension is reduced, this imbalance has deleterious effects on the lumbar spine during gait. To compensate for reduced hip extension, there is an increase in lumbar extension by the hypertonic thoraco-lumbar erector spinae, resulting in hypermobility in the lumbar spine in the sagittal plane and strain of the intervertebral discs and ligaments.[1,3]

In the frontal plane, an imbalance develops between the weakened gluteus medius and minimus and the tight tensor fasciae latae and quadratus lumborum muscles, creating excessive sway in the pelvis during walking.[3]

Lower Quarter Evaluation

To evaluate for muscle imbalances and faulty movement patterns in the lower quarter, the following tests may be used:

1. *Pelvic clock.* The patient is supine, with the hips and knees flexed and feet resting flat on the tabletop. The knees and feet are placed hip-width apart. The patient is asked to bridge and slowly lower the pelvis down to the table. The operator palpates under the inferior ledge of the anterior superior iliac spine (ASIS) on both sides and notes whether the ASISs are lying symmetrically in the transverse plane. The patient is instructed to visualize lying on the face of an imaginary clock, with 12 o'clock at the top and 6 o'clock at the bottom (see Figure 15-12). The patient is instructed to rotate the pelvis toward 12 o'clock (posterior pelvic tilt) and then toward 6 o'clock (anterior pelvic tilt), while the operator follows the movement with steady contact maintained at the ASISs by the operator's thumbs (Figure 14-19). A common observation is that the ASISs are asymmetrical to start with and remain asymmetrical throughout the range or improve when moving toward 12 o'clock or 6 o'clock. When moving the pelvis toward 12 o'clock, the operator assesses for bilateral and symmetrical lumbar flexion, posterior sacral base nutation, and posterior rotation of the innominates. When moving the pelvis toward 6 o'clock, the operator assesses for bilateral and symmetrical lumbar extension, anterior nutation of the sacral base, and anterior rotation of the innominates. Initially, a patient is rarely able to rotate symmetrically toward 12 o'clock and 6 o'clock and keep the ASISs level throughout the entire range. To assess rotational control of the lumbar spine and pelvis, the patient is instructed to rotate the pelvis toward 3 o'clock and then toward 9 o'clock, while the operator maintains thumb contact under the inferior ledge of the ASISs. Ideally, the patient

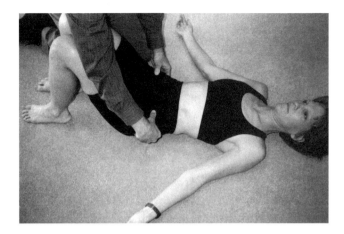

FIGURE 14-19
Palpation of the anterior superior iliac spines during the pelvic clock exercise.

should be able to rotate the pelvis toward 3 o'clock or 9 o'clock while maintaining the ASISs level in the transverse plane. Often, the operator will observe that the patient has great difficulty moving toward 3 o'clock or 9 o'clock and will substitute for the lack of pelvic rotation by moving the pelvis in the frontal or sagittal planes, or both. For example, when attempting to rotate toward 9 o'clock, the patient often hikes the hip on the left side (frontal plane) so that the left ASIS is pulled superiorly. When attempting to rotate toward 3 o'clock, the patient often excessively rotates the right innominate anteriorly (sagittal plane) so that the right ASIS moves inferiorly, when compared to the left side. Monitoring the movement of the ASISs with the operator's thumbs is crucial in evaluating neuromuscular control of the lumbopelvic region using the pelvic clock. Because the pelvic clock requires a sophisticated degree of motor control, it can be helpful not only in diagnosing faulty movement patterns in the lower quarter, but also in objectively measuring the success of treatment of the lumbar spine, sacrum, and innominates.

2. Hip abduction with external rotation. The patient is supine, with the knees bent and feet flat on the table (or floor), and performs a posterior pelvic tilt to 12 o'clock. The operator palpates under the inferior ledge of the ASISs to make sure the ASISs are level in the transverse plane at 12 o'clock. If the ASISs are not level, the operator instructs the patient to pull up on one side or lower the other side to make sure the test starts from a position of symmetry. The patient allows the knees to abduct while 12 o'clock is maintained. While the hips are abducting and externally rotating, the ASISs are continuously monitored by the operator's palpating thumbs, and then the patient is instructed to self-monitor using his or her own thumbs (Figure 14-20). If there is an

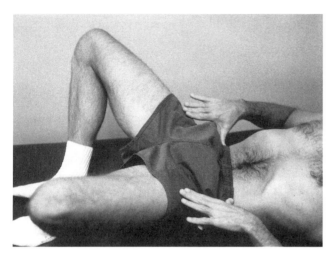

FIGURE 14-20
Palpation of the anterior superior iliac spines during hip abduction with external rotation.

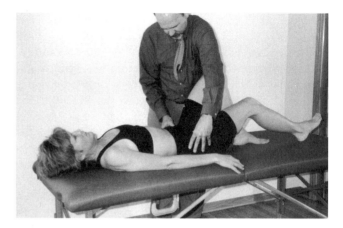

FIGURE 14-21
Pelvic tilt/heel slide, with the operator monitoring the position of the ASISs.

imbalance on one side of the pelvis with weak abdominal muscles and tight adductors, the posterior pelvic tilt (12 o'clock) cannot be maintained, and the ASIS is felt moving inferiorly on that side (i.e., the innominate is rotating anteriorly). Clinically, the most common pattern seen is a loss of control on the right side, with the right ASIS moving inferiorly while the left side remains in place. This muscle imbalance, with tightness of the hip adductors and inhibition of the abdominals, is often the cause or consequence of an inferior pubic dysfunction on the right side.

3. *Pelvic tilt/heel slide.* The patient is supine, with the knees bent and feet flat on the table, and is asked to flatten the lumbar spine by performing a posterior pelvic tilt to 12 o'clock. The operator palpates under the inferior ledge of the ASISs to make sure that the ASISs are level in the transverse plane when the pelvis is brought to 12 o'clock. If the ASISs are asymmetrical, with one side lower than the other, the patient is asked to pull the lower side up (superiorly) so that the ASISs lie in the same transverse plane. With his or her back remaining flat on the table, the patient is asked to slide one foot down along the table, while the operator monitors at the ASISs to make sure that neither side moves inferiorly during the test. Normally, if the posterior tilt and flattened lumbar lordosis are maintained, the ASIS should not move until the last 10–15 degrees of hip extension. This test challenges the ability of the abdominals to maintain a posterior pelvic tilt, while the iliopsoas muscles are activated eccentrically (Figure 14-21). Clinically, a commonly observed dysfunctional pattern is the inability to slide the right leg down without the

right ASIS prematurely moving inferiorly, indicating an imbalance between the abdominals and hip flexors on the right side of the pelvis. This pattern often presents itself in the presence of an anteriorly rotated innominate on the right side, a tight anterior hip capsule on the right side, tight hip flexors on the right side, or a combination of all three.

Note: Failure to monitor the ASISs with the operator's thumbs negates the sensitivity of these last two tests. Visually, without monitoring the ASISs, the patient may appear to be able to adequately stabilize the lumbar spine and pelvis during these tests. However, palpation of the ASISs frequently reveals that one or both innominates are indeed rotating anteriorly during either test, indicating a loss of pelvic stabilization.

4. *Straight leg raising (hamstrings).* The operator palpates with one hand on the ipsilateral ASIS to monitor for recruitment of posterior pelvic rotation during straight leg raising, assessing both the medial and lateral hamstrings of each leg. Normally, a straight leg raise should reach 70 degrees before noting any movement of the ASIS.[10] A straight leg raise with the hip in external rotation and abduction tests the length of the medial hamstrings, whereas a straight leg raise with the hip in internal rotation and adduction tests the length of the lateral hamstrings (Figure 14-22). It is important to monitor for pelvic rotation, because an additional 10- to 15-degree range of straight leg raising can occur when posterior rotation of the pelvis is allowed.[11]

5. *Hip abduction (gluteus medius and minimus).* The patient lies on one side, with the bottom leg flexed and top leg extended. The examiner observes

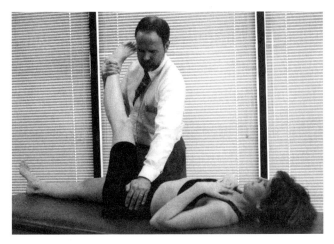

FIGURE 14-22
Straight leg raising with internal rotation and adduction of the hip to test the length of the lateral hamstrings.

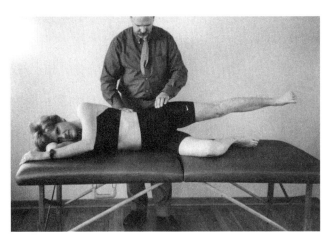

FIGURE 14-23
Testing left hip abduction.

and palpates the firing pattern of the quadratus lumborum, gluteus medius, and tensor fasciae latae while the patient abducts the upper leg (Figure 14-23). A common substitution pattern is for the tensor fasciae latae to predominate the movement when the gluteus medius is weak. This pattern produces flexion and internal rotation of the hip during active hip abduction. Another common substitution pattern is excessive hiking up of the hip by an overactive and hypertonic quadratus lumborum. These substitution patterns can be minimized during testing and retraining by asking the patient to elongate (i.e., reach away) and externally rotate the leg slightly as hip abduction is initiated.

6. *Hip extension (gluteus maximus).* The patient is prone, with the knee straight, and is asked to extend the hip actively. Both visually and by palpation, the "firing pattern" of the muscles involved in this movement is observed. Disagreement exists as to the correct sequence of muscle firing with hip extension.[11,12] Therefore, the primary questions to be answered with hip extension are whether the gluteus maximus fires, how well the spine stabilizes itself during the movement, and whether there is a major difference in control from right to left sides. Failure to activate the gluteus maximus may be noted, with hip extension achieved by the hamstrings and erector spinae musculature. This substitution pattern by the hamstrings and erector spinae muscles may be strong enough to produce active hip extension, with little weakness noted on manual muscle testing of hip extension. Chronic hamstring tightness and resultant hamstring strains may occur as a result of this substitution pattern and

reoccur, unless this muscle imbalance is corrected. Also to be noted in this test is the tendency for the lower thoracic and upper lumbar spine to rotate toward the contralateral side when the gluteus maximus fails to participate in active extension of the hip and when the pelvis is not adequately stabilized by the abdominals (Figure 14-24). To compare further the right and left sides during hip extension, the operator can palpate the inferior ledge of the posterior superior iliac spines (PSISs). Normally, the ipsilateral PSIS moves slightly craniad during active hip extension, but when it is dysfunctional, the operator may palpate or observe excessive movement of the PSIS cranially or no movement of the PSIS at all.

Failure to activate the gluteus maximus during prone hip extension does not necessarily mean that the muscle is weak; rather, this loss of recruitment should be thought of in terms of the muscle being inhibited from participating in terminal hip extension. More importantly, inhibition of the gluteus maximus may result in a loss of the dynamic force closure needed to stabilize the sacroiliac (SI) joint. The role of the operator is to find and treat the cause of the gluteal inhibition, rather than attempting to strengthen the gluteus maximus by resistance training. In our experience, dysfunction of the SI joint (particularly the posteriorly nutated sacral bases), dysfunction of the lower lumbar spine (i.e., FRS dysfunctions at L4-5 or L5-S1), and dysfunction of the hip (with a tight anterior hip capsule) all contribute significantly to inhibition of the gluteal musculature. Bullock-Saxton et al.[13] also have reported residual gluteus maximus inhibition secondary to a history of spraining the ankle.

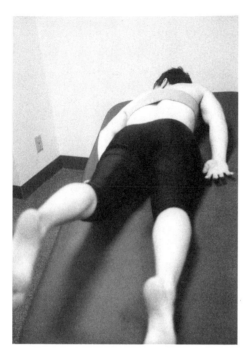

FIGURE 14-24
Abnormal left hip extension firing pattern. Note the hypertonicity of the right thoraco-lumbar erector spinae and rotation of the thoraco-lumbar junction to the right.

Lower Quadrant Treatment, Mobilization and Stretching

Mobilization for Treatment of Faulty Movement Patterns

The movement tests presented not only give the operator information regarding motor control and muscle function in the lower quarter, but also help in identifying associated areas of joint dysfunction in the hips, pelvis, and lumbar spine. The ability to activate a muscle is influenced by the summation of the afferent information coming into the nervous system. Consideration of the influence of joint dysfunction on muscle function gives the operator an additional tool to use in reprogramming motor control. For example, asymmetry in neuromuscular control, as revealed by assessing the supine pelvic clock, helps to diagnose non-neutral lumbar spine dysfunctions, sacral dysfunctions, and innominate rotations.[14] Inhibition of the gluteal musculature is often related to SI dysfunction, lower lumbar non-neutral dysfunctions, or a tight hip capsule. Treatment of the associated joint dysfunction(s) often has a dramatic effect on the ability to recruit a previously weakened (inhibited) muscle within the same treatment session, and the movement test can then become the exercise given to the patient to maintain self-correction.

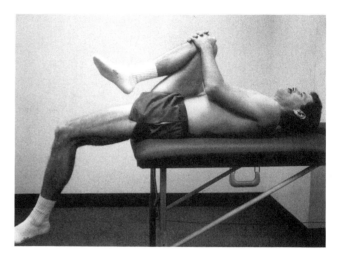

FIGURE 14-25
Left iliopsoas length test. Note the visible tightness of the left iliotibial band.

Stretching for Treatment of Faulty Movement Patterns

Once again, the tight muscles are stretched before initiation of any strengthening or movement re-education program.

The following muscle groups are commonly tight and can be treated by a sustained stretch held for 20–30 seconds and repeated two to three times or by postisometric relaxation techniques, in which the patient contracts the muscle against resistance for 5–7 seconds before relaxation and engagement of a new motion barrier.

1. *Iliopsoas.* The patient is supine, with the hips at the edge of one end of the table. One knee is drawn to the chest to flatten the lumbar spine, and then the other leg is allowed to hang freely. Assessment is made of the length of the iliopsoas. Normally, the hip should extend to neutral or slightly beyond. By observing if there is 90 degrees of knee flexion, the length of the rectus femoris is assessed. If there is adduction or abduction of the femur, the relative tightness of the adductors and tensor fasciae latae are assessed, respectively (Figure 14-25). The iliopsoas can be lengthened by maintaining this supine stretch position for 30–60 seconds; the stretch is repeated two to three times. A more dynamic self-stretch in half-kneeling has been described by Evjenth and Hamberg.[15] This exercise requires active (rather than passive) stabilization of the pelvis and recruitment of the gluteus maximus and hamstring musculature, as illustrated in Figure 14-26. In the half-kneeling exercise, the side to be stretched is positioned with internal rotation and extension of the hip. There is active contraction of the gluteus maximus muscle on the ipsilat-

FIGURE 14-26
Self-stretch of the right iliopsoas muscle in the half-kneeling position.

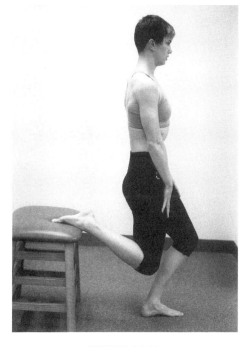

FIGURE 14-27
Right rectus femoris stretch, achieved by sitting back toward the heel, bending the left knee, and keeping the right knee pointed toward the floor.

eral side and the hamstring muscles on the contralateral side, stabilizing and maintaining the pelvis in a posteriorly rotated position during the stretch. The patient is taught to lead with the hip on the side to be stretched as the pelvis is brought forward, extending through the hip joint rather than arching (i.e., extending) through the lumbar spine. Restriction in extensibility of the iliopsoas muscle can influence lumbar spine mobility in all directions and, typically, needs to be addressed in almost every patient with low back pain.

2. *Rectus femoris.* The rectus femoris muscle can be stretched with the patient standing. The knee is flexed so that the foot on that side is supported on the back of a chair, which is placed behind the patient. The pelvis is rotated posteriorly, and the patient sits back toward the heel, maintaining the pelvic tilt and allowing the opposite knee to flex. This stretch is ideal because it teaches dynamic control of the pelvis while isolating the stretch specifically to the rectus femoris (Figure 14-27).

3. *Hip adductors.* The hip adductors can be stretched with the patient sitting up against a wall, with the feet together and hips abducted and externally rotated (Figure 14-28). The hands are placed on the floor behind the hips, and the patient is instructed to roll the pelvis forward toward 6 o'clock to deepen the stretch and toward

12 o'clock to relax. The patient can press the hands down on the floor to assist in extending the lumbar spine when rolling the pelvis toward 6 o'clock. The patient is instructed to repeat this 12-o'clock–to–6-o'clock rocking motion six to eight times, dropping the knees further out to the side with each movement toward 6 o'clock.

4. *Quadratus lumborum.* The stretch is done with the patient on the hands and knees. The ipsilateral arm on the side to be stretched is brought diagonally across the body, and the hand grasps a secure object with the thumb pointing down. If internal rotation of the arm bothers the shoulder, the thumb can be turned upward to externally rotate the shoulder, which then also stretches the latissimus dorsi on that side. The patient is instructed to sit back diagonally toward the hip on the side to be stretched (Figure 14-29). The stretch is sustained for 20–30 seconds and repeated two to three times, alternating sides.

5. *Piriformis.* The piriformis muscle arises from the anterior surface of sacral segments 2, 3, and 4 and attaches to the greater trochanter of the femur. From extension to 60 degrees of hip flexion, the piriformis acts as an external rotator and abductor of the hip. Beyond 60 degrees of hip flexion, the piriformis acts as an abductor

FIGURE 14-28
Hip adductor stretch in the sitting position.

but also is an internal rotator.[16] Balancing the pull of the piriformis on the sacrum is believed to be important when treating any SI joint dysfunction. Because the muscle has two distinctly different actions, there is no singular exercise that adequately addresses this muscle. Two stretches that are believed to address length restrictions of the piriformis are the buttock stretch and the supine hip-rotation stretch. The buttock stretch is described in Chapter 15 as a self-mobilization stretch for a forward sacral torsion (see Figure 15-14). The supine hip-rotation stretch is used to address tightness in the piriformis when the muscle is acting as an abductor and external rotator. For treatment of the right piriformis, the patient is supine, and the right hip is flexed less than 60 degrees. The right hip is adducted to place the right foot on the lateral side (outside) of the left knee. The patient grasps the right knee with the left hand and adducts and medially rotates the right hip (Figure 14-30). Through a series of isometric contract-relax cycles, the hip is brought progressively into further adduction and internal rotation to stretch the right piriformis.

6. *Hamstrings.* The patient is supine, with a small towel roll maintaining the lumbar lordosis. The hip on the side to be stretched is flexed to 90 degrees and held there by the patient clasping his or her hands behind the thigh. The other leg is actively held straight. The stretch is performed by active quadriceps contraction with the foot dorsiflexed, as in the instruction "reach toward the ceiling with your

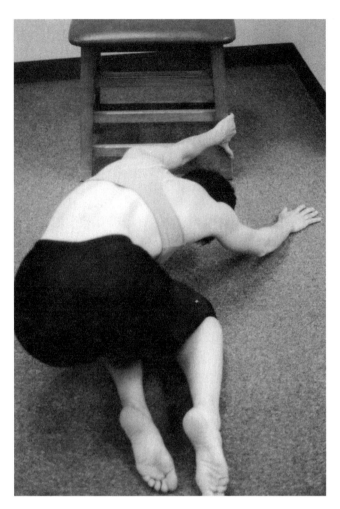

FIGURE 14-29
Kneeling quadratus lumborum stretch on the left. This position also stretches the left latissimus dorsi, especially if the thumb is pointed upward to externally rotate the shoulder.

heel" (Figure 14-31). The stretch is held momentarily and repeated 10 times in an on-and-off fashion.

Lower Quarter Treatment, Retraining

Patients with low back pain are commonly found to have weakness (inhibition) of the gluteus maximus, medius, and minimus muscles. In addition, there is evidence supporting the important stabilizing function of the transversus abdominis muscle,[8,9] which has been given very little attention in traditional abdominal strengthening programs. Exercises are prescribed specifically for these muscles in the hope of decreasing the biomechanical stresses placed on the lumbar spine and pelvis. Any of the movement tests initially used to assess for faulty movement patterns and poor neuro-

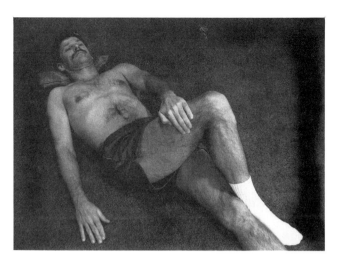

FIGURE 14-30
Supine stretch for the right piriformis.

FIGURE 14-31
Supine stretch for the right hamstrings.

muscular control of the lower quarter can be modified, as needed, to become a retraining exercise.

1. *Abdominals.* Strengthening exercises for the abdominal muscles start with isometric activation of the transversus abdominis muscle in various positions (i.e., supine and on hands and knees), while maintaining a neutral lumbar spine.[17] To assist the supine patient, the operator monitors the ASISs with the thumbs and asks the patient to rock the pelvis from 12 o'clock to 6 o'clock. The operator finds the midpoint (neutral) between these two extremes of pelvic rotation, while keeping the ASISs lying in the same transverse plane, and continues to monitor the ASISs to make sure the pelvis is held symmetrical during the muscle recruitment (see Figure 14-19). The patient is instructed to pull the umbilicus toward the spine while maintaining a neutral lumbar spine position. Common substitution patterns to be avoided include activating the external obliques with compression of the lower rib cage and failure to maintain a neutral lumbar spine position caused by the patient inadvertently performing a posterior pelvic tilt. Initially, the focus is on proper activation of the transversus abdominis and the patient's ability to hold an isometric contraction for up to 10 seconds while breathing normally. Once the muscle is properly recruited and has some endurance capacity, additional loading of the spine can be added by lifting or sliding a leg in the supine lying position (see Figure 14-21) or lifting a hand when the patient is positioned on the hands and knees (see Figure 14-17).

Note: A distinction needs to be made between retraining abdominal control and when testing for faulty abdominal control with the supine heel slide and with the hip abduction and external rotation movements.

When testing for abdominal control, a posterior pelvic tilt (12 o'clock) is maintained throughout the test to maximally challenge the abdominals. However, when initially retraining the abdominals, a neutral lumbar spine (i.e., midway between 12 o'clock and 6 o'clock) is advocated. Retraining the abdominals in a neutral lumbar spine position is thought to be more functional, as well as less stressful to the noncontractile elements of the spine.

To retrain the abdominal obliques, the patient is supine, with both knees up and feet resting flat on the table. The patient is instructed to drop both knees off to one side, just enough to lift the hip, pelvis, and lumbar spine off the table on one side. The patient is instructed to slowly rotate back to the midline by rotating the spine segmentally back to the table from the mid-thoracic region down to the pelvis (Figure 14-32), rather than rotating back from the hips.

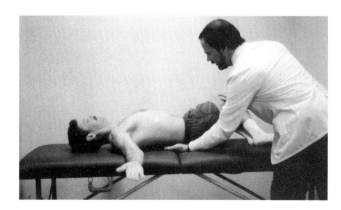

FIGURE 14-32
Abdominal oblique retraining exercise.

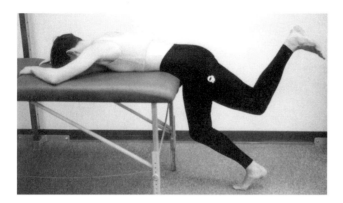

FIGURE 14-33
Gluteus maximus retraining exercise, maintaining a neutral lumbar spine.

FIGURE 14-34
Supine bridging, maintaining a neutral lumbar spine with transversus abdominis activation.

The inability to rotate the spine back to the table is frequently due to non-neutral ERS dysfunctions in the lower thoracic spine and thoraco-lumbar junction that inhibit abdominal oblique activation. Consequently, stretching the thoraco-lumbar erector spinae, which tends to be tight, and treating ERS dysfunctions of the thoraco-lumbar spine can assist in regaining abdominal oblique activation.

2. *Gluteus maximus.* Clinically, weakness of the gluteus maximus is seen in patients with SI joint dysfunction, non-neutral lumbar spine dysfunctions, and tight anterior hip capsules. The muscle may be inhibited by articular reflex mechanisms, a tight and shortened ipsilateral iliopsoas muscle, or both. Therefore, the iliopsoas should be assessed and stretched, if indicated, before attempting to strengthen the gluteus maximus. Strengthening exercises are usually initiated in the prone position, with the hips and lower extremities off the end of the table and a neutral lumbar spine stabilized by activation of the transversus abdominis. The patient is instructed to find the neutral spine position by rocking the pelvis from 12 o'clock to 6 o'clock and find the midpoint between these two extremes of motion. The transversus abdominis is activated before extending the hip with the knee flexed. The hip is extended only so far as the patient is able to maintain a neutral lumbar spine (Figure 14-33). Emphasis is placed on the quality of the movement and the patient being able to *feel* the muscle contract, rather than on multiple repetitions. Usually, the patient fatigues surprisingly fast (e.g., after only three or four repetitions) if the exercise is done properly.

Many patients fail to recruit the gluteus maximus in active prone hip extension, substituting with the lumbar erector spinae and the hamstring musculature. If this substitution pattern is not recognized, the patient may be performing an exercise that only reinforces the dysfunctional movement pattern.

Once the patient knows how to recruit the gluteus maximus properly, a bridging exercise may be added. The patient is supine, with the knees flexed and feet flat on the table or floor. He or she finds a neutral lumbar spine position (i.e., midway between 12 o'clock and 6 o'clock), activates the transversus abdominis to maintain the neutral position, and lifts the buttocks off the table by a strong active gluteus maximus contraction, being careful to avoid lumbar spine extension (Figure 14-34). Initially, with this exercise, cramping of the hamstrings may occur due to substitution of the hamstrings for lack of active hip extension by the gluteus maximus. Once the gluteus maximus is properly activated, cramping of the hamstrings with the bridging exercise ceases.

3. *Gluteus medius and minimus.* The patient is in the side-lying position and up against a wall, with the shoulders, hips, and the foot of the supporting lower leg against the wall. The dysfunctional side is uppermost, and the transversus abdominis is activated to maintain a neutral lumbar spine. The patient abducts the leg and, to avoid substitution with the tensor fasciae latae, slightly externally rotates the leg. Hip flexion is prevented by having the patient raise the top leg while maintaining heel contact with the wall (Figure 14-35). The patient also is instructed to avoid hiking the hip by elongating and reaching with the leg during abduction.

This chapter has introduced the use of functional movement tests to evaluate neuromotor control in patients with

FIGURE 14-35
Gluteus medius retraining, with the patient side lying against a wall.

musculoskeletal pain and dysfunction. Treatment of the muscle imbalances associated with frequently observed abnormal movement patterns assists in restoring normal neuromotor control and helps prevent the recurrence of joint dysfunction. We can then use an improvement of neuromotor control as an objective measurement of the patient's progress and response to treatment.

REFERENCES

1. Janda V. Muscles as a Pathogenic Factor in Back Pain. In The Treatment of Patients, Proceedings of the 4th Conference of International Federation of Orthopaedic Manipulative Therapists. Christchurch: 1980;1–23.
2. Janda V. Muscles, Central Nervous Motor Regulation and Back Problems. In I Korr (ed), The Neurobiologic Mechanisms in Manipulative Therapy. New York: Plenum Press, 1977;27–41.
3. Lewit K. Manipulative Therapy in Rehabilitation of the Motor System. London: Butterworth, 1985.
4. Janda V. Muscle Weakness and Inhibition (Pseudoparesis) in Back Pain Syndromes. In GP Grieve (ed), Modern Manual Therapy of the Vertebral Column. Edinburgh, UK: Churchill Livingstone, 1986;197–201.
5. Janda V. Muscles and Motor Control in Cervicogenic Disorders: Assessment and Management. In R Grant (ed), Physical Therapy of the Cervical and Thoracic Spine, Clinics in Physical Therapy. New York: Churchill Livingstone, 1994;195–216.
6. Warmerdam A. Manual Therapy: Improve Muscle and Joint Functioning. Wantagh, NY: Pine Publications, 1999;191.
7. Jull G. Management of cervical headache. Man Ther 1997;2(4):182–190.
8. Hodges PW, Richardson CA. Inefficient muscular stabilization of the lumbar spine associated with low back pain: a motor control evaluation of transversus abdominis. Spine 1996;21:2640–2650.
9. Hodges PW, Richardson CA. Altered trunk muscle recruitment in people with low back pain with upper limb movement at different speeds. Arch Phys Med Rehabil 1999;80:1005–1012.
10. Kendall FP, McCreary EK. Muscle Testing and Function (3rd ed). Baltimore: Williams & Wilkins, 1983;148.
11. Janda V. Manipulative Medicine in the Management of Soft Tissue Pain Syndromes. Presented at the Annual Meeting of the North American Academy of Manipulative Medicine; October 19–20, 1983; Alexandria, VA.
12. Vogt L, Banzer W. Dynamic testing of the motor stereotype in prone hip extension from neutral position. Clin Biomech 1997;12:122–127.
13. Bullock-Saxton JE, Janda V, Bullock MI. The influence of ankle sprain injury on muscle activation during hip extension. Int J Sports Med 1994;15:330–334.
14. Bookhout MR, Greenman P. Exercises for Musculoskeletal Dysfunction. Butterworth–Heinemann. In press.
15. Evjenth O, Hamberg J. Autostretching: The Complete Manual of Specific Stretching. Alfta: Alfta Rehab Forlag, 1989;88–89.
16. Kapandji IA. The Physiology of the Joints, Vol II. Edinburgh, UK: Churchill Livingstone, 1970;68.
17. Richardson C, Jull G, Hodges P, Hides J. Therapeutic Exercise for Spinal Segmental Stabilization in Low Back Pain: Scientific Basis and Clinical Approach. Edinburgh, UK: Churchill Livingstone, 1999.

15

Exercises as a Complement to Manual Therapy

Like Chapter 14, this chapter was an entirely new addition to the fifth edition of *Spinal Manipulation*. Over the years, the authors have learned that exercise not only helps to improve aerobic capacity and cardiovascular function and assist in stress reduction, but also should be used as an adjunct to manual therapy intervention. Generalized exercises have their place in overall conditioning programs, but more specific exercises are thought to improve a patient's self-management capability for some of the more chronic and commonly recurring dysfunctions previously discussed in this book.

An understanding of the functional anatomy and biomechanics of the spine is essential to the development of an individualized, specific home exercise program. A positional diagnosis of spinal or pelvic dysfunction delineates which movements need to be restored (Table 15-1) and forms the basis for the selection of the specific self-mobilizing exercises described in this chapter. Failure to assess and adequately treat biomechanical dysfunctions of the vertebral column and pelvis before the initiation of an exercise program may be one of the main reasons why some patients do not improve with exercise alone or report that exercise makes their condition worse.

Controversy exists as to what tissues serve as restrictors of spinal mobility. Since the 1960s, theories have been advanced describing meniscal entrapment,[1] joint capsule adhesions,[2] and hypertonicity in the deep spinal musculature due to abnormal afferent activity.[3] In theory, any of these restrictors could limit single segment mobility. Lewit[4] believes that the most frequent cause of the restriction, which he terms *joint blockage*, comes from faulty movement patterns due to muscle imbalances and postural strain. Theoretically, correc-

tion of muscle imbalances through a specific home exercise program may help to prevent faulty movement patterns and, therefore, prevent further segmental joint dysfunctions (see Chapter 14). This concept serves as the basis for the selection of exercises described in the previous chapter.

The exercises in this chapter are designed as self-mobilizing exercises to complement manual therapy treatment for specific joint dysfunctions found in the spinal column and pelvis. The exercises are presented by region, even though many have multiregional implications.

LUMBAR SPINE

The design of the lumbar spine allows motion to occur primarily in the sagittal plane (i.e., flexion and extension). Consequently, most exercise programs for patients with low back pain advocate restoration of flexion (Williams[5]) or extension (McKenzie[6]) mobility as their major emphasis. McKenzie also advocates the use of side-gliding (translation) maneuvers in select patients as a necessary component in lumbar spine self-treatment, and he should be credited with recognizing the importance of self-mobilizing exercises in the treatment of low back pain. The reader is referred to McKenzie's book, *The Lumbar Spine: Mechanical Diagnosis and Therapy*, for further information regarding his specific home exercise approach. In 1984, one of the authors (M. R. B.) noted the biomechanical similarities between McKenzie's approach to a patient with an acute lumbar scoliosis and lateral shift and the osteopathic muscle energy approach to a patient with an FRS lumbar dysfunction. McKenzie treated patients presenting with an

TABLE 15-1
Positional Diagnosis versus Motion Restriction

Positional Diagnosis	Motion Restriction
Flexed	Extension
Extended	Flexion
Side bent right	Left side bending
Rotated right	Left rotation

acute right lateral shift and lumbar kyphosis with shift correcting movements (i.e., left side gliding in standing) followed by prone press-ups to restore lumbar extension (Figures 15-1 and 15-2). From a manual therapy perspective, these same patients would most likely be treated for an FRSrt dysfunction by using a muscle energy technique with the patient in right side lying; this technique incorporates left side bending and left rotation coupled with lumbar spine extension (see Figure 8-2). The McKenzie approach (i.e., side gliding in standing, followed by prone press-ups) can then be used as part of the home exercise program for patients treated manually for lumbar spine FRS dysfunctions. The challenge was to develop additional, specific exercises to complement manual therapy for other spinal and pelvic dysfunctions.

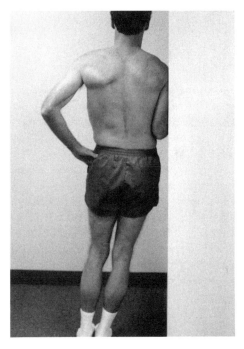

FIGURE 15-1
Left side gliding in the standing position.

FIGURE 15-2
Prone press-ups for lumbar spine extension.

EXERCISES FOR LUMBAR SPINE DYSFUNCTIONS

Exercises for Flexed, Rotated, and Side-Bent (FRS) Dysfunctions

Described for Restricted Extension and Side Bending

In a lumbar FRSrt dysfunction, the positional diagnosis is flexed, rotated right, and side bent right. Therefore, the motion loss is of extension, left rotation, and left side bending at that spinal segment. Exercises for this dysfunction include side gliding in standing, performed against a wall (see Figure 15-1) or facing a wall, which allows the patient to vary the amount of lumbar extension introduced before performing the side glide (Figure 15-3). The extension component can be addressed separately by prone press-ups (see Figure 15-2) or backward bending when the patient is standing (Figure 15-4) or sitting (Figure 15-5), allowing the exercise to be carried out easily at work or home.

Described for Restricted Rotation

The muscle energy and McKenzie types of exercises address the flexion, extension, and side-bending components, assuming that the rotation follows as a coupled movement. To address the rotation more specifically, the patient is instructed in one exercise for self-mobilization and another exercise for neuromuscular re-education, particularly for the deep spinal rotators and abdominal oblique muscles. Both exercises are performed with the patient supine.

1. *For restoration of rotation through the hips, pelvis, and lumbar spine.* The supine patient crosses one flexed leg

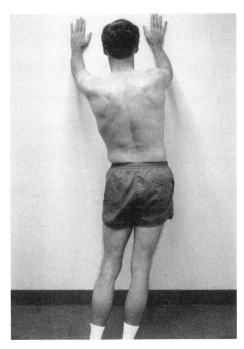

FIGURE 15-3
Left side gliding in the standing position, facing the wall.

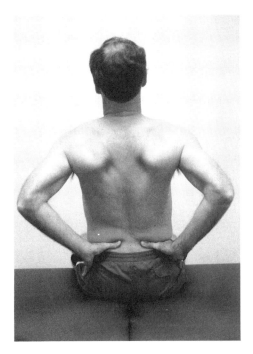

FIGURE 15-5
Self-mobilization for lumbar spine extension in the seated position.

over the other and rotates the legs and pelvis toward the side of the top leg (Figure 15-6).

The position is maintained as a static stretch for 20–30 seconds and repeated two to three times to each side, or the patient is instructed to pull the bottom leg back toward the midline, which is resisted isometrically by

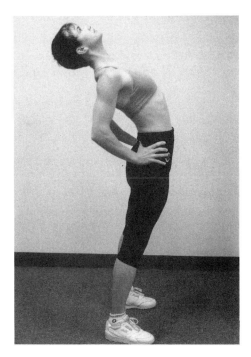

FIGURE 15-4
Backward bending in the standing position.

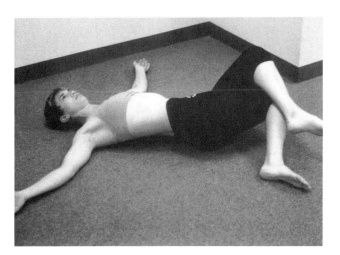

FIGURE 15-6
Self-mobilization exercise to restore right rotation through the lumbar spine by dropping the legs to the left.

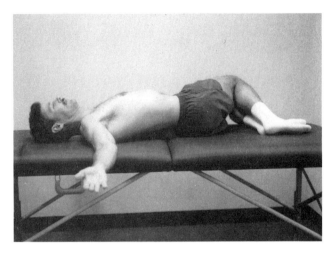

FIGURE 15-7
Neuromotor retraining for lumbar spinal rotation.

the top leg. The contraction is held for 5–7 seconds. On relaxation, the top leg pulls the bottom leg further over past the midline. This stretch is repeated three to four times progressively, first to one side and then the other.

2. *For restoration of rotational control by the spinal and abdominal muscles.* The patient is supine, with knees flexed and feet flat on the floor. The legs are dropped to one side and then the other, but when bringing the knees back to the starting (midline) position, the patient tries to bring each spinal segment, in turn, back to the floor, working from craniad to caudad (Figure 15-7). The purpose of this exercise is to re-educate the deep rotators of the spine and the abdominal oblique muscles so that control of rotational movement occurs through the trunk, rather than through the hips and lower extremities.

FIGURE 15-8
"Prayer stretch" to promote lumbar flexion.

FIGURE 15-9
Diagonal "hip sink" to the right to promote flexion, left rotation, and left side bending of the lumbar spine and posterior nutation of the right sacral base.

Exercises for Extended, Rotated, and Side-Bent (ERS) Dysfunctions

With an ERSrt dysfunction, the positional diagnosis is extended, rotated right, and side bent right so that the motion loss is of flexion, left rotation, and left side bending.

Described for Restricted Flexion
To restore flexion, the following exercises are suggested:

1. Single knee to chest, supine
2. Bilateral knee to chest, supine
3. "Prayer stretch," hands-and-knees position (Figure 15-8)

Described for Restricted Flexion, Left Rotation, and Left Side Bending
To restore flexion, left rotation, and left side bending together, the following exercises are suggested:

1. Diagonal "hip sink" movements from the hands-and-knees position, with the right hip directed toward the outside of the right ankle to elongate the right side of the spine and open the facet joints on the right side (Figure 15-9).

FIGURE 15-10
Forward bending in the left step standing position.

FIGURE 15-11
Elongation to the right in the sitting position.

2. Forward bending in left step standing, as described by McKenzie.[6] The patient stands with the left foot on a chair or stool and places both hands around the left knee. He or she slides the hands down the leg to the ankle and rests the middle of the chest on the left knee. The stretch is maintained for 5–10 seconds, then the patient brings the trunk back to the upright position. The stretch is repeated five to six times (Figure 15-10).

Exercises to Address the Long Restrictors of the Lumbar Spine

The multisegmental muscles also may be tight and need to be treated. This is particularly true in the presence of group (type I) dysfunctions, in which the primary restriction is of side bending. The most important long restrictor muscles in the lumbar region are the erector spinae, quadratus lumborum, and iliopsoas. These muscles can be screened for tightness by observing for a loss of the smooth symmetrical curve during active side bending of the spine in standing or by using the muscle length and movement tests previously described in Chapter 14.

Exercises to stretch these three muscle groups are described in Chapter 14.

Described for Restricted Lumbar Side Bending

A nonspecific exercise to improve lumbar side bending uses weight shifting with elongation in the seated position. To stretch the right side, the patient lifts the left buttock, shifting his or her weight to the right ischial tuberosity and, at the same time, abducting the right arm (Figure 15-11). This movement is repeated several times in a rhythmic, rocking motion. This exercise is also useful in facilitating the quadratus lumborum to fire on the contralateral side of shoulder abduction while lengthening the quadratus on the ipsilateral side (right).

Exercises to Restore Neuromotor Control of the Lumbar Spine

Pelvic Clock

The pelvic clock exercise, originally described by Feldenkrais,[7] is useful for self-mobilization and neuromuscular re-education of the pelvis, as well as the lumbar spine. The pelvic clock can also be used to evaluate and diagnose non-neutral lumbar spine dysfunctions.

The patient is supine, with the hips and knees flexed and the feet flat and approximately a hip's width apart. The patient is instructed to visualize the movements of the pelvis as taking place on an imaginary clock (Figure 15-12). Movement toward 6 o'clock creates lumbar spine extension, whereas movement toward 12 o'clock creates lumbar flexion. Movements across the clock (i.e., from 3 o'clock to 9 o'clock and from 9 o'clock to 3 o'clock) promote lumbar and pelvic rotation. When the patient is asked to move selectively around the face of the clock, three-dimensional

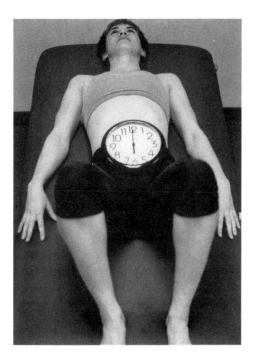

FIGURE 15-12
Starting position for the pelvic clock.

motion occurs. For example, movement around the clock in an arc from 3 o'clock to 6 o'clock promotes extension, right side bending, and right rotation of the lumbar spine. This particular movement is characteristically found to be restricted if there is an FRSlt dysfunction present in the lumbar spine. If the clock is restricted for movement toward 1 o'clock or 2 o'clock, an ERSlt lumbar spinal dysfunction is present. When a patient can perform a symmetrical, full-circle pelvic clock in both a clockwise and counter-clockwise direction, the lumbar spine is fairly clear of any non-neutral dysfunctions. For a patient who has been manually treated for an FRSrt in the lumbar spine and given the self-mobilizing exercises previously discussed (i.e., left side gliding in standing and prone press-ups), the pelvic clock exercise is given to reinforce active neuromuscular control. In this example, the patient can be instructed to rock the pelvis specifically toward 7 o'clock or 8 o'clock or around an arc from 6 o'clock to 9 o'clock to help maintain the correction.

EXERCISES FOR PELVIC DYSFUNCTION

Pubic Symphysis Dysfunctions

The superior and inferior pubis dysfunctions and specific manual treatments are detailed in Chapters 4 and 7, respectively.

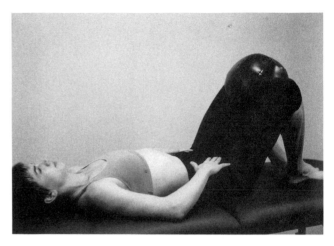

FIGURE 15-13
Self-correction for pubic dysfunction.

The symphysis is stabilized by strong ligaments and balanced by muscular attachments from above and below. The superior muscle attachments to the crest and symphysis are the abdominal wall muscles—specifically, the rectus and transversus abdominis and the internal and external obliques. The inferior attachments to the pubic ramus include the adductors magnus, longus, and brevis and the gracilis. Imbalance between the abdominals and hip adductors can influence and perpetuate symphysis dysfunction.

A self-mobilizing exercise for the pubic symphysis is similar to the "blunderbuss" treatment described in Chapter 7. The patient is supine, with feet flat on the floor and the knees bent and separated at least 15 cm (6 in.) by an incompressible object. The patient makes a firm effort to bring the knees together (Figure 15-13). The bilateral symmetrical action of the hip adductor muscles slightly decompresses the symphysis, allowing correction to occur. This exercise should be followed by appropriate exercises to balance the abdominal and hip adductor musculature, as previously described in Chapter 14.

Sacroiliac Dysfunctions

Dynamic stability of the sacroiliac (SI) joint is provided by the posterior SI, sacrospinous, and sacrotuberous ligaments and the supporting muscular slings. Clinically, the muscle groups that appear to have the most influence, directly or indirectly, on SI joint function are the piriformis, iliopsoas, glutei (maximus, medius, and minimus), hamstrings, latissimus dorsi, and lumbar erector spinae—all of which are addressed in Chapter 14.

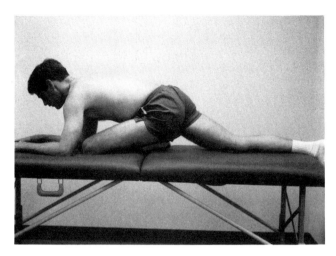

FIGURE 15-14
Buttock stretch to stretch the left piriformis and help promote posterior nutation of the left sacral base.

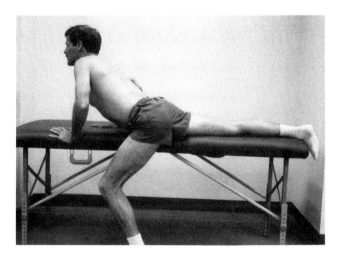

FIGURE 15-15
Self-mobilization to correct a posteriorly nutated right sacral base.

Four primary dysfunctions of sacral mechanics are described in Chapters 4 and 7. These dysfunctions include the anterior sacral torsions and unilateral anterior nutations, which have a major restriction of posterior nutation and superior translation of the sacral base. The more debilitating sacral dysfunctions are the posterior sacral torsions and unilateral posterior nutations, which have a major restriction of anterior nutation and inferior translation of the sacral base. In all four sacral dysfunctions, the primary restriction is of anterior or posterior nutation of the sacral base. Therefore, anterior or posterior nutation of the sacrum is the primary movement that the self-mobilizing exercises attempt to restore.

Described for Correction of an Anteriorly Nutated Sacral Base

1. *Buttock stretch.* The patient is in the hands-and-knees position, with the leg on the dysfunctional side externally rotated, flexed, adducted, and tucked underneath. The opposite leg slides directly backward, while maintaining a level pelvis and a straight spine. The stretch should be felt in the buttocks or posterior thigh. This position stretches the piriformis and gluteal fascia on that side, opens the posterior aspect of the SI joint, and induces slight flexion of L5, which encourages the sacrum to nutate posteriorly (Figure 15-14).

2. *Hands and knees diagonals.* For a left on left forward sacral torsion, the patient starts in the hands-and-knees position and is instructed to sit back diagonally toward the right hip (see Figure 15-9). This diagonal movement results in flexion, left side bending, and left

rotation of the lumbar spine and posterior nutation of the right sacral base. For a left unilateral anteriorly nutated sacrum, the patient sits back diagonally toward the left hip to posteriorly nutate the left sacral base.

3. Flexion exercises previously described for ERS dysfunctions of the lumbar spine also encourage posterior nutation of the sacral base.

Described for Correction of a Posteriorly Nutated Sacral Base

1. The patient is prone. For restriction of anterior nutational movement of the right sacral base, the right leg is abducted slightly and rotated externally to loose pack the right SI joint and open its anterior aspect. The left leg is dropped off the table and flexed at the hip and knee. The foot is on the floor so that the left side of the pelvis is stabilized by posterior rotation of the left innominate (Figure 15-15). The instruction is to perform a prone press-up while maintaining a relaxed lumbar spine and pelvis. By the selective positioning of the legs and the pelvis, the press-up encourages anterior nutational movement of the right sacral base.

2. Extension exercises (prone press-ups) are given to patients for self-treatment of lumbar spine FRS dysfunctions (see Figure 15-2) and often are used in treating patients with a herniated lumbar disc.[5] In patients with a posteriorly nutated sacral base, extension exercises are often ineffective and pain provoking, unless manual therapy is first directed to the SI joint for correction (see Figures 7-11, 7-12, 7-13, and 7-15).

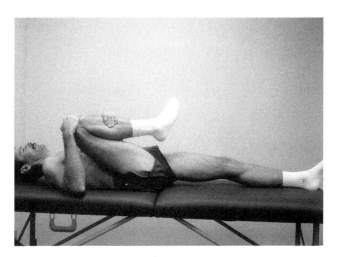

FIGURE 15-16
Correction of a right anteriorly rotated innominate.

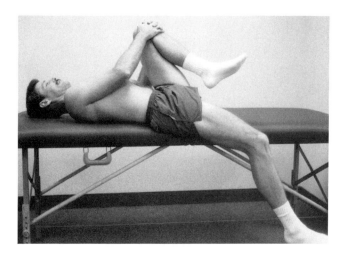

FIGURE 15-17
Correction of a right posteriorly rotated innominate.

Innominate Dysfunctions

In this text, the innominate bone is considered part of the lower extremity, and it is believed that imbalances of muscle length and strength in the lower limbs are often the cause of innominate rotations. Addressing lower extremity muscle imbalances, as discussed in Chapter 14, often corrects any innominate dysfunction, except for the nonphysiological inferior (downslip) or superior (upslip) innominate shears that need to be treated manually. If an innominate rotation persists after addressing the lower extremity muscle imbalances, the following exercises are given to the patient:

Described for Correction of an Anteriorly Rotated Innominate

For an anterior innominate correction, the patient is supine and rotates the innominate posteriorly by bringing the hip on the dysfunctional side into flexion, slight abduction, and external rotation, using both hands across the knee. The patient is instructed to contract the gluteus maximus by trying to extend the hip against the resistance of the hands for 5–7 seconds. After each contraction and subsequent relaxation, the leg is brought into further flexion, slight abduction, and external rotation. This isometric exercise is repeated three to four times progressively and is most commonly needed to treat the right side (Figure 15-16).

Described for Correction of a Posteriorly Rotated Innominate

For a posterior innominate correction, the patient is supine and drops the leg on the dysfunctional side off the table, while the opposite lower extremity is held in flexion

and posterior rotation with the hands. A series of isotonic contractions of the gluteus maximus on the involved side is made and held for 5–7 seconds to promote correction. Although it is illustrated on the right (Figure 15-17), this technique is most commonly needed on the left side.

EXERCISES FOR THORACIC SPINE DYSFUNCTIONS

Whereas lumbar spinal mechanics are influenced by the lower extremities, the thoracic spine is influenced by the upper extremities. For example, in the presence of hypertonicity and shortening of the latissimus dorsi and pectorals, the thoracic spine is postured in an exaggerated kyphosis, which predisposes the spine to FRS dysfunctions. A home exercise program that addresses the thoracic spine needs to include self-mobilizing spinal exercises and exercises that address muscular imbalances in the upper quarter, as described in Chapter 14.

Exercises for Multiple Stacked Non-Neutral Thoracic Spine Dysfunctions

Described to Promote Elongation of the Thoracic Spine

Because multiple, stacked ERS and FRS dysfunctions are common in the thoracic spine, an exercise to attempt to elongate the spine may be helpful before specific mobilization. The standing wall stretch is a suitable exercise.

The patient stands facing the wall, with the hands initially placed against the wall at approximately shoulder height. The feet are positioned 3–4 feet away so that, in the

FIGURE 15-18
Wall stretch for elongation of the spine and a posterior stretch of the legs.

stretch position, the arms are fully extended. The patient attempts to lengthen the spine by pressing the hips up and back, performing an anterior pelvic tilt while extending the elbows and dropping the chest toward the floor. As elongation of the spine occurs, the patient's hands can be lowered on the wall to approximately hip height (Figure 15-18). The stretch should be held for 30 seconds or longer and is repeated several times. This exercise also is an excellent method for stretching the hamstring muscles.

Described for Restricted Thoracic Spine Extension
Hands and Knees Exercise Extension can be localized to different areas of the spine in the hands-and-knees position by allowing the lumbar spine to sag and rocking forward or backward. When maintaining the sag, rocking forward promotes extension lower in the lumbar spine; rocking backward promotes extension higher into the lower thoracic spine (Figure 15-19).
Supine Bridging Exercise The patient is supine, with knees and hips bent and feet resting on a chair (Figure 15-20). The patient holds the front legs of the chair and, during exhalation, presses down with the feet on the chair to extend through the hips and lumbar region and up into the thoracic spine. At the same time, the patient retracts the shoulders to increase the stretch in the anterior rib cage and sternum. A blanket folded under the shoulders may be needed to prevent loss of the normal cervical lordosis during the effort. The position is held for a few seconds and repeated four to five times.[8] This exercise serves not only to mobilize the thoracic spine for extension, but also to strengthen the erector spinae

A

B

FIGURE 15-19
Extension of the spine in the hands-and-knees position. (A) Rocking forward to increase extension in the lower lumbar area. (B) Rocking backward to increase extension in the lower thoracic spine.

musculature to prevent recurrence of chronic, lower thoracic FRS dysfunctions.

Described for Restricted Thoracic Spine Flexion
Cat Back Exercise ERS dysfunctions in the thoracic spine can be mobilized with a "cat back" exercise in the hands-and-knees position, and some specificity can be obtained by varying the hand position. The further the hands are placed from the knees, the lower the apex of flexion motion induced in the spine (Figure 15-21).
Wall Press Exercise The wall press exercise, as described by Ward,[9] is an excellent exercise to promote flexion in the upper thoracic spine for correction of ERS dysfunctions. The wall press exercise also is useful for neuromuscular re-education of scapular control, particularly

FIGURE 15-20
Exercise to promote thoracic spine extension. This patient could benefit from a blanket folded under the shoulders to prevent a loss of the normal cervical lordosis.

FIGURE 15-21
"Cat back" exercise to increase thoracic spinal flexion. The further the hands are from the knees, the lower the apex of flexion induced in the thoracic spine.

in the presence of weakness of the serratus anterior and lower trapezius. The patient stands facing the wall, approximately 3 feet away with the hands placed on the wall at shoulder level. The scapulae are stabilized against the rib cage as the patient bends the elbows and leans forward to touch the nose to the wall without raising the heels from the floor. He or she then presses back, protracting the shoulders and extending the elbows. The patient maximally flexes the cervical and upper thoracic spine, while maintaining a neutral lumbar spine (Figure 15-22). The entire exercise is repeated four to five times, varying the hand position, as indicated, by placing the hands higher or

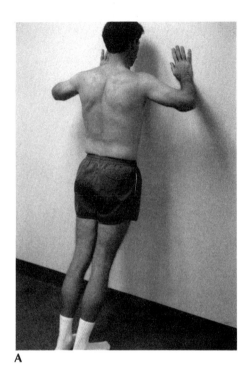

A

B

FIGURE 15-22
(A) The wall press exercise, starting position. (B) Maximal flexion is produced in the upper thoracic spine.

lower on the wall before repeating the sequence. For ERSlt dysfunctions, rotation of the head and neck to the right can be added for an additional stretch after the thoracic spine is flexed.

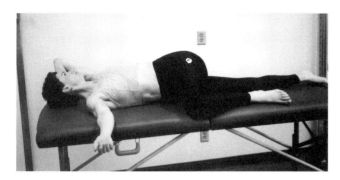

FIGURE 15-23
Thoracic self-mobilization for left rotation in the side-lying position.

Described for Restricted Thoracic Spine Rotation

Side Lying   To introduce rotation in side lying, the patient lies on one side, with the bottom leg straight, the top leg flexed less than 90 degrees at the hip, and the knee of the top leg resting on the table. The bottom arm is held straight out in front, resting on the floor or table, and the top hand is placed behind the head. The patient is instructed to roll backward and attempt to bring the ribs back toward the table (Figure 15-23). The stretch is repeated four to five times. The top hip is then flexed to 90 degrees, and the patient is instructed to rotate backward, again, four to five times. The rotation is repeated a third time, with the top hip flexed more than 90 degrees. The degree of hip flexion of the top leg determines where most of the rotation in the thoracic spine takes place (e.g., by increasing the degree of hip flexion, rotation occurs higher in the thoracic spine). Thus, the degree of hip flexion can be varied, depending on the area of the thoracic spine that has the greatest rotational restriction. The patient repeats this series of rotations on the opposite side, with the top hip flexed below, at, and above 90 degrees of flexion. Because placing the top leg on the table requires a considerable range of internal rotation of the hip, some patients may need to modify this exercise if hip mobility is restricted. This modification can be made by bringing both legs up together, rather than keeping the bottom leg straight.

Seated   Rotation in a seated position can be performed by working from below up to avoid strain of the cervical spine. To improve left rotation, the patient sits sideways on a chair, with the feet on the floor and the chair back to his or her left side. The patient grasps the chair back with both hands and initiates left rotation in the lumbar spine and then in the lower thoracic spine, working from below up. Breathing is used to enhance the movement: Inhalation lifts the spine (elongation), and exhalation is used to assist in making the turn. A series of four to five gentle turns is performed progres-

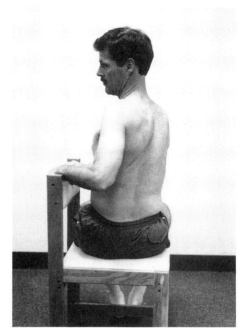

FIGURE 15-24
Self-mobilization for left rotation in the seated position.

sively, making sure that the shoulders remain down (i.e., relaxed) throughout each turn (Figure 15-24).

CERVICAL SPINE

Typical Joints C2-7 (T1)

In the typical joints of the cervical spine, rotation and side bending are always coupled to the same side. Therefore, there are only four patterns of dysfunction to be considered. The dysfunctional joint(s) may be flexed and left or right side bent or rotated, or they may be extended and left or right side bent or rotated.

Exercise for Flexed, Rotated, and Side-Bent (FRS) Dysfunctions

The patient sits and localizes to the dysfunctional segment by the index finger contacting the articular pillar of the lower vertebra at the level to be mobilized. The patient uses a combined active movement of extension, side bending, and rotation, attempting to look up and over the stabilizing index finger to mobilize at that segment (Figure 15-25).

Exercise for Extended, Rotated, and Side-Bent (ERS) Dysfunctions

The patient sits, with an index finger on the articular pillar of the superior vertebra of the dysfunctional seg-

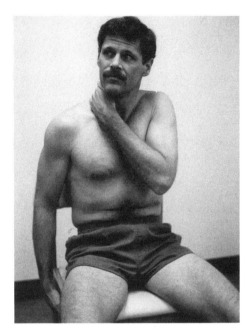

FIGURE 15-25
Self-mobilization for cervical spine FRS left dysfunctions.

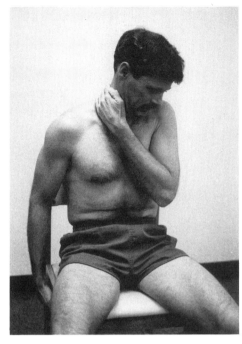

FIGURE 15-26
Self-mobilization for cervical spine ERS right dysfunctions.

ment. The patient directs and guides the combined movement of flexion, side bending, and rotation, pulling with the index finger to open the dysfunctional facet joint (Figure 15-26).

Exercise for the Long Restrictors

When multiple ERS dysfunctions are found in the cervical spine, the examiner must be suspicious of long restrictor muscle tightness, particularly if the dysfunctions involve the upper three or four cervical spinal segments. The levator scapulae and splenius cervicis produce extension, ipsilateral rotation, and side bending of the upper four cervical spinal segments and, if hypertonic, may contribute to the presence of multiple cervical ERS dysfunctions. For this reason, if multiple cervical ERS dysfunctions are found, these muscles should be stretched first, before attempting to treat individual cervical joints. The exercise for self-stretching of the levator scapulae, as previously described in Chapter 14, Figure 14-8, and the self-mobilizing exercise, as described for the ERS dysfunction, also are effective in lengthening the splenius cervicis.

Multiple FRS dysfunctions of the cervical spine also may implicate long restrictor involvement, particularly of the anterior and middle scalene muscles. These muscles are best stretched by placing the cervical spine in extension, combined with side bending away and rotation toward the tight side, as previously described in Chapter 14, Figure 14-10.

Altantoaxial Joint

Exercise to Restore Rotation at Cervical 1-2

The primary motion between the first two cervical vertebrae is rotation, and this exercise is performed easily with the patient sitting. The neck is flexed fully to bring the chin to the chest (i.e., to limit the available rotation in the lower cervical spine), and the patient is asked to rotate the head toward the restricted side (Figure 15-27). The rotation effort is repeated four to five times against the barrier.

Occipitoatlantal Joint

Exercises to Restore Flexion at the Occipitoatlantal Joint

The primary motion of the occipitoatlantal (OA) joint is flexion and extension, and a self-mobilizing exercise can be performed by flexing and extending the head on the neck (i.e., nodding) rather than moving the neck itself. This exercise is the active counterpart of the passive movement used in examination of this joint, and it involves rotation about an axis through the external auditory meatus (Figure 15-28). The facets at the OA joint are set at approximately a 30-degree angle to the sagittal plane. Therefore, this exercise can be made more specific to one OA joint by rotating the head 30

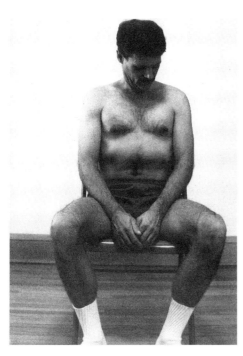

FIGURE 15-27
Self-mobilization for rotation of the atlantoaxial joint to the left.

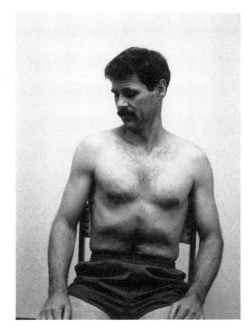

FIGURE 15-29
Self-mobilization for flexion of the right occipitoatlantal joint.

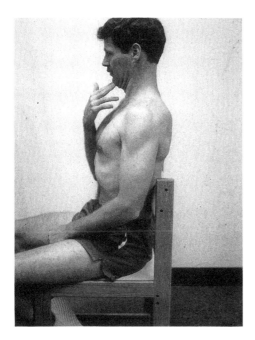

FIGURE 15-28
Self-mobilization for flexion of the occipitoatlantal joints.

degrees toward the joint that is to be mobilized before nodding (Figure 15-29).

The list of exercises included in this chapter is by no means exhaustive, but it provides suggestions for more specific directions to patients who take part in a home exercise program. If the goal is for patients eventually to be capable of managing their own conditions, it is essential for patients to understand where their dysfunctions are and how these dysfunctions can be addressed and controlled by exercises. This understanding gives the patient responsibility for his or her own well-being. Patient compliance seems to improve when exercises are designed in such a specific fashion.

It is hoped that this chapter stimulates further interest in the specificity of self-mobilizing exercises for musculoskeletal dysfunction.

REFERENCES

1. Bogduk N, Jull G. The theoretical pathology of acute locked back: a basis for manipulative therapy. Man Med 1985;1:78–82.

2. Stoddard A. A Manual of Osteopathic Practice. London: Hutchinson, 1961;43.

3. Korr I. Muscle Spindle and the Lesioned Segment. In Proceedings: International Federation of Orthopaedic Manupulative Therapists. Vail, CO: 1977;45:53.

4. Lewit K. Manipulative Therapy in Rehabilitation of the Locomotor System. London: Butterworth, 1985;22.

5. Williams PC. Conservative management of lesions of the lumbosacral spine. Instruct Lect Amer Acad Orthop Surg 1953;10:90–121.

6. McKenzie RA. The Lumbar Spine: Mechanical Diagnosis and Therapy. Waikanae, NZ: Spinal Publications Ltd, 1981.

7. Shafarman S. Awareness Heals: The Feldenkrais Method for Dynamic Health. Reading, MA: Perseus Books, 1997.

8. Tobias M, Stewart M. Stretch and Relax. Tucson: The Body Press, 1985;45.

9. Ward R. Myofascial Release: Continuing Medical Education Course Notes. East Lansing, MI: Michigan State University, College of Osteopathic Medicine, 1988.

Index